CONGRESS

A TO Z

CONGRESS *A* TO *Z*

CQ's
Ready Reference
Encyclopedia

Congressional Quarterly Inc.
1414 22nd St. N.W.
Washington D.C. 20037

Photo Credits

xiv - Ken Heinen; 5 - U.S. Department of Agriculture; 7 - Library of Congress; 10 - Charles Del Vecchio, *Washington Post;* 12 - Sue Klemens; 18 - Ken Heinen; 21 - Teresa Zabala; 24 - Ken Heinen

26 - Ken Heinen; 29 - Continental Illinois Bank & Trust Co. of Chicago; 32 - Paul Hosefros, *New York Times;* 33 - Library of Congress; 35 - National Portrait Gallery, Smithsonian Institution; 36 - Library of Congress; 39 - Teresa Zabala; 43 - AP/Wide World Photos

50 - Library of Congress; 53 - Library of Congress; 60 - Library of Congress; 62 - Architect of the Capitol; 67 - George Tames, *New York Times;* 68 - Congressional Black Caucus; 74 - Library of Congress; 76 - Library of Congress; 77 - *Eyes on the Prize,* PBS; 84 - Ken Heinen; 96 - Junior Bridge, National Organization for Women; 99 - AP/Wide World Photos; 100 - Library of Congress

104 - Ken Heinen; 107 - Library of Congress; 111 - Library of Congress

118 - Sue Klemens; 123 - Architect of the Capitol; 125 - Ken Heinen; 131 - Library of Congress; 138 - Lyndon Baines Johnson Library

142 - Rich Lipski, *Washington Post;* 145 - Strom Thurmond Institute; 148 - Jim Wells; 151 - AP/Wide World Photos; 156 - Associated Press; 160 - Sue Klemens (Conable), Debbie Jennings (Muskie)

166 - Ken Heinen; 168 - Bettmann Archive; 173 - AP/ Wide World Photos

174 - Architect of the Capitol; 178 - Library of Congress; 180 - Library of Congress; 181 - National Archives; 182 - Wide World Photos; 186 - Jim Wells; 188 - James K. W. Atherton, *Washington Post*

194 - AP/ Wide World Photos; 197 - UPI/ Bettmann Newsphotos; 205 - AP/ Wide World Photos (McCarthy), *Washington Post* (North); 212 - *Washington Post;* 214 - AP/ Wide World Photos

216 - United Press International; 220 - Library of Congress; 222 - Wide World Photos; 226 - Library of Congress (John), Senate Historical Office (Robert), Art Stein (Edward)

228 - Library of Congress (top), Teresa Zabala (bottom); 233 - Library of Congress; 237 - George Tames; 250 - C-Span; 258 - Library of Congress; 261 - Paul A. Schmick, *Washington Star;* 264 - UPI/Bettmann Newsphotos; 269 - Senate Historical Office; 270 - Ken Heinen

272 - Library of Congress; 275 - Library of Congress; 277 - National Archives; 280 - Teresa Zabala (Bradley), Stan Barouh (Glenn); 283 - Ken Heinen

286 - Architect of the Capitol; 289 - UPI/Bettmann Newsphotos; 291 - UPI/Bettmann Newsphotos

296 - Architect of the Capitol; 299 - George Tames, *New York Times;* 300 - *Washington Post*

302 - White House; 304 - Library of Congress; 306 - U.S. Postal Service; 308 - Jane Gilligan; 313 - Library of Congress; 320 - AP/Wide World Photos; 323 - AP/Wide World Photos; 328 - AP/Wide World Photos; 331 - Library of Congress; 335 - James K. W. Atherton, *Washington Post*

338 - Ken Heinen; 351 - Library of Congress; 354 - National Portrait Gallery, Smithsonian Institution; 355 - Copyright 1960 by Herblock in *The Washington Post;* 361 - Ken Heinen

364 - Architect of the Capitol; 373 - UPI/Bettmann Newsphotos; 377 - From *Herblock's State of the Union* (Simon & Schuster, 1972); 382 - James K. W. Atherton, *Washington Post;* 386 - Associated Press; 390 - Ken Heinen; 391 - Library of Congress; 396 - Jim Wells; 402 - Library of Congress; 404 - Associated Press; 410, 412 - Ken Heinen

414 - Ann Burrola, Democratic Senatorial Campaign Committee; 417 - Library of Congress; 421 - C-Span; 424 - Senate Historical Office; 426 - National Archives

428 - Library of Congress; 431 - Rich Lipski, *Washington Post;* 436 - Jack Kightlinger, White House; 439 - Wide World Photos; 444 - *U.S. News & World Report*

446 - Library of Congress; 450 - Associated Press; 461 - Library of Congress; 462 - White House; 465 - Library of Congress; 467 - Library of Congress; 468 - Art Stein; 470 - Ken Heinen

472 - Architect of the Capitol; 558 - Ken Heinen

Copyright © 1988 Congressional Quarterly Inc.

Printed in the United States of America

Library of Congress Cataloging-in-Publication Data

Congress A to Z.

Bibliography: p.
Includes index.
1. United States. Congress—Dictionaries.
I. Congressional Quarterly, inc.
JK1067.C67   1988   328.73′003′21   88-20336
ISBN 0-87187-447-4

PREFACE

Congress A to Z is a product of Congressional Quarterly's more than forty years of reporting on America's national legislature. The subtitle we have given the volume, *CQ's Ready Reference Encyclopedia,* describes exactly what we set out to create more than two years ago: a handy one-volume encyclopedic reference that will quickly and accurately answer questions about Congress.

This book is for all persons who have an interest in Congress, national politics, and the federal government, whether they are high school students doing research for a class paper, adults with a specific question about congressional operations, or simply political buffs who enjoy following activities on Capitol Hill in Washington, D.C.

The editors and writers have sought to provide, in a readily accessible form, all the basic information most readers will need to understand the structure and operations of the legislative branch of the federal government. *Congress A to Z* offers nontechnical explanations of congressional operations, as well as background on the development of the modern Congress.

The entries are arranged alphabetically and are extensively cross-referenced to guide you to related information elsewhere in the book. In addition, we have provided detailed name and general indexes to help you locate the proper entry quickly.

The core of the encyclopedia is a series of thirty essays that provide overviews of broad subject areas, such as the legislative process and the congressional committee system. Those essays are supported by nearly 250 additional entries. Many flesh out details of material covered in the broader essays or provide specific explanations of important technical matters such as recommittal motions and suspension of the rules. Others offer profiles of individual congressional committees and capsule biographies of selected members of Congress, past and present. A few brief historical entries help set the scene. A separate appendix provides statistical data and other material related to Congress. A general bibliography supplements suggested readings that accompany individual entries.

Lastly, we have attempted to go beyond information about how Congress works. You will find throughout the book a variety of helpful information on such matters as how to visit the Capitol, write your congressman, or order books from the Government Printing Office. We provide information about the White House and the Supreme Court, as well as maps of Capitol Hill and the central city to assist visitors to Washington.

This book is the result of the dedicated work of dozens of persons at CQ today and many more who have worked here before to make Congressional Quarterly the leading authority on Congress and politics. Most important are the reporters and editors for the CQ *Weekly Report* who provide the accurate information and the perceptive understanding of Congress on which we have so heavily drawn in preparing this volume. *Congress A to Z* has been written by a group of present and former CQ staffers who have followed the institution for many years. Associate Editor Ann Pelham prepared major portions of the manuscript. Other current and former CQ staff members who made important contributions to the content are Harrison Donnelly, Michael Wormser, Patricia Ann O'Connor, Julia McCue, Martha V. Gottron, Hoyt Gimlin, Richard L. Worsnop, Pam Fessler, 'and Jodean Marks. John Moore has assisted all of us by constantly checking and reviewing the work as it progressed. In addition, we are indebted to Walter Oleszek and Bruce Oppenheimer who reviewed much of the manuscript. The book's design was prepared by Harry Rinehart.

From manuscript to finished book is a huge step that requires the polished skills and hard work of many persons. Two who were especially important in producing *Congress A to Z* were Assistant Editor for Production Jane Gilligan and CQ's Typesetting Supervisor Jean Kight. Jane coordinated and tracked thousands of pieces of information to make sure all were in place at the correct time. Jean skillfully typeset the manuscript and prepared the layouts and composition for the pages that you will read in this volume.

We hope this book will meet the simple goal we established at the beginning and that has been CQ's hallmark since its founding: to provide readers with easily accessible, readily understandable, and accurate information about Congress.

Mary Cohn
Editor

CONTENTS

In this table of contents, primary essays are designated by a boldface type. Other text entries are in regular type. The entries in small capital letters will refer the reader to related entries elsewhere in the book. In addition, within many articles, the reader will find words in small capital letters indicating that significant additional information on that topic will be found elsewhere under that name.

CONTENTS

APPENDIX

Members of Congress

Congress at Work

Capitol and City

INDEXES

CONGRESS A TO Z

Abscam Scandal

Seven members of Congress were convicted on criminal charges as the result of an FBI undercover operation disclosed in 1980. The operation was known as Abscam, a combination of the words Arab and scam (a con man's trick).

In the Abscam operation, according to published accounts and subsequent court evidence, an undisclosed number of members of Congress were approached by intermediaries who offered to introduce them to representatives of wealthy Arabs interested in making investments in their districts. The Arabs' representatives were actually undercover FBI agents. Some of the members were asked if they could use their official positions to help the Arabs obtain U.S. residency. Others were asked to use their influence in government to obtain federal grants and gambling licenses or to arrange real estate deals.

Four of the six House members eventually convicted in the Abscam affair—Richard Kelly, a Florida Republican, and Democrats Raymond F. Lederer and Michael "Ozzie" Myers of Pennsylvania and Frank Thompson, Jr., of New Jersey—were videotaped accepting money. John W. Jenrette, a South Carolina Democrat, was tape-recorded saying he had been given the cash by an associate. John M. Murphy, a New York Democrat, allegedly told an associate to accept the cash. A seventh House member, Pennsylvania Democrat John P. Murtha, was named an unindicted co-conspirator.

The only senator to be convicted in the affair—New Jersey Democrat Harrison A. Williams, Jr.—turned down a cash bribe offered by undercover agents. But Williams was convicted for his participation in a complicated business scheme involving a hidden interest in a mining venture.

Williams and the six convicted House members served prison sentences. All seven claimed that the government had entrapped them. Williams maintained that the government had "manufactured" the crimes of which he was accused.

As a result of the scandal, all seven members were forced out of Congress. In October 1980 Myers became the first House member to be expelled for misconduct other than treason and the fourth to be expelled in history. Kelly, Murphy, and Thompson were defeated for reelection prior to their convictions and left Congress before disciplinary proceedings could be initiated against them. Jenrette, Lederer, and Williams resigned their seats. By leaving the Senate voluntarily in 1982, Williams avoided becoming the first senator to be expelled since the Civil War and the first to be ejected on grounds other than treason or disloyalty. *(See* DISCIPLINING MEMBERS.)   ~

Adams, John Quincy

John Quincy Adams (1767-1848), the sixth president of the United States, represented Massachusetts in both the Senate and House of Representatives during his long career in public life.

The son of John Adams, the nation's second president, he was a man of

John Quincy Adams

uncompromising rectitude and inflexible purpose. Adams entered the Senate in 1803 as a Federalist, but he soon ran into trouble for supporting Jeffersonian policies. He resigned his Senate seat in 1808. After holding various diplomatic posts, he served with distinction from 1817 to 1825 as President James Monroe's secretary of state. He was chiefly responsible for the Monroe Doctrine, which barred colonization in the Western Hemisphere by European nations.

Adams ran for president in 1824, in an inconclusive four-way race that ultimately had to be decided by the House of Representatives. Although Andrew Jackson was the leading candidate in both popular and electoral vote, the House chose Adams. Lacking political or popular support, Adams was not a successful president; Jackson defeated him in 1828.

In 1830 Adams was elected to the House of Representatives, where he served for seventeen years until his death. Known as "Old Man Eloquent," he conducted an almost single-handed attack on so-called gag rules that prevented discussion of antislavery proposals. The House repealed the rules in 1844. On February 21, 1848, the eighty-year-old Adams was stricken at his desk in the House chamber. He was carried to the Speaker's room, where he died two days later.

Adams was one of two presidents to serve in Congress after leaving the White House. Andrew Johnson, also a former senator, returned to the Senate for five months before his death in 1875. *(See* ELECTING THE PRESIDENT.*)* ～

Adjournment

Adjournment describes the action of Congress in bringing its meetings to a close. In the congressional context the word has several different meanings.

• End of session: The TERMS of Congress run in two-year cycles, and Congress must hold a regular series of meetings, called a session, each year. At the end of a year's session, the Senate and House adjourn *sine die*—literally, "without a day"; lawmakers do not intend to meet again in that particular session. Adjournment of the second session is generally the final action of a term of Congress. The president has authority under the Constitution to convene special sessions of Congress. Members frequently authorize their leaders to call them back into session as well.

• Mid-session: Within a session Congress may adjourn for holiday observances or other brief periods. That practice is known as adjournment to a day certain; lawmakers set a date for the session to reconvene. By constitutional directive neither house may adjourn for more than three days without the consent of the other.

• Daily: In the House of Representatives daily sessions almost always end in adjournment. The Senate may also adjourn, but it is far more likely to recess. By recessing it continues the same LEGISLATIVE DAY into the next calendar day, an arrangement that provides certain procedural benefits under Senate rules. A single legislative day may go on for weeks; it does not end until the Senate next adjourns. ～

Advice and Consent. See
APPOINTMENT POWER.

Aging Committees, House and Senate

Although congressional rules bar them from handling legislation, the two congressional Aging committees have served as effective platforms for advocates of the elderly. Their hearings, investigations, and reports have given the problems of the elderly increased visibility in Congress. The committees also keep tabs on bills affecting the elderly, which are handled by various legislative committees.

The Senate Special Aging Committee, set up in the early 1960s, survived a bid to disband it as part of an overall Senate reorganization in 1977. The senior citizens' lobby was so successful in arguing for the Aging Committee that only four senators voted against it.

The House Select Committee on Aging was launched in 1975. Its most prominent member has been Claude Pepper, an octogenarian Florida Democrat who fought ceaselessly for the elderly, with a special emphasis on Social Security. During three terms as chairman of the Aging Committee (1977-83), Pepper held well-publicized investigations of those he felt were preying upon the elderly. Many of the ideas he advocated, such as curbs on mandatory retirement, were later written into legislation by other committees and enacted by Congress. Pepper gave up the chairmanship in 1983, when he took over the House Rules Committee. ～

Agriculture Committee, House

The chief responsibility of the House Agriculture Committee is to oversee the federal government's many programs of support and assistance to farmers. Committee members, who mostly represent heavily rural areas, are the leading advocates in the House for the interests of farmers.

The most important elements of the committee's jurisdiction are federal farm price supports. Through a variety of mechanisms, such as government loans and direct cash payments, these programs determine the minimum prices farmers will receive for their wheat, corn, cotton, and other crops. The goal of these programs is to provide farmers with some protection against the wide swings in market prices for farm products.

In addition, the committee is responsible for other agricultural issues, such as the federal law regulating use of pesticides. Also under the committee's authority is the federal food stamp program, which helps poor people buy food.

Although the committee works on legislation in every session of Congress, its principal work comes in years when it must report a comprehensive "farm bill," establishing the overall shape of farm programs for the next four or five years. The year in which the farm bill comes up for renewal is usually a time of intense activity for committee members.

Most of the members of the Agriculture Committee come from southern and midwestern states, where issues involving farm interests are a prime concern. Some of the members are farmers themselves, or come from districts where farming remains an important part of the local economy. Few members come from big cities or industrial regions.

Farm Coalition

Politically, the most important aspect of the Agriculture Committee's work is the "farm coalition." The need for this coalition is based on the fact that no single crop is important everywhere in the United States. In the midwestern Farm Belt, wheat and corn are the dominant crops, and farmers there are most concerned with preserving federal assistance to those products. In the South, though, farmers care much less about wheat and corn than they do about price supports for the cotton and rice they mostly grow.

Each member is most concerned with protecting the interests of the crops most important to his or her own constituents, while paying less attention to the interests of crops that are grown in other regions. As a result, no one crop commands the allegiance of a majority of the committee or of the House as a whole. If each crop were considered separately, it would be politically weak and would have little chance of obtaining generous price-support levels.

So, long ago, committee members learned that it was in their interest to join together in a common front for all farm products. Groups supporting each crop found that they were better off supporting all the other crops, and receiving those groups' support in return. Members from Georgia, where peanuts are predominant, agreed to support, for example, special programs for Michigan potato growers. In turn, Michigan members voted in favor of peanut programs, even though that crop was not important in their state.

By sticking loyally to the overall farm coalition, Agriculture Committee members were able for many years to win House approval of legislation providing increasing federal support for their crops. If opposition developed to price supports for any one crop, committee members usually were able to overcome it by offering to increase federal aid to other crops as well, and so win over enough members to obtain a majority.

The growth of the food stamp program in the 1970s added significantly to the strength of the farm coalition. Food stamps are important to House members from big cities, who otherwise have little interest in supporting farm programs. By including generous funding for food stamps in farm legislation, Agriculture Committee members were able in return to win the support of many liberal, urban Democrats for crop-support programs.

However, several factors had by the 1980s begun to undermine the strength of the farm coalition in the House. The most basic was the decline in the political importance of farmers. The sharp decline in the number of people living in rural areas meant that there were many fewer House members who were primarily concerned with farm interests.

Moreover, the spiraling costs of federal farm programs during a time of massive budget deficits greatly increased the degree of opposition to the farm coalition and Agriculture Committee legislation. In the 1970s federal farm programs typically cost about $3 billion a year. By the mid-1980s that price-tag had swollen to more than $20 billion annually.

As a result, Agriculture Committee members found themselves under heavy pressure from other House members to hold down the cost of farm programs. By the 100th Congress (1987-89), it was clear to many observers that the Agriculture Committee would have great difficulty in the future in winning House approval of legislation that raised federal spending.   ~

Agriculture, Nutrition, and Forestry Committee, Senate

The Senate Agriculture Committee shares with its House counterpart the jurisdiction over federal farm programs. To a great extent, the amount of economic help the federal government pro-

Bringing in the Wheat
The House and Senate Agriculture committees represent farmers' interests in Congress. Their efforts depend on a coalition of members from the Midwest, where wheat and corn are the dominant crops, and the South, where cotton and rice predominate.

vides to farmers depends on the decisions made in the committee, and on the skill of committee members in guiding their legislation through the full Senate. The committee is formally known as the Agriculture, Nutrition, and Forestry Committee.

As is true in the House, the main work of the Senate Agriculture Committee occurs only every four or five years, when Congress considers renewal of legislation authorizing federal farm price supports, food stamps, and related programs. In between, the committee considers a variety of legislation responding to changes in the agricultural economy, from help for farmers hit by droughts or floods to emergency assistance for the banks that provide operating loans to farmers.

In many respects, the political situation of the Senate committee is similar to that of the House Agriculture Committee. The Senate panel is largely dominated by members from states where agriculture is a key factor in the local economy. Senate committee members also share with their House colleagues the primary goal of protecting the interests of farmers in the competition for federal resources.

Furthermore, the Senate committee traditionally has depended on the farm coalition, under which advocates of various crops band together for mutual political support. For many years, the Senate panel's work consisted largely of tallying up the requests of various special-interest lobbies, and so fashioning farm programs to cover each group's particular desires. The strategy used in the 1970s by then-Chairman Herman E. Talmadge typified the way in which farm bills were written. The Georgia Democrat simply asked each Agriculture member, "What do you need, Senator?" and compiled the answers into a farm bill.

However, the farm coalition on the committee came under increasing pressure in the 1980s, as the rapidly growing

costs of farm programs collided with the spiraling federal budget deficit. The strain on the coalition within the committee and the full Senate was shown clearly by action over the 1985 farm bill, which led to bitter debates over the Reagan administration's efforts to hold down the cost of farm programs.

Nevertheless, the farm coalition on Senate Agriculture remained a more potent political force than in the House, because of the differences in representation in the two bodies. In the House, lightly populated farm states, such as North Dakota, had very little voting strength. But the same states each had two votes in the Senate, giving them far more power and making farm issues considerably more important.

The continuing significance of the Agriculture Committee's work in the Senate was illustrated by the 1986 elections. Reagan administration efforts to hold down the cost of farm programs became a major campaign issue that year. Democratic Senate candidates in farm states sharply criticized their Republican opponents for supporting administration-backed farm-program spending cuts. Many farm voters agreed and helped the Democratic candidates to prevail in several states. Those results contributed greatly to the election of a Democratic majority in the Senate, ending six years of Republican rule. ~

Albert, Carl B.

Carl B. Albert (1908-—) was a Democratic member of the House for thirty years and its Speaker for six. An Oklahoma lawyer and former Rhodes scholar, Albert entered the House in 1947. On the day of his arrival, legend has it, the tiny (five feet, four inches) newcomer was mistaken for a congressional page by a veteran representative who called him over and directed, "Son, take these papers over to my office."

During his career in the House, Albert traveled a careful political road along which he made few enemies. He was a protégé of Speaker Sam RAYBURN, who tapped him to become majority whip in 1955. Albert moved on up the Democratic leadership ladder to become majority leader in 1962 and Speaker in 1971. He was acceptable to most factions of the party and won election as Speaker with only token opposition.

Because of his low-key style, Albert did little either to help or impede liberal reform efforts of the early 1970s, and his passive manner soon drew criticism. Some freshman Democrats talked openly of removing him after the House in 1975 upheld Republican President Gerald R. Ford's veto of a Democratic-backed strip-mining control bill. No effort was made to oust Albert, however, and criticism subsided by 1976. He did not run for reelection that year. ~

Nelson W. Aldrich

Aldrich, Nelson W.

Nelson W. Aldrich (1841-1915) was arguably the most influential member of the Senate from the 1890s until his retirement in 1911. Aldrich, a staunch conservative, allied himself with other like-minded Republican senators to control the first powerful party leadership organization in the Senate.

Aldrich was elected to the House of Representatives from Rhode Island in 1879. In 1881 he resigned from the House to fill a vacant Senate seat, and he subsequently won election to the Senate in his own right. A successful financier, Aldrich conformed to the contemporary stereotype of the Senate as a "millionaires' club." Wealth, however, was not his only claim to the job. He was accomplished at parliamentary tactics and had a strong interest in the economic affairs of the country.

Prior to the 1890s members of the Senate had only experimented with leadership by political party. In the last decade of the nineteenth century a group of Republican senators led by Aldrich and William B. ALLISON of Iowa pooled influence so that they might control the Senate. Calling themselves the School of Philosophy Club, members of the group cemented their ties during after-hours poker games. With the help of his friends, and through force of personality, Aldrich wielded tremendous power even though he held no leadership position and did not do so until 1899 when he became chairman of the Finance Committee.

With Allison, Aldrich effectively controlled committee assignments, the scheduling of legislation, and the business of standing committees. Loyalty to Aldrich and his cohorts was rewarded by good committee assignments and timely consideration of legislation. Rebellious Republicans were punished with the reverse treatment. The Aldrich "machine" was so effective that it was able to hinder the enactment of President Theodore Roosevelt's progressive policies and to force concessions from Roosevelt.

A champion of commercial interests, Aldrich opposed any substantive regulation of business and was able to temper restrictions imposed by the Interstate Commerce Act of 1887 and the Sherman Antitrust Act. He supported protective tariffs and clashed with Roosevelt over tariff reform. A protectionist tariff bill sponsored by the Aldrich party machine proved to be so unpopular with the public that it contributed to Republican defeats in the 1910 elections, and the backlash gave impetus to the formation of the Bull Moose or Progressive party. *(See* POLITICAL PARTIES.*)*   ~

Allison, William B.

William B. Allison (1829-1908) represented Iowa both in the House of Representatives and, from 1873 until 1908, in the Senate. He was counted among the most influential senators of his day.

Allison entered the House of Representatives in 1863 and continued there until 1871. As a representative he served on the Ways and Means Committee and championed the interests of the nation's railroads.

During his thirty-five years in the Senate, Allison was known more as a power broker than as a legislator. With Nelson W. ALDRICH of Rhode Island, Allison was a leader of the conservative Republicans who controlled the Senate around the turn of the twentieth century. Allison's influence and authority originally derived from his position as chairman of the Appropriations Committee. In 1897, as the most senior Republican in the Senate, he became chairman of the Republican Caucus. He was the first to realize that the position might be a useful tool in accruing and consolidating power.

Following his belief that "both in the committees and in the offices, we should use the machinery for our own benefit and not let other men have it," he took control of the Republican Steering Committee. Through the steering committee he took over the scheduling of legislation and the proceedings on the floor of the Senate. His authority over the Committee on Committees allowed him to fill committee vacancies to punish or reward fellow Republicans.

Under the leadership of Allison and Aldrich conservative Republicans were transformed into a cohesive political force that scored many victories over the more progressive Republican president, Theodore Roosevelt. On occasion Roosevelt was able to split the two senators, but for the most part Allison and Aldrich worked successfully together and with their supporters to challenge Roosevelt's policies.   ~

Amendments

Amendments are proposals to alter or rewrite legislation being considered by Congress. The amending process provides a way to shape bills into a form acceptable to a majority in both the Senate and House of Representatives.

Amending legislation is a three-stage process. It is, first of all, one of the chief functions of the legislative committees of Congress. Second, the amending process is at the heart of floor debate in both chambers. And third, amendments are vital to working out compromises on bills during House-Senate conference negotiations. *(See* LEGISLATIVE PROCESS.*)*

Amendments have many objectives. Members may introduce amendments to dramatize their stands on issues, even if there is little chance their proposals will be adopted. Some are introduced at the request of the executive branch, a member's constituents, or special interests. Some become tactical tools for gauging sentiment for or against a bill. Others are used to stall action on or to defeat legislation. In the House, where debate is strictly limited, amendments are often used to buy time; a member may offer a pro forma amendment, later withdrawn, solely to gain a few additional minutes to speak on an issue.

Amendments themselves are frequently the targets of other amendments offered by members having different points of view. The amending process becomes the arena for a tug-of-war among these diverse viewpoints and groups in Congress, and very frequently amendments become the most controversial elements in a bill.

Some amendments take on an identity of their own, regardless of the legislation to which they are attached. The Hyde amendment, a proposal to ban federal funding for abortions, touched off an emotional lobbying crusade in the 1970s. It brought fame to its sponsor, Rep. Henry J. Hyde, an Illinois Republican.

In Committee

Legislation comes under sharp congressional focus at the committee stage. A bill typically first undergoes section-by-section review and amendment by a specialized subcommittee, a process known as "marking up" the measure. The subcommittee may approve the legislation unaltered, but that is rarely the case; it is more likely to amend the bill, or substitute an entirely new version. The legislation then goes to the full committee, where the process may be repeated. The committee may accept the subcommittee amendments with little or no change, or it may make additional amendments.

If the changes are substantial and the legislation is complicated, the committee may introduce a "clean bill" incorporating the proposed amendments. The original bill is then put aside and

the clean bill, with a new bill number, is reported to the full chamber. If committee amendments are not extensive, the original bill is "reported with amendments." Later, when the bill comes up on the floor, the House or Senate must approve, alter, or reject the committee amendments before the bill itself can be put to a vote.

On the Floor

During floor action, members may seek to change the intent, conditions, or requirements of a bill; modify, delete, or introduce new provisions; or replace a section or the entire text of a bill with a different version. In the Senate, members may offer amendments that are entirely unrelated to the bill under consideration. Such nongermane amendments, or RIDERS, are usually not permitted in the House.

All of these attempts to alter legislative proposals fall within one of three basic types of amendments: those that seek to add additional text, those that seek to delete some or all of the existing text and substitute alternative language, or those that seek merely to delete some or all of the existing text.

Amendments that seek to revise or modify parts of bills or other amendments—for example, a single provision—are called perfecting amendments. SUBSTITUTE amendments aim at replacing previously introduced, or pending, amendments with alternatives. A variation of the substitute, referred to as an "amendment in the nature of a substitute," seeks to replace the pending bill with an entirely new version.

Though they are interpreted somewhat differently, rules in both houses prohibit the offering of amendments past the "second degree." An amendment may be offered to the text of a bill—a first-degree amendment. An amendment to that amendment is also in order—a second-degree amendment. But an amendment to an amendment to an amendment—a third-degree amend-

Hyde Amendment
An amendment to ban federal funding for abortions touched off an emotional lobbying crusade in the 1970s. The amendment became known as the Hyde Amendment for its sponsor, Rep. Henry J. Hyde.

ment—is not permissible. The rule, simply laid out in JEFFERSON'S MANUAL in the late 1700s, is more complex than it sounds. In practice, it is possible to have four or more amendments pending at one time, depending on how each chamber interprets the first- and second-degree requirement.

Skilled legislators may turn the rule to tactical advantage: By offering innocuous second-degree amendments, they may protect their first-degree amendments from other changes they oppose.

Generally speaking, bills in the House are considered section by section, with floor amendments in order only to the section of the bill then being considered. In the Senate, amendments usually are in order to any section at any time, unless such practices are prohibited by unanimous consent. It is a basic concept of the amending process that once an amendment has been rejected, it may not be offered again in precisely the same form.

Committee amendments, those made by the committee that reported the bill, normally are considered before amendments introduced from the floor. However, committee amendments themselves are subject to floor amendments. Both chambers vote on second-degree amendments before voting on first-degree amendments, although the precise order varies from chamber to chamber because of differing interpretations of the rules.

In Conference

Legislation cannot go to the president for his signature until both houses of Congress approve it in identical form. When the two houses pass different versions of a bill, they usually appoint a CONFERENCE COMMITTEE to resolve the differences.

Sometimes House and Senate conferees are unable to reach agreement on every difference in a bill sent to conference; such differences are referred to as "amendments in disagreement." Differences on which compromises are reached are incorporated in a conference report, on which each chamber votes as a whole. But amendments in disagreement must be resolved separately in each house once the conference report itself is adopted. The bill will fail unless both houses reach compromises on all amendments in disagreement or agree to drop them altogether.

Conferees generally are able to reach agreement, and Congress approves the bill. On occasion there are irreconcilable disagreements over content, but more frequently amendments are reported in disagreement because the rules of one chamber prohibit its conferees from accepting certain provisions added by the other house. That frequently occurs when the Senate adds nongermane amendments to House-passed legislation. House rules require that such amendments be considered and voted on separately by the full House.

Rules in both houses require conference committees to reach compromises within the bounds of the subject matter on which the House and Senate versions of a bill differ. If conferees go beyond those bounds, they may report an amendment in "technical disagreement." This commonly occurs when conferees exceed both the House- and Senate-passed funding levels for some program in an appropriations bill. In such cases, conferees draft an amendment recommending that the House and Senate concur in the agreed-upon amount. ~

Appeal

In both the Senate and House of Representatives, a member may challenge a parliamentary ruling of the PRESIDING OFFICER if he believes it violates the chamber's rules. Such a challenge is known as an appeal. A senator appeals to his fellow senators to overturn the presiding officer's decision; it can be overturned by majority vote. In the House, the ruling of the Speaker tradi-

tionally has been final, and members are seldom asked to reverse his stand— to appeal a ruling is considered an attack on the Speaker. The Senate is more likely to overturn the rulings of its chair, often on political grounds that have little to do with the parliamentary situation. ~

Appointment Power

The Constitution gives the Senate the right to confirm or reject presidential appointments to many government positions. Senators frequently have used this "advice and consent" power to press for their own political beliefs and assert Congress's independence from the executive branch.

Like the authority to approve or reject treaties, the right to review presidents' choices for jobs within the government is given only to the Senate. The House does not vote on presidential nominations, and members rarely have much influence in decisions about which people the president will appoint. (See TREATY RATIFICATION.)

Senators participate in the selection of Supreme Court justices, cabinet officers, ambassadors, and other high-level government officials. Only the president has the formal right to select someone to fill one of those positions. But the Senate has often used its power over the years to turn down presidential appointments and pressure the president into selecting people more to the liking of senators. In some cases, such as certain federal judgeships, senators traditionally have dictated the selection of nominees.

The Senate's decisions on presidential appointments, political scientist Hugh Heclo has written, "add up to a cumulative act of choice that may be at least as important as the electorate's single act of choice for president every four years."

In the vast majority of cases, however, the Senate's power over appointments is little more than a bureaucratic chore. Technically, all military promotions and many middle-level appointments within the civilian side of the government are subject to Senate approval. But the number of those appointments is so vast—nearly 40,000 in 1986—that senators can do little but routinely approve them.

In addition, the president's nominations even for many high-level positions normally are approved by the Senate with little debate or objection. Most senators believe, for example, that the president has a right to pick his own people for his cabinet, unless one of his choices has committed some illegal or highly unethical action or holds beliefs that are repugnant to most Americans. Only eight nominees for cabinet positions have ever been rejected by the Senate. A similar argument is often made about Supreme Court nominations—that the president, who was endorsed by the people in the last election, has the right to name a justice who agrees with his own legal philosophy. That argument has less force, however, because Supreme Court justices serve for life, rather than just the term of the incumbent president. There have been twenty-eight men whose nominations to the Supreme Court were rejected or dropped due to Senate opposition. *(See* COURTS AND CONGRESS.*)*

The effect of the Senate's power is seen most clearly in the small number of cases in which a nominee encounters substantial opposition. In many instances presidents or the nominees themselves will withdraw an appointment when it becomes clear that a large number of senators are prepared to vote against it. Such opposition may crystal-

Troubled Appointment

Few cabinet appointees encounter substantial opposition in the Senate. One who did was Edwin Meese III, attorney general in the Reagan administration. Concern over Meese's personal financial dealings led to a thirteen-month delay between his nomination and confirmation. Further controversy marked his tenure at the Justice Department.

lize during committee hearings on a nomination. Less often, presidents will continue to press their appointment even though it is clear that it faces possible defeat on the Senate floor. An outright rejection of an important nomination usually represents a major political setback for a president.

There are a number of reasons why the Senate rejects presidential appointments. Throughout the history of the United States, the Senate frequently has turned down nominees because of partisan political considerations. Another important cause for rejecting a nomination is because questions arise about the nominee's past record of personal conduct and ethics.

Presidents have one way to get around the Senate confirmation process, although it works only temporarily. The Constitution allows the president to fill vacant positions between sessions of Congress, when the Senate is not meeting. These "recess appointments" are allowed to stand until the completion of the Senate's next session.

History

Senatorial confirmation of executive appointments is a distinctly American practice. It was included in the Constitution as the result of a compromise. Some delegates to the Constitutional Convention favored giving the Senate the exclusive right to select people to fill key nonelected offices. Others argued that the president should have complete control of appointments. The compromise gave the president the power to choose nominees, subject to the approval of the Senate. The president "shall nominate, and by and with the Advice and Consent of the Senate shall appoint" officials, the Constitution states.

The Founding Fathers disagreed on the consequences of the compromise. Alexander Hamilton thought it was not especially important, because the Senate would have no power to select of-ficeholders independent of the president. But John Adams thought that the Senate's power would inevitably be used for partisan political purposes. Adams was quickly proved correct, during his own term as president. By 1800 it was firmly established that Senate approval of nominations would depend on political considerations.

Virtually every president in the succeeding two centuries would face difficult confirmation battles with the Senate. Presidents with solid political support in the Senate generally fared better than those who had to contend with a hostile Senate. But even strong chief executives sometimes were subjected to embarrassing defeats of their nominees.

In many cases the confirmation battles of the past seem relatively trivial, even if their political consequences were significant. In the 1870s, for example, Senate Republican leader Roscoe CONKLING resigned from the Senate as a result of a dispute with President James A. Garfield over appointments within the port of New York.

Other confirmation battles have been important events in the life of the nation. The long and bitter fight that led to the confirmation of Louis D. Brandeis to the Supreme Court in 1916 marked a crucial turning point in the direction of legal philosophy in the twentieth century.

Among all those many confirmation disputes, now mostly forgotten, two long-term trends are evident. One is the rise and decline of the president's PATRONAGE control over relatively minor but well-paying government positions. The other is the development of senators' power to control nominations that concerned their own states.

By 1820 the "spoils" system was solidly established in the awarding of government jobs. The term comes from the expression, "To the victor belong the spoils." This principle held that the party that had won the last presidential

SENATE REJECTIONS OF CABINET NOMINATIONS

Nominee	Position	President	Date	Vote
Roger B. Taney	Secretary of Treasury	Jackson	6/23/1834	18-28
Caleb Cushing	Secretary of Treasury	Tyler	3/3/1843	19-27
Caleb Cushing	Secretary of Treasury	Tyler	3/3/1843	10-27
Caleb Cushing	Secretary of Treasury	Tyler	3/3/1843	2-29
David Henshaw	Secretary of Navy	Tyler	1/15/1844	6-34
James M. Porter	Secretary of War	Tyler	1/30/1844	3-38
James S. Green	Secretary of Treasury	Tyler	6/15/1844	Not recorded
Henry Stanbery	Attorney General	Johnson	6/2/1868	11-29
Charles B. Warren	Attorney General	Coolidge	3/10/1925	39-41
Charles B. Warren	Attorney General	Coolidge	3/16/1925	39-46
Lewis L. Strauss	Secretary of Commerce	Eisenhower	6/19/1959	46-49

Source: Adapted from George H. Haynes, *The Senate of the United States: Its History and Practice.* 1938.

election had a right to put its own people in government offices, regardless of whether or not the previous officeholders were doing a good job. That rule still holds for top-level government offices such as those in the cabinet and their ranking subordinates. But in those days the principle of party control of government jobs extended to lesser positions. Jobs such as postmaster and collector of import duties at a port were highly sought after, and victorious political candidates made sure to reward their supporters by distributing them.

The Senate soon moved to take over its own share of the patronage bonanza. In 1820 it enacted a law limiting the terms of federal officials to four years. That produced constant turnover, which in turn gave senators much greater opportunities to give jobs to friends and relations. The forty-year period from 1837 to 1877 marked the high point of Senate efforts to control executive appointments. During this period the spoils system reached its peak and all presidents were subject to intense pressure for patronage appointments.

The excesses of the spoils system eventually became so serious that Con-gress began to limit political patronage. President Rutherford B. Hayes began to fight against the system in 1877, and by 1883 Congress established a civil-service system, which awarded most government jobs on the basis of merit.

A key element of the Senate's confirmation power was the idea of SENA-TORIAL COURTESY. This rule, which was first seen as early as 1789, provided that the Senate would refuse to confirm a nomination within a particular state unless the nominee had been approved by the senators of the president's party from that state. In practice, that meant that senators usually were allowed to select many officeholders directly—a power that they used to add to their political strength within their state. When neither of the senators from a state was of the president's party, that right was often given to House party members, or to local party officials. The tradition of senatorial courtesy declined in importance as more government jobs were made to be based on merit rather than patronage. But senators still exert a strong influence over certain federal judgeships and other offices within their states.

Politics and Ethics

In recent decades confirmation debates have tended to be less concerned with patronage than with questions about the political beliefs and personal ethics of nominees. These debates often revolve around a fundamental constitutional issue: Whether the advice and consent role of the Senate was intended to allow it to affect government policy, or only to provide a screen for weeding out unqualified or corrupt appointments. With regard to cabinet nominees, the prevailing sentiment appears to be that if an individual is shown to be honest and competent, then the president is entitled to name his choice without regard to policy positions or political ideology.

A differing view holds that senators can and should inquire into the policy intentions and commitments of a nominee before confirming him. Senators who disagree with a nominee's views may try to block the nomination. More often, critics will use the confirmation process to try to focus public attention on the nominee's views, or try to pressure the nominee into promising to do or not do something once in office.

Confirmation debates that center on political opinions most often involve appointments to independent government boards and commissions. These commissions, such as the Tennessee Valley Authority or the Federal Election Commission, are frequently seen as agents of Congress, and so rightfully subject to greater Senate intervention in nominations.

Arguments over political views also crop up in relation to major appointments, such as cabinet offices or the Supreme Court. Between 1933 and 1945 several of President Franklin D. Roosevelt's cabinet nominees faced vocal opposition because of their allegedly radical views, although all were confirmed. Roosevelt also won confirmation of Supreme Court nominee Hugo L. Black in 1937, despite charges linking Black, an Alabama senator, to the Ku Klux Klan.

President Richard Nixon, on the other hand, lost a Supreme Court confirmation fight in 1970 when it was revealed that nominee G. Harrold Carswell had once publicly endorsed the principle of racial segregation. Robert H. Bork, who was nominated to the Supreme Court in 1987 by President Ronald Reagan, lost his confirmation battle at least in part because a majority of senators believed that his judicial views on subjects such as civil rights and privacy were so conservative as to be outside the "mainstream" of American legal philosophy. (See COURTS AND CONGRESS.)

Far more than in earlier years, present-day nominees also are subject to searching inquiry about every aspect of their personal and professional lives. Sometimes seemingly minor indiscretions many years before are enough to disqualify a nominee to an important position. Reagan's second Supreme Court nominee in 1987, Douglas Ginsburg, was forced to withdraw his name after it was learned he had smoked marijuana some years before.

The issue of conflict of interest is an even more frequent topic of concern. Present-day nominees are expected to avoid all situations in which their official decisions could benefit their own personal interests, or in which they receive money from people who stand to benefit from their actions. The concern covers both situations in which the officeholder was actually abusing his government position, and those in which there was only an appearance of a conflict of interest.

Nominees with financial holdings that could be affected by their new jobs usually can solve any concerns by selling their holdings before taking office. But past incidents in which the nominee seemed to have had a conflict of interest can be more damaging. Nixon's 1970 appointment of Clement F. Haynsworth, Jr., to be a Supreme

Court justice was defeated because of charges that Haynsworth had failed in the past to demonstrate sensitivity to ethical questions and the appearance of a conflict of interest—even though critics conceded that he was not personally dishonest.

Sometimes investigations during the process can turn up information in time to prevent a questionable nominee from taking office. President Lyndon B. JOHNSON appointed Supreme Court Justice Abe Fortas to be chief justice in 1969. Critics were able to block the nomination, partly on the grounds that Fortas had accepted money from past business associates, one of whom had a son who was involved in a federal criminal case. The next year Fortas was forced to resign from the Court because of renewed controversy over his extrajudicial actions—the first time a Supreme Court justice had resigned under threat of impeachment.

At other times, though, the confirmation process may overlook potential problems posed by nominees of popular presidents. In 1977 President Jimmy Carter's nomination of Georgia business associate Bert Lance to be director of the Office of Management and Budget was approved after only brief consideration. Eight months later Lance had to resign because investigations revealed a strong pattern of questionable banking practices. The affair resulted in more searching inquiries into nominees' personal finances before they are approved.

The Lance affair and others like it highlight the dilemma that the confirmation process poses for the Senate. Senators are likely to face criticism for their actions on nominees regardless of whether they take an active or passive role in reviewing those put forward by the president. "If it [the Senate] is too assertive in applying what it collectively believes to be appropriate standards for presidential appointees, it is criticized for interfering with the president's right

to run the government," political scientist G. Calvin Mackenzie has written. "But if it is too deferential to the president, challenging only the very worst of his nominations, it is criticized for being a rubber stamp, for not effectively carrying out its responsibilities in the appointment process."   ∼

ADDITIONAL READINGS

Harris, Joseph R. *The Advice and Consent of the Senate: A Study of the Confirmation of Appointments by the United States Senate.* 1968.

Heclo, Hugh. *A Government of Strangers.* 1977.

Mackenzie, G. Calvin. *The Politics of Presidential Appointments.* 1981.

Appropriations Bills

One of Congress's most important duties each year is to pass bills appropriating money to operate government agencies and programs. The Constitution says money cannot be drawn from the U.S. Treasury "but in consequence of appropriations made by law." If Congress did not provide money in appropriations bills, the government would have to shut down. Indeed, brief shutdowns do occur from time to time when Congress fails to appropriate funds in timely fashion.

Appropriations bills provide legal authority to spend money previously approved in AUTHORIZATION BILLS, but they need not provide all of the money authorized. By custom, the House acts first on appropriations bills; the Senate revises the House version, although on occasion it has written its own separate measure.

For years Congress passed thirteen regular appropriations bills annually, in addition to one or more supplemental measures. But in the 1980s it became common to fold each of the thirteen individual measures into one huge bill—called a CONTINUING RESOLU-TION—that provided funding for all or nearly all of the federal government. *(See* BUDGET PROCESS.*)*   ~

Appropriations Committee, House

The House Appropriations Committee is the largest permanent committee in Congress, and one of the most powerful as well. Its members—fifty-seven in 1987—play a crucial role in the annual process by which Congress determines funding levels for government agencies and programs.

By custom, all spending bills begin in the House of Representatives. The job of the Appropriations Committee is to write the first versions of the regular appropriations bills each year, as well as any emergency funding measures that may be required.

Because it is the starting point in the appropriations process, the House committee has an unusual degree of influence over Congress's final spending decisions. The full House normally accepts the funding levels proposed by the committee for most programs. The Senate may challenge the House spending levels for a few highly visible programs, but it generally does not attempt to rewrite the whole bill. As a result, Congress's final decisions about federal government spending for individual activities frequently are identical to those amounts first proposed by the House Appropriations Committee. The bulk of the spending decisions made by Congress are made in this committee.

The Appropriations Committee has lost some of its influence since the 1970s. The congressional BUDGET PROCESS now limits the freedom of the Appropriations Committee to set

spending levels. Moreover, an increasing share of the federal budget is consumed by entitlement programs, such as Social Security, which the government is legally required to pay for completely. The Appropriations Committee has little or no ability to alter the amounts required for entitlement programs. *(See* BUDGET PROCESS.*)*

One development in the 1980s has helped to shore up the committee's power to make decisions, however. This is the practice of bundling appropriations for most or all federal agencies into a single omnibus bill, known as a CONTINUING RESOLUTION. These comprehensive spending bills usually are passed toward the end of a congressional session in an atmosphere of haste and pressure. As a result, many of the committee's funding decisions go unchallenged at subsequent stages in the LEGISLATIVE PROCESS. In addition, committee members are often able to slip controversial items through with little or no attention or opposition.

Service on the Appropriations Committee continues to be one of the most sought-after positions for House members. Representatives lobby vigorously to be appointed to the committee, and only those who have the backing of important House leaders or strong regional support are likely to gain a seat there. Members who win a spot on the panel give up their chance to participate in the shaping of new government activities, since the Appropriations Committee does not have the power to prepare legislation establishing government programs. Instead, members get an opportunity to steer funds to activities that are important to themselves or their constituents.

Just as the full House defers to the committee on most spending issues, so too the full Appropriations Committee looks to its subcommittees to make most of the important decisions. The recommendations of the Appropriations subcommittees—one for each of the

Dollar Power
The bulk of the spending decisions made by Congress are made in the House Appropriations Committee. Committee members meet in this crowded room to consider funding requests of government agencies.

customary thirteen annual spending bills—are normally accepted without change by the full committee.

It is in the subcommittees that the real work of the Appropriations Committee is done. Subcommittee members each year listen to many hours of testimony from government officials, who come to explain the dollar amounts requested for their agencies in the federal government's budget as prepared by the president. Subcommittee members then meet, usually in private session, to go over programs line by line and decide the exact dollar amounts to be given to each.

Because they follow the activities of the agencies under their jurisdiction closely, year after year, subcommittee members often acquire extraordinary knowledge about and power over government programs. When Rep. Jamie L. Whitten became chairman of the full Appropriations Committee in 1979, he retained his chairmanship of the panel's agriculture subcommittee, which he had headed since 1949. The Mississippi Democrat was often referred to as the "permanent secretary of agriculture," because his influence went on and on while the real secretaries of agriculture came and went.

History

Until the Civil War, spending matters were considered along with tax legislation in the House WAYS AND MEANS COMMITTEE. Overseeing both revenues and spending became too large a task for one committee, however, and the Appropriations Committee was established in 1865.

The spending panel quickly assumed a large amount of power. Under Chairman Samuel J. Randall, D-Pa., the Appropriations Committee became the object of hostility from other members, who thought it displayed an excessively tight-fisted approach to spending. That resentment fostered a move to curb the committee's power. House members voted to take away the panel's jurisdiction over a number of government programs, including defense, river and harbor projects, agriculture, and the Post Office. By 1885 the committee had lost control over half the federal budget.

But dispersal of spending power to several different committees frustrated efforts to establish unified control over government budget policy. In order to centralize spending power, the House in 1920 restored to the Appropriations Committee the exclusive right to approve appropriations bills.

Appropriations Committee members took on more power and independence in the decades that followed. Committee members frequently were able to win reelection easily year after year. Because of their long years of service, the SENIORITY SYSTEM placed them in positions of power, as chairmen of the committee and key subcommittees, where they became politically entrenched. As a result, they were able to pursue their own goals with little interference from the House leadership. Committee meetings were almost always held in secret, and even the records of hearings were usually withheld from outsiders until shortly before the appropriations bill came to the floor. Consequently, few members who were not on the subcommittee were in a position to challenge the bill. Two of the most powerful committee chairmen of this period were Clarence CANNON of Missouri, chairman for most of the period between 1949 and 1964, and George H. Mahon of Texas, who held the post from 1964 to 1979.

House leaders took some steps during the 1970s to curb the autonomy of Appropriations. The Legislative Reorganization Act of 1970 led to the opening to the public of most Appropriations subcommittee hearings, although many bill-drafting sessions remain closed to the public. In 1971 the seniority system was attacked and changed by many younger and more recently elected House members, who wanted to share in the power then concentrated in the hands of their more senior colleagues. One major change allowed committee and subcommittee chairmen to be selected without regard to seniority. *(See* REFORM.*)*

In 1975 the Democrats, who were in the majority, emphasized the importance of the Appropriations subcommittees by requiring that the chairmen of those panels, like the chairmen of full committees, be elected by a secret vote of all House Democrats. This raised the threat that a senior chairman might lose his job by being voted out of the position by colleagues. That, in turn, tended to make chairmen more responsive to the needs and interests of other House members, including the elected party leadership. Another Democratic party action that year also was aimed at Appropriations. A rule barring members from serving on more than two subcommittees was intended to prevent senior Appropriations Committee members from monopolizing key positions. ~

Appropriations Committee, Senate

The Senate Appropriations Committee is the largest committee in the Senate, and one of the most important. But its role in the Senate is not as significant as that played by the House Appropriations Committee in the House. For decades the Senate Appropriations Committee existed in the shadow of its more powerful House counterpart. *(See* APPROPRIATIONS COMMITTEE, HOUSE.*)*

Like the House panel, the Senate committee is responsible for preparing the annual bills that provide money for federal government agencies. Committee members—twenty-nine in the 100th Congress (1987-89)—review executive branch spending proposals and can recommend to the full Senate changes in the amounts requested for various programs. A longstanding unwritten rule in Congress requires that the House be the first chamber to act on these annual spending bills, which are called APPROPRIATIONS.

The Senate Appropriations Committee normally takes up a spending bill only after it has passed the House, although preliminary subcommittee work on the bills often begins earlier. Instead of writing a bill from scratch, as the House committee does, Senate committee members usually find themselves in the position of reacting to a completed bill that has already been approved by the House. As a result, Senate members are more likely to allow the bulk of the House bill to go through unchanged, while focusing their attention on increasing or reducing funding for a few highly visible programs.

For many years, the Senate committee operated largely as a "court of appeals." Supporters of programs whose funding had been cut by the House would try to lobby Senate committee members to restore some or all of the money. Senators frequently sought to increase funding levels approved by the House, but they rarely proposed funding reductions.

The heavy and diverse workloads of senators frequently put the Senate Appropriations Committee at a disadvantage in dealing with the House spending panel. Senate committee members served on one or two other major committees in addition to Appropriations, while House Appropriations members served only on that committee. The consequence was that senators often did not have the time to master the details of spending bills in the way

that House committee members did.

In the 1980s, however, Senate committee members sought to strengthen their role. Members worked to bring cohesion to their committee, and to establish a more unified stance in CONFERENCE COMMITTEE negotiations with the House. On some occasions, the Senate committee even formally finished work on appropriations bills before the House had passed its own versions of the measures. The Senate committee also became a key arena for debate over a number of important issues, such as the Reagan administration's requests for funding of the contra rebels fighting the leftist government of Nicaragua.

The Appropriations Committee also fought for flexibility in setting spending levels for different programs, even if they exceeded limits set by other committees that had responsibility for establishing policy. One of the most vocal of these disputes was between Ted Stevens of Alaska, chairman of the Defense Appropriations Subcommittee, and Armed Services Committee Chairman John Tower of Texas. The two chairmen, both Republicans, waged several floor battles in the early 1980s over Stevens's efforts to appropriate more money for certain defense programs than the Armed Services Committee wanted to allow.   ~

Armed Services Committee, House

The House Armed Services Committee has jurisdiction over most aspects of U.S. national defense. Along with its Senate counterpart, the House committee each year prepares the two bills that set the upper limits on how much the Defense Department can spend for weapons, manpower, and military facilities.

The massive size of the defense

Weapons Power
The House and Senate Armed Services committees are the central arena for debate on arms
control and the defense budget. Committee
members spend much of their time reviewing
Defense Department requests for funding of
military programs. The House committee holds
hearings in this imposing room.

budget—some $300 billion in 1986, or
about 60 percent of all federal spending
that is reviewed through the appropriations process—makes Armed Services
one of the most important and powerful
committees in the House. Members
spend much of their time reviewing requests for funding of new and existing
weapons programs submitted by military and civilian officials in the Pentagon. As a result, the committee plays a
key role in determining the size,
strength, and fighting ability of the nation's armed forces.

The two bills reported by the committee each year are the defense authorization bill, which covers most military programs, and the much smaller
military construction bill, which funds
the building of new facilities on military
bases. Together, the two bills cover
about 75 percent of defense spending.
Pay levels and fringe benefits for military personnel, which are determined
by separate legislation, comprise the
remaining 25 percent of the defense
budget.

The committee does not have complete control over spending for defense.

The BUDGET COMMITTEE sets an overall
limit on the amount of money available
for defense each year, and the APPRO-
PRIATIONS COMMITTEE determines the
exact dollar amounts for individual defense programs. But the Armed Services Committee plays the most important role in determining how the money
will be spent.

The committee is also a significant
arena for debate over issues of strategic
defense, particularly those involving
nuclear weapons. In the 1980s committee members were deeply involved in
controversies over nuclear arms control
and President Ronald Reagan's proposals for new nuclear missiles.

The members of Armed Services
traditionally have been characterized
by a conservative, strongly prodefense
orientation. Both Democratic and Republican members worked closely over
the years with Pentagon officials and
supported their budget requests, sometimes at levels considerably higher than
those favored by a majority of the
House. As a result, there has been a
strongly bipartisan atmosphere on the
committee. It does not have separate

majority and minority staff members, as most other committees do.

History

The roots of the Armed Services Committee stretch back to the creation of the Military and Naval Affairs committees in 1822. But the modern history of the committee begins in the years after World War II, about the time that the unified Department of Defense was created. The committee itself was created by the Legislative Reorganization Act of 1946 out of the combination of the Military and Naval Affairs committees.

For more than three decades the committee was dominated by a solid core of conservative southern Democrats and Republicans, who ensured that the annual defense bills closely followed Pentagon recommendations. At the helm of the committee were a succession of powerful southern Democrats, who ran its business with an iron hand.

The first of the autocratic chairmen was Carl Vinson, a Georgia Democrat who controlled the committee from 1949 to 1965, except for 1953 to 1955, when Republican Dewey Short of Missouri was chairman. Next came South Carolina Democrat L. Mendel Rivers (1965-71), who was frequently accused of running the committee as his personal domain, dictating its agenda and rarely allowing junior members to play a significant role. Rivers worked hard to steer Pentagon spending projects, such as military bases and defense contracts, to South Carolina. Cynics said he was so successful that the entire state would sink into the ocean if another military base was established there. Rivers's strenuous efforts to bring job-creating military bases and contracts to his home state were typical of the concerns of many committee members during this period.

Major changes in the committee began to occur in the 1970s. One new factor was the arrival on the committee of a small number of liberal Democrats. These Democrats, who were strongly opposed to U.S. military involvement in Vietnam, soon became vocal critics of the committee's prodefense majority. Members such as Les Aspin of Wisconsin and Patricia Schroeder of Colorado used their committee positions to highlight their attacks on what they saw as wasteful and excessive military spending. But they were overwhelmingly outnumbered on the committee and rarely had the strength to influence committee decisions.

The other factor that began to affect the committee in the 1970s was the Housewide attack on the SENIORITY SYSTEM. Reform-minded Democrats sought at this time to replace the existing method of selecting committee chairmen according to length of service with one based on elections within the House Democratic Caucus. The Armed Services chairman at the time, F. Edward Hébert of Louisiana, was one of the prime targets of reformers. The House Democratic Caucus, the organization of party members, deposed Hébert in 1975, replacing him with seventy-year-old Melvin Price of Illinois.

Price chaired the committee for the next decade. During that time, the committee prepared legislation authorizing the massive buildup in military spending sought by President Reagan in the early 1980s. But Price was not a strong chairman. Many of his colleagues saw him as too aged and infirm to run the committee effectively. At the same time, the small group of liberals on the committee was slowly gaining influence.

The turning point in the history of the Armed Services Committee came in 1985. Arguing that the committee needed more effective leadership, Aspin challenged Price. Price was supported strongly by the House Democratic leadership but was defeated by widespread doubts among members about his continued ability to manage the committee as chairman. In a highly unusual move, the Democratic Caucus chose as his replacement Aspin, who jumped over five more senior Democrats to become chairman.

Aspin's tenure was not a smooth one. In the 99th Congress (1985-87), he angered many of the liberal Democrats who had initially supported him by supporting some of Reagan's key defense proposals. Early in 1987, Aspin was initially ousted as chairman by the caucus. However, he fought back and later won reelection over three opponents.

By the 100th Congress (1987-89), the Armed Services Committee was significantly different from what it had been twenty years before. The majority of the committee remained considerably more favorable to defense spending than many other House members, particularly Democrats. Liberal members remained in the minority. But the balance of power had shifted to a group of centrist Democrats who espoused "military reform" ideas. While strongly in favor of defense, these members showed skepticism about the value of many of the weapons sought by the Defense Department. Their approach was summed up by one of their members, John M. Spratt, Jr., of South Carolina: "Our role is to be defense advocates, but not Department of Defense advocates." 〜

Armed Services Committee, Senate

Like its House counterpart, the Senate Armed Services Committee has responsibility for most aspects of U.S. national defense. Because it has authority over the vast array of Defense Department programs, the committee usually is considered to be among the most influential committees in the Senate. *(See* ARMED SERVICES COMMITTEE, HOUSE.)

The work of the Armed Services Committee revolves around the annual Defense Department authorization and military construction authorization bills. These measures must be reported and passed each year to give the Defense Department authority to spend money. Once they are passed, Congress may approve appropriations bills for purchase of weapons, military operations, and construction of military facilities.

The Senate committee resembles House Armed Services in many ways. Not only are the jurisdictions of the two committees the same, but also they have a similar political approach to defense issues. The Senate committee historically has had a prodefense majority, which has tended to give strong support to Pentagon requests for funding of proposed new weapons systems.

Senate Armed Services also has faced challenges to its authority over defense spending similar to those that confronted the House committee in the 1970s and 1980s. The development of the congressional BUDGET PROCESS and a new attitude of assertiveness on the part of the APPROPRIATIONS Committee both posed threats to the Armed Services panel's control over the amount of money available for defense spending.

However, Senate Armed Services has not normally faced the kind of political problems that frequently plagued its House counterpart during the 1970s and 1980s. Senate committee members generally proposed defense policies and spending levels that enjoyed broad support in the Senate—a marked contrast with the House, where Armed Services Committee proposals often were opposed by a majority of Democrats in the whole House.

History
Since its creation by the Legislative Reorganization Act of 1946, the Senate Armed Services Committee has frequently been controlled by a strong

Influential Chairman
The Senate Armed Services Committee has frequently been controlled by a strong chairman who put his imprint on defense policy. Sen. Sam Nunn, a Georgia Democrat, had great influence on defense issues even before he became chairman of the committee in 1987.

chairman who has put his personal imprint on Senate defense policy. The first and most powerful of these was Richard B. RUSSELL, a Georgia Democrat who ran the committee for a total of sixteen years, from 1951 to 1953 and then again from 1955 to 1969.

Russell, whose Senate career had begun in 1933, was one of the most powerful senators, and a dominant force on defense policy for nearly two decades. He towered over Senate debates on defense bills, both because of his mastery of defense issues and the immense respect his colleagues had for him. He was rarely challenged either in the committee or on the Senate floor. His control of defense topics became even more firm in the 1960s, when he also became chairman of the Appropriations Committee's Defense Subcommittee.

Russell's successor, Mississippi Democrat John C. STENNIS, also wielded considerable influence, because he chaired both Armed Services and the defense spending subcommittee. Despite the personal admiration many senators felt for him, however, Stennis did not dominate defense debates the way Russell had. Another committee member, Washington Democrat Henry M. Jackson, was widely viewed as the Democrats' defense expert. His knowledge of defense issues and advocacy of a strong defense posture made him a major force in the Senate and a leader among the section of the Democratic party that favored a tough stance toward the Soviet Union.

Republican Chairmen
The GOP takeover of the Senate in 1981 put Texas Republican John Tower in the Armed Services chair. Tower, a strong-willed negotiator who favored a hard line toward the Soviets, played a critical role in guiding President Ronald Reagan's massive defense buildup through the Senate in the early 1980s. Later, when enthusiasm for defense increases cooled, Tower was a key force in protecting Pentagon spending requests from budget cuts. He was followed for two years (1985-87) by Arizona Republican Barry M. Goldwater, a blunt-spoken conservative who had been the GOP nominee for president in 1964.

Nunn Influence

Sam Nunn, who took over Armed Services in 1987, was a chairman in the Russell tradition. Nunn, also a Georgia Democrat, was universally recognized as the most knowledgeable senator on defense issues even before he became chairman. His expertise on both broad strategic questions and technical defense matters made him the Senate's dominant force on defense issues in the late 1980s.   ∼

Army-McCarthy Hearings.   See
McCARTHY, JOSEPH R.

At-Large Representative.   See
HOUSE OF REPRESENTATIVES.

Authorization Bills

Congress passes authorization bills to determine which programs and agencies the federal government is allowed to operate. Authorization bills may create legal authority for new programs or continue the operation of existing ones, either indefinitely or for a specific period of time. Some authorizations set a ceiling on the amount of money that may be appropriated for the programs; others simply permit the appropriation of "such sums as may be necessary." Authorization bills do not themselves provide money; that requires separate action through the appropriations process. Congressional rules stipulate that programs must be authorized before money can be appropriated for them, but the requirement is often waived. *(See* APPROPRIATIONS BILLS.*)*   ∼

Overleaf:
Capitol corridor.

Baker, Howard H., Jr.

Howard H. Baker, Jr. (1925-), who retired from the Senate in 1985, was a Republican senator from Tennessee for eighteen years and majority leader for four. Defeated in his first campaign for the Senate in 1964, Baker ran again and won in 1966, becoming the first popularly elected Republican senator from Tennessee. Baker had strong roots in Congress. Both of his parents served in the House of Representatives, and his father-in-law, Everett McKinley DIRKSEN, was minority leader of the Senate.

Baker first gained national prominence in 1973 for his participation in Senate hearings on the WATERGATE SCANDAL. Disclosure of administration efforts to cover up political sabotage in the Watergate affair ultimately drove President Richard NIXON out of office. As vice chairman of the Select Committee on Presidential Campaign Activities, Baker impressed his colleagues and the country at large with his calm and measured approach. His recurrent question of witnesses—"What did the president know, and when did he know it?" —entered the language.

In 1977, after a last-minute campaign and by a slim margin, Baker was elected Senate minority leader. He became majority leader in 1981, after Ronald Reagan was elected president and Republicans won control of the

27

Senate. Despite some philosophical differences with the president, Baker decided that he would become, in his own words, Reagan's "spear-carrier in the Senate." It was a role he played faithfully during his four years as majority leader. Baker's style was relaxed and effective. Under his leadership, the Republicans in the Senate became a cohesive voting bloc that handed Reagan significant tax and budget victories. As majority leader, he also played a major part in the Senate's decision to allow television coverage of Senate floor proceedings.

In 1984, saying "eighteen years is enough," Baker announced that he would retire from the Senate to practice law. He had run unsuccessfully for the Republican presidential nomination in 1980 and was widely expected to try again in 1988. But in February 1987, under pressure in the IRAN-CONTRA arms sales controversy, President Reagan asked Baker to become White House chief of staff. In accepting the appointment, Baker removed himself from the 1988 presidential contest. ~

Banking, Finance, and Urban Affairs Committee, House

The House Banking Committee focuses primarily on the rapidly changing financial world, spending little time on the urban problems that dominated its agenda in the 1960s. Responsible for regulation of the complex U.S. financial system, the House Committee on Banking, Finance, and Urban Affairs has had to adjust the rules in response to the now global world of finance.

The committee, usually about fifty members strong, deals with a wide range of authorizing legislation, from the Export-Import Bank to rehabilitation of rental housing, and it shares responsibility for overseeing interna-

tional trade. Troubles in the savings and loan industry, questions about high interest rates, and worries about bank mergers were some of the problems that faced the committee in the 1980s. The Banking Committee rarely approves major legislation, but when it does the bills are always complicated and guaranteed to catch members in the crossfire of special interests. Few members enjoy choosing between banks and securities companies, for example.

For years the major question before the committee was how to respond to revolutionary changes in the financial industry. When money-market funds offered high interest rates in the 1970s, banks had to wait for permission to compete. New computer technologies made interstate banking attractive, but federal rules kept banks from competing across state lines. Then corporations such as Sears, Roebuck, and Co. began to take deposits and offer bank services—eroding territory banks once had to themselves.

Banks argued they were hindered by Depression-era laws crafted to insulate the banking system from the more volatile world of stock trading and land transactions. They wanted the rules changed so that they could compete in the insurance, real estate, and securities businesses, arenas closed to them since the 1930s. At the same time, though, banks were failing in the 1980s in numbers unmatched since the 1930s. The congressional debate centered on how to free the banks to compete without threatening the soundness of the financial system.

The Banking Committee's other role, as monitor of urban affairs, has received little attention since the 1970s. Once sought after by liberal, big city legislators, and still popular among representatives from New York City, the committee in the 1980s drew moderates whose districts serve as regional banking centers. Despite the higher visibility of banking questions, though, the com-

Competitive Pressure
Proposals to overhaul the nation's banking system preoccupied the House and Senate Banking Committees in the 1980s. Banks sought relief from Depression-era laws that prevented them from competing in the insurance, real estate, and securities businesses. These fields had been closed to them since the 1930s.

mittee continued to advocate public housing. That role was particularly critical when the Republican-controlled Senate and the Reagan administration teamed up against funding for federal housing programs in the 1980s. House Banking Chairman Fernand J. St Germain, a Rhode Island Democrat, managed to thwart that coalition in 1983 by holding hostage another committee bill, dealing with the International Monetary Fund, which President Ronald Reagan wanted. Eventually St Germain prevailed.

Reagan and Jake Garn, the Utah Republican who chaired the Senate committee, also shared a desire to deregulate banks and allow them to enter the securities field. But St Germain wanted to keep a government handle on financial institutions. The result was a years-long stalemate.

History

Since its establishment in 1865, when the overloaded Ways and Means Committee was split into three parts, the Banking Committee has never matched the standing of Ways and Means or the other committee set up then, Appropriations. The panel was called Banking and Currency until 1975, when the word Housing was added. In 1977 it was renamed Banking, Finance, and Urban Affairs.

Wright Patman, the feisty Texan who chaired the panel from 1963 to 1975, was a consummate populist who used Banking as a pulpit to attack Federal Reserve Board restraints on credit. Patman ran the committee with a firm, autocratic fist until age made it difficult for him to keep the fractious panel in line. In 1975, when he was eighty-two years old, Patman was one of three chairmen ousted by the Democratic Caucus after a loosening of SENIORITY rules.

The next chairman, Wisconsin Democrat Henry Reuss, had an almost academic interest in both banking and urban affairs, spotlighting the latter with a special Subcommittee on the City. Reuss lacked political skills, however. He had trouble with the back-room bargaining needed to pass legislation, and he suffered some embarrassing floor defeats.

After Reuss stepped down for health reasons in 1980, the top post went to St Germain, who since 1971 had chaired the preeminent Banking subcommittee, on financial institutions. St Germain, considered to be politically shrewd, held on to the subcommittee chairmanship. The power play was typical of St Germain, who relished being able to orchestrate the committee's every move and seldom shared his plans.

Though always careful to speak for the consumer, St Germain was criticized for his close financial ties with the banking and housing industries. The House ethics panel in 1987 absolved him of allegations that he grew rich through abuse of his office. He was found to have violated financial disclosure rules, but no disciplinary action was recommended.   ~

Banking, Housing, and Urban Affairs Committee, Senate

Watching over the nation's banking industry is the chief responsibility of the Senate Committee on Banking, Housing, and Urban Affairs. The committee is responsible for legislation dealing with regulation of the U.S. financial system. The Federal Reserve System, the comptroller of the currency, the Federal Deposit Insurance Corporation, and the Federal Savings and Loan Insurance Corporation fall within its purview. The Banking Committee also shares oversight of international economic policy, including foreign trade.

Like the House Banking Committee, the Senate committee has spent less time since the 1970s on housing and urban questions. Federal spending in those areas was cut under the Reagan administration, and budget constraints left little hope of future expansion. Problems of the nation's largest cities, once a major congressional concern, were not a high priority.

While Republicans controlled the Senate, Banking Chairman Jake Garn of Utah led the fight for a massive overhaul of banking regulation, which dated

from the 1930s. The challenge was to make banks more competitive with money-market funds and other non-banking firms without sacrificing the safeguards that had been built into the system.

Banking is considered a second-tier committee, less sought after than Finance or Appropriations, for example. Most of its legislative business is handled in the full committee, instead of in subcommittees.

History

Probably the senator best known for drafting banking legislation was Virginia Democrat Carter Glass, coauthor of one of the major 1933 banking laws, the Glass-Steagall Act, which prohibited banks in the Federal Reserve System from selling stocks and bonds. Glass, who chaired a key Senate Banking subcommittee, also played a major role in creation of the Securities and Exchange Commission in 1934. A senator from 1920 until his death in 1946, Glass had previously served in the House; as chairman of the House Banking Committee, he helped establish the Federal Reserve System in 1913. That was the same year the Senate set up its Banking and Currency Committee. Like the House, the Senate changed its banking committee's name in the 1970s to reflect its role in housing and urban affairs.

William Proxmire, an independent-minded Wisconsin Democrat, chaired the Banking Committee in 1975-81 and 1987-89. Garn held the post during the intervening years, when Republicans controlled the Senate.   ~

Barkley, Alben W.

As majority leader of the Senate from 1937 to 1947, Alben W. Barkley (1877-1956) played an important role in the passage of President Franklin D. Roosevelt's NEW DEAL legislation. Barkley was a supporter of Roosevelt, but not blindly loyal, and on occasion he differed vehemently and publicly with the president.

Barkley began his career in Congress in 1912 when he was elected as a Democrat to represent Kentucky's First District. After seven terms in the House of Representatives, he was elected to the Senate in 1926, and there he spent the remainder of his congressional career.

In 1937, upon the death of Majority Leader Joseph T. Robinson of Arkansas, Barkley embarked on a hard-fought campaign to succeed him. He defeated his rival for the post, Pat Harrison of Mississippi, but the battle brought to the surface deep rifts in the party between conservative southerners and New Deal Democrats. Barkley's margin of victory was narrow—one vote—and his success was attributed to a perception that Roosevelt favored his candidacy. The division among the Senate Democrats, once revealed during the contest for majority leader, contributed to the subsequent defeat of some of Roosevelt's domestic initiatives, most notably his attempt to increase the number of justices on the Supreme Court.

As majority leader, Barkley loyally supported Roosevelt's policies and served as a spokesman for the president in his relations with Congress. In the fall of 1938, at Roosevelt's request, Barkley agreed to punish senators who worked to defeat FDR's court-packing scheme. But he was tried too far by Roosevelt's veto of a tax bill in 1944. Incensed by the unprecedented veto of a revenue bill, Barkley spoke forcefully against the president on the floor of the Senate. Calling the veto "a calculated and deliberate assault upon the legislative integrity of every member of Congress," Barkley said: "Other members of Congress may do as they please, but as

for me, I do not propose to take this unjustifiable assault lying down. . . . I dare say that during the last seven years of tenure as majority leader, I have carried the flag over rougher territory than ever traversed by any previous majority leader. Sometimes I have carried it with little help from the other end of Pennsylvania Avenue." Barkley promptly resigned as majority leader and was just as promptly reelected by a unanimous vote of the Senate Democrats.

In 1948 President Harry S Truman persuaded Barkley to leave the Senate and run for election as his vice president. A popular public figure, Barkley soon became known affectionately as "the Veep." After serving one term as vice president, Barkley was reelected to the Senate in 1954. A campaigner to the end, he died while making a political speech in 1956.   ~

Bells, Legislative

Business on Capitol Hill is often interrupted by the jarring noise of bells that signal a floor vote in the House or Senate. Committee hearings and bill-drafting sessions stop while representatives and senators listen to the signal; even the congressional handball court is equipped with a buzzer.

New members quickly learn that one ring has a different meaning from three—or five. Fast walkers can wait until the last minute to leave their office building for a vote, but others respond to the first warning. Usually a fifteen-minute period is set aside for votes, and slow-moving legislators need every minute to reach the Capitol, even with underground subways to speed their trip.

When five bells ring, that means only a few minutes remain on a recorded vote, and members race for the floor. Every policeman, doorman, and

Rushing to Vote
Congress uses a bell system to notify members when floor votes are about to occur. Capitol police and other staff members help clear the way for senators and representatives on their way to vote.

elevator operator helps clear the way for senators and representatives on their way to vote.

The system of legislative bells has been operating in Congress for decades, with a record of wiring for buzzers as early as 1912. Many legislators have now supplemented the buzzers with beepers and portable telephones. Neighborhood restaurants, which once rang dinner bells or buzzers to signal a vote, have mostly abandoned the practice.   ~

Benton, Thomas Hart

Thomas Hart Benton (1782-1858) served as one of Missouri's first senators upon its admission to the Union. A man of strongly held opinions and a colorful past, Benton represented western agrarian interests and championed equality of opportunity at a time when western expansion and the issue of slav-

ery preoccupied the Senate.

Benton was editor of the St. Louis *Enquirer* when he was elected as a Democrat to the Senate in 1821. A spokesman for popular democracy, he supported western expansion and the availability of cheap land. He led the fight in the Senate against rechartering the Bank of the United States; the bank, a private corporation, engaged in commercial banking activities as well as issuing currency and serving as official depository for federal funds. He opposed the use of paper currency and thereby acquired the nickname "Old Bullion."

Benton supported Andrew Jackson's unsuccessful bid for the presidency in 1824, even though he and Jackson had fallen out some years earlier. Benton had served on Jackson's staff during the War of 1812, but their friendship had ended in a brawl in which Jackson had attacked Benton with a horsewhip and had himself been shot in the shoulder. When Jackson won the presidency in 1828, however,

Benton became one of his most valuable supporters in the Senate. Jackson's withdrawal of government funds from the Bank of the United States led the Senate to censure him in 1834; Benton led a successful fight to expunge the censure resolution from the Senate *Journal.*

Although Benton himself owned slaves, he believed that economic influences, aided by the country's geographical expansion, would ultimately destroy the system. To this end, he supported new western states' constitutions barring slavery. During the heated debate on the floor of the Senate over the Compromise of 1850—which brought California into the Union as a free state— Benton so enraged Mississippi Sen. Harry S. Foote that Foote threatened him with a cocked pistol.

Benton's belief that slavery had reached its geographical limits, coupled with the expansion of business interests in Missouri that were unsympathetic to his populist ideals, caused him to lose his Senate seat in 1851. He later served

Thomas Hart Benton

one term in the House (1853-55) but was defeated for reelection over his opposition to the Kansas-Nebraska bill, which allowed settlers in those territories to decide whether or not they wanted slavery there.   ∼

Beveridge, Albert J.

Albert J. Beveridge (1862-1927), an Indiana Republican, entered the Senate in 1899. As a freshman senator, he pledged his support to the ruling Republican clique led by Nelson W. AL-DRICH of Rhode Island and William B. ALLISON of Iowa. Soon, however, Beveridge became one of a small group of Republicans who supported the policies of President Theodore Roosevelt and opposed the more conservative views espoused by powerful Senate Republicans.

Beveridge left the practice of law in Indiana to enter the Senate. Aware that Allison had absolute control over committee assignments, the new senator sent him a list of preferred committees with a statement of loyalty: "I feel that the greatest single point is gained in the possession of your friendship. I will labor very hard, strive very earnestly to deserve your consideration."

That loyalty was short-lived. When Roosevelt became president in 1901, Beveridge found a Republican leader more to his liking. Against the pressure of the majority of his Republican colleagues, Beveridge became an enthusiastic and vocal advocate of a strong federal government and the kind of domestic policies that were labeled "progressive."

Beveridge failed to win reelection in 1910. In 1912 he served as chairman and keynote speaker at the Progressive national convention, which nominated Roosevelt as its presidential candidate. Beveridge ran unsuccessfully for governor of Indiana and twice again for his Senate seat. He received the Pulitzer prize in 1920 for his *Life of John Marshall.*   ~

Bill.   See LEGISLATION.

Blacks in Congress

Blacks were shut out of Congress for most of its history. Except during the post-Civil War RECONSTRUCTION period, black faces in Congress were extremely rare until the 1960s and 1970s, when civil rights legislation and voting rights laws gave blacks a greater political voice. A record number of blacks were elected to the 100th Congress (1987-89); it had twenty-three black representatives, including several committee chairmen. *(List, p. 489)*

No longer on the fringes of the establishment, veteran black leaders also held spots on the most powerful House committees. A black, William H. GRAY III chaired the House Budget Committee, one of the most difficult and most visible posts in the House. Numerically, though, blacks were still underrepresented; they constituted 11 percent of the voting-age population but held only about 5 percent of seats in the House. Most blacks represented districts with a majority of black voters. No black sat in the Senate, where only one black senator, Massachusetts Republican Edward Brooke (1967-79), had served in the twentieth century.

Background

The first black member of Congress, Mississippi Republican Hiram R. Revels, entered the Senate in 1870. From 1870 through the opening of the 100th Congress in 1987, three black senators and fifty-nine black representatives served in Congress. The twenty-two blacks who served in the nineteenth century were all Republicans, the party that led the emancipation of slaves. In the twentieth century all but two black legislators were Democrats.

The key to election of blacks after the Civil War was that southern states were not allowed to reenter the Union until they had enfranchised black voters. The Fifteenth Amendment to the Constitution, adopted in 1870, barred states from denying voting rights on the basis of race. Sixteen of the twenty-two blacks who served in the nineteenth century were elected in the 1870s, primarily from the South, where most blacks lived. As federal troops were withdrawn, though, southern states began to erode black voting rights. By the end of the century, literacy tests, poll taxes, and other devices designed primarily to prevent blacks from voting had been effective. Between 1901 and 1929 no blacks sat in Congress.

The long period without a black in Congress ended when Chicago's South Side sent Republican Oscar DePriest to the House in 1929. The same Chicago area continued to provide Congress with its sole black legislator—DePriest and two successors—until 1945, when the Chicago envoy was joined by Democrat Adam Clayton POWELL, Jr., from New York City's Harlem. Powell, a flamboyant personality, chaired the Education and Labor Committee from 1961 until 1967 when the House stripped him of the post after finding he misused committee funds.

Another watershed in black politics came in 1965, when Congress approved the Voting Rights Act, an aggressive move to end literacy tests and other requirements that kept blacks off voter registration lists in the South. The Supreme Court had also boosted black influence in 1964, when it endorsed the principle of "one person, one vote." Eventually that decision ended the practice in southern states of diluting black voting power by drawing district

Entered according to act of Congress in the year 1872 by Turner & Ives in the Office of the Librarian of Congress at Washington
ROBERT C. DE LARGE, M.C. of S.Carolina.   JEFFERSON H. LONG, M.C. of Georgia
US. Senator H.R.REVELS of Mississippi   BENJ.S TURNER,M.C. of Alabama   JOSIAH T. WALLS, M.C. of Florida   JOSEPH H. RAINY, M.C. of S.Carolina.   R. BROWN ELLIOT, M.C. of S.Carolina.

THE FIRST COLORED SENATOR AND REPRESENTATIVES,
In the 41ˢᵗ and 42ⁿᵈ Congress of the United States.

Blacks in Congress

Congress had no black members until 1870. The key to election of blacks after the Civil War was that southern states were not allowed to reenter the Union until they had enfranchised black voters.

lines through black communities. Another step toward increased black voting was ratification in 1964 of the Twenty-fourth Amendment, which outlawed payment of any poll or other tax as a voter qualification in federal elections.

Southern voters, who had last elected a black in 1899, broke the long dry spell in 1972, when Democrats Barbara Jordan of Texas and Andrew Young of Georgia won seats in the House. Jordan was one of five black women who served in the House; the first elected was Shirley CHISHOLM, a New York Democrat who served from 1969 to 1983. In 1986 Mississippi elected its first black representative since Reconstruction. That same year thirteen blacks ran as Republicans; all lost.

Several Democrats, on the other hand, had been building seniority since the 1960s: Augustus F. Hawkins of California, John Conyers, Jr., of Michigan, Louis Stokes of Ohio, and William L. Clay of Missouri. Elected in 1971 and still serving in the 100th Congress were Californian Ronald V. Dellums, New Yorker Charles B. Rangel, and Walter E. Fauntroy, the nonvoting delegate from the District of Columbia.

Black Caucus

The formal organization of blacks in Congress is the Congressional Black Caucus, which was set up in 1969, when the number of blacks grew from five to nine.

Although at times confrontational, the caucus also sought a role in the House power structure. One step was to gain seats on the most powerful congressional panels: Appropriations,

Rules, and Ways and Means. "In the history of the Congress, no black had ever sat as a member of these committees. We were not in the system," said Stokes, who chaired the caucus in the early 1970s. The effort was successful, as was a later bid to put Dellums on the Armed Services panel.

As blacks fought for power, one irony was their strong endorsement of the SENIORITY SYSTEM, once a source of southern conservatives' strength as they fought civil rights legislation. In the politically charged contest in early 1985 for chairmanship of the House Armed Services Committee, black members endorsed the aging chairman, Illinois Democrat Melvin Price, even though their political outlook was closer to that of the successful challenger, Wisconsin Democrat Les Aspin. Price represented the same seniority system that had moved blacks into positions of authority.   ~

James G. Blaine

Blaine, James G.

Maine Republican James G. Blaine (1830-93) had a long and varied career in public life. An influential newspaper editor, he helped establish the Republican party in Maine. His congressional service, from 1863 to 1881, included three terms as Speaker of the House. Blaine was the unsuccessful Republican candidate for president in 1884; he twice served as secretary of state.

As Speaker (1869-75), Blaine reorganized committees to advance his party's legislative priorities. A powerful and effective leader, he spurred committee chairmen who were grateful to him for their positions to pass Republican legislation favorable to the railroads and business in general.

During Blaine's speakership, a corruption scandal came to light in the House of Representatives that cast a

shadow over his subsequent career. Blaine was accused of having received bribes from Crédit Mobilier of America and the company for which it was building railroad lines, the Union Pacific Railroad. Blaine was implicated in the scandal by a series of letters indicating that he had done legislative favors for railroads in return for gifts of stock. On the floor of the House, Blaine forestalled a move to censure him by reading (but refusing to show) excerpts from the letters.

In July 1876 Blaine left the House to fill an unexpired Senate term. He was later elected to a full term but relinquished his seat in 1881 to become secretary of state for the newly elected president, James A. Garfield. He left the cabinet post after Garfield's assassination the same year.

In 1884 the Republicans chose Blaine as their presidential candidate. The campaign against Democrat Grover Cleveland was characterized by ill feeling and bitter rhetoric. Blaine's involvement in the railroad bribery scandal hurt his candidacy, as Cleveland supporters chanted, "Blaine, Blaine, James G. Blaine! Continental liar from the state of Maine." Blaine lost the election but later reentered public life to serve as an able and effective secretary of state under Benjamin Harrison (1889-92). ∼

Bolling, Richard

Missouri Democrat Richard Bolling (1916-) was one of the most powerful members of the House of Representatives when he retired in 1983. Although he never reached the speakership he aspired to, Bolling may have influenced the House more than any other member of his generation, assembling coalitions to pass major domestic programs and serving as intellectual father of the REFORM movement that changed the institution in the 1970s.

Bolling was a master parliamentarian with a practical grasp of intricate House rules. He wrote several books on the workings of the House and led a bold but unsuccessful move in the early 1970s to restructure the jurisdictions of the House standing committees. He was a principal architect of the congressional BUDGET PROCESS.

Bolling was first elected to the House in 1948. A protégé of Speaker Sam RAYBURN, he joined the RULES Committee in 1955. As a loyal lieutenant to Rayburn, he plotted strategy against the Republicans and conservative Democrats who had effective control of the committee. In 1961 Bolling and fellow liberals talked Rayburn into enlarging the Rules Committee and adding more Democratic members to help outvote the old conservatives. By the time Bolling became chairman in 1979, the committee stood firmly with the Democratic leadership.

Bolling failed to win leadership elections in 1962, when Carl ALBERT defeated him for majority leader, and in 1976, when he fell three votes short in

a contest eventually won by Jim WRIGHT. He was excluded from the Democratic centers of power during the speakership of John W. McCORMACK (1962-71), but returned to the inner circles when Albert became Speaker in 1971. Bolling was a close adviser to Speaker Thomas P. O'NEILL, Jr., who succeeded Albert in 1977. ∼

Borah, William E.

William E. Borah (1865-1940) was a Republican senator from Idaho for thirty-three years. He is best known for his efforts in 1919 to prevent the United States from signing the Versailles Treaty after World War I and to keep it from joining the League of Nations and the World Court. A man of strong principle, Borah was not so much an isolationist as one opposed to international treaties enforced by anything more concrete than moral sanctions.

Borah, a Boise lawyer, was elected to the Senate by the Idaho legislature in 1907. Later he was a strong supporter of the Seventeenth Amendment to the Constitution, which provided for the DIRECT ELECTION OF SENATORS. During his first term, Borah sponsored legislation to establish the Department of Labor and strongly supported ratification of the Sixteenth Amendment, which cleared the way for the imposition of an income tax.

Although Borah supported President Woodrow Wilson during World War I, he vigorously opposed Wilson's peace proposals. He was one of the group of "irreconcilables" or "bitterenders" who objected to the treaty, with or without reservations. The irreconcilables feared that Article Ten of the League Covenant (which stated that League members would support each other against external aggression) would involve the United States in armed conflicts not central to its interests. Borah also viewed the League Covenant as a "scheme which either directly or indirectly, greatly modifies our governmental powers."

Borah was the author of a resolution calling for the Washington Conference on the Limitation of Armament, convened in 1921-22 to discuss naval disarmament. As chairman of the Senate Foreign Relations Committee from 1924 until 1933, he endorsed the Kellogg-Briand Pact of 1928, which sought to outlaw war, and supported U.S. recognition of the Soviet Union. He died in office on the eve of World War II.   ∼

Budget Committee, House

Of all House committees, the Budget Committee is the one most concerned with broad questions about the overall shape of federal spending and taxation. Established by the Congressional Budget and Impoundment Control Act of 1974, the committee has responsibility for ensuring that the House complies with the budget-planning process created by that law.

Like its Senate counterpart, the House Budget Committee does not have authority to directly approve substantive legislation or spending bills. Instead, its task is to set out guidelines and goals for bills approved by other committees. To do that, the Budget Committee has two main duties. One is to propose an annual budget resolution, which establishes targets for total federal spending and revenue, and the amounts that can be spent on broad categories of federal programs, such as defense or welfare. The other duty is to try to make other committees and the whole House comply with those spending targets.

The House Budget Committee's influence in the budget process comes from several sources. The committee's work on a budget resolution each spring is closely followed in the press and elsewhere, and some committee members have become prominent spokesmen for different points of view on budget questions.

The committee is also the first House committee to examine the president's proposed budget each year, and so influences the shape of the budget debate for the whole year. In addition, the committee prepares instructions, included in the annual budget resolution, that require other committees to cut programs to meet budget targets. The committee cannot tell other committees how to comply with savings instructions, but sometimes the options for meeting the targets are few. This procedure is known as reconciliation. (See BUDGET PROCESS.)

By the 100th Congress (1987-89), however, many observers had concluded that the House Budget Committee had not been successful in the budget-watchdog role given it by the 1974 law. Not only was the budget process as a whole failing to prevent massive federal deficits, but also the committee in particular appeared to be losing power and importance in the House's decision-making process on spending issues. Some members wondered whether the committee, and the budget process as a whole, would survive as an effective force.

The budget resolutions that were the committee's chief product each year could be easily breached whenever Congress decided it wanted to spend more money. The committee had no politically useful favors to give out to other House members, and no effective punishments for committees that violated the budget resolution. Frequently, committee members had more influence from moral persuasion of their colleagues than from institutional clout.

The relative weakness of the House Budget Committee was highlighted by

Declining Power?
The House Budget Committee is concerned with
the broad shape of federal spending and taxation. By the mid-1980s the committee appeared to be losing influence in the House on
these issues.

comparison with the Senate Budget
Committee. In contrast to the House
committee's growing irrelevance in budget debates, the Senate committee remained a major player in that body's
work on budget issues.

Political scientists identified several causes of the House committee's
poor showing. A basic difference between the House and Senate Budget
committees was that most members of
the House panel were allowed to serve
only six consecutive years. As a result of
that limited service, House committee
members usually did not have a chance
to build up experience and knowledge
of budget issues to match that of Senate
committee members, who had no membership limit.

Another major problem that confronted the House Budget Committee
throughout its history was its deep partisan divisions between Democratic and
Republican members. Unlike the Senate committee, where bipartisanship
usually was dominant, House committee members of the two parties rarely
were able to agree on anything. The
budget resolutions produced by the
House committee were largely written
by the committee's Democratic majority, with little Republican participation.

As a result, the budget resolutions frequently ran into trouble on the House
floor from a coalition of Republicans
and conservative Democrats.

Another difference between the
House and Senate Budget committees
was that the House panel had ten members who were specifically designated as
representatives of the Ways and Means
and Appropriations committees. These
members usually opposed any attempt
by the Budget Committee to assert its
jurisdiction over issues within the
realms of their primary committees.
This tended to lessen the impact of the
committee as an independent force in
the House. The importance of the designated members declined, however, as
the total size of the committee grew,
from twenty-three at its creation to
thirty-five in the 100th Congress.

History

The short-term nature of the Budget Committee chairmanship, along
with other factors, worked to reduce the
power of the panel's chairman from the
beginning. The first four Budget Committee chairmen struggled to assert
their influence in the budget process.

The first chairman was Washington Democrat Brock Adams, who served

for only two years before resigning to become President Carter's secretary of transportation in 1977. Adams steered a policy of accommodation to other committees, avoiding confrontation over spending limits. Adams established the tradition that the House committee would go over individual budget items closely in compiling a budget—in contrast with the Senate committee, which focused on larger budget questions and avoided specific issues.

The next chairman, Robert N. Giaimo, a Connecticut Democrat, more frequently found himself at odds with other House members. Particularly in the Ninety-sixth Congress (1979-81), Giaimo had the difficult task of fashioning controls on the rapid growth of federal spending, while at the same time putting together a coalition that could command a majority of the House. The pressure on Giaimo began to grow in the late 1970s, during a time when the public was displaying anger over inflation and high taxes, and a strong desire to cut federal spending programs. Giaimo's chief achievement came in 1980. In the face of raging inflation and the possible collapse of financial markets, Giaimo and other congressional leaders helped fashion a dramatic budget-cutting plan that, at least for a time, seemed to bring about a balanced budget.

The tenure of Oklahoma Democrat James R. Jones was even stormier. Jones had the misfortune of coming into the Budget chairmanship in the wake of Ronald Reagan's presidential victory and heavy losses by House Democrats in the 1980 election. Jones was quickly confronted with the new president's demands for drastic spending cuts in domestic social programs. In response, Jones tried to put together a coalition of moderates from both parties. However, he was overwhelmed by an alliance of conservative Republicans and "Boll-Weevil" southern Democrats, backed by Reagan's great popularity.

By his second term (1983-85), Jones was able to establish an effective relationship with House Democratic leaders to regain control of the budget process. That pattern was continued by William H. GRAY III, a Pennsylvania Democrat. The first black chairman of the committee, Gray was successful in guiding budget resolutions through the House, although less so in fashioning workable budget agreements with the Senate. ～

Budget Committee, Senate

Since its creation by the Congressional Budget and Impoundment Control Act of 1974, the Senate Budget Committee has become an important influence on Senate decisions on federal spending. Although their overall success has been limited, Senate Budget Committee members have been among the leaders of Congress's attempt to control federal spending and reduce the growing budget deficit. *(See* BUDGET PROCESS.)

Like its House counterpart, the Senate Budget Committee faces an exceptionally difficult task each year. The committee must prepare a budget resolution setting out goals for spending and revenues in the coming fiscal year. Committee members have to work hard to put together a resolution that will have enough political support to resist numerous changes on the Senate floor.

The committee's task is particularly difficult in times of budgetary stress, when the federal government consistently takes in less money than it spends. These conditions prevailed during the 1980s and put the committee under conflicting pressures. The committee was forced to try to resolve demands for limits on the growth of federal spending, and for protecting funding for popular programs.

The committee has only limited power to enforce its spending decisions. Congress can exceed spending limits set by budget resolutions if a majority of its members agrees. Despite all their efforts, Budget Committee members were not able to bring annual deficits under control by the mid-1980s. Still, the Senate committee has been far more successful in its history than the House Budget Committee. Senate Budget plays a greater role in shaping spending decisions, and has more power to make other committees accept its views.

There are several reasons for the Senate committee's greater influence. One is the fact that committee members serve continuously, and so build up considerable experience and knowledge about budget issues. This is not true in the House, where most committee members can serve for no more than six years.

The Senate Budget Committee also has had a strong tradition of bipartisan cooperation, which the House committee has not. The Senate committee chairman and ranking minority member usually have worked closely together to produce a centrist consensus on issues, which usually wins the backing of the full Senate. The committee also has had a tradition of strong leaders who are deeply committed to the budget process, including Maine Democrat Edmund S. Muskie and Oklahoma Republican Henry S. Bellmon in the 1970s and New Mexico Republican Pete V. Domenici and Florida Democrat Lawton Chiles in the 1980s.

Another way the Senate committee has sought to establish its influence is by focusing on broad budget issues, while staying away from specific policies that are under the jurisdiction of the authorizing committees. Instead of going over the budget line by line, as the House committee typically does, the Senate committee has concentrated on the overall shape of the budget and the long-term implications of budget policy.

Although it cannot propose substantive legislation to the Senate on its own, the Budget Committee has several ways to try to enforce the fiscal policies embodied in the budget resolution each year. One is a process known as reconciliation, under which spending programs are altered through legislation to reduce their costs. The Budget Committee can direct other committees to approve legislation reducing spending under their jurisdiction by a certain amount, although it cannot tell the committees exactly how to achieve those savings.

Senate Budget members have also been effective over the years in challenging spending proposals on the Senate floor. Under the 1974 Budget Act, legislation that calls for spending in excess of the amounts set by the budget resolution is subject to a POINT OF ORDER, or parliamentary challenge. Senate Budget leaders have frequently used this tactic, and usually have had the floor votes to make the spending limits stick.

By the second half of the 1980s, however, some committee members had become discouraged by the inability of the budget process to reduce the deficit substantially, and by the frequent deadlocks over fiscal policy that at times threatened to paralyze the budget process.

"I think we're getting very close to abandoning the notion of ever truly balancing the budget," Domenici said in 1986. Domenici lost the committee chairmanship to Chiles after Democrats won the Senate in the 1986 elections. Two years later Chiles decided not to run for reelection, at least in part because of frustrations over the budget process.

History

The Budget Committee was strongly shaped in its early years by Muskie, its first chairman. A veteran senator and one-time Democratic vice-presidential candidate, Muskie was a major figure in the Senate. His decision to devote much of his energy and influence to the committee was an important factor in solidifying its importance. Muskie was greatly aided in his efforts by his alliance with ranking minority member Bellmon, a conservative Republican who was deeply committed to the budget process.

The committee's role was easier in the early years because there was less pressure to cut spending. Instead of having to make painful choices about which programs to cut, the committee tried to accommodate the spending needs of most federal programs. But Muskie and Bellmon worked hard to ensure that Congress stuck with its budget by challenging spending proposals that exceeded its limits. The committee had less success, however, in making sure that tax bills written by the Finance Committee complied with the budget.

The Budget Committee began to play an even more assertive role in the late 1970s and early 1980s, as Congress confronted rising deficits and runaway inflation. First in 1980 and then again in 1981, the committee used the reconciliation process to direct other committees to recommend savings in politically popular programs. The 1981 bill, written by the committee's new Republican majority, embodied the Reagan administration's plan for major cutbacks in federal social programs for the poor.

In the years that followed, Domenici and colleagues struggled to keep the budget process alive. Each year they had to overcome seemingly insurmountable political obstacles to get a budget finally approved, even if months after the official deadline. One of Domenici's most dramatic victories came in 1985, when he and the new majority leader, Kansas Republican Robert DOLE, produced a budget that passed only after an ailing Republican senator was brought from the hospital by ambu-

lance in the middle of the night to cast the deciding vote.

Domenici and Chiles also made considerable headway in forcing closer adherence to spending targets in appropriations bills by staging parliamentary attacks on them on the Senate floor on the grounds that they exceeded budget resolution spending targets.   ~

Budget Process

The budget process is the system Congress uses to determine government spending requirements and decide how to pay for them. The process requires legislators to set overall goals for government spending and revenues—and then to tailor their actions to meet those goals. Congress makes many of its most difficult policy decisions during this exercise.

The budget process is a cyclical activity that starts early each year when the president sends his budget proposals to Capitol Hill. The president's budget lays out his priorities for the fiscal year that will begin October 1. Before Congress adjourns for the year, the Senate and House of Representatives will create their own budget and provide the money needed to carry it out. Negotiations with the White House may narrow the differences between the two plans, but the congressional budget is likely to differ in important respects from that proposed by the president.

Lawmakers set their own priorities, deciding how much the government should spend and on what, whom to tax and by how much, and what gap should be allowed between spending and revenues. These decisions often bring Congress into sharp conflict with the president, especially in periods when too little money is available to meet all of the nation's needs. If the government spends more money than it takes in—as

Budget Negotiations
Reaching agreement on a federal budget entails difficult House-Senate negotiations each year. In this 1985 conference the Democratic chairman of the House Budget Committee, William H. Gray III, left, consults with his Senate counterpart, Republican Pete V. Domenici. Sen. Lawton Chiles, standing at right, replaced Domenici as chairman when the Democrats gained control of the Senate in 1987.

it did routinely starting in the 1960s— it must borrow to cover the resulting gap, or budget deficit. *(See* BUDGET TERMS.*)*

Beginnings
Through most of its history Congress acted piecemeal on tax and spending bills; it had no way of assessing their impact on the federal budget as a whole. Although the Constitution entrusted Congress with the power of the PURSE, primary control over budget policy passed to the executive branch.

Congress first conferred budget-making authority on the president in passing the Budget and Accounting Act of 1921. That law required the president to submit to Congress each year a budget detailing actual spending and revenues in the previous fiscal year, estimates for the year in progress, and the administration's proposals for the year

ahead. The law also created a Bureau of the Budget (renamed the Office of Management and Budget in 1970) to assist him.

Congress was not bound by the president's recommendations. It could provide more or less money for particular programs than the president requested, and it could change tax laws to draw in more or less revenue. But half a century went by before lawmakers began drawing up their own comprehensive budget plans.

1974 Budget Act
The congressional budget process grew out of fights over spending control in the 1970s. Angry over President Richard NIXON's refusal to spend money it had appropriated—a practice known as IMPOUNDMENT—Congress decided to create its own budget system. The Congressional Budget and Im-

poundment Control Act of 1974 established a BUDGET COMMITTEE in each chamber to analyze the president's budget proposals and to recommend a congressional budget policy. The CONGRESSIONAL BUDGET OFFICE was created to provide data and analyses to help Congress make its budget decisions.

The law required Congress each year to adopt a budget resolution setting overall targets for spending and revenues and establishing congressional spending priorities. (Originally, two budget resolutions were required, but the second was eventually dropped.) Budget resolutions did not require the president's approval—but the president retained VETO power over legislation to carry out the congressional plans.

Once a budget resolution was in place, Congress was required to pass legislation making any changes in law needed to ensure that spending and taxing guidelines were met. These changes were made through the APPROPRIATIONS process and through reconciliation, a procedure under which individual committees were required to cut programs within their jurisdictions to meet assigned quotas. Appropriations bills were required to conform to priorities established in the budget resolution. The 1974 act set a timetable for action to be completed before the start of the fiscal year October 1.

Changes in Law

The process seldom worked as intended. Deadlines were rarely met, Congress's budgetary restraint was weak, and federal deficits ballooned to more than $200 billion annually. In 1985 reformers pushed through a drastic change in the procedure. The Balanced Budget and Emergency Deficit Control Act of 1985—known as the Gramm-Rudman-Hollings Act for its congressional sponsors—established annual deficit-reduction requirements leading to a balanced budget by fiscal 1991. The law invented a new weapon,

called sequestration, to make automatic the tough spending reduction decisions that members were unwilling to face. It accelerated the budget timetable and strengthened procedures to make Congress meet its schedule.

Gramm-Rudman-Hollings, too, did not work exactly as intended, and Congress voted a further revision in 1987. The new measure promised a balanced budget by fiscal 1993, two years later than required in the original law. And it revised the automatic spending-cut procedure to meet objections the Supreme Court raised the previous year.

Competition for Dollars

In the early years of the process, congressional budget making was largely a process of accommodation. House and Senate leaders, anxious to keep the process going, proposed budget resolutions that left room for new programs and additional spending. As long as Congress remained in an expansive mood, the House and Senate were able to construct budgets that satisfied the particular interests of various committees and groups.

When Congress tried to shift to more austere budgets in the 1980s, it encountered much rougher going. While acknowledging the need to hold down spending, members sought to avoid cuts in programs important to their constituents. That became increasingly difficult as the competition for federal dollars increased.

Budget battles with the White House consumed Congress during the administration of President Ronald Reagan. Upon taking office in 1981, Reagan seized control of the congressional budget machinery to carry out sweeping spending and tax cuts that he had promised in his election campaign. In subsequent years Congress routinely dismissed Reagan's budgets, but it had trouble developing plans of its own that also were acceptable to the president. Each year witnessed epic battles between the two branches over the federal deficit, which more than doubled during Reagan's first term.

"The budget process has ... made it plain that there is no such thing as a free lunch," wrote Sen. William L. Armstrong, a Colorado Republican, in 1984. "A lawmaker who wishes to spend more for some program—whether welfare or defense—must explain where he intends to get the money to pay for it: by reducing spending on other programs, by raising taxes, or by incurring a larger deficit."

Setting budget priorities became a tumultuous undertaking in the 1980s. Few were pleased with the process.

Guns vs. Butter In 1982 the House defeated a Republican-backed budget resolution following adoption of a Democratic amendment transferring funds from defense programs to Medicare, the federal health-care program for the aged. Democrats cast their Republican colleagues as people who would "choose a forty-year-old battleship over their eighty-year-old mother," as one Democrat put it. Republicans who opposed defense cuts were nonetheless reluctant to be portrayed as voting against the elderly in an election year. Some voted for the transfer, then turned around and helped kill the budget resolution.

Social Security vs. Taxes Budget negotiations in the early 1980s repeatedly were stalemated by two key players' rigid stands: Reagan's refusal to raise individual taxes and the adamant opposition of House Speaker Thomas P. O'NEILL, Jr., a Massachusetts Democrat, to any cutbacks in Social Security benefits. Social Security was the second largest item in the federal budget and growing rapidly, but cuts were politically sensitive with the voters back home. Congress ultimately decided to remove Social Security spending from the budget accounts, but the deficit calculation continued to include Social Security funds.

Summitry An October 1987 stockmarket crash propelled a reluctant President Reagan into a budget "summit" with congressional leaders of both parties. Congress approved their work—a two-year, $76 billion deficit-reduction package—but the experience won no new converts for summitry. Many senators and representatives felt they had been excluded from the most important decisions of the session. "You work all year in your committees and then end up with three-quarters of the government run by a half-dozen people locked up in a room for three or four weeks," said Rep. Marvin Leath, a Texas Democrat. "I resent that."

Sow's Ear Syndrome The Senate Agriculture Committee tucked a new farm subsidy program into a 1987 deficit-reduction bill. The program was removed in a Senate-House conference at the insistence of House Majority Leader Thomas S. FOLEY, a Washington Democrat.

"The Agriculture committees have been ingenious in figuring out how to build a sow's ear into a silk purse," said Foley, a former chairman of the House Agriculture committee. Farm-state members had continuously "outsnickered" and "outmaneuvered" the budget act, he said, causing urban members to become "cynical" about costly farm programs. ~

ADDITIONAL READINGS

Davidson, Roger H. and Walter J. Oleszek, eds. *Congress and Its Members.* 2d ed. 1985.

Shuman, Howard E. *Politics and the Budget: The Struggle Between the President and the Congress.* 1984.

Stockman, David A. *The Triumph of Politics: The Inside Story of the Reagan Revolution.* 1986.

DIVIDING THE FEDERAL BUDGET PIE

The figures below show the distribution of revenues and spending in President Ronald Reagan's budget for fiscal 1989. The budget estimated that the federal government would take in $965 billion and pay out $1.1 trillion during the fiscal year ending September 30, 1989.

Where It Comes From . . .

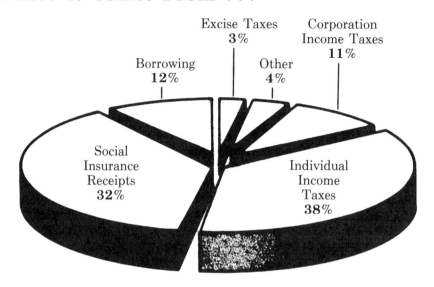

Excise Taxes
3%

Corporation
Income Taxes
11%

Borrowing
12%

Other
4%

Social
Insurance
Receipts
32%

Individual
Income
Taxes
38%

Where It Goes . . .

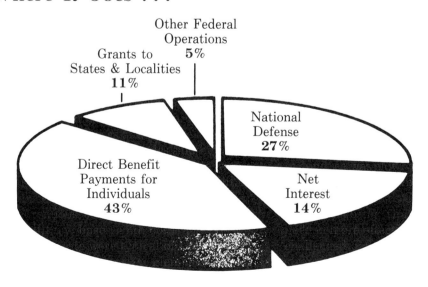

Other Federal
Operations
5%

Grants to
States & Localities
11%

National
Defense
27%

Direct Benefit
Payments for
Individuals
43%

Net
Interest
14%

Budget Terms

Appropriations Acts of Congress that provide actual funding for programs within limits established by authorizations. Appropriations usually cover one fiscal year, but they may also run for a specified or an indefinite number of years. *(See* APPROPRIATIONS BILLS.*)*

Authorizations Acts of Congress that establish discretionary government programs or entitlements, or continue or change such programs. Authorizations specify program goals and, for a discretionary program, set the maximum amount that may be spent. For entitlement programs, an authorization sets or changes eligibility standards and benefits that must be provided by the program. *(See* AUTHORIZATION BILLS.*)*

Budget A financial plan for the U.S. government prepared annually by the executive branch. It lays out in fine print how government funds have been raised and spent and where the president hopes to take the country in the fiscal year ahead. The budget provides for both discretionary and mandatory expenditures. Discretionary funds are appropriated by Congress each year. Mandatory spending is for entitlement programs such as Medicare and veterans' pensions. An entitlement can be changed only by a separate authorizing bill.

Budget Authority Legal authority to enter into obligations that will result in immediate or future government spending, called outlays. Budget authority is provided by Congress through appropriations bills.

Budget Resolution A congressional spending plan that does not require the president's signature. It sets binding totals for broad categories of spending—expressed in budget authority and outlays—and for revenues. Subsequent authorization and appropriations bills must observe these totals. The resolution assumes that certain changes will be made in existing law, primarily to achieve savings assumed in the spending totals. These savings are legislated in reconciliation and appropriations bills. Congress is supposed to complete action by April 15 on a budget resolution for the fiscal year that will begin October 1. *(See* BUDGET PROCESS.*)*

Congressional Budget and Impoundment Control Act The 1974 law that established the congressional budget process and created the Congressional Budget Office.

Deficit The excess of spending over revenues. A surplus exists if revenues are greater than spending. The government ran a budget surplus only once between 1961 and 1988. That was in fiscal 1969.

Entitlement A program—such as Social Security, Medicare, and Medicaid—that must provide specified benefits to all eligible persons who seek them. Generally, these programs are permanently authorized and are not subject to annual appropriations. Social Security, the largest entitlement, was removed from the budget in 1986, although its spending and revenue figures continued to be counted in deficit calculations.

Fiscal Year The federal government's accounting period, which begins on October 1 and ends on September 30 of the following year. A fiscal year is designated by the calendar year in which it ends. *(See* FISCAL YEAR.*)*

Gramm-Rudman-Hollings Act An act of Congress that set a timetable for achieving a balanced budget and specified a procedure designed to accomplish that goal through mandatory automatic spending cuts. As amended in 1987, the law called for a balanced budget by 1993. The Gramm-Rudman-Hollings Act—formally the Balanced Budget and Emergency Deficit Control Act of 1985—took the names of its three Senate sponsors: Phil Gramm of Texas and Warren B. Rudman of New Hampshire, both Republicans, and Ernest F. Hollings, a South Carolina Democrat.

Impoundment A president's refusal to spend money appropriated by Congress. The Congressional Budget and Impoundment Control Act of 1974 established procedures for congressional approval or disapproval of presidential impoundments. *(See* IMPOUNDMENT OF FUNDS.*)*

Outlays Actual cash expenditures made by the government. In passing appropriations bills, Congress does not vote on the level of outlays directly; each year's outlays derive in part from budget authority provided in previous years. Outlays also include net lending—the difference between what the government lends and what borrowers repay—payments on student loans, for example.

Receipts (Revenues) Government income from taxes and other sources such as user fees and sales of federal assets.

Reconciliation Legislation that revises program authorizations to achieve savings required by the budget resolution. Reconciliation bills usually also include revenue increases. The bills are based on instructions in the budget resolution that require authorizing committees to draft legislation specifying cost-cutting changes in programs under their jurisdiction. Authorizing committees do not have to make the program changes assumed by the reconciliation instructions; they may propose different methods of achieving their required savings. The committee proposals are rolled into a single bill for Senate and House action. Reconciliation bills are supposed to be completed by June 15.

Sequestration An automatic procedure for making spending cuts required by the Gramm-Rudman-Hollings law if Congress and the president fail to make them legislatively. Under the Gramm-Rudman-Hollings law, as revised in 1987, the president's Office of Management and Budget determines whether the estimated budget deficit will meet a target set in the law. If a target will not be met, OMB determines how much needs to be cut, or sequestered, from the budget. The Congressional Budget Office plays an advisory role. The law specifies that half the cuts must come from defense programs and half from nondefense programs. About two-thirds of federal spending is exempt in some way from the automatic cuts. If cuts are needed, they are imposed in a preliminary order August 25 and become permanent October 15, unless Congress enacts an alternative plan by that time. ~

Byrd, Robert C.

Robert C. Byrd (1918-), Democratic floor leader of the Senate from 1977 to 1989, performed his duties with old-fashioned courtesy and consummate parliamentary skills. But his sweep of silver hair and the stiff, formal cadence of his speech were poorly suited, some colleagues felt, to his role in the image-conscious Senate. In 1988 Byrd announced that he would not seek reelection to the LEADERSHIP post. The West Virginia senator would become the most senior member of the Senate in 1989 and—assuming Democrats retained control of the chamber—would be PRESIDENT PRO TEMPORE and chair-

man of the APPROPRIATIONS COMMIT-
TEE.

"West Virginia has suffered under
the economic policies of [the Reagan]
administration," Byrd said. "I believe I
can best serve the people of my state by
becoming chairman of the Appropriations Committee." His stated goal as
chairman was to get West Virginia its
fair share of the federal pie.

Raised by an aunt and uncle in the
coal fields of West Virginia, Byrd
worked for twelve years before he could
afford to start college. He was a gas
station attendant, grocery store clerk,
shipyard welder, and butcher. In 1946
he won election to the state legislature,
thanks in part to his talented fiddle
playing.

Byrd was elected to the House of
Representatives in 1952. Earlier, his
campaign had been threatened by disclosure that he had joined the Ku Klux
Klan when he was twenty-four. Byrd
explained the membership as a youthful
indiscretion committed because of his
alarm over communism.

Elected to the Senate in 1958, Byrd
combined his Senate duties with law
school, finally earning a degree in 1963.
In 1967 he won his first leadership post,
secretary of the Democratic Conference.

In 1971 he became majority whip, defeating Massachusetts Democrat Edward M. Kennedy. Byrd had assidu-
ously courted his colleagues—arranging
schedules to suit their convenience,
sharing campaign funds, sending birthday cards. "My role will be that of a
legislative tactician," he said. ". . . I
don't want to thrust an ideological position on anyone."

By the time Majority Leader Mike
MANSFIELD retired in 1977, Byrd had
made himself indispensable to numerous colleagues, and he had the votes
to succeed the Montana Democrat.
With President Jimmy Carter in the
White House, Byrd found himself cast
as the experienced insider. His legislative skills several times saved Carter's
programs, particularly his energy bills
and, in 1978, the Panama Canal treaties.

When Ronald Reagan assumed the
presidency in 1981, Republicans won
control of the Senate and Byrd became
minority leader. He tried to unite Democrats by holding weekly meetings and
weekend retreats, and he became more
aggressive in responding to Reagan.
When Democrats regained control of
the Senate in 1987, Byrd became majority leader for the 100th Congress.   ~

Overleaf:
House Speaker Joseph G. Cannon

Calendar

A list of business awaiting floor action by Congress is called a calendar. The House of Representatives has an elaborate system of calendars to help schedule its work. In the smaller Senate, the scheduling system is more flexible.

A House bill goes on one of five different calendars. They are collected in one document entitled *Calendars of the House of Representatives and History of Legislation.* The document, a valuable tool for congressional researchers, is published daily when the House is in session. The first issue of the week lists all House and most Senate measures that have been reported by committees, with a capsule history of congressional action on each. It also includes a general index. Midweek issues deal only with that week's action.

The five House calendars split up bills by broad category. The House CLERK assigns bills to one of the calendars when they are reported from committee. They are listed in the order in which they are reported, although they are not necessarily called up for floor action in that order.

Bills that have any effect on the Treasury—revenue bills, general APPROPRIATIONS bills, and AUTHORIZATION bills—go on the Union Calendar. Most other major bills, which generally

51

deal with administrative or procedural matters, go on the House Calendar. If all of these bills had to be taken up in the order in which they were listed on the calendars, as was the practice in the early nineteenth century, many would not reach the House floor before Congress adjourned. Instead, most major legislation reaches the floor by being granted a special RULE that allows it to be considered out of order. *(See* LEGISLATIVE PROCESS.)

Bills involving private matters are referred to the Private Calendar. They cover a range of purposes, from claims against the government to waivers of immigration requirements. Under House procedures, the Speaker is supposed to call up private bills on the first Tuesday of each month and may call them up on the third as well.

The CONSENT CALENDAR is reserved for noncontroversial measures. The first and third Mondays of the month are Consent Calendar days. Bills brought up under this procedure almost invariably pass without debate or amendment. A single objection is enough to block consideration the first time a bill is called up. If called up again, it may be blocked only if at least three members object.

The final House calendar, the Discharge Calendar, is rarely used. It comes into play only when 218 representatives (a majority of the total House membership) have signed a petition to take a bill away from the committee that is holding it. This practice, known as discharging a committee, makes it possible for the full House to act on measures that otherwise would remain buried in a hostile committee. Discharge measures may be considered on the second and fourth Mondays of each month. *(See* DISCHARGE.)

In the Senate, all bills go on a single legislative calendar, called the Calendar of General Orders. In addition, the chamber has an Executive Calendar listing treaties and nominations, which require the Senate's advice and consent. Senate floor action schedules are worked out informally, and bills need not be taken up in calendar order. ～

Calendar Wednesday

House rules provide a way for committee chairmen to force House debate on bills that have been reported by their committees but not scheduled for floor action by the RULES COMMITTEE. Under the procedure, known as Calendar Wednesday, bills may be brought directly to the floor on Wednesdays as the Speaker calls each committee in alphabetical order. Debate is limited to two hours. The procedure is vulnerable to delaying action and is seldom used. It is not observed during the last two weeks of a session and may be omitted at other times by a two-thirds vote. In practice, the House almost always dispenses with Calendar Wednesday by unanimous consent.

The procedure was adopted in 1909 in protest against the autocratic rule of Speaker Joseph G. CANNON, an Illinois Republican who maintained tight control over the House agenda. It had been used successfully only twice by 1988—in 1950 to bring a fair employment bill to the floor and in 1960 to call up a measure to aid economically depressed areas. ～

Calhoun, John C.

A brilliant philosopher and an eloquent champion of states' rights, John C. Calhoun (1782-1850) was the foremost spokesman for the South in the troubled period leading up to the Civil War. Lawyer, state legislator, U.S. representative, senator, secretary of war,

John C. Calhoun

secretary of state, and vice president, he played a critical role in the course of U.S. foreign and domestic policy in the first half of the nineteenth century.

Calhoun entered the House of Representatives in 1811. During his six years in the House he was a nationalist, supporting efforts to strengthen the central government. With Speaker Henry CLAY, he was one of a group known as the "War Hawks" who helped push the nation into the War of 1812.

Calhoun left Congress in 1817 to become James Monroe's secretary of war. In 1824 he was elected vice president under John Quincy ADAMS, a position that made him presiding officer of the Senate. More loyal to Andrew Jackson than to Adams, Calhoun assigned Jackson supporters to key committee posts. The Senate, which had only recently extended the assignment power to the presiding officer, quickly took it back.

Calhoun was reelected to the vice presidency in 1828, this time under Jackson, but he and Jackson soon were at odds. Jackson believed in a strong central government, while Calhoun had become an advocate of states' rights.

Angered by high protective tariffs, Calhoun became an eloquent advocate of the doctrine of nullification, which asserted that individual states had the right to annul federal laws they considered illegal.

Calhoun resigned as vice president in 1832 and returned to the Senate to defend his states' rights principles in a succession of dramatic debates with Daniel WEBSTER. He became an apologist for slavery and fought efforts to prohibit the practice in new states and territories. Except for a brief period (1844-45) as secretary of state under John Tyler, Calhoun remained a senator for the rest of his life. Shortly before his death in 1850, the dying Calhoun dragged himself into the Senate chamber to hear a colleague read his final speech.

Constant to the end, Calhoun in his speech attacked northern opponents of slavery and opposed Clay's final attempt to forestall the South's secession from the Union. Clay's proposals included, among others, a measure clearing the way for California's admission as a free state. They were subsequently adopted and became known as the Compromise of 1850.   ~

Call of the Calendar

Senate bills that are not brought up for debate by a motion, unanimous consent, or a unanimous consent agreement may be brought before the Senate for action when the CALENDAR listing them is "called." Under the procedure, which is used infrequently, bills must be called in the order in which they are listed on the calendar. Measures considered by this method are usually noncontroversial, and debate is limited to five minutes for each senator. *(See* LEGISLATIVE PROCESS.*)*   ~

Campaign Committees.   See
LEADERSHIP.

Campaign Financing

Getting elected to Congress requires money. To have any chance at all of winning a House or Senate election, a candidate will almost always require a large supply of funds to cover such expenses as campaign staff salaries, travel costs, mailings, print advertising, and, most important in recent years, radio and television commercials.

The ways in which candidates raise money is known as the system of campaign finance. Perhaps no other aspect of congressional politics and the American political system in general has aroused so much concern in recent years as the way in which the financing of campaigns takes place. Debate over campaign finance touches on the most basic issues of representative democracy and the integrity of Congress.

There are many potential sources from which congressional candidates can raise their money. Businesses, labor unions, individuals, political organizations, and candidates themselves have been important sources of funds at different times during the history of Congress. Today, businesses and unions are barred from contributing directly to campaigns. But they do so indirectly, through POLITICAL ACTION COMMITTEES of their employees and members. PACs and individuals have become the major sources of campaign funds. Spending by political parties has risen sharply since the 1970s, however. Party committees in each chamber raise and donate funds to party candidates. *(See* LEADERSHIP.)

The enormous expense of modern campaigns has made fund raising a crucial factor in political strength. In the 1984 Senate race in North Carolina, for example, Republican Jesse Helms, the incumbent senator, and James B. Hunt, Jr., his Democratic challenger, spent a total of $25 million, much of it raised from political allies outside the state. It is not uncommon for the two major-party candidates in a House race to spend a total of $1 million or more. In a 1984 House race in New York City, the Democratic and Republican candidates together spent $2.9 million, or nearly $15 for every vote cast in the election.

The ability to raise money is a key factor in determining a person's chances of getting elected. That is particularly true for challengers, who must work intensely to obtain enough money for the political advertising needed to become familiar to the voters. Incumbents, on the other hand, usually have less difficulty raising money. Particularly if they hold positions of influence in Congress, most incumbents can count on ample contributions from organized interest groups. Often incumbents are able to raise so much money in advance of the next election that potential challengers decide not even to try running against them.

The campaign finance system ultimately depends on the willingness of individuals and organizations to make donations. There are a number of reasons why people give to candidates. Ideally contributions are made because the giver thinks the candidate has the skill and experience to help run the government effectively, and the values and political beliefs to lead the nation in a positive direction. Viewed this way, political contributions are an important and valuable way in which people can participate in political life.

But there is another view, which sees political contributions and the current system of campaign finance in a considerably more negative way. Basically this perspective holds that contributions are intended to "buy" the vote of a successful congressional candidate on issues of economic importance

The 1988 Democratic Congressional
Dinner Co-Chairmen
Bob Graham   Steny H. Hoyer
The Democratic Senatorial
Campaign Committee
John Kerry, Chairman

and

The Democratic Congressional
Campaign Committee
Beryl Anthony, Jr., Chairman
cordially invite you
to participate in
The 1988
Democratic Congressional Dinner
Honoring The Honorable Thomas P. O'Neill, Jr.
on Wednesday evening, March the sixteenth
One Thousand Nine Hundred and Eighty-Eight
Reception at six o'clock p.m.
Dinner at seven-thirty o'clock p.m.
The Washington Hilton
1919 Connecticut Avenue, NW
Washington, D.C.

R.S.V.P. Card enclosed
$1,500 per Person

25th Anniversary
Democratic
Congressional
Dinner

The Money Factor
The ability to raise money is an important factor in determining who will be elected to Congress. Party organizations hold fund-raising events, such as this Democratic dinner, to raise money for party candidates.

to the giver. That does not necessarily mean—as used to happen regularly in past decades—that candidate and contributor engage in a straight trade of money for votes. Rather, candidates who become dependent on certain interests for financing their campaigns may feel obliged to vote for their interests, regardless of what they think is best for the country. While a member of Congress could vote against the interests of his major contributors, he would do so at the risk of losing their financial support in the next election.

Critics of the current campaign finance system worry that many members of Congress have become the captives of special interests, who pour massive amounts into campaign trea-

suries in return for favorable votes on legislation. Many politicians also are frustrated by the current system, which can force them into a never-ending, demeaning search for contributions, often at the expense of their congressional responsibilities.

Concern over the potentially corrupting influence of political contributions has led to numerous attempts since 1970 to reform the campaign finance system. Legislation passed in the 1970s set limits on amounts that could be given to each congressional candidate in each election—$1,000 from each individual and $5,000 from each PAC— and required candidates to disclose publicly the sources of their funds. But efforts to provide federal funding for congressional campaigns, as has been done in the presidential campaign since 1976, were rejected by Congress. Attempts to impose stricter limits on PAC contributions also were defeated repeatedly.

History

Campaign financing generally was not a major subject of controversy during Congress's first century. Fund raising was completely unregulated, with most candidates probably obtaining the money needed to pay for the lavish campaign rallies of the era from a few wealthy backers.

By the 1860s, however, the chief source of campaign money had shifted to federal government workers. The party that held the White House, and with it control of lucrative federal PA-TRONAGE, was able to persuade or require government jobholders to contribute to its campaign coffers. In the 1868 election, for example, an estimated three-quarters of the Republican Congressional Committee's campaign money came from federal employees.

The pressure on federal workers to contribute became one of the most criticized aspects of the "spoils system," under which the party in power was entitled to distribute jobs and contracts to its supporters. As early as 1867, Congress passed a law to protect workers in federal shipyards from having to make political contributions to keep their jobs. Agitation against the spoils system continued until 1883, when Congress passed the Civil Service Reform Act, which among other things barred mandatory political contributions for federal workers and made it a crime for a federal employee to solicit campaign funds from another federal employee.

As a result, political campaign managers turned for funds to the wealthy, and particularly to the giant corporations that began to exert increasing control over American economic life in the last decades of the nineteenth century. The high point of the increasingly lavish corporate involvement in political campaigns came in 1896, when financier Marcus A. Hanna raised $3.5 million, a staggering amount for the time, from corporations in order to finance the successful campaign of Republican presidential candidate William McKinley.

The unrestrained spending by big business on behalf of its favored candidates soon became a chief target of the reformist Progressive movement, which sought to end corruption and increase public involvement in political life. With the backing of President Theodore Roosevelt, Congress in 1907 passed the Tillman Act, which prohibited any corporation or national bank from making contributions to candidates for federal office.

In 1910 came the Federal Corrupt Practices Act, which established the first requirement that political committees backing candidates for the House publicly disclose the names of their contributors. The following year reporting requirements were extended to the Senate, which in 1913 became for the first time subject to DIRECT ELECTION by the voters. The 1911 law also set limits on the amounts that candidates could spend on their campaigns—$10,000 for Senate candidates and $5,000 for House candidates.

The next major overhaul of federal law governing campaign finance came in 1925, with passage of a new Federal Corrupt Practices Act. That law, which was to be the basis of federal campaign law for nearly half a century, limited the amounts that general-election candidates could spend to $25,000 for the Senate and $5,000 for the House. The act also continued the existing prohibitions on corporate contributions and solicitation of federal employees, and extended existing reporting requirements on campaign finance.

Subsequent laws in the following

decades expanded the scope of the 1925 act but left its basic structure intact. One change involved the extension of reporting requirements and spending limits to primary campaigns. Another was to make labor unions subject to the ban on political contributions that already applied to businesses.

The 1925 law proved to be almost totally ineffective in regulating the campaign finance system for congressional candidates. Although its spending limits and reporting requirements were widely violated over the years, no one was ever prosecuted under the act. Candidates soon learned that they could ignore the law with no risk, raising and spending money freely with only token efforts to comply. Indeed, there were so many ways that candidates could get around the statute that it was often said to be "more loophole than law."

Contributors and candidates developed a variety of ways to evade the law. The reporting requirement on contributions of $100 or more, for example, encouraged givers to make multiple contributions to candidates of $99.99. The law limited the amount an individual could give to a candidate to $5,000. So wealthy people channeled much larger sums to candidates through family members and friends, each of whom was allowed to contribute up to $5,000. Similarly, corporations were able to make contributions by awarding special bonuses to executives, who in turn gave the money to candidates.

For candidates the chief loophole was the provision of the law that applied coverage of the spending and reporting requirements only to financial activity made with the "knowledge and consent" of the candidate. As a result, candidates could receive and spend as much as they wanted simply by maintaining the legal fiction that they did not know it was taking place. Frequently candidates who conducted expensive campaigns were able to report that they had received and spent little or nothing.

Reform Efforts

Frustration with the weakness of the 1925 law and concern over the growing impact of television advertising on politics had fostered strong support in Congress for campaign-finance reform by the early 1970s. Within five years Congress passed major laws changing the way both presidential and congressional campaigns were financed and conducted.

The first major change in campaign law since 1925 was the Federal Election Campaign Act of 1971. That legislation combined two sharply different approaches to reform. One part of the law set strict limits on the amounts that federal candidates could spend on communications media. The law essentially limited spending on media advertising by House and Senate candidates to ten cents for each voting-age person in the congressional district or state. In addition, no more than 60 percent of the total media amount was allowed to go for television and radio advertising.

The other part of the law provided for the first time for relatively complete reporting requirements on contributions to candidates. Backers of the law hoped that full FINANCIAL DISCLOSURE would prevent abuses, by reducing excessive dependence by a candidate on any one giver. If the voters saw that a candidate got too much of his money from a single special interest, the theory went, they would vote against him.

The 1971 law was praised by many reformers for improving disclosure of campaign finances and limiting media spending. However, the law did little to prevent the pattern of widespread illegal campaign finance activities that was revealed by investigations into the WATERGATE political scandal. Although most of the abuses involved the presidential campaign—specifically the 1972 reelection campaign of President Richard Nixon—public outrage over the revelations led to pressure for further reforms in both presidential and congressional campaigns.

The result was the federal election law of 1974. That law, the most comprehensive such legislation ever enacted, substantially overhauled the existing system for financing federal elections. It established the Federal Election Commission, a six-member body responsible for overseeing campaign finance activities. The law also instituted a series of limits on the amounts that could be given to candidates in an election. Individuals were limited to a $1,000 gift to one candidate, and $25,000 to all candidates in a single year; political committees could give no more than $5,000 to one candidate, but were not limited in the total amount they could give to all candidates. In addition, the law tightened reporting requirements and established the system of public financing of presidential elections.

However, a key part of that law was soon overturned by the Supreme Court. In the landmark case of *Buckley v. Valeo* a diverse group of liberal and conservative plantiffs argued that the law represented an unconstitutional restraint on their right to spend money on behalf of political candidates. The Supreme Court, in a 1976 ruling, struck down the law's limits on the amounts that candidates could spend on campaigns. But the Court upheld provisions of the law limiting the amounts that individuals and PACs could contribute to specific candidates, as well as the law's reporting and disclosure requirements.

The Court also supported the presidential-election provisions of the law, which provided public financing for candidates, while limiting the amounts that candidates could spend. As a result, the focus of attempts to reform congressional campaigns shifted to proposals for public financing. Under such proposals congressional candidates in primary and general elections would receive federal funding, but they would have to limit the total amount they spent.

Backers of public financing argued that it would reduce what they described as the excessive influence of special interests in congressional campaigns. Presidential public financing had been successful, they said, in cleaning up a campaign finance system that had been filled with corruption in past elections. But opponents of public financing responded that it would make incumbents virtually unbeatable in most elections. If challengers were blocked by the law from outspending the incumbent, opponents of the law said, they would have little chance of overcoming considerable advantages enjoyed by the incumbent, such as free mailings under the congressional FRANKING PRIVILEGE and greater recognition among the voters. Although President Jimmy Carter supported them, public-financing bills were defeated in Congress several times in the late 1970s. Backing for the idea waned after that. In the 1980s reform efforts focused on attempts to limit total spending by PACs.

System in Operation

Despite those efforts to limit and control the campaign-finance system, spending on congressional elections has continued to grow at a steady pace. Each election year House and Senate candidates spend a combined total that exceeds the amount spent two years before. The ability to raise money remains an important factor in determining who will be elected to Congress. The insatiable money demands of congressional campaigns, particularly for radio and television air time, were shown by the Federal Election Commission's report on the 1986 election. For that election candidates spent $450 million on primaries and the general election. That figure was 20 percent higher than the previous record set in 1984, when the total was $374 million. In 1976 spending on congressional campaigns had amounted to only $66 million.

In 1986 House candidates spent $239 million. Senate candidates, who were running for many fewer seats, spent $211 million. As those figures indicate, Senate candidates frequently raise and spend much more than House candidates. That is understandable, considering that some Senate candidates are running in massive states like California and New York, with more than ten million residents, while all congressional districts have roughly half a million in population. In addition, Senate campaigns, which cover an entire state, generally are based heavily on media advertising. Individual House campaigns, which cover a relatively small congressional district, frequently rely less on advertising and more on personal campaigning by the candidate.

There are other differences between the House and Senate as well. House candidates tend to rely fairly heavily on PACs—34 percent of their contributions came from PACs in 1986, compared with 49 percent from individuals. Senate candidates received only 21 percent of their funds from PACs, with 65 percent of their contributions coming from individuals. House incumbents, who are eagerly courted by PACs, rarely have difficulty raising enough money. Senate candidates, who must raise larger amounts, often have to conduct vigorous fund-raising drives among individuals to obtain all the funds they need.

Access to large quantities of campaign money does not guarantee success in the election. Of the fifteen Senate candidates who spent the most money in 1986, eight were defeated. There were three House candidates who spent more than $1 million in losing efforts. Moreover, in some cases challengers were successful even though they were outspent by the incumbent. In 1986 six

Democratic Senate candidates managed to defeat better-financed Republican incumbents.   ~

ADDITIONAL READINGS

Alexander, Herbert E. *Financing Politics: Money, Elections and Political Reform.* 3d ed. 1984.

Stern, Philip M. *The Best Congress Money Can Buy.* 1988.

Cannon, Clarence

During his four decades in the House of Representatives, Democrat Clarence Cannon earned a reputation as a tough Appropriations Committee chairman and as the House's foremost authority on parliamentary procedure. He was the author of *Cannon's Procedure* and *Cannon's Precedents*, both still used by Congress.

Cannon (1879-1964) arrived in Washington in 1911, three years after receiving his law degree, to work as confidential secretary to House Speaker James B. "Champ" CLARK, also a Missouri Democrat. After Clark died in 1921, Cannon ran for his seat and won election to the House in 1922. He remained in the House until his own death in 1964.

Cannon was chairman of the Appropriations Committee from 1941 to 1964, except for two brief periods (1947-49, 1953-55) when Republicans controlled the chamber. He was one of the chief proponents of a move in 1950 to lump all regular appropriations for government agencies into a single bill. The experiment was unsuccessful, and in 1951 Congress returned to the practice of passing separate appropriations measures.

Cannon was a stickler for what he viewed as the prerogatives of the House.

Cannon Power
Joseph G. Cannon was the most powerful Speaker in history until Republicans and Democrats revolted against his arbitrary rule in 1910.

He reacted angrily in 1962 when the chairman of the Senate Appropriations Committee, Arizona Democrat Carl HAYDEN, demanded coequal status in the appropriations process—a field in which the House traditionally had claimed primacy. Feuding between the two chairmen, both then in their 80s, held up action on spending bills for much of the 1962 session.   ~

Cannon, Joseph G.

Joseph G. Cannon (1836-1926), a conservative Republican from Illinois, was the last in a succession of autocratic Speakers who dominated the House of Representatives during the late nineteenth century and the first decade of the twentieth. Cannon was the most powerful Speaker in history from 1903 until 1910, when Republicans and Democrats revolted against his arbitrary rule. He was stripped of most of his power by new rules that prohibited the Speaker from naming or serving on the

RULES Committee, through which Cannon had controlled the shape and fate of many bills; removed his authority to make committee assignments; and reduced his power to deny recognition to members during House floor debate. *(See* SPEAKER.*)*

"Uncle Joe" Cannon served in the House for half a century—from 1873 until 1923, with two short breaks (1891-93, 1913-15). He was never associated with any particular piece of legislation or cause, although he opposed the progressive policies of President Theodore Roosevelt. His seniority brought him the chairmanship of the Appropriations Committee in 1897, and he became Speaker six years later.

Cannon fully exploited the authority established by his predecessors. As Speaker, he was chairman of the Rules Committee, and he used this position to prevent legislation from coming to the House floor. He also took full advantage of his power over committee assignments; members loyal to Cannon could be confident of good committees, while dissidents were banished to unpopular ones. Using his power of recognition,

Cannon arbitrarily determined which members could speak on the floor. His counting of voice votes was suspect. "The Ayes make the most noise, but the Nays have it," he once ruled.

In 1909 the House rejected a resolution to curtail the Speaker's powers; it was introduced by James B. "Champ" CLARK, who was to succeed Cannon in the post two years later. Nebraska Republican George W. NORRIS introduced another in 1910. Although Cannon tried to prohibit debate on the measure, the House overruled him and adopted the resolution after twenty-nine hours of debate. Cannon then offered to resign as Speaker. Because he was well-liked by many, the House refused to consider his resignation, and he retained the speakership until the Sixty-first Congress ended the following year.   ~

Cannonism.   See SPEAKER OF THE HOUSE; CANNON, JOSEPH G.

Capitol Building

It was a "pity to burn anything so beautiful," a British officer reportedly said before setting fire to the United States Capitol during the War of 1812. Even then, at an early stage of its development, the seat of Congress was the most striking public building in Washington, D.C. It remains so to this day.

Though it may appear to the first-time visitor to be a unified whole, the Capitol is not one structure but several. The original building has been added to numerous times over its nearly two centuries of existence, and the process has by no means ended. A three-year-long restoration of the Capitol's West Front —the side that faces the Washington Monument midway down the Mall— was completed in November 1987.

The Capitol, constructed of sandstone and marble in the classic style, rests on an elevated site chosen by George Washington in consultation with Major Pierre L'Enfant, a young French engineer and city planner. In 1792 a competition was held to choose an architect, but William Thornton gained the president's approval with a plan submitted after the deadline. Washington praised Thornton's design for its "grandeur, simplicity, and beauty of the exterior." In 1793 the president set the cornerstone, with Masonic rites, and the building was begun.

The north, or Senate, wing of the Capitol was finished in 1800. Records, archives, and furniture arrived by ship from Philadelphia, the former seat of the federal government, in October of that year. Congress convened in the Capitol for the first time on November 21, 1800. President John Adams addressed the members the next day, congratulating them "on the prospect of a residence not to be changed." The Senate then consisted of 32 members from 16 states, while the House of Representatives numbered 105.

All three branches of the national government have had close association with the Capitol. For 134 years the building was the home of the SUPREME COURT. Most presidents have taken the inaugural oath of office in the Capitol or on its grounds, starting with Thomas Jefferson in 1801. Also, the Capitol long housed the LIBRARY OF CONGRESS, which now occupies three nearby buildings and is one of the largest libraries in the world.

Fire and Reconstruction

A British expeditionary force set fire to the Capitol on the night of August 24, 1814. Only the exterior walls were left standing. The damage might have been still greater if a violent thunderstorm, typical of that time of year in Washington, had not extinguished the flames.

Symbol of Union
Construction of the Capitol dome continued during the Civil War. "If the people see the Capitol going on," President Abraham Lincoln said, "it is a sign that we intend the Union shall go on."

Restoration work began in 1815 under the direction of Benjamin H. Latrobe, who had been appointed twelve years earlier as surveyor of public buildings. The central portion of the Capitol, with a low dome designed by Latrobe's successor, Charles Bulfinch, was completed in 1827.

After Bulfinch's appointment was terminated in 1829, his position remained vacant until President Millard Fillmore appointed Thomas U. Walter in 1851 to oversee an urgently needed enlargement of the building. By that time 62 senators and 232 House members were jammed into space designed to accommodate a much smaller number of legislators. Besides new Senate and House wings, Walter suggested the addition of a larger dome to replace the original one of copper-sheathed wood.

The present House chamber was occupied December 16, 1857. A little over a year later, on January 4, 1859, the Senate moved into its new quarters. The Supreme Court took over the former Senate chamber the following year, and in 1864 the old House chamber became Statuary Hall by act of Congress.

Even after the onset of the Civil War, work continued on the Capitol dome. "If the people see the Capitol going on," President Abraham Lincoln said, "it is a sign that we intend the Union shall go on." On December 2, 1863, a great crowd gathered to watch Thomas Crawford's sculpture of "Freedom" placed on top of the dome, fulfilling Lincoln's vision.

The Capitol Today
The Capitol has undergone only one major structural change since then. Under provisions of the Legislative Appropriations Act of 1956, a new marble East Front, faithfully reproducing the design of the old sandstone facade, was erected 32½ feet east of the original walls. The latter were retained to serve as interior walls. Work on the extension began in 1958 and was completed four years later, adding 100 rooms at a total cost of $11.4 million.

Then, controversy raged for two decades over a proposed extension of the Capitol's West Front. In 1983 Congress voted instead to restore the West Front, which includes the last remaining portions of the Capitol's original exterior. Unlike most other federally funded construction projects in the nation's capital, the West Front restoration was completed well ahead of time and under budget. The refurbished building, Architect of the Capitol George M. White said, "will look exactly like it did when it was new, but it will be structurally sound for the foreseeable future."

Important rooms in the Capitol that may be visited by the public without advance notice include the Rotunda, situated under the dome and decorated with statues and large-scale historical paintings, and Statuary Hall, which contains a collection of bronze and marble statues presented by the various states to commemorate distinguished citizens.

The bodies of a number of celebrated Americans have lain in state in the Rotunda. The list includes nine presidents—Lincoln, Garfield, McKinley, Harding, Taft, Kennedy, Hoover, Eisenhower, and Lyndon B. Johnson.

The Capitol is 751 feet, 4 inches long and 350 feet wide. It contains 16½ acres of floor space, an area slightly smaller than the White House grounds. The building's height at its tallest point, the top of the Freedom statue, is 287 feet, 5½ inches. The Senate and House occupy opposite ends of the building; the Senate chamber is in the north wing, the House in the south. The Capitol also includes committee chambers, offices, restaurants, repair shops, and other rooms. Tunnels and subways link the Capitol to Senate and House office buildings nearby.

Raising the Flags

Much of the Capitol's daily business is conducted in places inaccessible to the casual visitor—on the roof, for instance. It is there that employees of the Architect of the Capitol's flag office raise and lower thousands of American flags each year, all destined for shipment to citizens or organizations that request one in writing from their member of Congress.

The flag program began in 1937. In 1986 a total of 97,673—268 a day, on average—were run up a flagpole set aside for the purpose and lowered almost instantly. When mailed, each flag is accompanied by a certificate of authenticity. The recipient is charged a fee pegged to the type of fabric used, cotton or nylon. Each senator and House member may forward as many constituent requests as he or she wishes to the flag office.   ~

ADDITIONAL READINGS

Aikman, Lonelle M. *We the People: The Story of the United States Capitol.* 13th ed. 1985.
Brown, Glenn. *History of the U.S. Capitol.* 1903. Reprint ed. 1970.

Capitol Hill

When Pierre L'Enfant laid out the streets of Washington in the 1790s, he called the hill on the eastern end of town a "pedestal waiting for a monument." L'Enfant placed the CAPITOL there, housing the legislative and judicial branches a mile from the White House, which he located at the other end of Pennsylvania Avenue.

Known then as Jenkins Hill, the site had a sweeping view to the west of swampy land and the Tiber Creek, a finger of the Potomac first straightened into a canal and then captured in pipes and buried. Now Capitol Hill overlooks a formal panorama: the tree-lined lawn of the Mall, surrounded by museums and punctuated by the Washington Monument in the distance. Congress guaranteed its view in 1901, when it banned buildings higher than the Capitol dome—the equivalent of about thirteen stories.

The Capitol itself sits alone on a city block, its grounds a combination of gardens and parking lots. The grounds still reflect the design created in the 1870s by noted landscape architect Frederick Law Olmsted. Flanked on the north by Senate office buildings and on the south by House office buildings, the Capitol has on its eastern side the Supreme Court and the Library of Congress. Collectively, these buildings make up the area referred to as Capitol Hill.

Capitol Hill is also the name for the neighborhood of homes and commercial establishments radiating east of the congressional enclave. Developed to serve legislators and their families early in the nineteenth century, the village-like community serves the same function today. Restaurants and shops are flooded at lunchtime with congressional employees. Many senators and representatives live in the restored townhouses common in the area. Two lines of the Washington subway system serve the community.

As a neighbor, Congress has not always been popular. In the mid-1970s, plans to build a fourth House office building where homes already existed prompted an outcry from residents. Those plans were modified; since then schemes for expanding Congress have been replaced by concerns about controlling staff size and the legislative budget.   ~

Caucuses, Party

Party caucuses are the formal organizations of Democratic and Republican members within the House and Senate. At the start of each two-year term of Congress, representatives and senators vote in their party caucuses on party leadership, committee chairmanships, and committee assignments. Contests for House Speaker, Senate majority leader, and other top posts can be controversial, but many other caucus votes simply endorse the leaders' recommendations. *(See* LEADERSHIP.*)*

The Senate Democratic Conference and Senate Republican Conference, as the caucuses are known, meet about once a week to discuss legislation, though attendance varies and the sessions are informal. Meetings of House caucuses are more formal and usually well attended. The House Republican Conference gathers each week, and the House Democratic Caucus—the only one of the four organizations that for-

CAPITOL HILL

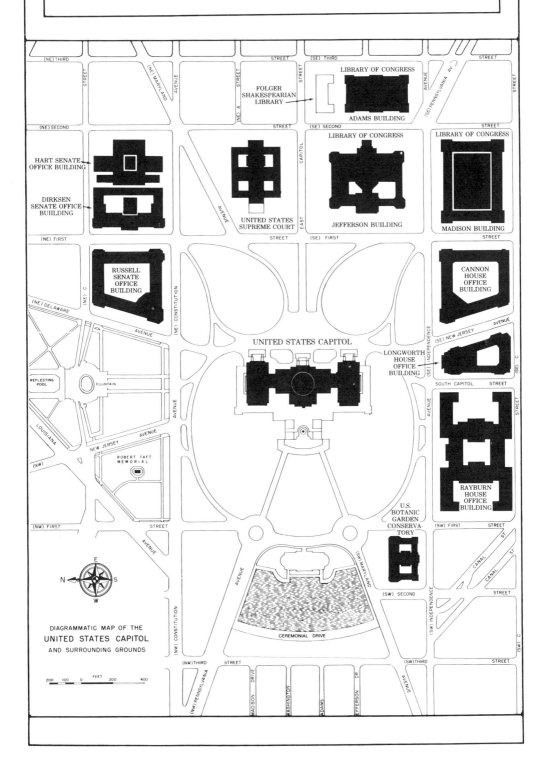

DIAGRAMMATIC MAP OF THE
UNITED STATES CAPITOL
AND SURROUNDING GROUNDS

mally calls itself a caucus—usually meets once or twice a month. Caucus sessions are closed to the public.

Within each caucus are committees that recommend party positions on bills, help schedule legislation, and make committee assignments. These groups handle most caucus business. Each caucus also has a campaign committee that raises and distributes money to candidates for congressional office.

The full caucus is rarely asked to settle questions about legislative policy. Instead the leadership and party committees try to help different factions reach a consensus. Budget questions, for example, often involve party task forces and hours of negotiations. If the leadership does bring a policy question to the caucus, the decision is often made by voice vote, which tends to suggest unity and mask any opposition.

Caucus votes have been a tool, though, when a large bloc of the caucus is unhappy with the leadership. That happened in the 1970s, when the House Democratic Caucus voted on the Vietnam War, Social Security, and other controversial issues. Such votes are divisive, however, and party leaders try to avoid them.

Changing Caucus Role

From 1800 to 1824 party caucuses in the House doubled as the national organizations for the major parties, choosing the nominees for president and vice president. By the 1830s, though, national party conventions had begun to select presidential nominees, and the importance of both major parties' caucuses had diminished. Late in the nineteenth century the caucuses became forums for discussion of legislative strategy.

The party caucus was overshadowed by strong SPEAKERS at the turn of the century. The caucus got new life after the revolt in 1910-11 against Jo-

seph G. CANNON, an Illinois Republican whose autocratic rule as Speaker (1903-11) caused him to be labeled "Czar." The House took away from the Speaker authority to name the floor leader, select committee chairmen, and make committee assignments. Those duties were shifted to the political parties. Democrats, when they gained the majority in 1911, used their caucus to solidify control of the House. George Galloway, in his classic *History of the House of Representatives*, described 1911 to 1920 as the time when "King Caucus supersedes Czar Cannon."

The caucuses were also a tool on political issues. Then, a two-thirds vote of the caucus could bind members to vote a certain way on legislation. House Republicans quickly abandoned this type of caucus, and even renamed their group a "conference" to clarify its role. Democrats let the binding vote fall into disuse.

The Democratic caucuses were particularly strong during President Woodrow Wilson's first term (1913-17). Wilson, a student of Congress, saw the caucus as an "antidote to the committees," providing unity and cohesion to counter those panels' independence.

The committees, though, grew more independent as the unwritten SENIORITY system became entrenched, beginning in the 1920s. The chairmanship of committees went almost automatically to the majority member with the longest record of service on that committee. The party leadership and the caucus were rarely involved and, as a result, were less able to hold the chairmen accountable.

The Democratic Caucus was also one step removed from another set of decisions: committee assignments. As part of the revolt against Cannon, that responsibility had been given to Democrats on WAYS AND MEANS, then chaired by Majority Leader Oscar W. UNDERWOOD of Alabama. Republicans used a Committee on Committees, which

Generation Gap
Party caucuses were the battleground for many institutional reforms in the 1970s, as junior members of Congress demanded a greater role in party decisions. In this 1975 picture two members of the Senate Democratic Conference debate a proposal to elect committee chairmen by secret ballot. Mississippi's John C. Stennis, left, appears unconvinced by the arguments of his younger colleague, Idaho's Frank Church.

included party leaders, to make assignments.

As the committees gained in power, the authority of the party caucus diminished. Party unity among Democrats also suffered because of political differences within party ranks, with conservative southern Democrats often voting with Republicans. *(See* CONSERVATIVE COALITION.*)*

The development of party caucuses in the Senate paralleled that in the House. In 1846 the caucuses won the power to make committee assignments. During the Civil War and Reconstruction Era, Republicans used their caucus frequently to discuss and adopt party positions on legislation. Republican leaders used the caucus extensively in the 1890s to maintain party discipline. Senate Democratic leaders adopted a binding caucus rule in 1903, but there is no record of its use.

More recently, caucuses have been used to collect and distribute information to members, to perform legislative research, and to discuss political and policy questions.

House Caucus Reborn

Liberal Democrats led a campaign in the late 1960s and early 1970s to revive the House Democratic Caucus, which they then used to make dramatic reforms in House procedures, including a sweeping assault on the seniority system. *(See* REFORM.*)*

Their first step was to get Speaker John W. McCORMACK, a Massachusetts Democrat, to agree in 1969 to hold regular monthly meetings of the caucus. Then in the early 1970s a wave of liberal Democrats was elected to the House, adding to the ranks of those sitting members who were frustrated with the rigid seniority system, which kept elder members, out of step with party politics, in top positions. The larger bloc of reformers made possible a number of changes.

The caucus voted to give responsibility for nominating committee chairmen to a new panel, the Steering and Policy Committee, a group of about thirty members headed by the Speaker. The panel, an arm of the leadership, also proposed committee assignments, a job previously handled by Democrats on the Ways and Means Committee. (Republicans since 1917 had given that role to a Committee on Committees; in the Senate, similar policy groups within each party recommended committee posts.)

Black Power
Among the most effective of all special
caucuses has been the Congressional Black
Caucus, which includes every black legislator.
Five of its members are shown here: from the
left, William L. Clay, Missouri; Julian C. Dixon,
California; Louis Stokes, Ohio; Walter E. Fauntroy,
nonvoting delegate of the District of Columbia;
and Mickey Leland, Texas. All are Democrats.

The caucus also decided to vote, by secret ballot, on nominations for committee chairmen and for chairmen of subcommittees of the Appropriations Committee. The caucus agreed to have Democrats on each committee, instead of the chairman, choose subcommittee chairmen. Worried that it might be resurrected after years of disuse, the caucus also repealed the rule on binding votes.

The reforms—and the new authority of the caucus—were dramatically illustrated in 1975, when the House Democratic Caucus unseated three incumbent chairmen. (The steering panel traditionally has followed the seniority system, nominating the senior member as chairman.) Two years later the caucus voted to oust a sitting subcommittee chairman from the Appropriations Committee.

Since then the Democratic Caucus has been more selective in using its authority. In 1985, though, the elderly chairman of the ARMED SERVICES Committee, Illinois Democrat Melvin Price, was replaced by Les Aspin, a Wisconsin

Democrat who ranked several places below the chairman in seniority. After his first term Aspin was himself challenged. Although it took several ballots, he eventually won reelection. The contest prompted promises from Aspin that, as chairman, he would be more responsive to others' views.

Reformers saw the Armed Services debate as evidence that the changes were working, making chairmen more accountable to the party and the party leadership more attentive to the caucus. Caucus politics, too, had grown more sophisticated, as the caucus's rank and file recognized that the power to remove chairmen was enhanced if used selectively.   ~

Caucuses, Special

Special caucuses are unofficial organizations that allow members of Congress to pursue common interests important to them and their constituents. More than a hundred special caucuses have been organized in the House of Representatives and Senate, and most legislators choose to join at least one of these groups. Representatives and senators also are automatically members of their own party caucus or conference. (See CAUCUSES, PARTY.)

A common denominator draws members to each informal caucus. The link can be as basic as race (the Congressional Black Caucus) or as straightforward as geographic location (the Long Island Congressional Caucus). The shared interest can be as specific as shoes (the House Footwear Caucus) or as broad as the future (Congressional Clearinghouse on the Future). Caucus members can be tied together by something as controversial as abortion (the Pro-Life Caucus) or as uncontroversial as tourism (the Congressional Travel and Tourism Caucus).

Some caucuses have only a handful of members, others more than a hundred. Membership is rarely selective, though the House Wednesday Group, a roundtable of Republicans that meets weekly,. invites its thirty-five or so members to join. Other caucuses by definition have criteria for membership, such as the one set up at the beginning of each Congress by new House members, or the caucuses with party affiliations. Even a few state delegations have evolved into formal organizations with staff.

Caucuses have thrived particularly in the House, where many members feel isolated and anonymous, even within their own parties. Many caucuses function almost as internal interest groups, lobbying committees and individuals for a particular cause. Caucuses sometimes send representatives to testify at hearings, and some draft specific legislative proposals. Critics, however, complain that caucuses disperse power in an already fragmented Congress and do little more than add to the swollen legislative bureaucracy.

Unlike legislative committees and the official party groups, which often have to mute conflict in order to build compromises, caucuses can endorse even the most controversial points of view. The staff director of the House Republican Study Committee, a conservatively oriented caucus, praised the cohesiveness of that group. "I've got a core group of people it would be hard to offend no matter how conservative I got," he said in 1987. In contrast, the Republican Conference, the party's official caucus, is constrained by the need to satisfy the wide range of political views represented in its membership.

Party Groups

Legislators have always formed alliances, but the modern special caucus dates from 1959, when liberal members of the House, frustrated by the successes of conservatives, revamped their own loosely knit group into a formal organization, the Democratic Study Group. With about a hundred members, a formal title, and annual dues then of $25, DSG was the prototype for the dozens of partisan and bipartisan caucuses organized since then.

The DSG provides background reports and daily bulletins on almost every legislative issue to more than 200 members. The Republican organization that mirrors DSG is the House Republican Study Committee, which was set up in 1973. In the 1980s it had about 120 members and was dominated by conservatives; like DSG, it produces background reports.

Dissatisfied, narrowly focused groups within a party have also used caucuses to draw attention to their demands. Conservative Republicans created the Conservative Opportunity Society in the 1980s; their relationship with House Democrats was more confrontational than the approach favored by Republican party leaders. A group of conservative Democrats organized the Conservative Democratic Forum, known informally as the Boll Weevils.

Some political caucuses are little more than a label for a loose coalition. The Gypsy Moths, also known as the Northeast-Midwest Republican Coalition, mobilized to fight Reagan administration budget cuts in the early 1980s. Another Republican-based caucus, the 92 Group, focused on having a Republican majority in 1992.

Minority Caucuses

Ethnic and minority groups have often banded together when Congress considered issues particularly important to them. Italian-Americans, Polish-Americans, Irish-Americans, and others have periodically spoken in unison. Blacks, Hispanics, and women have been represented by organized caucuses in the Congress of the 1980s.

Among the most effective of all caucuses has been the relatively small Congressional Black Caucus, which includes every black legislator. When it was formed in 1969, the caucus had only nine members, who had little role in the congressional power structure. By 1987 the Black Caucus had grown to twenty-three members and, thanks to seniority gains, included the chairmen of several committees and more than a dozen subcommittees. *(See* BLACKS IN CONGRESS.*)*

In addition, because of pressure by the caucus on the Democratic leadership, blacks had been appointed to the most powerful House committees. A measure of their success was the election in 1985 of William H. GRAY III, a black Pennsylvania Democrat, as chairman of the Budget Committee, an important and highly visible post. Legislatively, the Black Caucus lobbied for an economic agenda to help the poor, who are disproportionately black, and to strengthen and enforce civil rights laws. A major victory for the caucus was passage in 1986 of legislation imposing economic sanctions against South Africa.

The cohesiveness of the Black Caucus contrasted with the caucus of Hispanic members, which rarely took a unanimous position. The thirteen legislators in the Congressional Hispanic Caucus in 1987 ranged from conservative to liberal. On a 1986 immigration reform bill, a vital issue for HISPANICS, the bipartisan caucus split down the middle on the final vote.

WOMEN in the House formed a caucus in 1977, but they reorganized it in 1981 as the Congressional Caucus on Women's Issues and opened it to male members. In 1987 eighteen of the twenty-five women representatives belonged to the caucus, which had more than a hundred members in all. The women who did not join the caucus tended to be politically conservative. Among other activities, the caucus supported legislation to improve the economic status of women.

Other Alliances

Energy shortages in the 1970s sharpened simmering economic conflicts between southern and western states, dubbed the Sun Belt, and the older industrialized areas of the Northeast and Midwest. Forming a caucus was a simple, direct way to recognize these complex problems, and the Congressional Sun Belt Caucus and the Northeast-Midwest Congressional Coalition were established.

Industries such as steel, textiles, and automobiles have firm allies in their lobbying efforts: caucuses specifically to promote each industry. Primarily composed of legislators whose districts depend on a particular industry, the caucuses have focused on limiting imports and removing trade barriers to U.S. products abroad.

Funding

Unlike the official party caucuses, to which Congress directly appropriates funds, the unofficial caucuses depend on dues from members to cover their expenses. (Caucuses without separate offices or staff do not usually require dues.) The dues vary greatly. Among the more expensive as of 1987 were DSG, which charged $2,700, and the Congressional Black Caucus, with a $4,000 annual fee. Members have paid their favorite caucus as much as $20,000.

Dues are transferred to a caucus from a legislator's official allotment for office expenses and salaries. Some people have complained about using government money for that purpose. "These caucuses are financed by the federal Treasury and are by their nature lobbies," said Rep. Charles E. Bennett, a Florida Democrat, in 1985. "And I don't think the federal Treasury ought to be financing lobbying groups."

House Rules

The House put caucuses under close supervision in 1981. The new rules were prompted by concerns about groups that depended on both congressional and private funds. In addition to dues from members, several groups also received outside funds through donations, subscriptions to newsletters, and other activities.

Under the 1981 rules change, a special caucus seeking House office space and a share of congressional funds has to be certified as a legislative service organization by the House Administration Committee. Financial disclosure reports must be filed, and no private funds can be accepted.

Several groups that once depended on private funds have set up separate institutes or foundations that still accept donations and grants and have offices outside of congressional buildings. For example, the Congressional Black Caucus has a parallel Congressional Black Caucus Foundation; the Environmental and Energy Study Conference has a separate institute that conducts research and publishes a newsletter; and the Northeast-Midwest Coalition operates a research group. ~

ADDITIONAL READING

Cigler, Allan J., and Burdett A. Loomis, *Interest Group Politics.* 1983.

Censure. See DISCIPLINING MEMBERS.

***Chadha* Decision.** See LEGISLATIVE VETO.

Chaplain

Both the Senate and the House of Representatives have a chaplain, who is responsible for opening each daily session with a prayer and serves generally as spiritual counselor to members, their families, and their staffs. The chaplains are officers of the House and Senate and had annual salaries of $77,500 at the beginning of 1988.

The official chaplain does not offer the opening prayer every day. That honor occasionally goes to guest chaplains, who are often from members' home districts.

In 1983 the Supreme Court ruled that the practice of opening sessions with a prayer did not violate the ban on establishment of religion contained in the First Amendment to the Constitution.

The Court noted that the practice dated back to the First Congress, the Congress that adopted the First Amendment. "The practice of opening legislative sessions with prayer has become part of the fabric of our society," the Court said.

The Senate elected its first chaplain on April 25, 1789, and the House followed suit five days later. Each was paid $500 a year, comparable to the $6 received by members of Congress for each day of attendance. ~

Children, Youth, and Families Committee, House Select

Family issues were just emerging as a top concern of voters when the House in 1982 agreed to set up a select committee to focus on children, youth, and families. Since then, concerns about those issues have mushroomed, and the committee's studies and hearings have gained increased attention.

California Democrat George Miller pushed the House to approve the committee and then became its first chairman. He has used the panel to spotlight numerous problems and suggest solutions; one report showed improvements in infant mortality after a relatively modest investment in prenatal care. Miller has also argued that healthier babies would save society in the long run from higher costs of educating and caring for problem children.

The committee's authorization must be renewed at the beginning of each two-year congressional term. The panel has about thirty members. Like other special and select committees, it has no authority to write legislation. ~

Chisholm, Shirley

The first black woman to enter the House, New York Democrat Shirley Chisholm (1924-) never lost the independence that led her to title her autobiography *Unbought and Unbossed*. Her 1972 bid for the Democratic presidential nomination, which she hoped would "rattle the power structure," was quite in character; that she had no chance of winning did not deter Chisholm, who ended up with 151 votes at the party's national convention. By the time she retired from the House in

1983, though, Chisholm was no outsider. In 1977 she gained a seat on the RULES Committee, a position that gave her a chance to review virtually every major bill heading toward the House floor.

Chisholm's standing in the House had not come without a fight. When she first arrived in 1969, House Democratic leaders put her on the Agriculture Committee, a seat the Brooklyn Democrat did not want. She served instead on Veterans' Affairs until 1971, when she won the Education and Labor position she had sought in the first place.

Though the Democratic leadership gave her the seat on the Rules Committee, the ties were not binding. More than once Chisholm refused to agree to restrictions on floor action sought by Democrats. Chisholm was unpredictable in other ways. Despite her background as an educator, she opposed a separate Education Department, fearing it would mean less attention for special minority programs. She even had her differences with the largely male Congressional Black Caucus, which did not endorse her bid for the presidency. "Black males are no different than white males," Chisholm snapped when asked to explain the rift. "Since when do I have to clear it with them?"

Chisholm, born in Brooklyn in 1924, began her career as a nursery school teacher and director, and then headed a child-care center. She was elected to the state Assembly in 1964. When congressional district lines were redrawn in 1968, one result was a predominantly black district in Brooklyn. Chisholm, with strong support from church and civic organizations, was elected to the House.   ~

Christmas Tree Bill

Few sessions of Congress go by without passage of a "Christmas tree bill," so called because it is adorned with amendments like baubles on a holiday tree.

The traditional Christmas tree bill was a minor House-passed measure on which the Senate hung a variety of unrelated amendments providing benefits for special interests. The amendments most often involved tax or trade treatment. Enactment of these bills often came as Congress was preparing to adjourn for Christmas.

Russell B. LONG, chairman of the Senate Finance Committee from 1965 until Republicans gained control of the chamber in 1981, claimed fatherhood of the Christmas tree bill. The prototype was a measure passed in 1966, in the Louisiana Democrat's second year as Finance chairman.

The bill's original purpose was to help the United States solve its balance-of-payments difficulties. But Long's committee transformed it into a gem of legislative vote trading and congressional accommodation that aided, among others, presidential candidates, the mineral ore industry, large investors, hearse owners, and Scotch whisky importers.

1980s Measures

The Christmas tree bill in its traditional form became less common in the 1980s. Members of Congress preferred to tuck special-interest amendments into huge omnibus bills where their presence was unlikely to be noticed. Emergency funding measures, called CONTINUING RESOLUTIONS, became magnets for unrelated amendments because they had to be passed quickly to keep government agencies from shutting down. A prime example was a measure passed only days before Christmas in 1987. The huge package, appropriating money for the entire federal government, was riddled with special-interest provisions; some did not come to light for weeks after passage of the bill.   ~

Clark, James B. 'Champ'

Missouri Democrat James B. "Champ" Clark (1850-1921) was a member of the House of Representatives from 1893 until 1921 except for one two-year period (1895-97). From 1911 to 1919 he was SPEAKER of the House, succeeding Joseph G. CANNON, whose ouster he had helped engineer. In 1912 Clark was a candidate for the Democratic presidential nomination but lost to Woodrow Wilson after forty-six ballots.

Clark was elected Democratic minority leader in the Republican-controlled House in 1907. Opposed to the iron rule of Speaker Cannon, Clark proposed a resolution in 1909 to curtail the Speaker's powers. Although Clark's resolution was defeated, a measure based on his proposal won approval the following year.

In 1911, when the Democrats gained a majority in the House, Clark became Speaker—but without the sweeping powers Cannon had enjoyed. Oscar W. UNDERWOOD of Alabama was elected majority leader and chairman of the Ways and Means Committee. The Democratic Caucus decided that the party's members on Ways and Means would make up the Committee on Committees with responsibility for making committee assignments—a power previously exercised by the Speaker. As a result, Underwood, not Clark, functioned as the leader of House Democrats, and the power of the Speaker went into a fifteen-year decline.   ~

Clay, Henry

Henry Clay (1777-1852) of Kentucky was one of the giants of Congress

Henry Clay

during the first half of the nineteenth century. Gifted with charm and eloquence, Clay was known as the "Great Compromiser" for his efforts to resolve sectional disputes over slavery. His initiatives included two plans to curb the expansion of slave territory: the Missouri Compromise of 1820 and the Compromise of 1850. A spokesman for western expansion, Clay proposed an "American System" for economic development that featured a federally financed transportation network and high tariffs to protect American industry. Clay ran unsuccessfully for president as a Democratic Republican in 1824, as a National Republican in 1832, and as a Whig in 1844. *(See* POLITICAL PARTIES.*)*

Clay began his congressional career with two brief stints in the Senate, where he filled unexpired terms in 1806-07 and 1809-10. He was elected in 1810 to the House of Representatives, where he served for most of the next fifteen years. In the House he quickly joined other young "War Hawks" in pushing the nation into the War of 1812 against England. Clay was chosen as SPEAKER on the day he took office in 1811, and he remained Speaker as long

as he was in the House. Although he resigned his seat twice—in 1814, to help negotiate an end to the War of 1812, and again in 1820—he was reelected Speaker as soon as he returned to the House in 1815 and 1823. A formidable presiding officer and an accomplished debater, Clay exerted firm control over the House until he left the chamber for good in 1825.

Running for president in 1824, Clay wound up last in a four-way race that had to be decided by the House of Representatives. There Clay threw his support to John Quincy ADAMS, ensuring Adams's election. When the new president made Clay his secretary of state, critics charged that Clay was being paid off for his election support. *(See* ELECTING THE PRESIDENT.*)*

Debates Over Slavery

In 1830 Clay was elected to the Senate, where he played a leading role in the debates over slavery that preceded the Civil War. He left the Senate in 1842 but returned in 1849 and served until his death in 1852.

Clay's final effort to prevent the breakup of the Union, known as the Compromise of 1850, attempted to calm rising passions between slaveholding and free states. Among other measures, the Compromise of 1850 permitted California to be admitted to the Union as a free state and strengthened the federal law governing capture and return of runaway slaves.

Clay's proposals prompted a debate that has often been called the greatest in the Senate's history. It marked the last appearance in the Senate chamber of the "great triumvirate"—Clay; Daniel WEBSTER of Massachusetts, an apostle of national unity; and John C. CALHOUN of South Carolina, the South's foremost defender of slavery and states' rights. Calhoun, who was fatally ill, sat in the chamber while his final speech was read by a colleague.   ~

Clerk of the House

The Clerk of the House is the chief administrative officer of the House of Representatives. His Senate counterpart is known as the SECRETARY OF THE SENATE. The clerk's wide-ranging responsibilities include providing stationery supplies, electrical and mechanical equipment, and office furniture; paying salaries of House employees; attesting and fixing the seal of the House to SUBPOENAS; recording and printing bills and reports; reporting debates and keeping the official House *Journal*; certifying passage of bills; compiling lobby registration information; and preparing a variety of periodic reports.

The job pays well, $86,815 annually as of early 1988. Clerk of the House Donnald K. Anderson, who took over the post in 1987, had started out as a House PAGE in 1960 and worked his way up through PATRONAGE appointments by Democratic members.

The clerk is elected by the majority party in the House and generally remains in his job until that party loses control of the chamber. In 1967, however, the House replaced Clerk Ralph R. Roberts, who had served in the post since 1949. Roberts had been criticized for using the chauffeur and limousine that went with his job for trips to his home in Indiana and to racetracks. ∼

Cloakrooms

The locker rooms of the House and Senate are the cloakrooms, narrow L-shaped rooms along the sides and rear of the two chambers. Originally designed to hold coats, the hideaways now feature well-worn leather chairs, refrig-erators stocked with soda and candy, and televisions. When a series of votes is under way on the floor, legislators congregate in the cloakrooms, where they are able to relax while remaining only steps from the chamber. Cloakrooms are Democratic or Republican; each party oversees the cloakroom on its side of the chamber.

Employees assigned to the cloakrooms prepare messages several times a day describing floor action and floor schedules. These recorded updates are available by telephone.

Women members for many years chose not to use the cloakrooms, preferring the separate women's cloakroom set up in 1927. A special room for women members was still provided in the 1980s, though women were also frequent visitors in the majority and minority cloakrooms. ∼

Cloture. See FILIBUSTER.

Commerce Power

Congress has used its constitutional power over interstate commerce to justify a vast array of laws, ranging from civil rights to water pollution. What once was a controversial and disputed concept is now an accepted basis for laws governing the way Americans behave.

The federal authority over interstate commerce has been a key factor in the shift of power away from the states and toward the federal government. For many years the Supreme Court resisted a broad use of the commerce power, seeing it as an intrusion both on states' rights and on private property rights. But in the late 1930s, under pressure from President Franklin D. Roosevelt, the Court relaxed its stand. The interstate commerce power became almost

From Railroads . . .
The interstate commerce power is responsible for the bulk of modern federal regulatory activities. First to feel its regulatory bite were the railroads. Congress assumed authority over them in 1887.

limitless, matching at last the federal government's constitutional authority to oversee foreign commerce, which had never been questioned.

Since then, Congress has stretched the *interstate* commerce power to cover agricultural pricing, child labor, civil rights, consumer protection statutes, endangered birds, handguns, regulation of stocks and bonds, sewage treatment, minimum wages, worker safety laws, and more.

Authority over *foreign* commerce has allowed Congress to regulate trade with other nations, promoting exchange with some countries while using tariffs and embargoes to inhibit trade with others. The commerce clause has also made possible regulation of international shipping, aviation, and communications.

Cases involving the commerce clause still reach the Supreme Court. Now, however, the focus is not on what the federal government can do, but on what the states cannot do. Though clearly tilted toward awesome federal authority, the debate over the com-

merce power is not over. For example, the National League of Cities has argued that state and local government employees are not covered by federal minimum-wage laws, which are based on the commerce power. The Supreme Court agreed in 1982; in 1985 it reversed itself.

Few legal restraints remain on use of the commerce clause. Politically, though, expansive federal power has come under fire. Regulation of the transportation industry, one of the first uses of the commerce power, has been sharply curbed. Trucking deregulation in 1980 swept aside rules dating back forty-five years. That same year federal constraints on railroad rates and routes, a government concern since 1887, were largely lifted, leaving only limited rules.

Like the judicial debate over the commerce clause, the political debate is not over. Airline deregulation is one example. The strict government rules on routes and fares that had controlled the industry since 1938 were lifted in 1978. The changes unleashed a flurry of reduced fares and new routes; they also caused convulsions in the industry that saw some airlines combine and others fail. By the mid-1980s serious concerns about air safety had prompted many to argue for tighter government oversight. The same factor that had spurred the original broad application of the commerce clause—protecting the public interest—was once again at work.

Origins

The Articles of Confederation, adopted in 1777, set up a weak Congress, with little power over the states. Fights among the states were a primary reason for drafting a new constitution. They were taxing each other's goods, printing money, and generally bickering over how the economy would function. A stronger Congress, reasoned those gathered at the Constitutional Convention, was needed to resolve these conflicts and others. The clause giving Congress power to regulate interstate commerce was not extensively debated at the time. The Supreme Court first defined Congress's power to regulate interstate commerce in the case of *Gibbons v. Ogden* in 1824.

Congress moved gradually toward a broad application of the commerce clause. In the first part of the nineteenth century, as new frontiers opened up, Henry CLAY envisioned a strong federal role in developing roads and canals, which he called an "American System." Although Clay won support in Congress, President James MADISON vetoed the legislation in 1817. His successor, James Monroe, likewise argued that authority over interstate commerce was limited and did not give Congress the power to establish roads and canals.

Within Congress the federal role was also hotly debated. Southerners anxious to maintain slavery argued against broad federal power and in favor of states' rights. The opposition was led by John RANDOLPH, an acerbic Virginia representative who opposed Clay's American System. "If the Congress can do that," he argued, "it can emancipate the slaves."

Congress tried to get around the controversy by purchasing stock in private companies that were building roads and canals and by giving land grants to states. But even that approach

... To Civil Rights
The commerce power played an important role in congressional battles over civil-rights legislation in the 1960s. A landmark 1964 civil-rights law was rooted in the interstate commerce clause.

COMMERCE: STOCK FOR ALPHABET SOUP

Most modern federal regulatory agencies owe their existence to the Constitution's interstate commerce clause. A look at a few specific agencies shows how broadly the clause has been applied.

The oldest regulatory groups include the Interstate Commerce Commission (1887), Federal Trade Commission (1914), and Food and Drug Administration (1927). But it was during the New Deal era, with its rapid revamping of the federal role, that the "alphabet soup" of government regulatory agencies got its start. Among them were the Commodity Credit Corporation (1933), Securities and Exchange Commission (1933), Federal Communications Commission (1934), and National Labor Relations Board (1938). The Federal Power Commission, set up in 1920 to license construction of power plants in navigable waters, got new powers in the 1930s (and in the 1970s was renamed the Federal Energy Regulatory Commission).

Still operating under its commerce power and the duty to protect the general welfare, Congress has added other agencies, among them the Occupational Health and Safety Administration (1970), Environmental Protection Agency (1970), and Consumer Product Safety Commission (1972).

was unacceptable to President Andrew Jackson, who in 1830 vetoed the purchase of stock in the Maysville Road, a Kentucky turnpike. He argued the road was local, not national, in character. Congress was forced to draw back from roadbuilding; the coalition behind the American System fell apart.

Jackson's veto came just as railroad development was beginning in earnest; that same year the Baltimore & Ohio Railroad opened. The nation's transportation—and the focus of interstate commerce—shifted from canals and turnpikes to rails. Congress did not get actively involved in highway building again until 1916.

Regulation Begins

Railroad expansion led Congress to assume new power under the commerce clause. At first the legislators simply promoted the transportation system, giving generous land grants and government credit to the railroad companies as they crisscrossed the nation with tracks.

The complex network successfully linked the sprawling nation, but not without controversy. Railroad rate structures favored certain companies and regions over others, and rebates and price-fixing were common. Farmers were particularly vocal about what they considered to be unfair treatment. States tried to handle railroad regulation, but with limited success. In 1886 the Supreme Court severely limited the states' authority. The Court said they could not regulate an enterprise engaged in interstate commerce, even if it passed through the state, because interstate matters were a federal, not a state, concern.

With most major railroad companies already operating in more than one state, state regulation was essentially nullified by the Court decision.

Congress responded to the need for federal oversight of the railroads by passing the Interstate Commerce Act of 1887. With the new law, Congress began a decades-long expansion of federal regulation of interstate commerce. The Interstate Commerce Commission, established to oversee the regulation, was the prototype for later regulatory commissions.

The ICC was weak, though, and the Supreme Court within a decade had left the commission toothless. Congress found the Court equally reluctant to endorse congressional control over huge corporations. The anger at the railroads among farmers, consumers, and small-business owners in the late 1800s was matched by their outrage at the growing power of the trusts that controlled the steel, oil, sugar, meatpacking, and other industries. The trusts thwarted competition by combining smaller companies into huge corporations, and by controlling not only production of raw materials, but also manufacturing and distribution.

In an attempt to break up the trusts, and "protect commerce against unlawful restraints and monopolies," Congress passed the Sherman Antitrust Act of 1890. Within five years, though, the Supreme Court had narrowly limited application of the antitrust law, again reflecting the justices' conservative outlook. Congress did not fully address antitrust law again until 1914, when it passed both the Clayton Act and the Federal Trade Commission Act. By then the commerce power had become a very useful, though controversial, congressional tool.

As it endorsed an expansion of federal authority over railroads and corporations, Congress also began to experiment with broader federal "police power," a term used to describe protection of public health, safety, and even morals, a responsibility traditionally handled by the states. Again, the commerce power was the means for expanding congressional authority.

At first, Congress focused on tightening regulation of the railroads. For example, railroad workers responsible for coupling train cars were smashing their hands with alarming frequency. Congress responded by requiring that safety devices be installed on all cars used in interstate commerce. Another safety measure limited the hours that interstate railway employees could work.

Congress did not stop with the railroads. In 1895, upset about the prospect of nationwide gambling operations, the legislators made it illegal to transport lottery tickets across state lines. That expansion of federal police power ended up before the Supreme Court, as had so many other acts based on the commerce clause. This time, though, in 1903, the Court agreed with Congress that lottery tickets were commerce, thus upholding the power to regulate their transport.

'Stream of Commerce'

That the Court was gradually accepting a broader view of the commerce clause was clear two years later in a landmark decision, *Swift & Co. v. United States*, which introduced the term "stream of commerce." Justice Oliver Wendell Holmes, Jr., wrote that Congress still had authority over the production, marketing, or purchase of a product even if that exchange took place entirely within one state, because it was part of the overall stream of commerce.

Then Congress moved into new areas, enacting laws prohibiting the interstate transportation of explosives, diseased livestock, insect pests, falsely stamped gold and silver articles, narcotics, and prostitutes.

A major new realm—protection of the consumer's health and safety—was opened to federal control when Congress in 1906 passed the Pure Food and Drug Act, which banned all harmful substances from food and provided penalties for false labeling. Congress went on to require inspection of red meat being shipped across state lines and, in 1910, to authorize federal action against misbranded or dangerous poisons, such as insecticides. In 1914 deceptive advertising came under federal purview. In each case, Congress depended on the commerce clause.

Broader interpretation of the commerce power also took Congress into an arena the federal government had generally avoided since the Maysville Road veto: highway building. The 1916 Federal Aid Road Act, which provided federal money to states to help build major trunk highways, was a first, modest return to the role President Jackson had thwarted by vetoing aid to the Maysville Road. From that time on Congress steadily expanded its financial commitment, eventually paying for 90 percent of the nationwide interstate highway system.

New Deal Expansion

Never had the commerce power been extended so broadly or rapidly as it was by President Franklin D. Roosevelt. The nation's economy was in shambles when he took office in 1933, and Roosevelt launched a bold attack on the Great Depression. Spurred by the president, Congress invoked its commerce power and other authority to undergird his NEW DEAL programs.

Roosevelt was hampered, though, by the Supreme Court. By mid-1936 the Court had found unconstitutional eight of ten major New Deal statutes. Several decisions were handed down at once on May 31, 1936, known as Black Monday. Roosevelt responded: "Is the United States going to decide . . . that national economic problems must be decided only by the states. . .? We have been relegated to the horse-and-buggy definition of interstate commerce."

Roosevelt's famous battles with the Court eventually ended with victory for the president. From 1937 on, the Court consented to an unprecedented expansion of federal authority, beginning with its ruling in favor of the 1935 National Labor Relations Act, which gave workers the right under federal law to organize and bargain collectively. The Court had made a major shift since its earlier ruling that unions violated antitrust laws.

Civil Rights

The commerce clause played a special role in congressional battles over civil rights legislation in the 1960s. Although the Fourteenth Amendment had been added to the Constitution after the Civil War to clarify individual rights, its scope was limited. Supreme Court decisions had restricted its application to actions carried out by states, not those by individuals and private organizations.

To close that gap Congress turned to the commerce clause. The Supreme Court had already used the clause to restrict segregation. In 1946, for example, the Court upheld a black woman's refusal to make her bus seat available to a white by moving to the rear. Such rules burdened interstate commerce, the Court ruled.

Then President John F. KENNEDY used the commerce clause as the basis for his 1963 legislation to end discrimination in restaurants, hotels, and other public accommodations. It seemed the best legal route for requiring those outside of government to end racial discrimination. Using the commerce clause was also a tactical maneuver to keep southern opponents of the measure from blocking it in Congress. Because of its wording, Kennedy's bill was sent to the Senate COMMERCE Committee, thwarting the chairman of the JUDICIARY Committee, a southern foe of civil rights who had buried many civil rights measures. The Commerce Committee acted quickly on the measure, and its members served as key supporters on the floor. After various compromises, Congress passed the sweeping civil rights legislation in 1964.

Challenges to the law were quickly filed, but Supreme Court decisions upheld its application even to local enterprises. The classic case involved Ollie's Barbecue, a Birmingham, Alabama, restaurant that claimed not to be covered by the law because it had only local clientele. The federal government, seeking to enforce the law, successfully argued that 46 percent of the food served had been supplied through interstate commerce. The restaurant's refusal to serve blacks was declared illegal.

These civil rights decisions left little doubt regarding the about-face in the Supreme Court's view of the commerce power since the nineteenth century. Almost no restriction remained on federal authority under the commerce clause, which the Court had once limited in its efforts to leave most government up to the states and most business unregulated.   ~

ADDITIONAL READINGS

Gavit, Bernard C. *Commerce Clause of the United States Constitution.* 1970.

Swisher, Carl Brent. *American Constitutional Development.* 2d ed. 1954.

Walker, David B. *Toward a Functioning Federalism.* 1981.

Commerce, Science, and Transportation Committee, Senate

The Senate Commerce Committee spent most of the 1980s deregulating the transportation industry—and then reexamining what it had wrought. Faith in the magic of the free market was shaken by complaints about bad service and by mergers and bankruptcies. The Commerce Committee never considered turning back the clock, but its members did talk about tinkering with the remains of the regulatory structure in order to regain some federal control.

The committee has jurisdiction over all forms of transportation, from boats to jets. It also handles legislation dealing with consumer safety, oceans policy, interstate commerce, communications, management of fisheries and the coastal zone, and science, among other areas.

Nothing the committee did, however, matched the impact of its deregulatory moves. The changes began in 1978, when Congress lifted the strict government controls on airline routes and fares that had regulated the industry since 1938. In 1980 trucking deregulation swept aside Interstate Commerce Commission rules dating back forty-five years. That same year, regulation of railroads, a government concern since 1887, was reduced to a shadow of the once elaborate constraints on rates and routes. The committee also reviewed the breakup of the Bell telephone system ordered by federal courts.

The Commerce Committee, set up in 1816, was among the first created in the Senate. Its name was changed in 1961 from the Interstate and Foreign Commerce Committee, to simply Commerce. Reorganization in 1977 made it the Commerce, Science, and Transportation Committee.

Despite its longevity, the committee always ranked far below the Appropriations and Finance committees, both in attracting senators and in having a chance to handle major questions. One unintended effect of deregulation was to diminish further the Commerce Committee's ability to command the Senate's attention. Many of its concerns were, in the eyes of fellow senators, often minor.

For more than two decades the Commerce Committee was chaired by Warren G. Magnuson, a six-term Washington Democrat who was the most senior member of the Senate when he lost his seat to a Republican in 1981. Magnuson was named Commerce chairman in 1955; he finally gave up the post in 1977 to take over the Appropriations Committee. A close friend of Lyndon B. JOHNSON, Magnuson became the president's spear carrier in the 1960s on consumer issues, including automobile safety standards and the Consumer Product Safety Commission. He led an unsuccessful campaign to introduce federal rules for no-fault automobile insurance.

Nevada Democrat Howard W. Cannon was chairman from 1978 to 1981, years of difficult negotiations between the House and Senate over deregulation. He inherited the committee just as the Carter administration was focusing much of its domestic policy on deregulation of the transportation industries. Cannon quickly became known as a tough negotiator in conference who always carried enough proxies in his pocket to back up his position. But Cannon lost the 1980 election to one of the Republicans who tipped control of the Senate to the GOP.

Republican Bob Packwood of Oregon chaired the committee from 1981 until 1985, when he left to take over the Finance Committee. Packwood tried unsuccessfully to continue the wave of deregulation, focusing on loosening federal controls on the broadcasting industry, but his efforts failed. For the next two years, John C. Danforth, a Missouri Republican, held the top post. Skeptical of complete deregulation, he favored moves such as national licensing standards for truck and bus drivers. Danforth had trouble, though, when he tried to pass a product liability bill that set some limits on court awards for damages; he was thwarted by a filibuster led by Ernest F. Hollings, a South Carolina Democrat. When Democrats regained the Senate in 1987, Hollings became chairman of the Commerce Committee, promising to ride herd on the safety practices of the transportation industries.   ∼

Committee Action.   See
LEGISLATIVE PROCESS.

Committee of the Whole

The House of Representatives considers almost all important bills within a parliamentary framework known as the Committee of the Whole. This is one of the most important stages in the LEGISLATIVE PROCESS and comes after the House's legislative committees have studied and drafted the bills. The Committee of the Whole is not a committee as the word is usually understood; it is the full House meeting under another name for the purpose of speeding action on legislation.

The committee is formally known as the Committee of the Whole House on the State of the Union. It includes all 435 members of the House. Meeting on the floor of the House chamber and using special parliamentary rules, the Committee of the Whole debates and amends legislation. It cannot pass a bill. Instead it reports the measure to the full House with whatever changes it has approved. The full House then may pass or reject the bill—or, on occasion, return it to the legislative committee where it originated. Amendments adopted in the Committee of the Whole may be put to a second vote in the full House of Representatives.

Far fewer members must be on the House floor to conduct business in the Committee of the Whole than in a regular House session. This may be an advantage when busy representatives cannot be rounded up to attend a floor meeting. A quorum for doing business in the Committee of the Whole is only 100 members, in contrast to 218 in the full House. The Speaker does not preside but selects another member of the majority party to take the chair. AMENDMENTS are considered under a rule—frequently ignored—that theoretically limits debate to five minutes for those who favor the amendment and five minutes for those opposed.

Until 1971 many important issues were decided in the Committee of the Whole by VOTING methods that provided no record of how individual members stood. That was an attraction for representatives who wanted to avoid publicity about politically difficult issues. Under rules in force in the mid-1980s, a recorded vote must be ordered in the Committee of the Whole if twenty-five members (one-fourth of a quorum) demand it. An electronic voting system is used, and each member's vote is displayed beside his or her name on panels above the Speaker's desk. The vote is also published in the *CONGRESSIONAL RECORD.*

The Committee of the Whole has no counterpart in the Senate. The concept originated in the British House of Commons, where it was used during periods of strained relations with the king to evade the normal restrictions of a formal House of Commons session. ~

Committee on Committees. See
LEADERSHIP.

Committee System

Committees are the legislative workhorses of Congress. Almost every piece of LEGISLATION introduced in the Senate or House of Representatives initially is sent to a committee for review and recommendations. Committees do not have to wait for bills to be referred to them; they frequently write their own bills from scratch. Sometimes bills are prompted by committee INVESTIGATIONS that highlight national problems or disclose official wrongdoing.

Specialized subcommittees usually consider the legislation first, often making substantial changes before sending the bill to the full committee for action. A committee or subcommittee usually holds hearings at which those who favor and those who oppose a measure have an opportunity to express their views. The committee may decide to approve the bill, with or without change, and "report" it to the parent chamber. Or

the panel may decide to kill the measure altogether. It is very difficult for a bill to reach the Senate or House floor without first winning committee approval. The committee also manages the debate once the measure arrives on the floor. Later, after both the Senate and House have passed the bill, committee members from both chambers work together to put the measure into final form. *(See* LEGISLATIVE PROCESS.*)*

Congressional committees have changed dramatically in recent decades. Subcommittees have taken over much of the work once performed by full committees, and junior members now share the power once exercised by authoritarian committee chairmen. A rapid expansion of STAFF has eased the congressional workload; some observers now complain that committee aides have undue influence on legislative policy.

While the prestige of individual committees rises and falls as national issues change, some panels remain at the center of power. That charmed circle includes House WAYS AND MEANS and Senate FINANCE, which are responsible for tax legislation, and House and Senate APPROPRIATIONS, which have jurisdiction over federal spending. The House and Senate BUDGET committees exert influence by setting broad budget guidelines for Congress to follow. One of the most influential committees in either chamber is the House RULES Committee, which controls access to the House floor for all major bills.

Types of Committees
Congressional committees come in several forms, each with its own particular purpose:
• Standing committees handle most of the legislation considered by Congress. They are permanent bodies with responsibility for broad areas of legislation, such as agriculture or foreign affairs. The Senate has sixteen standing committees and the House has twenty-two; they are organized on roughly par-

CONGRESSIONAL COMMITTEES
100th Congress

Senate	House
Agriculture, Nutrition, and Forestry	Agriculture
Appropriations	Appropriations
Armed Services	Armed Services
Banking, Housing, and Urban Affairs	Banking, Finance, and Urban Affairs
Budget	Budget
Commerce, Science, and Transportation	District of Columbia
	Education and Labor
Energy and Natural Resources	Energy and Commerce
Environment and Public Works	Foreign Affairs
Finance	Government Operations
Foreign Relations	House Administration
Governmental Affairs	Interior and Insular Affairs
Judiciary	Judiciary
Labor and Human Resources	Merchant Marine and Fisheries
Rules and Administration	Post Office and Civil Service
Small Business	Public Works and Transportation
Veterans' Affairs	Rules
Select and Special:	Science, Space, and Technology
Aging	Small Business
Ethics	Standards of Official Conduct
Indian Affairs	Veterans' Affairs
Intelligence	Ways and Means
	Select and Special:
Joint Committees	Aging
	Children, Youth, and Families
Joint Economic	Hunger
Joint Library	Intelligence
Joint Printing	Narcotics Abuse and Control
Joint Taxation	

allel lines in each chamber. The number of members varies from committee to committee, and membership is generally proportionate to the overall party breakdown in the parent chamber. Thus the majority party in the chamber maintains a majority in its committees.

• Most standing committees divide their work among several subcommittees. As in the full committees, membership is weighted toward the majority party in the parent body. Subcommittees vary in importance from committee to committee. Some, such as the thirteen subcommittees of each chamber's Appropriations Committee, have great authority; the bills they draft are routinely endorsed by the full Appropriations committees without further review.

Subcommittees provide the ultimate division of labor within the committee system. They help Congress handle its huge workload, and they permit members to develop specialized knowledge in a particular field. But they are often criticized as fragmenting responsibility and increasing the difficulty of policy review, while adding substantially to the cost of congressional operations. An explosion of subcommittees since the 1970s has prompted calls to limit their growth. Some 230 subcommittees existed in 1987; a number of committees had as many as eight. Most subcommittees are offshoots of standing committees.

• Both chambers from time to time create select or special committees to study special problems or concerns, such as hunger or narcotics abuse. The Senate and House committees that investigated the IRAN-CONTRA AFFAIR were select committees. These committees may make recommendations, but they are not usually permitted to report legislation. In most cases they remain in existence for only a few years. Exceptions are the Select INTELLIGENCE committees in both chambers, which do consider and report legislation. They

are standing committees in everything but name.

• Joint committees are composed of members drawn from both the Senate and House; their party makeup reflects the party ratios in each chamber. Chairmanships generally rotate from one chamber to the other every two years, at the beginning of each new Congress. Of the four existing joint committees, only one has a policy role. That is the Joint ECONOMIC Committee, which studies economic problems and makes recommendations to Congress but cannot report legislation. The Joint Committee on TAXATION performs staff work for the House Ways and Means and Senate Finance committees. The two remaining joint committees—those on PRINTING and the LIBRARY—deal with administrative matters, such as the LIBRARY OF CONGRESS and the GOVERNMENT PRINTING OFFICE.

• CONFERENCE COMMITTEES, a special kind of joint committee, are temporary bodies that have important powers. Their job is to settle differences between bills that have passed the House and Senate in slightly different form. They go out of business when the job is done.

Development

The congressional committee system had its roots in the British Parliament and the colonial legislatures. In the earliest days of Congress, legislative proposals were considered first on the Senate or House floor, after which a temporary committee was appointed to work out the details. The committee then reported its bill to the full chamber for further debate, amendment, and passage. Once the committee reported, it was dissolved. Gradually, however, the temporary panels evolved into permanent committees, and legislation came to be referred directly to the committees without prior consideration by the full Senate or House.

By the closing years of the nineteenth century these small groups had developed such great power that Congress was frequently said to have abdicated its lawmaking function to its committees. Although committees were created by and responsible to their parent bodies, they functioned with almost total independence. The panels tended to be dominated by their chairmen, whose power resulted from rigid operation of the SENIORITY SYSTEM. Under that system the member of the majority party with the longest continuous service on a committee automatically became chairman.

The chairmen often did not share the prevailing views of Congress as a whole or the membership of their own party. Yet their powers were so great that Woodrow Wilson, in his 1885 study, *Congressional Government*, described the system as "a government by the chairmen of the standing committees of Congress."

One of the last old-time committee czars was Rep. Howard W. SMITH, a conservative Virginia Democrat who chaired the House Rules Committee from 1955 until 1967. The Rules Committee is the gateway through which major bills must pass to reach the floor, and Smith made the most of his power to censor the legislative program of the House. He regularly blocked civil-rights legislation sought by the Democratic leadership.

Congress did not take major steps to curb committee powers until the 1970s, when junior House members demanded and won fundamental changes in the way Congress—particularly the committees—operated. The changes diluted the authority of committee chairmen and other senior members and redistributed power among their younger and less experienced colleagues. Many of these junior members became chairmen of newly created subcommittees. By the 1980s the full committees had lost much of their influence to subcommittees, whose chairmen became

powers in their own right. *(See* REFORM.*)*

The most significant of the 1970s reforms was a decision by House and Senate Democrats to allow the CAUCUS of party members in each chamber to elect committee chairmen. Although most chairmen continued to be chosen on the basis of seniority, the election requirement made chairmen accountable to their colleagues for their conduct; its force was illustrated in 1975, when three House chairmen were deposed in caucus elections. Several others lost their posts in subsequent years.

Caucus election of committee chairmen was only one of the changes that restricted the chairmen's authority. Most House committees were required to establish subcommittees; House Democrats took the additional step of adopting a subcommittee "bill of rights" that transferred authority over subcommittee organization from committee chairmen to subcommittee Democrats. Committees were required to have written rules, and House Democrats were restricted in the number of chairmanships they could hold. Members were given their own professional staff to help them with committee work. Committee and subcommittee staff increased.

The diffusion of committee power ended the era of autocratic committee chairmen. From that time on a chairman's authority depended on the support of a committee majority and his own personal and legislative skills. In the 1960s, during his heyday as chairman of the House Ways and Means Committee, Arkansas Democrat Wilbur D. MILLS enjoyed almost unchallenged authority over his panel. But the political climate had changed by the time Oregon Democrat Al Ullman succeeded Mills in 1975.

Power Centers

Committees vary markedly in the power they exert. One panel may be powerful because of the subjects it handles. Another may become powerful when an aggressive chairman expands his turf. Yet another may be formally classified as a "minor" committee.

Money committees are enduring centers of power. The House Ways and Means and Senate Finance committees write tax bills that govern the flow of revenues into the federal Treasury. They also have jurisdiction over billions of dollars in federal spending for Social Security, Medicare, welfare, unemployment, and other programs. The House and Senate Appropriations committees, which prepare annual funding bills for government agencies, oversee the full range of federal activity. Control over federal spending gives Appropriations members important influence with their colleagues, as well as with the executive branch. The House and Senate Budget committees exert a more subtle power. They set broad spending limits that other committees are expected to observe. But the limits can be violated whenever the political will to meet them evaporates.

The power a committee wields may change with the times. Under an aggressive chairman with expansionist aims, the House ENERGY AND COMMERCE Committee emerged as a major power center in the 1980s. Chairman John D. Dingell, a Michigan Democrat, became known for his skill at capturing jurisdiction over additional areas of legislation. The committee laid claim to measures touching major regulatory agencies, nuclear energy, toxic wastes, health research, Medicaid and Medicare, railroad retirement, telecommunications, tourism, and others. It developed the largest staff and budget of any House committee.

As Energy and Commerce gathered influence, some power centers of an earlier era were in marked, though perhaps temporary, decline. The House EDUCATION AND LABOR Committee had its days in the sun in the 1960s, when Congress was enacting landmark school aid laws; the Senate ENERGY Committee shone in the 1970s, when energy policy was a major economic issue.

The House Rules Committee suffered a brief decline in the 1970s but remains one of the most influential panels in either chamber. With authority to draft ground rules for floor debate on most major bills, Rules can limit or bar amendments to a bill—or prevent its consideration altogether. The House seldom rejects the panel's recommendations on such matters.

Members' Assignments

A member's influence in Congress often is closely related to the committee or committees on which he or she serves. Assignment to a powerful committee virtually guarantees plentiful campaign contributions. While many members may seek a particular committee because they have an interest in that panel's jurisdiction, others' preferences are based on political need. Members from large agricultural districts gravitate toward the AGRICULTURE committees. Those with major military installations often seek out the ARMED SERVICES committees.

The political parties in each chamber assign members to committees. Those assignments are then routinely approved by the full House or Senate at the beginning of each two-year Congress. The specific process varies by chamber and party.

Just wanting to be on a committee is not enough to ensure assignment to it. In most cases members have to fight for assignments to the more influential panels. In each chamber a few powerful committees, such as Finance and Ways and Means, are difficult to get on. By contrast, congressional leaders often have to seek "volunteers" to serve on lesser panels, such as the House DISTRICT OF COLUMBIA Committee. A member's rank on a committee is determined by his length of service, or seniority, on the panel, and a new member must start at the bottom.

Representatives typically serve on only two committees. Senators often serve on four. Although some veteran members do switch committees, most keep their assignments throughout their careers, gradually advancing through the seniority system to the coveted position of chairman (or ranking minority member, depending on which party is in power).   ∼

ADDITIONAL READINGS

Davidson, Roger H., and Walter J. Oleszek. *Congress and Its Members.* 2d ed. 1985.
Fenno, Richard F., Jr. *Congressmen in Committees.* 1973.
Goodwin, George. *The Little Legislatures: Committees of Congress.* 1970.
Smith, Steven S., and Christopher J. Deering. *Committees in Congress.* 1984.
Unekis, Joseph K., and Leroy N. Rieselbach. *Congressional Committee Politics: Continuity and Change.* 1984.

Concurrent Resolution.   See
LEGISLATION.

Conference Committees

Conference committees play such an important part in the LEGISLATIVE PROCESS that they are sometimes called the third house of Congress. A bill cannot be sent to the president for his signature until it has been approved in identical form by both the Senate and House of Representatives. Frequently, however, the two chambers pass different versions of the same bill, and neither is willing to accept the version passed by the other. Enter the conference committee, a temporary Senate-House panel established solely to work out the differences between the two chambers on a particular bill. Although conferences are convened on a relatively small number of measures, these bills generally include the most important LEGISLATION before Congress.

Conference committee members are formally appointed by the Speaker of the House and presiding officer of the Senate. In practice they are chosen by the chairman or senior minority party member of the committee (or committees) that originally handled the bill. Conferees usually are selected on the basis of their SENIORITY, or length of service, and their knowledge of the legislation. Where a subcommittee has exercised major responsibility for a bill, its senior members may be chosen. Both political parties are represented on the conference committee.

There need not be an equal number of conferees, known as managers, from each house, because a majority vote determines the position of each chamber's delegation on all decisions made in the conference. Conference committees vary widely in size. The conference committee on a 1981 bill to control toxic substances consisted of eight members. By contrast, it took more than 250 members to shape that year's deficit-reduction measure; conferees broke up into small groups to consider separate sections of the complex legislation.

Senate and House conferees vote separately on each issue, and a majority of both delegations must agree before a compromise provision is included in the final bill. Conferees are supposed to defend their own chamber's provisions even if they disagree with them. They are not supposed to insert new material in a bill or reconsider provisions that are the same in both the House and Senate versions. In practice, however, many bills are substantially rewritten in conference. Conferees are not always able to compromise all of their differences; in that case they may leave final decisions on some matters to the full

Conferees at Work
Conference committees are often appointed to reconcile Senate and House differences on important bills. Traditional full-scale conferences, like this one on a 1986 education bill, sometimes give way to private negotiations between conference leaders.

House and Senate. A majority of conferees from each chamber must sign the conference report containing the compromise.

The Senate and House must approve the conference report and resolve any remaining differences before the compromise bill can go to the White House. Conference reports are rarely rejected and cannot be amended on the floor under ordinary procedures. The conference committee dissolves after approval by one chamber; should the conference report be rejected, a new conference could be required.

The conference system, used by Congress since 1789, had developed its modern practice by the middle of the nineteenth century. Until 1975 most conference committees met in secret, but House and Senate rules changes have broken down the secrecy and seniority that once were the norm. However, some conferences—such as those dealing with secret intelligence activities—still are closed, and others are settled by a small number of senior members negotiating behind closed doors. *(See* REFORM.) ~

ADDITIONAL READING

Volger, David J. *The Third House: Conference Committees in the U.S. Congress.* 1971.

Confirmation. See APPOINTMENT POWER.

Conflict of Interest. See ETHICS.

Congressional Budget and Impoundment Control Act. See BUDGET PROCESS.

Congressional Budget Office

Congress has its own office of budget specialists and economists to provide budgetary analyses and economic forecasts. The Congressional Budget Office is intended to give legislators nonpartisan information, setting out policy options without making recommendations. CBO acts as a scorekeeper when Congress is voting on the federal budget, tracking bills to make sure they comply with overall budget goals. The agency also estimates what proposed legislation would cost over a five-year period.

CBO works most closely with the House and Senate Budget committees, which like CBO were established in 1974 by a new congressional budget law. The intent of that law was to force Congress to consider the overall federal budget, with projected revenues, spending, and deficits. In the past legislators had made spending decisions haphazardly, rarely considering future costs or how new programs fit into the overall budget. *(See* BUDGET PROCESS.*)*

The new budget process was also an attempt to regain fiscal control that had been lost to the executive branch. Congress created CBO to give it the kind of expert budgetary support that the president received from his Office of Management and Budget.

The CBO director is appointed for a four-year term by the Speaker of the House and the president pro tempore of the Senate. Alice M. Rivlin was CBO director from 1975 to 1983. She was followed by Rudolph Penner, who left in 1987. Penner's successor had not been chosen by mid-1988.　　　　　∼

Congressional Directory

The *Congressional Directory* is the official who's who of Congress. The thick volume, published at the beginning of each two-year term of Congress, contains biographies of each senator and representative, as well as a hodgepodge of other information: lists of committees, telephone numbers, maps of congressional districts, diagrams of Capitol offices, staffs of executive agencies, and a roster of ambassadors, among other material.

The *Directory* has been published since 1821. The Postmaster printed the *Directory* until 1857, when the Joint Committee on Printing took over. The format of the book has changed little over the years, although it has grown larger. The 1877 edition had 160 pages; the 1987 edition had ten times that number. Single copies of the *Directory* can be purchased from the GOVERNMENT PRINTING OFFICE.　　∼

Congressional Record

The *Congressional Record* is the primary source of information about what happens on the floors of the Senate and House of Representatives. The *Record*, published daily when Congress is in session, provides an officially sanctioned account of each chamber's debate and shows how individual members voted on many issues.

By law, the *Record* is supposed to provide "substantially a verbatim report of the proceedings." Exchanges among legislators during debate can be quite lively and revealing. But senators and representatives are able to edit their remarks for the *Record*, fixing grammatical errors or even deleting words spoken in the heat of debate. Speeches not given on the floor are often included, though both the Senate and House have tightened rules about "inserting remarks," as the process is known. The full texts of bills and other documents, never read aloud on the floor, are often printed in the *Record*.

Because much of what Congress does takes place off the House and Senate floors, reading the *Record* gives only a limited sense of how Congress works. Despite its drawbacks, though, the *Record* is an essential tool for a general

Printing the *Record*
The *Congressional Record* comes off the presses at the Government Printing Office. The *Record* is published daily when Congress is in session.

student of Congress and for anyone following a specific issue. In addition to floor debate and vote tallies, the *Record* notes past and future committee meetings and hearings, as well as the next day's schedule for floor action. *(See* LEGISLATIVE PROCESS.*)*

The *Record* is not the official account of congressional proceedings. That is provided in each chamber's *Journal*, which reports actions taken but not the accompanying debate. However, the *Record* is used to determine what Congress intended when it passed a law; for example, federal agencies drafting regulations sometimes turn to recorded debate to get a better understanding of legislative intent.

The *Record* contains four separate sections: House proceedings, Senate proceedings, Extensions of Remarks, and the Daily Digest. An index published twice a month helps penetrate the gray pages, which typically have three columns of tightly spaced text. Tables and charts rarely appear. While newspaper articles are often inserted by legislators, editorial cartoons are taboo. Smaller type and other typographical

devices identify inserted articles and speeches not actually delivered on the floor.

Since 1979 time cues have marked House floor debate to show roughly what time a particular discussion occurred; Senate proceedings have no indication of time. Speakers during debate are identified by name, but not by party or by state, unless to distinguish between two legislators with the same last name.

The cost of printing the *Record*—about $21 million a year in the mid-1980s—has drawn criticism. About 27,000 copies of each day's issue are printed. Each senator is entitled to fifty free copies for constituents, and each representative to thirty-four. Additional copies are provided for office use. Twice as many free copies were provided until a rules change in 1977.

An annual subscription to the *Record* cost $218 in the mid-1980s; an individual copy cost $1.25. Until 1970 a subscription cost only $1.50 a month.

Rules require that any insert of more than two pages include an estimate of printing costs by the Government Printing Office, which has printed the *Record* since 1873. One of the most expensive inserts appeared in the issue of June 15, 1987, when Rep. Bill Alexander, an Arkansas Democrat, inserted 403 pages covering three and a half years of congressional debate on an amendment barring military aid to the antigovernment contra guerrillas in Nicaragua. Alexander defended the estimated $197,000 cost of inserting the debate.

"The cost of U.S. policy in Central America is more than a billion dollars," said Alexander, an opponent of aiding the contras. "If this information is used properly, it could save us billions of dollars." Republicans said they would object automatically to any future inserts costing in excess of $10,000.   ~

Congressional Research Service.
See LIBRARY OF CONGRESS.

Conkling, Roscoe

A skilled political operator, Roscoe Conkling (1829-88) always managed to keep his hand in power struggles, whether in the Republican party, Congress, or his home state of New York. Conkling seemed to relish conflict, almost inviting confrontation with his arrogant manner and back-room machinations. In the end, though, he pushed too far, and the political intrigue that fueled his career was his undoing.

Conkling first served in the House (1859-63, 1865-67). In the Senate (1867-81) Conkling led a Republican faction that usually controlled the Committee on Committees, rewarding supporters with valuable committee appointments. He eventually chaired the Senate FOREIGN RELATIONS Committee.

Control of appointments was also the key to the New York political ma-

chine that Conkling headed. Two of Conkling's allies ran the customhouse in New York, where U.S. customs revenue was collected and where hundreds worked at PATRONAGE jobs. When President Rutherford B. Hayes, a supporter of civil service reform, took office in 1877, he attempted to curb patronage abuses. Conkling's allies refused to comply with a ban on partisan political activities by federal employees, and Hayes called for their resignations. When they refused to resign, he nominated two other persons to replace them. The Senate declined to approve Hayes's nominees after Conkling invoked senatorial courtesy—a custom permitting senators of the party in office to control selection of local federal officials. The Senate confirmed two subsequent Hayes nominees, however. *(See* APPOINTMENT POWER.)

When James A. Garfield was elected president in 1880, Conkling expected a return to the patronage system. But Garfield was overwhelmed by competing Republican party factions, each demanding patronage slots. When Garfield did not accept Conkling's choices for the customhouse, Conkling tried to get the Senate to reject Garfield's nominations. The effort failed. In a risky power play, Conkling resigned his Senate seat in May 1881, as did his ally, fellow New York senator Thomas C. Platt. Conkling expected the state legislature to reelect them, thus strengthening his hand. But the legislature refused; Conkling's political career was over.   ~

Connally, Tom

Texas Democrat Tom Connally (1877-1963) was chairman of the Senate Foreign Relations Committee from 1941 to 1953, except for two years when Republicans controlled the Senate. He entered the Senate in 1929, after twelve years in the House of Representatives, and remained until his retirement in 1953. He played an important role in U.S. foreign policy in the post-World War II period.

Connally supported successive Democratic administrations on foreign policy. He helped Franklin D. Roosevelt plan the United Nations and was one of the eight representatives of the United States at the San Francisco Charter Conference in 1945. As a result of its membership in the United Nations, the United States became a member of the International Court of Justice. Connally also played an important part in persuading the Senate to accept membership in the court.

In 1946 the Senate considered a resolution allowing the court jurisdiction over all matters that it did not deem purely domestic. Although President Harry S Truman urged that the Senate agree to the resolution, members of the Senate were reluctant to let the court decide what was or was not a matter under domestic jurisdiction. As a compromise, Connally offered what became one of the most notable reservations to an international treaty. The Connally reservation provided that the Senate would decide what are matters "within the domestic jurisdiction of the United States."

Although he lost his chairmanship of Foreign Relations in 1947, when Republicans gained control of the Senate, Connally helped win Senate approval of the Marshall Plan for postwar European recovery. When he regained his chairmanship two years later, he championed the North Atlantic Treaty. ∼

Consent Calendar

Members of the House of Representatives may place on the Consent Calendar any bill on the Union or House CALENDAR that is considered to be noncontroversial. Bills on the Consent Calendar are normally called on the first and third Mondays of each month.

When such a bill is called up for the first time, its consideration may be blocked by the objection of a single member. If objection is made, the bill is carried over to the next day on which the Consent Calendar is called. If three members object the second time the bill is called up, it is stricken from the Consent Calendar. If fewer than three members object, the bill is passed without debate.

Official objectors are appointed by each party at the beginning of every Congress to guard against passage of important measures on which there may be substantial opposition. Objectors police bills on the Consent Calendar and act for absent members. ∼

Conservative Coalition

In 1937 President Franklin D. Roosevelt tried to persuade Congress to pass a bill "packing" the Supreme Court with liberal justices. He failed, even though his own Democratic party commanded overwhelming majorities in both the House and Senate. Roosevelt had discovered a new phenomenon—the "conservative coalition" of Republicans and southern Democrats.

For decades thereafter the conservative coalition was a force to reckon with in the legislative affairs of the nation. Often it was a controlling force. Liberal Democrats rarely were able to govern, even when their party had a clear majority in both the Senate and House of Representatives. They were not able to govern because conservative southerners in their own party, allied with Republicans across the aisle, mustered the votes to stop them.

By the mid-1980s, however, institutional changes in Congress and demographic changes in southern states had weakened the conservative coalition. Many southern Democrats had abandoned coalition politics, saying they did not expect to return to it any time soon.

The Changing South

For reasons that go back to the Civil War, the "solid South" evolved as a one-party region. That began to change as early as 1948, as the national Democratic party under President Harry S Truman added civil rights for blacks to its agenda and the South revolted. Over the next three decades, southern allegiance to the Democratic party steadily eroded, and the Republicans gained a firm foothold. It was in these years that the conservative coalition emerged, often to oppose civil rights. The coalition enabled southern Democrats to exercise power, if only blocking power, from their position as a dwindling minority.

Well into the 1960s most congressional districts in the South were overwhelmingly rural, with a one-party political system, and, in the Deep South, an all-white electorate. Southern members of Congress controlled most of the important committees. Sometimes they cooperated with their national party, but more often they frustrated its goals.

By the 1980s the South had changed, and the Democratic party in the South had changed with it. The South had become much less Democratic, less rural, more suburban, less poor, and more educated. As northern natives moved into the South, the region became less "southern." The upshot was that southern voters became less conservative.

The southern electorate changed in other ways as well. The enfranchisement of blacks in the 1960s and 1970s made southern politicians of both parties far more sensitive to civil rights and other liberal social issues. Blacks comprised a larger share of all southern voters. Republicans, meanwhile, gained a foothold in many parts of the South, although they remained far short of a majority. Many voters came to think of themselves as independents, not aligned with either party.

These changes were felt in Congress. Southern states elected a new breed of Democrats who showed little interest in following traditional conservative leadership. They moved closer to their party's national leadership and no longer cast many votes with Republicans. GOP members, for their part, made fewer attempts to promote unified positions with the southern Democrats.

Statistics compiled by Congressional Quarterly vividly demonstrate the coalition's decline. Beginning in 1957, each year CQ charted the percentage of floor votes on which a majority of southern Democrats and a majority of Republicans voted together against a majority of Democrats from outside the South. During the coalition's heyday in the 1960s and 1970s, it appeared on 20 percent to 30 percent of Senate and House floor votes. By 1987 coalition appearances had dropped to little more than 8 percent.   ∼

Constitutional Amendments

One of the most important functions of Congress is its role in amending the Constitution. The amendment process reflects the constitutional principle of checks and balances, the division of authority among the various branches of government. The power to alter the nation's fundamental law is divided between Congress, the law-making branch of government, and the states, whose ratification of the Constitution originally gave it force.

A major reason for calling the Constitutional Convention of 1787 was that the method of amending the Articles of Confederation, the nation's first legal charter, had proved to be impractical. Any change in that document required the consent of the Continental Congress and every one of the states.

Under the system devised in 1787, still in use today, Congress plays a leading part in proposing constitutional amendments. The final decision on approving amendments still rests with the states, but unanimity is not required. Amending the Constitution nonetheless remains very difficult, and only twenty-six amendments have been adopted over the past two centuries.

Thousands of proposed amendments have failed to make it through the constitutional process. Between 1787 and 1987, Congress submitted only thirty-three amendments to the states; seven of those proposals failed to win ratification.

The most notable recent failure was the proposed Equal Rights Amendment, which died June 30, 1982. Although Congress had extended the original 1979 deadline for ratification, the ERA fell three states short of the thirty-eight needed for ratification. The amendment, pressed by women's rights advocates, stated: "Equality of rights under the law shall not be denied or abridged by the United States or by any state on account of sex." Congress had approved the proposal in 1972, forty-nine years after it was first introduced.

An amendment that would have given the District of Columbia voting representation in Congress died in 1985; only sixteen state legislatures had ratified that proposal within the seven-year deadline set by Congress.

Several proposed amendments were circulating in Congress in 1988, including measures to require a balanced federal budget, permit prayer in public schools, ban abortion, and pro-hibit the use of busing to desegregate public schools.

Amendment Procedures

The Constitution provides two amendment procedures, but only one of them has ever been used. That process begins with Congress, which by two-thirds majority votes of the Senate and House of Representatives may send amendments to the states for ratification. Under the second—untried—method, amendments may be proposed by a constitutional convention, which Congress must convene if requested to do so by the legislatures of two-thirds (thirty-four) of the states.

In either case a proposed amendment becomes part of the Constitution if it is ratified, or approved, by three-fourths (thirty-eight) of the states. Congress has the power to determine which of two procedures states shall use to ratify a proposed amendment. In every case but one it has prescribed approval by state legislatures. The exception was the Twenty-first Amendment, repealing Prohibition; in that case Congress required ratification by state conventions.

The president has no formal authority over constitutional amendments; he cannot veto them. Nor can governors veto approval of amendments by their legislatures.

Convention Controversy

Backers of a proposed constitutional amendment that has been bottled up in Congress sometimes campaign for a convention to consider their proposal. While no such campaign has yet succeeded, the effort may spur Congress to act on the proposal. The Seventeenth Amendment was forced on the Senate in the early 1900s by popular pressure for a constitutional convention to take the selection of senators out of the hands of state legislatures. Fearing that such a convention might go too far, senators decided to submit a specific direct-election proposal to the states.

Trying Again
Supporters of the Equal Rights Amendment
have launched a new drive for the proposal,
which was just three states short of ratification
when its time ran out in 1982. Congress had
approved the ERA in 1972, forty-nine years after
it was first introduced.

Some convention campaigns have come close to success. In the 1960s thirty-three states petitioned Congress for a convention on a constitutional amendment permitting one house of a state legislature to be apportioned on some basis other than population. In the 1970s and 1980s thirty-three states petitioned for a convention on an amendment requiring a balanced federal budget.

No procedures have been established for determining what is a valid state call for a constitutional convention, or for actually running one. As a result, there is no guidance on what a convention could debate, who would be the delegates, how many there would be, and who would preside. Many people fear a convention could become a runaway session that would open up the entire Constitution for amendment.

The balanced-budget campaign il-
lustrates the concern the prospect of a convention can arouse. Responding to a convention drive launched in 1975, Congress began considering a balanced-budget amendment, while intensifying its own efforts to bring the budget under control. As insurance, the Senate JUDICIARY Committee drew up legislation establishing procedures for a convention should the need arise. The matter was set aside when the convention campaign appeared to stall short of its goal in the mid-1980s.

Successful Amendments

The Constitution has proved remarkably durable. Although the United States has changed dramatically in the past 200 years, only a handful of amendments have been required in the basic document devised in 1787.

The first ten amendments, known as the Bill of Rights, were there almost from the beginning. Omission of a bill of rights was the principal source of dissatisfaction with the new Constitution in the state ratifying conventions held in 1788. Congress and the states moved quickly, and the amendments were ratified in 1791. The Bill of Rights added explicit guarantees of fundamental civil liberties, such as freedom of speech and trial by jury, that had not been spelled out in the original document.

A Supreme Court decision and a crisis in presidential election procedures precipitated the next two amendments. The Eleventh Amendment (1795) stipulated that the power of the federal judiciary did not extend to private suits against states. The Twelfth Amendment (1804) provided for separate balloting for president and vice president in the electoral college.

Civil War Era

The Civil War prompted three amendments. The Thirteenth Amendment (1865) abolished slavery. The Fourteenth Amendment (1868) was designed to protect the basic rights of freed slaves, most significantly by forbidding states to deprive any person of life, liberty, or property without due process of law, or to deny anyone equal protection of the laws. The Fifteenth Amendment (1870) prohibited denial of the right to vote on the basis of race, color, or previous condition of servitude.

The Fourteenth Amendment's due process and equal protection clauses, both open to wide differences of interpretation, have served as the basis of controversial shifts in the role of American government. Until the mid-1930s, the amendment was little used to protect individual rights; it was more effective in protecting property rights from government regulations. But in the years following World War II, the Supreme Court began using the Fourteenth Amendment to restrict state action on civil and political rights. By invoking the due process clause, the Court gradually extended Bill of Rights guarantees to cover actions by state governments. Relying largely on the equal protection clause, the Court forced fundamental reforms in state policies of racial segregation and legislative malapportionment; the equal protection clause was the basis for the Court's historic 1954 decision outlawing racial segregation in public schools.

Twentieth Century

Four amendments were ratified from 1913 to 1920, largely as a culmination of the PROGRESSIVE movement. The Sixteenth Amendment (1913) gave the United States the income tax, the Seventeenth (1913) provided for DIRECT ELECTION OF SENATORS, the Eighteenth (1919) prohibited the manufacture, sale, or transportation of alcoholic beverages, and the Nineteenth (1920) cleared the way for WOMEN'S SUFFRAGE.

Two further amendments were ratified in 1933. The Twentieth Amendment altered the dates for the beginning of a new Congress and of the president's term. The Twenty-first repealed the Eighteenth Amendment, thus ending Prohibition.

Five amendments have been added to the Constitution since World War II. The Twenty-second Amendment (1951) limited presidents to two terms in office, the Twenty-third (1961) gave citizens of the District of Columbia the right to vote in presidential elections, the Twenty-fourth (1964) outlawed poll taxes in federal elections, the Twenty-fifth (1967) set procedures for handling presidential disability, and the Twenty-sixth (1971) gave eighteen-year-olds the vote. (See YOUTH FRANCHISE.)   ~

ADDITIONAL READINGS

Mansbridge, Jane J. *Why We Lost the Equal Rights Amendment.* 1986.
Swisher, Carl Brent. *American Constitutional Development.* 2d ed. 1954.

Contempt of Congress

A person who refuses to testify or to produce documents demanded by a congressional committee risks being cited for contempt of Congress, which is a criminal offense. This ability to punish for contempt reinforces the congressional INVESTIGATIONS process.

The Constitution did not specifically grant Congress the power to punish for contempt, except in the case of one of its own members. But from the beginning Congress assumed that it had power to jail persons who were judged in contempt; it even confined some in the Capitol. At first Congress imposed punishment itself, but since the 1930s contempt cases have been prosecuted in the courts.

When a committee wishes to start criminal proceedings against a balky witness, it introduces a resolution in the Senate or House citing the witness for contempt. If the full chamber approves the resolution, as it generally does, the matter is referred to a U.S. attorney for prosecution in a federal court. Contempt of Congress is a misdemeanor punishable by a fine of at least $100 and one to twelve months' imprisonment.

On rare occasions contempt citations stem from acts, such as bribery or libel, that obstruct the proper functions of Congress. Most contempt citations in recent decades have resulted from refusal to cooperate with congressional committees. The peak period for contempt citations came in the years following World War II, as the House UN-AMERICAN ACTIVITIES COMMITTEE conducted a zealous, if controversial, pursuit of people associated with subversive organizations such as the Communist party. In 1950 alone the House voted fifty-nine contempt citations, fifty-six of them recommended by the committee. Many cases involved private persons who invoked the Constitution's Fifth Amendment protection against self-incrimination.

More recently, most contempt disputes have been triggered by the refusal of executive branch officials to supply documents sought by Congress. These disputes have tested the limits of EXECUTIVE PRIVILEGE to withhold confidential information. They often have been settled through compromise. That was the case in 1982 when a House committee recommended that Interior Secretary James G. Watt be cited for contempt for refusing to turn over cabinet documents sought by committee investigators. President Ronald Reagan eventually settled the dispute by giving committee members limited access to some of the documents for one day.

A contempt citation against Anne M. Burford, former head of the Environmental Protection Agency, was canceled in 1983 after the White House agreed to meet subcommittee demands for access to EPA documents. Acting on Reagan's orders, Burford had refused to turn over the documents; she was the first person to be held in contempt of Congress for refusing to produce information because of executive privilege.   ~

Continuing Resolution

A continuing resolution is a measure to keep government agencies operating when regular APPROPRIATIONS bills have not been enacted by the beginning of the government's FISCAL YEAR. The resolution gets its name from the fact that if it does not become law, the agencies could not continue working because they would run out of money.

Congress has used continuing reso-

President Reagan Protests

lutions—CRs in Capitol Hill jargon—for more than a century as a temporary expedient to buy time for completing action on regular appropriations bills. Between 1954 and 1987 Congress approved at least one continuing resolution every year. Most continued funding for a few days, weeks, or months. In the late 1970s, however, Congress began putting into continuing resolutions the entire text of appropriations bills that had not cleared and to make the CRs cover the full fiscal year.

For decades the executive branch had shifted funds to bridge short gaps between the end of the fiscal year and the enactment of new appropriations. But in 1980 the attorney general prohibited that practice for all but essential costs; agencies had to shut down if their funding lapsed. The impact of the ruling was dramatically illustrated the following year, after President Ronald Reagan vetoed a full-year continuing resolution for virtually the entire government. Federal workers were sent home, the Statue of Liberty and Washington Monument were closed, and the Constitution was lowered into a protective vault at the National Archives. Congress and the president hastily agreed on a substitute measure.

Because of their urgency, continuing resolutions increasingly became magnets for controversial bills and amendments, or RIDERS, that might not pass on their own. Before 1986 continuing resolutions often bundled into a single package six or more uncompleted appropriations bills for the coming fiscal year. In 1986 and 1987 Congress swept all thirteen regular appropriations measures into huge OMNIBUS BILLS that provided $576 billion for fiscal 1987 and $604 billion for fiscal 1988.

Reagan Gesture

In 1988 President Reagan took aim at Congress's use of continuing resolutions in his televised STATE OF THE UNION address. Hoisting a copy of the huge fiscal 1988 spending measure, Reagan threatened a veto if lawmakers sent him such a bill again. And he challenged members of Congress to take back funding for such parochial projects as cranberry research and commercialization of wildflowers.

"A picture is worth a thousand words," Sen. John W. Warner, a Virginia Republican, said of Reagan's gesture. "It was probably the first glimpse Americans had ever had" of a continuing resolution.

Omnibus continuing resolutions have some advantages over individual bills. For one thing, they give a better sense of total appropriations and Congress's progress in holding down spending. But individual provisions of the mammoth measures may sail through unnoticed. The fiscal 1988 continuing resolution, approved as Congress rushed to adjourn for Christmas, contained many surprises. One of the most controversial was an $8 million appropriation for education of North African Jews in Paris. That funding surfaced only after the bill had become law; it was quickly rescinded. ~

Courts and Congress

The federal judiciary and Congress possess potent powers to check the authority of each other. Congress determines the courts' jurisdictions, confirms their members, and pays their bills. And the judiciary—most particularly, the Supreme Court—defines the limits of congressional authority.

Both branches have exercised these powers with restraint. Frequent disagreements and heated rhetoric aside, the instances of direct conflict between the judiciary and Congress have been few.

Judicial System

The framers of the Constitution left much unwritten when it came to the judicial branch. Unlike Articles I and II of the Constitution, which detailed the powers and prerogatives of Congress and the executive, Article III simply sketched the outline of a federal judiciary.

"The judicial power of the United States shall be vested in one supreme court, and in such inferior courts as the Congress may from time to time ordain and establish," the Constitution stated. Thus, other than the Supreme Court, the existence and structure of any lower federal courts were left entirely to the discretion of Congress.

Congress exercised that discretion early in its history. As one of its first acts, it passed the Judiciary Act of 1789, establishing the Supreme Court, three circuit courts of appeal, and thirteen district courts. Thereafter, as the nation grew and the federal judiciary's workload increased, Congress established additional circuit and district courts. By 1988 the system had grown to thirteen circuit courts and ninety-four district and territorial courts.

Judicial Review

The Constitution also was silent on the question of judicial review. Various powers were granted to the judiciary but no mention was made of the authority to declare a law passed by Congress unconstitutional and to nullify it.

Court-Packing Plan
President Franklin D. Roosevelt caused a furor in 1937 with his plan to increase the membership of the Supreme Court. The existing Court had struck down a series of New Deal statutes, and Roosevelt hoped to add six new justices who would support his programs. His Court-packing plan was strongly opposed within and outside of Congress and was never enacted.

Many constitutional scholars agree, however, that most of the framers intended the Supreme Court to assume the power of judicial review. Writing as Publius in *The Federalist Papers,* Alexander Hamilton contended: "[T]he courts were designed to be an intermediate body between the people and the legislature in order, among other things, to keep the latter within the limits assigned to their authority."

The question of whether the Court could nullify an act of Congress remained unanswered until 1803. In *Marbury v. Madison,* a case that had begun as a relatively unimportant controversy over a presidential appointment, the Court laid down the principle of judicial review. Chief Justice John Marshall declared that "a law repugnant to the Constitution is void." In so doing, he firmly asserted the power of the Supreme Court to make such determinations: "It is, emphatically, the province and duty of the judicial department to say what the law is."

Although *Marbury v. Madison* is perhaps the most famous decision in the Supreme Court's history, the Court's assertion of its power to nullify a law attracted little attention at the time and it would be more than fifty years before the power was exercised again.

Of the many thousands of acts passed by Congress in its first two centuries, few more than a hundred were declared unconstitutional. Most scholars agree that the primary significance of judicial review is the awareness of every member of Congress that the laws Congress passes can be nullified by the Supreme Court if they violate the Constitution. *(See* LAWS DECLARED UNCONSTITUTIONAL.*)*

Congressional Influence

Congress does not lack ways of influencing the judicial branch. It does so in three general ways—through selection, confirmation, and impeachment of

justices; through institutional and jurisdictional changes; and through direct reversal of specific decisions.

Individual Pressures The Constitution requires that the Senate give its "advice and consent" to appointments to the federal judiciary. Through the unwritten custom of SENATORIAL COURTESY, the Senate has wielded considerable influence over appointments to federal district courts. The Senate generally will refuse to confirm a nomination within a particular state unless the nominee has been approved by the senators of the president's party from that state. Once a candidate is selected, the nomination usually receives a perfunctory hearing and quick approval. *(See* APPOINTMENT POWER.*)*

While the Senate has little to say in the selection of Supreme Court nominees, it does play a significant role once the nomination is submitted for its approval. Of the 145 Supreme Court nominations submitted to the Senate by early 1988, 28 had failed to receive Senate confirmation. In contrast, only eight cabinet nominees had been rejected.

IMPEACHMENT is a rarely used congressional power, but it has been used most often against federal judges. Eleven of the fourteen officers impeached by the House of Representatives by early 1988 were federal judges, as were all five of the officers convicted by the Senate.

Only one Supreme Court justice—Samuel Chase—has ever been impeached by the House, but he was acquitted in 1805 following a sensational Senate trial. Two other Supreme Court justices have faced serious impeachment threats. William O. Douglas weathered impeachment inquiries in 1953 and 1970, but Abe Fortas retired from the Court in 1969 after the House threatened an inquiry.

Congress has even used its power of the PURSE to show displeasure with the Court. In 1964 legislation authorizing

SUPREME COURT NOMINATIONS REJECTED, DROPPED

Nominee	Year	President	Action[1]
William Paterson[2]	1793	Washington	Withdrawn (for technical reasons)
John Rutledge[3]	1795	Washington	Senate rejected
Alexander Wolcott	1811	Madison	Senate rejected
John J. Crittenden	1828	J. Q. Adams	Postponed, 1829
Roger B. Taney[4]	1835	Jackson	Postponed
John C. Spencer	1844	Tyler	Senate rejected
Reuben H. Walworth	1844	Tyler	Withdrawn
Edward King	1844	Tyler	Postponed
Edward King[5]	1844	Tyler	Withdrawn, 1845
John M. Read	1845	Tyler	No action
George W. Woodward	1845	Polk	Senate rejected, 1846
Edward A. Bradford	1852	Fillmore	No action
George E. Badger	1853	Fillmore	Postponed
William C. Micou	1853	Fillmore	No action
Jeremiah S. Black	1861	Buchanan	Senate rejected
Henry Stanbery	1866	Johnson	No action
Ebenezer R. Hoar	1869	Grant	Senate rejected, 1870
George H. Williams[3]	1873	Grant	Withdrawn, 1874
Caleb Cushing[3]	1874	Grant	Withdrawn
Stanley Matthews[2]	1881	Hayes	No action
William B. Hornblower	1893	Cleveland	Senate rejected, 1894
Wheeler H. Peckham	1894	Cleveland	Senate rejected
John J. Parker	1930	Hoover	Senate rejected
Abe Fortas[6]	1968	Johnson	Withdrawn
Homer Thornberry	1968	Johnson	No action
Clement F. Haynsworth, Jr.	1969	Nixon	Senate rejected
G. Harrold Carswell	1970	Nixon	Senate rejected
Robert H. Bork	1987	Reagan	Senate rejected
Douglas Ginsburg	1987	Reagan	Withdrawn

[1] A year is given if different from the year of nomination.
[2] Reappointed and confirmed.
[3] Nominated for chief justice.
[4] Reappointed and confirmed as chief justice.
[5] Second appointment.
[6] Associate justice nominated for chief justice.

Source: Library of Congress, Congressional Research Service.

federal pay increases, Supreme Court justices were given $3,000 less than the increase for other federal executives. There was little doubt in anyone's mind that the action was the result of congressional pique over recent Court decisions on such issues as obscenity, school prayer, desegregation, and loyalty-security programs.

Institutional Pressures Congress sometimes tries to influence the judi-ciary through institutional or proce-dural changes, but it has considered many more proposals than it has ap-proved.

Congress has the power to create judgeships, and it is in this area that politics historically has played a most important role. In 1801, for example, the Federalist-dominated Congress cre-ated additional circuit court judgeships to be filled by a Federalist president. But when the Jeffersonians came to power in the midterm elections, the new posts were abolished.

Congress has increased or reduced the number of justices on the Supreme Court seven times. Generally, laws decreasing the number of justices have been motivated by a desire to punish the president; increases have been aimed at influencing the philosophical balance of the Court itself.

While the size of the Supreme Court has remained at nine since passage of the Judiciary Act of 1869, proposals to change the number of justices have been put forward periodically. The most serious proposal in the twentieth century came not from Congress but from the president. Franklin D. Roosevelt in 1937 proposed legislation that would have made it possible to appoint six additional justices. Ostensibly to improve the efficiency of the Court, the increase was in reality designed to allow Roosevelt to appoint new justices who would support the constitutionality of his NEW DEAL programs. A series of New Deal statutes had been struck down by the existing Court. The Court-packing plan was strongly opposed within and outside of Congress and was never enacted. Nonetheless, it coincided with a change of heart on the part of the Supreme Court. Shortly after the proposal was made public, the Court upheld in quick succession revised versions of key statutes.

Proposals to require two-thirds of the Court to concur in order to declare an act of Congress or state statute unconstitutional have been made occasionally, but they have never been approved and seldom even seriously considered by Congress.

Congress once, in 1868, prevented the Supreme Court from deciding a pending case (*Ex parte McCardle*) by repealing its appellate jurisdiction over the subject matter of the case. Several other such attempts have been made, but they have been defeated, most of them by large margins. In 1802 Congress abolished a Court term altogether to delay a decision.

Reversals of Rulings Of all the methods of influencing the Supreme Court, Congress has had most success in reversing individual Supreme Court rulings either through adoption of CONSTITUTIONAL AMENDMENTS or passage of legislation.

Four of the twenty-six amendments to the Constitution were adopted specifically to overrule the Supreme Court's interpretation of that document. The amendments reversed rulings on the ability of citizens of one state to bring suit against another state (Eleventh Amendment), the application of the Bill of Rights to the states (Fourteenth Amendment), the income tax (Sixteenth Amendment), and the eighteen-year-old vote (Twenty-sixth Amendment).

But the most frequently used method of reversing the Supreme Court is for Congress to repass a statute after modifying it to meet the Court's objections. This kind of reversal through simple legislation is easily accomplished if the Court has interpreted a statute contrary to the construction intended by Congress. The House and Senate may then pass new legislation explicitly setting forth their intention. In many cases of this type, the Court will suggest the course the legislation should take to achieve its original purpose. ～

ADDITIONAL READINGS

Berger, Raoul. *Congress vs. the Supreme Court.* 1969.

Congressional Quarterly. *Guide to the U.S. Supreme Court.* 1979.

Warren, Charles. *Congress, the Constitution, and the Supreme Court.* 1925.

Overleaf:
Leadership offices.

Debt Limit

Bills to increase the national debt limit often serve as vehicles to get around the regular legislative process in Congress. Members whose pet proposals are languishing in committee frequently try to slip their proposals through as amendments to debt-ceiling bills.

Each year Congress approves one or more bills raising the statutory ceiling on federal government borrowing from the public. Conservative members often use debt-limit debates to protest high federal spending, and the bills may generate spirited political conflict. Yet Congress has little choice but to pass the bills: If the increases are not approved, the government will be unable to pay its bills. This gives debt-ceiling measures a special urgency that makes them a natural target for unrelated amendments, or RIDERS. Congress must act on them quickly, and a president is likely to think twice before vetoing them.

Many major proposals have become law as amendments to debt-limit measures. A 1985 debt-limit increase included a radical overhaul of the congressional BUDGET PROCESS. Known as the Gramm-Rudman-Hollings act, the budget measure swept through Congress without committee consideration or extensive floor debate. Two years later, another debt bill was used to make major repairs in the original Gramm-Rudman-Hollings law.

Although crises over debt-limit bills frequently bring the government to the brink of default, Congress has brushed aside suggestions that it eliminate the ceiling altogether. The House in 1979 adopted a system that permitted it to approve debt-limit increases through its budget process without voting separately on the issue. The new system was supposed to end recurrent House wrangling over debt bills, but squabbles continued to erupt from time to time. In the Senate, which chose not to go along with the House system, debt bills continued to provoke extended debates and streams of unrelated amendments.   ~

Deferral.   See BUDGET PROCESS; LEGISLATIVE VETO.

Deficit.   See BUDGET PROCESS.

Delegates, Nonvoting

In addition to its 435 voting members, the House of Representatives has five limited members who can make speeches, serve on committees, and hold chairmanships, but who are not allowed to vote on the House floor.

Four of the five represent islands that are closely linked to the United States: Puerto Rico, the Virgin Islands, Guam, and American Samoa. The fifth represents the DISTRICT OF COLUMBIA, the seat of the national government. All are known officially as delegates except the Puerto Rican, who is called a resident commissioner. Unlike the others, he serves a term of four years instead of two.

Nonvoting positions have existed in some form or other since 1794, when the House received James White as the nonvoting delegate from the Territory South of the Ohio River, later to become the state of Tennessee. Most of the current positions date from the 1970s. Only Puerto Rico's position has much longevity; it was granted in 1900.   ~

Dies Committee.   See INVESTIGATIONS.

Direct Election of Senators

Like members of the House, senators are chosen by a vote of the people in each state. But it has not always been that way. Only since 1913 have people had the right to vote directly for the men or women they want to represent them in the Senate.

Before 1913 senators were selected by the legislatures of each state. The voters had only an indirect voice in the choice of senators, through their right to elect members of the legislature. It required a decades-long battle, leading to the Seventeenth Amendment to the Constitution, before the direct election of senators was established.

Under the Constitution, states were given seats in the House according to the size of their population. But seats in the Senate were equally divided, with each state getting two senators. The Founding Fathers thought of the House and Senate in basically different ways. House members were to be representatives of the people, elected by the voters. Senators, by contrast, were to be representatives of the sovereign states —"ambassadors," in effect, to the federal government.

As a result the Founding Fathers believed that the people should not elect the senators. Instead they decided

THE MAKING OF A SENATOR.

WHEN WILL THE PEOPLE STAND FROM UNDER?

Election by Legislatures

By the early twentieth century the Senate was the most conspicuous case in which the people had no direct say in choosing those who would govern them. Legislative elections encouraged corruption.

that the legislatures would be more thoughtful and responsible in selecting the kind of persons needed to represent the interests of the states in Congress. The Constitution gave Congress the right to establish specific rules governing the election of senators by the legislatures. For more than seventy-five years, however, Senate election procedures were left up to the individual states.

The election system used by most states proved to have serious flaws. Most states required candidates to win majorities in both houses of the legislature. But since members of the two houses often disagreed on candidates, the system produced many deadlocks. Frequently all other legislative business ground to a halt as members of the legislature struggled without success to agree on a candidate. Sometimes the legislature was simply unable to elect anyone, leaving the state without full representation in the Senate.

Congress reacted to the problems by passing a Senate election law in 1866. The law required the two houses of a legislature first to vote separately on candidates. If no candidate received a majority in both houses, then members of both chambers were to meet together and vote jointly, until one candidate received a majority of all votes.

Unfortunately, the 1866 law did little to correct the problems surrounding Senate elections. Deadlocks and election abuses continued to occur as political factions in each state fought for control of its two Senate seats. The stakes were high because senators customarily controlled much of the federal PATRON-AGE—government jobs and contracts—available in the state. In many cases the election of a senator became the dominant issue in the legislature, causing other important state business to be virtually ignored.

A dispute in Delaware at the end of the nineteenth century illustrates how bitter and prolonged fights over Senate elections could be. Divisions in the state legislature were so fierce that no Senate candidate was elected for four years. For two years (1901-03), Delaware was left entirely without representation in the Senate because members of the legislature could not agree on candidates.

The system also encouraged corruption. Because of the importance of Senate seats, and the relatively small numbers of state legislators who controlled them, candidates frequently were tempted to use bribery and intimidation to win. Controversies over alleged election fraud often had to be resolved by the Senate.

The most basic criticism of legislative elections of senators, though, was that they did not reflect the will of the people. For more than a century the American political system had gradually been moving toward giving the mass of voters more power. By the early years of the twentieth century the Senate was the most conspicuous case in which the people had no direct say in choosing those who would govern them.

Reform Efforts

Efforts to establish direct election of senators followed two different strategies. One was through a constitutional amendment, which passed the House on five separate occasions. But the Senate, all of whose members were chosen by the legislatures, was adamantly opposed to direct elections. Even after the legislatures of thirty-one states petitioned for a direct-election constitutional amendment, the Senate did not consider the proposal for many years. *(See* CONSTITUTIONAL AMENDMENTS.*)*

The other approach was through changes in state laws. Although the legislatures were required by the Constitution to select senators, reformers sought ways to ensure that the will of the people would control the legislatures' choices.

Oregon, which had a strong tradition of political reform, made the most determined attempts to guarantee the popular choice of senators. In 1901 the state established a system in which voters cast ballots for Senate candidates. While not legally binding, the results were supposed to guide the legislature in selecting candidates. The system initially was unsuccessful. The first time it was used, the legislature selected a candidate who had not received any votes in the popular election.

Soon after, however, Oregon reformers devised a system in which candidates for the legislature promised to support the popular choice for Senate regardless of their own preference. Once most members of the legislature were committed to backing the candidate who won a majority of popular votes, the legislative election became a mere formality ratifying the choice of the people. Other states soon adopted the "Oregon plan," so that by 1910 nearly half the senators chosen by the legislatures had already been selected by popular vote.

The state reform plans put more pressure on the Senate to approve a constitutional amendment. Fearing that the states would demand a new constitutional convention, senators finally agreed in 1910 to vote on a direct-election constitutional amendment. But opposition in the Senate remained strong. After a long and heated battle in the Senate, Congress approved the amendment on May 13, 1912. The amendment became part of the Constitution on May 31, 1913, after the required three-fourths of the states had given their approval.

The direct-election amendment did not have dramatic consequences. Most of the senators who had been elected by the legislatures were reelected by the people. Over the years since 1913, though, the selection of senators by the people has become a key part of the American political system.   ∼

Dirksen, Everett McKinley

Illinois Republican Everett McKinley Dirksen (1896-1969) was one of the most colorful members of Congress in recent history. He was known as the Wizard of Ooze for his florid style. As minority leader of the Senate (1959-69), Dirksen proved himself to be a master of compromise and persuasion. He used his great skills as an orator and negotiator to unify and strengthen the Republican voting bloc. His remark that "the oil can is mightier than the sword" spoke both to his skill in managing his flock and his ability to bring Republican legislation before a Democratic Senate.

Dirksen began his congressional service in the House of Representatives, but illness forced him to leave the House after sixteen years (1933-49). Upon his recovery, in 1950 he ran successfully for the Senate, where he served until his death in 1969. Dirksen endorsed all of President Dwight D. Eisenhower's major policies and was elected minority whip in 1957, at the beginning of his second Senate term. Two years later he advanced to minority leader.

Dirksen was unpredictable, often switching positions at critical moments. He publicly opposed the Civil Rights Act of 1964 and the nuclear test ban treaty but subsequently voted for them. He played a critical role in the passage of the 1968 Civil Rights Act. "One would be a strange creature indeed in this world of mutation if, in the face of reality, he did not change his mind," the senator once said.

Dirksen was unable to persuade the Senate to approve two of his favorite legislative projects, both of which would have reversed Supreme Court decisions of the early 1960s. In the wake of the Court's "one person, one vote" decision, he worked for a constitutional convention to restructure legislative apportionment. He also repeatedly sponsored resolutions to allow voluntary school prayer.   ~

Discharge, Committee

Both the House of Representatives and the Senate have procedures by which committees may be relieved, or "discharged," of legislation under their jurisdiction. The discharge mechanism was designed as a way to keep committees from blocking action on controversial bills.

The House procedure, first adopted in 1910, works through a rarely used device called the discharge petition. If a bill has been held up by a legislative committee for at least thirty days, or if the RULES COMMITTEE refuses to clear it for floor action within seven days, any member may offer a motion to discharge the committee from the bill. The clerk of the House draws up a discharge petition and if 218 members (a majority of the House) sign on, the discharge motion goes on the Discharge CALENDAR. The names of members signing the petition are published in the *CONGRESSIONAL RECORD*. After a seven-day grace period, if the committee still has not acted on the bill, any member may move to call up the discharge motion on the floor. If that is approved, a motion to call up the bill itself follows. Discharge measures may be considered on the second and fourth Mondays of each month.

Discharge efforts are seldom successful—members are reluctant to disregard a committee's judgment and the committee review process—but the threat of such a move may spur a committee to act. That happened in 1983, when the House WAYS AND MEANS COMMITTEE cleared a controversial tax

withholding bill only after 218 members had signed a discharge petition to force the bill to the floor.

The Senate discharge procedure also is used infrequently, chiefly because it is cumbersome and rarely effective. Discharging a committee from a particular bill does not automatically bring the legislation to the Senate floor for immediate consideration—the primary reason for using this motion. Instead, in virtually all cases the legislation discharged is placed on the Senate calendar. Legislation listed on the calendar can be brought up on the floor only by unanimous consent or by MOTION, which is debatable and thus open to a FILIBUSTER.   ~

Disciplining Members

Congress is legally responsible for monitoring the behavior of its members, an authority so extensive that it permits legislators to oust a wayward colleague from the House of Representatives or Senate. The Constitution states that Congress should "determine the rules of its proceedings, punish its members for disorderly behavior and, with the concurrence of two-thirds, expel a member." On the basis of that disciplinary authority, the House and Senate have voted to expel, censure, or reprimand their erring colleagues. Other offenders have been stripped of chairmanships or fined. *(Lists, pp. 491-94)*

Until adoption of formal, enforceable ethics codes in 1977, Congress was guided by an informal set of rules. After charges were made against a member, a special investigation was usually carried out; then the full House or Senate acted on the results. The formal codes generally follow that same procedure, although responsibility for investigating charges and recommending penalties now falls to permanent House and Senate committees on ethics. The ethics committees also may express disapproval of a member's behavior without recommending formal sanctions by their parent chambers. *(See* ETHICS.*)*

The most serious—and rarest—rebuke has been expulsion, which under the Constitution requires support from two-thirds of those voting. Only a majority is required for a vote to censure, reprimand, or fine a member. Discipline involving a loss of chairmanship or committee membership is usually handled by the CAUCUS of party members, instead of the full House or Senate, because the caucus is responsible for those assignments.

Expulsion

Except for expulsions of Southerners loyal to the Confederacy during the Civil War, Congress has rarely used its powerful authority to remove a legislator from office for misconduct.

The first expulsion occurred in 1797, when Tennessee Sen. William Blount was ousted for inciting members of two Indian tribes to attack Spanish Florida and Louisiana. The expulsion followed a House vote to impeach Blount, the only time the House, which originates all IMPEACHMENT proceedings, ever voted to impeach a senator or representative. The Senate headed off the impeachment proceedings by voting to expel Blount, something the House had no authority to do.

During the Civil War fourteen senators and three representatives were expelled. On a single day, July 11, 1861, the Senate expelled ten Southerners for failure to appear in their seats and for participation in secession from the Union.

From the Civil War to 1988, formal expulsion proceedings were instituted

Assault on Sumner

The years leading up to the Civil War were marked by violence in Congress. In 1856 two South Carolina representatives entered the Senate chamber, where Rep. Preston S. Brooks bludgeoned Massachusetts Sen. Charles Sumner while he sat at his desk. The House censured Rep. Laurence M. Keitt for his failure to stop the assault. The drawing below, Winslow Homer's only political caricature, is entitled "Arguments of Chivalry."

"THE SYMBOL OF THE NORTH IS THE PEN; THE SYMBOL OF THE SOUTH IS THE BLUDGEON."— *Henry Ward Beecher.*

nine times in the Senate and eleven times in the House. However, Congress only once during that time agreed to expulsion: The House voted in 1980 to expel Pennsylvania Democrat Michael J. "Ozzie" Myers. Myers was caught in the ABSCAM political corruption scandal when he took money from an FBI agent posing as an Arab sheik. In most other cases the House shied away from expulsion and instead opted for a lesser form of punishment. Nine of the twelve House expulsion cases resulted in censure. Several members resigned to avoid expulsion proceedings.

Early in 1988 the House ethics committee recommended expulsion of Rep. Mario Biaggi, a New York Democrat who had been convicted on criminal charges in 1987. The House delayed action on the committee recommendation because Biaggi was about to undergo a second criminal trial.

The Senate Committee on ETHICS in 1982 recommended the expulsion of New Jersey Democrat Harrison A. Williams, Jr., another Abscam target. Senate floor debate had begun when Williams, aware that a vote to expel him was likely, announced his resignation.

Censure

Eight times in the Senate and twenty-two times in the House a majority of legislators by 1988 had voted to censure a colleague for misconduct. Censure is a formal show of strong disapproval that requires a legislator to face his critics in the chamber; the presiding officer reads aloud the condemnation of his actions while he and his colleagues listen. A censured House Democrat also automatically loses his committee or subcommittee chairmanship under rules adopted by the House Democratic Caucus in 1980.

A typical censure was the wording read aloud in 1967 to Sen. Thomas J. Dodd, a Democrat from Connecticut. In a dramatic moment Dodd, who had

been charged with pocketing for personal use more than $100,000 in campaign contributions, heard that his conduct was "contrary to accepted morals." The censure said Dodd's behavior "derogates from the public trust expected of a senator and tends to bring the Senate into dishonor and disrepute."

Censure has been prompted by a wide variety of actions, including disloyalty during the Civil War, a fist fight on the Senate floor, insulting remarks to colleagues, acceptance of stock for legislative favors, and use of campaign contributions for personal expenses.

Probably the most publicized was the censure of Sen. Joseph R. McCARTHY in 1954. Although his tactic of labeling colleagues and others as communists had long been controversial, the Senate for almost three years did nothing to curb the growing power of the Wisconsin Republican. Only after the nationally televised Army-McCarthy hearings, when McCarthy's arrogance and abuses were seen by the public, did the Senate act to "condemn" McCarthy, an action historians consider equal to a censure. *(See* INVESTIGATIONS.)

Among those censured have been:

• Laurence M. Keitt, censured by the House in 1856 for not acting to stop an assault on a senator, despite knowing of the plans in advance and witnessing the attack. Keitt, a South Carolina Democrat, allowed a fellow South Carolinian, Rep. Preston S. Brooks, to strike Sen. Charles SUMNER, a Massachusetts Republican. Brooks hit Sumner several times with a heavy walking stick while Sumner sat at his desk in the Senate chamber.

• Oakes Ames, a Massachusetts Republican, and James Brooks, a New York Democrat, censured by the House in 1873 for accepting stock in Crédit Mobilier, a railroad construction company, in return for legislative favors.

• South Carolina Democrats Benjamin R. Tillman and John L. McLaurin, censured by the Senate in 1902 for engaging in a fist fight in the Senate chamber.

• Hiram Bingham, a Connecticut Republican, censured by the Senate in 1929 for putting on his staff a manufacturing association employee whose assignment was to advise on tariff legislation.

• Charles C. Diggs, Jr., a Michigan Democrat, censured by the House in 1979 for taking kickbacks from the salaries of his office employees.

• Charles H. Wilson, a California Democrat, censured by the House in 1980 for using campaign contributions to cover personal expenses.

• Gerry E. Studds and Daniel Crane, censured by the House in 1983 in separate cases of sexual misconduct. Studds, a Democrat from Massachusetts, had admitted having a homosexual relationship with a teenager working as a congressional page. Crane, a Republican from Illinois, had an affair with a female page.

Reprimand

From its first use in 1976 until 1988, the House six times voted to reprimand a colleague for misconduct. A reprimand is a milder form of punishment than censure because the legislator need not be present to receive the rebuke.

The House ethics committee—formally known as the Committee on STANDARDS OF OFFICIAL CONDUCT, established in 1968—first suggested a reprimand instead of censure after investigating charges that Florida Democrat Robert L. F. Sikes maintained a business interest in companies dealing with the defense subcommittee he chaired. The House again opted for the lesser penalty in 1978, when John J. McFall, Edward R. Roybal, and Charles H. Wilson, all California Democrats, were reprimanded for mishandling cash contributions from South Korean rice dealer Tongsun Park. In 1983 the ethics committee recommended a reprimand

for two members charged in separate cases of sexual misconduct; the House instead chose the more severe punishment of censure for Studds and Crane. George Hansen, an Idaho Republican, was reprimanded in 1984 after being convicted of violating federal financial disclosure laws. The sixth member to be reprimanded was Pennsylvania Democrat Austin J. Murphy; the House said Murphy diverted government resources to his former law firm, allowed another member to vote for him on the House floor, and kept a "no-show" employee on his payroll.

The Senate has not used the term "reprimand," but did decide in 1979 to denounce, rather than censure, Georgia Democrat Herman Talmadge. Like the House, the Senate wanted to register its disapproval, but without the harsh condemnation historically associated with censure. The Senate had been through a painful fifteen-month-long probe into charges that Talmadge, a popular senator, had used public and campaign funds for personal expenses. The veteran senator had the longtime habit, he testified, of accepting from friends and supporters small amounts of cash, which covered daily expenses.

Loss of Chairmanship

Unseating a chairman did not become a common method for disciplining unethical behavior until the 1970s. Prior to that, loss of seniority or a chairmanship had been primarily a tool that party caucuses used to punish disloyalty.

By 1980, though, the House Democratic Caucus had made loss of a chairmanship automatic for members censured by the House, or those indicted or convicted of a felony carrying a sentence of at least two years. The rule had an unexpected effect in 1988 on Thomas Downey, a Massachusetts Democrat who was not under any investigation. Because he was next in seniority, Downey became head of two different subcommittees whose chairmen were charged with felonies.

In the mid-1970s two powerful House Democrats resigned their chairmanships to avoid having them taken away by the House Democratic Caucus. Wilbur Mills, an Arkansas Democrat who chaired the House WAYS AND MEANS COMMITTEE, came under fire after publicity about his affair with an Argentine strip dancer. Mills, who was eventually treated for alcoholism, gave up his influential chairmanship in late 1974 but served out the term to which he was reelected that year.

Two years later the spotlight was on Wayne L. Hays, a Democratic representative from Ohio who chaired both the HOUSE ADMINISTRATION COMMITTEE and the Democratic Congressional Campaign Committee. Hays was accused of keeping a mistress on his payroll; he was about to be stripped of both chairs by the Democratic Caucus when he gave them up. Hays resigned from the House before any further disciplinary action was recommended.

An earlier link between loss of a chairmanship and unethical behavior involved Adam Clayton POWELL, Jr., a Democratic representative from New York's Harlem district. Powell, under investigation for misuse of committee funds and other alleged abuses, was deposed as chairman of the EDUCATION AND LABOR COMMITTEE in a 1967 vote by the Democratic Caucus. The full House then voted to exclude Powell from membership, an action that the Supreme Court overturned two years later.

Exclusion

Exclusion is a disciplinary procedure that applies to those not yet formally seated in the House or Senate. One purpose of the procedure is to resolve debate over whether just-elected legislators meet the basic constitutional qualifications for office; Congress has found some who did not. Legislators have also tried, sometimes successfully, to exclude Mormons who practiced polygamy, colleagues considered disloyal because of the Civil War, and others charged with misconduct.

This broader use of exclusion as a disciplinary tool was apparently ended by the 1969 Supreme Court decision in the case of *Powell v. McCormack*, which limited exclusion only to cases where constitutionally set qualifications for office were not met.

Powell, who had challenged his exclusion from the House, had a flamboyant lifestyle that fueled his colleagues' anger at his frequent absences, his extensive use of public funds for travel, and his loose use of his payroll to hire relatives and friends. Powell's response to the criticism was to insist he was a victim of racism.

In his appeal to the Supreme Court, Powell argued that Congress could refuse to seat an elected legislator only if he did not meet the qualifications spelled out in the Constitution: age, citizenship, and residence in the appropriate state or district. The Supreme Court agreed with this argument and sharply limited the application of exclusion. However, the Court did leave to Congress the discipline of an already-seated member. Powell, who had been reelected in 1968, took his seat in 1969 after the Court decision. The House then voted to fine him $25,000 for his earlier misuse of government funds. ∼

District of Columbia and Congress

The framers of the Constitution gave Congress the exclusive right to legislate for the District of Columbia, the nation's capital. Lawmakers' exercise of that authority has fluctuated over the years.

Congress granted limited self-government to the District of Columbia in 1800, and it endured for nearly seventy years. Then, after a brief experiment with a territorial system, Congress took back virtually all government authority over the District in 1874. For the next century Congress acted as the city's governing council, while the president chose its administrators. The Senate passed home-rule measures six times between 1949 and 1965, but the chairman of the House DISTRICT OF COLUMBIA COMMITTEE, South Carolina Democrat John L. McMillan, consistently used the power of his position to block home-rule bills in the House.

Finally, after McMillan's primary defeat in 1972, Congress once more gave local residents limited control over their own affairs. Under the 1973 home-rule law, Congress retained veto power over legislation approved by the District's elected government, as well as control over the D.C. budget. In the years that followed, the House and Senate continued to intervene from time to time in District affairs.

District residents have had a nonvoting DELEGATE in the House of Representatives since 1971; they have been able to vote in presidential elections since 1964. In 1978 Congress approved a proposed CONSTITUTIONAL AMENDMENT that would have given the District of Columbia full voting representation in Congress—two senators and at least one House member. The proposal died, however, when it failed to win ratification by three-fourths of the states as required by the Constitution. Legislation to make the District a state remained stalled in Congress in 1988. ∼

District of Columbia Committee, House

Representatives do not scramble to sit on the House District of Columbia

Committee. The District Committee oversees the municipal affairs of Washington, D.C., which have little significance for voters elsewhere in the country. In any case, the committee's work has been sharply curtailed since 1973, when Congress granted the city limited self-government. (See DISTRICT OF COLUMBIA AND CONGRESS.)

The District's population is overwhelmingly black, and blacks play dominant roles in the District Committee. Its black members in the 100th Congress (1987-89) included Chairman Ronald V. Dellums, a California Democrat, and Walter E. Fauntroy, the District's nonvoting DELEGATE, also a Democrat.

Prior to 1973, southern conservatives dominated the committee for many years, maintaining iron control over the District and its large black population. Led by South Carolina Democrat John L. McMillan, the committee's chairman from 1949 until 1973, they blocked a succession of bills to grant self-government to D.C. residents.

The committee's makeup changed dramatically in the wake of the 1972 congressional elections. McMillan was defeated in a primary runoff, and five other southern Democrats on the committee either lost their bids for reelection or retired. When the committee convened in 1973, its chairman was Charles C. Diggs, Jr., a Michigan Democrat and a black. Under its new direction, the committee approved a home-rule bill, and a compromise version of the measure became law later that year. In 1987 the committee approved a bill to grant statehood to the District, but members were sharply divided on the proposal, which faced tough opposition in Congress as a whole.

The committee has no counterpart in the Senate, which dropped its D.C. committee after the District gained home rule. D.C. matters now fall within the broad jurisdiction of the Senate Governmental Affairs Committee. In addition, each chamber's Appropriations Committee has a separate D.C. subcommittee.   ∼

Dole, Robert

Through a combination of legislative skill and a forceful personality, Robert Dole (1923-) became a formidable figure in the Senate in the 1980s, first as a committee chairman and then as majority leader from 1985 to 1987. The Kansas Republican scored major legislative victories, proving that the Senate could, indeed, be led.

He was first elected to the House in 1961 and remained there until he moved to the Senate in 1969. When Republicans came to power in the Senate in 1981, Dole became chairman of the FINANCE COMMITTEE. In that position he guided difficult legislation through an often chaotic and recalcitrant Senate. Dole oversaw passage of three major tax bills—including President Ronald Reagan's sweeping 1981 tax-cut program—and an overhaul of the Social Security program.

Dole had the ability to count votes and—through a mixture of negotiation, compromise, arm-twisting, and verbal whiplashing—he frequently brought competing interests into line behind a controversial bill. He seasoned his legislative skill with a quick wit and a sharp tongue, which somewhat softened over the years.

His style was in marked contrast to that of the amiable Howard H. BAKER, Jr., the Tennessee Republican he succeeded as majority leader in 1985. Dole's strong will and aggressive use of power produced significant legislative victories and undermined the ability of small groups of senators to bring the chamber regularly to a standstill. Legislation passed with Dole's help included, among others, a major revision of the

tax code, a new farm bill, and aid to the contra rebels in Nicaragua.

Not all of Dole's efforts were successful during his tenure as majority leader, which ended when the Senate returned to Democratic control in 1987 and Dole became minority leader. Nor have all his political endeavors met with success. Dole, who was chairman of the Republican National Committee from 1971 to 1973, served in 1976 as Gerald R. Ford's vice-presidential running mate on the losing Republican ticket, and failed in his 1980 and 1988 bids for the Republican presidential nomination.   ∼

Doorkeeper, House

The House doorkeeper introduces at the door of the chamber official guests, visitors attending joint sessions, and the bearers of messages from the Senate and the president. He is responsible for House documents, publications distribution (folding rooms), CLOAKROOMS, and telephone service. He also supervises doormen, pages, and barbers; issues passes for seats in the House galleries; and performs a variety of custodial services (these functions are performed by the SERGEANT-AT-ARMS in the Senate). The annual salary of the House doorkeeper was $86,815 as of January 1988.   ∼

Douglas, Stephen A.

Called the "Little Giant" for his small stature and formidable talents, Stephen A. Douglas (1813-61) was a skilled and energetic orator. He is best remembered as Abraham Lincoln's opponent in the Lincoln-Douglas debates of 1858. At the time of the debates,

Douglas was campaigning for his third term in the Senate, where he had served as a Democrat since 1847. He also served in the House of Representatives for two terms (1843-47).

Chairman of the Senate Committee on Territories, Douglas opposed anything that would hinder the organization of new territories or the entrance of new states into the Union. Because slavery proved to be just such a hindrance, Douglas searched for a compromise on the issue. He became an advocate of popular sovereignty, under which new states and territories could decide whether or not to allow slavery. In 1854 he sponsored the Kansas-Nebraska bill, allowing those territories to determine for themselves whether to allow slavery within their borders. The measure angered both North and South and led to violence in the territories.

In 1857 the Supreme Court handed down the Dred Scott decision, *Scott v. Sandford*, which held that Congress did not have the power to curtail the expansion of slavery. In 1858 Douglas and Lincoln, his opponent for the Senate, debated the Dred Scott decision; Douglas insisted that although the national legislature could not limit slavery, state legislatures could do so. Douglas won the election, but his position angered many Southerners. In 1859, to punish him for his perceived opposition to slavery, the Senate Democratic Caucus voted to remove him as chairman of the Committee on Territories.

Douglas opposed Lincoln in the presidential election of 1860 and lost, in part, because the Democratic ticket was split. He loyally supported the new president, and in 1861 he undertook a trip at Lincoln's request to encourage support for the government's policies. He contracted typhoid during the trip and died at the age of forty-eight.   ~

Overleaf:
Tax lobbyists waiting outside committee room.

Economic Committee, Joint

Since 1946 the House and Senate have had a joint committee to monitor the nation's economy. Although it cannot write legislation, the Joint Economic Committee issues reports and holds hearings on a variety of topics, ranging from the Soviet economy to the price of beef. With a much broader focus than most congressional committees, the committee tries to provide an overview of the economy and a look at long-range trends.

Most widely known are the committee's annual March report and its midyear report, usually issued in August. The March report responds formally to the economic report issued early each year by the president's Council of Economic Advisers; both reports are mandated by the Employment Act of 1946, which set up the committee and the council. The act's goals are "maximum employment, production, and purchasing power."

Because Democrats and Republicans have traditionally had such different expectations for the economy, the two parties have often written separate reports. During the Reagan administration, Republicans usually predicted a healthy economy and Democrats forecast calamity. Since 1967 the committee has had ten members from the Senate and ten from the House, with six major-

ity and four minority members from each chamber.

The post of committee chairman rotates between the House and Senate every two years. The chairman often initiates studies, directing the staff to work on a particular topic.

Two men put their personal stamp on the committee in the 1950s and 1960s. Representative Wright Patman, a Texas Democrat, served as chairman five times between 1957 and 1975. An outspoken critic of powerful commercial banks and the politics of the Federal Reserve Board, Patman used the Joint Economic Committee as yet another platform for his attacks. On the Senate side, the chair was held three times in the 1950s and 1960s by Democrat Paul Douglas of Illinois, a prominent liberal who had been a well-regarded professor of economics at the University of Chicago.

Another longtime member of the panel was Senate Democrat William Proxmire of Wisconsin, who did not run for reelection in 1988. He served twenty-seven years on the joint committee, including two terms as chairman and two as vice chairman.   ~

Education and Labor Committee, House

The House Education and Labor Committee has responsibility for many of the programs established by the federal government to attack poverty and other social problems. Its jurisdiction includes federal spending for education and job training, as well as a wide range of efforts to aid children, the poor, and the disabled.

During the 1960s the committee was the originator in the House of much of the legislation sought by President Lyndon B. JOHNSON for his GREAT SOCIETY. Most importantly, it helped write the 1965 legislation that for the first time ever provided federal financial support for locally controlled elementary and secondary education. In later years the committee went on to approve legislation that greatly expanded financial aid to college students, set up health-and-safety programs in the workplace, and banned discrimination against the handicapped.

The committee continues to have jurisdiction over many of those programs. However, the political climate in the House has changed greatly since the 1960s, and the committee's degree of influence has been sharply curtailed as a result. By the 1980s many House members were far more skeptical about the value of federal involvement in social problems than they had been previously. Few members favored creation of new social programs, and many favored substantial reductions in spending on existing programs.

As a result, the members of the Education and Labor Committee found themselves increasingly isolated in the House. A majority of committee members, particularly on the Democratic side, continued to favor strong federal involvement in social issues. But, particularly during President Ronald Reagan's first term (1981-85), a majority of members of the whole House wanted to see tough measures to hold down the cost of existing social programs, even if it meant curtailing the federal role in combating problems.

The Education and Labor Committee for much of the 1980s was rarely able to get its new legislative proposals through the House. Those bills that were approved by the House frequently were killed in the Senate. Most Republicans, who controlled the Senate from 1981 to 1987, strongly opposed the social spending programs favored by the Democratic majority on House Education and Labor.

Instead of proposing new social programs, many members of the Educa-

Declining Force

The House Education and Labor Committee has lost influence since the 1960s, when it was the launch pad for many Great Society social programs. In 1965 it helped write legislation that for the first time ever provided federal financial support for elementary and secondary education.

tion and Labor Committee were forced to concentrate on defending existing programs. In 1981 the committee sought to defy budget-cutting requirements passed by Congress and supported by Reagan. The committee's efforts were unsuccessful, however, and Congress approved legislation cutting billions of dollars from programs under Education and Labor's jurisdiction. ~

Electing the President

For two centuries Americans have been choosing their presidents indirectly through what is known as the electoral college system. The authors of the Constitution conceived the system as a compromise between selecting presidents by Congress or by direct popular vote. Congress has two important responsibilities in the selection process.

Although the voters cast their ballots for president and vice president every four years, their choice is not final until Congress counts the electoral votes, which are determined by the popular-election results in each state. A majority of electoral votes (270 out of a total

of 538 in 1988) is needed to elect.

Counting the electoral votes is almost always a ceremonial function. But if no candidate for president or vice president wins a majority of electoral votes, the House of Representatives must choose the president and the Senate must choose the vice president. The House has chosen a president only twice. In the course of the nation's history, however, a number of campaigns have been designed deliberately to throw elections into the House, where each state has one vote and a majority of states is needed for election.

Few decisions of the Founding Fathers have been more criticized than the constitutional provisions governing the selection of the president. Thomas Jefferson called them "the most dangerous blot on our Constitution." A proposed constitutional amendment to reform the system was introduced in Congress as early as 1797. Since then hardly a session of Congress has passed without the introduction of one or more such measures.

Electoral Vote System

The Constitution provided that each state should appoint presidential electors, known collectively as the electoral college, equal to the total number of its senators and representatives. The electors, chosen as each state legislature directed, would meet in their separate states and vote for two persons. The votes would be counted in Congress, and the candidate who received the most votes, provided they were a majority of the total, would become president. The candidate who received the second highest number of votes would become vice president.

If no candidate won a majority of electoral votes, the House of Representatives was to select the president; each state would have one vote, and a majority of states would be required for election. Selection of the vice president would fall to the Senate, with a majority required.

Originally no distinction was made between ballots for president and vice president. That caused confusion when national political parties emerged and began to nominate party tickets for the two offices. All the electors of one party tended to vote for their two party nominees. But with no distinction between the presidential and vice presidential nominees, there was danger of a tie vote between the two. This actually happened in 1800, leading to adoption of the Twelfth Amendment to the Constitution, which required separate votes for the two offices.

The framers of the Constitution intended that each state choose its most distinguished citizens as electors and that they should vote as individuals. But with the development of strong political parties, the electors came to be chosen merely as representatives of the parties. Independent voting by electors disappeared almost entirely, although on a few occasions an elector has broken ranks to vote for a candidate other than his party's.

Counting the Electoral Vote

The Constitution provides that "The President of the Senate shall, in

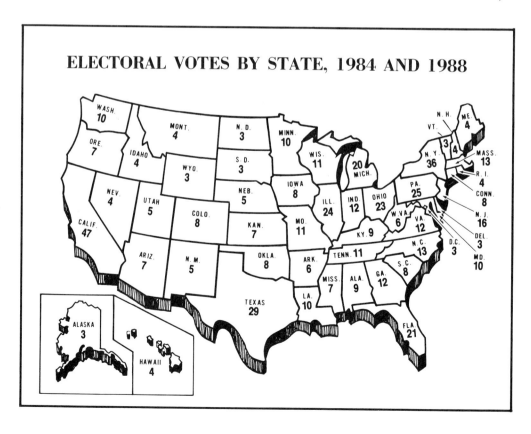

ELECTORAL VOTES BY STATE, 1984 AND 1988

Hayes-Tilden Contest
Counting electoral votes in Congress is not always just a formality. This picture shows a special congressional electoral commission taking testimony on disputed electoral votes in the 1876 presidential election. Congress gave the election to Rutherford B. Hayes even though Democrat Samuel J. Tilden had a majority of the popular vote.

the Presence of the Senate and House of Representatives, open all the Certificates, and the Votes shall then be counted. . . ."

Under modern practice, the electors meet in their states to cast their ballots in December following a presidential election. With rare exceptions, the party that carried the state's popular vote wins all of the state's electoral votes. The ballots of all the states are opened and counted before a joint session of Congress in early January, clearing the way for inauguration of the president on January 20.

The Constitution did not say what to do if there were disputes about electors' ballots. That became a critical concern following the 1876 election when, for the first time, the outcome of the election had to be determined by decisions on disputed electoral votes. The 1876 campaign pitted Republican Rutherford B. Hayes against Democrat Samuel J. Tilden. Tilden led in the popular-vote count by more than a quarter of a million votes but trailed by one vote in the electoral college; the votes of three southern states were in dispute. After Republicans agreed to withdraw federal troops from the South, a special commission awarded the disputed electoral votes to Hayes.

In 1887 Congress passed permanent legislation on the handling of disputed electoral votes. The 1887 law, still in force a century later, gave each state final authority in determining the legality of its choice of electors; majorities of both the Senate and House were needed to reject any disputed electoral votes.

Election by Congress

The election of 1800 was the first in which the House of Representatives elected the president. Candidates of what was then the Democratic-Republican faction had more electoral votes than the Federalists, but their electors unintentionally cast equal numbers of votes for Thomas Jefferson, their choice for president, and Aaron Burr, their choice for vice president. The tie vote threw the election into the House, where the losing Federalists insisted on backing Burr over Jefferson, whom they considered a dangerous radical. It took thirty-six ballots to arrive at a decision; on the final tally ten states voted for Jefferson, four for Burr. Thus Jefferson became president and Burr automatically became vice president.

The Jefferson-Burr contest clearly illustrated the dangers of the constitutional double-balloting system. The Twelfth Amendment, requiring separate votes for president and vice president, was proposed by Congress and quickly adopted by the states in time for the 1804 election.

The only other time the House elected a president was in 1825. There were four chief contenders in the 1824 presidential campaign: John Quincy ADAMS, Henry CLAY, William H. Crawford, and Andrew Jackson. When the electoral votes were counted, Jackson had 99, Adams 84, Crawford 41, and Clay 37. Jackson led in the popular vote, but he failed to win a majority of the total electoral vote. As required by the Twelfth Amendment, the names of the top three contenders—Jackson, Adams, and Crawford—were placed before the House. Clay threw his support to Adams, who narrowly won election. Adams in turn made Clay his secretary of state, thus lending credence to charges that Clay had agreed to support Adams in return for the appointment. Adams took office under a cloud from which his administration never recovered; he lost the presidency to Jackson four years later.

On one occasion the Senate was forced to decide a vice presidential contest. That happened in 1837 when Democrat Martin Van Buren was elected president with 170 electoral votes, while his vice presidential running mate, Richard M. Johnson, received only 147—one short of a majority. The Senate elected him, 33-16.

Vice Presidential Vacancies

The Twenty-fifth Amendment to the Constitution, adopted in 1967, gave Congress additional authority over vice presidential selection. The amendment, which established procedures to be followed if the president became disabled or died, also gave directions for filling a vacancy in the office of vice president. Whenever a vice president died, resigned, or succeeded to the presidency, the president was to nominate a successor. A majority vote of both houses of Congress was required to confirm the nominee. *(See* APPOINTMENT POWER; PRESIDENTIAL DISABILITY.*)*

The vice presidential selection system was used for the first time in 1973 after the resignation of Vice President Spiro T. Agnew, who was under investigation on criminal charges. President Richard Nixon nominated Michigan Rep. Gerald R. Ford, the House Republican leader, to succeed him. Ford easily won confirmation by the House and Senate in less than two months.

In 1974 the Twenty-fifth Amendment was used again, after Nixon resigned as president to avoid impeachment because of the WATERGATE SCANDAL. Ford succeeded to the presidency, thus becoming the first president in American history who had not been elected either president or vice president. Ford nominated Nelson A. Rockefeller, the governor of New York, to succeed him as vice president. Rockefeller's great wealth provoked controversy, but he, too, was confirmed.   ~

ADDITIONAL READING

Peirce, Neal, and Lawrence D. Longley. *The People's President.* rev. ed. 1981.

Enacting Clause

"Be it enacted by the Senate and House of Representatives of the United States of America in Congress assembled...." This imposing language is the standard opening for bills introduced in either chamber. Known as the enacting clause, it gives legal force to measures once they have been approved by Congress and signed by the president. During House floor action, opponents of a bill sometimes offer a motion to "strike the enacting clause." Such a motion, if approved, kills the measure.   ~

Energy and Commerce Committee, House

With its sweeping jurisdiction and collection of colorful personalities, the House Energy and Commerce Committee has been a ready stage for a never-ending stream of policy debates, political deals, and conflicts between individuals. Volatile topics such as controlling automobile fumes, cleaning up poisoned backyards, and overseeing the oil industry trigger showdowns both at the subcommittee and committee levels. The Commerce Committee is often where industry faces off against the consumer, and the committee always attracts more than its fair share of lobbyists. The high level of controversy means votes are often close, with the outcome in suspense until the last moment—in sharp contrast to many committees where consensus is the norm.

An octopus of a committee, Energy and Commerce is responsible not only for overseeing energy, but also for health, communications, consumer safety, part of the transportation industry, and numerous regulatory agencies. Its chairman in the 1980s, Michigan Democrat John D. Dingell, was tenacious about protecting his turf and never hesitated to reach for new territory. Few areas escaped being probed by the committee's Oversight and Investigations Subcommittee, which Dingell also chaired.

Although its primary Senate counterpart is the Energy and Natural Resources Committee, the two committees are not parallel in their jurisdictions. Senate Energy shares with the House Interior Committee, for example, oversight of federal lands, much of nuclear power, and the bulk of the coal industry. The environmental concerns of House Energy and Commerce, such as air pollution, are the responsibility in the Senate of its Environment and Public Works Committee, not the Energy Committee. When House Energy and Commerce tackles communications policy or transportation deregulation, it deals in conference with the Senate Committee on Commerce, Science, and Transportation.

History

The Interstate and Foreign Commerce Committee was set up in 1795, but Congress did not begin a broad application of its authority over interstate commerce until 1887, when it set up the Interstate Commerce Commission. Since then, federal oversight of the marketplace has become extensive, and the Commerce Committee has helped create a wide variety of regulatory agencies. The committee was renamed Energy and Commerce in 1980. (See COMMERCE POWER.)

The committee had high visibility in the 1950s because it investigated several scandals. A subcommittee probe revealed that a Boston industrialist had paid hotel bills and given a vicuna coat and oriental rug to Sherman Adams, a top Eisenhower administration aide who later resigned. Other topics were rigged television quiz shows and "payola" from the record industry to radio disc jockeys.

Among the longest running debates in the committee was that over energy pricing. In the 1970s top Democrats on the committee, including Dingell and then-chairman Harley O. Staggers of West Virginia, were a last bastion of resistance to deregulation of natural gas and oil.

Jurisdiction of the committee shifted in the mid-1970s. The Public Works Committee was assigned responsibility for all forms of transportation except railroads, which were a special interest of Staggers—who eventually got credit for the 1980 railroad deregulation, called the Staggers Act. The reforms also transferred to Commerce

Assertive Chairman
An octopus of a committee, Energy and Commerce is responsible not only for overseeing energy, but also for health, communications, and numerous other programs. Under the assertive chairmanship of Rep. John D. Dingell, the committee broadened its reach in the 1980s.

from Ways and Means health issues not related to taxes. Within the committee, that period in the 1970s was also one of change. Staggers's low-key style frustrated many other Democrats. While shifting more and more authority to the subcommittees, they voted in 1979 to take away Staggers's subcommittee chairmanship. Dingell, from his vantage point as chairman of the Energy and Power Subcommittee, ran the full committee in all but name.

Energy issues dominated the late 1970s, but action shifted away from the Commerce Committee. Instead, decisions were made by an ad hoc energy committee, which the House leadership set up to overcome the maze of conflicting committee jurisdictions over energy. A special study committee then recommended in 1979 that a permanent energy committee be established, but opposition was strong, particularly from Commerce members who saw their role being reduced. In the end, the House simply renamed the committee Energy and Commerce.

Health issues were also a key committee concern; the leader in that area

was California Democrat Henry A. Waxman, who in 1979 became chairman of the Subcommittee on Health and the Environment. Waxman was so politically aggressive that he organized his own campaign finance committee and contributed to liberal colleagues in hopes they would elect him subcommittee chairman.

Waxman had numerous feuds with Dingell over air pollution controls, which Dingell found constrained the automobile industry so important to his Detroit district. They also fought over controls on acid rain, which Dingell opposed because it threatened to limit the burning of coal. In 1987 Dingell got an edge when the House Democratic leadership put his choices on the committee: three new allies from coal country. ~

Energy and Natural Resources Committee, Senate

Managing federal lands and setting energy policy are the main tasks of the

Senate Committee on Energy and Natural Resources. The committee traditionally has been controlled by westerners whose states have vast amounts of federal parks and forests and it is attractive to senators whose states depend on oil and gas. But the committee also includes advocates of wilderness and proponents of energy conservation; though less volatile than the House Energy and Commerce Committee, Senate Energy is equally unpredictable.

For most of the 1970s the committee focused on energy, struggling to adapt price controls and other federal rules to an energy market dominated by a cartel of oil-rich Middle Eastern countries that limited supplies and kept prices high. By the 1980s the energy situation had changed drastically, with declines in prices, in imports, and in overall consumption; the Energy Committee was even considering relief for domestic oil and gas producers, such as an end to remaining controls on natural gas prices. Committee members were still talking about preparing for oil shortages, but no one was listening.

The committee was first organized in 1816 as the Committee on Public Lands and Survey. A 1977 Senate reorganization shifted jurisdiction of some environmental laws to the Environment and Public Works Committee; what was then the Interior and Insular Affairs Committee became Energy and Natural Resources.

Henry M. Jackson, a Washington Democrat, chaired the committee from 1963 until 1981. A leading senator, forceful and well-liked, Jackson managed to keep the committee's concerns in the Senate limelight. Although a foreign policy hawk, Jackson was a liberal on domestic issues and for years advocated price controls on oil and gas, a position that never caused conflict in his nonproducing state. But Jackson, too, had parochial concerns; for example, he always got the Bonneville Power Administration federal funding for ad-

ditional dams on the Columbia River. Jackson, who died in 1983, was also a dedicated environmentalist, with accomplishments that included creation of protected wilderness areas in Alaska and controls on strip mining, topics handled by the Senate Energy Committee.

When Republicans controlled the Senate from 1981 to 1987, James A. McClure of Idaho took the Energy chairmanship. McClure favored a completely free market for energy and in 1983 pushed a Reagan administration plan to remove all remaining federal controls from natural gas. It took him months to get the legislation out of committee, and the compromise that finally emerged had only lukewarm support. It lost decisively on the floor. Despite his opposition to controls, though, McClure did support federal subsidies for synthetic fuels, such as liquids made from coal. That program, created with great brouhaha in the late 1970s, died in 1985 because of budget constraints.

McClure's successor, Louisiana Democrat J. Bennett Johnston, shared his outlook, preferring a market-oriented approach to energy policy. Johnston was known for his solid grasp of the technical aspects of energy and for his ability to craft compromises. He bristled at the label "oil-state senator," arguing that his decisions were not automatically governed by the industry position. In 1984 Johnston got upset enough about proposed energy company mergers to push for a law that would temporarily halt them; he lost on the floor.   ~

Engrossed Bill

An engrossed bill is the final copy of a measure as passed by either the Senate or House of Representatives, including changes made during floor action. It must be certified in its final form by the secretary of the Senate or the clerk of the House. *(See* ENROLLED BILL; LEGISLATIVE PROCESS.*)*   ~

Enrolled Bill

The final copy of a bill that has been passed in identical form by both the Senate and House of Representatives is known as an enrolled bill. It is certified by the secretary of the Senate or the clerk of the House, depending on where the bill originated, and then sent on for the signatures of the House Speaker, the Senate president pro tempore, and the president of the United States. An enrolled bill is printed on parchment-type paper. *(See* ENGROSSED BILL; LEGISLATIVE PROCESS.*)*   ~

Entitlements.   See BUDGET PROCESS.

Environment and Public Works Committee, Senate

Two markedly different responsibilities fall to the Senate Committee on Environment and Public Works: watching over the nation's environment, and building its highways, dams, and sewers. Neither task was as easy or popular in the 1980s as it had been only a decade before.

The 1970s were probably the heyday of the committee, when landmark environmental laws were passed and federal money still flowed freely. In the 1980s efforts to clean the environment were stymied by more insidious problems, such as toxic waste disposal and acid rain. Glamorous public works

projects lost out in the federal budget squeeze—and gave way to new concerns about the nation's deteriorating dams and bridges.

North Dakota Democrat Quentin N. Burdick became chairman in 1987, his first top post in almost three decades as a senator. Never one to seek power or publicity, Burdick brought a low-key style to the Environment Committee. He gave great latitude to a host of active, aggressive subcommittee chairmen, such as George J. Mitchell of Maine and Frank R. Lautenberg of New Jersey.

While Republicans controlled the Senate (1981-87), Robert T. Stafford of Vermont chaired the commmittee. He was forced to take a defensive posture, deflecting attacks on environmental laws by industry; often Stafford was on the opposite side from the Reagan administration. Stafford also helped win extensions of water pollution controls and the "superfund" program to clean up toxic waste. Stafford concentrated on the environment instead of highways, reflecting years as a key player on the Environmental Protection Subcommittee.

Stafford had worked closely with Maine Democrat Edmund S. Muskie, who played a key role in passage of several major environmental laws in the 1970s. Chairman of the Environmental Protection Subcommittee, Muskie had key support from West Virginia Democrat Jennings Randolph, who chaired the full committee from 1966 to 1981. The growing importance of environmental concerns was reflected in a 1977 decision to change the committee's name, from Public Works to Environment and Public Works. Muskie left the Senate in 1980 to become secretary of state under President Jimmy Carter.

While Muskie was handling environmental problems, Randolph concentrated on public works projects. Roads had always been important to West Virginia, bringing jobs and businesses to poor communities otherwise isolated by hills and mountains. In the spirit of the 1930s NEW DEAL, Randolph embraced highways, dams, and other projects as valid ways to spread federal spending. But his attitude was out of step in the 1980s, and Republicans slowed to a trickle the flow of money to West Virginia. Randolph, at the age of eighty-one, retired in 1985.

Budget problems led to sharp cutbacks in one of the committee's most creative schemes for cleaning the environment. The centerpiece of the 1972 clean water law was a grant program giving local governments billions of dollars to upgrade their sewer systems. Congress agreed in 1981 to put tight limits on the expensive program; instead of the "carrot" of extra funds, the government was forced to use the "stick" of regulations and fines to clean up the nation's water.   ~

Ervin, Sam J., Jr.

Sam J. Ervin, Jr. (1896-1985), served twenty years as a Democratic senator from North Carolina. He is best remembered as chairman of the Senate WATERGATE committee, which investigated charges that led to the resignation of President Richard Nixon in 1974. During the committee's televised hearings, Ervin's knowledge of and respect for the Constitution, his courtly manner, and his pithy quotations made him an admired national figure.

Prior to his Senate service, Ervin practiced law in North Carolina, served in the state legislature, and sat on the bench of the criminal and supreme courts within the state. In 1946 Ervin served one year in the U.S. House of Representatives to finish the term of his brother Joseph, who died while in office.

Ervin was appointed to fill a vacant

Senate seat in 1954 and was elected to full terms starting in 1956. As a freshman senator, he was a member of the select committee that recommended Senate censure of Sen. Joseph R. McCARTHY, a Wisconsin Republican whose INVESTIGATIONS of communism had drawn great criticism.

Ervin construed the provisions of the Constitution strictly. On the grounds of protecting states' rights, he rejected civil rights legislation and other Democratic domestic programs such as health care for the elderly and school busing. But as a member of the Judiciary Committee he worked to strengthen the civil rights of government workers, Indians, and mental patients. He often inveighed against information gathered on private citizens by the government; "It is my belief that the Recording Angel drops a tear occasionally to wash out the record of our human iniquities," he said. "There is no compassion to be found in computers."

As chairman of Judiciary's Separation of Powers Subcommittee, Ervin recommended procedures to be followed in a convention held to consider CONSTITUTIONAL AMENDMENTS; although such a convention had never been held, the prospect troubled many leaders. Ervin's bill passed the Senate in 1971 and 1973, but the House did not vote on the measure.

In 1973 Ervin was chosen to head the Senate Watergate committee—formally known as the Senate Select Committee on Presidential Campaign Activities. He was selected because of his knowledge of the Constitution and because, earlier that year, he had declined to run for reelection in 1974. He was therefore unable to capitalize on the publicity generated by the committee's investigations. Quoting the Bible and Shakespeare, Ervin immediately caught the attention of the public. A self-described "old country lawyer," Ervin seemed the antithesis of the Watergate conspirators. He became a folk hero and retired in 1974 on a wave of public admiration.   ~

Ethics

Daniel Webster, a respected Massachusetts statesman in the nineteenth century, openly demanded money from the railroads in return for his support of a bill before the Senate. James A. Garfield, an Ohio representative who became president in 1881, accepted a gift of stock from Crédit Mobilier of America, a company seeking legislative favors. Emanuel Celler, a New York Democrat who chaired the House Judiciary Committee for almost twenty-five years, continued even in the 1970s to practice law alongside partners who handled cases before the federal government.

These actions, which went unpunished, would probably be scrutinized in the 1980s as blatant conflicts of interest by one—or all—of the three groups that monitor a legislator's behavior: the courts, his colleagues in the House and Senate, and the voters.

The courts handle indictments of legislators charged with bribery and other financial corruption prohibited by federal criminal statutes; they also review violations of the 1978 Ethics in Government Act. Also designed to expose, or at least discourage, corruption are federal CAMPAIGN FINANCING laws, which require public disclosure of donations and monitor use of funds. Regulation is handled by the Federal Election Commission, which can fine violators or take them to court.

The House and Senate ethics codes are the internal guidelines for how legislators behave. Personal finances must be disclosed, income earned outside Congress is restricted, and use of public funds is carefully monitored. The House Select Committee on STAN-DARDS OF OFFICIAL CONDUCT and the Senate Committee on ETHICS investigate allegations and make recommendations to the House and Senate, which then decide whether to discipline a legislator.

The remaining judge of representatives and senators is the electorate. Approval from the voters means the extension, or death, of an official's political life. Voters can be the toughest critics as they apply an invisible set of rules and standards to an official's performance and then hand down their verdict at the polls.

For a man like Webster, who openly complained when payments to him for favors were late, the modern guidelines would leave little room to operate. Yet, despite proper behavior by the majority, members of Congress continue to be accused of bribery, influence peddling, misuse of funds, sexual misconduct, violations of campaign disclosure laws, and breach of security. The standards for a politician's conduct are high; so are the temptations.

Punishing Misconduct

For most of its history, Congress operated under an unwritten ethics code, backed by a constitutional directive that legislators should oversee their own behavior. Thomas Jefferson set the tone in 1801, while he was vice president and presiding officer of the Senate. In JEFFERSON'S MANUAL he wrote, "Where the private interests of a member are concerned in a bill or question he is to withdraw." Jefferson was suggesting that a legislator avoid what is known today as a "conflict of interest," when the chance for personal gain influences a decision ostensibly made for the public good. Each chamber's rules permit members not to vote on matters affecting their personal interests.

The Constitution states that Congress should "determine the rules of its proceedings, punish its members for disorderly behavior, and, with the concurrence of two-thirds, expel a member." However, it was left to the legislators to determine the rules and decide who was breaking them. The policing of Congress has been done on an ad hoc basis. When someone complains about a colleague's behavior, the House or Senate usually investigates.

The most drastic step Congress can take is to expel a colleague, but that constitutional right has been used only nineteen times. The bulk of those cases occurred during the Civil War, when Southerners were expelled for disloyalty. Between 1861 and 1988, only one member was expelled: Rep. Michael "Ozzie" Myers, a Pennsylvania Democrat, who was expelled in 1980 after he took bribe money from an FBI agent posing as an Arab sheik.

Early in 1988 the House ethics committee recommended expulsion of

Rep. Mario Biaggi, a New York Democrat who had been convicted on criminal charges in 1987. The House delayed action on the committee recommendation because Biaggi was about to undergo a second criminal trial.

Congress has turned more often to another formal punishment: censure, in which a member's conduct is condemned in a formal hearing before the entire House or Senate. More recently Congress devised a new version of censure, a reprimand, which allows a member to avoid being present in the House or Senate chamber while his behavior is condemned. Loss of chairmanships and fines have also been used as punishment. *(See* DISCIPLINING MEMBERS.*)*

Politics, a member's personal popularity, and even the customs of the times play a part in the judgment. When one member of the House shot

Morgan's Creature

Congressional ethics have long been the subject of cartoonists' barbs. Here Congress is depicted as the creature of J. P. Morgan, the most powerful figure in U.S. finance and industry at the turn of the twentieth century.

another to death in a duel in 1838, the House declined to expel the murderer or to censure two colleagues who served as seconds in the duel. As another legislator noted, dueling by members had been frequent and generally had gone unnoticed by the House. In contrast, just six years earlier, when the House for the first time formally censured a member, the reason for the censure was simply a remark. The representative had told the Speaker his eyes were "too frequently turned from the chair you occupy toward the White House."

Congress has traditionally been reluctant to discipline its members. Many agree with Sam RAYBURN, House Speaker for most of the period between 1940 and 1961, who believed the voters, not fellow politicians, should be the ultimate judge of behavior. The House and Senate have often delayed their investigations and decisions until after an election; the voters often oblige by defeating the colleague under fire. House Democratic Caucus rules require that an indicted member step down from his chairmanship for the duration of the session or until the charges are dismissed.

Legislators have another way to avoid disciplining a colleague: his resignation. Two House members and one senator used resignation in 1980-82 to duck their almost certain expulsion following indictments for conspiracy and bribery during the FBI's undercover operation known as ABSCAM.

Representatives and senators have also retired in the midst of investigations or following disciplinary action. After the House ethics committee found in 1986 that Democrat James Weaver of Oregon had filed incomplete financial reports, Weaver amended the reports; the changes helped him avoid any disciplinary action, but so did his plans not to seek reelection. The Senate Republican leader, Pennsylvanian Hugh Scott, was accused in 1976 of receiving up to $100,000 in illegal campaign contributions from a Gulf Oil Corporation lobbyist. After Scott denied any impropriety, the ethics committee voted in closed session not to pursue its investigation; Scott retired from Congress three months later.

Congress's reluctance to discipline colleagues varies depending on the nature of their misconduct. Typically Congress, and the voters, have been more forgiving of personal problems and of those who admit their wrongdoing and repent. Criminal misconduct and a refusal to promise better behavior tend to result in disciplinary action—or election defeat.

Ethical Questions

The smell of money pervades most ethical questions, but legislators have also been disciplined for insults, questions of loyalty, sexual misconduct, and other offenses. Sen. Joseph R. McCARTHY, a Wisconsin Republican who became infamous for communist-hunting in the early 1950s, was condemned by the Senate in 1954 for making insulting remarks about his colleagues. The wording of the charge reflected a compromise; one colleague had wanted to condemn McCarthyism by charging the senator with "habitual contempt for people." Two House members were censured in 1983 for sexual misconduct. The many cases of censure during the Civil War were based on disloyalty; Southerners had favored the Confederacy over the Union.

But other charges pale alongside allegations of bribery, kickbacks, misuse of public funds, or improper campaign contributions. Public outrage is greatest when money is involved. Scrutiny of a legislator's financial accountability has centered on his income, including outside sources such as legal fees and honoraria (income from speeches and articles); on contributions to his campaign; and on his access to and use of public funds and privileges.

The criminal code has long prohibited a member of Congress from acts such as soliciting or receiving a bribe in return for a vote or other favor, benefiting from a contract with a federal agency, or promising to influence an appointment in return for something of value, including a political contribution. These laws are enforced by the Justice Department, which investigates and then can indict a legislator for illegal activity.

But such blatant influence peddling is just part of the picture. Critics have argued that a legislator can also be improperly influenced by a generous fee for giving a speech or writing an article, by a large retainer for legal services, or by a handsome salary for serving on a corporate board. The question of whether to limit such income has been the most controversial aspect of ethics reform, which culminated in 1978 in a formal federal-wide code of ethics. A parallel concern has been how large campaign contributions can affect a legislator's decisions; that, and worry about escalating costs, prompted several reforms of campaign financing laws, beginning in 1971.

Scandals Prompt Reforms

The move toward a formal code of conduct took twenty years. Congress first endorsed a list of ten guidelines in 1958; the formal codes finally took effect in 1978. The initial set of rules was simply advice about how to behave properly, with no enforcement mechanism. Only after a series of scandals did Congress slowly begin to move toward a formal ethics code and a way to enforce it. The Senate set up a permanent ethics committee in 1964; the House followed suit in 1967. Politicians found that votes in favor of ethics were a good way to quiet negative publicity.

Bad publicity plagued Congress in the 1960s and 1970s. Bobby Baker, the powerful secretary to the Senate majority leader, resigned under fire in 1963 after allegations that he used his office

to promote his business interests. The Senate then went through a painful examination of how Sen. Thomas J. Dodd, a Connecticut Democrat, had misused campaign contributions; he was censured in 1967. The House was rocked in 1967 by its decision not to seat New York Democrat Adam Clayton POWELL, Jr.

The WATERGATE SCANDAL provided a flood of examples of improper behavior by top officials, both in the White House and during President Nixon's reelection campaign. In 1973, in the midst of early Watergate exposures, Vice President Spiro T. Agnew resigned; he had been charged with taking money in return for government contracts. In 1974 the influential chairman of the House Ways and Means Committee, Democrat Wilbur D. MILLS of Arkansas, resigned his chair after a well-publicized escapade with an Argentine strip dancer.

One of the worst years was 1976. Rep. Robert L. F. Sikes, a Florida Democrat, was reprimanded for investing in companies with business before the defense subcommittee he chaired. Ohio Democrat Wayne L. Hays, another highly placed veteran representative, resigned his top posts and then left the House in the midst of an investigation into charges that he kept a mistress on his payroll. That year Congress was also stung by a report that Gulf Oil had illegally contributed more than $5 million to the campaigns of dozens of legislators during the previous decade.

In response, the House in mid-1976 appointed a special ethics study commission chaired by David R. Obey, a Wisconsin Democrat; the Senate then set up its own special group. Early in 1977 the House approved the Obey commission's recommendations almost intact, despite controversy over income limits and other key issues. The Senate somewhat reluctantly approved a similar code.

Formal Ethics Code

Senators and representatives now must answer to two separate ethics codes, one internal and another external. The internal House and Senate codes adopted in 1977 provide the framework for the enforcing committees: the House Committee on Standards of Official Conduct and the Senate Committee on Ethics, which each have equal representation from Democrats and Republicans. The external code is the Ethics in Government Act, passed in 1978, which wrote into law the financial disclosure requirements contained in the congressional ethics code. The new law applied those and other rules to top officials throughout the federal government. However, most of the Ethics in Government Act did not apply to Congress.

The key element in the 1978 law was FINANCIAL DISCLOSURE. Though the most extensive ever approved, the disclosure rules still fell far short of what many critics said were needed to ensure that top officials operated without any conflict of interest. The rules require that legislators, the president and vice president, Supreme Court justices, cabinet secretaries and other top federal officials report each year how much they earn from salaries, fees, honoraria, and gifts. The annual report must include property holdings and other assets, which do not have to be specifically valued but are instead assigned to a broad category of value, such as "$50,000 to $100,000," established by the law.

In its internal rules Congress went further and set a limit on *earned income*, restricting the amount a member could earn to supplement his congressional salary. The critical issue was time spent on noncongressional business. No limit was placed on *unearned income*, such as that from real estate holdings, bonds, or stocks.

The House and Senate have different ceilings on outside earned income. A senator can earn from speeches, salaries, legal fees, and other activities an amount equal to 40 percent of his legislative salary, while a representative is limited to 30 percent. Under the $89,500 annual salary in place in 1988, a senator could earn an additional $35,800, while a member of the House could earn $26,850. *(See* PAY AND PERQUISITES.)

The internal House and Senate ethics codes also prohibited unofficial office accounts, which had been financed with private contributions; banned personal use of campaign funds; restricted use of the FRANKING PRIVILEGE, which allows members to send mail to constituents at taxpayers' expense; limited government-paid FOREIGN TRAVEL by retiring members; and prohibited travel reimbursement if costs were met by other sources. A loophole allowed legislators elected before 1981 to convert to personal use any remaining campaign funds when they left office.

Congress already had prohibited nepotism by senators and representatives under a 1967 law. Nepotism—the hiring of wives, children, and other close relatives—had been a frequent source of critical press comment. Columnists over the years had charged certain members with padding their official staffs with relatives who did little or no work for their government paychecks.

Outside Income Controversy

The limit on outside earned income, by far the most controversial aspect of the ethics code, took several years to evolve. Congress had first set income limits in the 1974 campaign finance law, but applied the ceiling only to honoraria from speeches and articles. The objective was to reduce instances where a legislator was paid thousands of dollars for a half-hour speech to an association or industry lobbying Congress.

The ethics code proposed to Congress in 1977 made those limits tighter, both by lowering the allowed amount and by broadening the definition of honoraria to include all earned income. A respected advocate of reform, Rep. Morris K. Udall, was among those who objected. "You're saying that if I have all kinds of inherited wealth in stocks and bonds, it's okay," the Arizona Democrat told the House. "But if I get out on weekends and hustle and get some money from speaking engagements, it's not okay."

But the Speaker of the House, Massachusetts Democrat Thomas P. O'NEILL, Jr., argued that the limit was needed to restore the "collective integrity of the House." The House Democratic leadership, which had often protected members by preventing votes on controversial questions, in this case forced a public accounting. Another factor was a pay raise for Congress that took effect at the same time. In the end, reluctant to appear opposed to ethical reform and anxious to assuage voters upset about higher pay, a majority voted for income limits and eventually endorsed the full ethics code.

The limit the House approved was 15 percent of a member's salary; with a salary of $57,500, extra earnings could not exceed $8,625 a year. That restriction proved too much for the Senate, where almost half the senators had reported honoraria income over that amount in 1977. The senators voted in early 1979 to delay the income limits for four years. Still in force in the Senate then was a $25,000 ceiling on honoraria included in the 1976 campaign finance law. In other words, senators could earn three times as much outside Congress as representatives.

By 1981 the House had jumped its limit from 15 to 30 percent, without a recorded vote. But the Senate had gone further, voting to eliminate the $25,000 ceiling. Senators were left free of any control on earned income.

Not until mid-1983 did the Senate accept an income limit, and then only after the House tacked the 30 percent level on to a pay increase for the senators. The Senate found even a 30 percent limit too confining and in 1985 increased it to 40 percent.

In 1986 a 40 percent limit was proposed to the House, but members rejected the move. An advocate of the increase was Speaker O'Neill, who had had a change of heart since 1977.   ~

ADDITIONAL READINGS

Drew, Elizabeth. *Politics & Money: The New Road to Corruption.* 1983.
Simon, Paul. *The Glass House.* 1984.
Stern, Philip M. *The Best Congress Money Can Buy.* 1988.

Ethics Committee, House. See STANDARDS OF OFFICIAL CONDUCT COMMITTEE.

Ethics Committee, Senate Select

The six members of the bipartisan Senate Select Committee on Ethics have the often awkward responsibility of making sure their colleagues behave properly. They are charged with enforcing the Senate code of ETHICS, a formal set of rules adopted in 1977. The three Democrats and three Republicans are expected to act collectively as investigator, prosecutor, and jury. In practice, committee members rarely conduct an official probe, preferring to handle potential problems in private before they escalate into scandals.

Most ethics questions focus on finances. Senators are required to keep separate their personal, office, and campaign funds, and they must file FINANCIAL DISCLOSURE statements with the

Ethics Committee. Senators must also avoid situations where they benefit personally from their official acts; bribery is the most blatant example, but more subtle corruption also occurs, such as an inside financial deal with an industry seeking a legislative favor.

The Senate voted in 1964 to establish an ethics committee. By 1988 four disciplinary cases had been brought to the Senate floor. The Senate endorsed the committee's recommendation in each case except the last, when debate over expulsion of New Jersey Democrat Harrison A. Williams, Jr., was cut short by his resignation. The Senate had already indicated its reluctance to handle the controversy by delaying its debate until seven months after the Ethics Committee's unanimous recommendation. *(See* DISCIPLINING MEMBERS.*)*

Critics complain the Ethics Committee has not aggressively policed the Senate. But committee members have said they want to prevent scandals as much as uncover them. The committee has published a manual that contains about 400 questions senators have asked the Ethics Committee, along with answers compiled by the committee and its staff. If a complaint is filed against a senator, rules allow the Ethics Committee to investigate and, if no action is recommended, to keep the matter from public knowledge.

History

Though established in 1964, the committee did not organize until 1965; its first chairman was veteran Mississippi Democrat John C. STENNIS, a former judge with a reputation for fairness and integrity. Stennis chaired the panel until 1975, when Nevada Democrat Howard W. Cannon took over for the next two years. Adlai E. Stevenson III, an Illinois Democrat, then chaired the committee from 1977 through most of 1979, the year the Senate voted to denounce Georgia Democrat Herman Talmadge. Stevenson resigned in the fall, though, and Democrat Howell Heflin, a freshman from Alabama, was named chairman, the first time since 1910 such a new member had been given a committee chairmanship. A former judge, Heflin in 1979-81 demonstrated a judicious restraint that his colleagues appreciated; they gave him the job again when Democrats regained the Senate in 1987. While Republicans controlled the Senate (1981-87), the committee had two chairmen. Malcolm Wallop of Wyoming, who often criticized the Senate ethics code, held the post in 1981-85; Warren B. Rudman of New Hampshire took over in 1985-87. Rudman then served as vice chairman under Heflin, continuing the practice of having a minority member in that post.   ~

Executive Branch and Congress

The Constitution vested the president with "the executive power" and Congress with "all legislative powers." Yet, each branch has come to play a major role in the other's supposed domain. The president is sometimes referred to as the "chief legislator," and Congress has significant leverage over the executive branch through its legislative and oversight powers.

"The constitutional convention of 1787 is supposed to have created a government of 'separated powers,'" Richard Neustadt wrote in *Presidential Power.* "It did nothing of the sort. Rather, it created a government of separated institutions *sharing* powers." *(See* SEPARATION OF POWERS.*)*

Constitutional Deliberations

No question troubled the framers of the Constitution more than the powers and structure to be given the executive branch. How much authority and independence to give the national exec-

Presidential Lobbying
One of the most powerful presidential lobbyists was Lyndon B. Johnson, shown here with Senate Majority Leader Mike Mansfield, left, and Minority Leader Everett McKinley Dirksen.

utive remained in dispute until the very end of the Constitutional Convention.

The convention at first favored a single executive, chosen by Congress for a term of seven years, whose powers would be limited by the fact that Congress would appoint judges and ambassadors and would make treaties. This plan for legislative supremacy finally gave way to a more balanced plan, which called for a president to be chosen by electors for a four-year term without limit as to reelection. (The Twenty-second Amendment, adopted in 1951, set a two-term limit.) The president was to make appointments and treaties, subject to Senate approval, and was given other powers as well.

The framers did not attempt to elaborate on how the system would actually work. The provisions on presidential power were both brief and ambiguous.

President as Lawmaker

The president's role as lawmaker begins with the constitutional duty to "from time to time give to the Congress Information of the State of the Union, and recommend to their Consideration such Measures as he shall judge necessary and expedient." To these bare bones, Congress has added further requirements. For example, the president is required to submit an annual budget message and an economic report. *(See* BUDGET PROCESS.*)*

Other legislative powers granted by the Constitution to the president include the power to veto bills, the power to make treaties (subject to Senate consent), and the rarely used power to convene one or both houses of Congress. The president's role as lawmaker has been further enhanced through the authority to issue rules and regulations, proclamations, and executive orders—or administrative legislation.

The president traditionally sets forth his legislative agenda in his annual STATE OF THE UNION address be-

fore a joint session of Congress. He then sends his legislative proposals to Congress in the form of draft bills.

Where these administration bills go from there depends on a variety of factors, including who is in the White House, which party controls Congress, the times and mood of the country, and, of course, the issue itself.

The Constitution said little about how a president would go about persuading Congress to pass his proposals. Several tools are available.

Lobbying   One tool is to lobby Congress directly. Early presidents kept their lobbying discreet, either doing it themselves or through a few trusted helpers. In modern times, executive lobbying has become more open and more elaborate. *(See* LOBBYING.*)*

President Harry S Truman set up a small legislative liaison office in 1949, but the staff was inexperienced and the real lobbying still was done by Truman and a few top advisers. His successor, Dwight D. Eisenhower, in 1953 appointed full-time, senior staff to the task. Liaison operations continued to expand and grow in sophistication in succeeding administrations.

In addition to the White House operation, all federal departments also have their own congressional liaison forces. The practice began in 1945, when the War Department created the office of assistant secretary for congressional liaison, centralizing congressional relations that had been handled separately by the military services. The services and some civilian agencies have liaison offices on Capitol Hill today.

There are some legal limits on executive lobbying. The executive branch is prohibited by a 1919 criminal statute from spending money to influence votes in Congress. It is generally understood that direct pressure by the executive on Congress is acceptable, but that spending money to solicit outside pressure on Congress is not.

Public Pressure When direct appeals to Congress fail, presidents often turn to their vast constituency for help. Presidents can mobilize enormous public pressure to persuade Congress to act on legislative programs. Radio and television have been potent tools for shaping public opinion.

One of the most skillful users of the media was President Franklin D. Roosevelt. In 1933, at the end of his first week in office, Roosevelt went on the radio to urge support for his banking reforms. He addressed a joint session of Congress, too. His reforms were passed that very day. Similar radio messages, known as "fireside chats," followed.

With the dawning of the age of television, presidents acquired further clout. President Lyndon B. JOHNSON in 1965 made masterful use of television to win support for the most sweeping voting-rights bill in ninety years. Johnson "allowed full play to his sense of theater," wrote Rowland Evans and Robert Novak in their book *Lyndon B. Johnson: The Exercise of Power.* Instead of appearing before Congress at the customary hour of noon, he waited until evening—when the television audience would be greater—to deliver "the best, most genuinely moving speech [he] had made as president." Evans and Novak said Johnson "achieved that elusive rapport with the people that is so vital to any presidency."

President Ronald Reagan enjoyed great success with his use of television. His 1981 televised appeal to Congress for passage of his budget package, accompanied by vigorous lobbying for public support of the program, was labeled by House Speaker Thomas P. O'NEILL, Jr., a Massachusetts Democrat, "the greatest selling job I've ever seen."

Patronage Another means for exerting pressure on Congress is patronage. Over the years this has meant everything from the president's power to fill government jobs to the issuing of coveted White House invitations.

Although the civil service and postal reforms of this century dramatically reduced the president's patronage chest, the award of government contracts, selection of sites for federal installations, and other political favors remain a powerful lever in the hands of a president. *(See* PATRONAGE.*)*

Veto When all else fails, there is always the veto, the president's most powerful defensive weapon. A president uses the veto not only to try to kill unacceptable bills but also to dramatize his policies and put Congress on notice that he is to be taken seriously.

Short of a veto itself, a presidential threat to veto legislation is a powerful form of lobbying. In 1975 both the House and Senate passed a consumer protection bill, but they dropped the measure because President Gerald R. Ford threatened to veto it.

Although the Constitution permits the House and Senate, by a two-thirds vote in each chamber, to override a presidential veto, in reality vetoes are rarely overridden. *(See* VETOES.*)*

Congressional Role
Congress plays an important role in the functioning of the executive branch. Responsibilities range from counting electoral votes, to providing executive branch funds, to monitoring the implementation of laws.

The Constitution provides that Congress will count electoral votes for president and VICE PRESIDENT, and if candidates fail to win a majority, the House will choose the president and the Senate will choose the vice president. Congress also bears responsibility in the related areas of PRESIDENTIAL DISABILITY AND SUCCESSION. *(See* ELECTING THE PRESIDENT.*)*

The Senate has the power to confirm executive APPOINTMENTS. Both the House and Senate can launch INVESTIGATIONS into executive activities, and both chambers work together to seek the IMPEACHMENT and conviction of top officials accused of wrongdoing.

Congress also shares with the executive important WAR POWERS and responsibility for TREATY RATIFICATION. But no power gives Congress as much influence as its POWER OF THE PURSE. Through its AUTHORIZATIONS and APPROPRIATIONS, Congress can play a significant role in formulating and carrying out executive policies. It may use its taxing power both to raise money to run the country and to regulate government activities. *(See* STRUCTURE AND POWERS.*)*

Many of these powers help Congress in performing one of its primary responsibilities, that of OVERSIGHT. In the laws it passes, Congress often leaves much to the discretion of the president and the federal bureaucracy. Congress must, therefore, ensure that its legislative intent is being carried out and remedy the situation if it is not. *(See* LEGISLATIVE VETO.*)*   ~

ADDITIONAL READINGS

Davidson, Roger H., and Walter J. Oleszek. *Congress and Its Members.* 2d ed. 1985.
Fisher, Louis. *The Politics of Shared Power; Congress and the Executive.* 2d ed. 1987.

Executive Privilege

Presidents occasionally refuse congressional demands for information or for officials' testimony before committees by claiming executive privilege. The term is modern, but the practice is as old as the Republic.

Nothing in the Constitution specifically grants executive privilege, but presidents since Washington have asserted a right to withhold information from Congress based on the constitutional SEPARATION OF POWERS. Congress has been reluctant to seek a decisive court ruling on the validity of executive privilege. Instead it has tried to rally public opinion in support of congressional demands for information, and occasionally it has cited executive branch officials for CONTEMPT OF CONGRESS.

Presidents have offered a variety of reasons to justify denying information to Congress. Perhaps the most common is the need for secrecy in military and diplomatic activities. Other reasons for administrative secrecy include protecting individuals from unfavorable publicity and safeguarding the confidential exchange of ideas within an administration. Critics frequently charge that an administration's real motive for refusing to supply information is to escape criticism or scandal.

Watergate Clash

The most dramatic clash over executive privilege came during an inquiry into the WATERGATE SCANDAL, which brought down the presidency of Richard NIXON in 1974. The Watergate affair began with a 1972 break-in at Democratic National Committee headquarters in the Watergate office building in Washington, D.C. But the unfolding scandal disclosed administration political sabotage that went far beyond the original incident.

Claiming executive privilege, President Nixon tried to withhold tapes and documents demanded by congressional investigators. The Supreme Court ruled unanimously in July 1974 that Nixon must give up tapes showing his own involvement in the scandal. Days later the House JUDICIARY COMMITTEE recommended that Nixon be removed from office for, among other things, failing to comply with a committee SUBPOENA, or demand, for the tapes. The president resigned, however, ending the NIXON IMPEACHMENT EFFORT.   ~

Executive Session

An executive session is a meeting of a congressional committee—or occasionally the full Senate or House of Representatives—that only its members may attend. Witnesses regularly appear at committee meetings in executive session. Defense Department officials, for example, testify in executive session during presentations of classified defense information. Other members of Congress may be invited, but the public and press are excluded.   ~

Expulsion.   See DISCIPLINING
   MEMBERS.

Extensions of Remarks

Each issue of the *CONGRESSIONAL RECORD* has a special section that serves almost as a scrapbook of the day. Legislators who want to publicize articles, newspaper stories, or other information can submit the text for a section called "Extensions of Remarks," which is located in the back pages of the *Record*. Any statement expected to take up more than four pages must be accompanied by an estimate of printing costs.

Senators usually prefer to have their articles or undelivered speeches printed as part of the day's floor debate, instead of in "Extensions of Remarks." The extra section is popular with House members, who often fill several pages. A special symbol identifies speeches not actually delivered on the floor.   ~

Overleaf:
Preparing for an all-night filibuster.

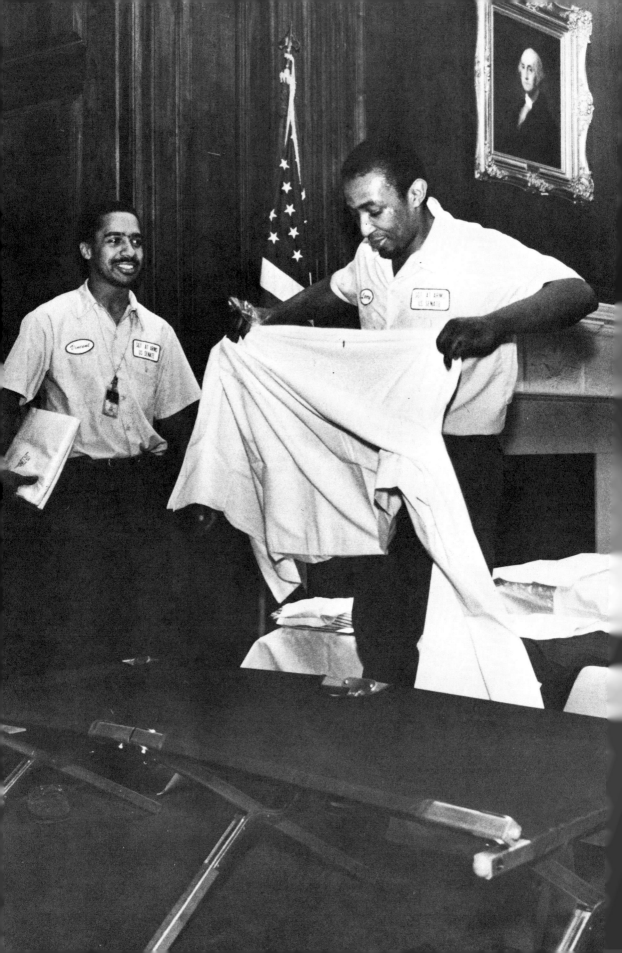

Federal Register

The *Federal Register* is a daily government publication that provides a wide variety of information on government operations. It contains presidential proclamations, executive orders, and other executive branch documents, including rules, regulations, and notices issued by federal agencies. The *Federal Register* spells out government requirements in many fields of public concern—environmental protection, food and drug standards, and occupational health and safety, to name just a few. It also includes proposed changes in agency regulations, on which the public is invited to comment. The *Federal Register* is published by the National Archives and Records Administration. ∼

Filibuster

The Senate has long been famous as the home of the filibuster: the use of prolonged debate and delaying tactics to block action supported by a majority of members. Filibusters have been mounted on issues ranging from peace treaties to internal Senate seating disputes. Editorial writers have condemned them, cartoonists have ridiculed them, and satirists have

caricatured them. But filibusters also have their admirers, who view them as a defense against hasty or ill-advised legislation. That view found expression in the classic 1939 film "Mr. Smith Goes to Washington."

Filibusters are permitted by the Senate's tradition of unlimited debate, a characteristic that distinguishes it from the House of Representatives. The term "filibuster"—derived from a word for pirates or soldiers of fortune—originated in the House, but the modern House seldom experiences delay that rises from a prolonged debate.

The Senate proudly claims to be a more deliberative body than the House. George Washington described it as the saucer where passions cool. But many people believe the modern filibuster impedes rather than encourages deliberation. Once reserved for the most bitter battles of historic dimension—slavery, war, civil rights—filibusters today have been trivialized, critics say.

Historically the rare filibuster provided the Senate's best theater; practitioners had to be ready for days or weeks of free-wheeling debate, and all other business was blocked until one side conceded. In the modern era drama is rare. Disappointment awaits visitors to the Senate gallery who expect a real-life version of Jimmy Stewart's climactic oration in "Mr. Smith Goes to Washington." They are likely to look down on an empty floor and hear only the drone of a clerk reading absent senators' names in a mind-numbing succession of QUORUM calls. Often the filibusterers do not even have to be on the floor, nor do the bills they are opposing.

In large part the change dates from 1975, when the Senate made it easier to choke off debate under a cumbersome procedure known as cloture. Despite the new rule, filibusters and threats of filibusters remain a common weapon of senators hoping to spotlight, change, delay, or kill legislation. Frequent resort to the filibuster, real or threatened, often impedes Senate action on major bills. Success is most likely near the end of a session, when a filibuster on one bill may imperil action on other, more urgent legislation.

Dramatic filibusters still occur on occasion, as demonstrated by a 1988 Republican filibuster against a CAMPAIGN FINANCING bill. To counter GOP obstruction, Majority Leader Robert C. Byrd, a West Virginia Democrat, forced round-the-clock Senate sessions that disrupted the chamber for three days. When Republicans boycotted the sessions, Byrd resurrected a little-known power last wielded in 1942: He directed the Senate SERGEANT-AT-ARMS to arrest absent members and bring them to the floor. In the resulting melee, Oregon Republican Bob Packwood was arrested, reinjured a broken finger, and was physically carried onto the Senate floor at 1:19 in the morning. Democrats were still unable to break the filibuster, and the campaign finance bill was pulled from the floor after a record-setting eighth cloture vote failed to limit debate.

As Old as the Senate

The Senate was just six months old in 1789 when delaying tactics were first used, by opponents of a bill to locate the nation's capital on the Susquehanna River. The first full-fledged filibusters occurred in 1841, when Democrats and Whigs squared off first over the appointment of the official Senate printers and then over the establishment of a national bank.

Slavery, Civil War, RECONSTRUCTION, and blacks' voting rights in turn were the sparks for the increasingly frequent and contentious filibusters of the nineteenth century. Opponents had no weapon against them; proposed rules to restrict debate were repeatedly rejected.

Minor curbs were adopted early in the twentieth century. But they did not hinder Republican filibusterers from killing two of President Woodrow Wil-

Record Setter

The longest speech in the history of the Senate was made by Strom Thurmond of South Carolina. Thurmond, a Democrat who later became a Republican, spoke for twenty-four hours and eighteen minutes during a filibuster against passage of the Civil Rights Act of 1957.

son's proposals to prepare the nation for World War I—a 1915 ship-purchase bill and a 1917 bill to arm merchant ships. As a political scientist in 1881, Wilson had celebrated "the Senate's opportunities for open and unrestricted discussion." After the 1917 defeat he railed, "The Senate of the United States is the only legislative body in the world which cannot act when the majority is ready for action. A little group of willful men . . . have rendered the great government of the United States helpless and contemptible."

Public outrage finally forced the Senate to accept debate limitations. On March 8, 1917, it adopted a rule under which a filibuster could be halted if two-thirds of the senators present voted to do so. The framers of this first cloture rule predicted it would be little used, and for years that was the case.

The first successful use of the rule, in 1919, ended debate on the Treaty of Versailles following World War I.

Nine more cloture votes were taken through 1927, and three were successful. The next successful cloture vote did not occur until 1962, when the Senate invoked cloture on a communications satellite bill.

Only sixteen cloture votes were taken between 1927 and the successful 1962 vote; most involved civil rights. Southern Democrats were joined by westerners and some Republicans in an anticloture coalition that successfully filibustered legislation to stop poll taxes, literacy tests, lynching, and employment discrimination.

Many filibusters turned into grueling endurance contests. South Carolina's Strom Thurmond set a record for the longest speech in the history of the Senate. Thurmond, a Democrat who later switched to the Republican party, spoke for twenty-four hours and eighteen minutes during a 1957 civil rights bill filibuster. Speakers did not always confine themselves to the subject under consideration. Democrat Huey P. LONG, the Louisiana "Kingfish," entertained his colleagues during a 15½-hour filibuster in 1935 with commentaries on the Constitution and recipes for southern "pot likker," turnip greens, and corn bread.

During a 1960 civil rights bill filibuster, eighteen southerners formed two-man teams and talked nonstop in relays. Supporters of the bill had to stay nearby for quorum calls and other procedural moves or risk losing control of the floor. Majority Leader Lyndon B. JOHNSON, a Texas Democrat, kept the Senate going around the clock for nine days in an effort to break the filibuster. That was a record for the longest session in history, but Johnson ultimately had to abandon the bill. Later in the year a weaker version passed.

"We slept on cots in the Old Supreme Court chamber [near the Senate floor] and came out to answer quorum calls," recalled William Proxmire, a Wisconsin Democrat who supported the bill. "It was an absolutely exhausting experience. The southerners who were doing the talking were in great shape, because they would talk for two hours and leave the floor for a couple of days."

Changing the Rule

Civil rights filibusters in the 1950s stimulated efforts to strengthen the cloture rule. As modified in 1949, the rule banned any limitation of debate on proposals to change the Senate rules, including the cloture rule itself. Since any attempt to change the cloture rule while operating under this stricture appeared hopeless, Senate liberals devised a new approach. Senate rules had always continued from one Congress to the next on the assumption that the Senate was a continuing body because only one-third of its members were elected every two years. Liberals now challenged this concept, arguing that the Senate had a right to adopt new rules by a simple majority vote at the beginning of a new Congress.

The dispute came to a head in 1959, when a bipartisan leadership group seized the initiative from the liberals and pushed through a change in the cloture rule. The new version permitted cloture to be invoked by two-thirds of those present and voting (rather than two-thirds of the full Senate membership, as the 1949 rule had required), and it also applied to rules change proposals.

Once cloture was invoked, further debate was limited to one hour for each senator on the bill itself and on all amendments affecting it. No new amendments could be offered except by unanimous consent. Nongermane amendments and dilatory motions, those intended to delay action, were not permitted. (See AMENDMENTS; RIDERS.)

While not addressing the continuing-body question directly, members added new language to their rules stating: "The rules of the Senate shall continue from one Congress to the next unless they are changed as provided in these rules."

The Modern Filibuster

In 1964 the Senate for the first time invoked cloture on a civil rights bill, thus ending the longest filibuster in history after seventy-four days of debate. Other civil rights filibusters were broken in 1965 and 1968. Liberal supporters of civil rights legislation, who had tried repeatedly to tighten controls on debate, became less eager for cloture reform in the wake of these victories. By the 1970s they themselves were doing much of the filibustering—against Nixon administration Vietnam policies, defense weapons systems, and antibusing proposals.

In 1975, however, the liberals tried again to tighten restrictions on debate, and they succeeded in easing the cloture requirement from a high of sixty-seven votes (two-thirds of those voting) to a flat sixty votes (three-fifths of the Senate membership). The old requirement still applied for votes on changes in Senate rules. The number of cloture votes continued to increase after the rule was eased, and the success rate nearly doubled.

Minorities still found ways to obstruct action on measures they opposed, however. The most effective tactic was the post-cloture filibuster, pioneered by Alabama Democrat James B. Allen, a frequent obstructionist. In 1976, when the Senate invoked cloture on a bill he opposed, Allen demanded action on the many amendments he had filed previously. He required that each be read aloud, sought roll-call votes and quorum calls, objected to routine motions, and appealed parliamentary rulings. Other senators soon adopted Allen's tactics.

As filibusters changed in character, the Senate's enthusiasm for unlimited debate eroded. At the mere threat of a filibuster it became a routine practice to start rounding up votes for cloture—or to seek a compromise—as soon as debate began. Most of that action occurred behind the scenes. If the first cloture vote failed, more were taken. Meanwhile, leaders often shelved the disputed bill temporarily, with members' unanimous consent, so the Senate could turn to other matters. That tactic, known as double-tracking, "kept the filibuster from becoming a real filibuster," as one senator said.

The television era prompted additional restraints on debate. When live televised coverage of Senate proceedings began in 1986, members gave new thought to their public image. Senators shied away from several proposals designed to quicken the pace and sharpen the focus of their proceedings for TV viewers. But they did agree to one significant change in Senate rules. They reduced to 30 hours, from 100, the time allowed for debate, procedural moves, and roll-call votes after the Senate had invoked cloture to end a filibuster. ～

ADDITIONAL READING

Burdette, Franklin L. *Filibustering in the Senate.* 1940.

Finance Committee, Senate

The most heavily lobbied committee in the Senate, the Finance Committee handles all federal taxation and about 40 percent of all federal spending. Because the tax code has so many special provisions, ranging from deductions for home mortgages to credits for child care, the committee has almost unlimited jurisdiction. Its responsibility for Social Security, health care for the poor and elderly, and welfare programs

Power Figures
The chairman of the Senate Finance
Committee is one of the most influential figures
in the Senate. Louisiana Democrat Russell B.
Long, left, ruled the committee from 1965 until
Democrats lost control of the Senate in 1981. He
was succeeded by Kansas Republican Robert
Dole, right, who held the post until 1985.

dwarfs the share of the federal pie assigned to most committees. The committee also handles tariffs and other restraints on international trade.

Although efforts to control the federal deficit have put limits on the Finance Committee's authority, it still operates with great latitude. Revenue
goals are set through the congressional
BUDGET PROCESS, but the Finance
Committee decides how the money
should be raised. Assignment to the
committee is keenly sought by senators.

Because the Constitution says revenue bills must originate in the House,
its WAYS AND MEANS Committee has
taken the lead on most tax bills, usually
operating under strict rules to get its
proposals safely through the House
without major amendments. The Senate Finance Committee is a stark contrast; committee members' special
wishes are accommodated, and other
senators are allowed to add a string of
amendments on the floor. In conference
the bills are rewritten again, often in
small, closed caucuses or, as in 1986, in
one-on-one meetings between the
House and Senate committee chairmen.
Although subcommittees have in many
cases diluted the power of full committees, the Finance Committee has resisted such a shift. Its subcommittees,
which do not have separate staff, have

almost no role in writing legislation.
That leaves the Finance chairman better able than most chairmen to steer the
committee toward his own ends. Senators often gather in an "exec room" behind the large hearing room, where they
discuss privately what will happen in
the public markup, or drafting, of the
legislation. When the chairman is ready,
but not before, they take up a matter in
formal session.

Because the tax code is extremely
complex, riddled with tax incentives
treasured by various industries, any effort to pass new tax legislation has always attracted a corridor full of lobbyists. That was particularly true in 1986,
when Congress passed a major tax law
designed to make the rules more equita-
ble. Members of the Finance Committee were often able to accommodate favored lobbyists or even fellow senators
by adding a sentence worded in a general way, but carefully crafted to benefit
a particular case. Russell B. LONG, the
Democratic senator from Louisiana who
chaired the committee from 1966 to
1981, once asked, "What is a loophole?
That is something that benefits the
other guy. If it benefits you, it is tax
reform."

Reform of the welfare system and
changes in health care benefits for the
poor and elderly also occupied the Fi-

nance Committee in the 1980s.

The breadth of its jurisdiction and the importance of its decisions, both financially and socially, have made the Finance Committee a most formidable group of senators. Campaign contributors agree; Finance members are consistently among those with the heaviest donations from POLITICAL ACTION COMMITTEES.

History

Among the first committees established in the Senate, the Finance Committee was set up in 1816. At first the committee handled all aspects of the federal budget, but it lost responsibility for spending during the Civil War, when a separate APPROPRIATIONS Committee was established. With the high costs of war, the job had simply become too large for one group to handle.

In the late nineteenth century, the Finance Committee was a bastion of protectionism, advocating tariffs on imports at rates often exceeding 50 percent. Among the committee's leaders were Republicans John SHERMAN of Ohio (1861-77, 1881-97), who chaired the committee, and William B. ALLISON (1873-1908), a senior member of Finance who also chaired the Appropriations Committee.

At the turn of the century, millionaire Rhode Islander Nelson W. ALDRICH (1881-1911), also a Republican, took the helm. One of the nation's leading conservatives, Aldrich consistently supported high tariffs. Politically astute, he won crucial votes from western senators by endorsing new tariffs to protect western-based industries. Often commodities in which Aldrich had personally invested, such as sugar, were beneficiaries of the tariff structure he helped create.

After the federal income tax was enacted in 1913, the importance of tariffs and excise taxes as a source of government funds diminished. The Finance Committee's focus shifted as

Congress began to write exceptions into the tax code, eventually creating a maze of rules. The push for special tax treatment never let up, and the Finance Committee has always been in the center of the clamor.

Two southern Democrats had long tenure as Finance chairmen after World War II. Harry Flood Byrd of Virginia chaired the committee from 1955 to 1965. One of the most conservative Democrats in the Senate, Byrd used his position as Finance chairman to block much of the social welfare legislation sought by Presidents John F. KENNEDY and Lyndon B. JOHNSON. After Byrd's death, Long, the Louisiana Democrat, took over as chairman; he proved more amenable to social programs—and to requests for special tax treatment from business and industry, particularly the oil industry. At first, in fights with the House, Long was overshadowed by the more experienced Wilbur D. MILLS of Arkansas, chairman of the House Ways and Means Committee. By 1987, though, when Long retired after almost forty years of service, he had become a legend in the Senate, confident in his command of complex subjects and skilled at breaking up tense negotiations with a funny story.

Robert DOLE of Kansas stepped into the chair when Republicans gained control of the Senate in 1981. That year he helped engineer passage of sweeping tax cuts sought by President Reagan. In 1982, in a break from the usual procedure, Dole's Finance Committee initiated a major tax bill, and the House did not vote on the measure until it emerged from a Senate-House conference. When Dole was elected majority leader in 1985, Bob Packwood of Oregon took over the Finance Committee, serving for just two years, until Democrats won back the Senate majority. Although at first not a supporter of tax reform, Packwood ended up presiding over a major overhaul of the tax code. In 1987 another oil-state Democrat,

Lloyd Bentsen of Texas, became Finance chairman.   ~

Financial Disclosure

Financial disclosure is a key principle behind two different reforms: federal ETHICS codes and CAMPAIGN FINANCING laws. Top federal officials are required to report annually the sources of their income, and candidates for federal office must file detailed reports of campaign contributions and expenditures.

The hope is that public scrutiny of financial records will discourage corrupt practices, ranging from conflicts of interest to outright bribery. The Supreme Court, upholding a 1925 law requiring reports on campaign spending, commented in 1934: "Congress reached the conclusion that public disclosure of political contributions, together with the names of contributors and other details, would tend to prevent the corrupt use of money to affect elections. The verity of this conclusion reasonably cannot be denied."

In actual practice, though, the soundness of the underlying concept made little difference. Until the reforms of the 1970s, the laws on disclosure simply did not work. President Lyndon B. JOHNSON, in proposing election reforms in 1967, described the campaign laws: "Inadequate in their scope when enacted, they are now obsolete. More loophole than law, they invite evasion and circumvention."

The requirements for financial disclosure, both in the ethics codes and in campaign financing laws, were greatly improved in later years, though critics still complained they were flawed and inconsistently enforced. The disclosure rules probably helped keep government officials honest, but no one was sure to what degree. The requirements in force in 1988 are described below.

Income Disclosure

Starting with passage of the Ethics in Government Act in 1978, top federal officials, both in Congress and in the executive and judiciary branches, had to file annual financial reports that covered salaries, honoraria, gifts, reimbursements, income from investments, and the value of assets and liabilities.

The disclosure requirements did not require specific amounts, but instead allowed reporting within a range of figures set in the law. This provided a rather vague picture of an official's financial situation but did give a sense of his wealth and how it was acquired, or of debt and how it was accumulated. However, the rules made it possible to omit the details of certain transactions, such as real estate deals. Mortgages, car loans, and other consumer loans did not have to be reported.

Members of Congress filed their reports with the CLERK OF THE HOUSE and the SECRETARY OF THE SENATE, and the House and Senate ethics committees reviewed them and investigated complaints. If the committees found omissions or false reports, they could recommend disciplinary action against the member in their report to the House or Senate. Expulsion, censure, reprimand, and denunciation were among the disciplinary actions the legislators could take. Sometimes the ethics committees recommended against any punishment, even when they concluded that the legislator had broken rules. (See DISCIPLINING MEMBERS; ETHICS.)

Executive branch employees filed their reports with the Office of Government Ethics, and judicial branch employees filed with the Judicial Ethics Committee.

The 1978 law provided for civil penalties of up to $5,000 against anyone who knowingly and willfully filed a false report or failed to file a report. For criminal penalties the 1978 law pointed to the general federal criminal statute

Penalties Imposed
Members of Congress are required to file reports annually disclosing the sources of their income. George Hansen, a Republican representative from Idaho, was convicted in 1984 for failing to report nearly $334,000 in loans and profits between 1978 and 1981. He was the first member to be convicted for failing to comply with financial disclosure rules. Hansen was fined and imprisoned for nearly a year.

prohibiting false reporting to the federal government. Breaking that law was a felony, for which the maximum fine was $10,000, and the maximum prison sentence five years.

Although several members were investigated for not complying with the financial disclosure rules, only one member of Congress was convicted between 1978 and 1987. George Hansen, a Republican representative from Idaho, was convicted in 1984 for failing to report nearly $334,000 in loans and profits between 1978 and 1981. Hansen was fined and imprisoned for nearly a year.

The ethics committees typically did not investigate or make recommendations while a Justice Department probe was under way, but they did review convictions to see if congressional disciplinary action was warranted. The House Committee on STANDARDS OF OFFICIAL CONDUCT, as the ethics panel is formally known, followed up Hansen's April 1984 conviction with a recommendation that he be reprimanded for the false reports. The House agreed. Hansen, who declined to change his reports when given a chance by the ethics com-

mittee and who maintained his innocence, was narrrowly defeated in his re-election bid in November 1984.

The House panel found inaccurate reporting by other members, but decided not to recommend disciplinary action against several Democrats, including: Geraldine Ferraro of New York, in 1984; James Weaver of Oregon and Dan Daniel of Virginia, both in 1986; Fernand J. St Germain of Rhode Island, in 1987; and Charlie Rose of North Carolina, in 1988. Inaccurate reports were part of the more serious charges of financial misconduct that resulted in the House censure of Democrats Charles C. Diggs, Jr., of Michigan, in 1979 and Charles H. Wilson of California in 1980, and the Senate reprimand of Georgia Democrat Herman Talmadge, in 1979.

Campaign Financing
Under campaign financing laws in effect in 1988, candidates for federal office were required to keep detailed records on who contributed to their campaigns and how the money was spent. A regulatory agency, the Federal Election Commission, made sure candi-

dates were complying with the law. Disclosure rules had a major impact on campaigning; the best evidence was that accountants and lawyers became a standard feature on campaign staffs of major candidates.

Financial disclosure was only part of the overall CAMPAIGN FINANCING law, which also limited the size of contributions by individuals and political committees. In presidential campaigns, candidates who accepted public financing also had to comply with spending restrictions. (The Supreme Court in 1976 ruled, in the case of *Buckley v. Valeo*, that spending limits are valid only when accepted voluntarily. Under the system in effect in 1988, for example, presidential candidates had to agree to limit spending in order to receive public financing. Congressional candidates did not receive public financing.)

History

The use of disclosure to keep tabs on campaign financing began in 1910 and 1911, when Congress passed and then amended the Federal Corrupt Practices Act. The law required congressional candidates and political organizations (operating in two or more states) to file financial reports, and limited spending to $10,000 for Senate candidates and $5,000 for House candidates.

Loopholes and lack of enforcement meant the law had little effect on campaigns; neither did an overhaul of the statute approved in 1925. A major flaw allowed congressional candidates to report they had received and spent nothing on their campaigns; the candidates maintained that campaign committees established to elect them to office had been working without their "knowledge and consent." No candidate for the House or Senate was ever prosecuted under the 1925 act.

Not until 1971 did Congress again address the financing of campaigns. The Federal Election Campaign Act of 1971 required, for the first time, relatively complete and timely public reports by candidates on who was financing their campaigns and how much they were spending. Less than three years later, rocked by misuse of campaign funds revealed during the WATERGATE investigation, Congress in 1974 extensively rewrote the existing campaign financing law. Although the Supreme Court overturned several features of that law, prompting yet another version in 1976, the financial disclosure requirements remained intact.

Still another revision, in 1979, was directed in part at reducing the red tape associated with financial disclosure. The changes reduced the frequency of required reports, raised the minimum contribution and expenditure that had to be itemized, and exempted candidates who raised or spent less than $5,000.

Requirements

A complex set of rules defined the various political committees that had to register and file financial reports with either the clerk of the House, the secretary of the Senate, or the Federal Election Commission. (Copies of all reports are on file at the FEC and in the relevant state.)

Each candidate designated a principal campaign committee that usually solicited and spent the bulk of his campaign funds. This committee had to report to the FEC; however, candidates who spent or received less than $5,000 were not required to file.

Also covered by the financial disclosure rules were political parties and their campaign committees, who had to report when $1,000 or more was spent or received in a year. POLITICAL ACTION COMMITTEES—organizations that distribute campaign contributions to candidates for Congress and other offices—also fell into that category. However, tighter restrictions applied to the PACs most closely tied to corporations, labor unions, trade associations, or certain other groups. Administration of these PACs, including bank accounts, was often handled by the corporation, union, or association, with the PAC funds kept in "separate segregated accounts," as the FEC called the setup. These PACs were required to report any expenditures, even if only $100 was spent in a year.

A separate rule applied to expenditures made without consulting the candidate. Such independent expenditures, either by individuals or political committees, had to be reported once they exceeded $250 in a year. Top independent spenders in the 1980s included Cecil R. Haden, a Texas industrialist and Reagan supporter, and Stewart Mott, a General Motors heir and liberal Democrat.

Among groups with large independent expenditures were the Congressional Club, spearheaded by conservative Republican Sen. Jesse Helms of North Carolina, and the National Conservative Political Action Committee, noted for its negative campaigns against several Democratic senators.

Reports

In addition to details of financial transactions, including total receipts and expenditures, the reports had to identify the source of all contributions in excess of $200. (This included a contributor whose smaller donations added up to $200 in a year.) Those paid more than $200 by the committee (for advertisements, transportation, management, or other campaign operating expenses) had to be listed by name and address.

Rules about when reports must be filed varied according to the type of campaign, whether an election was scheduled, and the amount of money involved. The focus of the rules, though, was on elections, with reports specifically required just before and just after elections.   ~

Fiscal Year

The financial operations of the federal government are carried out in a twelve-month fiscal year that begins on October 1 and ends on September 30. The president's budget and congressional spending bills are calculated on a fiscal-year basis. *(See* BUDGET PROCESS.*)*

The fiscal year carries the date of the calendar year in which it ends. The current fiscal calendar has been in use since fiscal 1977. From fiscal 1844 through fiscal 1976 the fiscal year began July 1 and ended the following June 30.   ~

Floor Debate.   See LEGISLATIVE PROCESS.

Floor Manager

The floor manager of a bill is responsible for guiding floor action on the measure in his chamber. The chairman of the committee or subcommittee that handled a bill usually acts as floor manager for its supporters. The committee's ranking member of the minority party or his designee leads the opposition.

In both the House and Senate the floor managers operate from designated aisle seats. Staff members, who rarely come onto the floor, are allowed to sit alongside.

Regardless of his personal views on a bill, a floor manager is under obligation to present the work of his committee in the most favorable light and to fend off undesirable amendments. The mark of a successful floor manager is his ability to get his bill passed without substantial change.   ~

Foley, Thomas S.

Widely regarded as a coalition builder, Washington Democrat Thomas S. Foley (1929-) became majority leader of the House in 1987. As a committee chairman and in various LEADERSHIP positions, he proved to be an effective bridge both between Democratic factions and to the Republicans.

Foley's negotiating skill and sense of detachment allowed him to reach the top levels of the House leadership without the aggressiveness it sometimes takes to make it that far in the chamber. In fact, Foley was so evenhanded that there was some question initially as to how effective he would be in the highly partisan job of House majority leader, which he took over from the hard-charging Jim WRIGHT of Texas.

Foley, first elected in 1964, earned a reputation as a good legislative manager and rose in Democratic ranks. In 1974 he chaired the Democratic Study Group, the strategy and research arm of liberal and moderate Democrats. As a veteran of numerous REFORM battles against secrecy and seniority in the committee system, Foley was the logical choice when the chairmanship of the Democratic Caucus opened up in 1977. He served in that position until 1981, when he became majority whip, the leadership's chief vote-counter. Thomas P. O'NEILL, Jr., who was then SPEAKER of the House, was looking for someone with parliamentary skills for the coming battles with House Republicans, and Foley, who had been the Democratic national convention's parliamentarian in 1980, fit the bill. Then Foley became majority leader in the leadership shake-up triggered by O'Neill's retirement at the end of the 99th Congress. *(See* CAUCUSES, PARTY*).*

As majority leader, Foley had to abandon the agriculture issues that pre-occupied him for much of his career. He was AGRICULTURE COMMITTEE chairman from 1975 until 1981.   ~

Ford, Gerald R.

Gerald R. Ford (1913-) is best known as the thirty-eighth president of the United States, but he came to that position after twenty-four years as a Republican representative from Michigan, including nine years as House Republican leader. He also served a brief stint as President Richard Nixon's vice president.

Ford was the first person to assume executive office under provisions of the Twenty-fifth Amendment to the Constitution governing presidential and vice-presidential succession. In 1973 Nixon chose Ford to replace Vice President Spiro T. Agnew, who resigned in the face of criminal charges. Ford became president in 1974 when Nixon himself resigned under threat of impeachment. *(See* PRESIDENTIAL DISABILITY AND SUCCESSION; WATERGATE SCANDAL; NIXON IMPEACHMENT EFFORT.*)*

Ford was first elected to the House of Representatives in 1948. From the beginning he compiled a strongly conservative voting record. He consistently voted against amendments to limit defense spending and was critical of Johnson administration policies during the Vietnam War. He voted against the 1973 War Powers Resolution, which sought to limit the president's war-making powers, and supported stepped-up bombing of North Vietnam.

On domestic issues, Ford backed attempts to limit federal spending and the expansion of the federal government. He opposed Medicare health care for the elderly and federal aid to education; while voting for the civil rights acts of the 1960s, he preferred milder substitutes. Angry over the Senate's rejection of two of Nixon's appointees to the Supreme Court, Ford launched an attack in 1970 on Justice William O. Douglas. Calling for his impeachment, Ford cited Douglas's financial connections with a private foundation and his defense of civil disobedience set forth in his book *Points of Rebellion.*

Ford's unwavering loyalty to his party led to his election as chairman of the House Republican Conference in 1962. He was elected House minority leader in 1965. He was admired by his peers for his honesty and frankness.

Popular in Congress and loyal to the administration, Ford was a logical choice for vice president upon Agnew's resignation on October 10, 1973. He was confirmed by the Senate on November 27, 1973, by a vote of 92-3.

On August 9, 1974, Nixon resigned and Ford assumed the office of president. His popularity with Congress and the country at large suffered after he pardoned Nixon on September 8, 1974. Ford ran unsuccessfully for president in 1976; defeated by Democrat Jimmy Carter, he retired from public life. ～

Foreign Affairs Committee, House

The House Foreign Affairs Committee is the primary committee in the House devoted to consideration of issues involving the role of the United States in the world. Throughout most of its existence, however, the committee has had a relatively small impact on the direction of U.S. foreign policy.

Traditionally, the House committee has been overshadowed by its Senate counterpart, the Foreign Relations Committee. To a great extent, this reflects the contrast between the foreign policy roles of the House and Senate established by the Constitution. Since the Constitution gives the Senate exclusive control over international treaties and nominations, the Senate Foreign Relations Committee is frequently at the center of debate over major international issues. The House has much less authority over foreign affairs under the Constitution, and so the House Foreign Affairs Committee has less authority as well.

The most important legislative topics that fall under the jurisdiction of the Foreign Affairs Committee are the many foreign aid programs. These provide economic assistance to poor and developing countries, as well as military equipment and training for U.S. allies around the world.

Traditionally, the Foreign Affairs Committee has ranked behind the Senate committee in public attention as well as constitutional authority. While Foreign Relations for many decades drew the best-known and most respected members of the Senate, the House committee frequently included many obscure junior members, who quickly left for a committee with more legislative and political importance. Nor, at least until the 1980s, did the chairman of the House committee have the political strength to play a major role in foreign policy debates.

The Foreign Affairs Committee also has been hit by the same forces that have reduced the once-great power of Senate Foreign Relations. The executive branch has assumed greater contol over foreign issues, thus reducing the foreign policy role of Congress as a whole.

Another problem for the Foreign Affairs Committee has been the political weakness of foreign aid programs. Although advocates of foreign aid say it can be an effective means of advancing U.S. interests in the world, these programs have long been highly unpopular among the public and a substantial section of Congress. In the 1980s foreign aid programs had become so controversial that Congress was able to complete final action on an annual foreign aid bill only once in five years. So the Foreign Affairs Committee rarely was able to have any legislative impact on how the programs were run.

The inability of Congress to pass foreign aid bills effectively transferred control over the shape and direction of foreign aid to the House Appropriations Subcommittee on Foreign Operations, which made many of the decisions about the programs during this period. So Foreign Affairs found itself facing an increasingly influential competitor within the House for influence over its most important areas of jurisdiction.

Nevertheless, the importance of the Foreign Affairs Committee grew in some important ways during the 1980s. A new chairman, Dante B. Fascell, a Florida Democrat, was seen by many as bringing stronger leadership to the com-

mittee. And a number of members who had arrived in the 1970s began to become more visible participants in foreign policy debates. New York Democrat Stephen J. Solarz, for example, was a leading congressional critic of deposed Philippine President Ferdinand E. Marcos. Illinois Republican Henry J. Hyde became widely known in the media for his spirited defense of the Reagan administration's Central America policy.   ~

Foreign Relations Committee, Senate

The Senate Foreign Relations Committee oversees most aspects of the relationship between the United States and other countries. It is one of the

Treaty Role

All treaties, regardless of their subject matter, are referred to the Senate Foreign Relations Committee. Secretary of State George Shultz, center, was the lead-off witness at the committee's 1988 hearings on a treaty banning U.S. and Soviet intermediate-range nuclear-force (INF) missiles. He is shown here with Foreign Relations Chairman Claiborne Pell, right, a Rhode Island Democrat, and committee member Jesse Helms, a North Carolina Republican.

most important forums through which members of Congress seek to exert influence in the field of international affairs.

Like its similarly named House counterpart, the FOREIGN AFFAIRS COMMITTEE, the Senate Foreign Relations Committee has jurisdiction over foreign aid and legislation concerning the operations of the State Department, which carries out most aspects of U.S. foreign policy. Unlike the House committee, Foreign Relations also has the right to recommend that foreign policy nominations and treaties submitted by the president be approved or rejected by the Senate. *(See* TREATY-MAKING POWER.*)*

Since the early nineteenth century, the Foreign Relations Committee has been one of the most prestigious and powerful committees on Capitol Hill. Throughout that time, committee members have played important roles in crucial foreign policy debates. Since the end of World War II in 1945, for example, the committee has been important in guiding U.S. policy through the Cold War of the late 1940s and 1950s, the Vietnam War in the 1960s, and the Panama Canal treaty in the 1970s. The committee was widely admired as a source of a bipartisan foreign policy consensus that for many years guided U.S. actions. Television coverage made its members familiar figures to many Americans.

However, by the 1980s the committee suffered a substantial loss in power and influence. For a variety of reasons, the committee no longer occupied the vital role in foreign policy decision-making that it had in previous decades.

One factor weakening the Foreign Relations Committee was the decline in Congress's foreign policy authority in general. A marked shift in power from Congress to the executive branch deprived the Foreign Relations Committee of a role in many key international issues.

The Foreign Relations Committee also lost part of its power to other congressional committees. The House Foreign Affairs Committee became a more important force during the 1980s, and so took away some of the Senate committee's influence. In addition the Senate Appropriations Subcommittee on Foreign Operations exerted a greater degree of control over foreign aid programs through its authority over annual spending bills.

The unpopularity of foreign aid programs also handicapped the committee. One of the committee's most important duties each year is to write a bill authorizing economic and military aid to other countries. But the bills approved by the committee rarely were able to win approval from the Senate or Congress as a whole. As a result, the committee had less of an impact on how those programs were run.

The political makeup of the Foreign Relations Committee also changed significantly in the 1980s. In its glory days, the committee was dominated by a coalition of moderate Democrats and Republicans, who usually were able to work out a common position on critical issues. By the 100th Congress (1987-89), the committee was deeply divided between mostly liberal Democrats and a group of very conservative Republicans. Debates on important issues, such as war in Central America and nuclear arms control, frequently were marked by bitter arguments between the two factions.

History

After its creation in 1816, the Foreign Relations Committee quickly became one of the most important in Congress, primarily because of its jurisdiction over treaties. All treaties, regardless of their subject matter, are referred to the committee.

The committee has attracted some of the most illustrious members of the Senate, including Daniel WEBSTER, John C. CALHOUN, Roscoe CONKLING, and Robert A. TAFT. Among its chairmen have been Charles SUMNER, Henry Cabot LODGE, William E. BORAH, Arthur H. VANDENBERG, and J. William FULBRIGHT.

The growing importance of the United States in world politics during the twentieth century has added to the importance of the Foreign Relations Committee. After World War I, for example, Lodge and other committee members played a crucial role in determining whether the United States would ratify the Versailles Treaty and thus join the League of Nations. The committee helped draft limitations on the treaty that were unacceptable to President Woodrow Wilson. As a result, the treaty was rejected, and the United States did not join the League.

After World War II, the committee was a major factor in committing the United States to a policy of heavy involvement in world affairs and the containment of communism. Before the war, Vandenberg and many other committee members had been "isolationists," who opposed U.S. entanglements with other countries. But Vandenberg, who chaired the committee in 1947-49, switched to an "internationalist" stance after the war. Along with other committee members, he helped create a bipartisan consensus in favor of a strong foreign policy.

The combination of television and the Vietnam War made Fulbright into the committee's most famous chairman. Fulbright, who served as chairman from 1959 to 1975, was an outspoken critic of President Lyndon B. Johnson's policy of expanding the U.S. role in the war in Vietnam. To dramatize his opposition, Fulbright held nationally televised hearings on the war in the mid- and late-1960s. The hearings were the subject of intense national interest and helped organize widespread public opposition to Johnson's policies.

Fulbright was defeated for reelection in 1974, however, and most of the

subsequent committee chairmen lacked his ability to lead the committee. Idaho Democrat Frank Church (1979-81) and Indiana Republican Richard G. Lugar (1985-87) were widely seen as strong chairmen able to restore the committee's influence. But Church was defeated for reelection in 1980, and Lugar lost his post when the Republicans lost control of the Senate in the 1986 elections. So each served as chairman for only two years.

Despite its loss of power, though, the Foreign Relations Committee in the late 1980s still was able to exert some influence over foreign policy. Media interest in the committee remained high, causing its hearings on arms control and other issues to attract considerable television and press coverage. Committee members also have learned to make use of their power over foreign policy nominations to influence policy. During the Reagan administration, conservatives as well as liberals on the committee sought to block presidential nominations to underscore opposition to various Reagan policies.

In addition, Lugar showed that a strong chairman could do much to restore the panel's importance. During his short term at the helm, Lugar was able to use his position to exert a considerable degree of influence over the Reagan administration's policies on two important foreign issues: the Philippines, where a popular movement ousted President Ferdinand E. Marcos, and South Africa, where the white minority government continued to deny basic human rights to the nation's black majority.   ~

Foreign Travel

Foreign trips by senators and representatives have been one of the most visible and controversial perquisites of serving in Congress. Defenders of foreign travel see it as a valuable way to educate legislators about world problems, particularly when many congressional votes deal with foreign affairs. But critics call the trips "junkets"—vacation trips at taxpayers' expense.

Some legislators are legendary for their traveling, among them Allen J. Ellender, a Democratic senator from Louisiana (1937-72), and Adam Clayton POWELL, Jr. (1945-67, 1969-71), a Democratic representative from New York. Legislators have since learned to be more discreet, but controversy still erupts. In 1985 Rep. Bill Alexander, an Arkansas Democrat, used a military plane at a cost of $50,000 for a solo trip to Brazil; Democratic colleagues later reacted by ousting him as chief deputy whip.

Most trips are made under the auspices of congressional committees, but House and Senate leaders get special travel allowances. House Speaker Jim Wright, a Texas Democrat, continued the Speaker's tradition of an annual spring trip, rewarding more than a dozen loyal colleagues in 1987 with an invitation to Spain, West Germany, and the Soviet Union. The excursion cost more than $145,000. Large delegations also go each year to meetings of the Interparliamentary Union and the North Atlantic Assembly, which get U.S. and foreign legislators together. Another popular trip is to the Paris International Air Show, where manufacturers display military hardware and other equipment.

Often congressional delegations travel on military planes, accompanied by Marines or other military escorts who help with baggage and act as flight attendants. Embassy personnel in each city they visit are expected to arrange meetings with local officials and arrange tours. "Control rooms" are set up in the hotels, where legislators are offered coffee in the morning and cocktails in the evening.

Senators and representatives have been required since the 1950s to file accounts of travel spending, but the rules have been rewritten several times since then. In 1973 Congress voted to stop requiring that travel reports be printed in the CONGRESSIONAL RECORD, but the rule was restored in 1976 after public protest. In the late 1980s committees, but not individual members, had to file quarterly travel reports with the CLERK OF THE HOUSE and SECRETARY OF THE SENATE. Other delegations had to file their reports within thirty days of the trip. All travel reports were published in the *Record*.

Reports do not have to be filed on trips funded by the executive branch or by private agencies.   ~

Former Members of Congress

More than eleven thousand people had served in Congress as of the late 1980s. Their activities after leaving the House and Senate, typically after eight or ten years, were as varied as those before they were elected. Many returned to the practice of law or to business. A few took prestigious posts outside government; former House member John Brademas, an Indiana Democrat, was named president of New York University in 1981, and New York Republican Barber B. Conable, Jr., also an ex-representative, became head of the World Bank in 1986. Still others simply retired, living on a congressional pension that in 1988 was about $21,000 a year after ten years of service.

Many members left Congress but stayed in politics. All but thirteen of the first thirty-nine presidents served in Congress or its predecessor, the Continental Congress. Thirty-three vice presidents had served in the legislative branch by 1988. Several contenders in the 1988 presidential campaign also had

LIFE AFTER CONGRESS
Former Members Find New Challenges

Sen. Edmund S. Muskie
Secretary of State

Rep. Barber B. Conable, Jr.
President, World Bank

Sen. Henry Bellmon
Governor of Oklahoma

Rep. Abner J. Mikva
Judge, Court of Appeals

Rep. John Brademas
President,
New York University

Sen. James Abourezk
Lobbyist, American-Arab
Anti-Discrimination Committee

congressional experience.

Former members of Congress have also been appointed to the cabinet or other top posts. After serving in the House and Senate, Albert Gallatin of Pennsylvania became Treasury secretary in 1801—and served a record thirteen years. Another veteran legislator, South Carolina's John C. CALHOUN, served as secretary of war and secretary of state, as well as vice president, in the pre-Civil War period. Tennessee Democrat Cordell Hull had spent almost twenty-five years in Congress when he was tapped as secretary of state by Franklin D. Roosevelt in 1933. In the 1980s President Ronald Reagan turned more than once to ex-legislators to staff his cabinet; in the White House itself, Tennessee Republican Howard H. BAKER, Jr., a former Senate majority leader, served as chief of staff.

Some members of Congress have given up congressional seats to take prestigious jobs in the executive branch. In the 1840s and 1850s Daniel WEBSTER, a Massachusetts Whig, twice left the Senate to become secretary of state. More recently, Maine Democrat Edmund S. Muskie stepped down as senator to become secretary of state; Stewart Udall, an Arizona Democrat, and Rogers C. B. Morton, a Maryland Republican, each left the House to become interior secretary—Udall in 1961, Morton ten years later.

Governors have often been elected to Congress, particularly to the Senate, but the path has gone both ways. Louisiana, South Carolina, Maine, and West Virginia were among the states whose governors in the 1980s had previously served in Congress. Republican Henry Bellmon of Oklahoma had an unusual résumé; first governor, then senator, in 1986 he was elected governor again.

Still another career choice for former members has been the judiciary. Although the pattern has been rare since the 1940s, about a third of all Supreme Court justices had previously served in Congress or the Continental Congress. More common recently have been other judicial appointments, such as the 1979 decision by Abner J. Mikva, a Democratic representative from Illinois, to accept a federal judgeship.

Among the most visible former members of Congress are those who stay in Washington as lobbyists, usually with law firms. They stalk familiar corridors and hearing rooms to win votes from former colleagues—or, in many cases, favorable wording from staff who draft the bills. Although ex-members have lifetime privileges on the House and Senate floors, the House has a rule against lobbying on the floor and the practice is frowned on in the Senate. Lobbying is not out of bounds, though, in the Capitol Hill dining rooms and gymnasiums still frequented by ex-members.

Often ex-member lobbyists handle the same issues they concentrated on as legislators. James Abourezk, a South Dakota Democrat, championed the Arab cause in the House and Senate in the 1970s; he later lobbied as chairman of the American-Arab Anti-Discrimination Committee. Florida Democrat Paul Rogers became an expert on federal health policy as chairman of a key House subcommittee; later, as a Washington lawyer, he was a director of Merck and Co., Inc., a major pharmaceutical manufacturer. J. William FULBRIGHT chaired the Senate Foreign Relations Committee for fifteen years until his 1974 reelection defeat; later he had clients from Saudi Arabia and Japan, among other countries. Richard S. Schweiker served in the Reagan administration's cabinet after he left the Senate in 1981 and then became president of the American Council of Life Insurance.

Several hundred ex-members belong to the U.S. Association of Former Members of Congress. The group, which has a variety of educational programs, hosts a reunion every spring on

Capitol Hill. Returning members meet in the House chamber, just before an official session, and have a chance, once again, to make a speech in the Capitol.   ～

Franking Privilege

The postman brings it, but instead of a stamp in the upper right-hand corner the envelope bears the signature of a member of Congress. For senators and representatives this facsimile of their handwriting, called the "frank," is an important privilege. Through newsletters and other mailings, sent at government expense, legislators can communicate directly with their constituents, informing them about congressional decisions and passing on useful news about the federal government. By the late 1980s Congress was spending about $90 million a year on its special postage.

The franked envelope might contain a legislator's response to a question or request, a copy of his newsletter, a survey, a press release, a packet of voting information, government publications, a seed report, or other printed matter that in some way relates to the legislator's "official duties." The frank cannot be used to solicit money or votes. Letters related to political campaigns, political parties, or personal business or friendships are not permitted. For example, a legislator cannot use the frank on a holiday greeting, a

Keeping in Touch
The franking privilege permits members of Congress to communicate directly with their constituents at government expense. Each member's facsimile signature, or frank, is used in place of a postage stamp.

message of sympathy, an invitation to a party fundraiser, or a request for political support.

Although Congress has limited use of the frank in the weeks preceding elections, the amount of franked mail still jumps dramatically in election years, prompting charges from challengers that the privilege is yet another advantage for incumbents.

Those authorized to use the frank include the vice president, members and members-elect of Congress, and certain officers of the House and Senate. Committees and subcommittees send mail under the frank of a committee member.

The concept of the frank is actually older than Congress itself. The first Continental Congress enacted a law in 1775 giving its members mailing privileges as a way of keeping constituents fully informed. It was also a way of reminding voters back home—between elections—that their legislator was thinking of them. A common practice in the nineteenth century was to send home packets of seeds, courtesy of the Agriculture Department. Congress enjoyed the use of the frank almost without restriction until 1973, when the first effort at self-policing began.

Although no stamp is needed, a franked letter is not actually mailed free of charge. The U.S. Postal Service keeps records on how many franked pieces of mail it handles and how much they weigh. At the end of the year the postal service sends Congress what amounts to a bill; Congress then transfers the funds to the postal service.

The cost of the mailing privilege jumped dramatically in the 1970s and 1980s, because of increases in both mailing rates and the amount of mail. In 1970 Congress sent 190 million pieces of franked mail at a cost of $11.2 million; by 1986 more than 750 million letters and packages were sent under the frank, and the cost had jumped to $96 million. If Congress spent more than it

appropriated for mailing costs, the practice was for legislators to vote more money halfway through the year.

But concerns about budget deficits prompted Congress to slow down the flood of mail. By 1988 annual costs were being kept below $90 million. The Senate used improved cost accounting to get a handle on its mailings. Beginning in 1986, each senator got a budget showing his share of the appropriation for postage, based on population; a contingency fund could bail out a senator who exceeded his budget. Each senator also received reports, twice a year, on his mass mailings and what they cost. The House resisted formal cost accounting, but still managed to hold down spending on postage. "We have, through jawboning Congress, restrained our use of the frank," said Californian Vic Fazio, a Democratic representative who chaired the subcommittee handling legislative appropriations.

Advantage to Incumbents

The advantage the frank gives to someone in office running for reelection has been the most controversial aspect of the traditional privilege. The debate intensified after the 1972 election campaign. Several mailings during the campaign were considered improper; what those in office mailed seemed too much like advertising for their political campaigns. Twelve cases reached the courts.

A blatant case of abuse took place in Georgia. A representative running for the Senate used the frank to send mail all over the state, not just to his congressional district. The mailing, which cost taxpayers more than $200,000, became a campaign issue—and a key factor in the representative's defeat. The winner, who made the franked mailing a campaign issue, was Democrat Sam Nunn, a future chairman of the Senate Armed Services Committee.

In response to the 1972 abuses, a public interest group filed a lawsuit in October 1973 charging that the frank was unconstitutional. The group, Common Cause, said the frank allowed incumbents—persons already in office—to use government funds to help their reelection efforts. That, Common Cause charged, gave incumbents an unfair advantage over those seeking their seats.

1973 Regulations

Within two months, anxious to set its own rules before the courts could interfere, Congress had passed a new law setting guidelines for use of the frank. These included tighter definitions of the types of mail eligible and a limit on mass mailings (defined as more than 500 pieces of identical mail) during the four weeks before an election. This was known as the "preelection cutoff," and applied to primary and general elections. A primary is one way political parties choose among two or more individuals who want to be the party's nominee for an office.

To oversee use of the franking privilege, the House set up a Commission on Congressional Mailing Standards; later the Senate gave its Select Ethics Committee a similar responsibility, although its Rules and Administration Committee handles routine administration of the frank.

Additional changes in 1977 and 1981 tightened the rules adopted in 1973. For example, the preelection cutoff was extended from twenty-eight to sixty days, making it harder to use the frank for political purposes.

By April 1983, with critics still charging the frank was used as a campaign tool, the House franking commission had proposed a tough new set of rules.

In early May, though, the Supreme Court declined to consider the decade-old Common Cause suit, thus finally bringing the case to a conclusion and removing the pressure for further reform. The proposed new rules received little attention.   ∼

Fulbright, J. William

Dean of foreign affairs in the Senate, J. William Fulbright (1905-) was a critic of U.S. foreign policy in the decades following World War II. From the beginning of his Senate career, Fulbright advocated the conduct of international relations based on understanding and the exchange of ideas rather than show of force. As chairman of the Senate Foreign Relations Committee from 1959 to 1975, Fulbright was at the forefront of Senate opposition to U.S. involvement in Vietnam.

An Arkansas lawyer and educator, Fulbright spent several years as president of the University of Arkansas before entering the House of Representatives as a Democrat in 1943. After one term in the House, he moved to the Senate in 1945 and remained there for thirty years.

In his first year in the House, Fulbright introduced a resolution advocating the establishment of a postwar organization to maintain world peace. In 1946 he sponsored legislation to establish the educational exchange program that bears his name. In later years, Fulbright saw the exchange program as his greatest contribution to international understanding.

In the Senate Fulbright was best known for his opposition to the Vietnam War. He voted for the Gulf of Tonkin resolution in 1964, but later regretted it; the resolution became the primary legal justification for prosecution of the war during the presidency of Lyndon B. JOHNSON. Fulbright criticized Johnson for his invasion of the Dominican Republic in 1965, and this so estranged the two that Fulbright had little influence over Johnson's conduct of the Vietnam War. Fulbright also was an outspoken critic of President Richard NIXON's handling of the war.

In 1973 Congress passed the WAR POWERS Resolution, designed to limit the president's powers to commit U.S. forces abroad without congressional approval; Fulbright had introduced the forerunner of the measure in 1967 and 1969.

Although liberal on international issues, Fulbright followed the more conservative domestic policies supported by his constituents. He opposed the Supreme Court's 1954 school desegregation decision and voted against the Civil Rights Act of 1964. In the end, though, Fulbright's concentration on international affairs distanced him from his constituents, and he was defeated for reelection in 1974.   ~

Overleaf:
Grand stairway of the Capitol.

General Accounting Office

Congress has its own agency, the General Accounting Office, to monitor executive branch spending. The largest congressional support agency, GAO has more than 5,000 employees who conduct investigations, perform audits, and offer legal opinions about financial disputes. GAO's basic role is to review how the executive branch spends the money Congress appropriates. Individual members of Congress, as well as committees, can ask GAO to investigate specific programs or broad policy questions.

When Congress revamped federal budget making in 1921, two new agencies were set up. The Bureau of the Budget (now the Office of Management and Budget) was to work with the president on his proposals for how and where federal funds should be spent. The General Accounting Office, an agency of the legislative branch, was to give Congress an independent review and audit of executive branch expenditures.

During World War II almost 15,000 people worked for GAO, handling masses of vouchers and routine claims related to the war. In 1950 GAO was freed from performing regular audits of agencies; the agencies themselves handled the audits, as well as the routine processing of vouchers and claims. As a result, instead of concentrating on de-

The Original Gerrymander
Gerrymandering is the practice of shaping voting districts to benefit one political party. It takes its name from a salamander-shaped legislative district created by the Massachusetts legislature under Gov. Elbridge Gerry in 1812.

tails of spending, GAO was able to review how agencies were managed, with a focus on uncovering waste and fraud. Some people maintain that GAO's reports are overly critical; others complain that the agency waters down its reports to avoid controversy.

Comptroller General

The comptroller general, who heads GAO, is appointed by the president and confirmed by the Senate. The comptroller serves a fifteen-year term. Seeking a larger role in filling the position, Congress in 1980 set up a special committee to suggest nominees to the president, though their list would be nonbinding.

The sixth head of GAO, Charles A. Bowsher, was chosen from the list. Bowsher, who took office in 1981, previously was a partner with the Arthur Andersen accounting firm.   ~

Germaneness.   See AMENDMENTS.

Gerrymandering

Gerrymandering is the practice of manipulating the physical shape of legislative districts to benefit a particular politician or party. The practice is probably as old as the Republic, but the word itself originated in 1812, when the Massachusetts legislature redrew the boundaries of state legislative districts to favor the party of Gov. Elbridge Gerry.

One of the redrawn districts was so peculiarly shaped that some critics said it looked like a salamander. An artist added a head, wings, and claws to the district map, and a Boston newspaper published the resulting drawing, which it called a Gerry-Mander. *Gerrymandering* quickly became part of the American political vocabulary, and the practice it describes is still in use. In 1986 the Supreme Court ruled that gerrymanders are subject to federal court review. *(See* REAPPORTIONMENT AND REDISTRICTING.)   ~

Government Operations Committee, House

Like its Senate counterpart, the House Government Operations Committee focuses primarily on how the federal government functions. Its sweeping jurisdiction—over the entire federal government—means an aggressive chairman can pursue almost any issue of interest. For the most part, though, Government Operations is detail-minded, tackling some of the less tantalizing subjects before Congess, such as computer security and the retirement system for civil servants. Until 1952 the committee was saddled with its original name, dating from 1816: Expenditures in Executive Departments.

Government Operations originates little legislation, with most bills written in the Subcommittee on Legislation and National Security. Among the legislation handled by the committee are proposals for government reorganization, including new agencies or departments, and intergovernmental relations. Other subcommittees concentrate on investigations, and exposure of waste and fraud is a theme that runs through many reports. The committee has often focused on procurement—what and how the government buys from private industry.

That Government Operations is seen by most as a backwater never fazed Jack Brooks, the feisty Texas Democrat who became chairman in 1975. After more than a dozen years in the post, Brooks was still verbally pushing and poking at the parade of bureaucrats who testified before the committee and its seven subcommittees. He once told a witness trying to protest Brooks's summation, "I think I've heard enough from you." Brooks also chaired the Subcommittee on Legislation and National Security.   ~

Government Printing Office

A barrage of documents generated daily by Congress and the rest of the federal government is produced by the

Rep. Jack Brooks, chairman, House Government Operations Committee

ORDERING FROM GPO

A wide range of information is provided in government publications. Although many are geared to a small audience and cover extremely technical matters, hundreds of publications are designed for general readers. Government publications are usually reasonably priced and often are available free of charge.

Questions about publications and orders are handled by the Superintendent of Documents, Government Printing Office, Washington, D.C. 20402. Telephone: 202-783-3238.

GPO publishes catalogs, including two free publications: *U.S. Government Books*, which lists about 1,000 best-selling titles, and *New Books*, a bimonthly list of all GPO publications placed on sale in the previous two months. These catalogs may be ordered from the Superintendent of Documents. Many libraries have in their reference section two other publications: *GPO Sales Publications Reference File (PRF)*, which is on microfiche, and the *Monthly Catalog of U.S. Government Publications*.

Payment must be received before orders are shipped. Checks or money orders should be made payable to the Superintendent of Documents. MasterCard and Visa are also accepted.

Government Printing Office. More than 5,000 people work for GPO, which is one of the largest printing operations in the world. For Congress, GPO prints—or contracts with commercial companies to print—thousands of publications each year, including bills, public laws, committee reports, the *CONGRESSIONAL RECORD* and *CONGRESSIONAL DIRECTORY*, legislative calendars, hearing records, and franked envelopes. Many books, pamphlets, and reports printed by GPO may be purchased by the public at the two dozen bookstores it operates throughout the country, or ordered by mail.

GPO also administers the depository library program. Selected libraries throughout the country receive copies from GPO of important government publications, including those that by law must be made public.

Congress agreed in 1860 to establish GPO, which has retained the old-fashioned title, public printer, for its top official. To set up GPO, buildings, equipment, and machinery were purchased from Cornelius Wendell, a private printer, for $135,000. A GPO building still stands on the site of the original plant. Oversight of GPO is handled by the congressional Joint Committee on PRINTING.   ~

Governmental Affairs Committee, Senate

Charged with overseeing how the federal government operates, the Senate Governmental Affairs Committee is able to probe almost every cranny of the bureaucracy. Although it is rarely responsible for major legislation, the committee's OVERSIGHT role is so broad that aggressive senators can use a seat on Governmental Affairs to pursue almost any matter that interests them, from telling the Defense Department it is a poor shopper to investigating nuclear safety.

Governmental Affairs looks at the federal government from a different perspective than most committees. Concerns about personnel management or maintenance of federal buildings give a nuts-and-bolts flavor to much of the agenda. But the committee also focuses at times on broader trends, such as the government's future role in health care or the effect of increased foreign economic competition.

The committee was established in 1842. It was known as the Committee on Expenditures in Executive Departments until 1952, when it was renamed Government Operations. In 1979 the title was changed to Governmental Affairs.

The committee usually operates outside the spotlight—except for its Permanent Investigations Subcommittee. Although formally created in 1948, the subcommittee grew out of a special committee that Sen. Harry S TRUMAN convinced the Senate to set up in 1941. The Special Committee to Investigate the National Defense Program, known as the Truman committee, concentrated on uncovering fraud and inefficiency as defense programs multiplied during World War II. The publicity the Missouri Democrat gained on the committee helped him win his party's vice presidential nomination in 1944. When the Senate in 1948 abolished all special committees, Vermont Republican George Aiken made the Truman committee part of his Committee on Expenditures in Executive Departments, giving it a broader mandate to investigate the management of all government agencies.

Often headed by the chairman of the full committee, who has first choice of assignments, Permanent Investigations is considered the most desirable Governmental Affairs subcommittee. In the 1950s it was the setting for Joseph R. McCARTHY's wide-ranging anticommunist INVESTIGATIONS. The Wisconsin Republican was chairman of the subcommittee, and full committee, in 1953-55. From 1949 until 1972, except during McCarthy's tenure, the full committee was chaired by Democrat John L. McClellan of Arkansas. Also chairman of the investigations subcommittee, McClellan instigated high-profile investi-

gations of organized crime that spotlighted, among others, the Teamsters Union and its head, Jimmy Hoffa. The panel also probed "white collar" crime, including Texan Billy Sol Estes and his paper empire of fertilizer and federal cotton allotments. The subcommittee's chief counsel then was Robert F. Kennedy, brother of future president John F. KENNEDY. McClellan left the committee in 1972 to become chairman of Appropriations.

Other chairmen of the Governmental Affairs Committee have included Connecticut Democrat Abraham A. Ribicoff (1975-81), Delaware Republican William V. Roth, Jr. (1981-87), and Ohio Democrat John Glenn, who took over the post in 1987. Georgia Democrat Sam Nunn, who had chaired the investigations panel in 1979-81, resumed that post in 1987.   ~

Gramm-Rudman-Hollings Act.   See BUDGET PROCESS.

Gray, William H. III

Smooth and witty, Pennsylvania Democrat William H. Gray III (1941-) plays inside House politics with a light touch and great success. His four-year term as chairman of the House Budget Committee, which began in 1985, gave him a chance to play the broker, satisfying different factions of the Democratic party and emerging as a national figure in the war on deficits. Liberal in his views, Gray used help from conservative and moderate elements within the party to pass his budget resolutions.

Like his father and grandfather before him, Gray was chief minister of the 4,000-member Bright Hope Baptist Church in North Philadelphia. Two Sundays a month he returned home to preach there. His predominantly black

district was overwhelming in its support
of Gray, who first won election to the
House in 1978. His work in Congress,
such as early support of economic sanctions against South Africa and advocacy
of funding for housing and mass transit,
further tightened his hold on the seat.

Gray jumped quickly into House
politics, winning choice assignments on
the Budget and the Democratic Steering and Policy committees. He campaigned quietly for the post of Budget
chairman, the most open of House
chairmanships because the committee
has a rotating membership and seniority is not a factor. Two other candidates
needed a loosening of limits on the
length of Budget Committee membership to be eligible for the chairmanship.
When the Democratic Caucus declined
to change the rule, Gray had already
lined up enough support to win.   ∼

Great Society

"Great Society" is the name given
to the sweeping array of social programs
proposed by President Lyndon B.
JOHNSON and enacted by the Democratic-controlled Congress in the mid-
1960s. In his 1964 speech launching the
Great Society, Johnson said it rested
"on abundance and liberty for all." It
demanded "an end to poverty and racial injustice," he said, but that was
"only the beginning."

The Great Society was the most
ambitious social agenda advanced by
any president since the NEW DEAL era
in the 1930s. Great Society programs
included medical care for the aged, a
historic voting rights law, the first comprehensive plan of federal aid to elementary and secondary education, the
War on Poverty, a Model Cities program, and housing, job training, and
conservation measures.

Johnson, who became president after John F. KENNEDY was assassinated
in 1963, opened his War on Poverty in
1964. But most Great Society programs
were enacted in 1965, following Johnson's landslide election to a four-year
term. By 1966 Johnson's Vietnam War
policy had sapped the president's popularity, and Congress became increasingly reluctant to support controversial
new domestic programs.

War on Poverty

The War on Poverty was the most
innovative of Johnson's Great Society
initiatives. It was launched under the
Economic Opportunity Act of 1964,
which established an Office of Economic Opportunity to direct and coordinate a wide variety of new and expanded education, employment, and
training activities. The ten separate
programs authorized by the law were
designed to make a coordinated attack
on the multiple causes of poverty; together the programs were to alleviate
the combined problems of illiteracy, unemployment, and lack of public services
which, according to the administration's
statistics, left one-fifth of the nation's
population impoverished.

Key sections of the law authorized
a Job Corps to provide work experience
and training for school dropouts, a
Neighborhood Youth Corps to employ
youths locally, a community action program under which the government
would assist a variety of local efforts to
combat poverty, an adult education
program, and Volunteers in Service to
America, or VISTA, which was billed as
a domestic Peace Corps.

The 1964 law was one of the most
controversial of Johnson's presidency.
The poverty program was plagued from
the beginning by charges of "boss rule"
and rule by the militant poor at the
local level, of rioting and excessive costs
in the Job Corps, and of excessive salaries in the OEO and at local levels.

Such reports, which distressed both
conservatives and liberals, eventually

Medicare Bill Signed
President Lyndon B. Johnson signs legislation establishing the Medicare program, as former President Harry S Truman looks on. Standing at rear are Lady Bird Johnson, Vice President Hubert H. Humphrey, and Bess Truman.

led Congress to take a stong hand in molding the program. Republicans made unremitting efforts to abolish OEO, and the agency was finally dis-

mantled during the presidency of Johnson's successor, Republican Richard Nixon. VISTA, part of the War on Poverty, continued in the 1980s.   ~

Overleaf:
House chamber.

Hayden, Carl

Carl Hayden (1877-1972) gave up his job as a county sheriff to become Arizona's first representative in 1912; he was sworn in five days after Arizona became a state. The Arizona Democrat remained in Congress for the next fifty-six years—a record unmatched by any other member of Congress through 1988. *(See* MEMBERS: SERVICE RECORDS.*)*

Hayden served fifteen years in the House before moving in 1927 to the Senate, where he served seven six-year terms. When Hayden retired in 1969, at the age of ninety-one, he was PRESIDENT PRO TEMPORE of the Senate and chairman of the Senate Appropriations Committee, a post he had assumed when he was seventy-eight.   ~

Hayne, Robert Y.

Almost by accident, Robert Y. Hayne (1791-1839) ended up participating in one of the Senate's most famous debates, the Webster-Hayne debate of 1830. Hayne, then a thirty-nine-year-old senator from South Carolina (1823-32), spoke boldly for states' rights, arguing that a state could reject a federal law it considered unconstitutional, a

concept known as nullification. His chief opponent, Daniel WEBSTER of Massachusetts, said the Union was not a compact of states but a creation of the people; the states, Webster said, had no authority to reject a tariff or any other federal law. The debate, which took place over a two-week period, packed the Senate galleries with spectators. Hayne gave a stirring defense of state sovereignty, a key proslavery position, but Webster, with a deep voice and a flair for drama, was more forceful in his defense of federal power over the states. *(See* STATES AND CONGRESS.)

Hayne had been elected to the Senate as a Tariff Democrat with help from fellow South Carolinian John C. CALHOUN, a leading proponent of nullification. While Hayne was advocating his mentor's position on the Senate floor, Calhoun, then vice president, was presiding. As South Carolina's resistance to high tariffs intensified in 1832, the state legislature named Hayne as governor, opening up the Senate seat for Calhoun, whom many considered the more effective statesman. Hayne, though ready to fight any federal troops enforcing the tariff laws, responded favorably to a congressional compromise, which Calhoun had crafted with Henry CLAY.

Before entering the Senate in 1823, Hayne served in the South Carolina state legislature and as the state's attorney general. He had only two years as governor; state rules prevented his serving an additional term. In 1834 Hayne became mayor of Charleston. He then devoted his energies to the establishment of a railroad that would link Charleston with the West.   ~

Hispanics in Congress

The swelling ranks of Hispanic-Americans—17 million people with roots to Mexico, Cuba, other Latin American nations, and Puerto Rico—remained substantially underrepresented in Congress in the 1980s.

Hispanic voting levels traditionally have fallen well below the national average. Hispanic activists say poverty, low education levels, language barriers, and alienation have discouraged voting.

Eleven Hispanic representatives served in the 100th Congress (1987-89), in addition to the nonvoting resident commissioner of Puerto Rico and nonvoting DELEGATES from Guam and the Virgin Islands. Hispanic members ranged from liberal to conservative. Although they banded together in the Congressional Hispanic Caucus, the group rarely took a unanimous position on issues. *(See* CAUCUSES, SPECIAL.)

Ten of the eleven Hispanic representatives with full voting privileges represented California, Texas, and New Mexico; one came from New York. Several Hispanics occupied important positions in the Democratic hierarchy of the House. The majority whip was Rep. Tony Coelho of California, and the chairman of the Agriculture Committee was E. "Kika" de la Garza of Texas, to cite two examples. Only one of the eleven Hispanic representatives was a Republican: Manuel Lujan, Jr., of New Mexico. *(List, p. 490)*

No Hispanic candidate had been elected to the Senate since 1970, when New Mexico Democrat Joseph Montoya won his second and last election; he was a senator from 1964 to 1977. The only other Hispanic senator—Dennis Chavez, who served from 1935 to 1962—was also a New Mexico Democrat.

In all, twenty Hispanics had held seats in Congress as of the 100th Congress, excluding nonvoting members. First to to serve was Rep. Romualdo Pacheco, a California Republican, who entered the House in 1877. After he retired in 1883, there was no Hispanic representation in Congress until Ladislas Lazaro, a Louisiana Democrat, entered the House in 1913.   ~

Historic Milestones

The history of Congress is studded with events that have helped to shape the legislative branch and define its relations with the nation as a whole. Some of these milestones in congressional history are listed below.

1787 Delegates to the Constitutional Convention agree to establish a national legislature consisting of two chambers: a HOUSE OF REPRESENTATIVES to be chosen by direct popular vote and a SENATE to be chosen by the state legislatures. Under the terms of the "Great Compromise" between the large and small states, representation in the House is to be proportional to a state's population; in the Senate each state will have two votes.

1789 The First Congress is scheduled to convene on March 4 in New York City's Federal Hall. The House does not muster a quorum to do business until April 1, however; the Senate, April 6. Congress will continue to meet in New York until August 1790.

President George Washington appears twice in the Senate to consult about an Indian treaty. His presence during Senate proceedings creates such tension that presidents never again participate directly in congressional floor proceedings.

1790 Congress moves to Philadelphia, where it will meet in Congress Hall from December 1790 until May 1800.

1800 Congress formally convenes in Washington, D.C., on November 17. Both houses sit in the north wing of the Capitol, the only part of the building that has been completed.

1801 In its first use of contingent election procedures established by the Constitution, the House of Representatives chooses Thomas Jefferson as president. The election is thrown into the House when Democratic-Republican electors inadvertently cast equal numbers of votes for Jefferson and Aaron Burr, their respective candidates for president and vice president. The Twelfth Amendment to the Constitution, requiring separate votes for president and vice president, will be ratified in time for the next presidential election in 1804. *(See* ELECTING THE PRESIDENT; CONSTITUTIONAL AMENDMENTS.*)*

The Supreme Court, in the case of *Marbury v. Madison*, establishes its right of judicial review over legislation passed by Congress.

1812 Using its WAR POWERS for the first time, Congress declares war against Great Britain, which has seized U.S. ships and impressed American seamen.

1814 British troops raid Washington on August 24, setting fire to the CAPITOL, the WHITE HOUSE, and other buildings. Congress meets in makeshift quarters until it can return to the Capitol in December 1819.

1820 House Speaker Henry CLAY negotiates settlement of a bitter sectional dispute over extension of slavery. Known as the Missouri Compromise, Clay's plan preserves the balance between slave and free states and bars slavery in any future state north of 36° 30' north latitude.

1825 The House settles the 1824 presidential election when none of the four major contenders for the office receives a majority of the electoral vote. Although Andrew Jackson leads in both popular and electoral vote, the House elects John Quincy ADAMS on the first ballot.

1830 The doctrine of nullification sparks one of the most famous debates in Senate history. The doctrine, as articulated by Vice President John C. CALHOUN of South Carolina, asserts the right of states to nullify federal laws

Short-Lived Compromise
Henry Clay's last great effort to hold the Union
together was known as the Compromise of
1850. The galleries were packed with visitors
when he addressed the Senate on behalf of his
proposals.

they consider unconstitutional. In a
stirring Senate speech, a fellow South
Carolinian, Sen. Robert Y. HAYNE, de-
fends the doctrine and urges the West
to ally with the South against the
North. Massachusetts Whig Daniel
WEBSTER responds with a passionate
plea for preservation of the Union.

1834 The Senate adopts a resolution
censuring President Andrew Jackson
for his removal of deposits from the
Bank of the United States and his refusal to hand over communications to
his cabinet on that issue. The censure
resolution will be expunged from the
Senate *Journal* in 1837 after Jacksonian Democrats gain control of the Senate.

1846 The House passes the Wilmot
Proviso, which would bar slavery in territories to be acquired from Mexico
in settlement of the Mexican War.
Southerners, led by Calhoun, defeat the
measure in the Senate. The proviso—
named for its sponsor, Rep. David Wilmot of Pennsylvania—deepens the sectional split in Congress over extension
of slavery.

1850 The Compromise of 1850,
Clay's final attempt to keep the South
from seceding from the Union, brings

together Webster, Clay, and Calhoun
for their last joint appearance in the
Senate. The dying Calhoun drags himself into the chamber to hear his speech
read by a colleague. Clay, in a speech
that extends over two days, urges acceptance of his proposals, which exact concessions from both the North and
South. The compromise package clears
the way for California to be admitted to
the Union as a free state, permits residents of New Mexico and Utah to decide in the future on slavery there, abol-
ishes the slave trade in the District of
Columbia, and establishes a strong fugitive slave law.

1854 Congress passes the Kansas-
Nebraska Act, repealing the Missouri
Compromise of 1820 and permitting
settlers in the Kansas and Nebraska
territories to decide whether or not they
want slavery. Opponents of the new law
establish the Republican party. Conflict
over slavery in Kansas leads to violence
in the territories—and in Congress.

1856 During debate on the Kansas
statehood bill, two South Carolina representatives attack Sen. Charles SUM-
NER at his desk in the Senate chamber.
They bludgeon him so severely that the
Massachusetts senator will not be able
to resume his seat until 1859.

1858 Abraham Lincoln, Republican candidate for the Senate from Illinois, challenges Sen. Stephen A. DOUGLAS, his Democratic opponent, to a series of debates on the slavery issue. Lincoln loses the election, but his moderate views recommend him for the presidential nomination two years later.

1859 The Thirty-sixth Congress convenes December 5, its members inflamed by the execution of abolitionist John Brown only days before. The House takes two months and forty-four ballots to elect a Speaker; its choice is William Pennington of New Jersey, a new member of the House and a political unknown. The session is marked by verbal duels and threats of secession. Pistols are carried openly in the House and Senate chambers.

1860 South Carolina secedes from the Union in the wake of Lincoln's election to the presidency. Ten other Southern states follow. The Civil War all but eliminates the South from representation in Congress until 1869.

1861 Congress establishes a Joint Committee on the Conduct of the War. The committee, a vehicle for Radical Republicans opposed to President Lincoln, uses its far-ranging inquiries to criticize Lincoln's conduct of the war.

1863-65 The Radicals, angry over Lincoln's mild policies for postwar RECONSTRUCTION of the South, pass a bill placing all Reconstruction authority under the direct control of Congress. Lincoln pocket vetoes the bill after Congress adjourns in 1864. Radicals issue the Wade-Davis Manifesto, asserting that "the authority of Congress is paramount and must be respected." They put their harsh Reconstruction policies into effect when Andrew Johnson becomes president after Lincoln's assassination in 1865.

1868 The House votes to impeach Johnson for dismissing Secretary of War Edwin M. Stanton in violation of the Tenure of Office Act. In the ensuing Senate trial, Johnson wins acquittal by a one-vote margin. *(See* JOHNSON IMPEACHMENT TRIAL.*)*

1870 The first black members take their seats in Congress, representing newly readmitted southern states. The Mississippi legislature chooses Hiram Revels to fill the Senate seat once occupied by Confederate president Jefferson Davis. Joseph H. Rainey of South Carolina and Jefferson F. Long of Georgia enter the House. All are Republicans. *(See* BLACK MEMBERS OF CONGRESS.*)*

1873 Several prominent members of Congress are implicated in the Crédit Mobilier scandal. A congressional investigating committee clears House Speaker James G. BLAINE, but two other representatives are censured for accepting bribes from Crédit Mobilier of America, a company involved in construction of the transcontinental railroad. *(See* INVESTIGATIONS.*)*

1877 Disputed electoral votes from several states force Congress for the first time to rule on the outcome of a presidential election. Congress determines that Republican Rutherford B. Hayes has been elected president by a one-vote margin over Democrat Samuel J. Tilden. Tilden led in the popular vote count by more than a quarter of a million votes, but Hayes wins the electoral vote, 185-184. He is sworn into office March 4.

1881 The Supreme Court, ruling in the case of *Kilbourn v. Thompson*, for the first time asserts its authority to review the propriety of congressional investigations.

1890 Republican Speaker Thomas Brackett REED puts an end to Democrats' obstructionist tactics that have paralyzed the House. The "Reed Rules" are adopted by the House after bitter debate. *(See* SPEAKER OF THE HOUSE.*)*

Speaker Dethroned
Rep. Joseph G. Cannon was the most powerful Speaker in the history of the House. But in 1910 the House revolted against his autocratic rule and stripped him of much of his authority.

1910   The House revolts against the autocratic rule of another Speaker, Joseph G. CANNON, and strips him of much of his authority. The power of the Speaker goes into a decline that will last nearly fifteen years.

1913   Ratification of the Seventeenth Amendment to the Constitution ends the practice of letting state legislatures elect senators. From now on they, like House members, will be chosen by direct popular election. The change is part of the PROGRESSIVE ERA's movement toward more democratic control of government. *(See* DIRECT ELECTION OF SENATORS.*)*

Also in 1913, President Woodrow Wilson revives the practice of addressing Congress in joint session. The last president to do so was John Adams in 1800.

1916   Four years before women win the franchise, the first woman is elected to Congress: Jeannette RANKIN, a Montana Republican. *(See* WOMEN'S SUFFRAGE.*)*

1917   A Senate FILIBUSTER kills the Wilson administration's ship purchase bill in the closing days of the Sixty-fourth Congress. "The Senate of the United States is the only legislative body in the world which cannot act when its majority is ready for action," Wilson rails. "A little group of willful men, representing no opinion but their own, have rendered the great government of the United States helpless and contemptible. . . ." The Senate quickly responds by adopting restrictions on debate through a process known as cloture.

1919   The Senate refuses to ratify the Versailles Treaty ending World War I. Senate opposition is aimed mainly at the Covenant of the League of Nations, which forms an integral part of the treaty. During consideration of the treaty, the Senate uses its cloture rule for the first time to cut off debate. *(See* TREATY RATIFICATION.*)*

1922-23   A Senate investigation of the TEAPOT DOME oil leasing scandal exposes bribery and corruption in the administration of President Warren G. Harding. His interior secretary, Albert B. Fall, ultimately is convicted of bribery and sent to prison.

1933   Franklin D. Roosevelt assumes the presidency in the depths of the

'Hundred Days'
Upon taking office in 1933, President Franklin D. Roosevelt called Congress into special session, the famous "Hundred Days," to enact his emergency economic proposals. Acting with breathless speed, Congress approved a number of highly controversial bills.

Great Depression and promptly calls Congress into special session. In this session, known as the "Hundred Days," lawmakers are asked to pass—almost sight unseen—a number of emergency economic measures. Roosevelt's NEW DEAL establishes Democrats as the majority party in Congress for most of the next half-century.

1934 For the first time Congress meets on January 3, as required by the Twentieth Amendment to the Constitution. The amendment, ratified in 1933, also fixes January 20 as the date on which presidential terms will begin every four years; that change will take effect in 1937 at the beginning of Roosevelt's second term.

1935 Sen. Huey LONG, the Louisiana "Kingfish," stages his most famous filibuster, on extension of the National Industrial Recovery Act. Long, a Democrat who has split with the president, speaks for a record fifteen and a half hours, filling eighty-five pages of the *Congressional Record* with remarks ranging from commentaries on the Constitution to recipes for southern "potlikker," turnip greens, and corn bread.

1937 Roosevelt calls on Congress to increase the membership of the Su-preme Court, setting off a great public uproar. The Court has ruled unconstitutional many New Deal programs, and critics claim the president wants to "pack" it with justices who will support his views. The plan eventually dies in the Senate. In the 1938 elections, Roosevelt will try unsuccessfully to "purge" Democratic members of Congress who opposed the plan. *(See* COURTS AND CONGRESS.)

1938 The House establishes the Dies Committee, one in a succession of special committees on Un-American Activities. The committee, whose chairman, Texas Democrat Martin Dies, is avowedly anticommunist and anti-New Deal, is given a broad mandate to investigate subversion.

1941 The Senate sets up a Special Committee to Investigate the National Defense Program. Its chairman is Missouri Democrat Harry S TRUMAN. The committee earns President Roosevelt's gratitude for serving as a "friendly watchdog" over defense spending without embarrassing the president. Truman will become Roosevelt's vice presidential running mate in 1944 and succeed to the presidency upon Roosevelt's death the following year.

Hunting Communists
Congressional committees conducted head-
line-grabbing investigations of communism in
the years following World War II. The most famous were those led by Sen. Joseph R. McCarthy,
shown here with committee aide Roy Cohn.

1946 Congress approves a sweeping legislative REFORM measure. The most important provisions of the Legislative Reorganization Act of 1946 aim to streamline committee structure, redistribute the congressional workload, and improve staff assistance. Provisions to strengthen congressional review of the federal BUDGET soon prove unworkable and are dropped. A section on regulation of LOBBYING has little effect.

1948 The House Un-American Activities Committee launches an investigation of State Department official Alger Hiss. Its hearings, and Hiss's subsequent conviction for perjury, establish communism as a leading political issue and the committee as an important political force. The case against Hiss is developed by a young member of the committee, California Republican Richard NIXON.

1953 Sen. Joseph R. McCARTHY, a Wisconsin Republican, conducts the most famous national investigations of communism during his two-year reign as chairman of the Senate Government Operations Committee's Permanent Investigations Subcommittee. His investigation of the armed services culminates in the 1954 Army-McCarthy hearings

and McCarthy's censure by the Senate that year.

1963 President John F. KENNEDY is assassinated, and Vice President Lyndon B. JOHNSON succeeds him. Johnson is elected president in his own right in 1964. Using political skills he honed as Senate majority leader (1955-61), Johnson wins congressional approval of a broad array of social programs, which he labels the GREAT SOCIETY. Mounting opposition to his Vietnam War policy leads to his retirement in 1968.

1964 Congress adopts the Tonkin Gulf Resolution, giving the president broad authority for use of U.S. forces in Southeast Asia. The resolution becomes the primary legal justification for the Johnson administration's prosecution of the Vietnam War. Congress will repeal it in 1970.

The Supreme Court, in the case of *Wesberry v. Sanders*, rules that congressional districts must be substantially equal in population. Court action is necessary because Congress has failed to act legislatively on behalf of heavily populated but underrepresented areas. *(See* REAPPORTIONMENT AND REDISTRICTING.*)*

1967 The House votes to exclude veteran representative Adam Clayton

POWELL, Jr., from sitting in the Ninetieth Congress. Powell, a black Democrat from New York's Harlem district, has been charged with misuse of public funds; he ascribes his downfall to racism. The Supreme Court rules in 1969 that the House improperly excluded Powell, a duly elected representative who met the constitutional requirements for citizenship. Powell is reelected to the House in 1968, but rarely occupies his seat. *(See* DISCIPLINING MEMBERS.*)*

1971 Congress passes the Federal Election Campaign Act of 1971, which limits spending for media advertising by candidates for federal office and requires full disclosure of campaign contributions and expenditures. It is the first of three major campaign laws to be enacted during the 1970s; major amendments will be enacted in 1974 and 1976. *(See* CAMPAIGN FINANCING.*)*

1973 The Senate establishes a select committee to investigate White House involvement in a break-in the previous year at Democratic National Committee Headquarters in the WATERGATE office building in Washington, D.C. The committee hearings draw a picture of political sabotage that goes far beyond the original break-in.

In its first use of powers granted by the Twenty-fifth Amendment to the Constitution, Congress confirms President Nixon's nomination of House Minority Leader Gerald R. FORD to be vice president. Ford succeeds Spiro T. Agnew, who has resigned facing criminal charges.

Congress passes the War Powers Resolution over Nixon's veto. The resolution restricts the president's powers to commit U.S. forces abroad without congressional approval.

1974 The House JUDICIARY COMMITTEE recommends President Nixon's impeachment and removal from office for his role in the Watergate scandal. Nixon resigns to avoid almost certain removal. Ford succeeds to the presidency; Congress confirms Nelson A. Rockefeller, his choice as vice president.

Seeking better control over government purse strings, Congress passes the Congressional Budget and Impoundment Control Act. The new law requires legislators to set overall budget levels and then make their individual taxing and spending decisions fit within those levels. *(See* BUDGET PROCESS.*)*

Watergate
Senate hearings on the Watergate scandal gripped the nation in 1973 and helped bring down the presidency of Richard Nixon the following year. The witness pictured here is Richard G. Kleindienst, who resigned as Nixon's attorney general in 1973 after heading a Justice Department investigation of the Watergate affair.

1975 The House Democratic Caucus elects committee chairmen for the first time and unseats three incumbent chairmen. It thus serves notice that SENIORITY, or length of service, will no longer be the sole factor in selecting chairmen. The chairmen's defeat is one of the most dramatic manifestations of the REFORM wave that sweeps Congress in the 1970s.

1977 The House and Senate adopt their first formal codes of ETHICS, setting guidelines for members' behavior. Personal finances must be disclosed, income earned outside Congress is restricted, and use of public funds is monitored.

1979 The House begins live radio and television coverage of its floor proceedings. The Senate will not begin gavel-to-gavel broadcasts until 1986.

1983 The Supreme Court invalidates the legislative veto, a device Congress has used for half a century to review and overturn executive branch decisions carrying out laws. Ruling in the *Chadha* case, the Court says the legislative veto violates the SEPARATION OF POWERS.

1987 Senate and House committees hold joint hearings on the IRAN-CONTRA AFFAIR, investigating undercover U.S. arms sales to Iran and the diversion of profits from those sales to "contra" guerrillas in Nicaragua. The committees conclude that President Ronald Reagan allowed a "cabal of zealots" to take over key aspects of U.S. foreign policy.   ~

ADDITIONAL READINGS

Galloway, George. *History of the House of Representatives.* 2d ed. 1976.

Haynes, George H. *The Senate of the United States: Its History and Practice.* 1938.

Josephy, Alvin M., Jr. *On the Hill: A History of the American Congress.* 1979. (Published in 1975 under the title: *The American Heritage History of the Congress of the United States.*)

House Administration Committee

Internal operations of the House are handled by the House Administration Committee. Details of committee budgets and decisions about allocating space—housekeeping matters, not the politics of leadership—are the committee's business.

Though committee chairmen are usually supreme in their own territory, the House Administration Committee holds a different view. To Administration members, chairmen are an annual parade of supplicants, asking for money to run their committees. Individual members, too, must deal with the committee, depending on it for office space and allowances, and approval for various expenditures.

Most spending requests are handled routinely. But House Administration has the potential to be a controversial, powerful committee. Of little consequence outside the House, the committee looms large in the world of Capitol Hill. Ohio Democrat Wayne L. Hays, who chaired the committee from 1971 to 1976, used his authority over money and office space to reward friends and punish enemies. Even petty matters, such as orders for new telephones, were reviewed to see whether the request had come from an ally, or someone who had irritated the prickly chairman. Hays's empire collapsed after revelations that he kept a mistress on the committee payroll; he resigned from the House in 1976.

Although never so manipulative as Hays, New Jersey Democrat Frank Thompson, Jr., also used his authority as chairman to tweak those who crossed him. Thompson was indicted as part of the ABSCAM scandal, and the controversy was a major factor in his 1980 election defeat.

In the 1980s committee budgets

were scrutinized as part of overall efforts to reduce the federal deficit. Republicans tried to limit staff and equipment, but, after bitter partisan battles, Democrats, whose ranks included all committee chairmen, usually prevailed. Frank Annunzio, an Illinois Democrat, became chairman in late 1984, after California Democrat Augustus F. Hawkins shifted to the top post at EDUCATION AND LABOR.

The Senate counterpart to House Administration is its Committee on RULES AND ADMINISTRATION. The Senate committee also handles legislative matters, such as questions of committee jurisdiction or floor procedure; in the House, those matters are in the purview of the RULES Committee.   ~

House Manual

The rulebook of the House of Representatives bears a formidable title: *Constitution, Jefferson's Manual, and Rules of the House of Representatives.* It is known informally simply as the House Manual. The House Manual is prepared for each two-year term of Congress by the PARLIAMENTARIAN of the House. In addition to the written rules of the chamber, the document contains the text of the Constitution, portions of JEFFERSON'S MANUAL, and the principal rulings and precedents of the House.   ~

House of Representatives

The 435 members of the House of Representatives share responsibility with the SENATE for writing the nation's laws and overseeing operation of the federal government. Elected every two years to represent districts of roughly half a million people, representatives work full time at a job that once took only a few weeks a year. A representative must attend committee hearings, draft legislation, keep up with floor debate, consider or offer amendments, vote on bills, and respond to constituents' problems. At the same time, he or she campaigns, because a new election is always less than two years away.

The structured rhythm of House procedures and the general hubbub caused by the sheer number of representatives contrasts sharply with the slower pace of the 100-member Senate, which is less than one-fourth the size of the House and prefers to operate informally. Senators' six-year terms allow them breathing space between campaigns, a luxury House members do not share. Most representatives travel home at least every other weekend, with the tab usually covered by official allowances.

Maintaining high visibility in their districts and raising campaign funds are part of the routine for most representatives. Newsletters are mailed out, letters answered, and individual problems with the federal bureaucracy handled, usually by the representative's staff in Washington and in the home district. POLITICAL ACTION COMMITTEES and individuals are asked to contribute campaign funds; the solicitation is often accompanied by an invitation to a cocktail party or a speech by the representative. In 1986 the average House member seeking reelection spent $334,000 on his campaign. *(See* CAMPAIGN FINANCING.*)*

With twenty-two standing committees, which have within them 140 subcommittees, the House is a complex institution, and decision making is spread broadly. The leadership controls the key gateways to floor action, but participation is open and usually democratic in the first stages of the LEGISLATIVE PROCESS, when members question witnesses at hearings or debate amendments during bill-drafting sessions. The

State of Union

The House chamber is the setting for the president's annual State of the Union address to Congress. Members of the Senate join the House for this ceremonial occasion. Administration officials, justices of the Supreme Court, and other dignitaries also sit in the chamber.

House has been most effective under strong leaders, who face the difficult task of satisfying a cumbersomely large and diverse body. Senate leaders have not been so crucial to that chamber's ability to function.

Two centuries of evolution have given the House thick volumes of rules and procedures, but the institution is far from rigid; its decisions can turn in a matter of minutes on what SPEAKER Sam RAYBURN, a Texas Democrat, called "rolling waves of sentiment." The basic principle in the House is that all points of view should be heard, but that minorities should not be able to block action. FILIBUSTERS, common in the Senate, are not allowed in the House. And the idea of delaying a vote to accommodate a single member, as the Senate sometimes does, is almost unheard of.

"Senate rules are tilted toward not doing things," said Speaker Jim WRIGHT, also a Texas Democrat, in 1987. "House rules, if you know how to use them, are tilted toward allowing the majority to get its will done." Senators who are ex-representatives are often frustrated with the slow pace of the Senate and long for the relative orderliness of the House. "Simply to come here and work in a museum is not my idea of a modern legislative process," said South Dakota Democrat Thomas A. Daschle, a senator who had served four terms in the House.

Despite its tight procedures, though, the House often leaves major questions unresolved for years as opposing sides scramble for votes and compromises are drafted. The lack of a national consensus on an issue is reflected in the House. The most difficult choices often are put off, and the last month of a session is a blinding whirl of legislative activity and night meetings. The habit is an old one. Davy Crockett, a legendary frontiersman who served three House terms (1827-31), said, "We generally lounge or squabble the greater part of the session, and crowd into a few days of the last term three or four times the business done during as many preceding months." Barber B. Conable, Jr., a New York Republican who served in the House from 1965 to 1985, was untroubled by disorderliness. "Congress is working the way it is supposed to work," he enjoyed saying, "which is not very well."

When the pace of voting is particularly frenetic at the end of a session, the House is filled with legislators who mill about, gathering in groups on the floor to talk, or streaming in and out of the chamber into the cloakrooms or nearby hallways. Veterans such as Richard BOLLING, a Missouri Democrat who served from 1949 to 1983, have watched their boisterous colleagues and muttered, "It's the silly season again." When a vote is close, representatives gather in the well of the chamber, near the rostrum, and watch the electronic voting chart, which displays how each member voted. Like spectators at a horse race, they wait expectantly for any vote switches and react with a collective gasp to any surprises. The Senate, which lacks a tally board, has no such sport.

Although many senators arrive at the Capitol already public figures, having served previously as representative or governor, members of the House face the prospect of anonymity among 400-plus colleagues. A new representative, called a freshman, jockeys for spots on favored committees and tries to develop expertise on a subject to avoid obscurity—and gain credibility in debate. His ability to act independently is also enhanced by STAFF; once reserved for senior members who ran committees, REFORMS in the 1970s gave additional staff even to the most junior members.

Despite its reputation as an open, democratic institution, the House as it approached the 1990s was struggling with a new set of concerns. Budget constraints dominated its agenda, and members not on the fiscal committees—

APPROPRIATIONS and WAYS AND MEANS —complained they were left out of major decisions. The opportunity to initiate new programs was almost nonexistent. Even floor amendments, once a way for individuals to influence the committee-driven system, were rarer in the 1980s as the Democratic leadership convinced the RULES COMMITTEE to restrict floor action. "In the retrenchment of the state, power is being concentrated," said California Democrat Vic Fazio in 1986. "There's a certain amount of resentment among members who thought they had achieved power and find it's a blind alley. They are presiding over the dissolution of the empire."

Origins and Development

The structure of the House was a victory for the more democratic-minded framers of the Constitution. The House "was to be the grand depository of the democratic principles of the government," said George Mason of Virginia. He and his colleagues prevailed over others who wanted state legislatures to elect the House, as they would the Senate until 1913. "The people immediately should have as little to do" with electing the government as possible, argued Roger Sherman of Connecticut, because "they want information and are constantly liable to be misled."

Though the House and Senate have equal standing on most matters, the Constitution gave each chamber special duties and responsibilities. The House has three special powers: to originate all revenue bills; to recommend removal of federal officials through the impeachment process; and to elect a president when the electors have failed to do so. *(See* PURSE, POWER OF; IMPEACHMENT; and ELECTING THE PRESIDENT.*)*

Originally a body of just sixty-five legislators, compared with twenty-six in the Senate, the House was at first more desirable. Gradually, though, legislators such as Henry CLAY, John C. CALHOUN,

Swearing In
The entire House of Representatives is up for election every two years. Here Speaker Jim Wright administers the oath of office to House members at the beginning of the 100th Congress in 1987.

and Daniel WEBSTER shifted to the Senate, cutting what became a well-worn path. The larger, more diverse House could not be easily swayed by an impassioned, eloquent speech. Rules, not orators, had already assumed control.

As early as 1841 the House limited debate, giving each representative an hour to speak on a bill. The rule prevails today, in contrast to the Senate, where a senator's right to speak for as long as he wants is curbed only rarely.

The House almost from the start delegated the drafting of bills to committees. At first, legislative debate took place on the House floor, and then a select committee was set up to write a specific bill based on floor discussions. The committee would return to the full House with its proposed language for a final vote. Often more than a hundred different select committees would be created in a session. *(See* COMMITTEE SYSTEM.*)*

Gradually, though, the House established "standing committees," with jurisdiction over particular subjects.

Among the earliest were the Ways and Means Committee and the Commerce and Manufactures Committee, today called ENERGY AND COMMERCE. What is now standard House practice began in this period, with committee members developing expertise in particular areas and thus gaining credibility to back their position on the House floor.

The Rules Committee, set up in 1789 and made a standing committee in 1880, provided further structure to the legislative process. It was responsible for deciding which legislation should reach the floor and what rules should cover floor debate. The Rules Committee usually works with the leadership of the majority party, although it operated independently in the 1940s and 1950s and held up action on an array of liberal programs.

Shifting Power Centers
The center of power in the House has shifted several times during the past two centuries. Strong individuals, such as Henry Clay, Thomas Brackett

A TYPICAL DAY IN THE HOUSE

A typical day in the House of Representatives might go like this:
- The CHAPLAIN delivers the opening prayer.
- The SPEAKER approves the *Journal*, the record of the previous day's proceedings. Often a member will demand a roll-call vote on the approval of the *Journal*.
- After some procedural activities—receiving messages from the Senate or the president and granting committees permission to file reports—members are recognized for one-minute speeches on any topic.
- The House then turns to its legislative business. Virtually every major bill is considered under a RULE setting guidelines for floor action. The rule is usually approved with little opposition, but the vote can be the first test of a bill's popularity. Those who want a less restrictive rule, so they can offer amendments, often work with opponents of a bill to defeat the rule.

After the rule is adopted, the House resolves into the COMMITTEE OF THE WHOLE to consider the bill. The Speaker relinquishes the gavel to a chairman, who presides over the Committee.

The debate time is controlled by the managers of the bill, usually the chairman and ranking minority member of the standing committee with jurisdiction over the measure. After time for general debate has expired, AMENDMENTS that are permitted under the rule can be offered. Debate on the amendments is conducted under a rule that limits to five minutes the time each side can speak. Members may obtain additional time by offering pro forma amendments to "strike the last word."

VOTING is by voice (the usual procedure); division (members stand to be counted); teller (a seldom-used procedure in which members walk past designated tellers); or by electronic device. When members vote electronically, they insert a plastic card into one of many voting stations on the House floor and press a button to record a "yea," a "nay" or a "present." Their vote is immediately recorded on a big screen on the wall above the Speaker's desk and tabulated, giving a running vote total. Most electronic votes last fifteen minutes.

After the amending process is complete, the Committee "rises," and the chairman reports to the Speaker on the actions taken. Acting once again as the House, the members vote on final passage of the bill, sometimes after voting on a motion by opponents to recommit the bill to its committee of origin.

- On many noncontroversial bills, the House leadership wants to speed up action, bypassing the Rules Committee and the Committee of the Whole. It can do that by waiving, or "suspending," the rules. Bills under SUSPENSION, sometimes as many as a dozen at a time, are usually brought up early in the week. Suspensions cannot be amended. Debate is limited to forty minutes. Then members are asked to vote on whether they want to suspend the rules and pass the bill. A single vote accomplishes both steps. A two-thirds vote is needed to suspend the House rules, making it a gamble sometimes to bring up legislation under suspension. Measures that are even less controversial are placed on the CONSENT CALENDAR or are passed by UNANIMOUS CONSENT.
- After the House completes its legislative business, members may speak for up to sixty minutes under SPECIAL ORDERS. They must reserve the time in advance but can speak on any topic—often to an almost deserted chamber.

REED, Joseph G. CANNON, and Sam Rayburn, have used their terms as Speaker to consolidate power in the House. At other times the House has been dominated by committee chairmen, party CAUCUSES, its Rules Committee, or voting blocs of members. For most of the twentieth century, the Democratic party has been in the majority, though it has not always been able to control House action.

The Speaker was the only House officer mentioned in the Constitution, which left undefined the rest of the organizational structure of the House. Only the Speaker is chosen by a formal House vote, though he is nominated, and effectively chosen, by the majority party. Each party votes in caucus to elect the majority and minority floor leaders. The whips, the next-ranking leaders, who are responsible for maintaining party loyalty, are also elected. These officials rank just below the Speaker in the House hierarchy. *(See* LEADERSHIP.*)*

The Speaker is usually chosen from among the most senior and loyal party members; since 1925 every Speaker has first served as majority or minority leader. The post of majority leader was not formally created until 1899, although prior to that the chairman of Ways and Means had been the floor manager and considered the deputy leader.

Forging a unified position is a difficult task with 435 members and the array of committees and subcommittees that are the first level of decision making in the House. Each panel competes to have its opinion heard—and its solution selected by the House. Most members serve on as many as six or seven different subcommittees; however, each can chair only one subcommittee.

Legislators also must ultimately answer to the voters in their districts. Though Democrats and Republicans have tried to strengthen party ties with campaign financing and other support, ideological differences within each party—and the need to "keep the voters back home happy"—make it difficult to keep the party voting together, particularly on controversial questions. The Democratic party has been in the majority in the House for most of the twentieth century.

The House membership, though accustomed to rules, has revolted when the power structure has grown too rigid and has failed to respond to changing demands. Cannon's autocracy, for example, spawned a coalition of Republicans and Democrats who in 1910 reduced the Speaker's powers. Rules changes in the 1970s were prompted by a SENIORITY SYSTEM that had grown more rigid because of the safe seats of conservative southern Democrats. Control of the House was in the hands of a few elderly men whose ideas about civil rights, conduct of the war in Vietnam, and other major questions were at odds with the views of a growing number of House Democrats.

By the mid-1970s a new generation of legislators, both Democrats and Republicans, had rewritten the rules to make the leadership more accountable to the Democratic Caucus and Republican Conference, the party organizations. The new members of the House, once kept meekly disciplined, suddenly had a voice in picking the leaders.

Membership

To serve in the House, a representative must have been a U.S. citizen for at least seven years and must be at least twenty-five years old. Members of the House must be residents in the state they represent, but not in the particular district.

In practice, few legislators need worry about the minimum age; the average House member is about fifty years old. Most have been citizens since birth. And the overwhelming pattern is for representatives to live in the district they serve.

Characteristics In the historic 100th Congress (1987-89) the House was dominated, as it had been since its inception, by middle-aged white men, with a background in law or business and a Christian upbringing. That landmark term did include twenty-three WOMEN, twenty-three BLACKS, and fourteen HISPANICS.

Only fifty legislators were new to the House, and only eight of those had defeated incumbents in primaries or the general election. *(See* MEMBERS OF CONGRESS: CHARACTERISTICS.*)*

Representation State legislatures redraw the lines of congressional districts every ten years, after the national census, to reflect population increases and shifts. Some states lose seats, while others gain, depending on shifts in the national population. Politics play a major role in the way the new district lines are drawn within each state. *(See* REAPPORTIONMENT AND REDISTRICTING.*)*

Under the 1980 census, six states with small populations were entitled to only one representative each: Alaska, Delaware, North Dakota, South Dakota, Vermont, and Wyoming. The largest House delegations were those from California, with forty-five representatives; New York, thirty-four; and Texas, twenty-seven.

Until the 1920s the House simply added seats to reflect population increases and to keep states from having the size of their delegations reduced. After a decade of dispute, Congress in 1929 agreed to 435 permanent seats, the number reached after the 1910 census. The legislators also voted in 1929 to reapportion the districts after the 1930 census, thus avoiding another lengthy protest from the states losing seats. The 1930 census eventually cost twenty-one states a total of twenty-seven seats in the House.

In addition to its voting members, the House has five NONVOTING DELEGATES.

Incumbency Though technically a new body every two years, the House in the mid-twentieth century changed only gradually, with old faces resuming the positions they had held for years. The situation contrasted sharply with statistics from the mid-nineteenth century; in 1869, 145 of 243 members were new to the House. Most elections since 1949 have brought fewer than eighty new members to the House. Turnover of seats averaged around seventy-five between 1973 and 1983; however, just forty-three new members were seated in 1985 and fifty in 1987.

Incumbents have a powerful edge in contests for House seats. Roughly three-quarters of all House members routinely win reelection with 60 percent of the vote or more. Since 1946 more than 90 percent of House members seeking reelection have retained their seats. In 1986 contests, only 8 of the 393 House members who sought reelection were defeated, giving incumbents a success rate of 98 percent. The House leadership makes it easier for the constantly campaigning members by giving them frequent four-day weekends, with most House business scheduled on Tuesday, Wednesday, and Thursday.   ~

ADDITIONAL READINGS

Bolling, Richard. *Power in the House.* 1968.
Fenno, Richard F., Jr. *Home Style: House Members in Their Districts.* 1978.
MacNeil, Neil. *Forge of Democracy: The House of Representatives.* 1963.
O'Neill, Thomas P., Jr., and William Novak. *Man of the House.* 1987.

Humphrey, Hubert H.

The Senate career of Hubert H. Humphrey (1911-78) spanned four decades, from 1949 until his death in 1978.

The Minnesota Democrat left the Senate in the 1960s to serve as vice president and ran unsuccessfully as the 1968 Democratic presidential nominee. But Humphrey ended up back on Capitol Hill in 1971, still the "happy warrior," as enthusiastic and irrepressible as ever.

Perceived as too liberal and garrulous when he first arrived in the Senate, Humphrey eventually became one of the most loved and revered senators in modern history. Many of his original goals, from civil rights to medical care for the elderly, became part of mainstream politics. But Humphrey's personal dream, to become president, was stymied; he was never able to overcome his identification with the war in Vietnam.

Humphrey learned his liberal politics in Minneapolis. He lost his first political race, for mayor of Minneapolis, in 1943, but then won in 1945 and 1947. The mayoral race was nonpartisan, but Humphrey was deeply involved in building the Democrat-Farmer-Labor party. In 1947 and 1948 he and his supporters wrested control of the DFL from a group of leftists who had ties to the Communist party. He became the DFL nominee for a Senate seat then held by a Republican.

Humphrey made a marked impression at the Democratic national convention in 1948 with his impassioned plea for a strong civil rights plank in the party platform. "The time has arrived for the Democratic party to get out of the shadow of states' rights and walk forthrightly into the bright sunshine of human rights," he said. When the convention adopted Humphrey's tough stand on civil rights, outraged southern Democrats walked out of the hall.

In the Senate, where southerners held the balance of power, Humphrey began his career at a disadvantage. Humphrey was tireless, though, and by 1961 he was majority whip, the second-ranking party leader. The culmination of his fight for equality came in 1964,

when he managed floor action on landmark civil rights legislation. He was in large part responsible for Senate ratification of the 1963 nuclear test ban treaty. The 1965 Medicare law built on a concept Humphrey proposed in one of the first bills he introduced in the Senate.

In 1964 President Lyndon B. JOHNSON chose Humphrey as his running mate. For Humphrey it proved an unhappy alliance. When he made his own bid for the presidency four years later, he was dragged down by his loyalty to Johnson over conduct of the Vietnam War. Still, Humphrey came very close to defeating Richard NIXON, with less than a percentage point of difference in the popular vote. After that defeat, he was out of public office for the first time in more than two decades. He reentered the Senate in 1971.

Humphrey made another run for the presidency in 1972 but, still haunted by Vietnam, he lost the Democratic nomination. Back in the Senate, in 1975 he became chairman of the Joint Economic Committee, a platform ideally suited to his advocacy of full employment programs. In 1976 he was reelected to the Senate for the last time. Early in 1977 the Senate created a new post, deputy PRESIDENT PRO TEMPORE, to honor Humphrey, now gravely ill with cancer. He died January 13, 1978. ∼

Hunger Committee, House Select

Increased concern about hunger and malnutrition in the United States and in foreign countries prompted the House in 1984 to set up a special hunger committee. Mickey Leland, a Texas Democrat, won bipartisan House support for his proposal and was later named committee chairman. The Hunger Committee, which must be reauthorized at the beginning of each two-year Congress, cannot write legislation but can make recommendations. It also holds hearings and makes reports.

The Senate had a special hunger committee from 1968 until 1977, when a reorganization shifted its duties to the Senate AGRICULTURE Committee. Sen. George S. McGovern, a South Dakota Democrat, chaired the Senate's hunger committee and used its hearings and studies to build support for the major expansion of federal food programs in the 1970s.   ~

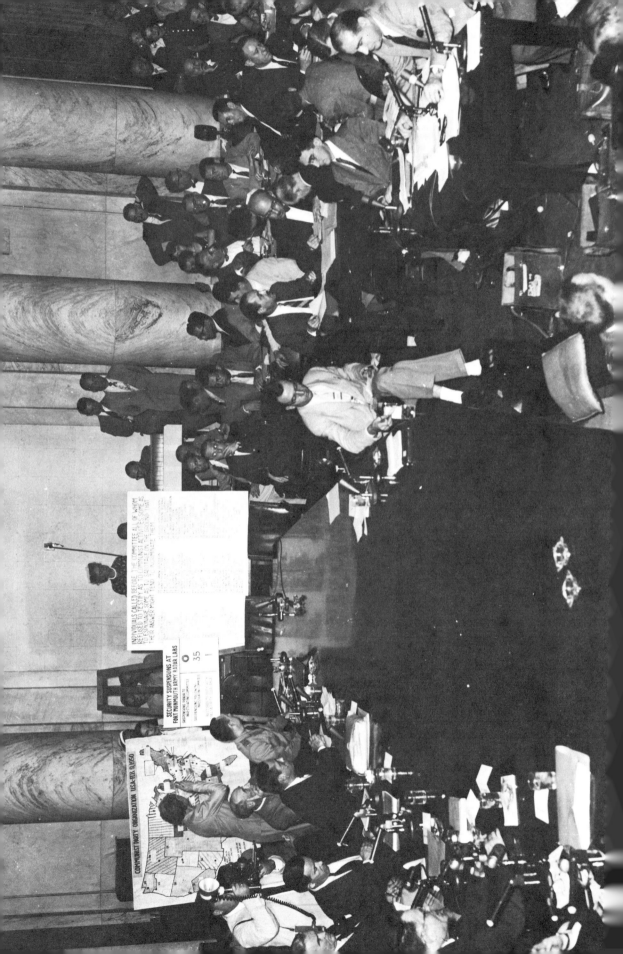

Immunity, Congressional

The Constitution shields members of Congress from lawsuits or criminal charges that relate to their legislative duties. This congressional immunity, provided by the "speech and debate" clause, was borrowed from British law. Questions persist, though, about where to draw the line between official and private acts, with courts giving different interpretations of the extent to which legislators' actions are protected from legal challenge.

By shielding lawmakers from retribution for official acts, authors of the Constitution hoped to guarantee the independence of the legislative branch. They wanted to keep Congress free from executive or judicial scrutiny inappropriate under the SEPARATION OF POWERS. The speech and debate clause states that senators and representatives "shall in all Cases, except Treason, Felony and Breach of the Peace, be privileged from Arrest during their Attendance at the Session of their respective Houses, and in going to and returning from the same; and for any Speech or Debate in either House, they shall not be questioned in any other Place."

The Constitution appears to give legislators immunity from being arrested while in the Capitol or handling congressional work. But the courts have decided the immunity applies only to

195

arrests for civil, not criminal, matters, leaving the privilege with limited practical application.

Members of Congress are still subject to criminal and civil charges for actions outside of Congress. Their behavior within Congress is monitored by their peers, who have authority to discipline colleagues for any unethical behavior. (See DISCIPLINING MEMBERS, ETHICS.)

Drawing the Line

The speech and debate clause has been controversial because of disputes about how to distinguish between legislative and nonlegislative actions. As one judge noted, a lawmaker can be immune from legal problems concerning a floor speech but not immune from charges related to circulating a copy of the same speech.

The rulings have not always appeared to be consistent. One legislator's bribery conviction was reversed because evidence against him was based on what he did, as subcommittee chairman, to prepare for an investigative hearing. The court agreed with him that such activity was shielded by congressional immunity. In another bribery case, though, prosecution continued because the court found the actions in question were not part of the legislative process.

Senators and representatives have also used congressional immunity as a shield against civil actions by private citizens. Sen. William Proxmire, a Wisconsin Democrat, was sued for libel in 1975 by a researcher who said his work was ridiculed by one of Proxmire's Golden Fleece Awards, which claimed to spotlight wasteful government spending.

The Supreme Court ruled in 1979 that congressional immunity covered Proxmire's statements on the floor of the Senate, but not his press release or newsletter. The case was eventually settled out of court.   ∼

Impeachment Power

August 9, 1974: President Richard Nixon relinquishes the office to which he was overwhelmingly reelected less than two years earlier. Nixon's resignation comes as the House of Representatives prepares to begin debate on impeaching him. By choosing to become the first president in history to resign, Nixon avoids almost certain impeachment and removal from office on charges arising out of the Watergate scandal. "Our long national nightmare is over," says Nixon's successor, Gerald R. Ford. "Our Constitution works."

The power of impeachment under the Constitution permits Congress to remove officials who are found guilty of grave misconduct. Congress has used that power sparingly. Only five federal officials, all judges, were removed from office through the impeachment process in the Constitution's first two centuries. Others, like Nixon, resigned voluntarily rather than risk impeachment. Thus the purpose of the impeachment process was realized, if not in the precise manner the Constitution envisioned.

The process is similar to an indictment and trial in the criminal court system. First, the HOUSE OF REPRESENTATIVES approves formal charges, called articles of impeachment, against an official accused of wrongdoing. House members then prosecute the case in a trial held in the Senate chamber. The SENATE is judge and jury. The penalty upon conviction is removal from office. There is no appeal.

The two most powerful officials actually impeached, or charged, by the House were Supreme Court Justice Samuel Chase in 1805 and President Andrew Johnson in 1868. Both were acquitted by the Senate after sensational trials. The overwhelming majority of

Historic First
Richard Nixon was the first president in history to resign his office. Nixon resigned in 1974 to avoid impeachment and removal from office for his role in the Watergate scandal. He is pictured here about to leave Washington on a White House helicopter.

impeachment proceedings have been directed against federal judges. Because they hold lifetime appointments "during good behavior," federal judges cannot be removed by any other means.

In 1986 the impeachment machinery was used to remove from office a federal judge, Harry E. Claiborne, who refused to resign his judgeship even though he was serving a prison sentence for tax fraud. Claiborne was the first person to be stripped of office through impeachment in fifty years.

Constitutional Background

The constitutional impeachment process had its origins in fourteenth century England, when Parliament sought to gain authority over the king's advisers. Impeachment was used against ministers and judges whom Parliament believed guilty of breaking the law or carrying out unpopular orders of the king. The king himself was considered incapable of wrongdoing and was therefore immune.

The framers of the U.S. Constitu-

tion embraced impeachment "as a method of national inquest into the conduct of public men," in the words of Alexander Hamilton. Details of the process were not settled until the closing days of the Constitutional Convention in 1787. Convention delegates at length determined that "the president, vice president, and all civil officers of the United States" should be subject to impeachment. Conviction was to be followed by "removal from office" and possibly by "disqualification to hold" further office.

The delegates had difficulty deciding who should try impeachments. They finally agreed to follow the pattern used by Parliament, where charges were brought by the House of Commons and tried before the House of Lords. Thus the House of Representatives was granted sole power to impeach, or charge, a federal official. The Senate was granted sole power to try impeachments.

Another difficult issue involved the definition of impeachable offenses. The language ultimately adopted—"treason, bribery, or other high crimes and misdemeanors"—left many questions unanswered. While treason and bribery have established legal definitions, the meaning of high crimes and misdemeanors remains in dispute to this day. As a Republican representative from Michigan, Gerald Ford took a sweeping view. In 1970, during an unsuccessful attempt to impeach Supreme Court Justice William O. Douglas, Ford declared: "An impeachable offense is whatever a majority of the House of Representatives considers it to be at a given moment in history."

The dispute over what constitutes an impeachable offense pits "broad constructionists," who view impeachment as a political weapon, against "narrow constructionists," who maintain that impeachment is limited to offenses for which a person may be indicted under the criminal code. During the Nixon impeachment inquiry in 1974, staff members of the House JUDICIARY COMMITTEE argued for a broad interpretation of high crimes and misdemeanors while the president's attorneys argued for a narrow view. As adopted by the committee, the first article of impeachment charged the president with obstruction of justice, a charge falling within the narrow view of impeachable offenses. Articles II and III reflected the broader interpretation, charging Nixon with abuse of his presidential powers and contempt of Congress.

Procedures

In modern practice, impeachment proceedings begin in the House Judiciary Committee, which holds hearings and investigates charges against an accused official. If its investigation supports the charges, the committee draws up articles of impeachment stating the reasons the official should be removed from office.

A resolution containing the articles of impeachment then goes to the full House of Representatives. The House may approve the committee's recommendations without change, or it may alter or reject the recommendations at will. The accused official is impeached if the House adopts the resolution of impeachment by a simple majority vote. Upon adoption of the impeachment resolution, the House selects several of its members to present the case to the Senate.

The Senate trial resembles a criminal proceeding, with the House "managers" acting as prosecutors. Senators take a special oath declaring that they will act impartially in the matter. If the president or the vice president is on trial, the Constitution requires the chief justice of the United States to preside. Both sides may present witnesses and evidence, and the defendant is allowed counsel, the right to testify in his own behalf, and the right of cross-examination. Breaking with tradition, the Senate in 1986 used a special committee to collect evidence in the Claiborne impeachment trial. The shortcut procedure had been authorized since 1935 but never before used.

The Senate votes separately on each article of impeachment, and the Constitution requires a two-thirds vote for conviction. If any article receives two-thirds approval, the defendant is convicted. If desired, the Senate may also vote to disqualify the person from holding future federal office. Only two of the five convictions have been accompanied by disqualification, which is decided by majority vote.

In addition, the removed officer remains subject to trial in the ordinary courts. President Ford granted a pardon to Nixon in 1974, protecting him from possible prosecution in the wake of the impeachment inquiry.

Notable Cases

Although impeachment proceedings were launched more than sixty times between 1789 and 1987, the

SENATE IMPEACHMENT TRIALS, 1798-1987

Between 1798 and 1987 the Senate sat as a court of impeachment thirteen times, as follows:

Year	Official	Position	Outcome
1798-99	William Blount	U.S. senator	Charges dismissed
1803-04	John Pickering	District court judge	Removed from office
1804-05	Samuel Chase	Supreme Court justice	Acquitted
1830-31	James H. Peck	District court judge	Acquitted
1862	West H. Humphreys	District court judge	Removed from office
1868	Andrew Johnson	President	Acquitted
1876	William W. Belknap	Secretary of war	Acquitted
1904-05	Charles Swayne	District court judge	Acquitted
1912-13	Robert W. Archbald	Commerce Court judge	Removed from office
1926	George W. English	District court judge	Charges dismissed
1933	Harold Louderback	District court judge	Acquitted
1936	Halsted L. Ritter	District court judge	Removed from office
1986	Harry E. Claiborne	District court judge	Removed from office

Source: Congressional Directory

Note: The House in 1873 adopted a resolution of impeachment against District Judge Mark
   H. Delahay, but Delahay resigned before articles of impeachment were prepared, so there
   was no Senate action.

House had impeached only fourteen officers: one president, one cabinet officer, one senator, and eleven federal judges. Thirteen cases reached the Senate. Six resulted in acquittal, five ended in conviction, and two were dismissed before trial after the person impeached left office. One case did not go to the Senate because the accused official had resigned.

Presidents Only two presidents have faced serious impeachment challenges.

In 1868 the House impeached Andrew Johnson, and the Senate subsequently came within one vote of removing him from office. The JOHNSON IMPEACHMENT TRIAL grew out of a power struggle between Johnson and Radical Republicans in Congress, who opposed his moderate policies toward the South after the Civil War. The president was formally charged with violating the Tenure of Office Act, which required Senate assent for removal of any official appointed through its advice and consent power. Johnson had fired the secretary of war, a holdover from the Lincoln administration. *(See* APPOINTMENT POWER.*)*

In 1974 the House Judiciary Committee recommended that Richard Nixon be impeached for obstruction of justice, abuse of power, and contempt of Congress. The NIXON IMPEACHMENT EFFORT stemmed from a 1972 break-in at Democratic National Committee headquarters in the Watergate office building in Washington, D.C., and subsequent efforts to cover up White House involvement in the burglary. Disclosure of taped conversations showing Nixon's participation in the cover-up made impeachment a virtual certainty. But he resigned ten days before the House was scheduled to begin debate on the matter, and the impeachment effort was dropped.

Judiciary In 1804 the House impeached Supreme Court Justice Samuel Chase, charging him with partisan behavior on the bench. The Senate trial in 1805 ended in acquittal. Chase, a Federalist, was a victim of attacks on the Supreme Court by Jeffersonian Democrats, who had planned to impeach Chief Justice John Marshall if Chase were convicted.

Between 1804 and 1986 five judges of lower courts were impeached by the House and convicted and removed from office by the Senate. The charges ranged from drunkenness to tax fraud. The Senate acquitted three other judges and dismissed charges against a fourth. Federal judges also have been the subject of most of the resolutions and investigations in the House that have failed to result in impeachment.

Cabinet   Secretary of War William W. Belknap was the only cabinet member to be tried by the Senate. He was acquitted in 1876 largely because senators questioned their authority to try Belknap, who had resigned several months before the trial. The House had impeached Belknap on charges that he had received bribes from a trader at an Indian post.

Congress   The House has impeached only one member of Congress. That was Sen. William Blount of Tennessee, who was impeached in 1797 on charges that he had conspired to carry on a military expedition intended to conquer Spanish territory for Great Britain. The Senate expelled Blount and subsequently dismissed impeachment proceedings for lack of jurisdiction. *(See* DISCIPLINING MEMBERS.)   ~

ADDITIONAL READINGS

Berger, Raoul. *Impeachment: The Constitutional Problems.* 1973.
Labovitz, John R. *Presidential Impeachment.* 1978.
Smith, Gene. *High Crimes and Misdemeanors: The Impeachment and Trial of Andrew Johnson.* 1985.

Impoundment of Funds

Presidential refusal to spend money voted by Congress, a practice known as impoundment, has been a nettlesome issue throughout the nation's history. Although the Constitution gave Congress complete authority to appropriate federal funds, it left vague whether a president was required to spend the appropriated money or whether he could make independent judgments on the timing and need for spending. *(See* PURSE, POWER OF.)

Impoundments go back to the administration of Thomas Jefferson, but they became a major dispute only in the late 1960s and 1970s when President Richard NIXON refused to spend billions of dollars of appropriated funds. Nixon argued that he was withholding the money to combat inflation, but opposition Democrats contended that the president was using impoundment primarily to enforce his own spending priorities in defiance of the will of Congress.

This conflict prompted Congress in 1974 to reassert its control over the federal budget by enacting the Congressional Budget and Impoundment Control Act. In addition to creating the BUDGET PROCESS used thereafter by Congress, the 1974 law established procedures for congressional approval or disapproval of presidential impoundments.

Under this system, the president must notify Congress if he intends to delay spending temporarily—a deferral—or cancel it altogether—a rescission. Rescissions require positive action by Congress: Unless it enacts a law approving the rescission, the president must spend the money. Deferrals work the opposite way: They take effect automatically unless Congress enacts a law, signed by the president or passed over his veto, forbidding him to delay the spending. The original 1974 budget act permitted either chamber of Congress to overrule deferrals, but that procedure was found unconstitutional under a 1983 Supreme Court decision outlawing the LEGISLATIVE VETO.

The Court said the legislative veto violated the SEPARATION OF POWERS doctrine by giving Congress "shared administration" of the laws.   ~

Indian Affairs Committee, Senate Select

The Indian Affairs Committee was created in 1977 in the midst of a Senate reorganization that was intended to consolidate and eliminate committees, not add new ones. That beginning, against all odds, and the several reauthorizations since then, reflect a recognition within Congress of Indian problems. Legislation related to Indian affairs is referred to the select committee for review, although the panel has no legislative authority. It also conducts studies and holds hearings.

Indians, or native Americans, have a unique relationship with Congress and the rest of the federal government. Although subject to federal laws and tribal regulations, Indians living on reservations are covered by state and local laws only when Congress gives its consent, as it has for criminal laws and in many other instances. Indian reservations have special status under which the federal government acts as trustee.

The primary advocate of establishing the committee in 1977 was Democrat James Abourezk of South Dakota, whose mother was an Indian. After Abourezk left the Senate in 1979, Montana Democrat John Melcher persuaded the Senate to continue the select committee, and Melcher became its chairman.   ~

Intelligence Committees, House and Senate Select

Most of their work is done in closed session, and even the legislation they report is usually kept secret. These habits of the House and Senate Intelligence committees reflect their role: oversight of the nation's espionage agencies. The relationship is uneasy, though; the intelligence agencies criticize Congress for leaking sensitive information, and the committees complain they are not kept informed.

Until the special committees were set up, jurisdiction over intelligence operations was scattered among several committees. Although shared jurisdiction is common on Capitol Hill, it particularly hindered oversight of intelligence activities. With so many people given access to classified information, executive agencies were reluctant to share data with Congress. Critics still say Congress is not careful enough about keeping classified information secret.

At the same time the intelligence agencies have often held information back from Congress. For example, Congress was not fully briefed about the extent of CIA involvement in the contra resistance to the Sandinista government in Nicaragua. When Robert McFarlane, then national security adviser, testified before the House Permanent Select Intelligence Committee in 1985, he denied that the Reagan administration was involved in illegal contra aid. Later investigations revealed that White House officials had orchestrated private donations to the contras despite a congressional ban on government involvement. McFarlane subsequently pleaded guilty to charges of withholding information from Congress. *(See* IRAN-CONTRA AFFAIR.*)*

Creation of the two special committees was prompted by revelations in the mid-1970s that intelligence agencies had run illegal covert operations, including plots to assassinate foreign leaders and surveillance of U.S. mail. The disclosures were detailed in news reports and later in investigations by two study committees set up temporarily by the House and Senate. Most notable was the fifteen-month probe headed by Sen. Frank Church, an Idaho Democrat, that chronicled a long list of intelligence abuses. Both the House and Senate decided they needed permanent intelligence committees to monitor how the United States conducted its espionage. The Senate established its permanent panel in 1976.

The House committee, set up on a temporary basis in 1975, had a shaky beginning. Its first chairman was replaced after members found out he had not shared inside information about illegal CIA activities. Then, in 1976, the House blocked release of the committee's final report in deference to objections from the Ford administration. But the report was leaked and published in the *Village Voice*, a New York City weekly newspaper, prompting an investigation by the House Committee on STANDARDS OF OFFICIAL CONDUCT. Not until 1977 did the House set up a permanent intelligence committee, and even that was controversial. Republicans argued, without success, that the ratio of nine majority members and four minority members would make the panel too partisan. (By 1988 the House panel had eleven Democrats and seven Republicans.) The first chairman was Edward P. Boland, a Massachusetts Democrat, who was a key opponent of undercover U.S. aid to the contras in Nicaragua.

Membership of the House committee must include a representative from each of the Appropriations, Armed Services, Foreign Affairs, and Judiciary committees. A member is allowed no more than six years of continuous service on the Intelligence Committee.

The Senate set up a special committee in 1975 and then voted in 1976 to create a permanent, fifteen-member panel. Like the House, the Senate limits service on the committee, allowing a senator to serve a maximum of eight years. In an effort to create a bipartisan spirit, the post of vice chairman is given to a member of the minority party. Membership on the committee must include two members from each of these committees: Appropriations, Armed Services, Foreign Relations, and Judiciary. In 1988 eight Democrats and seven Republicans served on the committee.

Although most special or select committees do not handle legislation, the intelligence committees each year approve the spending authorization for the intelligence agencies, including the Central Intelligence Agency, the Defense Intelligence Agency, the National Security Agency, the intelligence branches of the military services, and the Federal Bureau of Investigation. Except for the CIA, jurisdiction over the intelligence agencies is shared with other committees, but the select committees act first and have primary responsibility.

The Senate committee also handles the confirmation of top intelligence officials, such as the director of central intelligence. *(See* APPOINTMENT POWER.*)*   ∼

Interior and Insular Affairs Committee, House

The House Interior Committee oversees the nation's public lands, carrying out the decades-old philosophy that some land should be set aside and managed by the government for the good of all. Conflicts between preserving the land as wilderness and using it for logging, grazing, and mining often fall to the Interior panel, and then Congress, to resolve. Legislators from the West, where most federal land is located, dominate the committee. Interior also oversees the federal water projects that subsidize irrigation of arid western areas and make large-scale agriculture possible there. Among the oldest House committees, Interior was established in 1805 as the Public Lands Committee; its title was changed in 1951 to Interior and Insular Affairs.

The Interior Committee is not considered a major House committee. Many environmental issues, such as clean air and water, are not in its jurisdiction. Even federal lands are not entirely within its purview; it shares management of wildlife refuges with the MERCHANT MARINE Committee, and oversight of forestry with the AGRICULTURE Committee. Interior handles some aspects of energy policy, such as regulation of nuclear power and restrictions on the strip mining of coal, but the ENERGY AND COMMERCE Committee is the primary House energy panel.

Public Lands

Under Morris K. Udall, the Arizona Democrat who became chairman in 1979, Interior was a strong advocate of protecting public lands. Although many committee members still wanted to accommodate the timber and mineral industries, that attitude did not dominate the committee in the late 1970s and 1980s, as it had earlier, particularly under the lengthy chairmanship (1959-73) of Colorado Democrat Wayne N. Aspinall. Although Stewart Udall, interior secretary from 1961 to 1969 and Morris Udall's brother, won support from the Senate to close certain federal lands to commercial use, the proposals faced opposition from Aspinall and the House. Congress eventually passed the 1964 Wilderness Act; while a landmark bill, it included concessions to mineral leasing and other activities.

More than a decade later, the House, not the Senate, was the lead player on preservation issues. When Congress was considering what parks, forests—and energy development— were appropriate on the millions of acres of federally owned land in Alaska, the Senate pushed for less protection and more development. In contrast, the Interior Committee won House passage of a conservation-oriented bill. Eventually enacted in 1980, the Alaska lands measure fell short of House goals, but it did reflect earlier concessions by the Senate to the Interior Committee's proposals.

Reagan Years

Interior had a new role while President Ronald Reagan was in office (1981-89). James Watt, the Interior Department's secretary from 1981 to 1983, launched an aggressive campaign to allow private industry to develop wilderness areas before a 1984 deadline would close them to commercial use. That legacy, from Aspinall's era, had permitted an additional twenty years of development in areas designated as wilderness in 1964. Eventually, though, even Republicans on the Interior panel objected to Watt's plans, and Congress blocked him from acting. On many other issues, Interior took positions more proconservation than did the Republican-controlled Senate ENERGY AND NATURAL RESOURCES Committee, which also handles most public land questions.

Interior has a mixed record in one area: water projects. The committee oversees the Bureau of Reclamation, which since 1902 has provided water in the West at subsidized rates. Although sensitive to environmentalists' complaints in most areas, even Udall was a staunch defender of dams and waterworks, particularly the massive Central Arizona Project that promised to bring water to arid Tucson and Phoenix, which were in his district.   ~

Internal Security Subcom-
mittee.   See INVESTIGATIONS.

Investigations

Investigations serve as the eyes and ears of the legislative branch. They gather information on the need for possible future legislation and test the effectiveness of laws enacted in the past. They inquire into the qualifications and performance of government officials, including members of Congress themselves. They expose waste and corruption in government. They educate the public on great issues of the day.

All of these purposes have been served throughout the two-century history of Congress. Investigations have given Congress some of its finest—and some of its most deplorable—hours. Television has permitted millions of ordinary Americans to view a sampling of each without ever visiting the seat of Congress in Washington, D.C.

In 1974 the House Judiciary Committee won high praise for its conduct of an impeachment inquiry on President Richard Nixon. The committee recommended that Nixon be removed from office on charges of obstruction of justice, abuse of power, and contempt of Congress. The committee's work, concluding with a dramatic televised debate, helped prepare the nation to accept the resignation of the president it had overwhelmingly reelected less than two years earlier. A Senate committee investigation had helped set the stage for the NIXON IMPEACHMENT EFFORT by exposing administration efforts to cover up political sabotage in the WATERGATE SCANDAL.

In 1954 Sen. Joseph R. McCARTHY, a Wisconsin Republican, met his downfall as a result of his search for communist influence in American society. Mc-

Carthyism poisoned the political and social atmosphere of the early 1950s. The senator's power was felt, and feared, in Congress, the administrations of two presidents, the State Department, the armed forces, universities, and many other public and private institutions throughout the country. McCarthy's activities finally led to his censure, an official punishment, by the Senate. *(See* DISCIPLINING MEMBERS.*)*

As McCarthy and others have discovered, investigations can provide a fast ticket to fame for a little-known member of Congress. President Harry S TRUMAN won distinction during World War II when, as a Democratic senator from Missouri, he led a widely acclaimed investigation of the national defense program. NIXON, as a first-term Republican representative from California, made headlines in 1948 through his role in anticommunist investigations of the House Un-American Activities Committee.

Congress's investigative power became a major political issue in the 1940s and 1950s, largely as a result of communist-hunting investigations conducted by the Un-American Activities Committee, McCarthy's Senate Permanent Investigations Subcommittee, and a few other committees. To some people the threat to national security posed by communist activities was so great as to justify exceptional procedures. To others the threat to individual liberties from the behavior and authority of some committees appeared a more real danger than the threat of communism. The conflict resulted in Supreme Court decisions attempting to balance the powers of the committees and the rights of witnesses, and in modest congressional efforts to reform committee procedures.

The Investigative Process
Investigations are not mentioned anywhere in the Constitution, but the Supreme Court has upheld Congress's

Investigative Spectaculars

The ornate Senate Caucus Room has been the setting for many of Congress's most spectacular investigative hearings. At top, Sen. Joseph R. McCarthy is sworn in before testifying in the Army-McCarthy hearings in 1954. The faces, the issues, and the cameras have changed by 1987, when Lt. Col. Oliver L. North takes the oath in the Iran-contra investigation.

power to investigate as part of the LEG-ISLATIVE PROCESS. The Court first asserted its authority to review congressional investigations in the case of *Kilbourn v. Thompson* in 1881.

From the beginning Congress has delegated investigative functions to its committees. A major investigation typically begins when the Senate or House authorizes the investigation, often establishing a temporary committee (known as a "select" or "special" committee) to undertake the job. Following a preliminary inquiry by its staff employees, the committee holds hearings at which people with knowledge of the matter are called to testify. At the conclusion of the investigation the committee issues a report summarizing its findings and offering recommendations for future action.

Much of the information disclosed in investigations is uncovered during the staff inquiry. The formal hearings, at which witnesses appear, become dramatic spectacles intended to educate and influence the public through the media, particularly television.

The Senate committee that investigated the Watergate scandal was formed in February 1973. It spent several months interviewing people, including scores of Nixon administration officials, before the televised hearings began in May. Similarly, months of preliminary spadework preceded the May 1987 opening of joint Senate-House hearings on the IRAN-CONTRA AFFAIR, an investigation of undercover U.S. arms sales to Iran and the diversion of profits from those sales to the contra guerrillas in Nicaragua. Although the House and Senate each established a committee to investigate the affair, leaders of the two committees agreed to merge their investigations and hearings to avoid excessive duplication. That was an unusual procedure for the two houses of Congress, which traditionally have jealously guarded their powers.

Major investigations call for big staffs. At the height of the Watergate investigation sixty-four professional staff members were working for the committee. And the House Judiciary Committee employed a staff of nearly 100, including 43 attorneys, in its 1974 Nixon impeachment inquiry.

Sometimes people refuse to cooperate with congressional committees requesting their testimony or demanding that they produce records and documents. In such cases legislators can draw upon the SUBPOENA POWER to force them to comply. A subpoena is a legal order that requires a person to testify or to produce documents. Those who ignore subpoenas risk being punished for CONTEMPT OF CONGRESS.

When witnesses appear before a committee, they may be prosecuted as criminals if they do not tell the truth. Witnesses sometimes avoid testifying by citing the Fifth Amendment to the Constitution, which says a person does not have to be a witness against himself in any criminal case. Witnesses who invoke the Fifth Amendment as a basis for not testifying may be required to talk if they are granted limited immunity from prosecution.

On occasion government officials either refuse to testify or withhold information by order of the president. Refusal to cooperate with Congress on this basis is called EXECUTIVE PRIVILEGE. Presidents have had considerable success in using executive privilege to stymie demands for information.

Since many congressional investigations target mismanagement or wrongdoing by the administration in power, investigations tend to have partisan overtones. Votes on areas to be investigated, witnesses to be called, and the final committee recommendations may divide along party lines. Partisanship may be the reason why an investigation is undertaken in the first place, and this, of course, can influence how it is conducted.

A House investigation of federal

regulatory agencies in 1957-58 is a case in point. The Democratic chairman of the investigating subcommittee insisted that the inquiry was not a "political voyage." But its main result was the resignation of White House assistant Sherman Adams, right-hand man to Republican President Dwight D. Eisenhower (1953-61). Adams was accused of interceding with federal agencies on behalf of a Boston industrialist from whom he had received favors. Democrats used the Adams affair to embarrass the Republicans on the eve of the 1958 election campaign.

Investigative Milestones

Over the course of nearly two centuries Congress has investigated scandals, wars, national security threats (real and imagined), and any number of other topics that captivated inquiring minds on Capitol Hill.

Many of the earliest investigations involved charges brought against a senator or representative, but most concerned the civil and military activities of the executive branch. Between 1880 and World War I (1914-18) economic and social problems joined government operations as the principal fields of investigation. Between the two world wars (1918-39) subversive activities, those aimed at overthrowing the government, emerged as a major investigative concern.

Wartime Second-Guessing The investigative history of Congress began with an Indian massacre of troops sent into the Ohio territory in 1791. The following year the House established a select committee to inquire into the affair, thus launching the first congressional investigation. The committee absolved Maj. Gen. Arthur St. Clair, the troops' commander, of blame for the disaster. It said the War Department was at fault.

Seventy years later Congress set up its first joint investigating committee in response to another military action,

America's Civil War between the North and South. The Joint Committee on the Conduct of the War routinely second-guessed President Abraham Lincoln's military moves and attempted to plot its own course during the war.

The committee was controlled by Radical Republicans who were convinced that Lincoln was not acting aggressively enough to secure a Union victory against the Southern Confederacy. Its actions were welcomed by the Confederate military leader, Gen. Robert E. Lee, because of their divisive effect on Northern strategists. The committee, he observed, was worth about two divisions of Confederate troops.

Aware of the excesses of the Civil War committee, the World War II Truman committee—formally the Senate Special Committee to Investigate the National Defense Program—scrupulously avoided any attempt to judge military policy or operations. Created early in 1941, the committee sought to uncover and to halt wasteful practices in the war mobilization effort. It worked closely with executive branch departments and agencies.

Corruption Other investigations dealt with money and favors. There were many investigations during Ulysses S. Grant's two terms in the White House (1869-77). Probably the most famous scandal of the time was the Crédit Mobilier affair, which triggered inquiries in 1872-73 by Senate and House committees. The scandal involved wholesale corruption in the construction of the last portion of the transcontinental railroad, which had been completed by Crédit Mobilier of America, a company related to the Union Pacific Railroad, in 1869.

Attempting to head off a legislative inquiry into the affair, Rep. Oakes Ames, a Massachusetts Republican who was a principal shareholder in Crédit Mobilier, arranged to sell some $33 million of stock in the company at extremely low prices to members of Congress and executive branch officials.

Ames and another House member eventually were censured by the House. Others, including Vice President Schuyler Colfax and Rep. James A. Garfield, were implicated, but no action was taken against them. Garfield, an Ohio Republican, was elected to the presidency in 1880.

Another series of investigations in 1922-24 uncovered the TEAPOT DOME scandal, which ravaged the administration of President Warren G. Harding. That scandal involved Interior Department leasing of naval oil reserves on public lands to private oil companies. The reserves, at Elk Hills, California, and Teapot Dome, Wyoming, were natural deposits of oil that had been set aside for use by the Navy. As a result of the investigations, Harding's secretary of the interior, Albert B. Fall, was sent to prison for accepting a bribe. Two other cabinet members resigned, and other high officials resigned or were fired.

Finance and Industry Investigations of American business practices paved the way for several major regulatory laws in the early decades of the twentieth century.

A 1912-13 House investigation of the "money trust"—the concentration of money and credit in the United States—led to passage of the Federal Reserve Act of 1913, the Clayton Antitrust Act of 1914, and the Federal Trade Commission Act of 1914. A 1932-34 Senate investigation of the stock exchange and Wall Street financial manipulations paved the way for the Banking Acts of 1933 and 1935, the Securities Act of 1933, and the Securities Exchange Act of 1934.

The munitions industry was the focus of an investigation by a special Senate committee in 1934-36. The committee—chaired by Gerald P. Nye, a Progressive Republican from North Da-

kota—set out to prove that arms makers were merchants of death, linked together in a global ring, who promoted armed conflicts and reaped enormous profits. The evidence was thin, and the inquiry produced no legislation, but it established Nye as leader of the movement to curb the arms traffic and the nation's most eloquent isolationist.

Subversives After World War I, members of Congress frequently pushed for inquiries on threats to national security posed by antigovernment groups who were loyal to other nations. After World War II, rising tensions with the Soviet Union raised fears of communist subversion, and investigations of communist activities set the stage for enactment of various antisubversive laws.

In 1938 the House established the Special Committee to Investigate Un-American Activities and Propaganda in the United States. The committee was known popularly as the Dies Committee after its first chairman, Rep. Martin Dies, Jr., a Texas Democrat. The committee and its successors weathered nearly four decades of controversy.

In 1945 the Dies Committee was replaced by the House Un-American Activities Committee. Like its predecessor, the new committee carried on a crusade against persons and groups it considered to be subversive. The committee's aggressive style raised questions about abuse of Congress's investigative powers and the need to safeguard constitutional rights of those who appeared before or were investigated by the committee. Witnesses who agreed with the committee's activities accused hundreds of citizens of being communists or communist sympathizers.

A remark made to a witness by Rep. J. Parnell Thomas, a New Jersey Republican who was chairman of the House Un-American Activities Committee in 1947-1949, was a good indication of the committee's view of its power: "The rights you have are the

Un-American Activities

The year is 1948, and the House Un-American Activities Committee is preparing to launch a new investigation of communism in the United States. Chairman J. Parnell Thomas, center, poses with committee members and staff. Standing at left is Rep. Richard Nixon.

rights given you by this committee. We will determine what rights you have and what rights you have not got before the committee."

In 1947 the panel trained its sights on the movie industry. Hollywood personalities, including an actor named Ronald Reagan, testified about communist efforts to infiltrate the Screen Actors Guild. It was the year of the "Hollywood Ten," mostly screenwriters such as Dalton Trumbo, who defiantly challenged the panel's conduct and later went to jail after being arrested for contempt of Congress. Nervous studio executives responded with a "blacklist" of suspected communists, who were barred from Hollywood jobs. The blacklisting practice lingered into the 1950s and beyond.

The Un-American Activities Committee, with Nixon playing a key role, gained maximum attention in 1948 with a dramatic confrontation between Alger Hiss, a State Department official, and Whittaker Chambers, who accused Hiss of having been a communist years earlier. While Hiss professed his innocence, Nixon doggedly pursued the matter. He eventually succeeded in refuting Hiss's claim that he did not know Chambers, paving the way for Hiss to be convicted and jailed for perjury.

In the early 1950s the Un-American Activities Committee was overshadowed by Sen. Joseph McCarthy's more flamboyant hunt for communists. But McCarthy's investigation into alleged subversion in the U.S. Army—televised nationwide in 1954—ultimately convinced his Senate colleagues he had gone too far.

The Senate's 1954 vote to censure McCarthy for his tactics effectively ended his crusade, but the Un-American Activities Committee continued its work until the House abolished it in 1975.

The Age of Television   Televised hearings, first used spectacularly by the Un-American Activities Committee in 1948, were soon adopted by other committees as well. While television exposed witnesses to vast, often damaging, publicity, it enabled ambitious members of Congress to make a name for themselves in national politics.

In 1950-51 Sen. Estes KEFAUVER, a Tennessee Democrat, used televised hearings by his special investigating committee to spotlight racketeering, drug trafficking, and other organized crime. One of the highlights of the hearings was the appearance before the committee of reputed underworld king Frank Costello. Costello refused to have his face televised, so TV audiences viewed only his hands.

Hearings were followed by scores of citations for contempt of Congress and many local indictments for criminal activities. In a series of reports, the committee said crime syndicates were operating with the connivance and protection of law enforcement officials. Kefauver became a leading presidential candidate after the widely viewed hearings; he was the unsuccessful Democratic nominee for vice president in 1956.

In 1957 another special committee, chaired by Sen. John L. McClellan, an Arkansas Democrat, began investigating shady labor union activities. The panel's chief counsel was Robert F. Kennedy, brother of future president John F. Kennedy and himself a future senator and presidential candidate. The committee focused much attention on the Teamsters union and its president, James R. Hoffa, whom it characterized as a national menace running a "hoodlum empire." During the committee's 270 days of hearings, 343 witnesses invoked their Fifth Amendment right against self-incrimination. The inquiry led to the 1959 passage of the Landrum-Griffin Act, a measure designed to fight corruption in union affairs.

Abuses of Power   The Watergate scandal prompted a 1973-74 investigation by a Senate select committee that looked into widespread abuses of power by President Nixon and his top aides. The Senate committee was established early in 1973 to investigate White House involvement in a break-in the previous year at Democratic National Committee Headquarters in the Watergate office building in Washington, D.C.

The committee hearings drew a picture of political sabotage that went far beyond the original break-in. They also brought to light administration efforts to cover up the affair. The Watergate hearings led to the disclosure of tape recordings of Nixon's White House conversations and revelations that showed his role in the cover-up. In the summer of 1974 the House Judiciary Committee capped its own investigation by voting articles of impeachment against Nixon. He resigned on August 9, 1974, rather than face a House impeachment vote and probable conviction by the Senate. *(See* NIXON IMPEACHMENT EFFORT.*)*

Six months later a Senate select committee was established to look into charges of another form of government abuse: activities by the Central Intelligence Agency that exceeded its legal authority. The Senate committee conducted a fifteen-month inquiry that confirmed accounts of CIA spying on U.S. citizens, assassination plots against foreign leaders, and other abuses. In the wake of the Senate's CIA investigation, and a parallel one conducted by a House special committee, both chambers created ongoing INTELLIGENCE committees with oversight jurisdiction over the CIA.

The CIA also figured in 1987 hearings on the Iran-contra affair. Several witnesses testified that CIA officials had actively participated in a network of aid to the contra guerrillas in Nicaragua at a time when official U.S. assistance was barred by law. The Reagan administration's backing of the contras led Democrats to charge that the administration had flouted the will of Congress, endangering the constitutional system of government. In its November 1987 report, a bipartisan majority of the committee faulted the White House for "secrecy, deception, and disdain for the rule of law." ～

ADDITIONAL READINGS

Hamilton, James. *The Power to Probe: A Study of Congressional Investigations.* 1976.
McGeary, M. Nelson. *The Development of Congressional Investigative Power.* 1966.
Woodward, Bob, and Carl Bernstein. *All the President's Men.* 1987.
___. *The Final Days.* 1987.

Iran-Contra Affair

Startling revelations of secret U.S. arms sales to Iran and the diversion of some of the profits from these sales to U.S.-backed contra rebels fighting the Sandinista government in Nicaragua exploded on the public scene in late 1986.

The disclosures triggered multiple investigations and curtailed the political effectiveness of the most popular president in a generation, Ronald Reagan. The debate over Congress's proper role in foreign policy was rekindled.

The Iran-contra affair seemed to have faded from public view by the end of 1987, but it was back in front-page headlines a few months later when several key participants, including former White House aides, were indicted by a federal grand jury.

What Happened

Following the trails that brought two countries on opposite sides of the globe—Nicaragua and Iran—together in a U.S. foreign policy scandal was not an easy task for investigators or the American public. A bewildering array of charges, allegations, and facts emerged.

Contra Aid U.S. involvement with the Nicaraguan contras began in the early 1980s when the Reagan administration authorized the Central Intelligence Agency to form a paramilitary force to harass the leftist Sandinista government. Aid to the contra force grew, but in late 1982 a skeptical Congress began to restrict and ultimately cut off U.S. aid through a series of "Boland amendments," named after Rep. Edward P. Boland, a Massachusetts Democrat who was then chairman of the House Intelligence Committee.

As it became clear in 1984 that Congress would block further contra assistance, an aide to the president's National Security Council, Lt. Col. Oliver L. North, began to fill the void. Apparently working closely with CIA director William J. Casey, North provided the contras with intelligence information and advice on military tactics. Through private agents, including retired Air Force major general Richard V. Secord and his partner Albert Hakim, North arranged for the contras to buy covert shipments of arms. Administration officials solicited money for the contras from foreign allies. North worked closely with a group of conservative fund raisers who solicited money for the contras from wealthy Americans.

When questions about North's activities were raised on Capitol Hill in 1985, North prepared several letters, signed by his boss at the time, national security adviser Robert C. McFarlane, denying that the NSC staff was violating the Boland amendment or was fund raising for the contras. McFarlane's successor, Vice Adm. John M. Poindexter, sent letters in 1986 stating that the NSC was complying with the Boland amendment. North and Poindexter later contended to investigators that the Boland amendment barred involvement with the contras only by the U.S. intelligence agencies, not by the NSC staff.

In early 1986 the contra operation crossed paths with another covert operation, arms sales to Iran, when profits from the Iranian sales were used to help finance the contra-aid network.

Iran Initiative   Iran and the United States had been bitter enemies since 1979, when Iranian militants had taken over the U.S. Embassy in Tehran and held Americans hostage for more than a year. Aside from ritual denunciations of Iran's involvement in terrorism and calls for an end to the Persian Gulf war between Iran and Iraq, the Reagan administration appeared to be acting as if the radical Islamic regime in Tehran did not exist.

But, in fact, a policy reevaluation was under way. At Israel's suggestion, White House aides proposed to President Reagan that arms sales be part of a diplomatic move aimed at bolstering moderates in Iran. The aides got the president's attention by holding out the prospect of winning freedom for American hostages kidnapped in war-torn Lebanon by pro-Iranian groups.

Despite a U.S. embargo on direct arms sales to Iran and its own aggressive campaign to halt arms exports by all countries to Iran, the Reagan administration in 1985 approved Israeli sales of U.S. arms to Iran and in 1986 began selling directly to Iran. President Reagan in December 1985 signed a "finding" retroactively authorizing CIA participation in a November 1985 arms sale. Another finding was signed in January 1986 authorizing arms sales and containing an important and unusual provision directing that Congress not be told about it.

North and Secord, already working together on aid to the contras, became key participants in the Iran arms sales. Millions of dollars from the sales soon

Iran-Contra Hearings
Televised hearings give the public an insider's view of congressional activities. Committees headed by Sen. Daniel K. Inouye, seated left, and Rep. Lee H. Hamilton, seated right, held televised joint hearings in 1987 that filled in many of the details of the Iran-contra affair.

accrued in various Secord-Hakim accounts and Secord used some of the money to set up a sophisticated operation to deliver supplies to the contras inside Nicaragua. Secord later told congressional investigators that about $3.5 million was diverted to the contras from the Iranian arms sale profits.

Investigations

When the Iran-contra story broke in November 1986, investigators scrambled to find out what had happened. Conflicting recollections, contradictory statements from the White House, sloppy record keeping, a misleading chronology prepared by key participants, destruction and altering of documents, and the illness and death of former CIA director Casey complicated their job.

Attorney General Edwin Meese III conducted the first administration inquiry into the Iranian arms sales. Although it was much criticized for its investigative techniques, the inquiry did uncover a memo from North that mentioned the diversion of funds to the contras. In the aftermath of that revelation, North was fired and Poindexter resigned.

Reagan then appointed a prestigious board of inquiry, headed by former senator John Tower, a Texas Republican, and including former senator and secretary of state Edmund S. Muskie, a Maine Democrat, and former national security adviser and retired lieutenant general Brent Scowcroft. Under political pressure, the Reagan administration requested appointment of an independent counsel, or special prosecutor, and retired federal judge Lawrence E. Walsh, an Oklahoma Republican, was selected.

Congress began its own investigations. The House and Senate INTELLIGENCE and House FOREIGN AFFAIRS committees held hearings. House and Senate select investigating committees were appointed. (*See* INVESTIGATIONS.)

After a partisan battle, the Senate Intelligence Committee in January 1987 released a report chronicling the affair. A much more complete picture was provided the next month when the Tower Commission released its report. While cautiously worded, the Tower report served up a damning indictment of failures by Reagan and his aides throughout the events of the Iran-contra affair. The board criticized the president's inattention to detail—which they gingerly described as his "management style"—and the White House staff's failure to take compensating steps.

Following the Tower report's release, Reagan effectively fired his chief of staff and in a televised speech accepted responsibility for any failures and acknowledged for the first time that the United States had traded arms for hostages.

The select investigating committees, headed by Sen. Daniel K. Inouye of Hawaii and Rep. Lee H. Hamilton of Indiana, both Democrats, spent four months reviewing documents, privately interviewing hundreds of witnesses, and negotiating with independent counsel Walsh and witnesses' lawyers over the question of immunity for witnesses.

The committees' twelve weeks of joint public hearings filled in many of the details of the affair. For the American public, the focal point of the hearings was the combative and articulate North, who portrayed himself as a loyal soldier who had done only what was authorized and who had sought merely to serve his president. North's forceful presentation—aided by his appearance in a Marine Corps uniform adorned with medals—created a sensation, labeled "Olliemania" by the media. North was followed to the witness table by his former boss, Poindexter, who testified that he had never told Reagan about the diversion of funds to the contras.

In a strongly worded report released in November 1987, the bipartisan majority of the select committees

Celebrity Status
For many Americans, Marine Lt. Col. Oliver L. North was the star of the Iran-contra hearings. Reflecting North's celebrity status, reporters and photographers surround him as he leaves his Virginia home.

found that the failures of the affair stemmed from White House "secrecy, deception, and disdain for the rule of law." Reagan himself was responsible for setting loose a "cabal of zealots" and for failing to instill a respect for law among his subordinates, the committees reported.

The majority charged that the administration "violated," "disregarded," or "abused" a series of laws and executive orders. Among these were the Boland amendment, requirements that Congress be notified of all covert operations and transfers of U.S.-made weapons from the original purchaser to a third country, the criminal injunction against knowingly making "false statements" to Congress, and the requirement that all proceeds from the sale of U.S.-owned property be turned over to the Treasury and not be used for unauthorized purposes.

The majority devoted a chapter to a defense of the proposition that Con-

gress and the executive branch have shared power over foreign policy. North and Poindexter had bluntly told the committees that Congress should stay out of foreign policy, and even Secretary of State George P. Shultz, considered one of the officials most sensitive to congressional sentiment, had complained about Capitol Hill interference in the conduct of diplomacy. *(See* PRESIDENT AND CONGRESS.*)*

A Republican minority of the two committees issued a heated rebuttal to the report, acknowledging that Reagan made mistakes but saying that most of the fault rested with Congress for interfering with the president's policies.

Indictments
After nearly fourteen months of deliberation marked by legal challenges to the constitutional authority of independent counsel Walsh, a federal grand jury in March 1988 indicted North, Poindexter, Secord, and Hakim. In the

twenty-three count indictment, the four were charged with conspiracy to defraud the United States, theft of government property, and wire fraud.

Charges against North and Poindexter also included obstruction of Congress and making false statements. In addition, North was charged with obstruction of Meese's inquiry, falsifying and destroying official documents, accepting illegal gratuities, and conspiring to defraud the Internal Revenue Service. Secord and Hakim also were indicted on charges involving illegal gratuities to North.

A week before the indictments, former national security adviser McFarlane pleaded guilty to four misdemeanor charges of withholding informa-

tion from Congress. Walsh had obtained two earlier convictions, those of Carl R. "Spitz" Channell and Richard R. Miller, who in April and May 1987 had pleaded guilty to tax fraud charges for their role in raising private funds for the contras.   ~

ADDITIONAL READINGS

Brinkley, Joel, and Stephen Engelberg, eds. *Report of the Congressional Committees Investigating the Iran-Contra Affair with the Minority View: Abridged edition.* 1988.

Congressional Quarterly Almanac 1987.

Congressional Quarterly. *The Iran-Contra Puzzle.* 1987.

Overleaf:
Senate softball, 1954: Henry M. Jackson, batter; John F. Kennedy, catcher; and Mike Mansfield, umpire.

Jefferson's Manual

The Senate's first compilation of procedures was prepared by Thomas Jefferson for his own guidance when he was president of the Senate in the years of his vice presidency (1797-1801). Known as *Jefferson's Manual of Parliamentary Practice*, the work reflected English parliamentary practice of his day. *Jefferson's Manual* was adopted in part by the House of Representatives in 1837 and remains the foundation for many practices in the modern Senate and House. *(See* HOUSE MANUAL; SENATE MANUAL.*)*   ~

Johnson, Hiram

Hiram Johnson (1866-1945), a California Republican, was an isolationist leader in the Senate in the period embracing the first and second World Wars. Before entering the Senate in 1917, Johnson served six years as a reform governor of California. He was Theodore Roosevelt's running mate on the unsuccessful Progressive (Bull Moose) ticket in 1912. In the Senate, Johnson worked to block U.S. participation in the League of Nations and the World Court following World War I. He opposed U.S. participation in World

War II and the United Nations Charter in 1945.   ~

Johnson, Lyndon B.

Schooled in politics on Capitol Hill, Texas Democrat Lyndon B. Johnson (1908-73) used that expertise to build a working relationship with Congress considered the best of any president in modern times.

As Senate Democratic leader in the 1950s, Johnson transformed the job into a powerful, prestigious post. When he became president in 1963, he was able to win congressional support for civil rights and for GREAT SOCIETY programs on health, education, and welfare that were more sweeping than any since the NEW DEAL. Eventually, though, Johnson's conduct of the war in Vietnam strained his ties with Congress and split the Democratic party. Expected to seek a second full term as president, Johnson announced in March 1968 that he would not be a candidate.

Johnson first came to Washington in December 1931 to work for a House member from his home state. When a Texas representative died in 1937, Johnson won a special election to fill the vacancy. But he was impatient with the slow pace of the House, where power accrued to those with SENIORITY. When a Texas senator died in 1941, Johnson, then thirty-two, ran in a special election to fill the seat. He lost narrowly, despite support from President Franklin D. Roosevelt. He succeeded on his second try in 1948, winning the primary by a margin of eighty-seven votes—and earning the nickname "Landslide Lyndon."

Johnson's experience on the House Naval Affairs Committee helped win him a seat on the Senate Armed Services Committee, chaired by Georgia Democrat Richard B. RUSSELL. One of the most powerful members of the Senate, Russell led a coalition of Republicans and southern Democrats known as the CONSERVATIVE COALITION. Though friendly with Russell, Johnson avoided a close alignment with the southern bloc, a decision that later made it possible for him to work with both southern and northern Democrats.

While clearly ambitious and hard working, Johnson also benefited from a void in the top Democratic leadership ranks caused by election losses. In 1950 both the Democratic floor leader and whip—the second-ranking party leader—were defeated. Although he was still a freshman senator, Johnson, with Russell's support, was elected whip. He was elected minority floor leader in 1952, when the top post again fell vacant after an election that also cost the Democrats their majority in Congress. In 1954 the Democrats regained control of the Senate, and Johnson was elected majority leader, a job that had not tempted more senior colleagues away from their committee chairmanships.

Johnson had long been adept at building a network of loyal supporters. With committee assignments, campaign contributions, and a variety of other favors at his disposal, the new majority leader wove a complex tapestry of alliances with his colleagues. Johnson also had an extraordinary ability to persuade, in one-on-one encounters, through sheer force of will. The "Johnson treatment" became famous. To make a convert he might urge, threaten, beg, or cajole. "The only power available to the leader is the power of persuasion," he once said. "There is no patronage; no power to discipline; no authority to fire senators like a president can fire members of his cabinet."

Johnson was often described as crude and sometimes as cruel, but even his detractors had to acknowledge his talents for Senate leadership. As minority leader, he worked to maintain amicable relations between President

Dwight D. Eisenhower and Senate Democrats. He convinced the Democratic caucus in 1953 to give each senator, regardless of seniority, a seat on a major committee, a move known as the "Johnson rule" that presaged the congressional REFORM of the 1970s. In 1957 Johnson engineered passage of the first civil rights bill since Reconstruction. A testimony to Johnson's skill as majority leader, it passed without a FILIBUSTER and without causing a rift in the Democratic party.

Building on his eight years of success as majority leader, Johnson ran for the presidency in 1960. After an intense battle for the Democratic nomination, he surprised many by agreeing to run for vice president on a ticket headed by John F. KENNEDY. Like other vice presidents, Johnson was never comfortable in the role. His style and background were also markedly different from that of Kennedy and his top aides.

Kennedy's assassination on November 22, 1963, elevated Johnson to the presidency. In 1964 he won election to a full term in a landslide victory over Barry Goldwater. Johnson took advantage of an overwhelmingly Democratic Congress to complete action on Kennedy's legislative program and then to win passage of his own Great Society bills. Of the supportive Congress he remarked, it "could be better, but not this side of heaven." Johnson still suffered, though, from the feeling that he remained in Kennedy's shadow. "They say Jack Kennedy had style, but I'm the one who's got the bills passed," Johnson told a group of senators in 1966.

Johnson's good relationship with Congress was not to last. The 1966 midterm elections brought forty-seven additional Republicans to the House and three to the Senate. Concerned about the escalating war in Vietnam, the country's economic woes, and urban rioting, Congress and the public expressed growing dissatisfaction with the administration. Johnson announced

March 31, 1968, that he would not seek reelection. At the end of his term he retired to his Texas ranch, where he died of a heart attack on January 22, 1973.   ~

ADDITIONAL READINGS

Caro, Robert A. *The Years of Lyndon Johnson: The Path to Power.* 1982.

Evans, Rowland, and Robert Novak. *Lyndon B. Johnson: The Exercise of Power.* 1966.

Johnson, Lyndon B. *The Vantage Point: Perspective on the Presidency, 1963-69.* 1971.

Miller, Merle. *Lyndon: An Oral Biography.* 1980.

White, William S. *The Professional: Lyndon B. Johnson.* 1964.

Johnson Impeachment Trial

Only one president of the United States has ever stood trial on impeachment charges: President Andrew Johnson, who escaped removal from office in 1868 by a single Senate vote.

The IMPEACHMENT POWER granted by the Constitution permits Congress to remove federal officials it finds guilty of grave misconduct. The process requires two steps. An accused official must first be formally charged, or impeached, by the House of Representatives. The official then is tried in the Senate, where a two-thirds majority is required to convict.

Johnson was specifically charged with dismissing the secretary of war in violation of the Tenure of Office Act. But his impeachment was part of a larger political struggle with a hostile Congress. A Tennessee Democrat who had remained loyal to the Union at the outbreak of the Civil War, Johnson was chosen as Abraham Lincoln's vice presidential running mate in 1864. He be-

Presidential Impeachment
Andrew Johnson was the only president of the United States to stand trial in the Senate on impeachment charges. Here Rep. Thaddeus Stevens, right, and Rep. John A. Bingham appear before the Senate to read impeachment charges voted by the House. The Senate acquitted Johnson by a one-vote margin.

came president upon Lincoln's assassination the following year. Johnson tried to pursue Lincoln's moderate approach to the South, but that brought him into conflict with the Republican-controlled Congress—particularly the Radical Republicans, who favored harsh treatment of the defeated Confederacy.

On their first attempt to impeach Johnson, in 1867, the Radical Republicans suffered a crushing defeat. The House Judiciary Committee recommended impeachment on general charges, but the full House of Representatives rejected an impeachment resolution on a 57-108 vote.

A second impeachment effort was triggered early in 1868 when Johnson dismissed Secretary of War Edwin M. Stanton, a holdover from the Lincoln administration who had close ties to the Radical Republicans. In dismissing Stanton, Johnson defied the Tenure of Office Act, which required Senate approval for removal of government officials who had been appointed with Senate consent. The tenure law had been enacted over Johnson's veto in 1867. Its

purpose was to protect Republican officeholders from executive retaliation if they did not support the president.

Johnson's action infuriated Congress, which moved swiftly to impeach him. The House Committee on Reconstruction, headed by Rep. Thaddeus STEVENS of Pennsylvania, one of the Radical Republican leaders, reported an impeachment resolution on February 22, 1868, and the full House approved the measure two days later. The House acted on a 126-47 vote that divided along party lines.

In early March the House approved specific charges, called articles of impeachment, against Johnson and chose seven of its members to prosecute the charges before the Senate. There were eleven articles in all, the main one concerning Johnson's removal of Stanton in violation of the Tenure of Office Act.

The Senate trial ran from March 30 until May 26. Chief Justice Salmon P. Chase presided, as required in a presidential impeachment trial. The president did not appear. He was represented by a team of lawyers headed by

Henry Stanbery, who had resigned as attorney general to lead the defense.

After weeks of argument and testimony, the Senate on May 16 voted on a catchall charge considered most likely to produce a vote for conviction. The drama of the vote has become legendary. With 36 votes needed for conviction, the final count was guilty, 35, and not guilty, 19. Seven Republicans joined the twelve Democrats in supporting Johnson. Votes on two further charges were taken May 26, and again the tally was 35-19. The trial was abruptly ended to save Johnson opponents from further defeats.

The Tenure of Office Act was virtually repealed early in the Grant administration, once the Republicans had control of the appointing power. It was entirely repealed in 1887. In 1926 the Supreme Court declared that the tenure act had been unconstitutional.   ~

Joint Resolution.   See
LEGISLATION.

Joint Session

A combined meeting of the Senate and House of Representatives is called a joint session or a joint meeting of Congress, depending on how it is arranged. Joint sessions require adoption of a concurrent resolution by each chamber. Joint meetings are held when one chamber adopts a unanimous consent agreement to recess to meet with the other body.

A combined meeting to hear the U.S. president is called a joint session of Congress. Such sessions are always held in the House chamber, which has a larger seating capacity than the Senate chamber. A joint session usually is held early each year to hear the president's STATE OF THE UNION address. The pres-

ident may address joint sessions at other times as well.

From time to time foreign leaders are invited to address joint meetings of Congress. Strictly speaking, such occasions are not joint sessions, however. The first foreign leader to address Congress—in 1824—was the Marquis de Lafayette, the French hero of the American Revolution. Sixty-six foreign dignitaries had spoken to joint meetings by the end of 1987, according to the Congressional Research Service of the Library of Congress. Congress turned down a proposed address by Soviet leader Mikhail S. Gorbachev in 1987; critics said such appearances should be reserved for world leaders who were friends of democracy.

The Constitution requires that Congress meet jointly every four years to count electoral votes for president and vice president. These meetings are called joint sessions. If no candidate receives a majority of the electoral vote, the House and Senate must vote separately to decide the outcome: The House chooses the president, the Senate the vice president. *(See* ELECTING THE PRESIDENT.*)*   ~

Judiciary Committee, House

Many divisive issues—abortion, gun control, and civil rights, to name just three—must begin their path through the House in its Judiciary Committee. While most committees concentrate on programs or dollars and cents, Judiciary often deals with raw emotion.

For more than three decades, the panel's leadership has been firmly in liberal hands. In the 1960s, that gave civil rights legislation a boost; in the 1970s and 1980s, the liberal advantage foiled conservatives seeking constitutional amendments to outlaw abortion

Impeachment Role
The Judiciary Committee deals with many divisive issues, such as abortion, gun control, and civil rights. The committee gained celebrity status in 1974 when it recommended impeachment of President Richard Nixon.

and busing and to permit school prayer. Critics have called Judiciary a "legislative mortuary."

Still, widespread support for an issue can overcome a reluctant committee. That happened in 1986, when advocates of looser gun control laws used the threat of a DISCHARGE PETITION to force the Judiciary Committee into action. Then, on the floor, the committee's moderate bill was replaced with a progun measure.

The Judiciary Committee helped draft a variety of laws in the 1980s. Voting rights laws were extended, anticrime and antidrug programs were passed, and the nation's immigration laws were overhauled. The committee failed in 1983 to push through a proposed Equal Rights Amendment to the Constitution, which would guarantee equal rights for men and women. A previous ERA proposal had failed of ratification in 1982. (See CONSTITUTIONAL AMENDMENTS.)

The Judiciary Committee gained celebrity status in 1974 when it voted three articles of IMPEACHMENT against President Richard Nixon. Nixon resigned before the House could act on the articles. Although Judiciary Chairman Peter W. Rodino, Jr., was at first criticized for moving slowly, the New Jersey Democrat was later praised for his evenhandedness. By avoiding a partisan approach, Rodino was able to pick up impeachment votes from Republicans. (See NIXON IMPEACHMENT EFFORT.)

One of the first standing committees created by the House, the Judiciary panel was made permanent in 1813. Because of its responsibility for handling constitutional amendments, the committee has participated in a large share of Congress's most difficult and important decisions over the years.

Judiciary had only two chairmen between the mid-1950s and the late 1980s: Rodino, who announced his retirement in 1988, and New York Democrat Emanuel Celler. No other House committee could make that claim. Celler first chaired the panel from 1949 until 1953, when Republicans gained the House majority. Then Celler again served as chairman from 1955 until 1972, when, at age eighty-four, he lost a bid for renomination. Rodino took over in 1973; he had been chairman for barely a year when the WATERGATE SCANDAL put Judiciary in the spotlight.

Under Celler's leadership, the committee spent most of the 1950s focused on antitrust violations and monopolies and then shifted to civil rights legislation in the 1960s. Celler's support of civil rights was crucial because the Senate JUDICIARY COMMITTEE was led by an ardent opponent of the legislation. Celler also was a key advocate of immigration reform, passed in 1965, and gun control. Considered an autocratic chairman, he shared little authority with subcommittees.

Rodino continued the tradition of liberal politics and, like Celler, kept action under his control, in the full committee. Cautious and deliberate, he usually focused on just a few issues in each Congress. Although a more philosophical, aggressive chairman might have served as a visible counterpoint to the Reagan administration's conservative social agenda, Rodino preferred to be a relatively quiet obstructionist. But Rodino still had a spark that could save faltering legislation; he used it in 1986 on immigration reform, when he successfully pressured key negotiators to keep talking.

The Judiciary Committee in 1986 handled the impeachment of an imprisoned federal district judge in Nevada. Nine of its members, including Rodino, then served as managers, or prosecutors, during the Senate trial. The judge,

Harry E. Claiborne, was the first official in fifty years to be removed from office by impeachment and the fifth in the history of the country.   ~

Judiciary Committee, Senate

Ideological issues dominate the Senate Judiciary Committee, making it a volatile panel that attracts activists from both ends of the political spectrum. Although committee members manage to compromise on some issues, they also have bitter fights, and the nation's disputes about sensitive issues are often played out in the committee.

One of the oldest Senate committees, dating from 1816, Judiciary has never ranked among the most powerful. Its jurisdiction encompasses constitutional amendments, the federal judiciary, immigration, antitrust laws, and civil liberties. An important duty is recommending to the Senate whether to confirm presidential nominations to the Supreme Court. About one out of five nominees is rejected by the full Senate. (See APPOINTMENT POWER.)

In contrast with the House JUDICIARY Committee, which has had liberal leadership since the 1950s, the Senate committee has had numerous shifts in its top post, from a conservative southern Democrat to a liberal northern Democrat, and then to a conservative southern Republican. In 1988 Democrat Joseph R. Biden, Jr., of Delaware took over the committee.

The focus of the Judiciary Committee can shift drastically depending on which leader is in charge. While the Senate was in Republican hands (1981-87), the committee pushed through the Senate two bills high on the conservative agenda. But the measures, to reestablish the federal death penalty and to add a balanced-budget amendment to the Constitution, died in the

House—and had little chance of resurrection in a Democratic-controlled Senate. Democrats on Judiciary brought their ideological split with the Reagan administration to the forefront in 1987 when they rejected one Supreme Court nominee and forced the withdrawal of a second.

Despite its internal disagreements, the committee has managed to compromise on many issues. In the mid-1980s both a major revision of the criminal code and an overhaul of the nation's immigration laws reflected cooperation between Republicans and Democrats. Dozens of federal judicial nominees have generated little controversy, although there have been exceptions.

The committee has not always reflected the political makeup of the full Senate. Two of President Richard NIXON's nominees to the Supreme Court, Clement F. Haynsworth, Jr., and G. Harrold Carswell, were endorsed by the Judiciary Committee and then rejected by the Senate. In 1987 the committee was more in step with the full Senate, which agreed with the committee and rejected Robert H. Bork, Reagan's choice for the Court.

For more than two decades, from 1956 to 1979, the Judiciary Committee was chaired by James O. Eastland, a conservative Mississippi Democrat known for his fervent obstruction of civil rights legislation. When the Senate leadership began setting deadlines for committee action on voting rights and other bills in the mid-1960s, Eastland called the rules "legislative lynching." He never wavered in his support of conservative causes, endorsing school prayer, opposing the ban on poll taxes, arguing against immigration reform, and voting against gun control. He once claimed in a Senate address that the Supreme Court was biased in favor of communism. As committee chairman, though, Eastland mellowed over the years; autocratic and protective of his power at first, Eastland was pressured

into letting subcommittees have more authority. He eventually developed a reputation for fairness and evenhandedness.

After Eastland's retirement, Massachusetts Democrat Edward M. Kennedy had two years as chairman, from 1979 to 1981. Distracted by his campaign for president, he never took advantage of the chairmanship to promote the liberal causes he supported. Kennedy won credit for working well with Republican Strom Thurmond of South Carolina when the latter became chairman in 1981.

Thurmond was in a position to take the chairmanship because he opted in 1977 for the top minority spot on Judiciary instead of Armed Services. That prevented the Judiciary post from going to Charles McC. Mathias, Jr., of Maryland, whose liberal leanings made Republican leaders nervous. When Republicans took over the Senate, and Thurmond became chairman, he went so far as to abolish an antitrust subcommittee Mathias was in line to head.

Biden, who became chairman in 1987, was thrust immediately into the spotlight by the controversial Bork nomination. He won praise from both sides for his steady handling of the hearings and later debate.　　～

Junkets.　　See FOREIGN TRAVEL.

Jurisdiction

Jurisdiction is the word used to denote a congressional committee's area of legislative responsibility. Committee jurisdictions, spelled out in each chamber's rules or other documents, guide the assignment of bills to committees for preliminary consideration in the House and Senate. Many bills do not fall within the subject area of a single committee, however; in that case, they may be referred to two or more committees before going to the floor.

Because jurisdictional boundaries are not always precise, committees sometimes compete for referral of an important bill. Or one committee may try to usurp legislative territory that another committee considers its own. An aggressive chairman who became known for his skill at seizing new jurisdictional territory was Rep. John D. Dingell, a Michigan Democrat who became chairman of the House ENERGY AND COMMERCE Committee in 1981. ~

Kefauver, Estes

Estes Kefauver (1903-63) was an independent-minded Tennessee Democrat who served in the House of Representatives from 1939 to 1949 and in the Senate from 1949 until his death in 1963. Kefauver was known for his populist rhetoric and liberal voting behavior; his political trademark was a coonskin cap. He rose to national prominence as chairman of a Senate committee INVESTIGATION of organized crime. The resulting publicity fueled Kefauver's presidential ambitions. He was an unsuccessful aspirant to that office in 1952 and 1956.

Kefauver won his House seat in a special election in 1939. As a representative, his particular interest was legislative reorganization; he presented his case for REFORM in his popular book, *A Twentieth-Century Congress*, published in 1947. The Legislative Reorganization Act of 1946 contained several reforms espoused by Kefauver, including regulation of LOBBYING and expansion of congressional STAFF.

Kefauver won his Senate seat in 1948 by defeating the powerful Crump machine of Memphis. As a senator, he championed civil liberties—he was one

of only seven senators to vote against the Internal Security Act of 1950—and concerned himself with antitrust issues. He urged the Senate to investigate organized crime and in 1950 became chairman of the Special Committee to Investigate Organized Crime in Interstate Commerce. The committee heard testimony from Mafia figures and well-known criminals. Hearings were held all around the country; many were televised. While the investigation highlighted crime problems, little legislation resulted.

Kefauver did well in the 1952 presidential primaries and was considered the most popular Democratic contender, but he lost the nomination to Adlai E. Stevenson at the national convention; his independence appealed to voters, but not to his party. Republican Dwight D. Eisenhower won the presidency that year. Kefauver again entered the primaries for the 1956 election, but he withdrew to support Stevenson's nomination. He was chosen to be Stevenson's running mate after a hard-fought contest with Sen. John F. KENNEDY of Massachusetts.

Returning to the Senate after Eisenhower's landslide win in 1956, Kefauver played a critical role in the adoption of the Twenty-fourth Amendment to the Constitution, which banned poll taxes. He continued to head congressional investigations, most notably into antitrust violations.   ~

Kennedy, John F.

John F. Kennedy's (1917-63) congressional career has been overshadowed by his term as president. Kennedy, a Massachusetts Democrat, served in the House of Representatives from 1947 to 1953 and in the Senate from 1953 to 1960. Much of his career in Congress was spent building a legisla-

Dynasty
John F. Kennedy was the first of three Kennedy brothers to serve in the Senate. He was followed by Edward, top right, and Robert, bottom right.

tive record that would serve him well when he sought higher office. He was elected to the presidency in 1960 and served from 1961 until his assassination on November 22, 1963.

Kennedy was a World War II hero and a member of a powerful political family. After a brief career as a journalist, he ran for the House in 1946. An indefatigable campaigner, he won handily and was returned twice to that office. During his tenure in the House (1947-53), he was preoccupied by serving the needs of his Massachusetts constituents. Liberal in his defense of labor and support of low-cost housing and other domestic issues, he was more conservative when voting on foreign policy measures. He sharply criticized the Truman administration for allowing communist rule in China and gave only grudging support to foreign aid proposals.

In 1952 Kennedy made a successful bid for the Senate seat held by Henry Cabot Lodge, Jr. Although Dwight D. Eisenhower carried the state in that year's presidential election, Kennedy captured the Senate seat from the Republican incumbent with little difficulty. Once in the Senate, Kennedy began to emphasize national issues over northeastern concerns. In 1954 he voted for the St. Lawrence Seaway, a project that his general constituency opposed.

His seat on the Foreign Relations Committee, achieved in 1957, gave him a base from which to criticize the foreign policy of the Eisenhower administration. During his Senate tenure (1953-60), while convalescing from a grave operation, Kennedy wrote *Profiles in Courage*, sketches of senators who had followed their consciences over the wishes of their constituents.

Kennedy was denied the Democratic nomination for vice president in 1956 in a floor fight at the party's national convention. In 1960 his party nominated him for president, and he won over Richard NIXON by a very slim margin. As president, his most notable achievements were in the area of foreign affairs; his domestic program was planned but not fully implemented during his lifetime. He died, the victim of an assassination, in Dallas, Texas, in 1963.

Two of John Kennedy's brothers served in Congress after his death. Robert F. Kennedy, who had been attorney general in his brother's administration, was a senator from 1965 until his own death on June 6, 1968; he was assassinated while campaigning for the Democratic presidential nomination. Edward M. Kennedy entered the Senate in 1962; despite repeated efforts to win the Democratic presidential nomination, he was unable to capture the prize.   ～

Overleaf:
Lobbying then and now: civil rights, 1860s; MX missile, 1980s.

Labor and Human Resources Committee, Senate

Among the most liberal committees in the Senate, the Labor and Human Resources Committee has been a key advocate of the federal health, welfare, and education programs it helped create in the 1960s and 1970s. The committee's dogged defense of social programs has not always been successful. Congress cut some programs and consolidated others during the 1980s. But even Utah Republican Orrin G. Hatch, who chaired the committee from 1981 to 1987, was unable to win enough committee votes to carry out fully his—and the Reagan administration's—goals of curbing social spending and easing workplace rules.

More telling, though, as a measure of the committee's standing and power, was the bleak outlook for any new social programs. Democratic control of the Senate, regained in 1987, did not mean a return to the days when the Labor Committee could champion expansive—and expensive—social programs. Major new initiatives were simply not possible because of the growing federal budget deficit. Even popular ideas, such as aid for day care and protection against catastrophic health costs, prompted the question: Where will the money come from?

When concern mounted about the

37 million Americans without health insurance, the solution proposed by Labor Committee members was not national health insurance, though many approved of the idea. Instead, supporters such as Massachusetts Democrat Edward M. Kennedy suggested that employers be required to offer coverage to their workers, an approach that would not involve any cost to the federal Treasury.

It was ironic—and frustrating for the committee—that a broad consensus for social programs had been reached at the same time federal funds were drying up. Just three decades before, Congress had bitterly debated a limited federal commitment to education and health care. By the late 1980s the situation was much different; even Hatch and other conservatives had endorsed a federal role in providing child care. The price tag, though, was still a problem.

No similar consensus was reached on labor issues. Even traditional labor legislation such as an increase in the minimum wage was on hold during Hatch's chairmanship. Labor's star had been in decline since the late 1970s. In 1978 Hatch had been a major figure in a filibuster that killed a reform bill designed to make it easier for unions to organize.

On education and labor issues, the Labor Committee is the key Senate panel. On many health and welfare issues, though, it has been overshadowed by the Finance Committee. Finance has jurisdiction over Medicare, Medicaid, and Social Security, as well as Aid to Families with Dependent Children, the primary federal income program for the poor. These programs comprise the largest chunk of federal spending for health and welfare; only a portion remains for the Labor Committee, despite its overall responsibility for health and welfare policy. The National Institutes of Health, subsidized school lunches, and Head Start are among the variety of programs the committee handles.

One agency overseen by the committee, the Community Services Administration, was abolished by Congress in 1981.

History

The committee was set up in 1869 as the Education and Labor Committee. The 1946 Senate reorganization gave it a new title, Labor and Public Welfare. Another reform, in 1977, renamed the committee Human Resources. The new title was in effect only two years, though; labor advocates convinced the Senate to call the committee Labor and Human Resources.

The legacy of the NEW DEAL guided the Labor Committee as it pursued a gradual expansion of the federal social role. A key advocate of that view was Lister Hill, an Alabama Democrat who chaired the committee from 1955 to 1969. Although typical of southerners in his opposition to civil rights laws, Hill had a liberal view of social programs and often backed health proposals opposed by the medical establishment. He favored federal aid for medical research, hospital construction, and training of doctors and nurses. Hill's authority was enhanced because he also chaired the Appropriations subcommittee that handled labor, health, and welfare spending.

In the 1970s New Jersey Democrat Harrison A. Williams, Jr., chaired the committee, continuing the liberal tradition. An early proponent of safety in the workplace, Williams worked with labor leaders on a number of issues, not always with success. Williams's career in Congress was forever colored by his conviction on charges that included bribery and influence peddling. When a Senate vote to expel him seemed certain, Williams resigned his seat in 1982.

Hatch, who became chairman when Republicans gained control of the Senate in 1981, headed a committee that often deadlocked on votes, with Republicans Lowell P. Weicker, Jr., of

Connecticut and Robert T. Stafford of Vermont frequently voting with Democrats. Despite Hatch's reputation as a strident conservative, however, he worked with his colleagues to find acceptable compromises. He quickly learned that his more controversial proposals, such as establishment of a separate, lower minimum wage for young people, had no chance of approval. Kennedy, passing up the chairmanship of the JUDICIARY Committee, became chairman of Labor and Human Resources in 1987.   ~

La Follette, Robert M., Sr.

Robert M. La Follette, Sr. (1855-1925), was one of the founders of the progressive wing of the Republican party. Progressivism's basic themes of regulation of business, conservation, and dislike of machine politics surfaced in the late nineteenth century.

La Follette was elected to the House of Representatives as a Republican from Wisconsin in 1884. During his years in the House he was not distinguished for the independence and enthusiasm for reform that he later manifested. In 1890 La Follette lost his bid for reelection in a wave of Republican defeats, and he resumed practicing law in Wisconsin.

In the decade after his defeat, La Follette formulated a series of reform proposals that he worked to implement when he became governor of Wisconsin in 1901. He believed that businesses should bear a heavier burden of taxation consistent with that borne by other sectors. To challenge machine-ruled political conventions, he espoused political primaries. La Follette also supported increased regulation and oversight of the railroads. These proposals were eventually accepted by the state legislature; known as the "Wisconsin Idea," they were eventually copied by other states.

La Follette left the statehouse to become a U.S. senator in 1906. His brand of Republicanism was very different from that of the conservative ruling clique led by Nelson W. ALDRICH of Rhode Island. He opposed Aldrich on several occasions—including, spectacularly, his FILIBUSTER on an Aldrich currency bill in 1908. La Follette held the floor for eighteen hours and twenty-three minutes, one of the longest individual filibusters in the history of the Senate.

As a senator, La Follette championed public ownership of the railroads, once inserting a 365-page speech on railroad rates in the *CONGRESSIONAL RECORD*. Known as an "insurgent," La Follette so angered the "stalwart" faction of Senate Republicans that on one occasion they voted to elect a Democratic representative as chairman of the Interstate Commerce Committee rather than have La Follette assume that position. However, the Senate refused to expel him for sedition in 1917 when petitioned to do so by the Minneapolis Public Safety Commission. La Follette had given a speech in St. Paul criticizing U.S. involvement in World War I.

Twice an unsuccessful candidate for the Republican nomination for president, in 1908 and 1912, La Follette ran on the Progressive ticket in 1924. He lost but garnered 16 percent of the popular vote.

La Follette died in office in June 1925. Two months later he was succeeded by his son, Robert M. La Follette, Jr. ("Young Bob"), who served in the Senate until 1947.   ~

Lame-Duck Amendment

The Twentieth, or "Lame-Duck," Amendment to the Constitution estab-

Sen. George W. Norris

lishes the beginning date and frequency of sessions of Congress. The amendment requires the House and Senate to meet at least once a year, and it specifies January 3 as the opening date for each congressional session unless members select another date. Members' terms begin and end on January 3. *(See* TERMS AND SESSIONS OF CONGRESS.*)*

The amendment also sets the date for the inauguration every four years of the president and vice president: January 20 of the year following the election. Previously, both presidential and congressional terms had begun and ended on March 4. Other sections of the amendment outline Congress's authority in certain cases involving the death of a president-elect.

The Lame-Duck Amendment was added to the Constitution in 1933, after a decade-long struggle by its chief sponsor, Sen. George W. NORRIS, a Nebraska Republican. It got its nickname because it was an attack on the longstanding practice of "lame-duck" sessions of Congress. In congressional jargon, a lame duck is a member who serves out the balance of his term after being defeated or not seeking reelection.

From its earliest days, Congress followed a lopsided schedule that gave ample opportunities for lame ducks to wield considerable influence long after they had been rejected by their constituents. Under the traditional practice, which lasted more than 140 years, the first session of each two-year-long Congress began in December of odd-numbered years. That session, which opened more than a year following the election, customarily lasted for six months or so.

The second, "short" session of a Congress typically began in December of the even-numbered years. That session, which ran until March 4 of the following year, was known as the lame-duck session because it was conducted after the election for the succeeding Congress had already been held. As a result, many of the members who served in these sessions were lame ducks.

The traditional schedule had many drawbacks and was widely criticized for a century before finally being changed. The long delay in beginning each Congress slowed the government's response to public opinion as expressed through the elections. Presidents were able to make recess appointments and other moves without any interference from Congress. *(See* APPOINTMENT POWER.*)*

In addition to allowing defeated members to retain power for a few more months, the short sessions also were rarely productive. The fixed adjournment date was an invitation to FILIBUSTER, and members frequently took advantage of it as the session drew to a close. Merely by talking long enough, members could kill a bill by blocking action until the old Congress expired.

The short session survived for decades, however, because it was also advantageous to congressional leaders, particularly in the House. House leaders liked the short session because its automatic termination strengthened their ability to control the legislative output of the House. The House Republican leadership was to be the strongest opponent of the proposed Twentieth Amendment during more than ten years of congressional debate.

History

The practice of having long and short sessions of Congress evolved early in its history. The First Congress met for the first time on March 4, 1789, and soon decided that congressional terms would begin and end on that date each year. But the Constitution had directed that Congress should meet each year early in December. The congressional schedule soon accommodated both requirements by use of a schedule with long and short sessions.

Congresses in subsequent decades sometimes were called into special session by the president, and on numerous occasions they fixed earlier dates for meeting. But the basic pattern of long and short sessions did not change much.

Dissatisfaction with lame-duck sessions grew more intense in the early twentieth century. The use of the filibuster—greatly facilitated by the short session—was seen by reformers as a major obstacle to legislative progress. During the Wilson administration (1913-21), each of four second sessions of Congress ended with a Senate filibuster and the loss of important legislation.

Norris advocated a revision of the congressional schedule to abolish lame-duck sessions as a way of undermining use of the filibuster. His plan was in the form of a constitutional amendment, because the founding document specifically mentioned the first week in December as the opening date for a congressional session. Norris's amendment ended the gap between the start of congressional terms and the opening day of annual sessions, by putting both in early January.

The Norris amendment was popular in the Senate, which was searching at this time for ways to constrain the legislative havoc created by the filibuster tactic. The amendment was first passed by the Senate in 1923, on a 63-7 vote that far exceeded the two-thirds majority needed for approval.

However, the plan soon ran into trouble in the House. The Senate joint resolution was approved by the House Election Committee, and won the support of a majority of members of the RULES COMMITTEE, whose approval was necessary for floor consideration of the measure. But Rules Chairman Philip P. Campbell, a Kansas Republican who was himself a lame duck, refused to act on the resolution, and the proposal died for that session.

A similar pattern was evident in consideration of the Norris amendment for many years. The Senate approved the amendment six times before it finally won House approval. In the Sixty-eighth Congress (1923-25), the Senate-passed measure was again blocked in the Rules Committee, causing Norris to charge that his amendment was "being held up because machine politicians can get more out of this [legislative] jam than the people's representatives can get."

When the Norris amendment did reach the House floor, in 1929, a majority of members supported it. But the 209-157 vote for the proposal was short of the two-thirds majority required under the Constitution. In 1931 the House passed an amended version of the Norris plan, but the House and Senate could not agree on a final version, and it died.

The Democratic takeover of the House in the 1930 elections cleared the way for final approval of the amendment. The Senate adopted the joint resolution on January 6, 1932, and the House followed a month later with a 335-56 vote. The amendment became part of the Constitution less than a year later, when it had been ratified by three-quarters of the states. (See CONSTITUTIONAL AMENDMENTS.)

The amendment also acted to reduce the potential disarray produced by postponing a new president's assumption of office for four months after the November elections. It did so by moving the inauguration date to January 20, from March 4. The dangers created by that long delay were shown by the inauguration that took place even while the amendment was still in the process of being ratified. After the 1932 election, president-elect Franklin D. Roosevelt was not able to take over from defeated incumbent Herbert Hoover for four months. During that period, the Depression-wracked, nearly leaderless nation veered to the edge of economic catastrophe. *(See* NEW DEAL.*)*   ∼

Lame-Duck Session

A lame-duck session of Congress is one held after a successor Congress is elected in November of an even-numbered year but before it is sworn in the following January. Senators and representatives who have been rejected at the polls can vote in a postelection session, as can those who are about to retire from Congress by choice. Such members are known as lame ducks.

Lame-duck sessions are not noted for their legislative accomplishments. They frequently bog down in partisan bickering, especially if party control of one or both chambers is about to shift in the new Congress. Before adoption of the Twentieth, LAME-DUCK AMENDMENT to the Constitution in 1933, postelection sessions were a regular feature of the congressional calendar. The amendment advanced the starting date of a new Congress to January from March. No further postelection sessions were held until after World War II. Six were held between 1945 and 1988.

Among the notable lame-duck sessions since World War II was one in 1950, when Congress met in a marathon session to act on a "must" agenda presented by President Harry S Truman; the session ended only a few hours before the new Congress took over. In 1954 the Senate alone reconvened and voted to censure Sen. Joseph R. McCARTHY, a Wisconsin Republican whose anticommunist INVESTIGATIONS had rocked the nation. In a 1974 lame-duck session Congress approved the nomination of Nelson A. Rockefeller as vice president under President Gerald R. Ford and passed several major bills. *(See* APPOINTMENT POWER.*)*   ∼

Laws

Each bill that is passed and signed by the president, or passed over his veto, becomes a law. Eventually the law is incorporated into the *U.S. Code,* which is organized according to subject matter and divided into titles, chapters, and sections. The Code is updated annually by the Law Revision Counsel, a congressional office, and a new set of bound volumes is published every six years. *(See* LEGISLATION.*)*

Laws are also given numbers separate from their designation in the *U.S. Code.* A new series of numbers is assigned at the beginning of each two-year term of Congress; the first public law passed in the 100th Congress (1987-89) was labeled Public Law 100-1, or PL 100-1. Private laws, which deal with individuals and not the general public, have a separate numbering system: Private Law 100-1, etc. Laws are also referred to by their formal titles—the Legislative Reorganization Act of 1946, for example, or the Ethics in Government Act of 1978.

Although a bill technically becomes an "act" as soon as it is passed by one chamber of Congress, the term is generally reserved for measures that have become law. "Statute" is used interchangeably with "law."

At the end of each session of Congress, all of the public and private laws, as well as concurrent resolutions, are compiled and published as *U.S. Statutes at Large* by the Office of the Federal Register, which is part of the National Archives and Records Administration. Throughout the year, the same office publishes "slip laws," which are pamphlets containing the text of a bill as enacted and a summary of its legislative history. In the margin, alongside the legal language, are notes that identify a section as dealing with a particular subject.   ~

Leadership

Leadership is the term used to describe, collectively, the Democratic and Republican leaders in Congress and their lieutenants. The leaders are charged with getting Congress to support their party's goals; they also are responsible for operating Congress as an institution. Whichever party commands a majority in a chamber has primary direction of its operations.

In both the House and Senate, the organizations of party members, known as conferences or caucuses, vote on top leaders at the start of each two-year term of Congress. The elected leaders then make several key appointments to complete the leadership structure of each party. Committee chairmen, always from the majority party, are also part of the leadership. Nominated by party leadership groups, usually on the basis of seniority, they must win approval from the party caucuses. (*See* CAUCUSES, PARTY; COMMITTEE SYSTEM.)

Control over legislative activity is a powerful tool for leaders of the majority party. If they oppose a bill, they can usually keep it from coming to the floor, while a measure they favor gets top priority. Though the minority's influence declines with its share of House and Senate seats, minority leaders can also help, or hurt, the progress of legislation.

The power of the majority leadership is particularly pronounced in the House, where strict rules govern floor debate. Strong leaders are able to orchestrate the way the rules are applied and enforced in order to benefit party-backed legislation. In the Senate the rights of minority members are protected by tradition; they can bottle up legislative work with FILIBUSTERS and other delaying tactics. As a result, leaders of the Senate majority, anxious to avoid such obstructions, are usually more sensitive to the minority's viewpoint than those in the House.

The structure and practices of congressional leadership have evolved gradually. The Constitution established a PRESIDING OFFICER for each chamber, but other leaders have little written authority for their roles. Their positions and duties are based on tradition within the parties rather than formal rules that apply to Congress as a whole.

In acknowledgment of their special duties, top party leaders receive additional pay, enjoy spacious offices in the Capitol, and are allotted extra funds to hire staff. A car and driver are usually assigned to each. (*Leadership lists, see pp. 475-86*)

House
Speaker The most visible and prestigious officer within Congress is the SPEAKER OF THE HOUSE. The Constitution made him presiding officer of the House; custom has made him also the leader of the majority party in the chamber.

The Speaker is formally elected by the House at the start of each two-year term of Congress. The House chooses between candidates selected by the party caucuses, and the vote follows party lines. The majority's candidate becomes Speaker, and the minority's candidate becomes minority leader.

The modern Speaker is often the chief spokesman for his party nationally, as well as the leader of its members in the House. Most of the time he does not actually preside over floor debates but delegates that role to another member of his party. In practice, the Speaker takes the chair primarily when matters he considers important are before the House. Then his authority to recognize members, resolve disputes over rules, and oversee roll-call votes may be used to partisan advantage.

The Speaker traditionally gives up his seats on legislative committees. He rarely votes, except to break a tie.

In the 1800s the Speaker was often a forceful orator, elected because of his ability to command attention and articulate ideas. Seniority, or length of service—so much a factor in later years—was hardly considered. Henry CLAY was elected Speaker the day he entered in the House in 1811. In contrast, since 1925 every Speaker has first served as majority or minority leader.

Before the two political parties became dominant, the candidates' stands on certain issues often turned the contest. Slavery, in particular, had a role in several elections of Speaker. The 1855 race was so bitterly divided by the slavery question that resolving it took two months—and 133 ballots. By the twentieth century, with the Democratic and Republican parties well established, topical issues were rarely a factor in the contests, and the Speaker emerged from the most senior and most loyal party members.

Twice in this century the Speaker's role has undergone substantial changes. In 1910 the House revolted against the autocratic rule of Speaker Joseph G. CANNON and sharply curtailed the Speaker's powers. Power shifted to committee chairmen and the RULES COMMITTEE, which had been freed from the Speaker's domination. In the 1970s

the Speaker regained some of the authority he had lost sixty years earlier. *(See* REFORM; CAUCUSES, PARTY.*)*

Floor Leaders The floor leaders for each party are responsible for handling legislation once it reaches the full House; they oversee debate, amendments, and voting. Floor leaders traditionally give up their seats on legislative committees, but there have been exceptions.

The majority leader is the No. 2 official in the House. The post was not formally created until 1899. Previously, the chairman of the Ways and Means Committee served so often as floor manager that he was considered the deputy leader. The Speaker chose the majority leader until Democrats gained control of the House in 1911, when that authority was shifted to the Democratic Caucus. In most cases the majority leader has continued to be the Speaker's chief lieutenant, rather than a rival.

The minority leader is the minority party's top official. Since the post first became identifiable in 1883, the minority leader has always been that party's nominee for Speaker. The minority leader monitors floor activity but can only try to influence scheduling, as he has no direct control over it. He also serves as top party spokesman and performs other duties that the Speaker handles for the majority party.

Whips Ranking after the majority and minority leaders are the whips, first officially designated in 1899 with a term borrowed from the British Parliament. The whips try to convince party members to follow the leadership's program.

The whips also handle the mechanics of polling members on both their views on issues and their stands on specific floor votes. They inform members about upcoming floor action and make sure members are present for tight votes. Whips and their assistants sometimes stand at the door of the House chamber, signaling the leadership's

The Johnson Treatment
As Senate majority leader, Lyndon B. Johnson had an extraordinary ability to persuade, in one-on-one encounters, through sheer force of will.

position on a vote by holding their thumbs up—or down.

Whips are elected by each party. The Democratic whip was appointed by the Speaker and majority leader until 1987, when the Democratic Caucus voted to make the office elective. The Republican whip has traditionally been elected by the GOP conference.

Each party has designated numerous members as assistants to the whips. In the 100th Congress (1987-89) the Democratic whip had an organization of eighty-nine members, including a chief deputy whip, ten deputy whips, and nineteen zone whips, each of whom represented—and focused on—a specific area of the country. Republicans had a chief deputy whip, five deputy whips, and four regional whips; each regional whip had four assistant regional whips to share oversight of a geographic area.

Party Committees House Democrats have a Steering and Policy Committee, a thirty-one-member panel that makes committee assignments and helps develop party strategy and programs. The top elected leaders, chairmen of key committees, and several legislators appointed by the Speaker serve with twelve regional representatives on the policy committee.

Republicans split among three committees the duties handled by one Democratic panel. The minority leader chairs the Republican Committee on Committees, and two other legislators chair the Republican Policy Committee and Republican Research Committee.

Both parties also have congressional campaign committees that raise and donate funds to party candidates. In the House, these are the Democratic Congressional Campaign Committee and the National Republican Congressional Committee. The campaign committees, appointed in part by party leaders, solicit donations and then distribute the money, as they choose, to candidates for Congress. The first con-

gressional campaign committee was formed in protest against the national party committee in the mid-nineteenth century. Radical Republicans opposed to President Andrew Johnson, who ran the national committee, set up their own group. Democrats soon adopted the practice. *(See* CAMPAIGN FINANCING.*)*

Senate

Presiding Officers No post comparable to Speaker exists in the Senate. The Constitution named the vice president "president of the Senate" and authorized him to vote in case of a tie. But the vice president, who is elected as a member of the executive branch, is the president's man; his party affiliation may differ from that of the Senate majority. In modern practice, the vice president seldom visits the Capitol. He presides over the Senate on infrequent occasions, such as when it appears his vote might be needed to break a tie.

The Constitution also directed the Senate to elect a president pro tempore (president for the time being) to handle the vice president's duties in his absence. The Senate has not given much parliamentary authority to the president pro tem; he does preside or select a substitute to oversee floor debate. Until 1890 the post was filled, on a temporary basis, only when the vice president was absent. During some sessions no president pro tempore was appointed. Since 1945 custom has given the job to the member of the majority party with the longest record of Senate service.

Floor Leaders, Whips Both Democrats and Republicans developed a formal post of floor leader in the late 1890s, though official titles were not conferred until about 1911. The position of whip was established by Democrats in 1913, and by Republicans in 1915. Duties and roles are less institutionalized than they are in the House. The leadership's authority has been hampered by the Senate tradition of giving strong rights to individual senators, instead of to any group. The majority leader schedules floor action in consultation with the minority leader, and much of the Senate's business is conducted by unanimous consent of the members.

Party Committees The Democratic leader chairs the party's Policy Committee, Steering Committee, and Conference. However, the Conference secretary, who is elected by his colleagues, handles most aspects of that organization's business. Republicans elect other senators, not the top leader, to chair their Policy Committee and the Republican Conference.

Neither party has its top leader chair the campaign committees, known as the Democratic Senatorial Campaign Committee and the National Republican Senatorial Committee.

Leadership Tactics

Modern senators and representatives rarely follow their leaders blindly and often take pride in their independence. To encourage a strong party alliance, party leaders can use a number of rewards—and a few punishments. A legislator who votes with his party might be rewarded with a better committee assignment or a visit by party leaders to his district at campaign time. A pet program could be handled sympathetically by a committee or attached to an important bill heading for the floor.

Leaders are also aware of the local slant on everyday congressional business; they can steer to a loyal member what his district or state needs, whether it is a tax break for a key industry, a new flood control project, or an exemption from clean air rules. Campaign funds are also spread judiciously to encourage loyalty.

Punishment for disloyal behavior can be subtle. A member's bid for a local dam or his scheme to revamp na-

tional education grants could languish in an unresponsive committee. A request to switch committees or add another staff member could be denied. In rare cases, legislators have been stripped of committee seniority or a committee post for repeatedly betraying the party position. Democratic leaders removed Texas Rep. Phil Gramm from his seat on the House Budget Committee in 1983, after Gramm masterminded enactment of budgets proposed by Republican President Ronald Reagan. Gramm resigned his House seat, won reelection as a Republican, and soon rejoined the committee as a GOP member.

The need to satisfy diverse groups within their party has kept congressional leaders from taking bold political stands. An emphasis on ideology would split the party. Ironically, an almost apolitical role—sharing information—has become a vital way of building party unity. Background reports and whip advisories prepared by the leadership are a key link in the network of party members.

Congressional leaders often serve as national party spokesmen, publicizing their party's programs and achievements. Their role becomes especially visible when the president is of the opposing party. Critics have pointed to this role in complaining about the practice, particularly among Democrats, of promoting the next in line when the party's top leadership post is open. Party leaders are not always noted for their charisma or ability to articulate party policy, shortcomings less important within Congress than outside it.

Personal style can contribute or detract from a leader's effectiveness. In his ten years as House Speaker (1977-87), Massachusetts Democrat Thomas P. O'NEILL, Jr., depended on close personal relationships and a warm, friendly manner to win support. A game of golf with colleagues was O'Neill's way of building close ties. His Democratic counterpart in the Senate, West Virginian Robert C. BYRD, had a very different style. Byrd's management of the Senate was based on careful understanding of its procedures. "I did not get elected to be liked here," Byrd told the Senate in 1987. "I got elected because I thought I could do a job."

Jim Wright, a Texas Democrat who became Speaker in 1987, was a backslapper with a broad grin and confident manner. Wright's early handling of the job made it easy to forget how narrowly he won his first job on the leadership ladder in 1976. In an unusual public session of the Democratic Caucus, Wright needed three ballots to knock out three other candidates for majority leader, eventually winning by only one vote over Phillip Burton, a liberal California Democrat who served from 1964 until his death in 1983.

Among Senate Republicans, Howard H. BAKER, Jr., of Tennessee brought an open personal style to the floor leader's job, which he held from 1979 to 1985. His steady, low-key performance stood in sharp contrast to that of his father-in-law, Everett McKinley DIRKSEN of Illinois, who was Republican leader from 1961 to 1970. Dirksen's florid style and distinctive bass voice caused him to be called the "Wizard of Ooze."

As Senate majority leader from 1955 to 1961, Lyndon B. JOHNSON was known for his extraordinary ability to persuade colleagues to support him. In one-on-one encounters Johnson applied "the treatment," cajoling, touching an arm or shoulder for emphasis, leaning closer to make a point. The treatment, wrote Johnson biographers Rowland Evans and Robert Novak, was "an almost hypnotic experience [that] rendered the target stunned and helpless."

Johnson was a protégé of another forceful personality, fellow Texan and Democrat Sam RAYBURN, who served a record seventeen years as Speaker (plus four years as minority leader) between 1940 and 1961. Like Johnson, Rayburn demanded loyalty and responded ruthlessly to disobedience. He skillfully mixed political and personal relations, gathering favorite colleagues in a hideaway Capitol office to share a drink and stories. This "board of education," for teaching and learning, carried on a tradition begun by another House Speaker, Republican Nicholas LONGWORTH of Ohio, who ran the House from 1925 until 1931.   ~

ADDITIONAL READINGS

Cheney, Richard B., and Lynne V. Cheney. *Kings of the Hill: Power and Personality in the House of Representatives.* 1983.
Davidson, Roger H., and Walter J. Oleszek. *Congress and Its Members.* 2d ed. 1985.
Peabody, Robert L. *Leadership in Congress: Stability, Succession, and Change.* 1976.
Sinclair, Barbara. *Majority Leadership in the U.S. House.* 1983.

Legislation

Congress uses various types of legislation to differentiate how the thousands of bills and resolutions introduced each term are handled by the committees and scheduled for floor action. Different types of legislation receive different kinds of treatment. *(See* LEGISLATIVE PROCESS.*)*

Each chamber uses four parallel types of legislation. Two types, bills and joint resolutions, become law if passed in identical form by both houses and signed by the president. In the House of Representatives, these measures are labeled HR for a bill, and H J Res for a joint resolution. In the Senate, S denotes a bill and S J Res a joint resolution.

Every legislative proposal is given a number that reflects the order in which it is introduced during each two-year congressional term (HR 1, 2, 3, etc.; S 1, 2, 3, etc.). If passed and signed by the president, a bill that is public in nature gets another number—a public law (PL) number. Public law numbers also include the Congress in which they are enacted, as in PL 100-1, which identifies the first public law enacted in the 100th Congress. *(See* LAWS.*)*

The vast majority of legislative proposals—recommendations dealing with either domestic or foreign issues and programs affecting the United States government or the population generally—are drafted in the form of bills. These include both AUTHORIZATION and APPROPRIATIONS legislation.

Joint resolutions—the other form of legislation that can become law—have a more limited focus, though occasionally they may be used for omnibus legislation. Proposed CONSTITUTIONAL AMENDMENTS also are drafted in the form of joint resolutions, as are some emergency and catchall appropriations measures. In addition, routine, uncontroversial measures making technical or minor changes in existing law or correcting errors in newly enacted legislation may be drafted as joint resolutions.

There are no significant differences in consideration of joint resolutions and bills. Both must be passed in identical form by the House and Senate and signed by the president to become law. There is one major exception: Joint resolutions embodying proposed constitutional amendments are not sent to the president for his signature after they have been approved by Congress (by a two-thirds vote in each house). Instead, they are forwarded directly to the fifty states for ratification, which requires approval by a three-fourths majority (thirty-eight states).

One other form of legislation can be enacted into law: private bills (also labeled either HR or S), which, if enacted, have a separately numbered system of laws. Private bills deal primarily with matters for the relief of individuals or private parties and are not of a general nature affecting the nation. Immigration cases and grievances or claims against the United States comprise the largest categories of private bills today.

The other two forms of legislation are concurrent resolutions and, simply, resolutions. These are labeled H Con Res and H Res in the House, S Con Res and S Res in the Senate. Concurrent resolutions and resolutions, unlike bills and joint resolutions, are not signed by the president, do not become law, and thus do not receive PL numbers. Concurrent resolutions are internal measures of Congress and are considered only by the House and the Senate. Simple resolutions are considered only by the house in which they are introduced.

House and Senate concurrent resolutions address matters involving Congress itself as well as some wider issues that do not require the president's signature. An example of the former category are the so-called sense of Congress resolutions—expressions of congressional sentiment that do not have the force of law. Of potentially greater impact are the second category of concurrent resolutions, such as the annual congressional budget resolutions setting Congress's revenue and spending goals for the upcoming fiscal year. These are drafted as concurrent resolutions because they are not binding on the federal government and thus do not have to become law. Instead, they are only statements of congressional intent or expressions of Congress's budgetary priorities.

House and Senate resolutions deal with internal matters of each chamber, often of a housekeeping nature. For example, resolutions are used periodically to set the spending levels for the various legislative committees or to revise the standing rules of each chamber. In the

House, resolutions also embody the "rules" granted by the RULES COMMITTEE setting the guidelines for floor debate on each bill.

Introducing Bills

Legislation can be introduced only by senators and representatives and only when Congress is in session. All bills must be printed and made available to the public as well as to members of Congress. There is no limit on the number of cosponsors a bill or resolution may have or on the number of bills a member may introduce. Once introduced, assigned a number, and printed, a bill is referred to the appropriate legislative committee.

Frequently, identical legislation is introduced in both houses. So-called companion bills are employed primarily to speed the legislation through Congress by encouraging both houses to consider the measure simultaneously. Sponsors of companion bills also may hope to dramatize the importance or urgency of the issue and show broad support for the legislation.

Major legislation goes through changes in nomenclature as it works its way through the legislative process. When a measure is introduced and first printed, it is officially referred to as a bill, and so labeled. When the bill has been passed by one house and sent to the other body it is then reprinted and officially labeled an act. If cleared by Congress and signed by the president, it becomes a law (and also may still be referred to as an act).

When legislation is heavily amended in committee, all the changes, deletions, and additions, together with whatever is left of the original bill, may be organized into a new bill. Such measures, which are reintroduced and given a new bill number, are referred to as clean bills. For parliamentary reasons, this procedure is a timesaver once the bill reaches the floor of either house. If the original bill, with all the changes, is considered by the House or Senate, every change made in committee must be voted on individually. As a clean bill, all the changes made in committee become part of the new bill, with only one vote needed to approve it, unless additional amendments are introduced from the floor.

Treaties

In the Senate, a unique type of resolution known as a resolution of ratification is used for consideration of treaties. These resolutions have their own special labeling system. Instead of being identified by a number, resolutions of ratification are listed in alphabetical order: Exec (for Executive) A, B, C, etc., along with the Congress and the session in which they are submitted. For example: Exec A, 100th Cong., 2d Sess.

Of all the varieties of legislation used by Congress, resolutions of ratification are the only ones that do not lapse at the end of the Congress in which they are introduced. If not acted upon by the Senate, these resolutions are held by the Senate FOREIGN RELATIONS Committee and may be brought before the Senate during any future Congress. (The Senate also can show its lack of enthusiasm for a treaty by voting to return it to the president.) Approval of resolutions of ratification requires a two-thirds vote of senators present. The House does not participate in the ratification process. (*See* TREATY RATIFICATION.)   ~

Legislation Declared Unconstitutional

The right to review acts of Congress to determine whether they are constitutional was asserted by the Supreme Court early in its history and has been an accepted fact ever since. It serves as a constant reminder to Congress that the laws it passes will be measured against the provisions of the Constitution and nullified if found in conflict.

The Missouri Compromise, a federal income tax, child labor laws, New Deal statutes, and the LEGISLATIVE VETO—a device used by Congress to block executive branch actions—are some notable examples of laws struck down by the Court. But cases such as these are rare.

Of the thousands of federal laws enacted, only 123 had been invalidated in whole or in part by 1988. And of these, only a handful were laws of major significance for Congress, the Court, and the country.

The Court invalidated only two statutes from 1789 to 1865. But as Congress began to exercise its powers more fully in the late nineteenth century, the number of federal laws declared unconstitutional increased. Political scientist Lawrence Baum has identified two periods in which the Court has been in major conflict with Congress.

From 1918 to 1936, the Court overturned twenty-nine laws, many of which were important pieces of legislation. Included among these were statute after statute of President Franklin D. Roosevelt's NEW DEAL program.

From 1963 through 1988, fifty laws were overturned. In contrast to the earlier period, few of these were major laws, and much of the legislation was rather old. There were, of course, exceptions. In addition to the 1983 legislative veto decision, the Court struck down provisions of campaign finance legislation in 1976, a new bankruptcy court system in 1982, and an antideficit statute's method for automatic budget cuts in 1986. *(See* CAMPAIGN FINANCING; BUDGET PROCESS.*)*

Judicial Review

Although the Constitution made no mention of judicial review, many con-

stitutional scholars agree that most of the authors of the document intended the Supreme Court to determine whether acts of Congress conformed to the Constitution. But the question of whether the Court could actually nullify an act of Congress as unconstitutional remained unanswered until 1803. At that time, a rather minor political controversy over a presidential appointment turned into what many regard as the most important decision in the Supreme Court's history—*Marbury v. Madison. (See also* COURTS AND CONGRESS.*)*

After Democratic-Republican Thomas Jefferson had defeated Federalist John Adams for reelection to the presidency in 1800—but before the Republicans took office—Adams nominated a number of Federalists to judicial posts created by legislation passed by the lame-duck Federalist Congress.

The nominations were confirmed by the Senate and the commissions signed by Adams, but not all were delivered before Jefferson entered office. When Jefferson ordered that these commissions be withheld, William Marbury, who had been named justice of the peace for the District of Columbia, asked the Supreme Court to order Jefferson's secretary of state, James MADISON, to deliver the commission. Marbury filed suit under the Judiciary Act of 1789, which empowered the Court to issue writs of *mandamus* compelling federal officials to perform their duties.

The Supreme Court, led by Chief Justice John Marshall, held that Marbury should have received his commission but that the Court lacked the power to order that the commission be delivered. The Court ruled that the provision of the Judiciary Act empowering the Court to issue such an order was unconstitutional because Congress had no power to enlarge the Court's original jurisdiction.

Marshall's claim that it was "the

province and duty of the judicial department to say what the law is" was not seen as particularly important at the time. The Court's opinion that mandamus should have been granted if the Court had had jurisdiction attracted most of the attention.

Major Decisions

Significant laws declared unconstitutional by the Supreme Court include:

Missouri Compromise   Not until 1857—fifty-four years after the *Marbury* case—was a second act of Congress declared unconstitutional by the Supreme Court. In the infamous Dred Scott case (*Scott v. Sandford*), the Court held that the Missouri Compromise of 1820 was unconstitutional because Congress lacked the power to exclude slavery from the territories. That decision contributed to the intensification of the debate over slavery and its eventual explosion into civil war. The *Dred Scott* ruling was undone by the Thirteenth and Fourteenth Amendments.

Test Oath Law   The Court in 1867 declared invalid an 1865 law that required attorneys, as a condition for practicing in federal courts, to swear that they had never engaged in or supported the Southern rebellion against the Union. The Court's opinion in this case and other cases indicated that it would not review other federal RECONSTRUCTION legislation favorably. To avoid this possibility, Congress removed from the Court's jurisdiction cases arising under certain of those laws; it is the only time in the Court's history that Congress specified a group of laws the Court could not review.

Legal Tender Acts   The Court in 1870 struck down the 1862 and 1863 acts of Congress that made paper money legal tender in payment of debts incurred before the passage of the acts. Fifteen months later, two new appointees to the Supreme Court provided the votes needed to overturn the earlier decision (*Hepburn v. Griswold, Knox v. Lee*). Critics contended that the Grant administration had packed the Court to win the reversal and thus establish paper money as a legal currency.

Civil Rights Act   In 1883 the Court struck down the Civil Rights Act of 1875, which barred discrimination in privately owned public accommodations such as hotels, theaters, and railway cars. The decision was one in a series that vitiated Congress's power to enforce the guarantees given to blacks by the Thirteenth and Fourteenth Amendments. It would be almost a century before Congress and the Court effectively overturned this series of rulings.

Federal Income Tax   The Court in 1895 struck down the first general peacetime income tax enacted by Congress. The decision (*Pollock v. Farmers' Loan and Trust Co.*) was bitterly attacked by Democrats in Congress and was reversed in 1913 by the Sixteenth Amendment.

'Yellow-Dog' Contracts   Exhibiting its early antipathy to organized labor, the Court in 1908 invalidated a section of an 1898 statute that made it unlawful for any railway employer to require as a condition of employment that his employees not join a labor union, or so-called "yellow-dog" contracts. It was not until 1930 that the Court sanctioned a federal law guaranteeing railway employees collective bargaining rights.

Child Labor Laws   The Court in 1918 struck down a 1916 law that sought to end child labor. Congress responded in 1919 by passing a second child labor statute. When this law also was struck down in 1922, Congress adopted a constitutional amendment to overturn the decisions. But the amendment failed to win ratification by a sufficient number of states before the Court itself overruled its earlier decisions.

New Deal Laws   President Roosevelt's New Deal program provoked an unprecedented clash between the Court and the legislative and executive branches. At Roosevelt's instigation, Congress in the 1930s enacted a series of laws aimed at ending the Great Depression and restoring the nation's economic well-being. But of eight major statutes to come before the Court, only two were upheld. Laws struck down included the Agricultural Adjustment Act of 1933, the National Industrial Recovery Act of 1933, and the Bituminous Coal Conservation Act of 1935.

The Court came under heavy fire for its decisions, and Roosevelt proposed a controversial plan to increase the size of the Court, presumably to ensure a majority sympathetic to the New Deal. Shortly after the plan was proposed, the Court defused the issue by upholding a series of revised New Deal laws.

Legislative Veto   The Court in 1983 declared the legislative veto to be unconstitutional *(INS v. Chadha)*. Not since the New Deal collisions had Congress felt so keenly the power of the Supreme Court to curtail its actions. By denying Congress the use of the legislative veto, a device it had employed in more than two hundred laws since 1932, the Court seemed to alter the balance of power between Congress and the executive branch.

Gramm-Rudman   In 1986 the Court invalidated a key enforcement provision of the Balanced Budget and Emergency Deficit Control Act *(Bowsher v. Synar)*. It ruled that the law violated the constitutional SEPARATION OF POWERS by

requiring that the comptroller general determine how much federal spending needed to be cut to meet certain deficit goals. Congress responded by passing a revised version of the so-called Gramm-Rudman-Hollings law that essentially put that power in the hands of the White House Office of Management and Budget.   ∽

ADDITIONAL READINGS

Baum, Lawrence. *The Supreme Court.* 1985.
Berger, Raoul. *Congress vs. the Supreme Court.* 1969.
Congressional Quarterly. *Guide to the U.S. Supreme Court.* 1979.
Library of Congress, Congressional Research Service. *The Constitution of the United States: Analysis and Interpretation.* 1973. Supplement, 1982.
Warren, Charles. *The Supreme Court in United States History.* Reprint. 1987.

Legislative Day

In congressional usage, a legislative day extends from the time either chamber of Congress meets after an AD-JOURNMENT until the time it next adjourns. The rules in each chamber call for certain routine business at the beginning of each legislative day. *(See* MORNING HOUR.*)*

The House normally adjourns at the end of a daily session, so its legislative days usually correspond to calendar days. The Senate, however, sometimes goes weeks without an adjournment; it recesses instead. By recessing, it continues the same legislative day and avoids interrupting unfinished business. One of the longest legislative days on record, cited by congressional scholar Walter J. Oleszek, ran for 105 days in 1922, when the Senate was debating a tariff bill.   ∽

Legislative Obstruction.   See
FILISBUSTER.

Legislative Process

The legislative process is the procedure Congress uses to write the laws of the land. Through that process it transforms the ideas of presidents, members of Congress, political parties, interest groups, and individual citizens into national policy. The lawmaking function as set forth by the Constitution is complicated and time-consuming. It is governed by detailed rules and procedures, as well as 200 years of customs and traditions.

To become law a proposal must be approved in identical form by both the SENATE and the HOUSE OF REPRESENTATIVES and signed by the president— or, infrequently, approved by Congress over his veto. Legislative proposals usually follow parallel paths through the two chambers of Congress. Bills are referred to committees for preliminary consideration, then debated and passed (or rejected) by the full House or Senate. The process is repeated in the other chamber. When the House and Senate pass differing versions of a major bill, a Senate-House conference committee normally is appointed to work out a compromise. Both chambers must approve the conferees' changes before the bill can be sent to the president for his signature.

Not surprisingly, relatively few bills make it through this complex process. Members of the Ninety-ninth Congress introduced more than 11,000 bills and resolutions in 1985-86. They produced fewer than 700 laws.

Bills not passed die at the end of the two-year term of Congress in which they are introduced. They may be reintroduced in a subsequent Congress. *(See* TERMS AND SESSIONS.*)*

A typical bill that survives the many roadblocks to enactment generally travels the following route:

Introduction
All legislation must be formally introduced by members of Congress, although members themselves do not originate most bills. The vast majority of legislative initiatives today are proposed by the executive branch—the White House and federal agencies—and by special-interest organizations such as trade unions or business associations. But there are many other sources as well, including Congress itself, state and local government officials, and ordinary citizens.

LEGISLATION is drafted in various forms. Measures originating in the House are designated HR, H J Res, H Con Res, or H Res. Senate measures are designated S, S J Res, S Con Res, or S Res. Each measure carries a number showing the order in which it was introduced: HR 1 or S 1 would be the first bill introduced at the beginning of a new Congress. Many bills fall into one of two categories:

• AUTHORIZATION bills, which establish or continue government programs or policies and set limits on how much money may be spent on them.

• APPROPRIATIONS bills, which provide the actual funds to carry out authorized programs or policies or provide funds to operate government agencies.

Authorization bills may be valid for several years, but appropriations are valid for only one.

Committee Action
Once a bill is introduced by a member, it is generally referred to a committee that has specialized knowledge of the subject matter. Bills that involve more than one subject may be referred to two or more committees. Senators and representatives are far too busy to follow every bill that comes before Congress. They must rely on the committees to screen most of this legislation.

(*See* COMMITTEE SYSTEM.)

A bill usually faces sharpest scrutiny in committee. It is here that most of the detailed deliberation and rewriting is done. This is especially true in the House; in the Senate deliberation and revision by the full chamber sometimes are equally important in determining a measure's final shape.

Bills may be considered by the full committee initially or by a subcommittee—the more frequent method. Sometimes the major review of a bill occurs at the subcommittee level, and the full committee simply endorses the subcommittee's recommendations.

The committee or subcommittee generally holds hearings on legislation before taking further action on it. Comment is requested from administration spokesmen and federal bureaucrats who run the programs that might be affected by the bill. Heads of cabinet-level departments of the government testify on the most important proposals. Scholars and technical experts also may appear. LOBBYING groups and private citizens may testify for or against the legislation.

Committee hearings are very important in setting the legislative agenda and shaping its political tone. They are one of the most important forums for finding out what the public thinks about national problems and its views on how to solve them. Hearings also may serve an educational function. Members of Congress do not legislate in a vacuum. They need political support for the actions they take, especially when controversial issues or remedies are involved. Hearings assist Congress in developing a consensus on proposed legislation.

After the hearings are completed, committee members may meet to consider the provisions of the legislation in detail, a process known as "marking up" the bill. Many bills are heavily amended—that is, revised—or entirely redrafted in committee. Votes may be

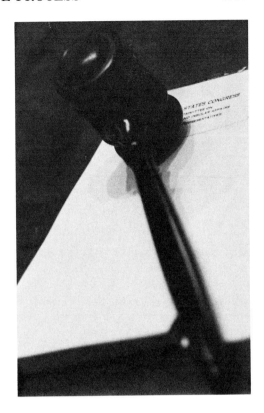

taken on controversial amendments and, finally, on whether to approve the bill and recommend that the full House or Senate pass the measure.

When committee action is completed, the panel prepares a written report describing the bill and its amendments, and explaining why the measure should become law. Both the members supporting the bill and those opposed may include their views in the report, which is filed with the parent chamber. At this point a bill is said to be "reported" to the House or the Senate.

The fate of by far the largest percentage of bills is sealed in committee. Bills that gain committee approval do not always win consideration by the parent chamber, but those that do are likely to pass—although they may be revised on the floor. Most bills simply die in committee. Procedures to remove a bill from an unsympathetic committee seldom succeed. (*See* DISCHARGE.)

Scheduling Floor Debate

House The House RULES COMMITTEE functions as sort of a traffic cop for bills reported from the legislative committees. Its power is considerable, even though it initiates little legislation on its own, and its role in the legislative process is crucial. The Rules Committee's power comes from its authority to control the flow of legislation from the legislative committees to the full House. Rules sets the terms of debate for almost every major bill that reaches the floor of the House. In today's greatly decentralized House, it is one of the few centralizing forces of the leadership. Generally, it acts on behalf of the Speaker in facilitating and promoting the majority party's program.

The Rules Committee chairman has wide discretion in arranging the panel's agenda. Scheduling, or not scheduling, a hearing on a bill will usually determine whether the measure ever comes before the House for debate. Under regular House RULES, bills must be brought up and debated in the order in which they are reported from the committees. The large volume of bills vying for action makes it necessary to have some system of priority selection. In the modern Congress there is just not enough time to act on all the legislation working its way through the legislative process.

Once the Rules Committee gives a bill the go-ahead for floor debate, it drafts a special RULE FOR HOUSE DEBATE, which is custom-made for each bill. The committee decides how many hours the House may debate the bill and whether all amendments, some amendments, or no amendments may be introduced from the floor. Although it has no authority to amend bills that come before it from other other committees, the Rules Committee can strike bargains on proposed amendments desired by various members in return for granting the rule.

For many years tax legislation was deemed too complex to entertain floor amendments. It was reasoned that the WAYS AND MEANS COMMITTEE, with expert knowledge of the subject matter, was in the best position to draft or amend such bills. They were given "closed" rules, prohibiting all floor amendments. Today few closed rules are granted by the Rules Committee. But there are many "modified" rules that allow amendments only to specific sections of a bill, or allow only amendments that have been drafted and printed in the *CONGRESSIONAL RECORD* in advance of the debate.

The drafting of legislation in the modern Congress is very complicated. In many cases, more than one committee works on a bill before it goes to the full House. Frequently their work involves fragile compromises, and the demands to keep these bills intact have mounted. Modified rules help to avoid hasty and sometimes ill-advised writing of legislation on the House floor. There also are political benefits for the leadership in controlling the amending process on the most controversial elements of a major bill. In the 1980s the Republican minority in the House skillfully used the amending process to frustrate the Democratic leadership's floor strategy. Modified rules can often head off embarrassing defeats or surprises during debates.

The rule from the Rules Committee also may waive POINTS OF ORDER—objections raised during the debate because something in the bill or a procedure used to bring the bill to the floor violates a House rule. Points of order often are used by a bill's opponents, who do not have enough votes to defeat the bill outright, to delay action and perhaps win concessions from the sponsors of the legislation. The Rules Committee can set aside temporarily any rule of House procedure—except those ordered by the Constitution—in order to facilitate action.

Like the bill to which it is attached, the rule for full House action requires the approval of a simple majority of the House. It is possible to amend the rule on the floor, but this occurs infrequently. Rules are seldom rejected. Once the rule is adopted, the bill itself can be debated.

There are special procedures for bringing up measures stymied in legislative committees or in the Rules Committee: the DISCHARGE PETITION and CALENDAR WEDNESDAY. In addition, the Rules Committee has a special power to draft rules dislodging bills from balky legislative committees. These procedures are seldom used.

There also are procedural shortcuts for bringing routine, relatively noncontroversial legislation to the floor. The bulk of legislation—probably 60-70 percent—is passed this way. The SUSPENSION OF THE RULES procedure is the most frequently used. Bills debated under this shortcut can be passed quickly if they can garner a two-thirds majority vote.

Senate Scheduling legislation for debate in the Senate is a more informal process. Senators have nothing comparable to the House Rules Committee. Nevertheless, the Senate faces the same problem of having to set priorities. Instead of trying to legislate by its cumbersome and rather archaic rules, the Senate legislates primarily through UNANIMOUS CONSENT AGREEMENTS. These are informal "gentlemen's agreements" geared to particular bills. They are the functional equivalent of the rules issued by the House Rules Committee.

Such agreements may limit debate time on the bill and on proposed amendments and may specify what amendments can be introduced and by whom. They may set a time and date to consider the bill and, leaving nothing to chance, may even set a time for a final vote. But unlike a House rule, unani-

mous consent agreements are drawn up privately, without committee hearings, by the majority and minority LEADERSHIP and other interested senators and cannot take effect if any senator objects. The drafters must be sensitive to the rights of all 100 members of the Senate. If the Senate did not have this mechanism, it would have to create its own scheduling committee.

Once an agreement is struck, the measure is brought to the floor at the prearranged time. Unless the agreement prohibits them, nongermane amendments, extraneous policy provisions also known as RIDERS, may be offered.

Bringing up controversial legislation by any other method, by offering a motion to do so, for example, is fraught with danger, since most Senate motions are debatable. Any senator can FILIBUSTER the motion; thus a time-consuming attempt to cut off "debate" can occur even before the bill is formally before the Senate.

As in the House, there are a number of ways of bringing to the floor legislation stalled in committee or never considered in committee: bypassing the committee stage and placing the bill on the legislative CALENDAR; suspending Senate rules; discharging the bill from the committee blocking it; or attaching the bill as a rider to another already on the floor. Of these, only the last is generally effective. Unlike the House, the Senate does not have a germaneness rule; there is nothing to prevent a senator from offering a water quality or civil rights measure as a rider to a health bill, for example.

Floor Action
There are marked differences between the way the two chambers debate and dispose of legislation—the floor action stage. The House, because of its size, must adhere strictly to detailed procedures. The House is organized to expedite legislative business. The SPEAKER is easily the most powerful

member in either chamber. He and his assistants control the agenda. The smaller Senate operates more informally. Power is less centralized, and no Senate leader wields the power the Speaker of the House possesses. Scheduling in the Senate traditionally has been the joint work of the majority and minority leaders.

The philosophy behind the rules also is different. Senate procedures are intended to give great weight to the minority, even at the expense of legislative efficiency. House rules emphasize majority rights.

Approval of bills and amendments in either chamber requires a majority of the members voting. Thus a tie vote spells defeat. In the Senate the VICE PRESIDENT of the United States, who under the Constitution is the Senate's PRESIDING OFFICER, may vote to break a tie. But this is the only circumstance in which he may vote. In the House the Speaker traditionally votes only to break a tie, although as an elected member of that chamber he may vote at any time on any proposal.

House House parliamentary procedures are the same for most major bills, except those handled under shortcut methods. The rule, presented in a resolution reported by the Rules Committee, is debated and adopted. The House debates most legislation in the Committee of the Whole House on the State of the Union, or more simply, the COMMITTEE OF THE WHOLE. This is nothing more than the House sitting in another form. When functioning as the Committee of the Whole, the House uses special rules designed to speed up floor action. On each bill there is a period for general debate, as regulated by the Rules Committee's rule, and separate debate and votes on all amendments that are introduced and allowed under the rule.

General debate is controlled by FLOOR MANAGERS for the majority and minority parties, who often are the chairman and ranking minority member of the committee that reported the bill. Most bills are debated and disposed of in one afternoon, although some bills take two or three days. Rarely is action drawn out over many days or even

weeks, as occurs in the Senate. House rules make filibusters and most other stalling tactics impractical. The House uses a parliamentary tool known as the PREVIOUS QUESTION to close debate and guarantee that a bill will come to a final vote.

After general debate, usually one or two hours, the bill is read section by section for amendment. The House considers amendments under guidelines that give the proponents and opponents at least five minutes to discuss each one. But a legislator can gain extra time by employing certain parliamentary MOTIONS.

Since the majority party sets the agenda, the minority party underlines its policy differences by trying to amend the bill. Amendments publicize the minority's positions even if there is little chance they will be adopted. Amendments also may be used as part of a strategy to defeat a bill: Opponents may attempt to weigh down the legislation with so many amendments that the bill will lose support. Some members, particularly on the minority side, develop great parliamentary expertise and act as self-appointed "watchdogs" of the rules and tactics of the majority.

Some votes in the House are taken by methods that make it impossible to tell how individual members voted. Others are taken by an electronic system that provides a public record of each member's vote and position on an issue. The Constitution spells out certain instances when votes must be individually recorded. (See VOTING.)

When all amendments have been disposed of, the Committee of the Whole dissolves and the bill is reconsidered by the members, now sitting as the House of Representatives. The House then proceeds through a series of parliamentary motions and votes that provide opponents a final opportunity to influence the outcome while guaranteeing that the proponents, assuming they are in the majority, will be able to pass the bill. Unlike the Senate, a determined House majority always can be expected to prevail on a particular bill.

Bills that reach a final passage vote are seldom defeated outright. By that time, the support or opposition has been clearly established, while attempts to revise the legislation have already been made during floor debate.

Senate In the Senate much of what goes on is planned in advance. Senators read speeches on legislation written by their staffs, and action on bills and amendments is by prior arrangement under unanimous consent agreements. Spontaneous debate is the exception. Normally there are few senators on the floor, except when crucial votes occur. Nevertheless, floor debate and procedural strategies are important in the Senate. One reason is that Senate rules make the legislative outcome less certain than in the House. The play of personalities and political influence affects the result to a much greater degree.

Floor action bears little resemblance to the procedures outlined in the formal rules. Scheduling is highly flexible. Debate is unstructured. No period is reserved, for example, for general debate. The Senate often conducts its business by setting aside its rules and operating through unanimous consent agreements. All senators can participate in scheduling. If there is broad backing for a bill, the Senate can act quickly. But without a political consensus, Senate action can be held up almost indefinitely.

On controversial bills for which agreements cannot be reached ahead of time, the majority leader may put the Senate on a "track" system. Tracking permits the Senate to have two or more bills pending simultaneously, with a specific time of the day designated for each bill. If one bill is being filibustered, the Senate can turn to another and thus not hold up all floor action.

HOW A BILL BECOMES LAW

This graphic shows the most typical way in which proposed legislation is enacted into law. There are more complicated, as well as simpler, routes, and most bills fall by the wayside and never become law.

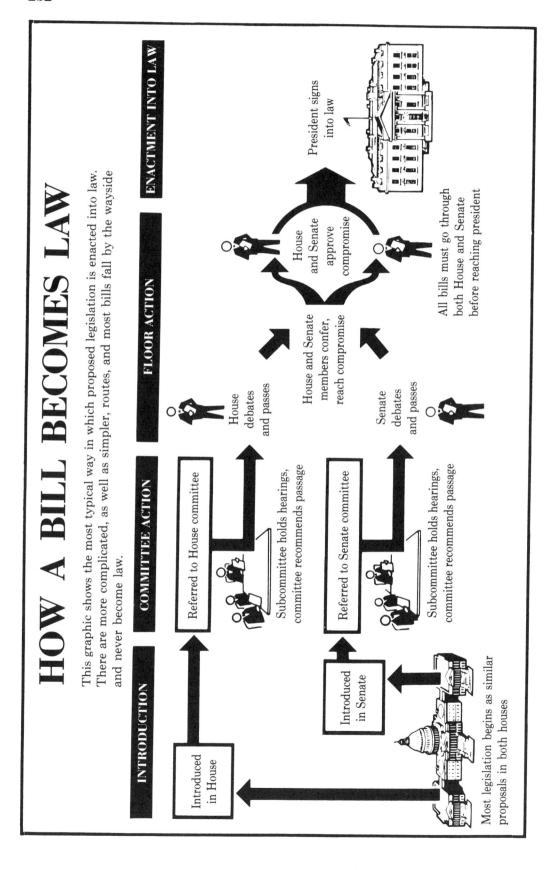

INTRODUCTION

Introduced in House

Introduced in Senate

Most legislation begins as similar proposals in both houses

COMMITTEE ACTION

Referred to House committee

Subcommittee holds hearings, committee recommends passage

Referred to Senate committee

Subcommittee holds hearings, committee recommends passage

FLOOR ACTION

House debates and passes

House and Senate members confer, reach compromise

Senate debates and passes

House and Senate approve compromise

All bills must go through both House and Senate before reaching president

ENACTMENT INTO LAW

President signs into law

The majority leader's greatest influence, therefore, comes from his control of the legislative agenda. He can schedule bills to suit certain senators, or the desires of the White House, or hold votes at times that benefit a bill's supporters or minimize the opposition's strength.

The Senate mostly relies on two types of votes, voice votes and roll calls. The roll sometimes is called slowly to give absent senators time to hustle to the floor from their offices in nearby buildings. Senators get a second chance to vote when the roll call is repeated. Much legislation is passed by unanimous consent. Even measures on which the Senate is closely divided may be passed without a roll call because the controversial issues already have been resolved, either by approval or rejection of key amendments or by procedural votes that reflect the Senate's positions before the bill itself is voted on.

Although there are alternative methods of bringing legislation to the floor, many of these may be subject to the filibuster. The Senate does not use such House parliamentary tools as the previous question to end debate. The only way to cut off debate is by informal agreement or invoking CLOTURE; for most legislation a vote of three-fifths of the entire Senate, or sixty members, is needed to end debate. Even without the filibuster, senators have many devices at their disposal for sidetracking legislation. There are rules that can delay consideration of a bill after it has been reported by a committee, and an informal practice allows senators to place "holds" on bills for varying lengths of time.

Action in Second Chamber

After a bill is passed by one chamber it is sent to the other. At this point several parliamentary options are available. The normal practice for all but the most routine legislation is for the measure to go to committee, where there will be more hearings, followed by markup, a vote to approve the bill, and the drafting of a committee report. It may then go to the floor. If passed by the second chamber, the bill in all likelihood has been substantially amended. It may be totally different from the first chamber's version. Both chambers usually agree to send these bills to a House-Senate CONFERENCE COMMITTEE to negotiate a compromise.

In certain situations the second body may approve the bill as passed by the first chamber, without further amendment, clearing the legislation for the president.

Conference Action

The House-Senate conference is the last major hurdle for most legislation. Everything the bill's sponsors have worked for, and all the effort exerted by the executive branch and private interests to help pass or defeat it, can be won or lost during these negotiations.

Either chamber may request a conference with the other to resolve the differences between the House- and Senate-passed versions. Conferees are appointed from each chamber. They are generally chosen by the chairman and highest-ranking minority member of the committee or subcommittee in which the bill originated.

Before House and Senate conferees begin their negotiations, each delegation meets separately to work out its positions on the key differences. They decide what they are willing to sacrifice and what provisions they will not bargain away.

Conferences are more informal than regular committee bill-drafting sessions. The staffs play a more obvious role in the final bargaining. Spokesmen for the administration usually are present, and lobbyists try to influence proposed compromises during breaks in the meetings. Theoretically conferees must observe certain rules: They may not amend or delete any section of the bill that is not in dispute, and they may not introduce new provisions not relevant to the differences already in the bills. In practice, however, many bills are substantially rewritten in conference.

If there are disagreements among House or Senate conferees, such disputes must be settled by majority vote. Each chamber's delegation may be of any size, but each side votes as a unit on each provision in disagreement. The political influence and skill of conference leaders play an important part in the outcome.

After conferees agree to a compromise bill, a conference report is written, explaining specific changes made by the conferees. The legislative intent of certain provisions may be written into the conference report rather than into the bill itself. The report is official once a majority of conferees from each house signs it.

Finally, after the report has been printed, the two houses vote on the compromise. Under legislative rules, bills that have been approved in conference are not supposed to be further amended by the House or Senate. But if conferees have been unable to agree on any of the amendments in disagreement, separate votes are taken in both houses to resolve the disputed provision. The House also must vote separately, in most circumstances, on any provision added by the Senate that is not germane to the bill. Sometimes bills are sent back to conference for further compromise efforts. The final version is rarely defeated, although it happens on occasion when wholesale changes are made in a long, controversial conference. Once the compromise is approved, the bill is sent to the White House for the president's review.

President's Role
When a bill reaches the president's desk, he has three choices. He may sign it, thus enacting the measure into law.

He may VETO it and return it to Congress with a statement giving his objections; Congress may override his veto by a two-thirds majority vote of both chambers. The bill then becomes a law without the president's approval. Finally, the president may take no action, in which case the bill will become law without his signature after ten days excluding Sundays—provided Congress does not adjourn during that period. Should Congress adjourn, however, the legislation does not become law. This is known as a pocket veto.   ~

ADDITIONAL READINGS

Birnbaum, Jeffrey H., and Alan S. Murray. *Showdown at Gucci Gulch.* 1987.
Davidson, Robert H., and Walter J. Oleszek. *Congress and Its Members.* 2d ed. 1985.
Oleszek, Walter J. *Congressional Procedures and the Policy Process.* 3d ed. 1988.
Redman, Eric. *The Dance of Legislation.* 1973.
Reid, T. R. *Congressional Odyssey: Saga of a Senate Bill.* 1980.

Legislative Veto

A device Congress used with increasing frequency in the 1970s and early 1980s to exercise greater control over the U.S. government was the legislative veto. This procedure allowed either one house or both houses of Congress, and in some instances even legislative committees, to reject regulations and policies recommended by the president or various federal departments and independent agencies.

In 1983 the Supreme Court ruled that most legislative vetoes were unconstitutional because they barred any role by the president in Congress's veto process. The high court said the Constitution requires final legislative decisions to be approved by both houses of Congress and presented to the president for his signature or veto. Congress's self-styled veto was criticized as a backhanded, even careless way of legislating that was outside the bounds of legitimate legislative procedures. And the Court maintained the legislative veto violated the Constitution's SEPARATION OF POWERS doctrine by expanding Congress's powers from lawmaking and OVERSIGHT to "shared administration" of the laws.

Nevertheless, the legislative veto served many useful purposes from the point of view of both lawmakers and presidents. Although presidents since Herbert Hoover had denounced the procedure as an infringement on executive powers, they accepted it in order to gain additional authority and flexibility in administering certain laws. Although the Court's decision outlawing the legislative veto was seen as buttressing the president's powers and curtailing congressional interference, many experts on Congress maintained it would have the opposite effect: Without their veto to closely monitor executive branch performance and regulations, lawmakers in the future would refuse to delegate broad powers.

Background

The legislative veto is a relatively recent congressional tool for controlling the executive branch. It was first written into law in 1932, when Congress passed legislation that gave President Herbert Hoover the authority to reorganize U.S. government departments but allowed either house of Congress, by majority vote, to "veto" his reorganization recommendations. Just a year later the House exercised that veto, blocking Hoover's plan. Hoover subsequently vetoed an emergency appropriations bill that would have allowed a single committee—the Joint Committee on Taxation—to exercise a veto over certain tax legislation.

Hoover's initial acquiescence in and subsequent opposition to the legislative veto set the pattern for future presidential views on the issue. All presidents since Hoover voiced strong objections to it, but most of them chose not to confront the issue directly. An exception was President Gerald R. Ford, who in 1976 dramatized his opposition by vetoing an environmental bill because it contained a veto provision. As a candidate for president in 1980, Ronald Reagan had given some support to Congress's use of the legislative veto, but once in office he reversed positions. In 1982 Reagan's solicitor general urged the Supreme Court to declare the veto unconstitutional.

The legislative veto was used infrequently until the early 1940s, when lawmakers saw it as an effective way to check the vast war-making and emergency powers Congress had granted the Roosevelt administration during World War II. Its use then declined in the 1950s and 1960s.

In the 1970s Congress began adding legislative veto provisions to a wide range of legislation, but especially in the fields of foreign policy/defense, energy, and environment. This trend was fueled by the Democratic Congress's growing distrust of President Richard Nixon's actions and by public criticism of excessive federal regulation.

The Vietnam War and the Watergate scandal weakened the presidency and helped to promote a more assertive Congress. It was no coincidence that this period saw a rapid expansion of the legislative veto. Some of the most important laws of the period contained legislative vetoes, including the 1973 War Powers Act, the 1974 Congressional Budget and Impoundment Control Act and the 1974 Federal Election Campaign Act. By the time the Reagan administration took office in 1981, there were well over 200 laws containing legislative veto provisions. Of these, more than one-third had been enacted since the mid-1970s. A bill enacted in 1980 to deal with future domestic energy shortages contained twenty-one separate veto provisions.

Types of Legislative Vetoes

Over the years Congress devised several types of legislative vetoes. Most of them had one feature in common: they allowed Congress, by one method or another, to block executive branch actions without the president having the opportunity to reverse the vetoes. Usually, Congress gave itself thirty to sixty days in which to consider and approve a veto. In some cases lawmakers were free to apply the veto at any time.

Probably the most common form of the veto procedure was the two-house veto, which required a majority vote in both the House and Senate to block an executive branch policy. Concurrent resolutions were used to approve two-house vetoes because they were not sent to the president for his signature or disapproval. (Some two-house vetoes were provided in bills requiring the president's signature.)

Congress also used one-house legislative vetoes. These allowed either chamber to block a government department's or independent agency's regulation by adopting a simple RESOLUTION of disapproval. A variation permitted either chamber to veto a federal regulation unless the other house overturned the first's action within a specified period.

Still another form of the veto gave certain House and Senate committees the power to block or delay a department's regulation.

All of the above veto procedures allowed federal departments or agencies to implement certain rules or programs unless Congress intervened to block them. However, another variation of the veto blocked or delayed certain regulations from taking effect unless lawmakers took the initiative and voted to approve them. This in effect constituted a veto in advance, which could be reversed only if one, or both, houses voted to let stand a proposed regulation or policy.

Supreme Court Ruling

The Supreme Court, in *Immigration and Naturalization Service v. Chadha,* June 23, 1983, and in followup decisions soon thereafter, ruled that all forms of the legislative veto that did not give the president the opportunity to respond to Congress's action were unconstitutional. The Court said the legislative process outlined in the Constitution demanded that all acts of Congress must include the president's participation—through his approval or veto—to be enforceable. Thus, if Congress gives federal departments and agencies the authority to issue certain regulations or make policy decisions, it "must abide by its delegation of authority until that delegation is legislatively altered or revoked." In the majority decision in *Chadha,* Chief Justice Warren E. Burger said it was beyond doubt "that lawmaking was a power to be shared by both houses [of Congress] and the president."

The only type of veto not affected by the Court's rulings was the two-house veto by JOINT RESOLUTION, which must be sent to the president for his signature or disapproval. This procedure essentially is the same as passing a new law.

Congress has taken steps to conform to the Supreme Court's decisions. But many legislative vetoes are still incorporated in current law despite their doubtful constitutionality. In any case, Congress can be expected to find innovative substitutes for the legislative veto.   ~

ADDITIONAL READING

Fisher, Louis. *Constitutional Conflicts Between Congress and the President.* 1985.

Library Committee, Joint

The Joint Library Committee oversees the Library of Congress, but it deals primarily with legal matters and general questions of policy. More detailed oversight of the library's budget and operations is handled by the House and Senate Appropriations subcommittees on the legislative branch. The Library Committee also rules on proposals to put statues or other memorials on the Capitol grounds.

The Joint Library Committee consists of five members of the HOUSE ADMINISTRATION Committee and five members of the Senate RULES AND ADMINISTRATION Committee; the chairmanship rotates between the House and Senate every two years. The Library Committee usually meets only once or twice in each two-year term of Congress, although members are frequently polled between meetings. Nominations for librarian of Congress are handled solely by the Senate Rules Committee, since that is a Senate duty. *(See* LIBRARY OF CONGRESS.)   ~

Library of Congress

The Library of Congress has the dual role of assisting Congress and serving as the nation's library. With more than 80 million items in its collection, the library is one of the largest in the world. More than a million new items are usually added each year.

The librarian of Congress oversees the library and its staff of more than 5,000 people. The annual budget exceeds $230 million. The librarian is a presidential appointee, confirmed by the Senate, but he reports to Congress, which has a ten-member Joint Commit-

tee on the LIBRARY. The thirteenth librarian of Congress, historian James H. Billington, was appointed in 1987.

Members of Congress are the most privileged users of the library. Their requests for books or background information are handled by a separate division, the Congressional Research Service. Its more than 800 employees handle a range of duties, answering simple queries or spending several months on a complicated analysis. CRS receives and answers more than 450,000 inquiries from Congress each year.

The library is housed in three sprawling buildings on Capitol Hill. Its extensive collections include one of three known perfect copies of the Gutenberg Bible (which is on display), a set of string instruments made by Antonio Stradivari, Thomas Jefferson's rough draft of the Declaration of Independence, a nearly complete set of Matthew Brady's photographs of the Civil War, and the personal papers of twenty-three presidents, from Washington through Coolidge. The earliest known motion picture, "Fred Ott's Sneeze," copyrighted in 1893 by Thomas Edison, is part of the library's collection, as is the world's smallest book, *Ant*, which is 1.4 millimeters square. Not every book published in the United States is part of the library's collection. Works in more than 460 different languages are included in the library's holdings; about two-thirds of its books are not in English.

Although the library buys books and subscribes to periodicals, its collection also benefits from copyright laws. Authors seeking U.S. copyright protection for books, music, photographs, art, movies, or other work must deposit one, and sometimes two, copies at the Library of Congress. The library does not keep every copyrighted work, but it adds to its collection thousands of the more than half a million items copyrighted each year.

A major library service is cataloging

USING THE LIBRARY OF CONGRESS

The main building of the Library of Congress is located across from the Capitol on First Street, S.E. Two additional buildings are located nearby. Visitors of any age may tour the library, which attracts more than two million people each year. The library also hosts concerts, poetry readings, and lectures.

Anyone over high school age is allowed to use the library's materials; high school students may do so if their principal writes that other searches for material have been unsuccessful.

The Library of Congress does not usually loan out its books. Instead, users request materials, and staff then retrieve them from the stacks. As a last resort, books can be checked out through interlibrary loan. That means the Library of Congress will lend a book, through another library, if it cannot be found anywhere else.

Visitors often wait for their books in the main reading room, an ornate, domed chamber decorated with stained glass, enormous pillars, and elaborate statues. The central card catalog is housed there—and spills into other nearby areas. Also available are terminals the public can use for searching records that the library has computerized.

The Library of Congress has several other reading rooms geared to particular subjects or collections; these are scattered throughout the library and are also open to the public. Library hours vary; each reading room has a separate schedule.

books published in the United States and abroad. U.S. libraries buy catalog cards, computer tapes, and other materials from the Library of Congress. The Library of Congress gives a catalog number to every book published in the United States (and many published abroad) that reflects the book's subject matter. The library also maintains the Dewey Decimal Classification System, which is used by most public libraries.

The library produces books in Braille and records books on tape for distribution to 160 cooperating libraries that provide services to the blind or partially sighted. About 2,500 book titles and a variety of music scores are selected each year for Braille transcription or for recording.

Scholars from all over the world are attracted to the Library of Congress and its extensive holdings. Their appreciation of its resources was given a rare public display in 1986, when more than 100 researchers protested new, early closing hours. Some protesters refused to leave the main reading room at the new closing time of 5:30 p.m., and several were eventually arrested. Others marched in front of the building. A public relations success, the protests prompted Congress to provide additional funds and earmark them for operating the library during evening hours. (Not all reading rooms are open during the evening, and many are closed on the weekend.)

Jefferson's Library

When Congress decided in 1800 to transfer the new United States government to Washington, D.C., the legislators set aside $5,000 to buy books and set up a congressional library. After a Joint Committee on the Library made a list, London booksellers supplied 152 works in 740 volumes. The new Library of Congress was given a room in the Capitol's north wing.

Most of the library's books were burned or pillaged in 1814 when British troops attacked Washington. After the war, Thomas Jefferson, then in retirement in Monticello, offered to sell Congress his distinguished collection of more than 6,000 volumes. Despite some grumbling from critics of Jefferson, the legislators agreed to pay about $24,000 for the library, pricing each book by size and format. Congress further boosted the library's status in 1815 by appointing James MADISON as librarian, the first person to hold the post on a full-time basis.

The library suffered from another major fire in 1851, when 35,000 of its 55,000 books were lost. After the Civil War, though, the library benefited from a new, stronger copyright law, passed in

1865. It required anyone applying for a copyright to deposit a copy of the publication in the library.

A major advocate of that law was Ainsworth R. Spofford, who in 1864 began thirty-two years of service as the librarian of Congress. A bookseller, publisher, and writer, Spofford had been assistant librarian. Under his tenure, the number of books and pamphlets the library owned grew from about 100,000 to more than one million. He was one of three librarians to serve more than three decades; the others were John S. Meehan (1829-61), a newspaper publisher, and Herbert Putnam (1899-1939), librarian of the Boston Public Library and member of a family of book publishers.

The twelfth librarian of Congress, Daniel J. Boorstin, a historian, was appointed in 1975 and served until 1987. Billington then took the post.

Three Library Buildings

While Spofford was librarian, in 1886, Congress agreed to construct a separate building for the library. The collection was moved in 1897 from crowded quarters in the Capitol to the new $6.36 million facility, modeled after the Paris Opera in the Italian Renaissance style and located across the street from the Capitol to the east. It has been called the Jefferson Building since 1980.

An annex was authorized by Congress in 1930 and occupied in 1939. The white marble building, which cost $9 million, is behind the main library. Originally it was called the Jefferson Building; Congress in 1980 renamed it the John Adams Building.

The third building, called the Madison Building, got congressional approval in 1965, but Congress for years put off appropriating the money to build it. Construction was finally completed in 1982 at a cost of more than $130 million, substantially more than the original $75 million estimate. About 80 percent of the library's employees work in the massive 1.5 million-square-foot building, which is across Independence Avenue from the main library. It is one of the largest buildings in Washington. *(See* CAPITOL HILL *for map of the area.)*   ~

Lobbying

A hiker writes his senator urging an end to logging in national forests. A teacher sends her dues to the National Education Association, which then fights cuts in federal education funds. A lawyer phones an old friend newly elected to the House and makes a pitch for a client's missile. An aide to the president stops by a committee meeting to suggest new wording for an amendment. An angry farmer brings his tractor to the steps of the Capitol to join a protest against low crop prices.

Each of these people is lobbying Congress, trying to win support for a certain point of view. Thousands of voices compete for congressional attention as laws are written and money provided for everything from health care to weapons. Individuals, organizations, corporations, and even governments can influence the way laws are made and carried out.

Lobbying is sanctioned by the Constitution. The First Amendment protects the right of the people to "petition the government for redress of grievances." Central to a democratic society is the freedom to ask questions, make suggestions, and debate results. Lobbying is an element of such widespread political participation. It allows competing points of view to be heard and provides information to those making decisions. Not guaranteed is whether all of the many voices will be heeded, or even heard. Unlike voters, who each get one ballot, lobbyists are not equal; some are clearly more powerful than others.

The most visible lobbyists are those who work full time in Washington. Their employers include trade or professional associations, law firms, public relations firms, large corporations, organizations with particular interests, and other groups. Political insiders populate the field; many lobbyists once held jobs on congressional staffs or in federal agencies. Former members of Congress frequently find jobs as lobbyists or as "rainmakers," valued by law firms because they attract clients eager for inside contacts and lobbying.

Some lobbyists focus on arcane details of specific laws; others concentrate on broader policy changes. Many handle a range of issues and a variety of clients; others tackle only one area. Whatever their approach, lobbyists are important players in the legislative process. Although representatives and senators still bristle at the notion of being "in someone's pocket," most would count a lobbyist or two in their circle of close advisers.

Often a lobbyist's best technique is simply to provide accurate information, either directly to a legislator or at a subcommittee hearing. The credibility gained then gives the lobbyist more influence when he argues his point of view. A record of reliability can also win a quick hearing should a lobbyist find a minor clause damaging to his or her client. Information packets, drafts of bills, and scenarios of how a bill would affect an industry are among the ways lobbyists approach legislators and their staff.

A century ago, lobbyists were widely portrayed as less than scrupulous characters, hanging out in the halls and lobbies of the Capitol. That reputation was enhanced whenever bribery and other improper practices were exposed. Industry's apparently excessive influence on the Senate was a major factor in the push for DIRECT ELECTION OF SENATORS; until 1913, senators were chosen by state legislatures.

But not all colorful lobbyists were corrupt. Among the most famous lobbyists of the past was the self-described "King of the Lobby," Samuel Ward, whose legislative successes in the mid-1800s were so dazzling that Congress decided to investigate him. When the investigating committee asked Ward about his well-known, elegant dinners for politicians, he replied, "At good dinners people do not talk shop, but they give people a right, perhaps, to ask a gentleman a civil question and get a civil answer."

At dinners and cocktail parties, at plush resorts where legislators combine speech-making and vacationing, well-heeled lobbyists continue to use Ward's methods. Other, less prosperous groups emphasize letter-writing and telephone calls. The White House can draw on the powerful allure of the president, as well as daily contacts on Capitol Hill by the president's "congressional liaison" staff, a euphemism for lobbyists. Federal agencies also have professionals as-

signed to monitor Congress.

Senators and representatives still find lobbyists waiting for them as they step off elevators, heading for votes on the Senate or House floor. Thumbs pointing up or down, to signal a yes or no vote, were once very common and can sometimes still be seen. But the bulk of lobbying is done long before a bill reaches the floor.

In addition to direct lobbying contacts, organizations can influence legislators by giving money to their political campaigns. Although CAMPAIGN FINANCING laws restrict donations, powerful lobbies make certain that responsive legislators get sizable contributions. Corporations and labor unions are not allowed to make direct campaign contributions, but their employees and members can form POLITICAL ACTION COMMITTEES, which then channel their donations to particular candidates. Trade associations and membership groups also form PACs. The largest PAC contributor in the 1986 election cycle was the Realtors Political Action

Farmers' Protest
Some groups have resorted to dramatic demonstrations to get the attention of Congress. Farmers brought their tractors and other farm machinery to Washington in 1979 to protest government farm policies.

Committee, a PAC affiliated with the National Association of Realtors; it contributed close to $2.8 million to candidates. Overall, PACs made about 28 percent of contributions to 1986 congressional campaigns.

Regulation of Lobbying

Lobbying is a constitutionally protected, legitimate activity, but the combination of special interests does not always add up to the public good. A frustrated Woodrow Wilson, campaigning for president in 1912, said, "The government of the United States is a foster child of the special interests. It is not allowed to have a will of its own."

Lobbyists have resisted efforts to regulate their activity. Congress has also found it difficult to restrain lobbying without infringing on the right to free speech. Rules on domestic lobbying were first considered in 1911 but not approved until 1946, when Congress passed the Federal Regulation of Lobbying Act.

The principle behind the 1946 law was disclosure, not regulation. The law simply requires lobbyists, both for corporations and organizations, to register their names and subjects of interest, along with what they spend. But loopholes mean that not all individuals and groups are listed, and that financial reports do not accurately reflect expenditures. The Supreme Court in 1954 upheld the constitutionality of the law, but its narrow interpretation made the statute even less effective. For example, the Court said the law applied only to funds directly solicited for lobbying; that exempted organizations that used general funds for lobbying. Another ruling required registration only for individuals whose primary job was contact with Congress; that definition allowed many lobbyists to avoid registering. The Court's interpretation made enforcement of the law almost impossible.

Critics of the 1946 law have fought for new rules. They came close to suc-

cess in 1976, when both the House and Senate passed revision bills, but senators and representatives could not resolve their differences. The legislation was unpopular with a broad group of lobbyists, many of whom found themselves working together for the first time as they fought the bill.

In the mid-1980s more than 7,000 individuals each year were registering as lobbyists under the law. Though the count was not complete, the registration rules did have some impact. After Rep. Charles Schumer, a New York Democrat, complained in 1987 to the Justice Department that lobbyists for the Airline Owners and Pilots Association had not registered, AOPA officials quickly listed their names with Congress.

Congress has dealt separately with lobbyists representing foreign governments and companies, whose ranks swelled in the 1980s. The Foreign Agents Registration Act of 1938, which has been amended several times, imposes tighter rules than the domestic law. As a result, it gives a fairly accurate picture of what foreign agents do. Since 1974 the Justice Department has added to the law's effectiveness by enforcing it more strictly.

Powerful Voices

Congress recognizes the role of interest groups in the first step of the legislative process: hearings. A trade association often sends its president to testify, instead of its Washington-based legislative representative. The assumption is that someone from outside Washington has more credibility. The witness spells out his organization's view of the legislation, and that basic position becomes the lobbyist's theme as he follows the bill through subcommittee, committee, onto the House or Senate floor, to a conference between the two houses, and then back to each house again for final passage.

In a parallel move, an interest group can have its members write directly to their states' legislators. This "grass-roots" lobbying can be extremely effective. Often an association, in its newsletter or a separate mailing, provides a sample letter or even a stamped postcard that members can sign and mail. Among the largest associations are the American Association of Retired Persons, with 24 million members, and the American Automobile Association, with 27.6 million members.

The credibility that a huge membership gives to an organization also accrues to groups with economic power. For example, the Business Roundtable, consisting of the chief executive officers of major corporations, always gets a respectful hearing on Capitol Hill.

Other groups, without such ready access, have resorted to dramatic demonstrations to get attention. More than 12,000 World War I veterans, angry about delays in payment of their bonuses and unable to find jobs during the Depression, gathered in Washington in May 1932. An estimated 200,000 blacks and whites massed before the Lincoln Memorial in August 1963 in support of civil rights legislation pending in Congress. Marchers gathered in November 1969 to press for an end to the war in Vietnam. Just a few months later, in April 1970, environmentalists held Earth Day, to galvanize support for clean air and water rules and other environmental laws.

Farmers borrowed the tactic in 1979, when they brought their tractors and other farm machinery to Washington to protest farm policies. One anti-abortion group has made an annual demonstration the heart of its lobbying effort. March for Life stages a rally on each anniversary of the Supreme Court's *Roe v. Wade* decision, the January 22, 1973 ruling that legalized abortion.

Certain groups have become almost legendary for their lobbying influence. The National Rifle Association, with three million members, has such a strong grass-roots organization that it can cost a politician votes to go against the NRA position. Those with pro-NRA records often get campaign contributions from the richly endowed NRA political action committee. Unlike many groups that focus on a broad range of issues, the NRA concentrates on opposing gun control. Other single-interest lobbying groups benefit from their members' passionate involvement in one issue. Anti-abortion groups fit that category, as does an organization, Mothers Against Drunk Driving, that successfully sought a higher legal age for consumption of alcohol.

Once known for its adamant opposition to federal health programs such as Medicare, the American Medical Association has softened its stand in recent years, a change that may have made it even more influential. The U.S. Chamber of Commerce follows a long list of business issues before Congress and backs up its position with an extensive network of local chambers. Geographically scattered membership is an important advantage for the AMA and the Chamber, as it is for organizations of pharmacists, insurance agents, teachers, and home builders, among others. The same large groups, though, are sometimes handicapped by the need to satisfy a diverse membership; trying to reach a consensus, to speak with one voice in Washington, can mute the organization's effectiveness.

Even within an industry, certain groups become more adept than others at presenting their point of view; the Independent Petroleum Association of America, for example, has often effectively opposed stands taken by the major oil companies. Because of the billions spent on defense by the federal government, the weapons industry has an array of Washington representatives who make up an extremely powerful group. Simple geography makes the American Trucking Associations influential; the group's headquarters build-

MADD: A GRASS-ROOTS SUCCESS STORY

Candy Lightner, whose thirteen-year-old daughter was killed by a drunken driver, led a parents' campaign that convinced Congress in 1984 to take steps to curb drunken driving. The grass-roots organization, Mothers Against Drunk Driving, or MADD, funneled the grief and anger of bereaved parents and others into a phenomenally successful lobbying effort. Spurred by MADD, Congress enacted a law penalizing states that failed to raise the minimum drinking age to twenty-one. The law also provided financial incentives for states that established tough drunken driving laws.

Lightner founded MADD in Texas after her daughter's death in 1980. Similar groups in other states were quickly organized, and by 1984 the organization claimed a half-million members in forty-four states. Parents used their own tragic stories to dramatize the problems; they lobbied their state legislatures for stiffer punishments for convicted offenders, monitored trials, and ran education programs to teach students the dangers of alcohol.

MADD said federal action was needed to establish a uniform drinking age because when one state raised its drinking age, students simply drove to nearby states where it was legal to drink. That created what MADD called "blood borders" as intoxicated teenagers drove home.

With support from key Senate and House members and a change of position by President Ronald Reagan, Lightner accomplished her goal. During Senate debate on the MADD bill, Wyoming Republican Alan K. Simpson referred to the "parents who have been literally crushed with sorrow by what has happened to their children." He continued: "We would not be here on this floor in this fashion and this swiftly if they were not effective."

Lightner, watching the final action, hugged a fellow MADD campaigner and yelled, "We got it!" Summing up her effort, she said: "It means a lot of lives saved, it means that grass-roots organizing works—and it means I can go home." When President Reagan signed the MADD bill, a jubilant Lightner was at his side.

ing near Capitol Hill has rooms readily available for campaign fundraisers. Knowing how to throw a good party is a special talent of some groups; the International Ice Cream Association throws a lavish—and popular—ice cream party every June.

Some groups develop a cozy relationship with a congressional committee or subcommittee and an executive agency or department. This set of lobbyists, legislators, and bureaucrats is sometimes called an "iron triangle," which provides a three-sided front against budget cuts or program changes. These lobbyists have more influence than "outsiders," who find it difficult to grasp the political nuances and technical jargon of an issue. Veterans' groups, for example, have always had a close relationship with key congressional committees, such as the House VETERANS' AFFAIRS Committee, and with the Veterans Administration. Few such triangles are so tightly knit, however, and complex issues keep the relationships fluid.

Labor unions, which once had enough clout to influence their members at election time, in recent years have found it harder to deliver voting blocs—and to have an impact on Capitol Hill. In the 1970s labor twice failed to win passage of an important picketing bill, losing first because of a veto by President Gerald R. FORD, and again when the House rejected a similar bill that President Jimmy Carter had promised to sign.

Lobbyists have also learned to form coalitions. As Congress prepared in the late 1970s to decide what parks and wilderness areas to create from federal lands in Alaska, environmental groups formed an alliance. Although the groups did not always agree on every point, they compromised on major areas and, together, presented their case to Congress. Their united front helped convince Congress in 1980 to accept many of their recommendations.

Governments have become lobbyists, too, with the National Governors Association, the League of Cities, and the National Conference of Mayors among the leading groups. States and cities also have their own representatives in Washington, many housed together in the Hall of the States just a few blocks from the Capitol. Though at first preoccupied with getting a bigger share of the federal budget, the associations have become sophisticated lobbyists on a variety of issues. In the 1980s, for example, the National League of Cities outflanked cable television operators, who wanted Congress to restrict a local government's ability to regulate cable. Each group of mayors and local officials contacted their own representative, making a hometown pitch that large cable companies found difficult to counter.

Foreign governments usually are most effective when U.S.-based groups argue their position. Israel, Greece, and Ireland have loyal friends in Congress in part because Americans of those heritages belong to strong, well-financed associations with political influence, such as the American Israel Public Affairs Committee.

Military officers and Pentagon officials often retire and then turn up as employees of defense contractors. Former White House officials also are popular lobbyists. Michael K. Deaver, once deputy chief of staff for President Ronald Reagan, moved quickly to set up his public relations firm and take on clients he had dealt with while at the White House—so quickly, in fact, that an independent counsel was assigned to investigate alleged unethical and illegal behavior. The investigation resulted in Deaver's conviction on charges of perjury. Another former Reagan political adviser, Lyn Nofziger, was convicted in 1988 of violating federal ethics laws that require officials to wait a year before lobbying former colleagues.

The influence that powerful groups

can exert on Congress was starkly illustrated in 1986 and 1987 when the House WAYS AND MEANS Committee voted several times to close its meetings—primarily, according to its members, to bar lobbyists. With wide-ranging authority over taxes, trade, Social Security, health, and welfare programs, Ways and Means is perhaps the most heavily lobbied committee in the House. "Members ought to have the courage to look the lobbyists right in the eyes and go against them," said committee member Don J. Pease, an Ohio Democrat who supported open meetings. "But as a practical matter, that's hard to do."

Standing above all other lobbyists is the president himself. The White House has its own legislative agenda, and the president dispatches his congressional liaison staff to Capitol Hill to try to win passage of his programs. The president also invites legislators to visit the White House; there representatives and senators feel the full effect of the aura of the White House—and have direct personal contact with the nation's most powerful politician.

Unlike other lobbyists, the president has a powerful tool on his side: the veto. By threatening to veto a bill he does not like, the president can quickly get the attention of the House and Senate and may win changes. For most presidents, though, the veto is a last resort; more important is their ability to persuade legislators to support their agenda. (See VETOES.)

The most successful presidential lobbyist was Franklin D. Roosevelt, whose legislative victories in the 1930s were the basis of the NEW DEAL. Another sweeping domestic program, the GREAT SOCIETY, was enacted in the 1960s at the behest of Lyndon B. JOHNSON, who had worked at the Capitol for thirty-two years—as a congressional aide, member of the House, senator, Senate minority leader, majority leader, and vice president. With President Johnson cracking the whip, Congress endorsed new federal programs on poverty, voting rights, and health care for the aged.

Group Against Group

A lobbying story can be found behind every major bill that goes through Congress. Most intriguing are those that pit powerful groups against one another.

Steamships and Railroads In the late 1850s Commodore Vanderbilt, the steamship king, found his lucrative contracts with the post office challenged by the railroads. Directing the lobbying effort himself, Vanderbilt successfully fought off the railroads, who wanted major help from Congress in building the transcontinental railroad. The railroad was put off until after the Civil War; by then Vanderbilt had sold his steamships and gotten into the railroad business, which Congress embraced with generous land grants and special financial treatment.

Prohibitionists and the Liquor Industry Convincing Congress to act on a controversial subject can take years, as the Anti-Saloon League found during its campaign for a national ban on alcoholic beverages. Impatient with the milder tactics of the Women's Christian Temperance Union, the Anti-Saloon League in the 1890s beefed up its own efforts and began to raise money, make campaign contributions, and rally local leaders. Eventually the League dispatched field organizers across the country to develop local groups. Opposing the League was the well-financed liquor industry, for which the fight against prohibition appeared to be a fight for life. The league's persistence finally paid off in 1919, when its supporters won ratification of a constitutional amendment banning the sale of alcoholic beverages. (The Eighteenth Amendment remained in effect until 1932, when another constitutional amendment repealing Prohibition was ratified.)

NRA and the Police After years of effort the National Rifle Association in 1986 won relaxation of gun control laws enacted following political assassinations in 1968. The victory came despite opposition from a coalition of police organizations, who labeled the NRA proposals the "cop-killer bill." During the House voting, groups of state and local police officers stood at parade rest in full-dress uniform at the doors of the chamber, staring silently at legislators as they filed in. Though unsuccessful in 1986, the police groups began to erode the traditional NRA power. They focused in 1987-88 on prohibiting plastic guns, which do not show up on metal detectors. The NRA opposed any laws against plastic guns, but that hard-line, hard-to-defend position began to cost the organization members, and a compromise became more likely.

Pesticide Free-for-All On rare occasions, opposing sides can put down their swords and compromise. That happened in 1986, when pesticide manufacturers and environmentalists both endorsed pesticide control legislation and helped move it through the House and Senate. The bill stalled, though, and differences between the House and Senate versions were never worked out. ~

ADDITIONAL READINGS

Birnbaum, Jeffrey H., and Alan S. Murray. *Showdown at Gucci Gulch: Lawmakers, Lobbyists, and the Unlikely Triumph of Tax Reform.* 1987.

Cigler, Allan J., and Burdett A. Loomis. *Interest Group Politics.* 2d ed. 1986.

Deakin, James. *The Lobbyists.* 1966.

Drew, Elizabeth. *Politics & Money: The New Road to Corruption.* 1983.

Levitan, Sar, and Martha R. Cooper. *Business Lobbies: The Public Good and the Bottom Line.* 1984.

Lodge, Henry Cabot

Henry Cabot Lodge (1850-1924) played an important role in the conduct of U.S. foreign policy from the Spanish-American War through World War I. An influential member of the Senate (1893-1924), Lodge was an intimate of Theodore Roosevelt and an enthusiastic imperialist. He believed that military strength, not law and moral suasion, was the determining factor in the conduct of international affairs. As chairman of the FOREIGN RELATIONS Committee and as Senate majority leader (1919-24), he mobilized opposition to the post-World War I Treaty of Versailles, which contained the Covenant of the League of Nations.

After receiving the first Ph.D. in political science granted by Harvard University, Lodge wrote several historical works and taught. Turning from theory to practice, he entered state politics and subsequently was elected to the U.S. House of Representatives in 1887. He served as a Republican representative from Massachusetts until 1893, when he entered the Senate.

As a representative, Lodge played an important role in support of the so-called "Force Bill" in 1890-91. The bill would have promoted black suffrage by authorizing the presence of federal officers at polling places from which blacks might be excluded during national elections.

Lodge supported, although without much enthusiasm, Roosevelt's domestic reforms. His real interest was in the conduct of foreign affairs. His enthusiasm for the Spanish-American War in 1898 led him to advocate the annexation of all of Spain's colonial holdings.

In 1919 Lodge gained international notoriety as the most powerful congressional opponent of the League of Nations. As chairman of the Senate Foreign Relations Committee, Lodge wrote the majority report on the committee's consideration of the Treaty of Versailles. In it he endorsed ratification but only with the addition of four reservations and forty-five amendments. The changes Lodge proposed strongly rejected any infringement on the sovereignty of the United States. Under his leadership, the Senate rejected the treaty and membership in the League of Nations in 1919 and in 1920. *(See* TREATY RATIFICATION.*)*

Lodge's grandson and namesake, Henry Cabot Lodge, Jr., served in the Senate in the World War II era (1937-44, 1947-53). He was an unsuccessful Republican vice presidential candidate in 1960.   ~

Logrolling

Legislation pending in the House or Senate can gather momentum as supporters pick up votes. One political tactic they use is known as logrolling: Senators and representatives anxious for passage of a bill win votes from colleagues by promising them support on future legislation. Logrolling can also describe the practice of adding amendments to induce fellow legislators to vote for a bill.

Mutual aid is the heart of logrolling. Often a string of minor arrangements among individuals helps push a bill towards victory. Less common are deals that put a solid bloc of legislators behind one measure in return for support from another group on a separate bill. That happened in 1964, when northern Democrats convinced southern Democrats to vote for a permanent food stamp program. In return, the northern Democrats agreed to vote for a wheat and cotton support bill sought by the southern Democrats. Republicans, who opposed the food stamp bill, were

not able to break up the Democratic coalition.

Logrolling is more common on legislation that benefits particular districts. The practice is also more likely when party discipline is weak, as legislators cross party lines to cast votes they believe are—or promise to be—of particular benefit to their home districts or states.   ~

Long, Huey P.

Huey P. Long (1893-1935) was governor of Louisiana when he was elected to the Senate in 1930. Determined to prevent his lieutenant governor, whom he disliked, from taking over, Long delayed entering the Senate until 1932, after his preferred successor had been elected governor. This determination to control politics in Louisiana was typical of the Kingfish, as Long was known.

Long, a Democrat and a populist, began his political career in 1918 as a member and later commissioner of Louisiana's railroad (or public service) commission, where he argued the consumers' case against the utilities. Unsuccessful in his first run for the governor's seat, he ran again and was elected in 1928. As governor, Long built roads and bridges, eliminated the poll tax, and provided free textbooks for school children. He also built a strong state organization through what many said was a combination of coercion and political favors. Even after he entered the U.S. Senate, Long continued to dominate Louisiana politics and government.

Championing the poor against the interests of big business and the wealthy, Long had a strong appeal for a populace battered by the Depression. He supported the campaign of Franklin D. Roosevelt but later opposed FDR's NEW DEAL, believing that it was not

The Kingfish
Huey P. Long was one of the most flamboyant figures in American politics until he was assassinated in 1935. Championing the poor against the interests of big business and the wealthy, Long had a strong appeal for a populace battered by the Great Depression.

radical enough. Instead, in 1934, he proposed a Share Our Wealth Society that would have put a limit on personal wealth and guaranteed a minimum income and homesteading allowance.

Regarded in Washington as an eccentric (he reportedly wore green pajamas to greet formal callers), Long was famous for his lengthy and colorful Senate FILIBUSTERS.

Furious with Roosevelt for withholding patronage prizes, Long threatened to leave the Democratic party and in August 1935 declared his candidacy for president. Before his campaign got under way, Long was assassinated on September 8, 1935, in the Louisiana state capitol in Baton Rouge. His son, Russell B. LONG, served in the Senate from 1948 to 1987.   ~

Long, Russell B.

When Russell B. Long (1918-) entered politics in 1948, he was simply fulfilling his destiny as a twentieth-century Long of Louisiana. His father was Huey LONG, a flamboyant governor and senator of that state, assassinated in 1935. One uncle and a cousin were members of the House of Representatives, and another uncle was governor of Louisiana. Unlike his father, an ardent champion of the poor, Long spent much of his career aiding home-state businesses—specifically oil and gas producers—through the Internal Revenue Code. In his thirty-five years on the Senate FINANCE Committee, Long became a master of the tax code and oversaw its many revisions.

A Democrat, Long was elected to fill a vacant Senate seat in 1948 shortly before his thirtieth birthday. He joined the Finance Committee in 1953 and was its chairman from 1965 to 1981. The committee has jurisdiction over almost half of the federal government's spending, including Social Security and many social programs, as well as jurisdiction over the federal tax code.

His style of leadership on Finance was based on rewards. In exchange for members' support of legislation, Long allowed them to add provisions benefit-

Destiny Fulfilled
The Long family of Louisiana has loomed large in 20th century American politics. Russell B. Long, son of the famed Kingfish, was thirty years old when he entered the Senate in 1948. As chairman of the Finance Committee from 1965 to 1981, he oversaw many revisions of the tax code.

ing interests in their states. Critics complained that this led to unwieldy—and not always the best—legislation. But Long's critics within the Senate were few. Wily, candid, and generous with fund-raising help, Long was well-liked by colleagues. Their affection for him did not blind them to his shortcomings, however. Elected majority whip in 1965, Long was judged unreliable in that post and was removed in 1969. He retired from the Senate in 1987.   ∼

Longworth, Nicholas

Nicholas Longworth (1869-1931) served as a Republican representative from Ohio from 1903 to 1913 and from 1915 to 1931. He was a conservative rather than a progressive Republican who, in 1912, supported the presidential candidacy of William Howard Taft over his own father-in-law, Theodore Roosevelt. This contributed to his defeat in the elections of 1912. Longworth had little sympathy for partisan squabbles, believing that order and a spirit of cooperation were essential for the smooth running of the House of Representatives. Elected SPEAKER in 1925, Longworth restored much of the power of that office that had been lost when the House revolted against the dictatorial rule of Joseph G. CANNON in 1910.

An Ohio lawyer, Longworth became involved in politics first in Cincinnati and then at the state level. In the U.S. House he was one of Speaker Cannon's trusted lieutenants, a member of Cannon's inner circle and poker group. Longworth became majority leader in 1923 and was elected Speaker two years later.

As Speaker, Longworth was determined to centralize authority in his office. One of his first acts was to demote thirteen progressive Republicans to the bottom of committee rosters. The loss of seniority was punishment for their votes in favor of a progressive candidate for Speaker and against a rules change that Longworth favored. Longworth by-passed the party steering committee and, like Cannon, relied on a few trusted colleagues to control the House. Unlike Cannon, however, Longworth did not rule through arbitrary interpretation of House rules but through persuasion and mediation. He prized and achieved the efficient and dignified conduct of the House.   ～

Overleaf:
House sergeant-at-arms bearing mace.

Mace, House

The most treasured possession of the House of Representatives is the mace, a traditional symbol of legislative authority. The concept, borrowed from the British House of Commons, had its origin in republican Rome, where the fasces—an ax bound in a bundle of rods—symbolized the power of the magistrates.

The mace was adopted by the House in its first session in 1789 as a symbol of office for the SERGEANT-AT-ARMS, who is responsible for preserving order on the House floor. The first mace was destroyed when the British burned the Capitol in 1814, and for the next twenty-seven years a mace of painted wood was used.

The present mace, in use since 1841, is a replica of the original mace of 1789. It consists of a bundle of thirteen ebony rods bound in silver, terminating in a silver globe topped by a silver eagle with outstretched wings. It is forty-six inches high and was made by William Adams, a New York silversmith, for the sum of $400.

There have been a number of occasions in the history of the House when the sergeant-at-arms, on order of the Speaker, has lifted the mace from its pedestal and "presented" it before an unruly member. On each such occasion, order is said to have been promptly restored. At other times the sergeant-at-arms, bearing the mace, has passed up and down the aisles to quell boisterous behavior in the chamber.

When the House is in regular session, the mace rests on a tall pedestal beside the Speaker's desk. When the House is sitting as the COMMITTEE OF THE WHOLE, the mace is moved to a low pedestal nearby. Thus it is possible to tell at a glance whether the House is meeting in regular session or as the Committee of the Whole.'   ~

Madison, James

When James Madison (1751-1836) was in his mid-twenties he suffered from melancholia, leading him to conclude that he was fated to die young and that, faced with eternity, earthly matters had little importance. When he died at age eighty-seven, he could look back on a life distinguished by extraordinary service to his country. Wide reading and observation combined with concern for the needs of the infant United States led him to formulate many of the precepts later set forth in the Constitution. His influence on this document was so great that he is often called the Father of the Constitution.

As a young man, Madison was caught up in the political affairs of Virginia. In 1776 he was a delegate to Virginia's Revolutionary Convention, serving on the committee responsible for the drafting of Virginia's constitution and bill of rights. In 1780 he was elected to the Continental Congress, where he became a leader of those who favored the interests of national government over state sovereignty. Returned to Virginia, Madison entered the Virginia legislature in 1784.

Convinced that the Articles of Confederation were inadequate, Madison called for a convention to resolve problems plaguing the union of states. He played a leading role in the Constitutional Convention held in Philadelphia in 1787.

Madison was one of the authors of the "Virginia Plan," which proposed a tripartite national government, reflecting his belief that the governing power should be shared among three separate but dependent branches of government. Madison also advocated representation in Congress on the basis of state population, the right of the government to raise revenue, and the popular election of national legislators and executives. He kept the most extensive diary of the proceedings of the convention, published in 1840 as the Journal of the Federal Convention. With Alexander Hamilton and John Jay, he wrote the *Federalist Papers,* a series of commentaries on the Constitution aimed at building support for its ratification.

Government Roles

In 1789 Madison entered the new U.S. House of Representatives, where he served four terms. He introduced the Bill of Rights, fought for revenue legislation, and took part in shaping the executive branch. Angry over John Jay's 1796 treaty with Great Britain, Madison left Congress in 1797.

Madison served as secretary of state under President Thomas Jefferson and was elected to succeed him in 1808. Madison's presidency was plagued by political dissension and his inability to organize the country and armed forces for the War of 1812. After ratification of the Treaty of Ghent in 1815, Madison turned his attention to domestic problems and retired in 1817 with restored popularity.   ~

Majority Party Control.   See LEADERSHIP.

Mike Mansfield

Mansfield, Mike

Mike Mansfield (1903-), a Montana Democrat who followed Lyndon B. JOHNSON as majority leader of the Senate, exercised a permissive style of leadership that contrasted sharply with Johnson's methods. A representative for ten years and a senator for nearly twenty-five, Mansfield brought a wealth of congressional experience to the leadership post. His sixteen-year tenure as leader (1961-77) was the longest in Senate history. After Mansfield retired, President Jimmy Carter named him to be U.S. ambassador to Japan; the Japanese respected Mansfield so highly that President Ronald Reagan kept him in the post throughout his administration.

Mansfield left a career as a professor of Latin American and Asian history to run for Montana's First District House seat. Unsuccessful in 1940, he won in 1942. He gained a seat on the Foreign Affairs Committee, and in 1944 President Franklin D. Roosevelt sent him to China on a fact-finding mission.

Moving to the Senate in 1953, Mansfield was given a seat on the Foreign Relations Committee. He was one of the first two freshman senators to benefit from Johnson's decision to place newcomers on key committees. In the Senate as in the House, Mansfield compiled a liberal voting record on domestic and foreign issues.

A taciturn man, Mansfield often answered questions with a laconic "yep" or "nope." But his spareness with words did not keep him from the leadership track. In 1957 he became majority whip under Johnson. When Johnson moved to the vice presidency in 1961, Mansfield took over the majority leader's post. Johnson had been assertive, powerful, and manipulative; Mansfield was known as "the gentle persuader," because he held that each senator should conduct his affairs with minimal pressure from the leadership. Besides, he said, "Sooner or later they'd just tell you to go to hell and do what they wanted to anyway."

Mansfield held the respect of his colleagues, but he was not an aggressive leader, and under him the Johnson system of rewards and punishment gave way to a collegial leadership pattern in which the Democratic Policy Committee and the legislative committees played important roles. He was one of the first Democrats to differ openly with Johnson on the Vietnam War—and he was a leader of efforts to cut off funds for the war and thus force President Richard NIXON into negotiations to end it.   ~

Marbury v. Madison.   See
COURTS AND CONGRESS.

Markup.   See LEGISLATIVE
PROCESS.

Martin, Joseph W., Jr.

A representative from Massachusetts for forty-two years, Joseph W. Martin, Jr. (1884-1968), was leader of the House Republicans from 1939 to 1959. For most of those twenty years he was minority leader. But in the two Congresses in which the Republicans controlled the House (1947-49, 1953-55), Martin served as SPEAKER. He was the only Republican Speaker of the House between 1931 and the end of the Reagan administration. Martin also served as chairman of the Republican National Committee (1940-42).

Martin was a newspaper publisher in North Attleboro before he got involved in Republican politics in Massachusetts. After six terms in the state legislature, in 1925 he entered the U.S. House, where he remained until 1967. He served on the Foreign Affairs Committee and, later, the Rules Committee. Martin's name is not associated with any major legislation, nor was he known as an orator. A consummate politician, he was much more interested in the day-to-day workings of the House. "We are not reformers, not do-gooders, not theorists. . . . We are just practical Americans trying to do a practical job to reach practical goals," he said of members of Congress.

In 1933 Martin became minority whip. In this position and later, as minority leader and Speaker, Martin worked to defeat the domestic initiatives of Franklin D. Roosevelt and Harry S Truman. To this end, he helped to form an alliance of southern Democrats and Republicans, known as the CONSERVATIVE COALITION, which proved both durable and powerful. His efforts to derail the NEW DEAL, together with the opposition of New York Republicans Bruce Barton and Hamilton Fish, Jr., so enraged Roosevelt that during his 1940 presidential campaign he referred sarcastically to the three men as "that historic trio . . . Martin, Barton, and Fish."

If Martin's relations with Democratic presidents were bad, those with House Democratic leader Sam RAYBURN of Texas were correspondingly good—too good for many House Republicans. Martin had an amicable and cooperative relationship with Rayburn, who both preceded and succeeded him as Speaker.

In 1959 Republicans took the unusual step of ousting Martin as party leader, complaining that he was too old for the post and too conciliatory to the Democratic leadership. They replaced him with Charles A. Halleck of Indiana, an outspoken conservative.   ∼

McCarthy, Joseph R.

Joseph R. McCarthy (1908-57), a Republican senator from Wisconsin from 1947 to 1957, was Congress's most notorious anticommunist investigator of the post-World War II period. He gave his name to the atmosphere of fear and intimidation that pervaded American politics in the 1950s and helped extend the Cold War into the 1960s.

As chairman of the Senate Permanent Investigations Subcommittee in 1953-54, McCarthy conducted a series of wide-ranging and controversial INVESTIGATIONS; the State Department and the armed services were primary targets.

The hearings were the high-water mark of the "McCarthy era." National television exposure of the senator's abrasive and aggressive character, particularly during the Army-McCarthy hearings, began to turn public sentiment against McCarthyism. McCarthy's behavior led to his censure by the Senate in 1954. *(See* DISCIPLINING MEMBERS.*)*

McCarthy's Tactics

In February 1950 McCarthy fueled worries about communism with a speech in Wheeling, West Virginia, that claimed many government officials were communists. He followed up with six hours of accusations on the Senate floor. McCarthy charged that fifty-seven people, "known to the secretary of state as being communists," were still working and shaping policy at the State Department. Democrats, forced to respond to attacks on a Democratic administration, set up a special subcommittee of the Foreign Affairs Committee to investigate. During the panel's thirty-one days of hearings, McCarthy charged ten people by name with varying degrees of communist activities. He claimed he was hampered by President Harry S Truman's refusal to release the confidential personnel files of federal workers. However, the investigating panel, chaired by Maryland Democrat Millard E. Tydings, found most of McCarthy's charges to be false and rejected others because the person charged had never worked for the government. In its report the panel said, "We have seen how, through repetition and shifting untruths, it is possible to delude great numbers of people." In response, the Republican Policy Committee said the report was "of a purely political nature and is derogatory and insulting to Senator McCarthy."

The investigation, one of the most bitterly controversial in the history of Congress, became an important issue in the 1950 elections. Charges of "softness" toward communism were a major factor in Tydings's defeat and in several other campaigns. McCarthy, who took an active role in the Tydings race, was criticized in a later Senate investigation that called it a "despicable, back-street type of campaign."

In 1951 and 1952 investigations of alleged communism were carried out by both the House Un-American Activities

Joseph R. McCarthy

Committee and the newly formed Senate Judiciary Subcommittee on Internal Security. In 1953, when Republicans gained control of Congress, McCarthy launched his own investigations and hearings as chairman of a third "anticommunist" panel—Government Operations' Permanent Subcommittee on Investigations.

McCarthy, who had just been reelected, focused on a wide range of topics, questioning the Voice of America, the condition of State Department personnel files, trade with China, the loyalty of a Harvard University professor, and Army operations in New Jersey. His aides toured Europe, checking out the holdings of State Department libraries, which they complained included thousands of books written by communists or "communist sympathizers." In its year-end report, the subcommittee included among its accomplishments several resignations from the government of what it called "Fifth Amendment communists."

Army-McCarthy Hearings

The subcommittee was continuing its probe of possible spies in the Army in 1954 when McCarthy hit an unexpected roadblock. McCarthy had told a brigadier general he was questioning that the general was "not fit to wear that uniform" and did not have "the brains of a five-year-old." Army Secretary Robert T. Stevens announced he would appear in the officer's place. Stevens said he was "unwilling to have so fine an officer . . . run the risk of further abuse."

Eventually the Army charged that McCarthy and his staff had used improper means to seek preferential treatment for a private, G. David Schine, who had been a consultant to the subcommittee and a friend of committee counsel Roy M. Cohn. McCarthy, in turn, claimed the charges were an attempt to force the subcommittee to call off its probe of the Army. The result was an investigation by the subcommittee of its own and the Army's charges. McCarthy temporarily resigned his chairmanship. The thirty-five days of televised hearings presented an unprecedented look at the phenomenon by then widely known as McCarthyism.

In charges and countercharges, Stevens, Army counsel John G. Adams, McCarthy, Cohn, and several other witnesses told their stories, often contradicting one another. McCarthy, who managed to convince his fellow Republicans that he personally was innocent, made a poor impression on the television audience and on the Senate as a whole. The committee's report said McCarthy should have kept better control of his staff, especially Cohn, who was "unduly aggressive and persistent." Democrats, in a minority report, said McCarthy "fully acquiesced in and condoned" the "improper actions" of Cohn.

Censure by the Senate

By then McCarthy was already the subject of a censure resolution. Sen. Ralph E. Flanders, a Vermont Republican, had introduced the resolution, which charged McCarthy, among other things, with "personal contempt" of the Senate for refusing to answer questions and with "habitual contempt of people." On August 31, the same day the investigations subcommittee filed its report, two weeks of censure hearings began before a special bipartisan committee. The special committee recommended censure on two counts: McCarthy's conduct during the investigation of the Tydings election and his treatment of the brigadier general in early 1954. The Senate, voting after the November elections, accepted the first charge, but rewrote the second to focus on McCarthy's conduct during the censure hearings. The vote to censure McCarthy was 67 to 22.

With the return of the Senate to Democratic control in 1955, McCarthy lost his subcommittee chairmanship. His influence and his ability to command publicity had already been curbed by the Senate censure. McCarthy died of a liver ailment on May 2, 1957.   ∼

McCormack, John W.

Seventy years old when he became House SPEAKER in 1962, Massachusetts Democrat John W. McCormack (1891-1980) never managed to get the House running smoothly. Frustrated liberal Democrats tried to oust him in 1969; though their attempt failed, such an attack on a sitting Speaker was unprecedented. McCormack retired the next year, after forty-three years in the House, the first casualty of an increasingly impatient crowd of young Democrats who went on to REFORM House procedures in the 1970s.

McCormack, whose home was Boston, never attended high school, but he read law books at the law firm where he worked as an office boy. At the age of twenty-one, McCormack passed the bar. After a stint in the state legislature, he lost his first bid for Congress in 1926, but then, after the incumbent died, won the seat in 1928.

McCormack was an early ally of Texas Democrat Sam RAYBURN, who was elected majority leader in 1936. McCormack became secretary and then chairman of the House Democratic Caucus. When Rayburn became Speaker, he backed McCormack as majority leader, a key factor in McCormack's victory.

McCormack's poor reputation as Speaker overshadowed his more effective performance as number-two Democrat. Rayburn decided when to bring legislation to the floor and how to craft it for a maximum chance of success; McCormack did the legwork, rounding up votes and speaking for the Democratic leadership during the debate.

McCormack was comfortable on the floor. "I believe in fighting hard, but I don't like personal fights," he once said. "I go down on the floor of the House and take on my Republican friends." Though he consistently backed liberal positions on domestic issues, McCormack was never passionate about his beliefs. Not naturally inclined to be forceful, he had little chance to act independently while Rayburn was in charge.

When Rayburn died in November 1961, McCormack was heir-apparent and succeeded him without challenge. But McCormack was seen as a weak leader, particularly by the increasingly active liberal Democrats who were frustrated by the CONSERVATIVE COALITION of conservative southern Democrats and Republicans. When Republican gains in the 1966 elections reduced the Democratic majority, McCormack drew even more criticism for not bringing southern Democrats into line. His enthusiastic support of the war in Vietnam also made him out of step with many younger members.

In 1969 Rep. Morris Udall, an Arizona Democrat in his forties, ran for Speaker against McCormack. Although Udall got only fifty-seven votes, the challenge was a sign of how the Speaker's authority had declined. McCormack did not run for reelection in 1970.   ~

Members of Congress: Characteristics

Congress has been dominated since its inception by middle-aged white men with a background in law or business and a Christian upbringing. An elite group, representatives and senators have income and education levels well above the national average.

Members' average age in 1988 was about fifty-three, although senators and representatives ranged in age from thirty (Rep. John G. Rowland, a Connecticut Democrat, born in 1957) to almost ninety (Rep. Claude Pepper, a Florida Democrat, born in 1900). Back in 1869 the average age was forty-four. Senators on average are usually about five years older than representatives.

Blacks and women, shut out of Congress for decades, were well integrated into Congress by the late 1980s, but their numbers remained small. Twenty-three blacks and twenty-three women served in the landmark 100th Congress (1987-89). *(See* BLACKS IN CONGRESS; WOMEN IN CONGRESS; *also lists of members, pp. 487-489)*

Most members of Congress have undergraduate degrees, and many have additional training. By occupation, senators and representatives are primarily from law or business. In the 1980s roughly two-thirds of the Senate and almost half of the House were lawyers, though the number of lawyers in Congress has gradually declined since the 1970s. For lawyers, serving in Congress has often meant an enhanced reputation; in contrast, to an employee of a

Celebrities
Members of Congress who built their careers on celebrity status included Democratic senators Bill Bradley of New Jersey, left, once a basketball star, and John Glenn of Ohio, an ex-astronaut.

corporation, a stint in Congress may look more like a hindrance to his climb up the promotion ladder.

For many legislators serving in the 1980s, these occupations represented past activity. Serving in Congress had become a full-time job; ETHICS rules limited income earned outside of Congress, though income from investments such as real estate or stock was not restricted. In the 1970s and 1980s a new type of legislator emerged: the career politician whose primary earnings had always come from political office at the local, state, or federal level. That pattern was possible because states and localities had begun to think of political positions as full-time jobs, and they had raised salaries to reflect that concept. In 1987 more than 100 members considered public service and politics to be their primary occupation.

The route to Congress typically begins with local or state politics. Senators have often served in the House or as governor, while representatives frequently emerge from state legislatures or city councils. The line on a candidate biography—"No previous political office"—is not uncommon, though. In 1987 two new representatives—Maryland Democrat Thomas McMillen, a former basketball player, and Kentucky Republican Jim Bunning, a former baseball player—joined several other ex-athletes in Congress. Others who built their careers on celebrity status included Democratic senators Bill Bradley of New Jersey, once a basketball star, and John Glenn of Ohio, an ex-astronaut; and Republican Rep. Fred Grandy of Iowa, who starred in the television series "Loveboat."

Protestantism has been the most common religious affiliation for legislators, with about half in that category; Catholicism has been next. The number of Catholics and Jews in Congress increased in the 1960s and 1970s.

Although the House and Senate in many ways do not mirror the electorate, the House does reflect geographic shifts in the nation's population. After each ten-year census, the 435 districts are reapportioned, with a few states gaining or losing representatives. The Congress of the 1980s had far more Californians, Texans, and Floridians than the Congress of the 1930s; New York and Pennsylvania, on the other hand, continued to lose seats. *(See* REAPPORTIONMENT AND REDISTRICTING.*)*

Change in the characteristics of members has come slowly on Capitol Hill, in part because turnover rates have been low in this century. Incumbents usually seek reelection—and usually win another term in office. In 1986 about 96 percent of veteran legislators had successful campaigns.

Once in Congress, members in the 1980s stayed an average of about ten years. New members comprised an average of 12.3 percent of the House and 13.5 percent of the Senate between 1976 and 1986.   ~

Members: Service Records

Senators and representatives by the 1980s were spending an average of about ten and a half years in Congress. None was ready yet to challenge the record for the longest service in Congress, held by Carl HAYDEN, an Arizona

LONGEST SERVICE IN CONGRESS

Member	Years of Service		Total Years*
Carl T. Hayden, D-Ariz.	House:	1912-27	57
	Senate:	1927-69	
Carl Vinson, D-Ga.	House:	1914-65	50
Emanuel Celler, D-N.Y.	House:	1923-73	50
Sam Rayburn, D-Texas	House:	1913-61	49
Jamie L. Whitten, D-Miss.	House:	1941-	47†
Wright Patman, D-Texas	House:	1929-76	47
Joseph G. Cannon, R-Ill.	House:	1873-91	46
		1893-1913	
		1915-23	
Adolph J. Sabath, D-Ill.	House:	1907-52	46
Lister Hill, D-Ala.	House:	1923-38	45
	Senate:	1938-69	
George H. Mahon, D-Texas	House:	1935-79	44
Warren G. Magnuson, D-Wash.	House:	1937-44	44
	Senate:	1944-81	
Justin S. Morrill, R-Vt.	House:	1855-67	44
	Senate:	1867-98	
Melvin Price, D-Ill.	House:	1945-88	44
William B. Allison, R-Iowa	House:	1863-71	43
	Senate:	1873-1908	
Henry M. Jackson, D-Wash.	House:	1941-53	43
	Senate:	1953-83	

* As of 1988. Totals are based on exact dates of service. Minor differences in days or months of service determine rankings of members with the same total years.
† Service record as of June 1988. Whitten was seeking reelection.

Source: Congressional Research Service

Democrat who served in the House (1912-27) and Senate (1927-69) a total of fifty-seven years.

Hayden's record as longest-serving member of Congress was longer by seven years than any colleague's. Second place went to Rep. Carl Vinson (1914-65), a Georgia Democrat and long-time chairman of the House Armed Services Committee, who served for fifty years. Close behind Vinson, with just short of fifty years' service, came Rep. Emanuel Celler (1923-73), a New York Democrat who chaired the Judiciary Committee. Sam RAYBURN (1913-61), a Texas Democrat and House Speaker, served for almost forty-nine years.

The only member seeking reelection in 1988 who approached Rayburn's record was Rep. Jamie L. Whitten, a Mississippi Democrat who began his career in 1941. By the end of the 1987-89 term, Whitten's service would total forty-eight years.   ~

Merchant Marine and Fisheries Committee, House

An odd mix of legislation makes Merchant Marine and Fisheries a hybrid committee, where apologists for the shipping industry rub shoulders with environmental activists. A primary activity has been to keep in place the massive subsidies and cargo preference rules that have supported the ailing U.S. shipping industry since 1916. But the committee has not had the clout to expand support of the industry, which has been swamped by international competition and hampered by dissension among unions, shipbuilders, and ship operators.

Merchant Marine's standing has not been been helped by charges of unethical behavior against committee leaders. New York Democrat John M.

Murphy was chairman of Merchant Marine in 1980 when he was caught up in the ABSCAM scandal on charges of influence peddling. He lost his reelection bid that year.

Mario Biaggi, also a New York Democrat, was vice-chairman of Merchant Marine in 1988 when he was convicted on bribery charges; the House ethics panel recommended his expulsion. *(See* DISCIPLINING MEMBERS.*)*

History

Merchant Marine was set up in 1887. Considered a secondary committee, it attracts members from coastal and Great Lakes districts. In addition to shipping, the committee oversees the oceans, including fishing policy, wildlife and fisheries, and the Coast Guard. On many environmental issues it shares jurisdiction with other committees. Its Senate counterpart on most questions is the COMMERCE, SCIENCE AND TRANSPORTATION Committee.

Because of Merchant Marine's relatively narrow jurisdiction, advocates of reorganization proposed eliminating the committee in the 1970s. The chairman at the time, Missouri Democrat Leonor K. Sullivan, managed to defeat attempts to abolish her committee.

North Carolina Democrat Walter B. Jones took over the committee in 1981 after Murphy's election defeat. High on the seniority list was Gerry E. Studds, a Massachusetts Democrat from a district with fishing and shipping interests.

Merchant Marine in the 1980s was successful in fighting user fees for recreational boaters and in passing toxic cleanup legislation. The committee also managed to resist efforts by agricultural interests to win an exemption for their products from existing "cargo preference" rules, which required shippers to use U.S.-operated vessels, instead of less expensive foreign-flag ships, for half of all government-generated exports.   ~

Michel, Robert H.

Robert H. Michel (1923-), elected House minority leader in 1981, steered his party to victories no one expected the Republicans to win. His successes earned the Illinois Republican a reputation among many as the most impressive House leader of either party since Democrat Sam RAYBURN of Texas.

While some of his victories were due in part to President Ronald Reagan's popularity, Michel knew how to work the Reagan factor for every vote it could produce. His instinct for House politics enabled him to maintain unity in a Republican bloc driven frequently to quarreling by its semi-permanent minority status.

The White House depended on Michel's skills during the months of negotiations in 1981 over Reagan's budget and tax bills—skills that delivered virtual Republican unanimity on key votes. The package of anticrime bills that became law in the 98th Congress (1983-85) and the continuation of aid to the Nicaraguan contras in the 99th (1985-87) could be attributed to Michel's quiet intervention at key moments.

It was also a measure of his ability that he survived as a leader in the Reagan years. With what he called "gentle persuasion," Michel balanced the demands of junior conservatives, urging confrontation with the Democrats, against those of moderates in the party. Having maintained good relations with the Democrats, he was able to win victories that would have been impossible without their votes.

Michel was first elected in 1956 and spent much of his congressional career as a member of the APPROPRIATIONS COMMITTEE. During his quarter-century on that committee, Michel became a top-flight negotiator, skilled in the

Robert H. Michel

trade-offs and compromises that are the hallmark of the APPROPRIATIONS process.

Michel became minority whip in 1974, a position he held until his election as minority leader, when House Republicans opted for his "workhorse" campaign arguments over the oratorical flourishes of opponent Guy Vander Jagt of Michigan. (See LEADERSHIP.)   ~

Mills, Wilbur D.

An expert on U.S. tax law, Wilbur D. Mills (1909-) skillfully used his knowledge and political savvy during seventeen years as chairman of the House WAYS AND MEANS Committee (1957-74). Mills's preeminent position made his fall in 1974 even more dramatic. After well-publicized escapades with a striptease dancer, he resigned as chairman and, acknowledging problems with alcoholism, entered a hospital for treatment. Mills served the term he had just won and then retired in 1977.

Mills was a judge in White County, Arkansas, when he first ran for Congress in 1938. Friendship with Democratic leader Sam RAYBURN won Mills a seat in 1943 on the Ways and Means Committee, a coveted spot usually reserved for more senior members. Mills studied the tax code and by the time he became chairman was well known for his grasp of even minor details. Colleagues were awed by his ability to speak, without notes, in favor of his committee's work.

An authoritarian chairman, Mills kept control over all tax measures by bringing them before the whole committee and refusing to establish subcommittees to consider different issues. Mills solidified his power by accurately sensing what the House would support and drafting legislation accordingly. He took tax bills to the floor under ground rules that barred floor amendments, and the full House regularly passed the measures by wide margins.

Mills's personal prestige was enhanced by his role as chairman of the Democratic Committee on Committees; since 1910 the chairman of Ways and Means, along with the panel's Democratic members, had made Democratic committee assignments. Mills was the last chairman, though, to have the double responsibility; the Democratic CAUCUS in 1974 shifted committee assignments to the Democratic Steering and Policy Committee. The caucus also tried to dilute the authority of the Ways and Means chairman by expanding the panel from twenty-five to thirty-five members.

Conservative in his politics, Mills still managed to work with Presidents John F. KENNEDY and Lyndon B. JOHNSON, though not on every issue. Opposition from Mills was enough to kill a bill; his resistance to Medicare stalled the legislation for several years.

By the 1970s Mills was a target of Democratic reformers, who considered his accumulation of power improper and a roadblock to a more democratic House. His personal indiscretions simply bolstered their position. In October 1974 police stopped Mills's car near the Tidal Basin, a shallow part of the Potomac River not far from the Washington Monument. One of the passengers, later identified as stripteaser Fanne Fox, jumped from the car and ended up in the water. Several weeks later Mills appeared briefly on stage with Fox in Boston.

Although he had just been reelected, his standing in Congress was never the same. After his retirement in 1977, Mills stayed in Washington, working for a law firm, Shea and Gould, and lobbying his former colleagues.   ~

Morning Business.   See
MORNING HOUR.

Morning Hour

The morning hour is a time set aside by the Senate at the beginning of a daily session for transaction of routine business. Under Senate rules, the morning "hour" may actually extend for up to two hours. During that period members conduct what is known as morning business—introducing bills, filing committee reports, and receiving messages from the House of Representatives or the president. Senators may make brief speeches by unanimous consent. A senator also may move to consider any bill on the CALENDAR, but such motions must be decided without debate. That tactic is rarely used.

The Senate's rules do not call for a morning hour every day—only if its previous session ended in ADJOURNMENT. Even then, the morning hour may be limited or dropped by unanimous consent. Between adjournments, the Senate conducts morning business by unanimous consent. *(See* LEGISLA-TIVE DAY.*)*

Although House rules also provide for a morning hour, the arrangement is almost never used there.   ~

Motions

Motions play as important a role as VOTING in Congress. In fact, without the use of motions members could never reach the stage where votes take place. Virtually every step in the LEGISLATIVE PROCESS is initiated and completed by motions of one type or another. Put another way, motions enable senators and representatives to consider and dispose of legislation in a deliberate and orderly manner. Certain motions are especially important to the opponents of a bill, giving the minority side on any issue an opportunity to be heard and to present its policy choices.

Motions have specific functions, and their use is governed by the parliamentary situation. Among others, there are motions to adjourn, recess, postpone debate, end debate, withdraw other motions, proceed to the consideration of a bill or conference report, TA-BLE a bill, RECONSIDER a bill, strike out and insert SUBSTITUTE provisions in a bill, RECOMMIT a bill to a committee, DISCHARGE a committee from consideration of a bill, move the PREVIOUS QUESTION to bring a measure to a vote, SUSPEND the rules, and make a POINT OF ORDER. A few are used only in one chamber.

Under normal circumstances, members can offer motions or initiate other legislative business only when they are recognized by the chair (the presiding officer). Once a member who has the floor offers, or "moves," a motion or introduces an amendment, he or she gives up the floor.

The standing rules of each house recognize certain motions as having precedence over others. A formal hierarchy is necessary to avoid confusion and disputes when several members desire to offer different, and sometimes conflicting, motions at the same time. A tabling motion supersedes a motion to reconsider a previous vote on a bill. A vote therefore would be held on the tabling motion first; if adopted, the motion to reconsider would be nullified. A motion to adjourn in either house takes precedence over all others.

Some motions are more important than others—even indispensable—to the everyday operations of the House and Senate. Others are clearly dilatory in intent. Some are offered merely to gain extra debate time when the House is sitting as the COMMITTEE OF THE WHOLE and debate on amendments is limited to five minutes for each side. Pro forma motions "to strike the last word" or "to strike the enacting clause" of a bill give proponents and opponents each five additional minutes to debate an amendment. However, delays cannot go on indefinitely. A member who thinks debate is dilatory can always offer his own motion to end debate immediately or at a specified time. This procedure for ending debate does not apply in the Senate.   ~

Overleaf:
Raising flags over the Capitol to be sent to constituents.

Narcotics Abuse and Control Committee, House Select

Back in 1977, before "Just Say No" campaigns and proposals for mandatory drug testing, the House set up a select committee to study drug problems. The Select Committee on Narcotics Abuse and Control focused then on marijuana and heroin; by the late 1980s its primary concern was cocaine.

Like other select committees, the panel has no legislative jurisdiction but holds hearings and conducts investigations; it must be reauthorized at the beginning of each two-year term of Congress.

Several other House committees, including JUDICIARY, FOREIGN AFFAIRS, and ENERGY AND COMMERCE, have legislative jurisdiction over various aspects of drugs. When Congress passed a massive antidrug bill in 1986, eleven House standing committees contributed to the measure, which also included some proposals made by the Narcotics Committee.

Democrat Charles B. Rangel became chairman of the Narcotics Committee in 1983; he was the third New Yorker in a row to head the committee. Rangel, whose Harlem district was plagued with some of the country's worst drug problems, had worked on the narcotics issue for most of his House career.   ~

New Deal

The period in U.S. history known as the New Deal generally refers to the first two terms (1933-41) of President Franklin D. Roosevelt. An aggregate of hundreds of individual programs, the New Deal was designed to rescue the United States from the greatest economic depression in its history. The recovery programs of the Roosevelt administration in turn brought about major changes in American society, economic relationships, and government.

Roosevelt coined the term "New Deal" in his acceptance speech at the 1932 Democratic National Convention in Chicago. Breaking with tradition by attending the convention in person to accept the party's presidential nomination, Roosevelt pledged "a new deal for the American people." He was the overwhelming winner in 1932 against President Herbert Hoover. That election also gave FDR large Democratic majorities in both houses of Congress, providing the new president with a clear mandate to initiate his recovery programs. Roosevelt vowed in his presidential inaugural speech "to treat the task as we would treat the emergency of a war."

Philosophy

Roosevelt's governing philosophy rested on a dynamic role for the federal government, including Washington's responsibility to relieve the nation's poverty and unemployment. His New Deal called for massive changes in agriculture to improve the lot of the farmer through a variety of assistance programs; conservation and development of the nation's resources for the widest benefit of the nation's population; new protections for the working man and reform of labor-management relations; rehabilitation of American industry to establish a more productive as well as a more humane economy; wholesale changes in the nation's financial system, including tighter federal regulation of banking and securities exchanges; and, internationally, lower tariffs and reciprocal trade agreements to stimulate business activity.

Although a long list of innovative domestic programs and reforms are associated with the New Deal, Roosevelt did not assume office with an overall plan to remake the U.S. economy or institute a welfare state. Rather, the New Deal began with a series of stopgap relief measures aimed at revitalizing free enterprise, which was near collapse after four years of massive economic dislocation. Pragmatic rather than doctrinaire, FDR drew on the ideas of experts in many fields in and out of government. Many of his proposals originated in the PROGRESSIVE ERA and in the Wilson administration's experience in mobilizing the country in World War I. But the New Deal went far beyond any earlier American government involvement in the affairs of its citizens.

Strategy

Immediately upon taking office, Roosevelt convened a special session of Congress—the famous "Hundred Days" session—to deal with the economic emergency. Congress, acting with breathless speed and virtually without debate, enacted some fifteen landmark bills proposed by the administration, most of them highly controversial. The president himself delivered ten major speeches. He assumed the role of a bipartisan leader reaching out to all groups and interests in a time of crisis. That strategy could not last indefinitely, especially as the New Deal in later years concentrated on fundamental long-term reforms and programs directed at groups and economic interests that threatened its success. Conservative southern Democrats as well as northern industrialists, whom the president called "economic royalists," in-

Launching the New Deal
Franklin D. Roosevelt's landslide victory in the 1932 presidential election provided a clear mandate for his New Deal recovery programs. Here Roosevelt confers with Sen. Joseph T. Robinson of Arkansas, Senate majority leader from 1933 to 1937.

creasingly felt uncomfortable and insecure. And by early 1935 the more innovative New Deal laws were being challenged directly by the Supreme Court. In the next year and a half, the Court overturned six of the New Deal's most sweeping laws. *(See* COURTS AND CONGRESS.*)*

In his second term Roosevelt began to focus the New Deal on structural reform and was more outwardly supportive of organized labor, the unemployed and the rural poor, the aged, and small business. At the same time he called for more stringent federal regulation of big business and higher taxation on the more affluent. He tried to meet head-on the Supreme Court's challenge by introducing his so-called "Court-packing" idea. Having just won reelection in the greatest presidential landslide in U.S. history, FDR early in 1937 called for increasing the Court's size as a way to

dilute the influence of several old, conservative justices on the nine-member bench. In this he suffered one of his most humiliating defeats in Congress. He miscalculated public reaction, and the plan divided the ranks of the New Deal coalition.

Though he lost the battle, FDR won the war. Even before Congress debated the controversial proposal, the Court began to show a willingness to accept New Deal policies. Newly passed legislation similar to that declared unconstitutional just a year or two earlier was now upheld. And changes in the membership of the Supreme Court, beginning with the appointment of Hugo Black in August 1937, ensured that a majority of the justices would be sympathetic to the expansive legislation of the New Deal.

Between March 1937 and February 1941 the Court upheld revised versions of virtually all the legislation it had declared unconstitutional in Roosevelt's first term. In doing so, it reversed many of the doctrines it had espoused in curtailing state and federal power over economic matters. The Court's new direction culminated in a 1941 decision upholding the Fair Labor Standards Act of 1935, commonly known as the Wagner Act. That law prohibited child labor, set a maximum forty-hour work week and established the first national minimum wage (forty cents an hour) for workers engaged in, or producing goods for, interstate commerce. Child labor was prohibited, and severe limits were placed on teenage employment in hazardous occupations. *(See COMMERCE POWER.)*

Nevertheless, the political costs of Roosevelt's defeat on the Court bill had lasting effects on the New Deal. After 1938 a CONSERVATIVE COALITION of southern Democrats and Republicans repeatedly blocked administration initiatives. At the same time, the administration was forced to turn its attention to mobilization for war. Still, as late as 1939 FDR could point to enactment of an impressive list of administrative reforms for controlling the expanded federal bureaucracy.

Legislation

The National Industrial Recovery Act (NIRA) was the centerpiece of the New Deal's recovery plan. Enacted in 1933, the measure established a National Recovery Administration that encouraged cooperation among industry trade groups under exemption from antitrust laws. It also set maximum daily working hours and minimum wage rates, and it guaranteed workers the right to join a labor union and bargain collectively. Other provisions of the law established a Public Works Administration to organize and supervise a network of public works projects. This landmark law was overturned by the Supreme Court in 1935, only to be re-

placed by the even stronger Wagner Act.

The NIRA was only one of the major New Deal bills. The Agricultural Adjustment Act aimed to increase farm income by holding down production. The Wagner-Steagall Act established the Federal Housing Authority and authorized several billion dollars—an unheard of amount in those days—to supervise and finance slum clearance and construction of low-income housing. The Home Owners' Loan Act set up the Home Owners' Loan Corporation to help avert foreclosures by refinancing home mortgages at very low interest rates. The Glass-Steagall Banking Act barred commercial banks from operating in the investment banking business and established the Federal Deposit Insurance Corporation. The Securities Exchange Act established a commission to fight fraud and misrepresentation in the securities business. Probably the best known and most lasting New Deal accomplishment was federal old age and unemployment insurance: the Social Security Act of 1935.   ~

Nixon, Richard

The stormy career of Richard Nixon (1913-) reached heights and fell to lows remarkable in American political history. After two terms in the House as a Republican representative from California, he moved to the Senate. Before he could complete his first term, he was put on the Republican ticket with Dwight D. Eisenhower in 1952 and became the second youngest vice president in the nation's history.

In 1960 Nixon lost a close race for the presidency to John F. Kennedy. Two years later he lost a bid for the California governorship and bade a bitter farewell to politics. "You won't have Nixon to kick around anymore," he told

Inside Story
A new member of Congress soon learns the ins and outs of life on Capitol Hill. In this 1947 picture rookie Rep. Richard Nixon gets an insider's glimpse of the House chamber from House Clerk Ralph Roberts.

members of the press, which he blamed for his two losses. Six years later Nixon was elected president; he was reelected in 1972. Midway through his second term he was forced to resign in the wake of the WATERGATE SCANDAL.

Nixon viewed his career in terms of crises and setbacks (he wrote *Six Crises,* a political memoir, in 1972). His rise to high political office was swift, impelled by political rainmakers who chose him as a candidate before, it seemed, he had declared himself. Nixon was a lieutenant in the Navy in 1946 when a California Republican group asked him to run for the House of Representatives. He accepted and was successful, accusing his opponent, Jerry Voorhis, a NEW DEAL Democrat, of communist sympathies.

As a freshman representative, Nixon served on the Education and Labor Committee, where he helped to draft the Taft-Hartley Act of 1947, a landmark labor law. His career in the House is most notable, though, for his activities on the House Un-American Activities Committee. Over the objections of some committee members, Nixon persuaded the committee chairman to allow him to reopen an investigation into charges that Alger Hiss, a former State Department official, had communist affiliations. The investigation led to Hiss's indictment for perjury, the first indictment to result from the committee's investigation into communist activities. The case brought Nixon national recognition, and, as he himself acknowledged in *Six Crises*, "it also left a residue of hatred and hostility toward me" that was to wax and wane throughout his public career. *(See* INVESTIGATIONS.)

Nixon used the country's fear of communism to his advantage in his 1950 Senate bid, linking the voting record of his Democratic opponent, incumbent Helen Gahagan Douglas, with that of an allegedly procommunist representative. Nixon won handily, but

many observers called his campaign the dirtiest on record, and Nixon's later reputation as a ruthless campaigner stemmed from his conduct then.

Nixon was in the Senate less than two years when he caught the eye of New York governor Thomas E. Dewey, who was promoting Eisenhower's 1952 bid for the presidency. Soon Dewey also was promoting Nixon for the vice presidency. Nixon came close to being forced off the ticket when charges surfaced that he had used the proceeds of a secret campaign fund to supplement his Senate salary. On September 23, 1952, he went on national television to rebut the charges, referring at one point to his wife's "respectable Republican cloth coat," and to a dog, Checkers, that had been given to his children.

Nixon's own presidency was notable for his achievements in foreign relations, particularly improved relations with the Soviet Union and China and the ending of the war in Vietnam. His domestic programs, however, suffered gravely from poor relations with the Democratic Congress. With the revelations brought to light by the investigations into the break-in at the Watergate headquarters of the Democratic National Committee, his administration faltered to a standstill. In the face of almost certain IMPEACHMENT and removal from office for obstruction of justice, Nixon left the White House on August 9, 1974, the first American president to resign the office. *(See* NIXON IMPEACHMENT EFFORT.)   ～

Nixon Impeachment Effort

Dusting off its rarely used impeachment machinery, Congress in 1974 began impeachment proceedings against President Richard Nixon for his role in the WATERGATE SCANDAL. Nixon's resignation from the presidency cut

Telling Evidence
Release of taped White House conversations concerning Watergate led directly to President Richard Nixon's departure from office. The Supreme Court ordered Nixon to release the tapes, which made clear that the president had participated in efforts to cover up the Watergate burglary.

short the effort, thus sparing him almost certain impeachment and removal from office.

Under the IMPEACHMENT POWER granted by the Constitution, Congress may remove the president and other officials for "treason, bribery, or other high crimes and misdemeanors." The process requires two steps. An accused official must first be formally charged, or impeached, by the House of Representatives. The official then must be convicted on those charges in a Senate trial. Only one president before Nixon had faced a serious impeachment threat: Andrew Johnson, who was acquitted by the Senate in 1868. *(See* JOHNSON IMPEACHMENT TRIAL.*)*

The House JUDICIARY Committee adopted three charges, called articles of impeachment, against Nixon in late July 1974. The articles charged him with abuse of his presidential powers, obstruction of justice, and contempt of Congress. The full House never voted on these articles; Nixon resigned, on August 9, after Republican House and Senate leaders told him that the evidence against him virtually ensured that he would be impeached, convicted, and removed from office.

The chain of events that ended in Nixon's resignation began with a 1972 break-in at Democratic National Committee headquarters in the Watergate office building in Washington, D.C. A national scandal unfolded with discovery of White House involvement in the burglary and other political sabotage, as well as subsequent cover-up efforts. The extent of White House activities was spelled out in 1973 hearings before a special Senate committee headed by Sen. Sam J. ERVIN, a North Carolina Democrat who was noted for his knowledge of the Constitution.

A House impeachment inquiry was triggered in October 1973 when Nixon fired a special prosecutor who had been appointed to investigate the Watergate affair. The prosecutor, Archibald Cox, had tried to force Nixon to release tapes of conversations concerning Watergate. In July 1974 the Supreme Court ordered Nixon to release the tapes, which made clear that the president had participated in efforts to cover up White House involvement in the burglary. The Supreme Court action came as the House Judiciary Committee was preparing to vote on impeachment charges against Nixon.

The Judiciary Committee approved three articles of impeachment in a series of votes July 27-30. The first, adopted 27-11, charged Nixon with obstruction of justice. The second, adopted 28-10, charged him with abuse of power. The third, adopted 21-17, charged him with contempt of Congress.

House debate on impeachment was set to begin August 19. Adoption of the charges was considered a certainty, and the Senate began preparing for a trial. It was at this point that Republican congressional leaders told Nixon the evidence against him almost guaranteed that he would be impeached, convicted, and removed from office. On August 8 Nixon went on television to announce that he would resign. The following day, his resignation effective, Nixon left the White House.

The House Judiciary Committee was still preparing its report recommending Nixon's impeachment, and the report was later filed in the House. But the impeachment proceedings themselves went no further. A month after succeeding Nixon, President Gerald R. FORD granted his predecessor a "full, free and absolute pardon ... for all offenses against the United States which he ... has committed or may have committed" during his years as president. ~

Norris, George W.

George W. Norris (1861-1944) entered Congress as a Republican, became a Progressive Republican, and ended his congressional career as an Indepen-

dent Republican. No matter what his party label, Norris was and remained a reformer. His zeal led him to advocate changes in the House of Representatives, the electoral system, the ownership of utilities, and the resolution of labor disputes.

Norris entered the House of Representatives from Nebraska in 1903. He joined with Democrats in 1908 to try to curtail the powers of the SPEAKER so abused by Joseph G. CANNON, a Republican. The attempt was unsuccessful, and Norris's constituents were unimpressed; he was reelected by a margin of twenty-two votes. Norris and his Democratic allies eventually won their goal, however, and in 1910 the Speaker was stripped of much of his power.

Norris moved to the Senate in 1913, the year that the Seventeenth Amendment, calling for DIRECT ELECTION OF SENATORS, was ratified. Norris had backed that change and continued to push for presidential primaries and the abolition of the electoral college. He supported President Woodrow Wilson's domestic policies but was one of six senators to vote against entry into World War I. He voted against the Treaty of Versailles, which ended the war and created the League of Nations.

Concerned by filibusters that slowed the proceedings of the Senate, Norris proposed doing away with the "lame-duck" session at the end of every Congress (held after the election of a new Congress but before it began on March 4). The Senate was most vulnerable to filibuster during the short session. Norris wrote the Twentieth Amendment to the Constitution, ratified in 1933, which abolished the short session by advancing the first day of a Congress to January. (See LAME-DUCK AMENDMENT.)

A supporter of organized labor, Norris sponsored legislation restricting the use of federal injunctions against striking workers. He believed that hydroelectric power should be publicly owned, and he sponsored the legislation establishing the Tennessee Valley Authority.

Never one to take party ties too seriously, Norris endorsed the candidacy of Franklin D. Roosevelt in 1932 and subsequent elections. Norris was defeated for reelection in 1942.   ~

Overleaf:
The Speaker's Lobby in the Capitol.

Oath of Office

Article VI of the Constitution stipulates that senators and representatives, as well as the president and other public officers, "shall be bound by Oath or Affirmation to support this Constitution; but no religious Test shall ever be required as a qualification to any Office or public Trust under the United States."

The form of the oath of office was established by law:

"I, A B, do solemnly swear (or affirm) that I will support and defend the Constitution of the United States against all enemies, foreign and domestic; that I will bear true faith and allegiance to the same; that I take this obligation freely, without any mental reservation or purpose of evasion, and that I will well and faithfully discharge the duties of the office on which I am about to enter. So help me God."

The oath of office is administered to newly elected members at the start of each new Congress in January of odd-numbered years. Because the entire House is up for election every two years, all representatives take the oath each time. Members first elect their chief presiding officer, the SPEAKER, and he is sworn in by the CLERK OF THE HOUSE; the Speaker then administers the oath to all other members as they stand together in the chamber. In the Senate,

297

one-third of whose members are elected every two years, the vice president administers the oath to senators-elect as they come to the front of the chamber in small groups.   ~

Omnibus Bills

A noteworthy feature of the modern Congress has been its tendency to package many, often unrelated, proposals in a single, very long piece of legislation.

Although omnibus bills have been used throughout the nation's history, they assumed new importance after Congress adopted its BUDGET PROCESS in 1974. Using that process, each year the Senate and House of Representatives adopt an omnibus budget resolution setting an overall plan for government spending and revenues. They follow up with another omnibus measure revising government programs to conform to the overall plan.

In addition, it became common practice in the 1980s for Congress to provide funding for most or all government departments and agencies in a single, omnibus bill known as a CONTINUING RESOLUTION.

These omnibus bills accounted for a large share of legislative action in the 1980s, as Congress struggled to reduce the federal budget deficit. Critics complained that individual provisions of the bills often received little debate, and members were forced to vote on the mammoth measures without fully understanding what they were doing.

Others defended the omnibus approach, however, arguing that members benefited from the broad overview of government activities it provided. Some noted that many politically unpopular actions, however necessary, might be impossible unless they were buried in an omnibus bill.   ~

O'Neill, Thomas P., Jr.

As SPEAKER of the House of Representatives from 1977 until his retirement in 1987, Thomas P. O'Neill, Jr., (1912-) found himself playing a role that could not have been more alien to his background. In his twenty-seven years as a Democratic representative from Massachusetts prior to becoming Speaker, "Tip" O'Neill had practiced a closely held insider's politics, talking strategy with close friends over poker or golf. The speakership in those years was similarly an inside office. O'Neill's three predecessors sought to win key showdowns on the House floor by quietly building coalitions within the chamber.

O'Neill became Speaker just as House members began to put more stock in independence, rather than party loyalty, and to take their cues from constituencies outside the chamber. O'Neill soon found that he could win more votes by influencing public opinion than by twisting arms. And—as the one visible Democratic officeholder at the national level during the first six years of the Reagan administration—O'Neill inevitably became the party symbol to the national press.

O'Neill came to the House in 1953, a cigar-smoking, poker-playing Red Sox fan from Cambridge, proud of his great success in state politics, where he had been his party's first Speaker of the Massachusetts House in the twentieth century. In Congress O'Neill joined the PUBLIC WORKS COMMITTEE to make sure that Massachusetts got its share of federal jobs and projects. In his second term he moved to the RULES COMMITTEE, which controls access to the floor for major legislation. During his eighteen years on Rules, O'Neill nearly always supported the Speaker; he was

Talking Strategy
Presiding over the House is only part of the Speaker's job. In this 1985 picture Speaker Thomas P. O'Neill, Jr., meets with Democratic floor leaders to discuss budget strategy.

viewed more as a loyal soldier than as a potential House leader.

Two events helped change that perception. In late 1967 O'Neill broke with President Lyndon B. JOHNSON and publicly opposed the war in Vietnam, thus drawing the attention of younger House liberals. Three years later O'Neill worked with many of these same liberals to pass a major reform of House procedure. In 1971 O'Neill won a place on the leadership ladder as majority whip, and in 1973 he became majority leader. When Carl ALBERT retired as Speaker in 1976, Democrats made O'Neill Speaker by acclamation.

Strongly partisan, more interested in the politics of the House than the content of legislation, O'Neill carried the Democratic banner during the Carter and Reagan administrations. Although he had no particular enthusiasm for President Jimmy Carter's programs, O'Neill worked hard to get them through Congress. He pushed through

tough ethics legislation and speedily delivered House approval of Carter's massive energy package. But by the end of Carter's term O'Neill was having a difficult time, often unable to break up a united Republican front or to prevent Democratic defections.

With the election in 1980 of a Republican president and a Republican-controlled Senate, O'Neill fell victim to the rising level of partisan tension on the House floor and was unable to block House approval of President Ronald Reagan's economic package. Democrats regained effective control of the House in the 1982 elections. In his final years as Speaker, O'Neill nearly always had the votes to prevail when he wanted. ~

ADDITIONAL READING

O'Neill, Thomas P., Jr., and William Novak. *Man of the House: The Life and Political Memoirs of Speaker Tip O'Neill.* 1987.

Winning Ways
Effective oversight requires the cooperation of the executive branch, but Congress can bring pressure to bear on agency officials. A contempt citation against Anne M. Burford, former head of the Environmental Protection Agency, was canceled in 1983 after the White House turned over documents sought by congressional investigators. Burford had refused to provide the documents.

Oversight Power

Congress has delegated to the executive branch broad authority over agencies and programs it has created. Its oversight power helps it make sure that the executive branch performs as Congress intends it to do.

Hearings and INVESTIGATIONS, the most publicized form of oversight, provide some of the most colorful moments on Capitol Hill. The protracted 1987 hearings on the IRAN-CONTRA AFFAIR exposed a web of covert activities involving members of President Ronald Reagan's National Security Council. There were moments of high drama as Marine Lt. Col. Oliver L. North, a former NSC staff member, defended his role in U.S. arms sales to Iran and the diversion of profits from those sales to antigovernment guerrillas in Nicaragua.

Oversight takes less spectacular forms as well. The most effective may stem from the power of the PURSE. Because Congress controls the federal purse strings, it is able to review agencies' performance and demand changes before providing the money needed to operate agency programs. House and Senate Appropriations committees make searching inquiries into agency activities before voting annual APPROPRIATIONS. Other committees review agency performance as they consider renewal of AUTHORIZATIONS, without which programs cannot be funded.

Lawmakers also exercise their oversight function through informal contacts with executive officials. The GENERAL ACCOUNTING OFFICE and other support agencies help Congress keep tabs on what is going on in the executive branch. In addition, many agencies are required to make regular reports to Congress on their activities. Staffs of individual members of Congress conduct ongoing oversight through casework—the handling of constituent questions and problems regarding agency actions.

The Supreme Court in 1983 ruled unconstitutional another widely used oversight device. That was the LEGISLATIVE VETO, by which one or both houses of Congress—or sometimes even a committee—could overrule executive actions. The Supreme Court decision, in the case of *Immigration and Natural-*

ization Service v. Chadha, was a major victory for the executive branch, which had traditionally opposed the legislative veto as an intrusion on executive branch responsibility for carrying out the laws. The decision was a major defeat for Congress, whose attorneys had argued that the legislative veto was a useful and necessary modern invention that enabled Congress to delegate authority without abdicating responsibility. Congress had included legislative veto provisions in more than 200 laws since 1932.

The *Chadha* decision did not end the use of legislative vetoes, which continued to be included in bills passed by Congress. Legislators and executive branch officials also explored informal alternatives to the legislative veto. The device had been useful to both branches, permitting Congress to give the executive branch broad leeway over administration of programs while retaining ultimate control.

Developing Role

Congress did not officially acknowledge an oversight role until it enacted the Legislative Reorganization Act of 1946. That law directed the House and Senate standing committees to exercise "continuous watchfulness of the execution by the administrative agencies" of the laws and programs under their jurisdiction. Another reorganization act approved in 1970 called for regular reports on oversight activities. Better oversight of fiscal and budgetary matters was the aim of the Congressional Budget and Impoundment Control Act of 1974. Committee reorganization measures in the mid-1970s required many House committees to set up oversight subcommittees and certain Senate committees to carry out "comprehensive policy oversight."

This new interest in oversight investigations came about in part because of revelations of executive branch abuses, beginning with the WATERGATE SCANDAL that drove President Richard Nixon from office in 1974. Following its investigation of the Nixon White House, Congress investigated the performance of the Central Intelligence Agency. The fifteen-month inquiry confirmed that the CIA had spied on U.S. citizens, participated in assassination plots against foreign leaders, and engaged in other abuses of its authority. In the wake of the investigation, both the Senate and the House set up permanent Intelligence committees with oversight jurisdiction over the agency. Other congressional investigations faulted the performance of the FBI and major regulatory agencies.

Oversight investigations are not always effective means of monitoring agency performance. The reason may be as simple as inadequate work by committee staff. Sometimes the investigating committee has developed a close working relationship with the agency being investigated; that relationship may color the committee's view of the agency's performance and make criticism unlikely. Then again, effective oversight requires the cooperation of the executive branch, and occasionally the White House may refuse to provide information to Congress during a politically sensitive investigation. Officials may justify their refusal to cooperate by citing EXECUTIVE PRIVILEGE to withhold confidential information. However, Congress may win their cooperation by threatening to cite them for CONTEMPT OF CONGRESS or by granting them IMMUNITY from prosecution.   ~

ADDITIONAL READING

Fisher, Louis. *The Politics of Shared Power: Congress and the Executive.* 2d ed. 1987.

Overleaf:
Congressional leaders breakfasting at the White House with the president.

Pages

Visitors to the Capitol often see young people in dark blue suits hurrying through the corridors with messages or handing out documents on the House or Senate floor. Called pages, the boys and girls are juniors in high school who attend school early in the morning and then run errands for Congress the rest of the day. About sixty-five pages work for the House and about thirty for the Senate. They are housed on two floors of a congressional office building.

Pages are PATRONAGE appointees. Those nominated by the more senior representatives and senators have the best chance of being selected. Pages serve for at least one semester; some stay for a full year. There is also a summer program for pages. Pages do not work directly for those who appoint them, but instead report to the House DOORKEEPER and the Senate SERGEANT-AT-ARMS.

By 1988 Congress was paying pages about $850 a month, of which $300 went for room and board (five evening meals a week). Pages are required to follow a dress code. A House description of the page program, noting the extensive walking required on the job, says, "We cannot stress enough that pages bring well broken-in, comfortable shoes."

Congress revamped the page program in the early 1980s after criticism that pages were poorly supervised and schooled. Housing for pages, called the Page Residence Hall, was set up in early 1983. Congress also agreed that only juniors in high school should serve as pages; previously pages had ranged in age from fourteen to eighteen, making it difficult to provide an appropriate curriculum. The House began to operate its own school for pages in fall 1983. The Senate opted to extend its contract with the District of Columbia, which once operated both schools.

Scandal twice shook the page program in the early 1980s. In news reports in 1982, two unidentified pages told of sexual misconduct on the part of House members. Later, after a House investigation, they recanted their stories. Joseph A. Califano, Jr., a former cabinet secretary who headed the investigation, said most of the "allegations and rumors of misconduct were the product of teenage exaggeration, gossip, or even out-and-out fabrication that was often repeated mercilessly in a political capital that thrives on rumor."

More painful for the House was its 1983 censure of two representatives who had sexual relationships with pages. Daniel B. Crane, an Illinois Republican with a wife and six children, admitted that he had had an affair in 1980 with a seventeen-year-old female page. Gerry E. Studds, a Massachusetts Democrat, was found to have had a homosexual relationship in 1973 with a seventeen-year-old male page. (See DISCIPLINING MEMBERS.)

History

Records as early as 1827 show that boys worked as messengers. The name "pages" first appeared a decade later in the *Congressional Globe*, a predecessor of the *CONGRESSIONAL RECORD*.

Youthful Aides

The page program permits selected young people to study Congress from within. The pages shown here were photographed on the Capitol steps with House Speaker Frederick H. Gillett in 1920.

Sen. Jacob K. Javits, a New York Republican, appointed the first female page in 1970, but her employment was delayed until the following May, when the Senate voted to permit girls as pages. The House appointed its first girl pages in mid-1973. Javits also broke the color barrier when he appointed the first black page in 1965.

Some pages have returned to the halls of Congress as legislators. Rep. John D. Dingell of Michigan and Sen. David Pryor of Arkansas, both Democrats, were once pages.   ∼

Pairs. See VOTING.

Parliamentarian

Two of the most powerful employees of Congress are the Senate and House parliamentarians. These officials are the arbiters of legislative practice in each chamber. Their interpretations of the body's rules and precedents can have a profound impact on the shape of legislation and the course of floor action.

The parliamentarian or an assistant is always on the floor during House and Senate sessions, whispering advice to the PRESIDING OFFICER. The parliamentarian does not officially make rulings. But presiding officers rarely ignore the parliamentarian's advice, especially in the Senate, where freshman senators traditionally take the chair. The parliamentarian can often anticipate the POINTS OF ORDER and parliamentary inquiries likely to be raised. When he cannot do so, he must be able to offer authoritative on-the-spot advice to the presiding officer.

Parliamentarians also play an important role behind the scenes. As masters of the procedural and technical skills that are the backbone of success-

ful legislating, they are consulted by members of both parties and their staffs. They are acknowledged experts in suggesting ways to route legislation to a sympathetic committee, preparing it for floor debate, and protecting it from opposition attacks. The parliamentarians customarily are responsible for referring bills to the committees with appropriate jurisdiction. They also prepare and maintain compilations of the precedents in each chamber. House parliamentarians build on work prepared earlier in the twentieth century by two House members, Asher Hinds, a Maine Republican, and Clarence A. CANNON, a Missouri Democrat. Senate precedents were compiled by Floyd M. Riddick, Senate parliamentarian from 1965 to 1974.

Parliamentarians are chosen by the leadership of the House and Senate. In the House the parliamentarian is the Speaker's man. Lewis Deschler, parliamentarian from 1928 to 1974, was a member of Speaker Sam RAYBURN's "Board of Education"—a group of the Speaker's House friends who met with the Texas Democrat at sundown for drinks and strategy talks. In the Senate, where power is more diffused, parliamentarians have occupied a less central position.   ∼

Party Discipline. See LEADERSHIP.

Patronage

Patronage is the term for the use of political power to place favored individuals in jobs. On Capitol Hill, doorkeepers, elevator operators, and PAGES are among the support jobs filled by senators and representatives who make patronage appointments. Only veteran legislators have the chance to fill pa-

Political Loyalty
The practice of considering political loyalty when filling jobs began with President George Washington.
The list of patronage jobs controlled by Congress was once very broad, extending even to the choice
of rural mail carriers.

tronage slots. All members of Congress, though, hire their own office STAFF, and committee and subcommittee chairmen have even more slots to fill. These legislative jobs are not considered to be patronage.

The majority party in the House or Senate handles the bulk of patronage slots, although the minority party staffs its own CLOAKROOM and other posts that have a party designation. When control of the House or Senate changes hands, to either a new leader or party, the tradition has been to let those in patronage jobs stay on.

In the 100th Congress (1987-89) Rep. Jack Brooks handled House patronage, in consultation with his fellow Texas Democrat, Speaker Jim Wright. Brooks chaired the House Democratic Personnel Committee, which dealt with patronage; in fact, he was the only member of the panel, which in the past usually had five members.

In the Senate the arrangement has been less formal, with the two party leaders, and their staffs, allocating the patronage among fellow senators. Although seniority is a factor, party leaders can also make patronage slots available to colleagues in return for favors—such as crucial votes on legislation.

Patronage attracted little controversy by the 1980s. The list of patronage jobs had been gradually shortened; in 1969, for example, President Richard Nixon removed from congressional influence 63,000 postmaster and rural carrier jobs. Congress had also eliminated patronage from most jobs where skill and training were important, such as the Capitol Hill police force. Although about forty-five police officers on the House side were still patronage appointees by the late 1980s, those individuals had to meet the same standards and undergo the same training as other members of the force.

Most patronage posts are supervised by the House DOORKEEPER and the Senate SERGEANT-AT-ARMS, whose jobs are also dependent on personal ties and party loyalty. The House and Senate vote at the beginning of each two-year term of Congress on those and several other positions; the nominees, who usually spend several years in the same job, are chosen by party leaders and elected on strict party-line votes.

The practice of considering political loyalty when filling jobs began with President George Washington. It was Andrew Jackson, though, who first provoked public criticism of the practice, known as the "spoils system." *(See* APPOINTMENT POWER.*)* ~

Pay and Perquisites

Members of Congress earn income in three main ways.

First, members receive a salary, which in 1987 was $89,500 a year for both senators and representatives. Salary levels are subject to change, however. *(See p. 502)*

Secondly, members may earn outside income, often in the form of honoraria—payments for speeches and articles, usually by interest groups concerned with legislation before Congress. Congressional rules allow senators to earn up to 40 percent of their salaries (in 1987, $35,800) in outside income. House members may earn up to 30 percent of their salaries ($26,850 in 1987).

Finally, members have other benefits and perquisites, such as an excellent pension program. The exact value of those benefits is difficult to calculate.

Pay: Political Football

Disputes over pay levels have been a constant feature of congressional politics since Congress began in 1789. The Constitution settled one key question concerning pay, by decreeing that members would be paid by the federal government, rather than by the states they represented. But it left up to members themselves the delicate question of the exact level of pay.

Members have tried repeatedly over the past two centuries to raise their pay. Frequently their efforts have been successful, as salaries have climbed from $6 a day in 1789 to $89,500 a year in 1987. But attempts to raise pay have also encountered strong opposition from members' political opponents and many taxpayers. At different times in the past, pay raises have led to the defeat of many incumbents at the next election. On other occasions economic problems and political criticism have forced members of Congress to reduce pay levels, or to keep them at the same level, even though inflation was drastically reducing their purchasing power.

Fear of criticism from the voters has made members of Congress very reluctant to go on the record in support of a pay raise. As a result in recent decades Congress has attempted to develop automatic mechanisms for providing pay increases.

One method has been to establish an independent commission to recommend pay levels for members and other high-ranking federal officials. Established in 1967, the Commission on Executive, Legislative, and Judicial Salaries reviews and makes suggestions for changes in salaries every four years.

The commission has worked differently from the way sponsors intended, however. Only twice since 1967—in 1969 and 1977—have increases proposed by the panel gone into effect. In other years political opposition has blocked proposed increases.

In 1986 a commission recommended that congressional pay be increased to $135,000 a year. President Ronald Reagan proposed a smaller increase, from $77,400 to $89,500. Reagan's proposal went into effect in early 1987, despite strong opposition from some members of Congress.

The other method for raising pay has been through an automatic adjustment for inflation. This cost-of-living

Privileged Parking
Members of Congress enjoy many special perquisites in addition to their salaries. Among the most controversial are special parking privileges at crowded Washington National Airport.

adjustment, which also covers other federal employees, raised pay from $75,100 to $77,400 at the start of 1987.

The terms of debate over congressional pay have not changed much over the years. Supporters of higher pay stress the importance of paying enough to attract talented people to run for Congress. Without adequate pay, they add, only the rich will be able to afford to serve in Congress.

Despite their seemingly high pay, in comparison with most workers, members of Congress argue that they are hard-pressed to meet their needs. They must support two residences, one in Washington and one in their home state, on salaries that are frequently much less than what they could earn as lawyers or business executives.

Opponents of pay raises traditionally have argued that it is wrong for members to be able to act to raise their own pay. Congressional salaries normally are several times the average wage-earner's income, they say, and should be enough to attract qualified people. Opponents also contend that members should not be able to protect themselves during times of economic difficulties, while their constituents are struggling to cope with inflation or unemployment.

Outside Income

Traditionally, service in Congress was a part-time job. Members attended sessions for a few months each year, and then returned to their regular jobs, from which they earned most of their income. In recent years, however, Congress has tended to meet for most of the year. The demands of legislating and constituent service make it difficult for members to hold other jobs.

As a result, members have come increasingly to rely on honoraria as a source of outside income. Most of the honoraria earned by members come from speeches to conventions held by trade associations and labor unions.

Honoraria are particularly valuable to senators, who usually are better-known and more in demand by organizations than most House members. According to Common Cause, the self-styled citizens' lobby, two-thirds of senators received honoraria equal to 40 percent of their salaries, the maximum allowed by Senate rules, in 1985. In the House, by contrast, only one-fifth of members earned the maximum 30 percent of their salaries allowed by

House rules in 1985.

Members frequently donate to charity any honoraria income in excess of the limits. Rep. Dan Rostenkowski, chairman of the House WAYS AND MEANS Committee, reported that he received $250,000 in fees for fifty-one speeches in 1987. The Illinois Democrat donated most of the money to charities.

Although honoraria are perfectly legal, many people are concerned about their effect on congressional decisions. Most honoraria come from groups with an interest in legislation before Congress. Critics of honoraria, such as Common Cause, argue that the payments are little more than legalized influence buying. Members who receive payments from special interests are more likely to vote in favor of those interests in Congress, critics say.

Concern over the effects of honoraria on the legislative process has led Congress to impose restrictions on the amounts individual members can earn. The first such limits went into effect in 1975. Since then Congress has imposed a number of different limits on honoraria, often after bitter battles between House and Senate members over the issue. House members, who normally have less of an opportunity to earn honoraria, usually favor tighter restrictions on such outside income. Senators, for whom honoraria may be a major source of income, favor looser limits. The House established its 30 percent honoraria limit in 1981. The 40 percent Senate limit on honoraria went into effect in 1985. Members of Congress are also required to file annual FINANCIAL DISCLOSURE statements reporting their income from various sources.

Other Income and Perquisites

The list of other financial benefits available to members of Congress is a long one. For example, senators and representatives participate in a federal pension program. Members contribute 8 percent of their salaries, and the federal government matches their contribution. Members who retire after some years of service can receive a generous pension income.

Many other benefits are provided to members. These include such things as health and life insurance, access to health and recreation facilities, and free Capitol Hill and airport parking. Others are minor, or old-fashioned holdovers from an earlier day. For example, members can receive free plants for their offices and discounts on office supplies, as well as goatskin-bound copies of publications issued by the Government Printing Office.

Another type of congressional benefit is related more closely to members' performance of their jobs. Members receive allowances to pay the salaries of their STAFF, and to cover the expenses of offices in Washington and their home districts. They can send postage-free mail to constituents, a practice known as the FRANKING PRIVILEGE, and they receive a travel allowance, which varies according to how far their home states are from the nation's capital. In addition, they can engage in FOREIGN TRAVEL at government expense.

Although such benefits are intended to help members carry out their duties, they can also aid members personally. Most importantly, members can use their staff work and travel allowances to build up their political strength at home, thus improving their chances of reelection.   ~

Petition

The First Amendment to the Constitution guarantees the right of the people "to petition the Government for a redress of grievances."

Organizations or private citizens' groups from time to time exercise this right, petitioning one or both houses of

Congress to support particular legislation or to give favorable consideration to a matter not yet receiving congressional attention. Petitions are referred to committees with legislative jurisdiction over the subject matter.   ~

Point of Order

If a member of the Senate or House of Representatives believes that the chamber is violating rules governing its conduct of business, he or she may enter an objection. Such action, known as raising a point of order, usually stops all parliamentary proceedings, except a recorded vote, until the chair sustains or overrules the member's objection. Before ruling, the chair frequently will allow debate on the point of order, giving both sides the opportunity to explain their positions. The chair's rulings are subject to APPEAL and may be overturned by the chamber's membership. That occurs more frequently in the Senate than in the House. Some House bills go to the floor under ground rules that prohibit points of order.

When a member in either chamber raises a point of order that a QUORUM—the minimum number of members required—is not present to conduct business, no further legislative activity can take place until enough absent members have been rounded up.   ~

Policy Committee.   See
LEADERSHIP.

Political Action Committees (PACs)

Political action committees (PACs) are organizations that raise and distrib-

ute campaign contributions to candidates for Congress and other offices. Their rapid growth in wealth and power during the 1970s and 1980s has made them one of the most controversial aspects of the CAMPAIGN FINANCING system.

There are two main types of PACS. Some are connected with specific economic interests in society, such as business or organized labor. These groups help elect candidates who will encourage favorable treatment for their members by the government. Examples of this type of PAC are the AFL-CIO's Committee on Political Education and the Business-Industry Political Action Committee.

Other PACs are independent organizations formed to promote the political beliefs of the members. (Some members form their own PACs.) These groups typically support candidates who agree with them on key issues, such as abortion or nuclear arms control. Such PACs include the National Right to Life PAC (anti-abortion) and the Council for a Livable World (pro-arms control).

Under federal law PAC contributions to individual candidates are limited to $5,000 per election. But PACs are not limited in the total amount they can give to all candidates. They can also spend as much as they want to help candidates—for example, with heavy television advertising—as long as they operate independently of the candidates' campaigns.

Although PACs had existed in the past, their real growth began with the passage in 1971 and 1974 of laws to reform campaign financing. These laws, and subsequent court decisions, provided the legal basis for the rapid growth of PACs, particularly in business. Corporations and labor unions are barred from contributing directly to campaigns. But they are allowed to form PACs to collect voluntary contributions from employees, stockhold-

TOP PAC CONTRIBUTORS
1985-86 Election Cycle

Realtors PAC	$2.8 million
American Medical Association PAC	2.1 million
National Education Association PAC	2.1 million
UAW-V-CAP (United Auto Workers)	1.6 million
National Association of Retired Federal Employees PAC	1.5 million
Committee on Letter Carriers Political Education	1.5 million
D.R.I.V.E. (Teamsters)	1.5 million
Build PAC (National Assn. of Home Builders)	1.4 million
Association of Trial Lawyers PAC	1.4 million
Machinists Non-Partisan Political League	1.4 million

Source: Federal Election Commission

ers, and members for distribution to candidates.

Within little more than a decade PACs developed into a major factor in the financing of congressional elections. In 1974, 608 PACs were registered with the Federal Election Commission. The PACs donated a total of $12.5 million to House and Senate candidates in that election year. By 1986 the number of PACs had increased to over 4,000, donating a total of $132 million to all congressional candidates.

Perhaps even more significantly, PACs have provided a growing share of all funds available to congressional candidates. As recently as 1978, PACs supplied only 17 percent of all campaign contributions. By 1986 they were providing 28 percent of campaign funds. PAC contributions are particularly important in the House, where many candidates regularly receive more than half of their campaign funds from PACs. Senate candidates usually are less reliant on PACs, filling an average of about 20 percent of their campaign coffers with PAC money.

PACs play a much less important role in presidential elections. They provide only a small share of funds needed by candidates seeking their party's presidential nomination, and are barred from contributing to the publicly financed general-election campaigns.

Incumbents' Advantage

Campaign contribution statistics show that PACs have a strong preference for incumbent legislators who are running for reelection. PACs give most often to current members of Congress because they are already able to vote and speak out for PAC interests. That is particularly true with committee chairmen, who have more power than other members to get legislation approved.

Some PACs show clear preferences for Democratic or Republican candidates. But their partisan leanings are usually not as strong as their preference for incumbents. PACs tend to support current members regardless of their party. Business PACs, for example, are usually considered more likely to favor Republican candidates. But in 1984 business PACs gave 44 percent of their House contributions to Democrats—almost all of whom were incumbents. Labor unions usually favor Democratic candidates, both as challengers and incumbents.

Challengers, by contrast, are a gamble for a PAC. Only a few candidates who run against current members each year are successful. By giving to a challenger PACs could anger the incumbent, who might vote against them in the future. Business- and labor-related PACs gave incumbents 80 percent of their House contributions and 65 percent of their Senate contributions in 1984.

Challengers have to work especially hard to overcome the PACs' preference for incumbents. Many travel to Washington more than a year before the election, hoping to generate enough financial support from PACs to get their campaigns off to a strong start and increase their chances of defeating the incumbent.

PACs that are organized around political beliefs are more likely to give to challengers. In addition they are very active in conducting independent campaigns for and against candidates, sometimes to great effect. In 1980, for example, the National Conservative Political Action Committee waged intensive advertising campaigns targeting key liberal Democratic senators. A number were defeated, including George McGovern of South Dakota, who had been the unsuccessful Democratic presidential candidate in 1972. In other cases, however, those efforts can be ineffective, and even generate sympathy for the candidate being attacked.

Critics and Supporters

Many people are sharply critical of the role played by PACs. PACs have been called "the toxic waste of American politics" and accused of "destroying the electoral process." The basic criticism of PACs is that they are allowing organized, well-financed groups to gain too much influence. By accepting contributions from PACs, critics say, members of Congress and other politicians become dependent on them. That may make them reluctant to vote against the interests of the PAC—either from fear of losing the PAC's contributions or fear of having the PAC help finance

challengers against them.

There have been a number of legislative proposals to curb the influence of PACs over the years, but none of them have become law. One way would be to provide public financing of congressional candidates, such as now exists in the presidential election; a public financing proposal was lost in a Senate FILIBUSTER in 1988. Another would be to limit the total amount that a PAC could give to all congressional candidates in an election.

Defenders of PACs say that they are a legitimate means by which people voluntarily join together to back candidates. PACs encourage people to enter politics, they say, adding that there is no real difference between contributions from separate individuals and those that are from the combined support of a number of people. PACs are a more efficient way of delivering financial support to candidates, they add.

PACs also stress that they are not trying to "buy" members' votes. Instead their aim is to gain access to the member, to ensure that the member will listen to their point of view when an issue affecting them arises.   ~

ADDITIONAL READINGS

Cigler, Allan J., and Burdett A. Loomis. *Interest Group Politics.* 2d ed. 1986.

Malbin, Michael J., ed. *Parties, Interest Groups, and Campaign Finance Laws.* 1980.

Sabato, Larry J. *PAC Power.* 1984.

Political Parties

Political parties are vital elements in the life and work of Congress and its members. Although they are not specifically mentioned in the Constitution, political parties have been important in Congress almost since it was created.

The chief functions of the parties in Congress are to help select members, through the electoral process, and to organize and distribute power within the institution. The party that has a majority of seats in each chamber controls all key positions of authority.

In the broadest sense, a political party is a coalition of people who join together to try to win governmental power by winning elections. Members of a party supposedly share a loosely defined set of common beliefs, although there are often extremely wide differences of opinion and outlook among members of the same party. Citizens rely on political parties to define issues, to support or oppose candidates on the basis of those issues, and then to carry out the agreed-upon policies when the party is in power.

Political parties in America serve many functions in addition to selecting and organizing members of Congress. Most importantly, they help elect the president, by nominating candidates for the office and then working to get them elected. They also put forward candidates for most state and local offices, and help elected leaders mobilize political support for their programs.

Since the mid-nineteenth century there have been only two major political parties in Congress, the Democratic and the Republican. For more than a century almost all members of Congress have belonged to one of these two coalitions. But it has not always been that way. In the nineteenth century a number of different parties were significant in Congress. It was not until after the Civil War that the Democrats and Republicans began to share complete control of Congress between themselves. Even since then, however, some members of other parties—the Progressive

Nominating Power

Members of Congress always figure prominently in their parties' presidential nominating conventions. Pictured here is the 1868 Democratic convention in New York's Tammany Hall. Earlier in the nineteenth century, party caucuses in Congress chose presidential nominees.

party in the early 1900s, for example—occasionally have been elected. Sometimes a member declines to join either party and is called an independent.

The Democrats and Republicans each have been dominant at different times during the history of Congress. For much of the period between the Civil War and the Great Depression of the 1930s, Republicans held majorities in both the House of Representatives and the Senate. Since the election of 1932, however, Democrats usually have been in control of both chambers. They have been particularly strong in the House, where for decades they have held a majority solid enough to withstand periodic Republican gains produced by landslide GOP presidential victories.

One essential function of the parties is to provide a mechanism for choosing and supporting congressional candidates. Without the parties, a congressional election could be a confusing process in which a large number of individual candidates sought votes with only the aid of their friends and personal connections. Instead, the parties help to narrow the choice facing voters to the more manageable number of two candidates, and provide each with money and organizational support to ensure that their messages are heard.

Parties normally choose congressional candidates through primary elections. During a primary campaign, aspiring candidates seek the support of fellow party members. The candidate who receives the most votes in the primary then becomes the party nominee and goes into the general election campaign with, at least in theory, the united support of local party members and assistance from national party organizations.

Parties also play an essential role in the internal organization of Congress. Without structures for bringing together like-minded members for common action, Congress might find itself in constant chaos, as 100 senators and 435 representatives each fought solely for his or her individual agenda. Instead, the parties help to create a system in which leaders and followers can work together in pursuit of their common program.

All formal authority in Congress is arranged according to party. The party that holds a majority in each chamber has the votes to select leaders, such as the Speaker of the House and the president pro tempore and the majority leader in the Senate. Majority party leaders control the legislative agendas. All committee and subcommittee chairmen are members of the majority party. Within each party there is a whip system, which enables party leaders to bring pressure on party members to vote in support of the party position on key issues. (See LEADERSHIP.)

Still, it is important to keep in mind the weaknesses of the congressional parties. Although the parties choose general-election candidates for Congress, those candidates frequently campaign on their own, seeking to appeal to voters without reference to party labels. Once in Congress, members are under no obligation to support party positions or obey party leaders. Other than a few procedural questions, votes in Congress are rarely on a party-line basis. The voting records of many members—for example, conservative Democrats or liberal Republicans—often more closely resemble those of the other party's majority than their own. (See CONSERVATIVE COALITION.)

The relative weakness of the current congressional parties is shown by the contrast to other times and other countries. In the early part of this century, for example, the party CAUCUSES often exercised significant control over all aspects of Congress. Parties also are often far more important in other parliamentary democracies than they are in Congress. In England, for example, leaders of the Conservative, Labor, and

Liberal parties hand-pick candidates for parliamentary seats. Members are usually required to vote for the party position on key issues in Parliament.

Development of the Party System

The Founding Fathers never envisioned the importance that political parties would develop in Congress and the nation. The authors of the Constitution had little understanding of the functions of political parties; they were ambivalent, if not hostile, to the new party system as it developed in the early years of the Republic. "If I could not go to heaven but with a party, I would not go there at all," said Thomas Jefferson in 1789.

The Constitution did not mention parties, either to authorize them or prohibit them. It made possible a permanent role for parties, however, by giving citizens civil liberties and the right to organize. At the same time it erected safeguards against partisan excesses by creating a system of checks and balances within the government.

Parties emerged soon after the adoption of the Constitution. Those who favored the strong central government embodied in the Constitution came to be called Federalists. Led by Treasury Secretary Alexander Hamilton, they were drawn mostly from merchants and bankers of the Northeast, who favored strong government action to prevent the money from losing its value through inflation. They were opposed by a group that later became known as the Democratic-Republicans. Led by Thomas Jefferson and James Madison, the Democratic-Republicans were largely southern and western farmers, who opposed a strong central government and sought government policies to make it easier to borrow money.

Party lines were fluid in the first Congresses, with members drifting between one loose coalition and the other. By the mid-1790s, however, the factions had hardened enough for one senator to observe that "the existence of two parties in Congress is apparent." Federalists generally held the upper hand in these early years, controlling the Senate and contending equally for power with the Democratic-Republicans in the House. By 1800 Jefferson's supporters had become a majority. Their control of Congress continued to grow in the ensuing years. The 1816 elections signaled the effective end of the Federalist party, whose representation in Congress dropped off to a small minority.

Along with the dominance of the Democratic-Republicans, the first twenty years of the nineteenth century saw growth in the power of the party caucus over Congress's operations. Important decisions were made in private meetings of the Democratic-Republicans, and members were pressed to follow the party's position. The power of the party caucus was increased by its role as presidential nominating committee. Party members in the House and Senate had the authority to name the Democratic-Republican presidential candidate, who at that time was virtually assured of being elected. Caucus nominations continued through 1824.

The size and power of the Democratic-Republican party soon led to the development of internal factions, as different regional groups struggled for influence within the only national political organization. By the mid-1820s two groups emerged: the National Republicans, who favored internal economic development projects and a protective tariff against foreign goods; and the Democrats, who represented agrarian interests from the South and West and held that the common people, not the rich, should have the dominant voice in government. The Democrats captured control of Congress in 1826.

The Democrats, who took over the White House in 1828 with the election of Andrew Jackson, were to remain the dominant party in Congress for the next three decades. The National Republicans, who soon took the name of Whigs, twice won the presidency and always held a substantial number of seats in Congress. But the Whigs were able to capture a majority of either body on only a few occasions—the 1840 and 1846 elections in the House and the 1840 and 1842 elections in the Senate.

The Whigs faded rapidly during the 1850s and went out of existence in 1856. In their place rose the Republican party of today, which was initially composed of Democrats and Whigs who opposed the extension of slavery. The Republicans won control of the House in 1854, lost it in 1856, and then regained it in 1858. They were not able to muster a majority in the Senate until 1860, on the eve of the Civil War. The young party held a solid majority throughout the war. The Democratic presence in Congress was sharply reduced after its many members from the South quit to join the Confederacy.

Party Dominance

The Republican party controlled Congress and the presidency for most of the next seventy years. Democrats sometimes were able to win a majority of House seats, and on occasion won a Senate majority. But the Republicans, who soon gained the nickname of "Grand Old Party" (GOP), dominated the era. They were backed by eastern business interests and favored high tariffs and tight controls of the amount of money in the economy. The Democrats were the party of the South, and of disaffected agricultural interests from the West. They generally sought low tariffs and liberal credit.

The role of the parties became much more important during this period. Although the Congress of the pre-Civil War period tended to be dominated by brilliant individuals, the postwar Senate and House were the are-

nas of powerful party leaders. This trend was particularly apparent in the Senate, where many of the members were "party bosses" who had gained power through political organizations in their own states. These men placed a high value on party loyalty and the need for party discipline. They were often ready to compromise their ideals to maintain harmony within the party.

The first attempt at developing a strong party structure came in the 1870s, when New York Republican Roscoe CONKLING organized a faction that controlled the Senate on procedural matters. Conkling's group had little effect on legislation, however, and the Senate returned to individualistic ways after Conkling left the Senate.

The true birth of modern party discipline came in the 1890s. Republican Sens. William B. ALLISON of Iowa and Nelson W. ALDRICH of Rhode Island organized an informal group of senators, who at first met only for poker and relaxation. After Allison was elected chairman of the Republican Caucus—the organization of party members—in 1897, the group assumed control of the Senate. Allison used his office to solidify his own control of his party, and his party's control of the Senate. "Both in the committees and in the offices, we should use the machinery for our own benefit and not let other men have it," Allison said.

Allison controlled the Steering Committee, which directed floor proceedings, and the Committee on Committees, which made committee assignments. Although chairmanship of committees was determined solely by SENIORITY, or length of service, Allison had great leeway to appoint members to committees who would follow his wishes. Access to positions of influence soon depended on the favor and support of the party leaders.

Republicans used the caucus to work out party positions in private and then to speak with a unified voice on the Senate floor. Although they were not bound to obey the party position, members who ignored it risked losing most of their power in the Senate. The Democrats soon followed the Republicans by organizing their own internal power structure. In the House majority party control solidified under two powerful Republican Speakers: Thomas Brackett REED and Joseph G. CANNON.

By the end of the nineteenth century, the two major political parties had assumed a decisive role in the LEGISLATIVE PROCESS. The parties named the committees that initially considered legislation and determined what bills would be brought to the floor. Party members worked out their differences in caucus meetings, and then went forth in disciplined ranks to ratify caucus decisions on the floor.

The system of strict party control was not popular among many people outside of Congress, who saw it as violating the principles of representative democracy. There were also critics of the system within Congress, including the Liberal Republicans of the 1870s and the "Mugwump" antileadership Republicans of the 1880s. In addition, representatives of third parties attacked the system.

The most important of these were the Populists, who represented an agrarian-reform movement based in the Midwest. The Populists won three Senate seats and eleven House seats in 1892. They reached their peak in the crucial election of 1896, when they and their allies won seven Senate seats and thirty House seats. Much of their program, which stressed loosening of controls on the amount of money circulating in the economy, was adopted by the Democrats, and the Populists soon faded from the scene.

The cause of reform was soon picked up by the progressives. This movement sought both economic changes, such as antitrust legislation and introduction of the income tax, and

political measures aimed at opening up the system to public pressure, such as DIRECT ELECTION OF SENATORS and laws against corrupt election practices. The progressives were composed of reformist Republicans and members of the separate Progressive party. The Bull Moose-Progressives, as they were called in honor of their leader, former president Theodore Roosevelt, elected seventeen House members in 1912. The progressives played key roles in the congressional reform movement of the early 1900s, working to reduce the autocratic power of House Speaker Cannon, and pushing curbs on the FILIBUSTER and a proposal for direct election through the Senate. (See PROGRESSIVE ERA.)

Even so, the system of party control of Congress that had grown up in the last decades of the nineteenth century developed into a formal institution in the first two decades of the twentieth century. In 1911 Senate Democrats elected a single member to serve both as chairman of the party caucus and as floor leader. Republicans soon followed suit, and by 1915 the majority and minority leaders were the acknowledged spokesmen for their parties in the Senate. In the House the revolt against the power of the Speaker led to a great increase in the power of the party caucuses. The Democrats, who controlled the House from 1911 to 1919, worked out most legislative decisions within the "King Caucus." Members were obligated to vote for the party position if endorsed by a two-thirds majority. The dominant force in the chamber was Democratic Majority Leader (and WAYS AND MEANS Committee Chairman) Oscar W. UNDERWOOD of Alabama, who had far more power than Speaker James B. "Champ" CLARK of Missouri.

Republicans regained control of both houses of Congress in 1918, and they maintained their power until the early years of the Great Depression. However, the party was torn by deep divisions between regular forces and the progressives, who often cooperated with the Democrats in pushing legislation favorable to the economic interests of western farmers. Progressive Republicans who tried to challenge their party leadership were quickly punished by the loss of seats on important committees.

Democratic Dominance and Party Decline

The Republicans lost their exclusive control of Congress in 1930, when Democrats gained a narrow majority in the House. That election proved to be a warning sign of what was to come two years later. The 1932 elections were a watershed in the history of partisan divisions in Congress. Led by presidential candidate Franklin D. Roosevelt, who promised relief from the economic disaster that had befallen the nation, the Democrats swept to commanding majorities in both House and Senate. By the 1936 elections, the Republicans had been reduced to a small minority. The Democrats held 331 House seats as a result of that election, compared with 89 seats for the Republicans. The Democratic majority in the Senate was an overwhelming 76-16.

With few exceptions, the Democrats remained in control of Congress from then on. Between the 1930s and the late 1980s, they lost their House majority only twice, in the 1946 and 1952 elections. Senate Republicans had brief interludes in power as a result of the same elections, as well as a more significant period of ascendency in the 1980s. The GOP controlled the Senate during the first six years of President Ronald Reagan's administration (1981-87). However, Democrats regained a substantial majority in the 1986 elections.

A number of conflicting reasons have been put forward for the long-term Democratic dominance of Congress. The remarkable thing about the Demo-

crats' continuing status as the majority party is that it has survived even in the face of periodic strong shifts in popular sentiment to the Republicans, as shown by a number of landslide GOP presidential victories.

Many Democrats and political scientists argue that their longstanding hold on power reflects their party's superior ability to attract top-quality congressional candidates, who have the ability to appeal to voters and are willing to carry out the time-consuming tasks of constituent service that help ensure an incumbent's reelection. Republicans, on the other hand, frequently attribute the Democratic domination of the House to the Democratic control of the redistricting process. This theory holds that the Democrats, who control most state legislatures, have been able to draw the lines of many congressional districts in a way that guarantees the election of Democrats. *(See* REAPPORTIONMENT AND REDISTRICTING.*)*

Still, the significance of the Democratic lock on Congress has been reduced by another important trend in the years since World War II. This is the decline of the parties as the most important forces in Congress. Parties and party leaders have much less power in Congress in the modern era than they did at the beginning of the century. Members of Congress now usually function as individuals rather than loyal party members, both in their electoral campaigns and in the way they vote in committee and on the floor.

The growth of primaries as a means for selecting congressional candidates has added to the decline of the importance of parties. The aim of primaries, when they were introduced early in this century, was to reduce the power of corrupt party bosses, by giving the choice of the party nominee to party members as a whole. But primaries have also had the unintended effect of undermining the parties as institutions. Congressional candidates today often bypass the established party leadership in their area and appeal directly to voters.

Republicans and Democrats in Congress have made strong efforts in recent years to restore some of their influence in electoral politics. Each party has a House and Senate campaign committee, which provides national help for party congressional candidates. The committees play key roles in recruiting, training, organizing, and funding campaigns. The Republicans in particular have developed their campaign committees into wealthy, high-technology centers able to wage a coordinated, national campaign for GOP candidates. *(See* CAMPAIGN FINANCING.*)*

Other factors have contributed to the decline of the parties within Congress. In the 1950s and 1960s the CONSERVATIVE COALITION of Republicans and southern Democrats effectively controlled both House and Senate, and it was able to frustrate efforts by the Democratic leadership to push through civil rights and other legislation. In the 1970s the congressional reform movement stripped away much of the power of old-line party leaders. That has made it possible for members to ignore the position of the party leadership, and to vote according to their own interests, without fear of much punishment.

Still, the parties in Congress are not always divided and relatively weak. Sometimes party members coalesce into a powerful voting bloc. In the early years of the Reagan administration, for example, Senate Republicans maintained a high degree of unity on key votes. That enabled Reagan to push through his controversial spending- and tax-cut proposals. House Republicans have also been relatively united, and Democratic unity has been increased by the replacement of many very conservative southern Democrats by a new breed of southerners who are more in line with the national party position.

The modern era has seen the al-most total extinction of third-party and independent members of Congress. The last significant block of House members from outside the two major parties was in the Seventy-fifth Congress (1937-39), when thirteen Progressives and Farmer-Labor Party members were elected from the upper Midwest. In the Senate the last such members were James L. Buckley, a Conservative from New York (1971-77), and Virginia's Harry F. Byrd, Jr. (1965-83), who entered the Senate as a Democrat but became an independent in 1971.   ~

ADDITIONAL READINGS

Chambers, W.N., and Walter D. Burnham, eds. *The American Party System.* 2d ed. 1975.

Schlesinger, Arthur M., Jr., ed. *History of U.S. Political Parties.* 1973. Reprint 1981.

Wattenberg, Martin P. *The Decline of the American Political Parties, 1952 to 1984.* 1984.

Pork-Barrel Politics

Congress has been putting a local twist on decisions since its inception. Legislators from farm states agitate for price supports, while those from the arid West endorse water reclamation projects. Attention to special interests has made trade and tax laws particularly complex; representatives and senators often try to add a clause to benefit important industries and businesses in their districts or states. When the aid is most specific—with a certain amount of federal money going to a particular local project or interest—the practice is known as pork barrel.

Few legislators can resist taking credit for a new park, post office, dam, or sewage treatment plant. With much

Pork Protest
Most legislators see delivering federal funds back home as a legitimate role. But critics complain that political clout, rather than need, too often determines where the money goes. Rep. Silvio Conte donned this pig mask to let colleagues know what he thought of a 1983 water projects bill.

of their work in Congress focused on broad national questions, senators and representatives enjoy the chance to show something concrete to their constituents. Distributing federal largess qualifies as pork-barrel politics when the outcome depends on political clout, instead of on an impartial, objective assessment of need.

Capital improvement projects, such as dams and bridges, are traditionally considered pork-barrel spending. Congress also earmarks for particular districts or states other types of spending: parks, pollution control research, solar energy laboratories, academic grants, and contracts for submarines or other defense-related items.

Most legislators see delivering federal funds back home as a legitimate role. But critics complain that Congress is too influenced by parochial concerns and should be more attuned to national needs. Presidents often share that view. Jimmy Carter angered legislators in 1977 with his "hit list" of water projects he said were wasteful and environmentally unsound. It was a major setback to his budding relationship with Congress.

Ronald Reagan saved his most vociferous complaints for late in his presidency. In his 1988 STATE OF THE UNION address, Reagan complained about items "tucked away behind a little comma here and there" in an omnibus appropriations bill he signed in late 1987. "For example there's millions for items such as cranberry research, blueberry research, the study of crawfish, and the commercialization of wildflowers," he told Congress.

As efforts to trim federal spending intensified in the 1980s, less money was available for traditional pork-barrel spending. The list of projects was shorter, and the fight to get a favorite item on it was even more intense. Those not on the APPROPRIATIONS committees and not in the party hierarchy have often found their requests ignored. "Those with the clout use the clout to get what they want, and merit selection never enters into the thinking," said Republican Rep. Robert S. Walker of Pennsylvania in 1987, when several members agreed to talk about pork-barrel politics. By then members of the Appropriations committees, once able to accommodate favored colleagues, had little left over to share after the lists of top legislators were taken care of. "You're not in a position to say, 'Anything I can do for you,'" said Vic Fazio, a California Democrat on the panel. "What you'd really like is for members to go away."

Still, enough members are usually pleased with the legislation to make passage easy. "All of us go begging to the Appropriations Committee for water projects or different things we want in our district," said Rep. Douglas H. Bosco, a California Democrat. "It isn't easy to vote to cut one of these bills because a lot of times you're fearful that the next time you go asking for something, the door will be slammed in your face."

A classic pork-barrel bill was passed in 1987. Congress added 120 specific "demonstration" projects to a major highway bill, a ploy that gave legislators credit for particular items in addition to the lump sum given to each state. President Reagan vetoed the legislation, but Congress, in a lopsided bipartisan vote, overrode the veto. Even leaders of the president's own party, including House Republican leader Robert H. MICHEL of Illinois and Whip Trent Lott of Mississippi, refused to support the president.   ~

Post Office and Civil Service Committee, House

The policies of the federal bureaucracy—hiring, firing, and retiring—are the concern of the House Post Office and Civil Service Committee. Although agencies and departments usually have little contact with the committee, it does handle salary levels and major personnel questions, such as a 1978 civil service reform and a 1986 revamp of the federal retirement system. The committee is heavily lobbied by the unions that represent federal employees.

The Post Office Committee also oversees the U.S. mails, as it has since 1808. It lost much of its control in 1970, when the Postal Service became an independent corporation. But the committee still provides a forum for complaints about deliveries and postal rates, and it continues to influence postal operations. Companies with large postal budgets, such as those advertising with mass mailings or sending material by subscription, keep in close touch with the committee.

Among the most controversial topics handled by the Post Office Committee is compensation of federal employees and members of Congress. Legislators are reluctant to vote in favor of higher salaries for themselves because of criticism that they are feathering their own nests.

The Post Office Committee handles national holidays; in 1983 it won that designation for the birthday of the Rev. Dr. Martin Luther King, Jr., the black civil rights leader who was assassinated in 1968. The committee also has jurisdiction over political activity by government workers.

Within the House, the committee has little appeal. Few members who sit on the panel put much effort into its activities. In the Senate, the Postal Service and federal personnel are among the subjects handled by the GOVERNMENTAL AFFAIRS Committee.   ~

Powell, Adam Clayton, Jr.

Rep. Adam Clayton Powell, Jr. (1908-72), a flamboyant Democrat from New York, triggered a storm of controversy over congressional powers and ethics in the 1960s. A House vote to exclude Powell from Congress because of misconduct led to a Supreme Court decision prohibiting Congress from adding to the constitutional qualifications for membership. The Powell case was also a key factor in the development of congressional codes of ETHICS.

Powell—the pastor of the Abyssinian Baptist Church in Harlem, one of the largest congregations in the country—was first elected to Congress in 1944. He rose in seniority to become the chairman of the House EDUCATION AND LABOR COMMITTEE in 1961 and was considered by many to be the most powerful black in the United States.

But Powell came under fire on a variety of issues—his involvement in court cases concerning income tax evasion and libel; his numerous well-publicized trips at government expense; and his employment of his wife as a member of his congressional staff while she lived in Puerto Rico.

His downfall began in 1966 as a result of a revolt in his own committee over legislative business. When his long absences delayed passage of antipoverty legislation in 1966, the committee adopted new rules that limited his power as chairman.

Following an investigation into Powell's use of committee funds, he was stripped of his committee chairmanship in 1967 and temporarily denied a seat in the House. In March 1967 the House, rejecting the recommendations of a select committee that Powell be punished but seated, excluded Powell from the 90th Congress. *(See* DISCIPLINING MEMBERS.*)*

Powell was reelected at a subsequent special election and again in 1968. He was seated in January 1969, although he lost his seniority and was fined. Following his swearing in, Powell told a press conference: "I'll behave as I always have."

The Supreme Court in 1969 ruled (*Powell v. McCormack*) that the House had acted unconstitutionally in excluding Powell. The Harlem Democrat was defeated in a primary election in 1970 and died in 1972.   ∼

President and Congress.   See EXECUTIVE BRANCH AND CONGRESS.

President Pro Tempore

Officially the highest ranking senator, the president pro tempore is in practice a largely ceremonial leader. By tradition, since 1945, the post has gone automatically to the senator in the majority party with the longest service record. Because of his seniority, the president pro tempore usually chairs a committee and is counted among the top decision makers in the Senate. However, he has far less influence than the party floor leaders. There is no Senate post comparable to the House SPEAKER. *(See* LEADERSHIP.*)*

The Constitution calls for the president pro tempore to preside when the VICE PRESIDENT, the constitutional president of the Senate, is absent. The president pro tempore has never become a politically powerful position, in part because the vice president at any point is able to take the chair, unseating the president pro tempore. One ceremonial task of the president pro tempore is to sign the final version of legislation passed by Congress.

In the nineteenth century the post was filled on a temporary basis, whenever the vice president was not present. But the Senate never let the vice president be an active participant in its affairs; often he was of a political party different from that of most senators. As the vice president spent less time in the Senate chamber, the president pro tempore evolved into a long-term position. In 1890 the Senate decided the president pro tempore should serve until "the Senate otherwise ordered." In effect, it gave tenure to the person elected.

Although the president pro tempore occasionally presides over the Senate, the job is usually handled by the more junior members of the majority party. Senators rotate as PRESIDING OFFICER, usually spending less than an hour at a time in the chair.

Republican Strom Thurmond of South Carolina was seventy-nine years old when he became president pro tempore in 1981. Unlike many of his predecessors, Thurmond clearly enjoyed the ceremony of the office and presided over the Senate at the beginning of each day. Democrat John C. STENNIS of Mississippi became president pro tempore in 1987. His physical frailty, including the loss of a leg in 1984 to cancer, limited his role as presiding officer. But Stennis, born in 1901, was warmly regarded by his colleagues, who appreci-

ated the dignity he brought to the top-ranking Senate post. ∼

Presidential Disability and Succession

Congress has broad responsibility for maintaining the continuity of the presidency. The Constitution provides (Article II, Section 1) that Congress should decide who is to succeed to the presidency if both the president and vice president die, resign, or become disabled. Congress enacted a presidential succession law as early as 1792. But for nearly 200 years legislators avoided the question of presidential disability, because they were unable to decide what constituted disability or who would be the judge of it. Those ques-

Historic First
The Twenty-fifth Amendment to the Constitution provides a way to replace a vice president who dies, resigns, or succeeds to the presidency. The first vice president to take office under the amendment was Gerald R. Ford, right, who was nominated by President Richard Nixon and confirmed by Congress in 1973. Ford succeeded Spiro T. Agnew, who resigned under fire.

tions were not resolved until adoption of the Twenty-fifth Amendment to the Constitution in 1967.

Meanwhile, two presidents sustained serious disabilities. James A. Garfield was shot in 1881 and was confined to his bed until his death two and a half months later. Woodrow Wilson suffered a serious stroke in 1919 but remained in office until his term ended in 1921. In each case the VICE PRESIDENT did not assume any of the duties of the presidency for fear he would appear to be usurping the power of that office; that left in doubt, especially in Wilson's case, the question of who actually was running the country.

The Twenty-fifth Amendment permits the vice president to become acting president under either of two circumstances. If the president informs Congress that he is unable to perform his duties, the vice president becomes acting president until the president says he is able to take over again. The vice president can also become acting president if he and a majority of the cabinet (or another body designated by Congress) decide that the president is disabled. The vice president will remain acting president until the president informs Congress that he is able to resume his duties; however, Congress can overrule the president's declaration that he is no longer disabled by a two-thirds vote of both the Senate and the House of Representatives.

Another section of the Twenty-fifth Amendment spells out what to do if the vice president dies, resigns, or succeeds to the presidency. In such a case the president is to nominate a replacement, who requires confirmation by a majority vote of both the Senate and House.

The presidential disability procedures first came into play in 1985 when President Ronald Reagan underwent cancer surgery. Reagan transferred his powers to Vice President George Bush just before receiving anesthesia and signed papers reclaiming them less than eight hours later. The president did not formally invoke the Twenty-fifth Amendment, however. A bipartisan advisory commission, in a 1988 report, criticized Reagan's reluctance to do so; it urged routine use of the disability mechanism in such cases.

The first vice president to be confirmed under the Twenty-fifth Amendment was Gerald R. FORD, who was nominated by President Richard Nixon in 1973; Ford succeeded Spiro T. Agnew, who resigned under fire. The second was Nelson A. Rockefeller, whom Ford nominated in 1974 after he replaced Nixon in the White House. *(See* ELECTING THE PRESIDENT.*)*   ~

Presidents Who Served in Congress

Nearly two-thirds of the nation's presidents over the past two centuries came to the White House by way of Congress. Of the thirty-nine presidents between 1789 and 1988, twenty-three had prior service in one or both chambers: eight had served in the House of Representatives, six in the Senate, and nine in both. In addition to the eight presidents who sat in the House before assuming the presidency, one served there after leaving it. Another ex-president returned briefly to the Senate, in which he had previously served.

The move from Congress to the White House began early. James MADISON, the fourth president, had served in the House, and his successor, James MONROE, had served in the Senate. Both Madison and Monroe also had been members of the Continental Congress, as had their predecessors— George Washington, John Adams, and Thomas Jefferson.

Few persons have moved directly from Congress to the White House, al-

CONGRESS: STEPPING STONE TO THE WHITE HOUSE

President	Congressional Service
James Madison (1809-17)	House (1789-97)
James Monroe (1817-25)	Senate (1790-94)
John Quincy Adams (1825-29)	Senate (1803-08)
	House (1831-48) [1]
Andrew Jackson (1829-37)	House (1796-97)
	Senate (1797-98, 1823-25)
Martin Van Buren (1837-41)	Senate (1821-28)
William Henry Harrison (1841)	House (1816-19)
	Senate (1825-28)
John Tyler (1841-45)	House (1817-21)
	Senate (1827-36)
James K. Polk (1845-49)	House (1825-39)
Millard Fillmore (1850-53)	House (1833-35, 1837-43)
Franklin Pierce (1853-57)	House (1833-37)
	Senate (1837-42)
James Buchanan (1857-61)	House (1821-31)
	Senate (1834-45)
Abraham Lincoln (1861-65)	House (1847-49)
Andrew Johnson (1865-69)	House (1843-53)
	Senate (1857-62, *1875*) [1]
Rutherford B. Hayes (1877-81)	House (1865-67)
James A. Garfield (1881)	House (1863-80)
Benjamin Harrison (1889-93)	Senate (1881-87)
William McKinley (1897-1901)	House (1877-84, 1885-91)
Warren G. Harding (1921-23)	Senate (1915-21)
Harry S Truman (1945-53)	Senate (1935-45)
John F. Kennedy (1961-63)	House (1947-53)
	Senate (1953-60)
Lyndon B. Johnson (1963-69)	House (1937-49)
	Senate (1949-61)
Richard Nixon (1969-74)	House (1947-50)
	Senate (1950-53)
Gerald R. Ford (1974-77)	House (1949-73)

Source: Adapted from the *Biographical Directory of the American Congress, 1774-1971.*

[1] Italics indicate post-presidential service.

though John F. KENNEDY made that leap in 1961, as did James A. Garfield and Warren G. Harding before him. Others have advanced through the vice presidency: John Tyler, Millard Fillmore, Andrew Johnson, Harry S TRUMAN, and Lyndon B. JOHNSON all succeeded presidents who died in office. Martin Van Buren was vice president when he ran for president. Gerald R. FORD, Richard Nixon's vice president, became president when Nixon resigned. Others held intervening posts in government: Madison, Monroe, and John Quincy ADAMS were secretaries of state, for example, while James K. Polk, William McKinley, and Rutherford B. Hayes were governors.

Success in one branch of the government has not always been matched by success in the other. Lyndon Johnson, a Senate majority leader of legendary skills, was a powerful and effective chief executive until his presidency foundered on the Vietnam War. But Abraham Lincoln's single term in the House did not foreshadow his immense stature as president, while Ford's years of House leadership did not translate into White House triumphs. More consistent was the performance of Harding, an ineffectual senator who became an ineffectual president.

The two presidents who served in Congress after leaving the White House were John Quincy Adams and Andrew Johnson. Adams pursued a seventeen-year career in the House of Representatives; earlier in life he also had served in the Senate. Johnson, with a background of service in both chambers, returned to the Senate for five months before his death.

Members of Congress without number have sought the presidency in vain. Aaron Burr, Henry CLAY, Stephen A. DOUGLAS, James G. BLAINE, Robert A. TAFT, Hubert H. HUMPHREY, and Robert DOLE are only a sampling of those who have tried and failed to win the high office.   ~

Presiding Officer

Members of the Senate and House of Representatives take turns presiding over floor debate, a job that is viewed by some as drudgery, by others as an honor requiring finesse and skill. Members may speak on the floor only if the presiding officer permits, or "recognizes," them. The presiding officer also rules on POINTS OF ORDER and delivers other pronouncements that regulate floor debate; the script is usually written by the PARLIAMENTARIAN, who cannot directly address the chamber but can prompt the member in the chair. Members may APPEAL, or challenge, the presiding officer's decisions, and his rul-

ings can be overturned by majority vote.

In the Senate it once was common for the VICE PRESIDENT, its constitutionally designated president, to preside over floor debates. In the modern Senate the vice president seldom is called in unless his vote might be needed to break a tie.

The PRESIDENT PRO TEMPORE (president for the time being)—usually the senior member of the majority party in the Senate—may preside in the absence of the vice president, but generally the Senate puts a freshman member in the chair. That relieves more senior members of a time-consuming task and gives newcomers first-hand lessons in Senate rules and procedures. Not surprisingly, new senators are heavily dependent on the parliamentarian for advice.

The House puts no premium on giving new members experience in the chair. Its formal presiding officer is the SPEAKER, the leader of the majority party in the chamber. But the Speaker must appoint other representatives to preside when the House is considering bills for amendment in the COMMITTEE OF THE WHOLE. When sensitive bills are under consideration, his choice turns to senior members who are skilled parliamentarians—such as William H. Natcher, a Kentucky Democrat who entered the House in 1953. While senators tend to view presiding as drudge work to be avoided, some House members actively seek the duty. In an institution as large as the House, it is one way for members to increase their visibility.

In both the House and Senate only members of the majority party preside. Until 1977 members of each party took turns presiding in the Senate. The practice was abandoned following an incident in which the presiding officer, a member of the minority party, broke with Senate custom by denying recognition to the majority leader.   ~

Press and Congress

Congress conducts its business all over Capitol Hill, all at once. Much of its activity is open to the public. Tourists crowd corridors as they wait to watch Senate and House floor action, students attend hearings, and lobbyists wait to press members for a vote. The most privileged observers, though, are print and broadcast journalists, who sit in reserved seats to watch floor action and hearings, work in special rooms in the Capitol, and enjoy close contact with senators and representatives.

For reporters, Congress is an extremely valuable and accessible source of information. Senators and representatives, in turn, appreciate the publicity that news coverage can give them, particularly at election time. Most legislators have a staff member whose sole, or primary, responsibility is to deal with the press.

Covering Congress

Reporters do not cover every event on Capitol Hill or follow every legislative issue. Choices are made, often informally and quickly, to skip floor debate and focus on a hearing or wait outside a roomful of negotiators who might reach agreement. Certain issues get more attention from the press because they affect more people or cost more money, or because they are interesting or controversial. Reporters talk to certain legislators instead of others because they are more involved in a particular issue, more accessible, more articulate, more powerful within Congress, or more representative of different parts of the country. Reporters say covering Congress is like watching a twenty-ring circus with no clue about where or when the most dazzling act will be.

Print and broadcast journalists cover Congress from both a national and a local perspective. While major news organizations, such as the *New York Times* or CBS, report on the national or international implications of a congressional decision, dozens of reporters look first at how legislators from their area voted. Instead of seeking comments from the key committee chairmen who handled a bill, reporters for regional newspapers interview local representatives and senators. Even congressional leaders who deal often with national reporters maintain a close relationship with reporters from their region. Regional reporters far outnumber those from the major news organizations.

To some legislators, local coverage is preferable to appearing on a national program. "I can be on Tom Brokaw," said Rep. Dan Glickman, a Kansas Democrat, in 1987, referring to the NBC evening news anchor. "But it is not as important to my reelection as being on the NBC affiliate in Wichita.... On national TV, you don't get more than a short bite. On local TV, it's often two or three minutes."

Attracting the Press

Senators and representatives try in numerous ways to influence news coverage. Congressional offices issue press releases and newsletters that point out a legislator's accomplishments. Well-equipped Capitol Hill recording studios make it possible for senators and representatives to tape statements, making a video version of a press release that can even be beamed via satellite to home television stations. Many members are given space on newspaper editorial pages for columns.

Within Congress traditions have evolved that put the spotlight on individual members, giving them a chance to attract press attention. Both the House and Senate set time aside for floor statements by members on topics that need not relate to the day's legisla-

Press Conference
More than 7,000 people from the news business
are accredited to work on Capitol Hill. In this
1988 picture, reporters cluster around Senate
Majority Leader Robert C. Byrd as he announces
that he will give up his leadership position.

tive debate. Just before committee meetings begin, chairmen often give each member a chance to make a statement that is typically directed not at fellow members but at reporters. *(See* SPECIAL ORDERS.*)*

More than 7,000 people from the news business are accredited to work on Capitol Hill. Congress has given reporters themselves responsibility for deciding who qualifies for membership in the Senate and House press galleries. For working journalists, accreditation is straightforward, but rules prohibit gallery members from doing paid promotion work or lobbying. The restrictions date from the 1880s.

There are four separate press galleries in each chamber: for daily newspapers and news services, periodicals, radio and television correspondents, and photographers. Each is staffed by congressional personnel and furnished by Congress with telephones, typewriters, and other equipment.

Congress is a very open institution, but meetings and even floor debate may be closed to the public. Public access to floor action was greatly enhanced by live TELEVISION coverage, which the

House allowed in 1979 and the Senate in 1986. Employees of the House and Senate operate the cameras. C-SPAN, a cable network, provides continuous coverage to its subscribers, and national and local news programs often show brief excerpts from debate. But members have voted to hold secret discussions of sensitive national security matters.

Although committee hearings have been open to the public for decades, the writing of legislation was done primarily in private until the 1970s. Then REFORM efforts opened up committee sessions unless the members specifically voted to close them. By the mid-1970s even conference committees, which resolve differences in House and Senate versions of bills, were open to reporters. Often those meetings, held in cramped rooms in the Capitol, are able to accommodate only two or three reporters. Some committees, such as the Appropriations committees, meet in such small rooms that public access is always limited.

By the mid-1980s the push for openness, or "sunshine," on Capitol Hill had begun to fade. Among the committees that frequently closed meetings was the House WAYS AND MEANS Committee, which shut the press and public out of its tax-writing sessions. Ways and Means Chairman Dan Rostenkowski, an Illinois Democrat, was asked in 1987 about closed-door sessions. "It's just difficult to legislate [in open meetings]," he said. "I'm not ashamed about closed doors. We want to get the product out."

"I hate to say it, but members are more willing to make tough decisions on controversial bills in closed meetings," acknowledged Ways and Means Democrat Don J. Pease of Ohio, who usually voted against closing meetings..

Being able to attend hours-long meetings, though, often has not made it easier for reporters to write news stories. Legislation must pass through several stages before it becomes law, and the process of crafting compromises and adding detailed amendments is often murky. Only a small part of what Congress does actually gets reported.

The difficulty of portraying what 535 different people are doing on a given day is a sharp contrast to the straightforward nature of most reporting on the president. Scholars have argued that television has enhanced the power of the presidency, while Congress has suffered because its activities are diffuse and difficult to present concisely in a brief news story.

For reporters Congress can be an excellent source of information, particularly when the White House has decided not to talk about a subject. Presidents have criticized Congress for news leaks, but legislators are independent-minded and unlikely to end their mutually beneficial relationships with reporters.   ∼

Previous Question

The previous question motion is one of the fundamental rules of general

parliamentary procedure. Its use is indispensable to the legislative process in the House of Representatives because it is the only way to bring debate to a formal close.

The previous question is adopted, or "ordered," by a majority vote. Adoption of a motion ordering the previous question brings the House to a direct vote on the pending question. The motion itself is not debatable but must be put to a vote immediately. The motion is used not only to bring debate to a close, but also to foreclose the opportunity to revise, or amend, the question or legislation pending before the House. The previous question is used only when members are sitting as the House; it is not permitted in the COMMITTEE OF THE WHOLE, where other debate limitations apply. When the RULES COMMITTEE grants a special rule for floor debate on a bill, it routinely adds language "ordering the previous question" in advance of the debate. (See LEGISLATIVE PROCESS.)

The motion normally is offered by the FLOOR MANAGER of the bill. Adoption of the previous question means essentially that the House thinks the legislation or parliamentary question has been debated adequately and that members are ready to vote. If the House defeats the previous question, debate continues and amendments are in order. In addition, control of the debate passes to those who successfully opposed adoption of the previous question.

The House's use of the previous question motion most distinguishes its debates from those in the Senate. Since it is a debate-limiting device, the previous question is not permitted in the Senate, which cherishes "extended debate." Senate debate can be shut off in only two ways: by unanimous consent or by a two-thirds vote to invoke cloture. (See FILIBUSTER.)

An example of the importance of ordering the previous question occurred in 1981 on the eve of debate on a $35 billion package of budget cuts that had been proposed by President Ronald Reagan and House Republicans. The rule supported by the House Democratic leadership would have forced the House to vote separately on each proposed cut, making it very difficult for the Republicans to sustain their budget package. But the procedural vote ordering the previous question on the rule, which would have cleared the way for the Democrats' ground rules, failed on a vote of 210-217. That vote opened the rule to amendment, and the Republicans then rewrote the rule to allow a single vote on the entire package of budget cuts; their version was adopted 216-212.   ∼

Printing Committee, Joint

Although the Joint Printing Committee rarely meets, its staff closely monitors the printing operations of the entire federal government. Unlike most congressional committees, which oversee the operations of executive agencies and how they carry out congressional mandates, the Joint Printing Committee actually approves or disapproves specific agency decisions about printing. The purchase of a press by the GOVERNMENT PRINTING OFFICE or plans by the Defense Department to buy new data-processing equipment can be vetoed by the Joint Printing Committee. A mandate to reduce inefficiencies and waste in public printing guides the committee, but it also makes sure agencies are complying with laws that require public access to government information.

The Joint Printing Committee has authorized more than two hundred government printing plants (outside of GPO), but it also keeps business coming to GPO that many agencies would rather do themselves or buy from private companies. Critics say GPO rates and schedules for completing work are not competitive. Congress, though, created GPO to handle congressional publications, and the Joint Printing Committee has operated from the premise that GPO, since it exists, should also be used for other federal printing.

The Joint Printing Committee is responsible for the style and format of the *CONGRESSIONAL RECORD* and for the contents of the *CONGRESSIONAL DIRECTORY*. When the House and Senate each decided to mark in the *Record* those speeches that were not actually delivered, the Joint Committee chose the mechanism for making that distinction. The committee acts as the ombudsman for Congress, overseeing the way GPO handles the printing of the *Record* and other congressional publications.

The committee consists of the chairmen of the HOUSE ADMINISTRATION and the Senate RULES committees, and four other members from each panel.   ∼

Private Bill.   See LEGISLATION.

Privilege

Privilege relates to the rights of members of Congress and to the relative priority of the motions and actions they may make in their respective chambers.

"Privileged questions" deal with legislative business. The order in which legislative measures are considered by Congress is governed by strict priorities. A motion to table, for instance, is more privileged than a motion to recommit; thus it would be voted on first. *(See* MOTION.*)*

"Questions of privilege" concern legislators themselves, and they take precedence over almost all other proceedings. Matters affecting the rights, safety, dignity, and integrity of proceedings of the House or Senate as a whole are questions of privilege in both chambers. Questions involving individual members are called questions of "personal privilege."   ~

Progressive Era

The Progressive Era usually is thought of as the period in U. S. history from about 1900 to 1917, when Americans concluded that the government and economic affairs of the country were being run by unscrupulous politicians and powerful corporate interests. Much legislation enacted by Congress was designed to further the influence and financial advantage of these interlocking groups.

The national economy was largely the province of the railroads, manufacturing and mining corporations, and the large banks and financial institutions. Nor was the collusion limited to big business and the federal government. Almost all state governments and large cities in the decades before the turn of the century had fallen under the control of these same economic interests.

The Progressive movement was basically a revolt against this conspiracy of politics and economic power. Its roots were in the rural populist protests of the Midwest during the final third of the nineteenth century. Concerned citizens feared that democratic government and the basic well-being of vast numbers of Americans were threatened by this concentration of wealth and political power in a privileged few. Exploitation of the underprivileged, women, and children was widespread. The Progressive Era, therefore, was both a culmination of reform pressures that had been building since the 1880s and the beginning of a new political activism directed at bringing government and economic institutions under genuine popular control. The Progressives sought reform of existing structures rather than revolutionary change.

Progressive Agenda

The Progressives became an influential force at various levels of American society. The initial targets were the injustices and political corruption in the cities. Cleaning up the cities required

Father and Son
Progressive activists of the early twentieth century sought to bring government and economic institutions under genuine popular control. Sen. Robert M. La Follette, right, was a leader of Progressive forces in the Senate. He is shown with his son Robert, Jr., who succeeded him in the Senate in 1925.

the wresting of power from boss-ridden machines. This led to campaigns to capture control of state governments, since reformers found that in most cases the big-city machines were tied into statewide political networks. Inevitably, the reform pressures were to affect the two national political parties.

At the local level, the Progressive movement sought to relieve problems such as the substandard living and health conditions in urban areas, unemployment, child labor, exploitation of women and immigrant workers, and the high incidence of industrial accidents. At the state level, it tried to break the stranglehold of the giant trusts and corporations—such as the railroads—on economic life, to end the exploitation and abuse of natural resources by business interests, and to reform state constitutions.

At the national level, the Progressives' concerns centered on the need for a fairer distribution of the country's wealth and an end to social and class divisions along economic lines. Specific proposals included DIRECT ELECTION of U.S. senators; direct primaries; the Australian, or secret, ballot; the initiative, referendum, and recall to give voters more direct control over government; the graduated income tax; postal savings banks; protective labor laws; and regulation of economic power generally.

The quest for social justice, urban rehabilitation, and the health and welfare of the working man and the disadvantaged did not always center on economic, political, or administrative solutions. The Eighteenth Amendment to the Constitution, outlawing the sale or manufacture of alcoholic beverages, was in part a Progressive concern.

Progressivism in Politics

The influence of the Progressives in Congress began with attempts to open up the LEGISLATIVE PROCESS. Politically, the Progressives were an insurgent element within the Republican

party. For a couple of years before U. S. entry into World War I, they held the balance of power. Joining forces with a majority of Democrats in the House, they were able in 1910 to strip the autocratic and conservative Speaker, Illinois Republican Joseph G. CANNON, of most of his power. The revolt against "Cannonism," led by Progressives George W. NORRIS of Nebraska and John M. Nelson of Wisconsin and Democrats James B. "Champ" CLARK of Missouri and Oscar W. UNDERWOOD of Alabama, was consolidated in 1911. That year House Democrats returned to power and won approval of meaningful reforms in the rules that made it easier to bring to the floor for debate legislation that had been blocked by the conservative leadership. Clark was elected Speaker, but Underwood became the real leader of the House.

Speaker Cannon had opposed much of the Progressive agenda sought by President Theodore Roosevelt (1901-09). Roosevelt's reputation as a Progressive rested on his policies toward "trust-busting," railroad regulation, conservation, his "Square Deal" for labor, and other efforts in which his administration took the first tentative steps nationally to grapple with the complex social and economic problems of a modern industrial nation.

In the Senate, the Progressives were led by Robert M. LA FOLLETTE of Wisconsin, Albert J. BEVERIDGE of Indiana, Albert B. Cummins and Jonathan P. Dolliver of Iowa, and by Norris and Underwood, both of whom went from the House to the Senate.

A split in Republican ranks between the Progressives and the conservative backers of President William Howard Taft led Roosevelt in 1912 to form the Progressive (Bull Moose) party. The division among Republicans gave Democrat Woodrow Wilson a landslide victory in that year's presidential election. Wilson, who initially had championed traditional free enterprise and rejected the activist government role espoused by Roosevelt, eventually supported a dynamic federal role to solve the nation's social and economic problems. By 1916 Wilson had won enactment of most of the demands the rural Populists and Progressives had advocated.

Progressives' Accomplishments

The Progressives achieved an impressive record of social, economic, and political reforms. But many of these programs were disrupted by U. S. entry into World War I, by the disillusionment that followed the failed peace settlement and, later, by Supreme Court rulings and the conservative presidential administrations of the 1920s. Many of the changes the Progressives fought for had to be won anew in the 1930s. To an important degree, the philosophical and political foundations of the NEW DEAL had their origin in the Progressive Era.

A few of the landmark initiatives identified with the Progressives and enacted during the Wilson administration were the Federal Reserve Act, Federal Trade Commission Act, Clayton Antitrust Act, and Rayburn Securities Act. Others included the Adamson Act, which created the first eight-hour workday on interstate railroads, and the first federal law regulating child labor. Although not ratified until 1920, the Nineteenth Amendment, granting suffrage to women, also was a consequence of the Progressive Era. *(See* WOMEN'S SUFFRAGE.*)*   ~

Public Works and Transportation Committee, House

The federal government has spent billions of dollars building roads, airports, dams, and subways—and the House Public Works Committee has had a say in most of those decisions. Even the politics of tight federal budgets have not dimmed the panel's enthusiasm for road building and channel dredging.

Labels like PORK BARREL are not welcome on the Public Works Committee. Although less sought after than WAYS AND MEANS, APPROPRIATIONS, or RULES, Public Works has always been popular with legislators eager to show concrete evidence of their work. When the committee is choosing special projects, those located in the districts of committee members usually get top priority. But Public Works also accommodates other members, on a bipartisan basis, by including dams or roads for those who comply with the unwritten rule: Give full support to bills that contain something for your district.

Despite budget constraints in the 1980s, Public Works chalked up several successes. Congress in 1987 overrode presidential vetoes of both a highway bill and a measure providing sewage treatment grants. For the first time since 1970 legislators authorized new dams, port dredging, and other water projects. In 1986 clean water laws were extended. The victories, though, often came after setbacks and years of work. In 1986, for example, Congress failed to reauthorize highway and mass transit programs, leaving a serious gap in the flow of federal funds to state highway departments. The next year disputes between the House and Senate were resolved.

Public Works is also responsible for the aviation and trucking industries and played a key role in ending regulation of airlines in 1978 and trucking in 1980. (Railroad deregulation was handled by the ENERGY AND COMMERCE Committee.) In the 1980s the committee raised safety concerns with both industries; pressure for profits has in many cases led companies to postpone buying new equipment, cut back on maintenance, and ask employees to work extra hours at their jobs.

Public Works has faced criticism for its commitment to capital improvements. President Ronald Reagan complained that the 1987 water treatment bill was "loaded with waste and larded with pork." But Public Works Chairman James J. Howard, a New Jersey Democrat who held the post from 1981 until his death in 1988, argued that Public Works "has probably done more economic good for more people than any other committee in Congress." Intense and skilled at negotiating, Howard shepherded several major bills through Congress. Though committed to traditional public works, Howard also showed flexibility; after years of opposition, he agreed in 1978 to package mass transit with highway funding. That ended years of second-class status for buses and subways—and won new urban votes for the legislation in the process.   ~

Purse, Power of

The Constitution entrusted to Congress the power to tax and spend. For two centuries the "power of the purse" has given the legislative branch paramount authority to command national resources and direct them to federal purposes. No other congressional prerogative confers so much control over the goals of government, or so much influence on the nation's well-being.

Since the 1930s Congress has made broad use of its taxing, spending, and borrowing powers to vastly enlarge the government and expand its influence over the U.S. economy. The way the government spends its money—and raises it through taxes or borrowing—carries enormous consequences for the nation's economic performance and its political and social balance. Under congressional direction, the federal govern-

ment provides income to the poor and health care to the elderly, builds highways and space shuttles, encourages economic development with subsidies and tax advantages, and pays for weapons and soldiers to operate them.

Through the years the House and Senate have jealously guarded most congressional powers to finance the machinery of government. But Congress has had trouble using its taxing and spending powers to shape a coherent federal budget policy. The result has been mounting gaps between spending and revenues and constant battling between Congress and successive presidents for final authority to set budget policy.

Much as it wanted to control the purse strings, Congress rarely bothered until the mid-1970s to tie its separate legislation to tax and spending totals. (Since 1921 the executive branch had drawn up yearly federal budgets setting forth revenue, spending, and deficit or surplus targets.) But in the early 1970s a heavily Democratic Congress fiercely resisted when Republican President Richard NIXON refused to spend billions of dollars already appropriated to federal agencies, a practice known as IMPOUNDMENT.

Congress responded in 1974 by setting up its own elaborate BUDGET PROCESS, which forced it to weigh spending against expected government revenues and to establish limits for each. Lawmakers continue to make actual decisions on spending and revenues through separate legislation, written by different House and Senate committees. BUDGET committees in each chamber draw up overall budget plans, but the actual spending bills are written by the House and Senate APPROPRIATIONS committees within limits set by AUTHORIZATION bills that have been drafted by various other committees. The House WAYS AND MEANS and Senate FINANCE committees control the complicated process of writing tax legislation.

Appropriations Conference
The way the government spends its money
carries enormous consequences for the nation's
well-being. Spending decisions are made in
conferences such as this one between members of the House and Senate Appropriations
committees.

Power to Tax

Without sufficient revenues, no
government could function effectively.
The Constitution granted Congress the
right to enact almost any taxes, except
for duties on exports. That power was
enlarged in 1913 by adoption of the Sixteenth Amendment to the Constitution,
authorizing a federal tax on incomes.

Tariffs During the nineteenth century
the federal government derived the
bulk of its revenues from tariffs on imports and other customs duties. Limited
funds were also provided by estate or
excise taxes.

Disputes over tariff policy were
common. At times the nation was divided by region, with protective tariffs
popular in the North and East, where
manufacturing was important to the
economy, and unpopular in the agricultural West and South. Critics were so
upset by duties imposed in 1828 that
they called the law the "tariff of abomi-
nations." In the last part of the century
tariff policy split the major political

parties; Republicans generally favored
high tariffs, while Democrats supported
low tariffs.

Customs duties provided a smaller
share of federal revenue after taxation
of incomes began. Politically, though,
the debate continued. Thinking higher
tariffs would boost the badly ailing domestic economy, Congress in 1930
passed the Smoot-Hawley Tariff Act,
which raised duties to the highest levels
in U. S. history. The misguided effort
was repealed in 1934.

Congress finally delegated virtually
all of its tariff-making power to the
president, beginning with the Reciprocal Trade Agreements Act of 1934. By
then individual and corporate income
taxes had begun replacing customs receipts as the main source of government
revenues. In 1910 customs duties still
brought in more than 49 percent of federal revenues; by the 1970s they had
dropped to less than 1 percent.

Income Tax Congress first passed
taxes on income to finance the Civil

War, but the levy expired in 1872. The income tax was renewed in 1894, with the rate set at 2 percent on personal incomes in excess of $3,000. The next year, though, the Supreme Court ruled the tax unconstitutional; it violated a requirement that direct taxes be apportioned among states according to population.

That roadblock was removed by the Sixteenth Amendment, and a new income tax system was established in 1913. Congress exempted families with low incomes from the income tax; over the years a complicated sliding scale evolved that set higher tax rates on higher incomes. Tax deductions, allowed from the start, encourage specific activities; among the best known is the deduction for interest on home mortgages, a subsidy to encourage home ownership that "costs" the government more than $20 billion a year in lost revenues.

Congress had no constitutional difficulty with the corporate income tax it first levied in 1909. The Supreme Court let the tax stand as an excise on the privilege of doing business as a corporation. An outright corporate income tax was enacted in 1913.

Federal taxes on individual incomes now comprise well over half of all federal revenues, totaling nearly $393 billion in fiscal 1987. Corporate income taxes amounted to $84 billion.

Excise, Other Taxes The power of Congress to tax in other areas is well established. Excise taxes—taxes on the sale of products or services—have always been a part of the federal tax system. The excises levied upon ratification of the Constitution included taxes on carriages, liquor, snuff, sugar, and auction sales. Modern excise taxes extend to telephone service and diesel fuel.

Another important area of taxation is payroll taxes, which financially underpin the Social Security and unemployment compensation systems. Payroll taxes are the second largest source of government revenues: $303 billion in fiscal 1987.

Power to Spend

The Constitution gave Congress the basic authority to decide how the government should spend the money it collects. It set few specific limits on the spending power. And by authorizing Congress to collect taxes "to pay the debts and provide for the common defense and general welfare of the United States," the Constitution opened the way for an expansive interpretation of the power.

The new national government spent $5 million in fiscal 1792, its fourth year in operation. Peacetime spending grew slowly until the 1930s, when President Franklin D. Roosevelt and Congress launched massive federal programs to pull the economy out of the worst depression in U.S. history. During World War II federal spending multiplied tenfold, reaching $92.7 billion in fiscal 1945. Spending dropped off after the war ended, only to rise again during the Korean War. It continued upward in an almost uninterrupted spiral for the next three decades.

Federal spending mounted to more than $1 trillion in fiscal 1987, accounting for more than a fifth of the nation's total output of goods and services. As recently as 1978, less than half that amount was spent annually; in 1974, less than a third. A combination of factors swelled the federal budget and kept spending at high levels even when revenues, though also increasing, fell behind. Annual deficits, the gap between revenues and spending, first broke the $200 billion mark in 1983.

Since the 1970s the largest portion of spending has been for payments to individuals—retirement benefits, welfare, disability insurance, and other programs. When inflation in the 1970s made fixed benefits seem unfairly small, Congress provided automatic cost-of-living increases for many programs, a process known as indexing. That increased the government's costs, as did the growing ranks of participants. Many benefit programs were established as entitlements, which required payments to everyone who met legal requirements. Once these programs were in place, Congress found it politically impossible to dismantle them. Payments to individuals were expected to make up 43 percent of federal spending in fiscal 1989, far outstripping defense spending, the second largest category, which accounted for 27 percent.

Congress was also obligated to fund contracts from previous years; in 1987 such contracts amounted to about 18 percent of spending. Interest on the national debt was an uncontrollable element of the budget, consuming more than 14 percent of spending.

Only about 25 percent of federal spending remained under direct congressional control through the annual appropriations process. Reducing those programs by substantial amounts proved very difficult for the House and Senate. The bureaucracy that operated the programs, and the groups that benefited from them, created a powerful momentum against budget cuts.

Power to Borrow

There is no constitutional restriction on the government's power to borrow money on the nation's credit. Congress by statute has set a DEBT LIMIT since 1917, but it has regularly raised the limit, though often with political difficulty. Funds to pay interest on the debt have been permanently appropriated since 1847. Congress protected that obligation from political uncertainty, thus enhancing the nation's credibility as a borrower.

Debt has been incurred by the federal government when it has found it necessary to spend more than it has collected in tax and other forms of revenue. Then the deficit must be made up by borrowing.

Throughout most of the nation's history, government has tried to assure that revenues were sufficient to meet spending requirements. This philosophy, which in application meant an approximate balance between revenues and spending, was generally accepted until the early 1930s. But then Congress approved major federal projects to stimulate economic recovery. In the process the government began following an economic philosophy, developed by British economist John Maynard Keynes, that justified peacetime deficits to ensure stable economic growth.

As a result, the government abandoned its former insistence on balancing revenues and spending. The practice of using the federal budget to help solve national economic problems was increasingly accepted. Budget deficits and a rapidly increasing national debt were the result. By 1988, the national debt—money the government owed to others—exceeded $2.8 trillion. Paying interest on those loans cost more than $100 billion a year; this was the third largest component of the federal budget, exceeded only by defense and Social Security.   ~

ADDITIONAL READINGS

Fenno, Richard F., Jr. *The Power of the Purse.* 1966.
Schick, Allen. *Congress and Money.* 1980.
Stockman, David. *The Triumph of Politics.* 1986.

Overleaf:
Capitol subway.

Quorum

A quorum is the minimum number of members who must be present for the transaction of business. In both chambers of Congress it is a majority of the total membership: 51 in the Senate and 218 in the House of Representatives, provided there are no vacant seats. Only 100 members are required when the House is sitting as the COMMITTEE OF THE WHOLE, the parliamentary framework it adopts when it considers bills for amendment.

A quorum is assumed to be present, even when only a handful of members are on the floor, unless a member suggests otherwise. In that case the roll is called, and absentees stream into the chamber to make up a quorum. Quorum calls are frequently used in the Senate to kill time while groups of senators informally negotiate legislative or procedural disputes.   ~

Randolph, John

John Randolph (1773-1833) represented Virginia in the House of Representatives intermittently from 1799 to 1833. His tenure there was interrupted four times, once to allow service in the Senate from 1825 to 1827. Randolph

was a State Rights Democrat who opposed legislation that he believed would strengthen the national government at the cost of state sovereignty. Despite his difficult personality, many in Congress were in awe of his brilliant oratory and his uncompromising beliefs. Henry Adams described him standing to speak to the House "with the halo of youth, courage, and genius around his head—a sort of Virginian Saint Michael, almost terrible in his contempt for whatever seemed to him base or untrue."

Randolph entered Congress as a supporter of Thomas Jefferson and almost immediately became chairman of the WAYS AND MEANS Committee. He supported Jefferson's purchase of the Louisiana territory but later broke with the president over his attempts to acquire Florida.

A constitutional purist, Randolph refused to bow to necessity if it conflicted with principle. He opposed protective tariffs, roads built by the national government, the chartering of the Bank of the United States, and federal interference in the issue of slavery. Randolph also was a prominent opponent of the Missouri Compromise of 1820. Ill feeling over this issue between Randolph and Henry CLAY, another great orator, went beyond words in 1826. That year, the two men met in a duel over Randolph's denunciation of Clay's support for John Quincy ADAMS's selection as president. Neither man was harmed. Clay had been a losing candidate for the presidency in the 1824 election, which had been decided by the House of Representatives. *(See* ELECTING THE PRESIDENT.*)*

In 1830 Randolph traveled to St. Petersburg as Andrew Jackson's minister to Russia. He was forced to leave shortly after his arrival due to illness. Plagued all his life by ill health, Randolph died in 1833 after periods of dementia, alcoholism, and opium use.   ∼

Rankin, Jeannette

Jeannette Rankin (1880-1973) was the first woman to serve in Congress. A suffragist and pacifist, she ran for the House at a time when only a handful of states allowed women to vote and as the nation was about to enter World War I. *(See* WOMEN IN CONGRESS.*)*

Born into a family that believed in education for women and political activism, Rankin was graduated from the University of Montana and went on to study social work at the New York School of Philanthropy. She then returned west and lobbied for the enfranchisement of women in the states of Washington, California, and Montana.

Rankin ran as a Republican for one of Montana's House seats in 1916 on a platform favoring Prohibition, women's rights, and federal suffrage (the Nineteenth Amendment giving women the right to vote was not ratified until 1920). When elected, Rankin said: "I knew the women would stand behind me. I am deeply conscious of the responsibility. I will not only represent the women of Montana, but also the women of the country, and I have plenty of work cut out for me."

In the House Rankin worked to further the cause of women. She introduced legislation to grant women citizenship independent of their husbands and sponsored a bill providing for federally supported maternal and infant health instruction. She helped to set up a House committee on women's suffrage and tried to ensure that employment generated by legislation would include women.

In 1917 the House voted on the United States' entry into World War I. With forty-nine other representatives Rankin voted no, saying, "I want to stand by my country but I cannot vote for war." Her vote brought her a national notoriety not given to her forty-nine male colleagues.

After her first term in the House, Rankin ran unsuccessfully for the Senate. Out of office, she continued to work for women's rights, and in 1940 she was reelected to the House. Ironically, she was again faced with a vote on the United States' involvement in a war. This time Rankin was the only member to vote against entry into World War II. Few shared the view of Kansas newspaper editor William Allen White, who said of her pacifist stand: ". . . It was a brave thing! And its bravery somehow discounted its folly." After the vote, she was forced to lock herself in a phone booth to escape the curious and angry crowds.

In 1968 when she was in her late eighties, Jeannette Rankin led a Jeannette Rankin Brigade to the Capitol to protest the war in Vietnam. She died at the age of 92.   ∼

Sam Rayburn

Rayburn, Sam

Sam Rayburn (1882-1961) served as SPEAKER of the House of Representatives longer than any other member in history. He wielded great authority through a combination of personal prestige, persuasiveness, and an almost uncanny sense for the institution and how it worked.

A Texan and a Democrat "without prefix, without suffix, and without apology," Rayburn entered the House in 1913. In 1931 he became chairman of the Interstate and Foreign Commerce Committee, where he managed the regulatory measures of the New Deal. In 1937 he became majority leader and in 1940 Speaker. Except for stints as minority leader in 1947-49 and 1953-55, he retained the speakership until his death in 1961.

Rayburn's oft-quoted advice to younger members, "To get along, you've got to go along," reflected a House in which it was no longer possible to exercise the kind of power earlier Speakers had enjoyed. "You cannot lead people in order to drive them," he said. "Persuasion and reason are the only ways to lead them. In that way the Speaker has influence and power in the House." Rayburn used all the power he had available to him. He rewarded members who were sympathetic to the goals of the Democratic party with good committee assignments. In 1961 he gave way to the pressure of party liberals and orchestrated the expansion of the RULES Committee to ease the passage of liberal legislation. Occasionally he could be more autocratic. In 1941, for example, he was "suspected of wielding a quick gavel," to prevent reconsideration of a military draft extension that had passed by a 203-202 vote. More than anything, Rayburn ruled behind the scenes through conciliation and compromise. Although plagued by a CONSERVATIVE COALITION of southern

Democrats and Republicans that stymied much Democratic domestic legislation, Rayburn was very successful in getting legislation through the House. He oversaw the passage of the Civil Rights Acts of 1957 and 1960 and was able to gain approval for much foreign affairs legislation.   ∼

ADDITIONAL READINGS

Champagne, Anthony. *Congressman Sam Rayburn.* 1984.
Hardeman, D. B., and Donald Bacon. *Rayburn: A Biography.* 1987.

Readings of Bills

House and Senate rules require that all bills be read three times before passage, in accordance with traditional parliamentary usage. The original purpose was to make sure legislators knew what they were voting on, but in modern practice only the bill's title is usually read.

When legislators need a delaying tactic, they sometimes object to requests for UNANIMOUS CONSENT to dispense with a reading. Then the drone of the text being read aloud is added to the usual hum of noise on the House and Senate floors. Few listen to the words.

Senate rules require bills and resolutions to be read twice, on different LEGISLATIVE DAYS, before they are referred to committee. The third and final reading follows floor debate and voting on amendments.

In the House the first reading occurs when the bill is introduced and printed by number and title in the *Congressional Record.* The second reading occurs when floor consideration begins; often the bill is read section by section for amendment. The third reading comes just before the vote on final passage.   ∼

Reapportionment and Redistricting

Reapportionment and redistricting are the two processes that determine distribution of the 435 seats in the House of Representatives. Because they decide the number of voting members in the House that each state will have, as well as the voting strength of various regions, population groups, and political parties within each state, they are often among the most important and controversial issues within the American political system.

In brief terms, reapportionment is the redistribution of House seats among the states to reflect shifts in population as indicated by the national census, which is carried out every ten years. States whose populations grew quickly over the previous decade are given additional House seats, while those that lost population or grew more slowly than the national average have seats taken away.

Redistricting, in turn, involves the redrawing of congressional district lines within each state, based on the number of House seats allotted to it and population changes within the state. Almost every House member represents a specific area within a state. (Six states elect only one House member, who represents the entire state.) The exact shape of each House district determines which voters will be able to vote in elections for that House seat. Redistricting usually occurs in the two years following reapportionment and is normally controlled by the governor and legislature of the state. The courts sometimes order another round of redistricting in the middle of a decade, and on occasion even draw new district maps on their own.

Reapportionment and redistricting have been subjects of debate throughout U.S. history because the Constitution did not specify how they should be carried out. The Founding Fathers decreed that House seats would be divided among the states on the basis of population, and that House members would be elected by the people. Beyond that, however, the Constitution gave little useful guidance on these subjects, leaving Congress, the courts, and state governments to wrestle with them for 200 years.

After many decades of debate, the basic goal of reapportionment and redistricting was settled by Supreme Court rulings in the 1960s. The guiding principle of the two processes is "one person, one vote." For the system to be fair, each citizen must have approximately the same representation in the House. That means that the 435 congressional districts should be as close to equal in population as possible.

Many other key questions about reapportionment and redistricting have yet to be settled. Most importantly, the courts have not decided definitively whether the Constitution allows states to GERRYMANDER, or draw House district lines to favor one party over the other.

In contrast to the House, the Senate never undergoes reapportionment or redistricting. The Constitution gave each state two Senate seats, and senators are always chosen on a statewide basis.

Reapportionment

In general, reapportionment is less politically controversial than redistricting. Although the results of reapportionment can have major political effects in determining the relative strength of states and regions in the House, the process is ultimately based on a mathematical formula that distributes House seats to states on the basis of their populations.

It has not been easy to pick the best formula for distributing House seats. Congress has tried a number of different methods over the years. None of them, including the one currently in use, has worked perfectly. Many experts believe it is impossible to devise a method of allocating House seats that does not give some states more or less representation than they deserve on the basis of their population.

The basic reason for the problems of reapportionment is simple: No state can have a fraction of a representative. Each state must have a whole number of House members, from one to as many as forty-five in the mid-1980s. Yet states are rarely entitled to a round number of representatives based on their population. Consider, for example, a state with 1 percent (roughly 2.4 million) of the nation's population. Strictly on percentage terms, that state would have a right to 1 percent of the House, or 4.35 members. If that state is given only four House members, it is underrepresented. If it gets five members, it is overrepresented.

Even with the complex reapportionment formula now in use, there are wide variations in the amount of representation states receive, based on their population. Maine and Nevada, for example, both send two representatives to the House, even though Maine (1.1 million) has many more people than Nevada (787,000). South Dakota gets only one House member, despite the fact that its population (690,000) is only a little less than Nevada's. Population variance also arises from the Constitution's requirement that each state have at least one representative. So Alaska, which had only about 400,000 residents in 1980, gets as much representation as South Dakota.

The Founding Fathers settled the difficult question of distribution of House seats for the first Congresses by specifically listing how many seats each of the thirteen original states were to receive. That was necessary because there were no accurate statistics on the

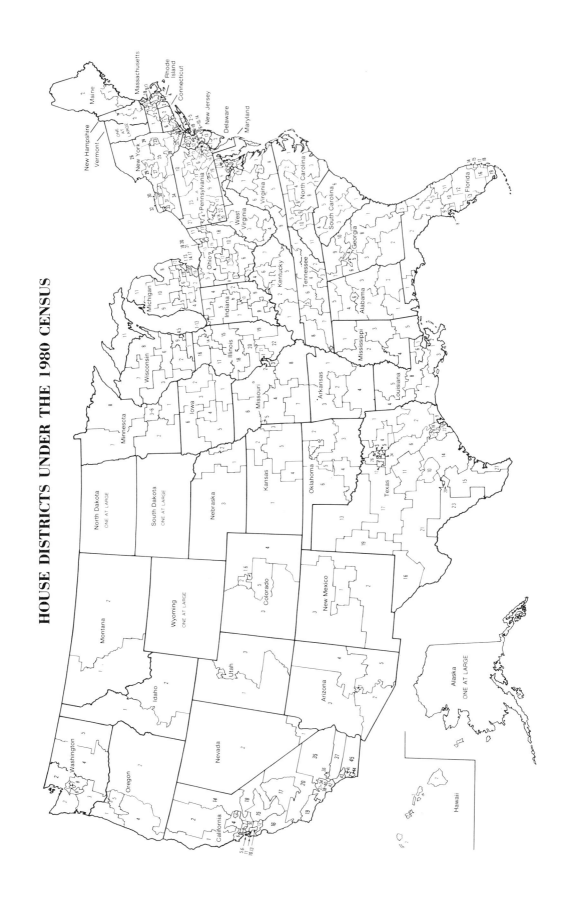

HOUSE DISTRICTS UNDER THE 1980 CENSUS

populations of the states. Once the first census was undertaken, in 1790, the Constitution directed that each congressional district have at least 30,000 residents, except for small states, which were guaranteed at least one representative no matter what their population. In a compromise between the slave-owning South and the rest of the country, the Constitution provided that each slave would be counted as three-fifths of a person in determining the size of each state's House delegation.

In the early decades Congress followed the Constitution in basing representation on an ideal population size of a congressional district. As a result the total number of House members at any one time varied widely. In 1832, for example, the standard size of a congressional district was set at 47,700 people, producing a House of 240 members. None of the different allocation methods used in those days could solve the problem of fractional representation, however, resulting in congressional districts of widely varying size.

Moreover, the early reapportionment methods were inadequate to cope with the rapid growth in the nation's population. No matter what method was used, there seemed to be unanticipated effects that went against common sense. One method was subject to the "population paradox," under which an increase in the total population would lead to a decrease in the size of the House. Another technique produced the "Alabama paradox," which at times resulted in a decrease in a state's delegation even as the total number of House seats was increased.

Finally, around 1850, Congress settled on a method that seemed to solve many reapportionment problems. The size of the House was supposed to be fixed, although Congress regularly voted to add more members as new states entered the Union. That avoided the difficult problem of cutting back on the representation of existing states to

make room for new ones. By the beginning of the twentieth century, however, that process threatened to make the House too large to be a workable legislative body. In 1911 Congress fixed the size of the House at 435, where it remains today.

The decision to freeze the size of the House set the stage for the reapportionment battles of the 1920s. The 1920 census was a landmark event in the nation's history, because it showed for the first time that there were more people living in cities than in rural areas. As a result states with large cities were entitled to many more representatives, while rural states faced sharp cutbacks in their House representation. Arguing that people who lived on farms and in small towns were the heart and soul of America, rural representatives fought hard to prevent their loss of power. They managed to block reapportionment throughout the 1920s. Redistribution of House seats did not take place until after the 1930 census. The reapportionment produced drastic shifts in power, with California nearly doubling its House delegation, from eleven to twenty, while twenty-one states lost a total of twenty-seven seats.

Since 1950, when the current method of reapportionment ("method of equal fractions") was adopted, arguments over reapportionment methods have declined. Nevertheless, reapportionment every ten years has continued to exert a major influence on political strength in the House. Because Americans move so often, the populations of many states can change substantially over the course of ten years. The political strength of those states in the House can change considerably as well.

The most important change in state populations in recent years has been the shift of people away from the older, industrial states of the Northeast and Midwest (the Frost Belt) to the newly developing states along the nation's southern tier, from Florida to

California (the Sun Belt). The 1980 census illustrates how great a change that trend has made in the House. As a result of the 1980 census, seventeen House seats shifted from the Northeast and Midwest to the Sun Belt. The biggest gainer was fast-growing Florida, which picked up four seats. With nineteen seats, Florida had more than twice as many seats as it had had in 1960, when it had eight. Texas gained three seats, and California two, while eight states gained one seat each.

New York, by contrast, lost five seats—the sharpest drop in House representation for any state since 1840. New York's population had fallen by 700,000 since 1970, while most other states were gaining population. Illinois, Ohio, and Pennsylvania lost two seats each, while six states lost one seat each.

Many political analysts predicted that the 1980 reapportionment would substantially alter the political makeup of the House. Most of the states that lost seats tended to favor liberal Democrats, while the states that gained seats were more likely to favor Republicans or conservative Democrats. Because of Democratic successes in the state redistricting battles that followed reapportionment, however, the effects were much less significant than expected. In the 1982 congressional elections the Democrats suffered a net loss of only two seats as a result of reapportionment.

Redistricting

Unlike reapportionment, the redistricting process has grown more, rather than less, controversial in recent decades. The combination of Supreme Court decisions in the 1960s, major population shifts within states, and the advent of computer-based technology has made redistricting a subject of intense dispute. The national Republican and Democratic parties devote immense resources to the effort to persuade state legislatures and the courts to approve state district plans favorable to their own candidates.

Indeed, some political analysts believe that redistricting is the single most important factor determining political control of the House. Specifically, they argue that the dominance of the Democratic party, which has controlled the House continuously since 1955, is due to Democratic control of the redistricting process. Democratic-dominated state legislatures have devised district plans that give all the advantages to Democratic House candidates, Republicans argue, making it difficult for Republican candidates to win even when they are favored by a majority of the voters. Other political experts disagree with that argument. But there is no question that redistricting is crucial to the outcome of many House elections.

The early years of debate over redistricting were dominated by the fundamental question of whether there needed to be congressional districts within states at all. The Constitution had not said so, and several states favored use of at-large House elections. Under the at-large system all voters in a state choose all of the state's House members. Use of the system declined because it did not encourage the close ties between representative and citizens that developed when a member of Congress represented a specific area. Congress banned at-large House elections in 1842, except in one-member states, although the ban was frequently violated until the 1960s. That law also established the basic principle that House districts should be contiguous—that is, a single, connected area, not several separate areas scattered across a state.

For a hundred years redistricting questions were not very prominent. State legislatures had to draw new district lines when reapportionment cost the state House seats, and occasionally there was a heated dispute over a single congressional district. Generally speaking, though, state legislatures ignored the question of redistricting. They rarely acted to change district lines. That tendency had important consequences—notably, a failure to give cities additional representatives as their populations grew. But partisan fights over district lines were rare, and there was little pressure for major alterations in the shape of most districts.

That was radically changed when the Supreme Court began considering redistricting issues in the 1960s, after refusing for decades to interfere in districting questions. By the time the Court began to act, there was clear evidence that something was wrong with the way legislative districts were drawn. Particularly in state legislatures, rural areas were vastly overrepresented, while cities did not have nearly as much representation as their populations warranted. In every state the most populous state legislative district had at least twice as many people as the least populous district. Things were not as bad in congressional districts, but there were still wide differences in rural and urban representation. In Texas one urban district had four times as many people as one lightly populated rural district.

The state legislatures, which were dominated by members from rural areas, refused to change the existing districts. Frustrated urban dwellers turned to the courts, arguing that they were being denied fair representation by the legislatures. In its historic decision on *Baker v. Carr*, the Supreme Court ruled in 1962 that the districts used in the Tennessee state legislature were unconstitutional, because they violated the principle of one person, one vote. In 1964 the Court extended that doctrine to the House in the case of *Wesberry v. Sanders*, which concerned congressional districts in Georgia. That decision stated that congressional districts should be as nearly equal in population "as is practicable."

Since then the Court has continued to tighten the requirement that con-

gressional districts be of equal populations. In the 1969 case of *Kirkpatrick v. Preisler*, the Court struck down the district plan of Missouri, whose largest district was 3.1 percent more populous than its smallest. Any population difference, "no matter how small," the Court declared, was unacceptable in all but a few cases. The Court set an even more rigorous standard in the 1983 case of *Karcher v. Dagget*, in which it ruled against a New Jersey district plan that had a population difference between districts of .69 percent—about 3,600 residents in districts of 526,000.

Although the one-person, one-vote principle is now widely accepted in American politics, some political experts are critical of the strict standard of population equality set by the Court in recent years. For one thing, the census figures for district populations are not entirely accurate, and they usually are out of date within a year or two after the census is taken. Moreover, district lines that are drawn to ensure equal population often cross traditional political boundaries, such as cities, counties, or regions, that help voters develop a sense of identification with and interest in their congressional district. Finally, critics have pointed out that the Court's standard could be satisfied by a district plan that was a grossly unfair case of political GERRYMANDERING—as long as each district had the same number of people.

The issue of gerrymandering is at the center of current debate over redistricting. While the subject is complex, it ultimately boils down to one basic idea: Certain areas within each state show a long-term preference for one party over the other. In each election the majority of voters in these areas have a strong tendency to vote for the candidate of one party, regardless of who is running or what issues are being debated. An area with many working-class people and blacks, for example, in many cases will favor Democratic candidates year after year. A wealthy area in the suburbs, on the other hand, may back Republicans in almost every election.

Because these voting habits are well known to political experts in each state, it is possible to create districts that are almost certain to favor candidates of one party. A district composed solely of blue-collar and inner-city neighborhoods will almost always elect a Democrat, while one made up entirely of well-to-do suburbanites will be a "safe" Republican seat.

But state legislators and party strategists have learned over the years to play even more subtle redistricting games. If an incumbent barely survived a tough reelection fight, his friends in the state legislature might agree to add to his district areas filled with voters who favored his party, while taking out some neighborhoods that usually voted against him. On a larger scale the "A" party might try to "dilute" the "B" party's voting strength, by spreading B voters among several districts, preventing B candidates from winning a majority in any one. Or, A strategists could concentrate all possible B voters in one district, creating a safe district for the Bs but making all the others in the state favorable to A candidates.

Another potential type of gerrymandering involves race. By dividing up black or other minority voters among several districts, a legislature might be able to ensure that no more than 50 percent of the voters in any district were minorities, and so prevent election of a minority representative. When blacks in the South began to vote in large numbers in the 1960s, civil rights groups feared that they might be subjected to racial gerrymandering by white-dominated legislatures. So the 1965 Voting Rights Act contains provisions barring redistricting plans that dilute the voting strength of blacks, Hispanics, or other minorities. The law required that nine states, and parts

of thirteen others, submit their redistricting plans to the U.S. Justice Department to see if they were racially biased. The department and the courts have required changes in redistricting plans in a number of states to make sure they did not prevent black candidates from having any chance of being elected.

Unresolved Question

The constitutionality of gerrymandering is an important unresolved question in American politics. By one argument it is unconstitutional, since it deprives voters in a gerrymandered district of the right to make an effective choice between candidates of both parties. If a district is set up to make election of a Democrat inevitable, then Republicans in the district have lost the right to cast anything more than a symbolic vote for their candidate. The Supreme Court has traditionally been reluctant to rule on the question of gerrymandering, which it has considered a political question out of its jurisdiction. As long as the districts were sufficiently similar in population, the Court has not been willing to judge whether they were unfairly gerrymandered.

In 1986 the Court handed down its first significant decision on gerrymandering. In a case involving Indiana's state legislative districts, the Court ruled that political gerrymanders were subject to constitutional challenges for unfairly discriminating against political parties. The case was expected to open the door for a large number of cases challenging allegedly gerrymandered district plans.   ~

ADDITIONAL READINGS

Congressional Quarterly. *Congressional Districts in the 1980s.* 1983.

Mann, Thomas E., and Norman J. Ornstein, eds. *The American Elections of 1982-1983.*

Recess. See ADJOURNMENT.

Recess Appointment. See APPOINTMENT POWER.

Recommittal Motion

Motions to recommit are used extensively in the House of Representatives, infrequently in the Senate. Although a motion to recommit a bill may be offered for several reasons, the most common purpose is to kill the legislation pending in the full House or Senate. Motions to recommit also may be offered to resolutions, House-Senate conference reports and, in the House, amendments added to legislation by the Senate. *(See* LEGISLATIVE PROCESS.*)*

In the House the motion cannot be used during consideration of a bill for amendment in the COMMITTEE OF THE WHOLE, but it may be offered before a vote on passage of the bill in the full House. If the motion is successful, the bill is returned to the committee that reported it. There are two kinds of recommittal motions. A simple motion to recommit, if adopted, kills the bill for all practical purposes. A motion to recommit "with instructions" contains language instructing the committee to report the bill back "forthwith" with certain amendments (or sometimes after a study is completed or by a certain date). If the instructions to report forthwith are adopted, the instructions automatically become part of the legislation; usually the bill is not actually returned to the committee.

The motion to recommit is a standard parliamentary procedure in the House, one of the final steps toward passage of legislation. As such, it is guaranteed by the rules. Opponents must be given preference in offering the motion; only one such motion is permit-

ted on each bill. If made with instructions to add or amend certain provisions, recommittal motions give opponents of a bill a final opportunity to revise the legislation. They are an important strategic and policy tool of the minority, especially on bills considered under ground rules that bar floor amendments. *(See* RULE.*)*

The Senate does not routinely use recommittal motions because opponents have many other ways to defeat or amend legislation. Occasionally the Senate will vote to recommit legislation with certain instructions and report it back to the Senate within a specified period of time. From time to time the Senate entangles itself in such a parliamentary morass that it uses the recommittal motion to extricate itself. That happened in 1982 when the Senate was considering a bill to raise the national DEBT LIMIT. Majority Leader Howard H. BAKER, Jr., a Tennessee Republican, had promised senators for months that they could offer their pet proposals as amendments to the debt bill. But when the measure reached the floor, it became bogged down in a debate on controversial amendments dealing with abortion and school prayer. After five weeks, and with more than 1,400 amendments still pending, the Senate recommitted the measure to the FINANCE Committee, which immediately stripped it of all but the debt limit provisions and returned it to the floor for a final vote. ~

Reconciliation. See BUDGET PROCESS.

Reconsider, Motion to

The motion to reconsider is a necessary procedure for the final disposition of legislation in both the Senate and House of Representatives. A principle of parliamentary law is that floor action on bills and amendments is not conclusive until there has been an opportunity to reconsider the vote by which the question was approved or rejected. This step is routine in the House, where the motion to reconsider usually is followed immediately by a motion to TABLE. The SPEAKER usually makes the tabling motion by stating that "without objection a motion to reconsider is laid on the table."

Once the motion to reconsider is tabled, the earlier action on the bill or amendment is final since the act of tabling blocks any future attempt to reverse the result. Under the rules of both houses, the motion to reconsider must be made by a member on the prevailing side of the original vote (approving or rejecting the bill or amendment) or by someone who did not vote.

Besides its importance as a pro forma procedural step in the passage of legislation, the motion to reconsider, followed by a tabling motion, also is used routinely after amendments and other parliamentary questions have been voted on. In the Senate, the results are not always pro forma. On close votes in particular, switches can occur, and bills and amendments are reconsidered, giving members another chance to vote on the original question.

The rules in both houses set a time limit for entering motions to reconsider, and the parliamentary situation determines when such motions are in order. For example, a motion to reconsider a vote rejecting an amendment after the bill itself has been passed would come too late.   ∼

Reconstruction Era

The period immediately following the Civil War is known as the Re-construction Era. It refers to the policies implemented by the victorious Union government in the eleven war-torn and economically prostrate Confederate states. But Reconstruction, encompassing roughly the years 1865 to 1877, connotes more than merely a sectional administrative matter. It represents a period of unprecedented radical national leadership dominated by Congress at the expense of the presidency and the judiciary.

Lincoln's Lenient Policy

Even before the Civil War ended, President Abraham Lincoln had outlined a policy for dealing with the Southern states once they capitulated to the Union armies. As early as 1862 he began appointing military governors in areas that had fallen to the Union. He first outlined his Reconstruction policy in December 1863 and eloquently reiterated his views in his last public address April 11, 1865. Lincoln's primary goal was to return the seceded states to the Union as quickly and painlessly as possible. Except for a relatively few Confederate civilian and military leaders, amnesty and restoration of property rights were to be granted to everyone who gave an oath of loyalty to the Union. Whenever 10 percent of the electorate of any state made such a pledge, a state government could be established, and the president was prepared to recognize that state as once again a loyal entity of the United States. The states of Louisiana and Arkansas promptly accepted Lincoln's terms and had adopted new constitutions abolishing slavery even before the president was assassinated.

Such magnanimous treatment of the South was at odds with the will of Congress, which during and after the war was controlled by the Republicans, the most influential of whom were radical abolitionists. They did little to disguise their hatred of Southerners and their institutions and refused to accept

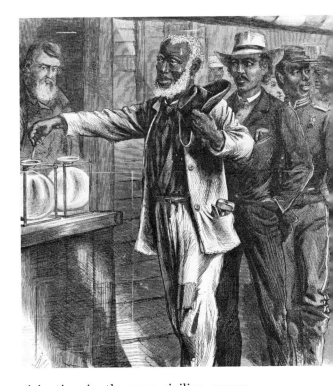

The First Vote
The collapse of the Confederacy resulted in the emancipation of some four million slaves. The Radicals' aim was to use the former slaves' votes to ensure Republican domination in Southern state governments and in Congress.

the validity of Lincoln's terms. In their view Reconstruction was solely the jurisdiction of Congress. When the two readmitted Southern states sent their newly elected representatives to Washington, Congress refused to seat them.

Radical Reconstruction

To the Radical Republicans, the Southerners remained traitors and rebels, who could not be restored to citizenship of a country they had repudiated without first undergoing rigid tests of loyalty. They devised a punitive plan of their own for implementing Reconstruction. Embodied in the Wade-Davis bill—named for Sen. Benjamin F. Wade of Ohio and Rep. Henry W. Davis of Maryland—the bill required a majority of the electorate in a state, rather than 10 percent, to swear their allegiance to the federal government before the state could be readmitted to the Union.

The Radicals' amnesty excluded even common Confederate soldiers from holding federal office. Such a policy had the effect of excluding from participation in the new civilian governments of the South the natural leaders and experienced statesmen of the region. But that was just the beginning. Behind all the invective and passion, the Radicals' real motive was to force upon the South immediate, full equality of all former slaves and use Negro votes to ensure Republican domination in Southern state governments and in Congress. The collapse of the Confederacy had resulted in the emancipation of some four million slaves. Rep. Thaddeus STEVENS of Pennsylvania, leader of the Radicals and implacable enemy of President Andrew Johnson, saw in the Fifteenth Amendment to the Constitution the means of ensuring a permanent Republican majority. The amendment guaranteed universal male suffrage, stipulating that the right to vote "shall not be denied or abridged by the United States or by any State on account of race, color, or previous condition of servitude." Stevens's policies were not based on sympathy for the Negro but rather on political advantage and cold hatred of the Southern gentry.

Lincoln was convinced that leniency was the only way to build loyalty to the Union and establish intersectional peace. Although he pocket-vetoed the Wade-Davis bill, the bill's authors issued the legislation as a manifesto of congressional sentiment and intent. "The president . . . must understand that the authority of Congress is paramount and must be respected," they asserted, ". . . and if he wants our support he must confine himself to his executive duties—to obey and execute, not make the laws—suppress by arms armed rebellion, and leave political reorganization [of the South] to Congress." Confrontation between the legislative and executive branches over Reconstruction now was inevitable and was not resolved until President Johnson had been impeached, harsh and constitutionally questionable Reconstruction laws enacted, and the Constitution itself amended to suit the Radicals' purposes.

After Lincoln's assassination, the less politically astute Johnson played into the hands of the Radicals. He had the disadvantage of being the nominal leader of a party in which he was not a member. A War Democrat added to the Republican ticket in 1964 to emphasize unity, he had no personal following in either the North or the South. After a brief period of vindictiveness that appeased the Radicals, Johnson reversed positions and adopted Lincoln's mild policies.

Committee of Fifteen

Though not its chairman, Thaddeus Stevens dominated a joint committee of the House and Senate—the Joint Committee of Fifteen—that was the outgrowth of the Committee on the Conduct of the War that had tried to force its views on Lincoln. The joint committee officially investigated and reported on the credentials of Southern members-elect to Congress. But it was this committee that wielded the real power in Congress at the time. The Radicals' Reconstruction policies and the tactics used against the president were formulated by this group.

The Radicals' leader in the Senate was Charles SUMNER of Massachusetts. He was not on the Committee of Fifteen, but next to Stevens he was the most powerful figure in the Reconstruction policy. Doctrinaire, he too believed the Confederate states had committed political suicide and that Congress had exclusive jurisdiction over postwar administration of these outlaw states. As an idealist, without any personal knowledge of the Negro's condition, Sumner insisted on giving the freed slaves immediate equality. He gave the Radical cause a tinge of idealism and respectability.

In 1866 Johnson vetoed the first of two Freedmen's Bureau bills, designed to provide services for and protect the rights of the ex-slaves. The Radicals were unable to override that veto, but the veto of a civil rights bill as unconstitutional was overridden soon thereafter. Even Radicals had doubts about the bill's constitutionality. To allay any doubts they drafted the Fourteenth Amendment, which, among other things, guaranteed the civil rights of Negroes against state interference, reduced the Southern states' representation in Congress in proportion to the denial of Negro suffrage, and disqualified from holding federal or state office ex-Confederates who formerly held such offices. But the most important provision was the first clause: "No State shall make or enforce any law which shall abridge the privileges or immunities of citizens of the United States; nor shall any State deprive any person of life, liberty, or property, without due process of law; nor deny to any person within its jurisdiction the equal protection of the laws."

The congressional elections of 1866, in which the Radicals were reelected, proved to be critical to the direction

Reconstruction policy would take. Using the results as vindication of their policy, the Radicals pushed through Congress a series of punitive laws, including the First Reconstruction Act of 1867. This law declared there were no legal governments in the Southern states (except in Tennessee) and divided the South into five military districts supervised by Union officers. There followed a harsh military occupation of some 20,000 men, including a force of Negro militia. The military commanders' primary tasks were to create new electorates and establish new state governments. In South Carolina, Alabama, Florida, Mississippi, and Louisiana black voters outnumbered whites. New constitutions were drafted enfranchising blacks, disenfranchising ex-Confederate leaders, and guaranteeing civil and political equality to the freedmen.

Separation of Powers

The Reconstruction policies threatened more than the South. The Radicals' goal, ultimately, was to establish a government dominated by Congress and, within Congress, by the Radical Republicans themselves. With pliant executive and judicial branches, the constitutional principle of SEPARATION OF POWERS was in jeopardy. This was the inescapable implication of passage, over Johnson's veto, of the First Reconstruction Act of 1867, as well as two other laws passed at the same time. The first, the Command of the Army Act, barred the executive from exercising any control over the army by requiring the president to issue all military orders through the General of the Army. Nor could the president fire or suspend this officer from office. The second, the Tenure of Office Act, prevented the president from removing civilians in the executive branch, including members of his own cabinet, without the consent of the Senate. This, of course, made it impossible for a president to control his administration. Johnson refused to recognize the constitutionality of the law and dismissed his secretary of war, Edwin M. Stanton. This action provided the Radicals with the excuse they needed to attempt to remove Johnson from office through the IMPEACHMENT process. In a Senate trial the president escaped removal by a single vote. If the Radicals' effort had succeeded, the presidency would have gone to Wade, next in the line of succession as Senate PRESIDENT PRO TEMPORE since the vice presidency was vacant. (See JOHNSON IMPEACHMENT TRIAL.)

Congressional Republicans remained in control of most of the reconstructed states, in varying degrees, well into the 1870s. Control was maintained by an alliance of Negroes and Radical Republicans. The latter consisted of two types: "carpetbaggers"—Northerners who came South for political and economic profit, and "scalawags"—Southern white renegades. This led to a dreadful record of misrule, political corruption, human exploitation, and economic dislocation, including staggering budget deficits.

By the early 1870s the country's appetite for the Radicals' drastic policies toward the South gradually abated. In 1874 Democrats gained control of the House of Representatives, and the policy of Reconstruction was finally repudiated. The last Union troops were withdrawn from South Carolina and Louisiana in 1877 by order of President Rutherford B. Hayes.   ~

Reed, Thomas Brackett

Thomas Brackett Reed (1839-1902), known as "Czar" Reed, was one of the most powerful SPEAKERS in House history. Determined to put an end to the obstructionist tactics of the minority party, Reed made a series of

'Czar' Reed

Thomas Brackett Reed was one of the most powerful Speakers in the history of the House of Representatives. Although resented for his assumption of power, "Czar" Reed was admired for his wit.

rulings from the chair that allowed the Republican majority to conduct the business of the House without hindrance. His biting wit, determination, and sheer size made Reed impressive and aided him in forming a cohesive Republican voting bloc.

After practicing law in Portland, Maine, and serving in city and state offices (including the state legislature), Reed was elected to the House of Representatives in 1876. In 1882 he was appointed to the RULES Committee, where he acquired power and the respect of fellow GOP members. When Republicans assumed control of the House in 1889, they elected Reed Speaker. He led Republicans when they were out of power from 1891 to 1895 and resumed the job of Speaker from 1895 to 1899.

The House over which Reed took control was plagued by filibusters that slowed the conduct of business. Democratic representatives refused to answer quorum calls (even though present and visible on the House floor) and introduced a flurry of dilatory motions to harry their opponents and delay the passage of legislation. Reed's insistence that all members present—whether answering or not—be counted towards a quorum caused pandemonium on the floor. Members tried to hide and were prevented from leaving by the SERGEANT-AT-ARMS, who was ordered to lock the door. Reed ruled further that the chair would not entertain motions whose purpose was to delay business. These and other "Reed Rules" were formally incorporated into the rules of the House in 1890.

The rules revisions and Czar Reed's exercise of power allowed the House to pass an unprecedented number of bills during the so-called "Billion-dollar Congress" of 1889-91. Although resented for his assumption of power, Reed was admired as an epigrammatist and wit. (When a member stated that he would rather be right than president, Reed replied: "The gentleman need not be disturbed, he never will be either.")

Reed was an unsuccessful candidate for the Republican presidential nomination in 1896. He resigned from Congress in 1899 in protest over U.S. involvement in the Philippines and Hawaii.   ~

Reform, Congressional

Making Congress work better is a never-ending process that has preoccupied senators and representatives ever since reformers turned the Continental Congress into the House of Representatives and Senate. Once institutional reforms are in place, they may turn out to be ineffective or cause new, unexpected problems—prompting another set of institutional reforms.

Reforms are changes that have been deliberately put in place, but the House and Senate have also changed incrementally, adapting to new circumstances and to new members. The story of the evolving Congress encompasses far more than reorganizations and formal revisions of rules. *(See* HOUSE OF REPRESENTATIVES*;* SENATE.*)*

Changing the Rules

Like many institutions, Congress is biased toward maintaining the status quo. Reform does not come easily, and it frequently threatens the existing power structure. In 1910 the House ended the autocratic rule of SPEAKER Joseph G. CANNON, a conservative Illinois Republican, but only after a two-year struggle by Democrats and insurgent Republicans. They finally succeeded in stripping the Speaker of his

"I Said I Had Him Trained — Notice How He Sits Up?

Unruly Beast
For many years conservative members of the House Rules Committee were able to block legislation sought by Democratic leaders. Speaker Sam Rayburn assured liberals in 1959 that their legislation "would not be bottled up in the committee." But he was often unable to deliver on his promise.

power base on the RULES Committee and removing his authority to appoint House COMMITTEE members and their chairmen.

The Rules Committee, which controls access to the House floor for major bills, has been the focus of extended reform efforts. For many years the committee was dominated by a coalition of conservative Democrats and Republicans who repeatedly blocked or delayed liberal legislation. In 1959 Speaker Sam RAYBURN, a Texas Democrat, headed off a liberal effort to curb the Rules panel by giving his "personal assurance" that civil rights and other social legislation "would not be bottled up in the committee." Rayburn often was unable to deliver on his promise, however, and two years later the House voted to add three additional members to the committee, thus diluting the power of its conservative members. The dramatic 217-212 House vote in January 1961 was an early signal of the wave of reform that would come in the next decade.

In the 1970s the party CAUCUSES in each house voted institutional reforms that enabled junior members to share power held by their older and more experienced colleagues. Among the changes was a sweeping attack on the SENIORITY system, which used length of service to determine committee chairmanships. Democrats and Republicans in both chambers agreed to elect their committee leaders, using secret ballots in most cases. The most vivid evidence of the new system at work came in 1975, when House Democrats deposed three chairmen. Seniority, however, remained a major factor in choosing leaders.

The House rejected proposals for wholesale reorganization of its committee structure, but the Senate approved substantial changes in its committee system in 1977. Several of the most important Senate reforms centered on the FILIBUSTER, the use of unlimited debate to block the will of the majority. The

reforms aimed to strengthen Senate restrictions on the filibuster, first adopted in 1917.

Reformers of the 1970s also sought to increase members' accountability by opening to the public and press the inner workings of Congress. Committees generally were required to meet in open session, and VOTING reforms in the House exposed members' floor votes to greater public scrutiny. The House began gavel-to-gavel TELEVISION broadcasts of its floor proceedings in 1979, a step the Senate did not take until 1986.

Statutory Changes

Other major reforms have been achieved by statute. The Legislative Reorganization Act of 1946 streamlined the committee structure, reduced and redistributed the workload of Congress, and improved staff assistance. Budget control provisions included in the act soon proved unworkable and were dropped. A section on lobby regulation was too weak to be effective. While there were fewer committees under the new structure, subcommittees proliferated.

Another Legislative Reorganization Act, this one in 1970, was intended to improve Congress's deliberative process in the House and Senate chambers as well as in the committees. The 1970 law authorized additional staff, strengthened Congress's research and information sources, and required the administration to provide Congress with more information about the federal budget. The act also included changes in Senate rules that limited the ability of the most senior members to monopolize choice committee assignments.

The Congressional Budget and Impoundment Control Act of 1974 established a process that for the first time forced lawmakers to coordinate their spending and revenue decisions in a single budget package. It also curbed presidential IMPOUNDMENT of funds appropriated by Congress. The 1974 act was less effective than its sponsors had hoped; in the 1980s, as budget deficits rose to alarming levels, lawmakers made substantial changes in the BUDGET PROCESS. Also revised were laws dealing with CAMPAIGN FINANCING and ETHICS.

Two important twentieth-century reforms were achieved through constitutional amendments. The Seventeenth Amendment, ratified in 1913, provided for DIRECT ELECTION OF SENATORS; they previously had been chosen by state legislatures. The Twentieth Amendment, ratified in 1933, advanced to January from March the date for the beginning of a new Congress; that ended the regular practice of LAME-DUCK sessions that ran from December after an election until the new Congress convened the following March.

1980s Concerns

Despite the reforms of the 1970s, few legislators were satisfied with the way Congress worked in the 1980s. Within each chamber members debated further changes in congressional procedures.

Many senators were vocal about their dissatisfaction with Senate procedures, which have depended more on unwritten custom and civility than on written rules. The eleven senators elected in 1986 made a formal proposal for changes. Washington Democrat Daniel Evans, a former governor and university president, said frustration with the Senate was a major reason he chose not to seek reelection in 1988. "Somehow we must reach a happy compromise between the tyranny of autocratic chairmen and the chaos of a hundred independent fiefdoms," Evans said, adding later, "There's a sense that the whole system is breaking down." Arkansas Democrat Dale Bumpers argued for a new structure: "What we need is something like the House Rules Committee."

"In an era of fast-moving, globalized issues, the possibility that the world could pass the Senate by increases immeasurably," warned Sen. Thomas A. Daschle, a South Dakota Democrat.

In the House representatives talked less about the diffusion of power and more about its concentration. The emphasis on budget making, and the need to curb spending, left authorizing committees on the sidelines and enhanced the standing of already elite taxing and spending panels. Omnibus spending bills, used in 1986 and 1987 to consolidate a dozen appropriation bills, meant fewer legislators could influence the outcome. "What we have now is a technique for returning to a closed system where a few people make all the decisions," said Indiana Democrat Philip R. Sharp.

House Republicans, in the minority for most of the twentieth century, escalated their complaints in the late 1980s. They argued, some with bitterness, that the Democratic leadership was restricting floor debate and amendments in ways that trampled minority rights.

Frustration with House and Senate operations even prompted criticism of open meetings, a basic tenet of the 1970s reforms. The House WAYS AND MEANS Committee was one of many panels that began closing doors again in the 1980s. "It's just difficult to legislate," said Illinois Democrat Dan Rostenkowski, chairman of Ways and Means. "I'm not ashamed about closed doors. We want to get the product out." ~

ADDITIONAL READINGS

Davidson, Roger H., and Walter J. Oleszek. *Congress Against Itself.* 1977.
Hinckley, Barbara. *Stability and Change in Congress.* 1988.
Rieselbach, Leroy N. *Congressional Reform.* 1986.
Sheppard, Burton D. *Rethinking Congressional Reform.* 1985.

Removal Power

The Senate can approve or reject presidential nominations through its APPOINTMENT POWER, but the congressional role in removing individuals from office is limited. The Constitution does not speak to the question of removal, and presidents have resisted numerous efforts by Congress to restrict their ability to dismiss officials.

The Supreme Court has generally sided with the executive but did rule in 1935, in the case of *Humphrey's Executor v. U.S.*, that Congress can restrict the president's authority to remove officials from independent agencies or regulatory bodies.

What constrains presidents more than legalities, though, is politics. Congress and the public usually react negatively when presidents make blatant use of their authority to fire personnel. When Harry S TRUMAN in 1951 relieved General Douglas MacArthur of his command, the president's public approval rating dropped to less than 30 percent.

President Richard NIXON's popularity dropped to an all-time low in 1973 after he dismissed Archibald Cox, the special prosecutor investigating the WATERGATE SCANDAL. The event was known as the "Saturday night massacre" because the attorney general resigned and the deputy attorney general was fired for siding with Cox. The firings spurred the NIXON IMPEACHMENT EFFORT that led to Nixon's resignation in 1974.

Congress was most aggressive in claiming the removal power in 1867, when it passed the Tenure of Office Act. Since the 1830s, when President Andrew Jackson made political loyalty a requirement for many federal offices, Congress and the president had been haggling over control of federal PATRONAGE. The 1867 act said officials appointed by the president and confirmed by the Senate could not be removed without senatorial consent. The dispute came to a head when President Andrew Johnson suspended his secretary of war and the Senate refused to concur.

Early in 1868 Johnson dismissed the secretary, Edwin M. Stanton. The House responded by voting articles of IMPEACHMENT, charging the president with violating the Tenure of Office Act. In a Senate trial on the House charges, Johnson escaped removal from office by a single vote. The Tenure of Office Act was repealed in 1887. *(See* JOHNSON IMPEACHMENT TRIAL.*)*   ~

Report.   See LEGISLATIVE PROCESS.

Reprimand.   See DISCIPLINING MEMBERS.

Rescission.   See IMPOUNDMENT OF FUNDS.

Resident Commissioner.   See DELEGATES, NONVOTING.

Resolution.   See LEGISLATION.

Rider

Amendments that are not germane, or pertinent, to the subject matter of a bill are called riders. They are most frequently used in the Senate, where nongermane amendments are considered fair play. But they also turn up in the House of Representatives, even though House rules prohibit them.

A rider is often a proposal that would be unlikely to become law as a separate bill, either because one chamber would not pass it or because the president would VETO it. Riders are more likely to be accepted if they are attached to urgent LEGISLATION, such as bills providing funds to operate the federal government. Emergency funding bills, called CONTINUING RESOLUTIONS, have become magnets for unrelated amendments because they must be passed quickly to keep government agencies from shutting down. A continuing resolution approved in 1984 included, almost as a footnote, a sweeping revision of federal criminal law.

Sometimes a rider is used as a "sweetener" to win the president's approval of a measure he opposes. A tax bill President Ronald Reagan had vowed to veto became law in 1983 after Congress attached a Reagan trade plan to the measure. Other riders have been used to rescue bills that became stalled in hostile committees. A notable example occurred in 1960 when Senate Majority Leader Lyndon B. JOHNSON made good on a promise to act on civil rights legislation. When the Senate JUDICIARY Committee failed to produce any, Johnson called up a minor House-passed bill, and a landmark civil rights measure was added on the Senate floor. But riders may also obstruct the passage of a bill. An urgent debt ceiling measure had to be pulled from the Senate floor in 1982 after a five-week filibuster over unrelated amendments involving abortion and school busing. Some 1,400 additional amendments had been prepared on these and other issues.

Tax legislation is frequently subject to riders. The Constitution says tax bills must originate in the House, but the Senate FINANCE Committee has learned how to initiate major tax proposals by attaching them to minor House-passed bills. That happened with a sweeping tax increase in 1982.

The Senate also has a fondness for loading tax or trade bills with nongermane amendments that benefit special interests. Such measures are known as CHRISTMAS TREE BILLS.

Even though House rules prohibit nongermane amendments, members have found ways to get around the restrictions. Antiabortion riders became a regular feature of annual government appropriations bills in the 1970s and 1980s; they met the House germaneness standard because they were worded to restrict the use of federal funds for abortions. The House may also waive its germaneness rule, a practice that sometimes creates strange legislative bedfellows. A 1980 House bill simultaneously set new nutritional requirements for infant formulas and increased federal penalties for marijuana trafficking. ~

Rule for House Debate

Most major legislation that reaches the House floor is debated and amended under a resolution, known as a rule, that governs floor consideration of the measure. The rule establishes time limits for debate and determines what amendments, if any, may be offered; it may include other provisions as well. A bill goes to the RULES COMMITTEE after it has been reported by a legislative committee. The Rules Committee then writes the rule and presents it to the full House. House approval of the rule precedes floor debate and amendments. *(See* LEGISLATIVE PROCESS.*)*

In devising rules for floor consideration, the Rules Committee works closely with the House leadership. Prior to 1975 reforms, the committee frequently was able to frustrate leadership goals. ~

Rules, House and Senate. See LEGISLATIVE PROCESS.

Rules and Administration Committee, Senate

The task of overseeing Senate operations is handled by the Senate Rules and Administration Committee. Its focus is usually on the nuts and bolts of running the Senate—committee budgets, assignment of office space, and other housekeeping matters. The panel also has jurisdiction over election law, including restrictions on CAMPAIGN FINANCING; corrupt practices; presidential succession; and contested elections. Although the committee is responsible for Senate rules and organization, most efforts to reform Senate procedures have been handled by special, temporary committees. Rules, at the center of the Senate establishment, has had little enthusiasm for change. The committee has two House counterparts, the HOUSE ADMINISTRATION and RULES committees.

Although rarely in the limelight, Senate Rules has had a role in several key Senate decisions. In the 1950s, reacting to Sen. Joseph R. McCARTHY's abusive treatment of witnesses before his subcommittee, the Rules panel pushed committees to adopt safeguards giving witnesses a chance for rebuttal. A 1960s investigation into misconduct by Bobby Baker, secretary of the Senate from 1955 to 1963, was handled by Rules; Republicans on the panel said Democrats limited their probe to protect Lyndon B. JOHNSON, who had hired Baker while he was the Democratic leader.

Various REFORMS went through the Rules Committee in the 1970s, though it often did not originate the changes. The panel endorsed opening the Senate chamber to TELEVISION cameras in the early 1980s; the rest of the Senate went along in 1986.

While Republicans controlled the Senate (1981-87), Charles McC. Mathias, Jr., of Maryland chaired the committee. Wendell H. Ford of Kentucky assumed the post when the Democrats took control of the Senate in 1987. ~

Rules Committee, House

The House Rules Committee occupies a unique place in the congressional COMMITTEE SYSTEM. Almost all major legislation that is debated on the floor of the HOUSE OF REPRESENTATIVES must first win the committee's blessing. Its opposition can kill a bill that another House committee spent months preparing.

Rules is frequently described as a traffic cop for the House, determining which bills get to the floor, which amendments—if any—can be considered, and in what order they will come up. By controlling the amendment procedure, the Rules Committee is able to influence the substance of legislation. In addition, the panel has broad jurisdiction over House rules of procedure and House reorganization issues.

The committee is strictly partisan. It is an agent of the SPEAKER, who is both the presiding officer of the House and the overall leader of the majority party in the chamber. Democrats have held almost unbroken control of the House since 1931. As the majority party, they occupy more seats on the committee than the Republicans do—in fact, a disproportionate ratio. Nine Democrats and only four Republicans served on the panel in 1987. The committee's Democrats are put there by the Speaker, and with rare exceptions they do what he wants. The outnumbered Republican members have little say in the matter.

Granting a Rule
All but the most routine legislation passes through the Rules Committee. A

House Traffic Cops

Membership on the Rules Committee carries great weight. Almost all major legislation that is debated on the floor of the House must first win the committee's blessing.

bill goes to Rules after it has been considered and approved by a legislative committee that specializes in the subject involved. During a hearing before the Rules Committee the legislative committee's chairman, senior minority party member, and others explain the bill and how they want it to be handled on the floor.

After the hearing the Rules Committee generally approves a resolution, known as a rule, that sets time limits for general debate on the entire bill and establishes ground rules for considering amendments to it. Some rules permit any germane, or relevant, amendment to be offered from the floor. These are known as "open" rules. Others, called "closed" rules, prohibit all floor amendments. Frequently, bills are given "modified closed" rules that allow only

specified amendments to be introduced or permit floor amendments only to certain sections of the bill.

The rule must be adopted on the House floor before the bill is debated. Infrequently rules are amended or defeated when they reach the floor, but most receive routine approval. *(See* LEGISLATIVE PROCESS.*)*

Shifting Role

The Rules Committee was established on a temporary basis in 1789, but originally it had jurisdiction only over House rules. Its influence over legislation did not develop until after the Speaker was made a member of the panel in 1858. It began issuing rules for floor debate in 1883. Until 1910 the committee worked closely with the House leadership in deciding what legislation could come to the floor. But it was made independent of the leadership in the Progressive revolt of 1909-10 against Speaker Joseph G. CANNON.

A coalition of conservative Democrats and Republicans took control of the committee in the late 1930s and frustrated the Democratic leadership for decades. Under the twelve-year chairmanship of Virginia Democrat Howard W. SMITH, 1955-67, the panel repeatedly blocked or delayed civil rights measures sought by the Democratic majority. Because the committee had no regular meeting day and could be called together only by the chairman, it was frequently unable to clear any bills for floor action during the final days of a session when Smith simply "disappeared" to his Virginia farm.

Several attempts to break the conservative grip on the committee proved unsuccessful. Finally, in 1975, the House Democratic CAUCUS gave the Speaker the power to name all Democratic members of the panel, subject to caucus approval. Rules thus returned to leadership control.

A seat on the Rules Committee still carries great weight. Sometimes it is a springboard to House leadership. Rules member Thomas P. O'NEILL, Jr., earned a place on the leadership ladder for his role in a House reorganization effort advanced by the Rules Committee in 1970. O'Neill, a Massachusetts Democrat, went on to become Speaker in 1977.

Rules members also have an opportunity to leave their imprint on bills that come before them. The committee may require changes in one measure as the price of granting a rule; it may bar a floor amendment that would transform another. Legislative committees sometimes woo votes for their bills in the Rules Committee by appealing to the interests of individual Rules members—adding a flood control project in one member's district, perhaps, or revising a foreign policy provision opposed by another.

For these reasons, among others, Rules Committee assignments are highly prized. Rules members tend to represent the dominant political currents of the House. They come from politically safe districts; what little turnover there is on the panel typically results from death or retirement, not election defeat. Most members do not serve on other major committees.   ~

Russell, Richard B.

Richard B. Russell (1897-1971) was at the heart of the Senate power structure for most of his long career (1933-71). Even before seniority made him chairman of two top committees, ARMED SERVICES and then APPROPRIATIONS, the Georgia Democrat was leader of a tightly knit bloc of southern conservatives who dominated the Senate for years. He also worked closely with Lyndon B. JOHNSON, who had been a freshman senator when Russell backed him for the Democratic leadership in the early 1950s. For his own leadership role, Russell preferred working behind the scenes and on the Democratic Policy and Steering committees, where he usually held sway.

Patrician in his demeanor and gracious in his dealings with others, Russell built his reputation on what he called "doing homework." His byword was caution. "When I am in doubt about a question, I always vote 'no,'" Russell once said. His assessment of leadership was straightforward: "Any man who dares to vote independently is a leader ... and any man who can persuade three or four men to vote with him is a power."

Russell was an opponent of civil rights legislation, but he avoided racist statements, invoking instead the traditional states' rights arguments against federal interference. His politics, though generally conservative, could not be neatly categorized; for example, Russell opposed U.S. involvement in Vietnam from the beginning.

As chairman of Armed Services (1951-53, 1955-69), Russell never took as gospel the military policies proposed by the executive branch; he questioned and criticized without hesitation. Russell also learned how to steer defense contracts toward Georgia, which became a major center of the military industry. Russell chaired the Appropriations Subcommittee on Defense in the 1960s, giving him a powerful dual role, with control over the authorization of military programs and then over the actual spending.

Born and raised in Winder, Georgia, Russell was the fourth of thirteen children. His father, who had made unsuccessful bids for governor and senator, served as chief justice of the Georgia Supreme Court. Russell, who practiced law in Winder, was elected in 1921 to the Georgia legislature; in six years he was chosen Speaker. The next step for the young politician was the governor's mansion; he won a two-year term as governor in 1930. When he took office in 1931, he was the youngest chief executive in the state's history. But his tenure was brief. When a Georgia senator died, Russell was selected to fill the unexpired term, and he joined the Senate in January 1933. Except for a bid for the Democratic presidential nomination in 1952, which he lost on the third ballot, Russell, a bachelor, focused his life on the Senate for the next thirty-eight years.

Russell became the most senior senator in 1969, a standing that gave him the title PRESIDENT PRO TEMPORE. His health was poor, though, and he died from emphysema in 1971. His colleagues the following year marked their affection and respect by naming one of two existing Senate office buildings in his honor. ～

Overleaf:
Senate chamber.

Science and Technology Committee, House

Once preoccupied with space exploration, the House Science and Technology Committee by the late 1980s focused on a wide array of government research and development programs. Energy, aviation, transportation, and environment were among the research topics within the jurisdiction of the committee, which also reviewed overall government science policy.

Most legislators consider Science and Technology their secondary committee. Frequently the legislation written by the committee becomes part of a broader measure that other committees have also helped draft. In floor action on major bills Science often ends up as partner of a more aggressive committee that dominates the debate. For example, nuclear waste disposal is an issue shared with the INTERIOR and COMMERCE committees, which have usually overshadowed Science.

Within its own territory—research and space—Science was showing more independence by the late 1980s. The committee was often lobbied by the aerospace, energy, and high-technology companies competing for government support. Committee members sought to keep research compatible with overall government science policy. They even began more critical questioning of the

365

National Aeronautics and Space Administration.

"Because of its great success story, Congress has been too shy in finding fault with NASA," said Robert A. Roe, the New Jersey Democrat who became chairman in 1987. "As a result of the *Challenger* [space shuttle] accident, Congress and NASA must begin a new era, one in which Congress must apply the same strong oversight to NASA that it does to any other government agency."

The committee evolved over the years from a panel set up in 1958 as the Select Committee on Astronautics and Space Exploration. In 1959 it became the Science and Astronautics Committee. When reorganization proposals became commonplace as part of REFORM efforts in the 1970s, Science at first seemed vulnerable to efforts to streamline committee jurisdictions. But the committee ended up with a broader mandate, a move that improved its standing within the House. It was renamed Science and Technology in 1975. ∼

Seating Disputes

The Constitution made each house of Congress the judge of the elections of its members. Under that authority the Senate and House of Representatives have settled hundreds of contested elections. Defeated candidates have challenged election results after close tallies or apparent voting irregularities. Although Congress has tried to put a judicial tone on its decisions, usually the result is partisan—the party in power gives the seat to its candidate.

The House is governed by the Federal Contested Election Act of 1969. No comparable law guides the Senate, but it handles far fewer disputes because it oversees about 33 elections every other

November, while the House oversees 435. The entire membership of the House, but only a third of the Senate, is elected every two years. The Senate has been elected by popular vote only since 1913. Previously, senators were chosen by state legislatures. *(See* DIRECT ELECTION OF SENATORS.)

The closest race in Senate history was a 1974 New Hampshire contest that was ultimately settled by a new election. The initial tally was so close that one count showed only two votes separating the contenders. Senators spent seven months wrangling over the results. After forty-one roll-call votes on the question, John A. Durkin, the Democratic candidate, finally relented and asked for a new election. The Senate declared the seat vacant and set the second election for September 1975. It was the first time senators had ever declared a vacancy because they could not make up their minds. Durkin handily defeated Republican Louis C. Wyman.

The closest House contest of the twentieth century was resolved in 1985 by a vote along party lines. The decision, which came after an acrimonious, four-month-long struggle, made Republicans so angry they walked out of the House chamber in protest. For the next several days they used parliamentary tactics to disrupt proceedings on the House floor. The dispute centered on Democratic incumbent Frank McCloskey, who appeared to have narrowly lost his Indiana House seat in November 1984 to Republican Richard D. McIntyre. After a recount of votes, though, McCloskey claimed the seat. The House in early 1985 declared the seat vacant and called for an investigation. A special investigating committee then declared McCloskey the winner by four votes. The House, dominated by Democrats, voted to accept the committee recommendation, triggering the Republican walkout. In a 1986 rematch, McCloskey beat McIntyre by a comfortable margin. ∼

Secretary of the Senate

The secretary of the Senate is the chief administrative officer of the Senate. His responsibilities are similar to those of the CLERK OF THE HOUSE: providing equipment and supplies, disbursing payroll, and making periodic reports, among others.

Like his House counterpart, the secretary of the Senate is elected by the majority party in the chamber and generally continues in the post as long as that party maintains its majority. As of early 1988, the secretary's annual salary was $88,000.   ~

Senate

The Constitution says they are two equal chambers, but members rarely leave the Senate to run for the House of Representatives. The two bodies share the jobs of legislating, overseeing the federal government, and representing their constituencies. But the Senate, once known as the "world's most exclusive club," projects an image of influence and prestige that the House does not match.

There are striking differences between the two legislative bodies and how they go about their work. The Senate has 100 members—two from each state—while the House has 435 members. Senators are elected for six years, House members for two. Senators have a broad, state-wide constituency, while most House members represent comparatively narrow districts within states.

These differences have shaped the practices and procedures of the two chambers. The smaller Senate is more informal and flexible, in contrast to the highly structured House. It is more individualistic, with power more evenly distributed. The Senate shares certain executive powers with the president, which contributes to the chamber's greater prestige.

With fewer members to share the limelight, senators enjoy more attention. But, on the downside of that, there are fewer members to share the workload, which is as heavy in the Senate as in the House. As a result, senators tend to be policy generalists, while representatives develop specialties. It takes the Senate longer to consider legislation, in part because it sees its paramount function as deliberation.

Representatives who move to the Senate face the political equivalent of culture shock upon exposure to their freewheeling, disorganized new environment. They welcome the Senate's tradition of deference to individual senators. But some look back with nostalgia on the efficient procedures of the House, where it was routinely possible for members to have four-day weekends at home. Many miss the fraternity of the House, though few wish to go back.

"Rules and tradition make it possible for every member of the Senate to play a significant role in legislating," said Colorado Republican William L. Armstrong, who was elected to the Senate in 1978 after six relatively obscure years in the House. "It's possible even for a brand new member to jump right in."

"A senator has greater access to virtually anyone inside or outside of government," remarked Paul Simon, an Illinois Democrat who moved from the House to the Senate in 1985. "There are very few people who won't return a phone call from a U.S. senator."

Senators who have served in both chambers say they are far busier than they were in the House. "There is a constant press of time...," said House transplant William S. Cohen, a Maine Republican. "The lack of time con-

A TYPICAL DAY IN THE SENATE

A typical day in the Senate might go like this:
- The Senate is called to order by the PRESIDING OFFICER. The constitutional presiding officer, the VICE PRESIDENT, seldom is in attendance. Usually the PRESIDENT PRO TEMPORE presides over the opening minutes of the Senate session. During the course of the day, other members of the majority party take turns presiding for an hour at a time.
- The Senate CHAPLAIN delivers the opening prayer.
- The majority leader and the minority leader are recognized for opening remarks. The majority leader usually announces his plan for the day's business, which is developed in consultation with the minority leadership.
- Senators who have requested time in advance are recognized for SPECIAL ORDERS; they may speak about any topic for five minutes.
- After special orders, the Senate usually conducts morning business. During morning business—which need not be in the morning—members conduct routine chores. They introduce bills and receive reports from committees and messages from the president. (See MORNING HOUR.)
- After morning business, the Senate considers legislative or executive matters. If the majority leader wants the Senate to begin work on a piece of legislation, he normally asks for unanimous consent to call up the measure. If any member objects, the leader may make a debatable motion that the Senate take up the bill. The debatable motion gives opponents the opportunity to launch a FILIBUSTER, or extended debate, even before the Senate officially begins considering the bill. A few measures—such as budget resolutions and reports from Senate-House CONFERENCE COMMITTEES— are privileged, and a motion to consider them is not debatable.

After the Senate begins work on a bill, floor debate is generally handled by managers, usually the chairman and the ranking minority member of the committee with jurisdiction over the measure. Some measures are considered under a time agreement in which the Senate unanimously agrees to limit debate and to divide the time in some prearranged fashion. In the absence of a time agreement, any senator may seek recognition from the chair, and, once recognized, may speak for as long as he or she wishes. Unless the Senate has unanimously agreed to limit amendments, senators may offer as many as they wish. Generally, amendments need not be germane, or directly related, to the bill.

Most bills are passed by a voice vote with only a handful of senators present. Any member can request a roll call, or recorded vote, on an amendment or on final passage of a measure. Senate roll calls are casual affairs. Few members answer the clerk as their names are called. Instead, senators stroll in from the cloakrooms or their offices and congregate in the well (the area in the front of the chamber). When they are ready to vote, senators catch the eye of the clerk and vote, often by indicating thumbs-up or thumbs-down. Roll-call votes are supposed to last fifteen minutes, but some have dragged on for more than an hour.
- Often, near the end of the day, the majority leader and the minority leader quickly move through a "wrap-up" period, during which minor bills that have been cleared by all members are passed by unanimous consent.
- Just before the Senate finishes its work for the day, the majority leader will seek unanimous consent for his agenda for the next session— when the Senate will convene, which senators will be given special orders and, sometimes, specific time agreements for consideration of legislation.

straints makes the institution itself timeless. You have no set time for anything. You're constantly in motion. . . . It's a bizarre situation."

Origins

The differences between the two chambers were not an accident of history, but rather the result of a carefully crafted plan of the framers of the Constitution in 1787.

The Senate was born of compromise—one so significant it was called the "Great Compromise" of the Constitutional Convention. Without it, the convention would have collapsed. When it was decided that representation in the House would be proportional to a state's population, the small states sounded the alarm. Fearful of domination by the more populous states, they insisted that states have equal representation in the Senate. The large states resisted until agreement was reached that, in return for equality of state representation in the Senate, the House would be given sole power to originate money bills, which the Senate could accept or reject but could not modify. (This was changed later to allow the Senate to alter or amend revenue bills.)

The convention also decided that voters would elect House members but that the Senate should be insulated from popular sentiments. To this end, the convention directed that senators be elected by the state legislatures and for six-year terms.

James MADISON explained the delegates' thinking: "The use of the Senate is to consist in its proceeding with more coolness, with more system, and with more wisdom, than the popular branch."

State legislatures no longer elect senators—the people do. Senators are now spending an enormous amount of time and energy running for reelection, despite their longer terms. And there are those who would question whether the Senate has stayed aloof from popular legislative battles.

Nonetheless, the Founding Fathers' views can still be heard two centuries later. During a 1986 debate over whether to televise Senate proceedings, the discussion was laced with references to the differences between the two chambers, with the Senate depicted as the slow, quiet voice of reason and the House as the more impulsive voice of popular demands. Words of George Washington were repeated on the Senate floor: "It's important to this institution and to the nation for the Senate to play the role of the saucer where the political passions of the nation are cooled."

The Senate ultimately decided to let the nation's passions cool coast to coast. It voted in 1986 to allow TV cameras into the chamber, as the House had done earlier.

Powers

Contrasting views over the roles of the Senate and House were apparent in the Constitutional Convention's debates over congressional powers. For the most part, the two chambers were given equal powers, but there were several important exceptions. *(See STRUCTURE AND POWERS.)*

Power of the Purse One of the most significant instances in which one chamber was given precedence over the other was in the exercise of the power of the PURSE. The Constitution required that the House originate tax legislation. The convention's debate over the question of whether the Senate should be allowed to amend the House tax bills reflected the contrasting concepts of the Senate as likely to be either the most responsible branch or the most aristocratic one, to be strengthened or checked accordingly. The question eventually was resolved in favor of the Senate's right to amend.

And it is a right the Senate does not hesitate to use, particularly toward the end of the session. Because the Senate has no procedures or rules to ward off amendments, the Senate often has turned tax measures into "CHRISTMAS TREE BILLS" that bestow benefits on various economic interests.

The Senate has even on occasion circumvented the constitutional stricture on originating tax bills. In 1982 it wrote the largest peacetime tax increase in the nation's history by attaching the plan to a minor House-passed tax bill that went straight to a House-Senate CONFERENCE COMMITTEE.

Counterbalancing the House's precedence in money matters are the Senate's executive powers that it shares with the president. These are the powers of confirmation of APPOINTMENTS and approval of TREATY RATIFICATION.

Power of Confirmation The Constitution requires that the president appoint government officials with the advice and consent of the Senate. The vast majority of nominations involve routine confirmation, but those for top positions in the federal government and judiciary are closely scrutinized by Senate committees and sometimes hotly debated on the Senate floor.

Recent examples were the grueling battles over President Ronald Reagan's SUPREME COURT nominations in 1987. One nominee was defeated and a second withdrew under intense Senate scrutiny before a third finally received Senate approval. *(See* APPOINTMENT POWER.*)*

Treaty Power The Constitution requires that the Senate give its advice and consent to a treaty. A two-thirds vote of those senators present is necessary for approval of TREATY RATIFICATION.

The Senate's voting record on treaties has been overwhelmingly favorable. Outright rejection is rare, the classic example being the prolonged debate and ultimate rejection in 1920 of the Treaty of Versailles, which embodied not only the World War I treaty of peace with Germany but also U.S. membership in the League of Nations.

Congressional involvement in the treaty process reached an unprecedented level in modern times during negotiation in the late 1970s of the SALT II agreement with the Soviet Union and during consideration of the Panama Canal treaties and related legislation. The Panama Canal treaties were eventually approved by the Senate, but the arms agreement was shelved after the Soviet invasion of Afghanistan.

Impeachment Power The Senate and House share the awesome power of IMPEACHMENT of high federal officials. The House conducts the investigation, brings charges (called articles of impeachment) against an official, and argues for impeachment during a trial conducted in the Senate.

The final decision is the Senate's. The Constitution requires a two-thirds vote of the senators present to convict on any article of impeachment. Between 1789 and early 1988, the Senate had sat as a court of impeachment thirteen times. Five cases ended in conviction and six in acquittal. In two cases the Senate dismissed the charges.

Election Power Both chambers have the responsibility of counting the electoral votes for president and vice president. If no candidate for the presidency has a majority of the electoral votes, the House chooses the president. If no vice presidential candidate has a majority, the Senate makes the choice. *(See* ELECTING THE PRESIDENT.*)*

Only once has the Senate resolved a vice presidential contest. In 1837, when Martin Van Buren was elected president, his running mate, Richard M. Johnson, was one vote short of a majority because Van Buren electors from Virginia had boycotted Johnson. The Senate elected Johnson vice president.

The Senate of 1975 included at least a dozen once and future contenders for the presidency. None was elected president, but two served as vice president: Hubert H. Humphrey (1965-69) and Walter F. Mondale (1977-81).

Development

The framers of the Constitution assumed that the House would be the pre-eminent chamber, with the Senate functioning as a revisory body and a restraining influence. And, initially, the House did overshadow the Senate. In fact, it was reported that, in the First Congress (1789-91), the Senate often adjourned its own tedious sessions so that its twenty-six members could go and listen to the livelier floor debates in the House.

But the Senate's influence was soon to be felt. The importance of its treaty and appointment powers, in which the House had no share, was a factor in the Senate's rise. In addition, serving in the smaller Senate became more desirable than membership in the rapidly expanding House. The Senate's longer term and more stable membership also made it more attractive.

The Senate's legislative importance increased gradually. In the early years, the House dominated the great debates, such as those surrounding the War of 1812. But the Senate took the lead in the struggle over the Missouri Compromise of 1820 and succeeded in imposing on the House an amendment barring slavery in future northern states.

In the years leading up to the Civil War, the Senate inevitably became the chief forum for the great antislavery debates. Illustrious figures such as Daniel WEBSTER of Massachusetts, Henry CLAY of Kentucky, and John C. CALHOUN of South Carolina emerged during this "Golden Age" of the Senate.

Alexis de Tocqueville, French aristocrat, scholar, and astute observer of American life, was inspired to write in 1834: "... the Senate is composed of eloquent advocates, distinguished generals, wise magistrates, and statesmen of note, whose arguments would do honor to the most remarkable parliamentary debates of Europe."

De Tocqueville had harsher words for the House of Representatives:

"... One is struck by the vulgar demeanor of that great assembly. Often there is not a distinguished man in the whole number...."

Legislative Process Courtesy, dignity, and informality marked the proceedings of the early Senate. Sometimes on a chilly morning members would leave their seats and gather around the fireplace to conduct Senate business.

There was little need for elaborate procedures or for a formal division of labor because there was not much labor to divide. But, as the duties of Congress grew and as legislation increased in volume and complexity, a discernible LEGISLATIVE PROCESS began to evolve.

"Rules are never observed in this body; they are only made to be broken. We are a law unto ourselves," claimed Republican Sen. John J. Ingalls of Kansas in 1876. And Ingalls had a point. In the smaller, more individualistic Senate, rules have been far less important than in the larger House. The Senate today operates largely by UNANIMOUS CONSENT, suspending or adjusting its rules as needed.

Because the early Senate saw its primary function as deliberation, no restrictions were placed on debate, and thus was born the Senate's cherished tradition of unlimited debate.

There was little obstruction in the early Senate, but the FILIBUSTER—the practice by which a minority employs extended debate and dilatory tactics to delay or block action on a bill—became increasingly common in the nineteenth century, reaching a virtual epidemic in the 1880s and 1890s.

A rule to cut off filibusters was finally adopted in 1917 and was first used several years later during the seemingly interminable debates on the Treaty of Versailles. Further reforms to curtail obstructionism in the Senate were adopted over the years. Yet the filibuster—or even the threat of one—remained a potent weapon.

Moving Up
John F. Kennedy was one of many senators who began their congressional careers in the House of Representatives. The future president is shown here as he announced that he would challenge Sen. Hubert H. Humphrey in 1960 presidential primaries.

The Senate originally conducted most of its deliberations in its chamber. Senators would consider questions brought before them and indicate the line of action to be followed before appointing a temporary committee to work out the details of proposed legislation.

Ad hoc select committees soon grew to an unmanageable number (there were nearly 100 in the 1815-16 session), and the Senate established permanent legislative committees.

Committees developed into powerful, autonomous institutions during the nineteenth century. The important practice of having the majority party's most senior member of a committee serve as chairman was begun at this time. These committee chairmen often served as floor managers of bills until formal floor leaders were established. (See COMMITTEE SYSTEM; SENIORITY SYSTEM.)

The Constitution mentioned only two Senate officers: the VICE PRESIDENT of the United States was to serve as the president of the Senate and a PRESIDENT PRO TEMPORE was to act in his absence. But neither officer was given any real power and, as a result,

neither has done much more than preside over the Senate.

Eventually the Senate had a formal LEADERSHIP hierarchy, but a tradition of strong leadership would never develop in the Senate the way it did in the House. As Senator Webster put it in 1830: "This is a Senate, a Senate of equals, of men of individual honor and personal character, and of absolute independence. We know no masters, we acknowledge no dictators. . . ."

Leadership was provided by powerful individuals or groups until political parties began to dominate. Modern party discipline made its appearance in the Senate in the 1890s, and formally designated majority and minority floor leaders followed in the early 1900s.

These leaders would come to play an important role in organizing the Senate to carry out their parties' programs. Senators would reach top leadership positions after years of spending time on the floor, mastering parliamentary rules, and constantly doing favors for members.

No Senate leader in modern times has rivaled the effectiveness of Lyndon B. JOHNSON, a Texas Democrat who served as minority leader in 1953-54 and as majority leader from 1955 until he resigned to become John F. KENNEDY's vice president in 1961. His influence was the accumulation of hundreds of intense one-to-one relationships. He got his way by subjecting senators to his legendary "treatment"—cajoling, accusing, threatening, and promising—until he had won. *(See p. 237.)*

Johnson's power was not something that could be passed on to successors, partly because it was so uniquely his but also because the climate in the Senate was changing.

Organizational and procedural changes in the 1970s enabled less senior members of the Senate to gain power at the expense of older and more experienced legislators. With more staff, more money, and more power, individual senators were able to maintain their independence from party leaders and more easily pursue their own interests and legislative goals.

The Modern Senate By the 1980s members were increasingly frustrated by the legislative system and the Senate's bouts of legislative paralysis. A few highly publicized retirements focused attention on the problems of the modern Senate.

"We are legislators. Like baseball players who like to play nine innings, like farmers who like to plant all of their fields, we like to pass laws," said South Dakota Democrat Thomas A. Daschle, who moved from the House in 1987. "In an era of fast moving, globalized issues, the possibility that the world could pass the Senate by increases immeasurably."

Complaints about the Senate's cumbersome processes are as old as the institution itself. Because of its privileges of unlimited debate and virtually unlimited amending powers, the Senate may well spend days considering a measure that the House debated and passed in one afternoon. To keep things moving, the Senate in the early 1970s began operating on a two-track system, with a certain period of time reserved daily for particularly controversial bills. In this way, a much-debated bill theoretically would not interfere with other business.

Nonetheless, delays and obstructionism continued to grow. Filibusters, reserved a generation ago for civil rights and a handful of other historically divisive issues, were used on dozens of less important subjects. A few intransigent senators—one, if he or she was determined enough—could block action on any bill that did not have the sixty votes required to end a filibuster.

Probably no one voiced the growing frustration felt by many senators better than Barry Goldwater, who retired in 1987 after thirty years as a Republican senator from Arizona. "If this is the world's greatest deliberative body," he told a colleague one day in 1982, "I'd hate to see the world's worst."

Efforts to streamline procedures and pick up the pace were mounted in the 1980s. Yet, in an institution as steeped in tradition as the Senate, those seeking changes in procedures and organization inevitably faced an uphill battle. Senior members jealously guarded their power bases. Others resisted change because they thought the Senate's constitutional role and its identity as a "deliberative" body were inextricably linked to its inefficiency. They feared that changes would weaken the power of the minority party—and even individual senators—to affect the outcome of legislation. The burden of proof rested heavily on those seeking procedural revisions.

The leadership in the 100th Congress inaugurated a new system to answer one frustration of senators: the chamber's erratic schedule. The new plan called for the Senate to be in session for three five-day work weeks and then off for a week. Until then, the Senate generally had floor business four days a week. Members had complained that the unpredictable schedule interfered with family events, meetings with constituents, and campaign fundraisers.

Senate Majority Leader Robert C. BYRD, a West Virginia Democrat, encouraged efforts to improve efficiency, but he cautioned against expecting too much. "There is no magic solution that will automatically make the Senate a 9-to-5 job," Byrd said in 1987. "We could make it a 9-to-5 job but it would no longer be the United States Senate."

Elections

Senators were elected by state legislatures until the early twentieth century. But with the PROGRESSIVE ERA's movement toward more democratic control of government, public opinion increasingly favored popular election of senators, and eventually the Senate was forced to participate in its own reform. The Seventeenth Amendment, approved by Congress in 1912 and ratified by the states the following year, provided for DIRECT ELECTION OF SENATORS.

The six-year terms of senators are staggered. One-third of the Senate seats are up for election every two years rather than all the seats being open at one time. In the event of a vacancy, a state governor may make a temporary appointment until the vacancy can be filled by a special election.

The length of a senator's term has always been considered a real advantage, especially by House members who face elections every two years. Historically, senators were able to act as statesmen for the first half of their terms and deal with politics in the last few years. But Senate seats are not so secure as they once were, and senators are increasingly becoming permanent candidates, like their House colleagues. Senate races are not only more competitive but also more costly, with multimillion-dollar campaigns no longer uncommon. According to Majority Leader Byrd, one of his biggest problems as leader was accommodating the senators' need for

time away from the floor to raise campaign money. (See CAMPAIGN FINANCING.)

Qualifications To serve in the U.S. Senate, the Constitution requires that a person be at least thirty years of age, have been a citizen of the United States not less than nine years, and live in the state he or she is to represent.

Characteristics Few senators in modern times have found the age requirement to be a problem. The average senator in the 100th Congress was 54.4 years old. (See MEMBERS OF CONGRESS: CHARACTERISTICS.)

The Senate in 1987 counted two WOMEN among its ranks, and no BLACKS or HISPANICS. These statistics were hardly surprising, given the fact that only sixteen women had been elected or appointed to the Senate since its beginning. (Of these, one served just a day and another never was sworn in because Congress was not in session.) Only three blacks had served in the Senate.

One telling statistic from the 100th Congress was the number of former representatives serving in the Senate: thirty-eight, more than a third of the Senate's membership. Although representatives tend to bristle when the House is referred to as the "lower chamber," the Senate's greater prestige and publicity, longer term, larger staff, and more generous perquisites; the opportunity for increased effectiveness in the smaller Senate; a greater role in foreign affairs; and the challenge of dealing with a statewide constituency can be compelling incentives to make a run for the Senate.

Only one former senator sat in the House in the 100th Congress: Florida Democrat Claude Pepper, who, after serving as a senator from 1936 through 1951, became a House member in 1963. Yet even after Pepper's several decades in the House, people still called him by his more prestigious title—"Senator."   ~

ADDITIONAL READINGS

Drew, Elizabeth. *Senator.* 1979.
Evans, Rowland, and Robert Novak. *Lyndon B. Johnson: The Exercise of Power.* 1966.
Haynes, George H. *The Senate of the United States: Its History and Practice.* 2 vols. 1938.

Senate Manual

The *Senate Manual* is a handbook of rules and other requirements for Senate operations, comparable to the HOUSE MANUAL in the House of Representatives. In addition to the forty-two standing rules of the Senate, it includes other orders and resolutions dealing with Senate operations, as well as the sections of U.S. laws on Senate business. Among the matters covered are FINANCIAL DISCLOSURE requirements, CAMPAIGN FINANCING rules, senators' salaries, and rules for IMPEACHMENT trials. In the back of the document is an appendix that includes charts of electoral votes and lists of every senator, cabinet secretary, and Supreme Court justice who has ever served.   ~

Senatorial Courtesy

The Senate has derived from its APPOINTMENT POWER a custom that gives senators additional influence over presidential nominations to federal positions within their own states. Under the custom, called "senatorial courtesy," the full Senate usually goes along when a senator from the president's party objects to a nominee in his state.

The rule primarily affects nominations of judges, U.S. attorneys, federal marshals, and other federal officials based locally.

The custom dates from 1789, when President George Washington replaced his nominee for a post in Georgia with the candidate endorsed by the state's two senators. Among the most aggressive advocates of senatorial courtesy was Roscoe CONKLING, a New York Republican who served in the Senate from 1867 to 1881. The importance of senatorial courtesy diminished as positions once filled by PATRONAGE were brought into the civil service.

Another aspect of senatorial courtesy is the "hold" a senator can place on a nomination. A hold, considered a temporary delay, is possible even when a job has national significance. Usually the leadership of a senator's party will honor the hold, delaying the vote on the nomination. The senator may be waiting for written answers to questions or other information; when he receives it, he releases the hold. Like other aspects of senatorial courtesy, the hold is not always honored by a senator's colleagues.   ~

Seniority System

For many years positions of authority in Congress were routinely given to those members who had served in the institution the longest. The practice of reserving power to the most veteran senators and representatives is known as the seniority system.

A form of the seniority system still exists in the Congress of the late twentieth century. However, seniority is a less important factor than it was in earlier decades in selecting members for leadership positions.

The seniority system has been a unique aspect of Congress's internal organization. In no other major legislative body in the world has sheer length of service determined which members will have power and influence. Even when it was followed most closely in Congress, the seniority system was not a formal law or rule of the House of Representatives or Senate. Rather, it has always been an informal custom or tradition voluntarily observed by members.

There are two types of seniority. The first is seniority within the House or Senate as a whole. Each member is ranked within his own party according to when his current period of continuous service began. This type of seniority is of only limited significance, however. Senior members have access to the most desirable office space, and a few other privileges. The most senior member of the majority party in the Senate occupies the virtually powerless office of PRESIDENT PRO TEMPORE. But the most important positions—House SPEAKER and majority and minority leaders in each chamber—have never been filled on the basis of seniority. (See LEADERSHIP.)

It is within committees that the seniority system has had its greatest effect. Seniority on a committee is determined by when a member joined that committee, not when he or she became a member of Congress. During its heyday the seniority system ensured that the member with the longest service on each committee became the chairman. Other veteran committee members automatically became subcommittee chairmen. (See COMMITTEE SYSTEM.)

Congress did not always follow the seniority system. The practice of determining committee chairmanships solely on the basis of length of service evolved slowly in the late nineteenth and early twentieth centuries. It reached its peak in the decades after World War II. From 1949 to 1963 there was only one instance in which a House committee chairmanship was not awarded on the

The Godfather

1970s Reform Issue

basis of seniority.

The revolt against the seniority system began in the early 1970s. Many younger House members, who resented the iron control of a handful of veteran members, pushed through a series of reforms that greatly weakened the importance of seniority—for example, choosing committee chairmen on a secret-ballot vote by members of the majority party. The reforms did not obliterate the seniority system, however. Today, the most senior member of the majority party on a committee or subcommittee usually will be chosen chairman, unless there is strong political or personal opposition to him.

Efforts to change the seniority system have provoked heated debate. One argument for the system is simple: Experience counts. It often takes many years for members thoroughly to master the difficult subjects before their committees. The most experienced members also often have more of the political skills needed to provide strong leadership for a committee. Moreover, the practice of automatically awarding posts according to seniority prevents the periodic occurrence of debilitating internal battles for power.

Critics of seniority view it as a rigid, inefficient system that deprives vigorous younger members of influence while reserving power to a small group of senior members. In some cases the system produced very elderly chairmen whose talents and intellect had faded with the years. In others it encouraged chairmen to run their committees in an arrogant, autocratic manner that ignored the wishes of other members.

History

Several factors led to the development of the seniority system. One was the trend toward longer congressional careers that became evident in the early part of the twentieth century. In earlier times, when most members served for only a few terms, seniority meant little. But the arrival on Capitol Hill of a substantial number of members who viewed Congress as a lifetime job tended to emphasize the importance of seniority.

The seniority system also developed as a result of conflicts between leaders and the congressional rank and file. In the last decades of the nineteenth century, all-powerful leaders—the House Speaker and the chairman of the majority party caucus in the Senate—had total control over committee assignments and chairmanships. The revolt against that system led to the use of seniority to fill key posts. *(See* SPEAKER; CAUCUSES, PARTY.*)*

The Legislative Reorganization Act of 1946 solidified the rule of seniority. The act consolidated many committees into a smaller number of panels, thus giving a small number of seniority-selected chairmen wide power over every aspect of congressional activity. At the peak of the power of seniority, one congressional expert has written, "it seemed that Congress was ruled by a relatively small coterie of powerful committee chairmen."

A key consequence of the seniority system was to give members from the South an unusual amount of power. The Democrats, who were the majority party throughout most of this period, had a monopoly on southern House and Senate seats. Individual members from the South tended to win easy reelection for decades. As a result, the senior members on most committees were southern Democrats, who were able to exercise total control over their committees for many years.

The seniority-based power of the southern Democrats became a major point of conflict at the time when national Democratic leaders were seeking to push civil-rights and social legislation through Congress. The ability of the committee chairmen to block such legislation led to many bitter disputes. James O. Eastland, a Mississippi Democrat who chaired the Senate Judiciary Committee from 1956 to 1979, was notorious for bottling up civil-rights bills sought by party leaders.

The rule of the veteran members also caused intense frustration on the part of less senior members. By the 1970s most committee chairmen were over age sixty-five and had decades of service. That left many middle-aged members, who might otherwise have been at the peak of their careers, with little more power than the most junior members.

The revolt against the seniority system was a major element in the RE-FORM movement that transformed Congress in the 1970s. The key battleground for this movement was the House Democratic Caucus, which over the course of a few years took a series of actions that greatly reduced the importance of seniority in allocating power. (As the minority party, the Republicans had far less power to allocate, but seniority remained a dominant factor in their ranking of committee and subcommittee members.) The Senate also acted to reduce the iron-clad rule of seniority at about this time, although the changes there were less marked than in the House.

The changes approved by the House Democratic Caucus during the 1970s made it possible for party members to reject committee chairmen, and chairmen of Appropriations subcommittees, by secret ballot. Another change barred members from chairing more than one subcommittee, thus opening up the posts to more junior members.

As a result of the 1970s changes, senior members are no longer guaranteed chairmanships, if they have angered their colleagues for some reason. A key development in this movement came in 1975, when House Democrats defeated three incumbent committee chairmen. Ten years later they deposed a fourth: Eighty-year-old Melvin Price, who had taken over the Armed Services Committee in the 1975 revolt, was himself replaced by the committee's seventh-ranking Democrat, Les Aspin of Wisconsin. Price, a representative from Illinois since 1945, was considered too old and infirm to provide adequate leadership to the committee. ～

Separation of Powers

The Constitution established a national government comprising three independent branches: legislative, executive, and judicial. Each has distinct functions and powers derived directly from the Constitution. The resulting arrangement is generally referred to as the separation of powers.

Having experienced forms of arbitrary rule under both the British monarchy and various state legislatures under the Articles of Confederation, the framers of the Constitution were preoccupied with ways of avoiding a repe-

tition of either executive or legislative tyranny. They feared despotism by an elected legislature almost as much as by an autocracy. By fragmenting the powers of government among three separate bodies, the framers believed that no one branch would be able to dominate the government.

Such an arrangement has its price, however. To some extent government efficiency and speed are sacrificed to protect individual liberties.

Constitutional Structure

Article I outlines in considerable detail the powers and limitations of the legislative branch—which itself is divided into two chambers, the HOUSE OF REPRESENTATIVES and the SENATE. Of the three branches, the Founding Fathers were most familiar with the legislature, and its importance is reflected in the attention given it. Almost half of the Constitution is devoted to the operation and powers of Congress. The framers of the Constitution viewed Congress as the "first branch" of the government because they believed strongly in the need for a representative body to formulate national policy.

Article II outlines the powers of the executive branch, headed by the president. The organization and powers of the presidency are not described in nearly the detail provided for the legislature. The ambiguities, ironically, have helped to give the modern president great latitude in running the executive branch, particularly in foreign affairs.

The authors of the Constitution had serious reservations about establishing a strong executive. At the same time, however, they realized that it was primarily the lack of a strong national executive under the Articles of Confederation that had doomed the United States' first experiment in representative government. Indeed, under the Confederation there was no independent presidency; the legislature controlled and directed executive functions. At the Constitutional Convention in 1787, the delegates gradually were won over to the necessity of a stronger chief executive, though the extent of the president's powers remained a matter of dispute until the final days of the Convention.

Article III describes the powers and organization of the national judiciary, including the Supreme Court.

The other articles of the Constitution confer additional powers on the legislative and executive branches and spell out various government procedures and guarantees.

Sharing of Powers

The American system may be based on separation of powers, but those powers are not neatly divided into three separate and distinct entities. The Constitution is replete with instances where executive, legislative, and judicial powers overlap. Mixing the various powers of government among the three branches was another way of checking arbitrary rule. Thus the framers saw a network of checks and balances as an essential corollary to the separation of powers.

Separation of powers, to be effective as a governing doctrine, requires officials of the three branches, particularly legislators and the president, to work together in making national policy. From time to time in the nation's history, executive-legislative cooperation has broken down. Particularly divisive eras, such as the periods immediately before and after the Civil War, resulted in the near collapse of this necessary cooperation.

Since no one branch or political party can govern alone under this system, senators and representatives of the two major political parties must work out compromises with each other as well as with the executive branch. And the president must become involved in the LEGISLATIVE PROCESS by formulating a legislative agenda and working

hard to get it enacted. Since the early years of the twentieth century, and particularly since the administration of Franklin D. Roosevelt (1933-45), the president has in large part set the legislative agenda. Congress more often than not reacts to presidential initiatives. The president, nevertheless, is dependent on members of Congress to help promote and sell his legislative program.

Division of Powers

Despite the blending of government powers and functions among three branches, the separation of powers has real meaning. The Constitution grants many powers and responsibilities to one branch exclusively. All appointed and elected officials of the U.S. government are prohibited from serving in more than one branch simultaneously—with the one major exception of the vice president. As second in command, he is next in line of succession as the nation's chief executive. But the VICE PRESIDENT also has an important legislative role as president of the Senate. (See EXECUTIVE BRANCH AND CONGRESS; PRESIDING OFFICER.)

A provision of the 1985 deficit-reduction law known as Gramm-Rudman-Hollings was declared unconstitutional by the Supreme Court in 1986 on separation-of-powers grounds. The Court struck down the law's automatic spending-cut provision because it assigned certain executive powers and duties to the General Accounting Office, an agency controlled by the legislative branch, and thus violated the separation of powers. The separation of powers also figured in a 1983 Supreme Court decision declaring Congress's use of the LEGISLATIVE VETO unconstitutional.

Checks and Balances

As an additional safeguard against the exercise of arbitrary power, the framers incorporated in the Constitution provisions in which the legislative, executive, and judicial branches were checked by overlapping functions of one or both of the other branches. For example, the president wields two important legislative functions: formulation of a legislative agenda, and thus the ability to set national priorities; and the VETO power—allowing him to kill legislation he opposes, subject to the congressional power to override such vetoes. The president also exerts influence on the judicial branch through his power to appoint judges and Supreme Court justices, subject to congressional confirmation.

Many powers granted Congress infringe upon executive branch functions, including the power to declare war and to organize and maintain the armed forces. And Congress is given the power to impeach (in the House) and to try IMPEACHMENTS (in the Senate) of executive and judicial branch officials, including the president and federal judges. Congress exerts influence on the judiciary through its power to confirm APPOINTMENTS. Legislators also are granted the power, in Article III, to establish lower courts—the district and appeals courts—and to reorganize the federal court system.

The judicial branch has the ultimate check on Congress. Soon after the new Republic was in place, the Supreme Court declared and exercised the right to decide the constitutionality of laws passed by Congress.

Problems

Throughout the nation's history, the separation of powers has worked well in protecting the people against arbitrary rule and domination by any branch of government. But whether separation of powers provides effective government in an increasingly complex age is debatable. Many political scientists believe the present system fails to provide enough concentrated authority and harmony to ensure decisive governmental action. They also worry that a system of fragmented powers does not clearly identify responsibility for setting government policies or make officials accountable for their actions.

In such a system, for example, how can the nation's voters apportion responsibility between the executive and legislative branches and between Democrats and Republicans in Congress for the staggering budget deficits of the 1980s?

The U.S. system of two-year House terms, four-year presidential terms, and six-year Senate terms, another form of checks and balances, tends to diffuse power and responsibility.

For four of the eight years of the Republican administration of President Ronald Reagan, the Democratic party controlled both houses of Congress; the House of Representatives was in Democratic hands for all eight years. The period was marked by repeated conflict between the executive and legislative branches, resulting in frequent deadlocks in policy making and confusion about the role of the two branches in foreign policy.   ~

Sequestration.   See BUDGET PROCESS.

Sergeant-at-Arms

The House and Senate sergeants-at-arms are the police officers of their respective chambers. They attend all sessions and are responsible for enforcing rules and maintaining decorum, ensuring the security of buildings and visitors, and supervising the Capitol police force. Each was paid at an annual rate of $86,815 in early 1988.

The House sergeant-at-arms is in charge of the MACE, the symbol of legislative power and authority. He carries

the mace before him when he has to enforce order in the House chamber.

The sergeant-at-arms is also responsible for rounding up members for floor votes. This authority, unused since 1942, became an issue during a 1988 filibuster in which Republican senators boycotted votes on campaign-finance legislation. Senate Majority Leader Robert C. BYRD, a West Virginia Democrat, directed the sergeant-at-arms to arrest absent members and bring them to the Senate floor. Carrying out this order, Sergeant-at-Arms Henry K. Giugni tracked down Bob Packwood, an Oregon Republican, who was arrested and carried feet first into the Senate chamber. Packwood, whose broken finger was reinjured in the escapade, took his arrest in good humor. But other Republicans expressed deep bitterness over the incident.   ~

Sessions of Congress.   See
TERMS AND SESSIONS OF CONGRESS.

Sherman, John

John Sherman (1823-1900) became a fixture of the Republican party in the nineteenth century, serving both in Congress and in the executive branch. As an influential member, and later chairman, of the Senate Finance Committee, the Ohio Republican played a major role in formulating national financial policies. And later in his Senate career he sponsored antitrust legislation that carries his name to this day.

Sherman was elected to the House of Representatives in 1854 as part of the wave of antislavery sentiment that had led to the founding of the Republican party that year. In 1859 he was involved in a hotly contested race for House SPEAKER. Sherman led in the early voting, but he was anathema to the proslavery camp. The Republicans finally concluded he could not be elected, and he withdrew on the thirty-ninth ballot. Sherman became chairman of the House WAYS AND MEANS COMMITTEE instead.

When he moved to the Senate in 1861, he was assigned to the Senate FINANCE COMMITTEE and became its chairman in 1867. From this base, Sherman played an important role in the nation's finances during the Civil War and in the Reconstruction period. He supported wartime legislation authorizing paper money, or "greenbacks," and helped plan a new national banking system. In the postwar period he backed legislation calling for the redemption of paper money in gold.

Sherman's efforts were rewarded when he was named secretary of the Treasury in 1877. After his failure to win the Republican presidential nomination in 1880 (as happened again in 1884 and 1888), Sherman returned to the Senate in 1881. His legislative achievements included the Sherman Antitrust Act of 1890, a basic antitrust statute that is still on the books today, and the Sherman Silver Purchase Act of 1890. He was named PRESIDENT PRO TEMPORE of the Senate in 1886, the year he also became chairman of the Senate FOREIGN RELATIONS COMMITTEE.

Sherman left the Senate to become President William McKinley's secretary of state in 1897. Ineffectual in the role, Sherman resigned the next year in protest against the Spanish-American War. He died two years later.   ～

Small Business Committees, House and Senate

Popular with legislators, whose districts always include small businesses, the House and Senate Small Business committees have survived several attempts to reorganize them out of existence. Usually bipartisan in their actions, the two committees often serve as advocates, reminding other congressional panels of the special problems of small businesses.

The committees' main focus in the 1980s was on preserving the Small Business Administration, which the Reagan administration wanted to make part of the Commerce Department. Another concern was to guarantee the participation of small businesses in federal procurement and government contracts.

The Senate committee was set up in 1950 as a select committee. It gained standing committee status in 1980. Alabama Democrat John J. Sparkman was the panel's first chairman and had a long tenure in the post (1950-53, 1955-67). Connecticut Republican Lowell P. Weicker, Jr., chaired the committee from 1981 to 1987, when Arkansas Democrat Dale Bumpers took over.

The House committee was set up in 1947 as the Select Committee to Conduct a Study and Investigation of the Problems of Small Business. Two men served several terms as chairman: Texas Democrat Wright Patman (1949-53, 1955-63) and Tennessee Democrat Joe L. Evins (1963-79). The panel became the Small Business Committee in a 1974 reorganization.   ～

Smith, Howard W.

Howard W. Smith (1883-1976) served as a representative from Virginia from 1931 to 1967. A leader of the conservative southern Democrats, or "Dixiecrats," and chairman of the RULES Committee, Smith often was called the second most powerful man in the House of Representatives.

Smith began his career as a lawyer and went on to become a circuit judge and a banker. He became a foe of Franklin D. Roosevelt's NEW DEAL and opposed social welfare programs throughout his career. Smith also spoke out against legislation aiding organized labor and voted against the 1935 National Labor Relations Act. He sponsored a bill in 1939 that called for the imprisonment of resident foreigners who recommended changes in the U.S. system of government. In 1940 he authored the Smith Act, which made it a crime to be a communist. The act was later struck down by the Supreme Court.

Roosevelt called Smith "the greatest obstructionist in Congress," and it was as a dissenter that Smith made his career. From his seat on the Rules Committee, Smith harried opponents from both political parties. By forming an alliance with conservative Democrats and Republicans on the committee, Smith was able to bottle up legislation, which had to move through Rules before going to the House floor. In 1939 this CONSERVATIVE COALITION began demanding changes in bills before it would approve a rule. Under the dominance of these conservatives, the committee often flouted the wishes of the Democratic Speaker.

Smith became chairman of Rules in 1955. He once held up consideration of legislation for days by disappearing to Virginia because, he said, his barn had burned down and it had taken a while to repair. The committee could meet only when convened by the chairman. In 1958 liberals sought to restructure the Rules Committee; but the proposal was rejected by Speaker Sam RAYBURN, who promised that the committee would not bottle up civil rights and welfare legislation. But in 1961 Rayburn himself recognized the need to reorganize the committee and supported a successful attempt to increase its membership. The addition of loyal Democrats to the committee diminished Smith's authority. He was defeated for reelection in 1966.   ∼

Smith, Margaret Chase

Margaret Chase Smith (1897-), a Maine Republican, entered the House of Representatives in 1940 after the death of her husband, Rep. Clyde H. Smith. In 1948 she was elected to the Senate, where she served until 1973. An independent-minded Republican, Smith was the first of her party to denounce Sen. Joseph R. McCARTHY on the Senate floor for his virulent anticommunist activities.

Before her marriage, Smith worked as a teacher and then as an executive with a newspaper and a woolen mill. After Smith's husband entered Congress, she worked as his assistant in his congressional office. Her husband encouraged her to run for his House seat after he suffered a heart attack in 1940. He died later that year, and she was elected to the seat in a special election.

In the House Smith served on the Naval Affairs Committee, where she was a strong advocate of military preparedness. Her reputation as a "hawk" was borne out by her 1961 speech in the Senate criticizing President John F. KENNEDY's seeming reluctance to use nuclear weapons. She charged that this reluctance put the United States at a disadvantage with the Soviet Union. The speech prompted Nikita S. Khrushchev, then Soviet premier, to call her "the devil in the disguise of a woman."

In 1950 Smith presented a "declaration of conscience" on the Senate floor. The declaration, supported by six other Republican senators, criticized McCarthy's anticommunist campaign. She said, "I am not proud of the way we spear outsiders from the floor of the Senate.... I do not want to see the party ride to political victory on the Four Horsemen of Calumny—fear, ignorance, bigotry, and smear."

Smith was proud of her congressional attendance record and late in her career introduced measures to regulate senators' attendance on the floor. From June 1955 to July 1968 she never missed a Senate roll-call vote. Smith was defeated for reelection in 1972.   ∼

Speaker of the House

The Speaker is both the PRESIDING OFFICER of the HOUSE OF REPRESEN-

TATIVES and the overall leader of the majority party in the chamber. The Constitution says the House "shall choose their Speaker," but it does not describe the Speaker's duties. His role has developed over two centuries of parliamentary give-and-take.

The formal duties of the Speaker are broad. He officially has authority to refer bills to committees for preliminary consideration and to schedule LEGISLATION for House floor action. When presiding over the House, he has the power to recognize members wishing to speak, subject to certain limitations spelled out in the House rules. With the advice of the PARLIAMENTARIAN he also may decide POINTS OF ORDER, objections raised by members who think House rules have been violated. The Speaker chooses members to chair the COMMITTEE OF THE WHOLE, a parliamentary framework the House adopts when it considers bills for amendment. And he appoints members to various special House committees, as well as to conference committees, which work out the differences between House- and Senate-passed bills. *(See* COMMITTEE SYSTEM.)

These are usually routine tasks, governed by House customs and rules that limit the Speaker's options. Skillful Speakers nonetheless find ways to make the rules work to their advantage.

The Speaker's formal powers are less critical than his political mastery in determining his influence in the House. A successful Speaker enjoys personal prestige as head of the party LEADERSHIP structure and commands a high degree of party loyalty. He combines a deep understanding of the LEGISLATIVE PROCESS with strong persuasive skills.

The Constitution does not specify that a Speaker must be a member of the House, but no nonmember has ever been elected to the post. Speakers are chosen by the CAUCUS of the majority party's members, whose decision is confirmed by the full House at the beginning of each new Congress. In this cen-

tury only relatively senior members have been chosen, and they have retained the post as long as their party held a majority in the House or until their own retirement.

Like any other member, the Speaker may participate in debate and vote. Modern Speakers occasionally speak from the floor; they rarely vote except to break a tie. They do not serve on legislative committees.

Under the Twenty-fifth Amendment to the Constitution, adopted in 1967, the Speaker follows the vice president in the line of presidential succession. *(See* PRESIDENTIAL DISABILITY AND SUCCESSION.)

Historical Highlights

In the early years of Congress the Speaker was largely a figurehead. The first Speaker, Frederick A. C. Muhlenberg of Pennsylvania, was necessarily a nonpartisan presiding officer because political parties had not yet been formed when he assumed the post in 1789. *(List of Speakers, p. 475)*

The authority of the speakership ebbed and flowed during the nineteenth century, but by the 1880s the Speaker had become the dominant leader of the House. The stature of the office reached its peak in the early 1900s under a series of autocratic Speakers, but their arbitrary use of power led to a 1910 "revolt" that stripped the Speaker of most of his formal authority. In the 1960s and 1970s party discipline weakened in Congress, and Speakers found that to lead the House they had to rely chiefly on their own persuasive arts.

Clay The first really influential Speaker of the House was Henry CLAY, a popular Kentuckian who held the post for six terms between 1811 and 1825. The seven Speakers before him had presided over the House only ceremonially; Clay was the first to lead it.

Clay was elected Speaker the day he arrived in the House at age thirty-

Speaker Thomas P. O'Neill, Jr.,
With Portrait of Speaker Sam Rayburn

four. He promptly set out to assert the supremacy of Congress over the other branches of government and of the speakership over the affairs of the House. Clay owed his election as Speaker to a faction of young representatives known as the War Hawks, and he used the influence of his office to push the nation into the War of 1812. He stacked key House committees with supporters of his war policy, exploited House rules to reinforce his control of the chamber, and used his great oratorical skills to pressure President James MADISON into declaring war against England.

Reed   The next great expansion of the Speaker's power came under Thomas Brackett REED, who won the nickname "Czar Reed" for his efforts. Reed, a Maine Republican, served as Speaker in 1889-91 and 1895-99. When he assumed the post, delaying tactics by the Democratic minority often prevented the majority from working its will. Through a succession of floor rulings, Reed firmly established the right of the majority to control the legislative process.

The minority's chief stalling tactic was the "disappearing quorum." A majority of the chamber's members, known as a QUORUM, was required to transact business. But when the roll was called to establish the presence of a quorum, minority members who were present in the chamber refused to answer their names. Thus the vote fell short of the number required. Reed solved the problem of the disappearing quorum by counting all the members who were present, not just those who answered the roll. The Democrats were furious, but the Speaker held firm. Asked to explain the function of the minority, Reed is said to have replied: "The right of the minority is to draw its salary, and its function is to make a quorum."

Reed's rulings later became part of a new set of House rules, which was drafted by the RULES COMMITTEE under his chairmanship. Speakers had chaired the Rules Committee since 1858, and much of their power resulted from that arrangement.

Cannon   The power of the Speaker reached its peak when Illinois Republican Joseph G. CANNON held the post in 1903-11. While "Uncle Joe" Cannon instituted few parliamentary changes in the House, he used fully those made by his predecessors. His dictatorial rule ended in 1910 when insurgent Republicans joined Democrats in a revolt against him, stripping the Speaker of his authority to chair—or even to serve on—the Rules Committee, to appoint committee members, and to control all floor action.

Longworth   During his 1925-31 tenure, Nicholas LONGWORTH, an Ohio Republican, tried to restore the centralized authority of the Speaker that had been lost in the revolt against Cannon. Aided by a small group of trusted associates,

Longworth personally assumed control of the House. He was able to achieve through persuasion what Cannon had done by arbitrary interpretation of the rules.

Rayburn Legend surrounds the speakership of Sam RAYBURN, who served in the post from 1940 until his death in 1961, except for two short stints as minority leader when the Republicans controlled the House in 1947-49 and 1953-55. Rayburn exerted such influence during his tenure that the Texas Democrat was said to run the House out of his hip pocket.

Confronted after World War II with a party badly split over civil rights and other domestic issues, Rayburn found he could minimize disunity by making party decisions himself and bargaining with individuals rather than with the party as a whole. "To get along, you've got to go along," he routinely advised House freshmen, and they generally complied.

Rayburn's leadership style demonstrated the profound changes that had occurred in Congress since Cannon's reign. As party discipline declined, the Speaker found he had to rely on his personal style to achieve his goals. "The old day of pounding on the desk and giving people hell is gone," Rayburn said as early as 1950. "A man's got to lead by persuasion and kindness and the best reason—that's the only way he can lead people."

O'Neill A continuing decline in party discipline weakened the leadership of Thomas P. O'NEILL, Jr., a Massachusetts Democrat who was Speaker from 1977 until his retirement in 1987. O'Neill himself was known for his party loyalty and partisanship. But younger and generally more liberal Democrats criticized him for failing to crack down on conservative members who voted against positions supported by a majority of the party. O'Neill maintained that the party's diversity made it nearly impossible to discipline or even threaten to discipline disloyal members.

On one of the rare occasions when discipline was attempted, it backfired. Texas Democrat Phil Gramm was removed from his seat on the BUDGET COMMITTEE in 1983, in reprisal for his two-year collaboration with the White House on President Ronald Reagan's budget. Gramm promptly resigned his House seat, won reelection as a Republican, and returned to the Budget Committee under GOP auspices. He was elected to the Senate in 1984.

Wright Controversy surrounded Jim WRIGHT, a flamboyant Texas Democrat who succeeded O'Neill in 1987. Early in his tenure Wright crossed swords with the Reagan administration over his role in Central American peace negotiations. Later, the propriety of Wright's financial dealings was called into question, forcing the House Committee on STANDARDS OF OFFICIAL CONDUCT in 1988 to grapple for the first time with formal allegations of impropriety by a Speaker.   ~

ADDITIONAL READINGS

Hardeman, D. B., and Donald Bacon. *Rayburn: A Biography.* 1987.

O'Neill, Thomas P., Jr., and William Novak. *Man of the House: The Life and Political Memoirs of Speaker Tip O'Neill.* 1987.

Sinclair, Barbara. *Majority Leadership in the U.S. House of Representatives.* 1983.

Special Orders

Legislators who want to address the House or Senate on a topic not necessarily part of the day's legislative agenda can reserve a block of time in advance. This is called a "special order."

In the House members who have requested special orders are allowed to speak for up to sixty minutes at the end of the day's session—before the House adjourns but after legislative business has been completed. TELEVISION cameras record the speeches, which often are made to an almost empty chamber.

Controversy about the routine practice erupted in 1984, after Republicans repeatedly used special orders for speeches attacking the Democratic leadership. An angry Speaker Thomas P. O'NEILL, Jr., ordered the TV cameras to pan the House chamber, showing viewers that few were present to hear the emotional speakers. The practice has been continued; periodically during the period reserved for special orders, the cameras show the House chamber— and its rows of empty seats.

In the Senate members are recognized for special orders at the beginning of a day's session; they may speak for five minutes. Fifteen-minute speeches were permitted until 1986, when Senate sessions began to be televised and requests for special orders increased. Some senators ask for special-order time almost every day.

The term "special order" also refers to the resolution approved by the House RULES COMMITTEE setting guidelines for floor consideration of a bill. The resolution is more commonly known as a "rule." (See LEGISLATIVE PROCESS; RULE FOR HOUSE DEBATE.) ~

Speech or Debate Clause.   See
IMMUNITY, CONGRESSIONAL.

Staff

Thousands of people work for Congress, and its elected members depend heavily on these employees. Staff members cannot vote, but their imprint is on every other step in getting a bill passed. They draft legislation, negotiate with lobbyists, and plot strategy for floor action.

The influence of congressional staff is vast. Critics complain the staff exercises too much power and costs too much money. But legislators are asked to debate and vote on a wide range of complex issues, and they need staff to provide the expertise that one person alone simply could not master.

The congressional bureaucracy is well entrenched. More than 18,000 people work for the House and Senate, and another 3,000 handle security, maintenance, and other support services. Also considered to be working directly for Congress are an additional 3,000 employees at the four legislative service agencies: the Congressional Research Service of the Library of Congress, the Congressional Budget Office, the Office of Technology Assessment, and 30 percent of those working at the General Accounting Office. These 24,000 employees far outnumber the five-hundred-plus representatives and senators.

By the late 1980s Congress was spending five times as much on its operations as it did in 1970. Legislative branch appropriations, which include some nonlegislative activities, are nevertheless the best measure of its cost that Congress has provided over the years. That figure rose from more than $361 million in fiscal 1970 to more than $1.7 billion in fiscal 1988. The largest share goes to pay salaries.

Growth in Staff Size
The size of the House and Senate staff tripled between 1955 and 1975. That enormous growth changed the fabric of life on Capitol Hill. It crowded existing offices, prompted expansion into "annex" buildings formerly used as hotels or apartments, and spurred construction of a third massive Senate of-

fice building. The presence of so many employees made Capitol Hill more and more like a small city, bustling with restaurants, barbershops, stationery stores, gymnasiums, and its own subways linking office buildings to the Capitol. By the early 1980s the growth of staff slowed as Congress, trying to cut overall federal spending, responded to criticism about increases in its own budget.

After World War II, and again in the 1960s and 1970s, the federal government expanded rapidly and grew increasingly complex. Congress wanted its own sources of information, independent of the executive branch and interest groups, so it added staff. Changes within Congress also spurred the hiring of more people. In the 1970s erosion of the SENIORITY SYSTEM shifted new authority to junior and minority members; they wanted aides to help with their new responsibilities. Subcommittees were given new status, and by the late 1970s as many people worked for subcommittees as had worked for full committees in the 1960s.

Congress also became the last resort for those dealing with the federal bureaucracy. Each legislator usually had several employees whose sole job was answering voters' complaints, a task known as "casework" or "constituent services." Casework is usually the primary function of district and state offices. A measure of its importance is that more than a third of members' personal staffs work outside of Washington.

Partisanship

Congressional employees are drawn from a mix of backgrounds, but most are young, male, and well educated. Campaign workers can still end up on a legislator's payroll, but jobs also go to others with no ties to the politician or the district. An economist might be hired for a committee post, for example. Many veteran "Hill" employees outlast

the legislator who originally hired them; they simply get a job with someone else.

Sometimes staff members become politicians themselves. President Lyndon B. JOHNSON began his career as a congressional aide; later he was elected to Congress and served twenty-four years in the House and Senate, including six years as Senate majority leader.

Traditionally, many nonlegislative posts were PATRONAGE jobs. The chauffeur, the elevator operator, the parking garage attendant, and even jobs closer to legislative action, such as the doorkeepers, were controlled by party leaders and their top aides. The system began to erode in the 1960s, when Secretary of the Senate Bobby Baker, a Johnson protégé, was convicted of using his office—and his control of numerous Senate jobs—for personal gain. Since then the number of patronage jobs has been drastically reduced, although not eliminated. Merit, not friendship with a legislator, is usually the basis for being hired.

The political parties, however, still maintain control over numerous jobs. The top leaders of both parties have their own staff. Party affiliation is usually a factor when legislators hire their personal aides. Committee hiring is also partisan, with the majority usually responsible for about two-thirds of the jobs and the minority for about one-third. In reality, though, other qualifications often take precedence over party allegiance, and some committees have removed partisanship from their hiring practices. The nonpartisan staff of the Joint Committee on TAXATION serves tax-writing panels in both houses, and the House and Senate BUDGET committees consider most of their professional staff to be nonpartisan.

Despite partisanship in hiring, a line is drawn between congressional work and campaign work. House rules allow a House employee to work on a campaign if assigned congressional duties are also being fulfilled. The Senate

Staff: 1980s
Congressional employees are drawn from a mix of backgrounds, but most are young, male, and well educated. Staff members cannot vote, but their imprint is on every other step in getting a bill passed.

has no formal procedures to govern the practice. Sometimes staff members take a leave from their congressional posts and become campaign workers, paid by the campaign. Another practice is to divide duties, with a staff member's congressional pay reduced to reflect time spent on the campaign.

Hiring Practices
Although members of Congress follow voluntary rules against discrimination on Capitol Hill, they have exempted themselves from most labor and equal rights laws, including those guaranteeing a minimum wage, the right to organize unions without harassment, safety in the workplace, and equal pay for equal work.

Some critics call Congress "the last plantation." They complain that women employees on Capitol Hill receive less pay than men in comparable positions, that women and blacks are clustered in lower-paying jobs, and that blacks are underrepresented on the con-

gressional payroll. The Supreme Court ruled in 1979 that congressional employees have the right to sue for damages if they believe they are victims of job discrimination.

Many members who support federal antidiscrimination laws oppose their application to Congress because they do not want executive branch agencies to oversee operation of the legislative branch, no matter how noble the cause.

Congress did make specific rules in 1967 against hiring relatives, a practice known as nepotism. The ban on nepotism was slipped into a House bill and, once under consideration, was politically impossible to oppose. A senator or representative can still recommend a relative for employment in another office, and a legislator's relatives can still work in his office, but without pay. For example, Heather Foley for years has been a top, unpaid assistant to her husband, Washington Democrat Thomas S. Foley, who served as chairman of the

House Agriculture Committee before becoming House majority leader in 1987.

Personal Staff

Clerks were hired by Congress even in its earliest years, for jobs such as recording floor debate and handling committee paperwork. But authority—and funding—for a member's personal staff was not provided until 1885 in the Senate and 1893 in the House.

By 1919 a ceiling had been placed on the number of personal staff members each legislator could hire (committee staff were handled separately). In 1946 a House member could hire a maximum of five people, and a senator, six. By the 1980s representatives could hire eighteen full-time, permanent employees. Senators had no limit on the size of their personal staff, but most employed thirty to forty people. Each representative was allotted more than $400,000 to pay salaries. Senators got about $1 million, with the most populous states eligible for more than $1.6 million.

Legislators divide their personal staff between their Washington and local offices. Representatives usually have at least one district office; senators often have three or more spread across their state.

For their Washington office, most legislators hire an administrative assistant (A.A.) responsible for overall operations, including casework, and a legislative assistant (L.A.) who concentrates on committee action, floor votes, and a member's own political agenda. Often a press secretary handles questions from reporters and writes newsletters. Other employees report to these top aides. Hiring policies, job descriptions, pay scales, and vacations differ from office to office.

Committee Staff

Each committee, like each legislator, sets its own hiring policies. Most have a professional staff and a clerical staff, with staff director, legislative counsel, and chief clerk among the top posts. Reporting to them are legislative aides, researchers, investigators, and secretaries. Although those on a legisla-

Staff: 1920s
Congressional employees from an earlier era are shown below. These five sisters worked as secretaries for members of Congress in the 1920s.

tor's personal staff must focus on re-election efforts and casework, committee staff concentrate on legislation and can be very influential. The House since 1946 has restricted committee staff to handling committee business.

Authority for hiring full-time committee staff was in place by 1900, but the Legislative Reorganization Act of 1946 provided the funding for each committee to hire a roster of aides. In the 1970s the size of the committee staffs was greatly increased. The House in 1974 tripled the size of each committee's professional staff, from six to eighteen, and doubled the clerical staff, from six to twelve. No strict limits apply in the Senate, where committees usually employ forty or more people, with another five or more often working for each subcommittee. In 1975 the Senate gave each member authority to hire three legislative aides to help with committee work.   ∼

ADDITIONAL READINGS

Fox, Harrison W., Jr., and Susan Webb Hammond. *Congressional Staffs: The Invisible Force in American Lawmaking.* 1977.
Malbin, Michael J. *Unelected Representatives: Congressional Staff and the Future of Representative Government.* 1982.

Standards of Official Conduct Committee, House

Commonly known as the House ETHICS committee, the Committee on Standards of Official Conduct investigates representatives charged with ethical misconduct, such as misuse of campaign funds, failure to disclose personal finances, or improper acceptance of gratuities. The committee then reports to the full House and in some cases recom-

mends punishment, such as reprimand, censure, or, in rare cases, expulsion from the House. The Senate has a Select ETHICS COMMITTEE that monitors senators' conduct. *(See* DISCIPLINING MEMBERS.*)*

Unlike most House committees, where the majority party dominates, the ethics panel is bipartisan, usually with six members from each party. The chairman is from the majority party. The committee has its own investigative staff and counsel but has hired outside attorneys; former Watergate special prosecutor Leon Jaworski handled allegations of influence-peddling by Korean businessmen in the late 1970s. Committee investigations are usually triggered by complaints from colleagues or news stories. The committee also gives advice to members confused about ethics rules; by the late 1980s committee offices were getting twenty to thirty questions a day.

Few representatives seek a seat on the panel, which has the awkward responsibility of passing judgment on colleagues' behavior. In 1988 the committee assumed the most uncomfortable task it had ever faced—an investigation of Republican charges that the Speaker of the House, Texas Democrat Jim WRIGHT, had abused his office to enrich himself. The committee vote to undertake the investigation was unanimous.

Critics complain the committee is too lenient, reporting violations and then recommending no punishment. But California Democrat Julian C. Dixon, who became chairman in 1985, said, "I think the committee does a good job of, one, being nonpartisan and, two, investigating facts, evaluating facts, and taking appropriate action. But is the committee on a constant search for improprieties by members of Congress? The answer is no. I think the members of Congress have a right to feel the committee is not on a witch hunt."

The committee was established in 1967 in response to public outcry at a series of congressional scandals. The first chairman was Illinois Democrat Melvin Price. The House gave the panel only a limited mission at first: to write a code of conduct. Approved in 1968, the code expanded the committee's responsibility, giving it authority to enforce the new rules.

But the code was couched in general terms and FINANCIAL DISCLOSURE was confined to sources, not amounts, of income. The House and Senate each revamped its code in 1977, and in 1978 Congress applied ethics codes to the entire federal government.

Although the House usually goes along with the recommendations of the ethics committee, it has acted independently. In 1983 the committee recommended that two legislators be reprimanded because of improper relationships with teenage pages; the House opted for the stiffer penalty of censure.   ～

State of the Union

Early each year the president addresses a joint session of Congress, spelling out his legislative program and goals for the year in a State of the Union message. The annual address is the traditional way presidents comply with a constitutional directive to "from time to time give to the Congress Information of the State of the Union. . . ."

The evening session of Congress, usually in late January, brings a rare mood of pageantry to the House chamber, which is seldom so filled with people. Seated in the front rows are the Supreme Court justices, wearing their judicial robes, and members of the president's cabinet. Nearby are foreign diplomats. Galleries are packed with family members, visitors, and reporters. A special escort committee, dispatched by the Speaker, greets the president and accompanies him down the aisle.

The president's speech is usually interrupted several times with applause. On rare occasions members of an opposing party groan to indicate their disagreement with a statement. More typical is the reaction of the Democratic-controlled Congress to Republican President Ronald Reagan in 1988. Even when he was criticizing Congress for its catchall spending bills, and hefting a forty-three pound stack of documents to demonstrate their unwieldiness, the legislators reacted with applause and cheers.

The nation's first two presidents, George Washington and John Adams, delivered their annual messages as speeches to Congress. The third president, Thomas Jefferson, chose in 1801 to avoid what was an elaborate, formal ceremony, complete with a chair called "the president's throne." Instead he had his private secretary carry the message to Capitol Hill.

No president addressed Congress again until 1913, when Woodrow Wilson renewed the custom of delivering the message in person, a decision that was quite controversial. He eventually appeared before Congress twenty-six times, a record that still held in 1988. Since Wilson's time, only President Herbert Hoover has declined to visit Capitol Hill at all.

President Lyndon B. JOHNSON in 1965 shifted the time of the State of the Union address from midday to evening, a move designed to attract the large television audience during prime time. The next year Republicans got a half-hour slot from each network to offer their own assessment of national affairs. By 1976 television time was available to the opposing party immediately following the State of the Union broadcast.

In 1986 the State of the Union address was postponed for the first time.

On the morning of President Reagan's scheduled January 28 address to Congress, the space shuttle *Challenger* exploded, taking the lives of all seven crew members. Reagan delayed the speech until February 4.				~

States and Congress

Their relationship uneasy from the beginning, Congress and the states have never agreed on how to share—or divide—responsibility for governing the nation.

The ongoing conflict, which erupted once into civil war, has spawned numerous political disputes. Certain areas, such as national defense, are clearly in the federal domain. But the Constitution left many gray areas, with no clear rules about what level of government was in charge. Often the Supreme Court has been forced to referee, deciding whether the federal government or the states are ultimately responsible.

The sharing of responsibility for governing is called federalism, with a national government, fifty state governments, and thousands of local governments operating at different levels. By the 1980s the federal government clearly dominated the relationship; several Supreme Court decisions had enhanced federal authority, as had the enormous flow of federal money to state and local governments.

State and local officials found it almost impossible to refuse their share of tax dollars, even when the money came with rules and regulations that encroached on their autonomy. Congress, for its part, became accustomed in the 1960s and 1970s to setting national goals and giving other governments money to carry them out.

By the 1980s constraints on the federal budget made that pattern increasingly difficult to sustain. Sweeping new programs simply were not possible, and existing policies were at risk. Congress continued to set national goals but could no longer be counted on to couple the rules with federal money—"carrots"—for state and local governments to use in carrying them out. Governors and mayors, who developed an extensive LOBBYING apparatus in Washington in the 1970s and 1980s, began to call these policies "mandates without money." They were asked to spend their own money to implement federal goals. Even worse, from their point of view, was the use of the federal "stick"—potential loss of federal funds in other areas if they failed to comply with new national policies. Clean air laws, for example, called for cuts in federal highway funds for states that failed to meet national goals.

What had been a beneficial relationship with the federal government suddenly became less attractive to state and local governments, and they began to resist federal demands. Old arguments about states' rights had a new appeal, two centuries after the Constitution tried to divide local and national responsibilities.

Constitutional Responsibilities

The Constitution enumerated several powers of Congress, including authority over the federal PURSE, interstate COMMERCE, taxes and tariffs, and WAR. But it left untouched a wide area for the states to handle, such as education, property transactions, marriage, inheritance, contracts, and maintenance of domestic order, called the "police power." *(See* STRUCTURE AND POWERS.*)*

The Tenth Amendment spoke directly to the division of state and federal authority: "The powers not delegated to the United States by the Constitution, nor prohibited by it to the states, are reserved to the states respectively, or to the people."

Federal authority got an early test in Maryland, where opponents of the national bank tried to tax it into ruin. The Supreme Court, in an 1819 decision, *McCulloch v. Maryland*, sided with the federal government, saying its law prevailed over any conflicting state laws or constitutions because of the Constitution's "supremacy clause."

But numerous Court decisions after that gave the upper hand to the states. Not until 1937, in a landmark case upholding the Social Security system (*Helvering v. Davis*), did the Court elaborate the power of the "general welfare" clause. That was followed by other decisions endorsing a broad application of the interstate commerce clause, opening the door to broad federal regulations. Since then, federal authority has rarely been checked. *(See* COMMERCE POWER.*)*

In setting up the national government, the Constitution protected state interests in several ways. Each state was to be represented in Congress by two senators and one or more representatives. States were to govern the election of presidents and vice presidents through the electoral college system. No changes could be made in the Constitution itself without the approval of three-fourths of the states. *(See* STRUCTURE AND POWERS; ELECTING THE PRESIDENT; CONSTITUTIONAL AMENDMENTS.*)*

The Constitution left voter qualifications up to the states, but it has been amended five times to overrule state restrictions on voting rights. Congress and the Supreme Court have also acted against state attempts to limit voting. Males without property, blacks, women, and young people were among those benefiting from the changes.

Three constitutional amendments ratified after the Civil War were designed to guarantee individual rights, even against action by states. The Thirteenth, Fourteenth, and Fifteenth amendments outlawed slavery; affirmed that voting was a right regardless of race, color, or previous condition of servitude; and promised due process and equal protection to all citizens. Not until the 1960s, though, did Supreme Court decisions and congressional action on civil rights laws put the full authority of the federal government behind the concept of equal rights.

Highways
Highway legislation passed by Congress in 1916 became the model for subsequent federal grant programs. Highway aid still comprises more than 15 percent of total federal transfers to state and local governments.

States' Rights

The philosophical debate over states' rights influenced the drafting of the nation's first documents. Statesmen such as Alexander Hamilton, who favored a strong national government, and Thomas Jefferson, who favored the states, continued the dialogue even after the Constitution appeared to resolve many issues.

Virginia, Kentucky Resolutions The discussion was rekindled in 1798 when states resisted a move by Congress to squelch pro-French sentiment. Under the Sedition Act, the most vigorously enforced of four new laws, twenty-five people were arrested, including Republican newspaper editors who argued against the Federalist policies. Virginia, with a resolution drafted by James MADISON, and Kentucky, with a protest written by Jefferson, reacted to the restrictive law, asserting the right of states to resist laws they considered unconstitutional.

Seven northern states protested the resolutions, particularly the Kentucky Resolution's advocacy of "nullifi-

cation." Under that theory, a state—as opposed to the Supreme Court—could declare null and void any federal law it found to violate constitutional rights. In 1814 Massachusetts, Connecticut, and Rhode Island borrowed the theory when they met at the Hartford Convention to consider secession as a protest against the War of 1812.

Nullification South Carolinian John C. CALHOUN embraced the concept of "nullification" in the late 1820s and used it to support the proslavery argument of the southern states. The theory was the subject of a famous Senate debate in January 1830 between Daniel WEBSTER of Massachusetts and Robert Y. HAYNE of South Carolina. Calhoun, then vice president, presided over the chamber. "The Constitution is not the creature of the state government," said Webster, arguing against states' rights. "It is, sir, the people's Constitution, the people's government, made for the people, made by the people, and answerable to the people." He summed up his argument: "Liberty and union, one and inseparable, now and forever."

South Carolina in 1832 voted to nullify a new federal tariff act and to prohibit its enforcement in the state. Southern opposition to protective tariffs, internal improvements, and the national bank were all connected; anxious to avoid a federal ban on slavery, southerners argued for states' rights in other areas, too.

President Andrew Jackson responded by denouncing nullification, contending that states had surrendered a part of their sovereignty to the federal government. "Disunion by armed force is treason," Jackson said. A compromise on the tariff averted a direct confrontation, but the debate continued. Georgia in the 1830s tried to nullify a Supreme Court decision favoring the Cherokee Indians in its western territories.

Civil War The southern states took their concept of states' rights to its ultimate test in 1860 and 1861 when eleven states voted to secede from the Union. Their action was triggered by the election of President Abraham Lincoln; he opposed slavery and argued that the states, by joining the Union, had given up certain rights.

The victory of the Union in 1865 made the national government supreme and settled the argument about secession. But other aspects of the debate remained in dispute. The concept of states' rights continued to be identified with those reluctant to end racial discrimination.

Dixiecrats, Desegregation Champions of states' rights renewed their battle in the late 1940s and 1950s, as federal efforts to end racial discrimination intensified. When the Democratic National Convention in 1948 adopted a pro-civil rights platform, disgruntled southerners from thirteen states established a States' Rights, or Dixiecrat, party. They nominated for president Strom Thurmond, a South Carolina governor, who eventually won in Alabama, Louisiana,

Mississippi, and South Carolina. (Thurmond, who entered the Senate as a Democrat in 1954, became a Republican in 1964.)

Southern states also rallied around the states' rights cry in 1954, when the Supreme Court outlawed racially segregated public schools. For the next decade, congressional opponents of civil rights laws often leaned on the contention that states had constitutional rights to resist federal policy. A 1956 "manifesto" signed by 101 southern members of Congress declared, "We commend the motives of those states which have declared the intention to resist forced integration by any lawful means." In 1957 President Dwight D. Eisenhower sent federal troops to enforce civil rights in Little Rock, Arkansas, where black students enrolled at the previously all-white Central High School.

Grants-in-Aid

While debate over states' rights has at times been deeply philosophical, a more powerful factor in the federal-state relationship has developed with little such deliberation. Federal grants-in-aid to state and local governments have been steadily increasing in this century, with annual spending increasing from $12 million in 1913 to more than $100 billion by the mid-1980s. Conditions on use of this money have given the federal government increasing control over local matters.

The patchwork of grant programs has developed piecemeal, as Congress has responded to various problems. Conditions have been devised, too, in a fragmented way. An early rule was that states use the merit system to select those handling Social Security funds. Since then, requirements have grown increasingly complex. To be eligible for federal health funds, for example, states must have overall plans for how health care is delivered. Federally insured mortgages are available only to states with flood control programs. Highway grants come with a host of rules not only about how roads and bridges must be built, but also with links to other federal policies, such as speed limits and the minimum legal age for drinking alcoholic beverages.

Applicable to all grants are several "cross-cutting" rules on civil rights, affirmative action, environmental impact, labor, and accessibility for the handicapped.

Land Grants The earliest federal grants consisted of land; as western territories were divided, a portion of every parcel, often one-sixteenth of each township, was set aside, with proceeds used to support local education. Applying the same approach to roads and canals, though, met resistance. Several presidents, from James Madison to Andrew Jackson, opposed as improper a federal role in "internal improvements," despite the idea's popularity in Congress.

Even land grants were sometimes controversial. President Franklin Pierce in 1854 vetoed Congress's plan to provide land to states for facilities aiding the mentally handicapped. In 1859 President James Buchanan vetoed a congressional attempt to fund agricultural colleges. Both presidents argued that such federal funding was unconstitutional. Lincoln, though, supported a stronger federal role and in 1862 signed the Morrill Act, which provided grants of federal land to establish agricultural colleges.

Highways A new era began in 1916 with federal highway legislation. Matching grants and formulas for distributing funds were among the procedures devised then that became standard practice for decades afterward. To qualify for the aid, states were required to establish a highway department; by 1917, every state had managed to do so. (Highway aid still comprises more than

15 percent of total federal transfers to state and local governments.) It was no coincidence that the highway bill passed just three years after enactment of a federal income tax, which for the first time guaranteed a steady flow of funds into federal coffers.

New Deal, 1950s Coping with economic upheaval during the Depression of the 1930s, President Franklin D. Roosevelt proposed an array of federal programs, many of which were based on grants to states and also to cities. The most sweeping new law was the Social Security Act, which set up programs to benefit dependent children, the blind, and the elderly; these were administered by the states. Annual federal grants quadrupled between 1932 and 1940. By 1950, $2.3 billion was being spent on grants-in-aid.

Although the NEW DEAL clearly changed the framework of federal-state relations, debate about the proper federal role had not ended. Congress spent years in the 1950s arguing about federal aid to elementary and secondary education, a task traditionally handled by state and local governments. Some critics fought any federal aid, while churches insisted that funds also be channeled to parochial schools. The deadlock was broken, ironically, by the Soviet Union's 1957 launching of the first artificial satellite; Congress approved the National Defense Education Act the following year.

Great Society Democratic Presidents John F. KENNEDY and Lyndon B. JOHNSON led Congress on a sweeping expansion of federal welfare programs that required state and local governments to handle billions of additional federal dollars—according to federal rules. "This administration today here and now declares unconditional war on poverty in America," Johnson proclaimed in 1964. Food stamps, urban housing programs, community development, health care for the poor (Medicaid), health care for the elderly (Medicare), and education geared to disadvantaged children (such as Head Start) were among the bills passed in the 1960s and 1970s. Johnson called his policy "creative federalism." *(See* GREAT SOCIETY.*)*

New Federalism President Richard NIXON urged a "new federalism" that would return responsibility to the state and local levels. He wanted to accompany that with an infusion of federal money, which he called "revenue sharing." Congress in 1972 approved the revenue sharing program, which provided virtually unrestricted grants to state and local governments, but it resisted Nixon's efforts to combine most "categorical grant" programs, aimed at specific problems, into "block grants," a move designed to give more flexibility to local administrators.

Reagan Revolution The 1980s brought another attempt at "new federalism," this time by President Ronald Reagan, who argued that "our nation of sovereign states has come dangerously close to becoming one great national government." Reagan saw block grants as the first step in the redirection of money and power to state and local governments. But Congress, anxious to have national policy carried out uniformly in every state and city, resisted major shifts of responsibility back to the local level. As part of his program, Reagan sought sweeping cuts in federal payments to states and cities; Congress cut funding, though not so deeply as Reagan proposed in each annual budget request.

The Reagan years also brought an end to revenue sharing, which between 1973 and 1986 transferred more than $80 billion to state and local governments with few strings attached. More than 39,000 local governments benefited from the program; states did not receive revenue sharing funds after

1980. Revenue sharing money was used to pay police and fire personnel, provide health care to residents, buy library books, build and repair highways, support education, and meet dozens of other needs.   ~

ADDITIONAL READINGS

Elazar, Daniel J. *American Federalism: A View from the States.* 1984.
O'Toole, Lawrence J., Jr., ed. *American Intergovernmental Relations.* 1985.

Steering and Policy Committee.   See LEADERSHIP.

Stennis, John C.

By the time he announced his retirement in 1988, Mississippi Democrat John C. Stennis (1901-) had become an anachronistic figure in the Senate, a link to another era. But his physical frailty never diminished the dignity and rectitude that marked more than forty years of Senate service. His colleagues always held him in high esteem, as they demonstrated when, barely a month after he lost a leg to cancer in late 1984, Stennis returned to the Senate floor in a wheelchair. He was greeted by prolonged applause and embraces from his fellow senators, a display of affection they repeated when he became PRESIDENT PRO TEMPORE in 1987.

Born in 1901 on a Mississippi cotton and cattle farm, Stennis served in the state legislature and as a prosecuting attorney. He then spent ten years on the bench as a circuit judge. Stennis was elected to the Senate in 1947 after the death of Sen. Theodore G. Bilbo, a race-baiting demagogue. Two of the five candidates in the special election copied Bilbo's white supremacist style; Stennis, while ready to preserve "the southern way of life," did not make race the center of his campaign.

Stennis brought a judicial bearing to the Senate. A member of the committee that investigated the conduct of Sen. Joseph R. McCARTHY in 1954, Stennis was the first Democrat to take the Senate floor to denounce him, charging that McCarthy had poured "slush and slime" on the Senate. When the Senate ETHICS Committee was established in 1965, Stennis was immediately chosen to head the panel, even though he had not advocated establishing it. He chaired the committee until 1975.

In 1973 Stennis suffered critical gunshot wounds during a holdup in front of his Washington, D. C. home. He was absent from the Senate for several months.

Stennis voted as a southern Democrat, advocating fiscal conservatism and opposing civil rights legislation. But he was overshadowed by more aggressive southern senators, among them his Mississippi colleague, Sen. James O. Eastland; Stennis was junior senator until Eastland's retirement in December 1978.

Most of Stennis's career was focused on the ARMED SERVICES COMMITTEE, which he chaired from 1969 to 1981. He was also able to promote defense spending on the APPROPRIATIONS COMMITTEE, where he chaired the Defense Subcommittee. Stennis usually supported presidents in their military policies, even when his Democratic colleagues did not. But he also defended congressional prerogatives. In 1971 Stennis introduced WAR POWERS legislation to require congressional approval of sustained military action, and he supported the law enacted two years later over President Richard Nixon's veto. "The decision to make war is too big a decision for one mind to make and too awesome a responsibility for one man to bear," Stennis said. "There must be a collective judgment given and a collective responsibility shared."

When Democrats regained control of the Senate in 1987, Stennis, as the party's senior senator, became president pro tempore. He also became chairman of the Appropriations Committee. "I want to plow a straight furrow," he once said, "right down to the end of my row." ~

Stevens, Thaddeus

Thaddeus Stevens (1792-1868) served in the House of Representatives as a Whig (1849-53) and as a Republican (1859-68). An accomplished orator, Stevens held several important committee chairmanships, and on occasion his power surpassed that of the Speaker. Above all, Stevens hated slavery, and his career was devoted to its eradication and to the punishment of the rebellious southern states.

Before entering national politics, Stevens practiced law, owned a forge, and served in the Pennsylvania state legislature. Once in Congress he allied himself with the Free Soilers, who opposed the spread of slavery to western states. Stevens spoke and voted against the Compromise of 1850 because it failed to prohibit slavery in the territories of Utah and New Mexico. He also opposed the Fugitive Slave Act, which required the return of fugitive slaves to their owners. An uncompromising man, Stevens left Congress in 1853 to protest what he considered to be his party's indecisive stand on slavery.

Returning to the House in 1859, Stevens served as chairman of the WAYS AND MEANS COMMITTEE from 1861 until he became chairman of the new APPROPRIATIONS COMMITTEE in 1865. During the Civil War Stevens controlled the House, unchecked by a weak Republican Speaker.

Stevens often spoke of the South with bitterness and vindictiveness. He objected to Lincoln's plans for RE-CONSTRUCTION, declaring that the South had put itself beyond the protection of the Constitution. Stevens hoped to reduce the South to territorial status, thereby preventing an influx of southern representatives who would almost certainly be Democrats.

When President Andrew Johnson pursued Lincoln's plan for Reconstruction, conservative and radical Republicans joined together to impeach him on the pretext that his firing of Secretary of War Edwin M. Stanton violated the Tenure of Office Act. Stevens was a manager of the case against Johnson. Suffering from ill health and disappointed by Johnson's acquittal, Stevens died in 1868.

He was buried in a biracial cemetery; the inscription on his tombstone states that he chose to be buried there "...that I might illustrate in my death the principles which I advocated through a long life—Equality of Man before his Creator." ~

Structure and Powers

Under the Constitution Congress is charged with carrying out the legislative functions of government. The framers of the Constitution wanted the lawmaking role to be in the hands of a representative body; they considered Congress, the collective name for the SENATE and HOUSE OF REPRESENTATIVES, to be the "first branch" of the U.S. government, the primary maker of national policy. The powers, structure, and procedures of the national legislature, unlike those of the presidency and the judiciary—the other independent branches in the American system of SEPARATION OF POWERS—are outlined in considerable detail.

Checks and Balances Each branch is structured so it may restrain the others' excesses, resulting in a form of institutionalized "checks and balances." And within Congress itself the legislative power is checked in many ways. To a degree the House and Senate are competitors, even when both are controlled by the same party. Each seeks to protect its own turf and prerogatives. The Constitution helps to create the competition—the checks—by giving some powers to the Senate alone, like the powers to approve treaties and confirm presidential nominations, and others to the House, including the authority to originate all revenue-raising bills and, by custom, all appropriations bills.

While competition and conflict are built into the system, cooperation between House and Senate is an essential corollary, because legislation must be passed in identical form by both chambers before it can be sent to the president for his approval or VETO.

A form of checks and balances between branches comes into play once Congress finishes acting on a bill. The president may veto any bill that Congress sends him, forcing legislators to consider the chief executive's views and priorities; however, Congress may override the president's action by a two-thirds vote of both chambers. And the actions of both the legislative and executive branches are at least implicitly checked by the review functions of the national judiciary.

Another form of checks and balances derives from the system of federalism, the countervailing forces of the state and federal governments. Federalism is a factor to be reckoned with in the legislative process. Because members of Congress are elected either by states or by congressional districts within the states, local and regional interests strongly influence how the laws are drafted; this often creates tensions between the House and Senate and between Congress and the executive

The 'First Branch'
The framers of the Constitution considered Congress to be the "first branch" of the U.S. government, the primary maker of national policy. In modern times the president has assumed the lead role.

branch. Members are seldom dependent on their national party apparatus for their election. Senators or representatives who are popular back home usually cannot be forced to heed the wishes of the president or their party's congressional leaders. *(See* STATES AND CONGRESS.*)*

Congress's Many Roles Congress by design is untidy, unwieldy, and unrestrained. But an independent, decentralized, and deliberative legislature is just what the drafters of Article I had in mind. Members' constituents are not united on most issues most of the time, and a halting, indecisive Congress usually mirrors the public at large.

The framers of the Constitution did not look upon efficiency in lawmaking as the primary goal. Sensitive to what they viewed as the denial of basic human rights under British rule, and other failings of eighteenth-century governments, they were more concerned with ensuring individual rights and liberties. Within the federal government they feared the potential excesses or domination of one branch over the others, and in Congress the domination of a majority over the minority.

The Constitution, then, provides the framework of a complicated system of government. Some of the complexities become quickly apparent when tracing the steps involved in the LEGISLATIVE PROCESS.

Legislation must follow an intricate course before it can become law. Each step presents potential barriers to passage and gives legislators opportunities to kill or modify bills or provisions they oppose. Many experts on Congress have observed that the legislative process resembles an "obstacle course" that favors the opponents of legislation over the proponents. There are many points at which bills can be stymied or delayed and very few effective tools for speeding passage through Congress, particularly when members have strong differences over issues. But while opponents have the upper hand in most situations, members also are under great pressure to get legislation enacted, especially programs in the domestic field that can benefit their districts, states, or regions—a public works project, for example, or a Navy shipbuilding contract. Therefore, bargaining, compromise, and LOGROLLING are necessary to offset the institutional bias against speedy enactment of bills.

President as Legislative Leader The modern president plays the principal role in setting the legislative agenda. Congress expects the White House to submit proposals for new laws dealing with the whole spectrum of foreign and domestic policy. When existing programs come up for renewal, Congress generally waits for the executive branch to present its recommendations before setting the legislative wheels in motion. Though the Constitution implies that the president should play the leading role, this was not the general practice during the nineteenth century.

The president uses a variety of vehicles and forums to present his program to Congress and the nation. Best known is the annual STATE OF THE UNION address, which is a constitutional requirement. Article II, Section 3 directs the president periodically "to give to the Congress Information of the State of the Union, and recommend to their Consideration such Measures as he shall judge necessary and expedient."

Equally important is the president's annual budget message, with its accompanying documents. That message contains many of the president's legislative goals for the coming year, as well as his requests for money to run the federal government. The agenda also is shaped by periodic messages and statements proposing new measures or changes in pending bills. Even presidential veto messages may contain recommendations for future legislation.

Structure
The legislative branch is bicameral, meaning that it consists of two houses, or chambers. The terms of service in the House and Senate differ. Representatives are elected for two-year terms, senators for six years. Before adoption of the Seventeenth Amendment to the Constitution in 1913, senators were elected by their state legislatures. (See DIRECT ELECTION OF SENATORS.)

Senators represent entire states; House members represent population-based districts within the states. States having very small populations relative to the others qualify for only one representative in the House. For these, the entire state is the congressional district and is referred to as an at-large district. In the 100th Congress (1987-89) there were six at-large districts. Congress has passed a law prohibiting House members from being elected at large in states having more than one representative.

The traditional view has been that House members more closely represent the people than do senators because of their short two-year terms and smaller constituencies. While the greater frequency with which members of the House must face reelection does tend to force representatives to view their roles somewhat differently from senators, this distinction is fast disappearing. The pervasive influence of television today—including gavel-to-gavel coverage of both Senate and House floor debates—and other media coverage, and the ease with which members can return to their states and districts, make senators and representatives equally accessible to the public and aware of the views of the citizens they represent. Of course, senators already had been drawn closer to their constituents when they became subject to direct election.

The complexities of the legislative

process require Congress to operate through elaborate rules as well as informal practices that have been refined, modified, and changed over the years. Except where the Constitution delineates the powers and parliamentary procedures, each chamber has developed its own set of RULES from the body of traditions and precedents that has developed during 200 years of legislating. Size alone accounts for many of the differences in the organization of the two bodies and in the rules and customs each has adopted. The House requires a more formal structure and detailed rules; the smaller Senate legislates in an informal setting and may not follow its formal rules if it prefers not to.

Qualifications The Constitution sets only three qualifications for membership in Congress. They are:
- Age—A House member must be at least twenty-five years old, a senator at least thirty.
- U.S. citizenship—A House member must have been a citizen for at least seven years, a senator for at least nine.
- Residency—A senator or representative must be a resident of the state from which he is elected.

Since adoption of the Twentieth Amendment in 1933, members' terms have begun on January 3 of the year following their election. That amendment also made January 3 the beginning of each new two-year term of Congress and January 20 the date that newly elected presidents take office. *(See* TERMS AND SESSIONS OF CONGRESS; LAME-DUCK AMENDMENT.*)*

The original constitutional language regulating when sessions of Congress began, and the precedents Congress followed in its first 140 years, proved inefficient for timely lawmaking and unrepresentative of the most recent general-election results.

Elections are held on the first Tuesday following the first Monday in

Shared Powers
Congress most clearly shares its powers with the executive branch in the field of foreign affairs. During a 1987 summit meeting with President Ronald Reagan, Soviet leader Mikhail Gorbachev, right, took time out to confer with members of Congress.

November in even-numbered years.

Size The Senate, as mandated by the Constitution, consists of two senators from each state. Senators' terms are staggered. Only thirty-three or thirty-four Senate seats—one-third of the membership—are at stake in each biennial general election. For this reason the Senate considers itself a continuing body, and its rules continue in effect from one Congress to the next. The House adopts its rules at the beginning of each Congress.

The size of the House is determined by members of Congress themselves, within certain constitutional prescriptions. Throughout the nineteenth century the membership of the House was increased to reflect the growth of the nation's population and the addition of new states to the Union. In 1910 the size of the House was set at 435 members and it has remained at 435 ever since, except for a brief period (1959-63) after Alaska and Hawaii were admitted to statehood, when it was increased to 437.

The size of each state's House delegation is determined by the results of the decennial census. The Constitution specifies that House seats must be reapportioned among the states after every census to reflect population growth and shifts in population from one state to another in the ten-year interval since the last census. (There was no reapportionment after the 1920 census because Congress could not agree on any plan to reapportion House seats.) Ever since the House decided to keep its membership at 435, REAPPORTIONMENT has resulted in some states gaining seats at the expense of others. After the reapportionment following the 1980 census, House districts averaged about 520,000 constituents.

In addition to its 435 voting members, the House has five nonvoting DELEGATES. They represent the District of Columbia, Puerto Rico, the Virgin Islands, Guam, and American Samoa.

Powers of Congress

The many explicit powers of Congress enumerated in the Constitution reflect in part the Founding Fathers' experience with the woefully weak Congress under the Articles of Confederation, the nation's original plan of government. Under the Articles Congress was practically powerless to protect the national interest because of its inability to limit encroachment on the federal government's authority by the thirteen independent states. The Constitution's detailed, precise enumeration of many of Congress's powers reflects the fears and distrust between the various states and blocs of states at the time the document was drafted. Though these powers are extensive, most of them are shared with the other two branches, particularly the executive. Thus the Constitution really established a system not of separate powers, but one of separate institutions sharing powers and functions.

The Tenth Amendment specifies that powers not expressly delegated to Congress or the other branches, nor prohibited by the Constitution, are reserved to the states or to the people.

Domestic Powers Foremost among Congress's powers, enumerated principally in Article I, Section 8, is the right "to lay and collect taxes, duties, imposts and excises, to pay the debts [and] . . . to borrow money on the credit of the United States." Section 9 stipulates that no federal funds can be spent except "in consequence of appropriations made by law. . . ." Three key powers are involved here: taxing, borrowing, and spending. They are known collectively as the power of the PURSE.

The bulk of the time members spend on legislative work is occupied with measures that either directly or indirectly involve these three powers. Although there are certain limitations on how Congress can legislate under these powers, raising and spending money, or committing the federal government to spend money in the future, lie at the heart of congressional decision making. *(See* BUDGET PROCESS.*)*

Congress also is charged with providing for the "general welfare." These two words have provided the underpinning for the whole list of public assistance programs enacted by the modern Congress that are taken for granted today: Social Security, agricultural subsidies, workers' unemployment and disability insurance, food stamps, Medicare and Medicaid, and many other programs.

Also very important is Congress's power to regulate foreign and domestic COMMERCE. The power to regulate foreign trade through tariffs, import quotas, and licenses and trade embargoes has been vigorously exerted since the earliest days of the Republic. It is in the area of domestic commerce that Congress has vastly expanded its powers to cope with national problems in areas never imagined by the Founding Fathers.

The Constitution simply states that Congress shall have the power to regulate commerce with foreign countries "and among the several states. . . ." This general and rather innocuous language gave Congress the latitude it needed, beginning in the 1880s, to expand its power over commerce to meet the needs of an increasingly industrialized and urbanized society. In the early and mid-nineteenth century the Supreme Court accepted congressional regulation of interstate commerce, but viewed this power narrowly. It accepted regulation of common carriers such as the railroads, but not private property rights, states' rights, and most businesses, or social evils such as child labor. Only in the late 1930s and 1940s did the Court embrace Congress's broad interpretation of interstate commerce to include business activity, even where it had only an indirect effect on inter-

state commerce. The power was expanded further in the 1960s to deal with racial discrimination and other social problems and in the 1970s to encompass conservation and environmental issues. Now, congressional power in this area is practically limitless.

Congress sets the rules conferring citizenship on foreign-born persons as well as rules for their denaturalization, and it regulates the admission into the country and the deportation of aliens. Congressional power extends to bankruptcy, patent and copyright issues, regulation of the U.S. currency, the right to set standard weights and measures, and authority to establish a national postal system.

Foreign Policy Powers   It is in foreign affairs that Congress most clearly shares its powers with the executive branch. The Constitution presupposes that the two branches will maintain a delicate balance in exercising their foreign policy prerogatives. Nevertheless, the scope of and limits on Congress's power in the formulation of U.S. foreign and defense policies are still vigorously debated by both branches today. The extent of Congress's involvement in and influence over foreign policy has varied throughout American history. Since the early years of the Vietnam War in the 1960s, Congress and the White House have actively competed with each other for control of foreign policy.

Certain specific foreign policy powers granted to Congress are not disputed. These include: the power to raise, support, and regulate the armed forces; the power to declare war and, through its power of the purse, to finance or withhold financing for U.S. participation in foreign wars; and the requirement that the Senate give its consent to all treaties and executive branch nominations of diplomatic officials.

Although these powers have been important in ensuring that the legislative branch would remain an independent force in U.S. foreign affairs, their role in some cases has been altered or diminished by international developments since World War I.

Probably the most important factor is that the power of Congress to declare war has been drastically eroded; perhaps it is now obsolete. The nuclear age, when decisions about war must be made in minutes, rather than in days or weeks, makes the power of the national legislature to declare war seem impractical. Presidents in the post-World War II period have intervened with U.S. armed forces without first asking Congress's consent. World War II was the last in which Congress exercised its power to declare war. Since then American military forces have engaged in several major armed conflicts, including Korea and Vietnam.

Reacting to its inability to stem or, ultimately, end U.S. involvement in the Vietnam War in the 1960s and early 1970s, Congress in 1973 enacted the War Powers Resolution, over President Richard NIXON's veto, in an effort to reinvigorate its war-making—or war-curtailing—power. The effectiveness of that measure remained unclear in 1988.

Nor has congressional control of the purse strings been very effective in preventing U.S. armed intervention abroad. Once presidential decisions are made deploying U.S. military personnel overseas in hostile situations, it is difficult for Congress to force a halt to such operations, and possibly jeopardize the lives of Americans stationed in those areas. Congress did, however, use the power of the purse to wind down the Vietnam War. *(See WAR POWERS.)*

Another factor altering Congress's foreign policy powers has been the increasing reliance on executive agreements—compacts with other nations informally drawn up and agreed to by the executive branch alone, without any requirement for Senate consent. In certain areas of U.S. foreign policy, executive agreements have largely replaced treaties. *(See TREATY RATIFICATION.)*

While some of Congress's formal constitutional powers in foreign affairs have waned in importance, lawmakers' influence in this field has greatly expanded in other ways. Congressional backing is indispensable for the array of foreign economic and military aid and international lending programs the United States launched after World War II. These have expanded greatly in the intervening years, giving Congress enormous leverage over presidential policies. For example, when Congress approves such aid programs, it often writes laws giving itself a voice on how they are funded and administered, and mandating what actions the White House can and cannot take.

Institutional Powers Congress employs a wealth of institutional powers to buttress its position as an equal branch of government.

In the procedure for amending the Constitution, Congress and the states act alone; the president may propose constitutional amendments, but he has no formal role in their ratification. Article V provides that Congress, "whenever two-thirds of both Houses shall deem it necessary, shall propose ... " amendments to the Constitution, which take effect when ratified by three-fourths of the states. Alternatively, the states themselves, if two-thirds agree, can call a constitutional convention to propose amendments. However, the latter route has never been used successfully. *(See CONSTITUTIONAL AMENDMENTS.)*

The Senate alone possesses the key power to confirm or reject presidential appointments to many government positions. Most are confirmed routinely, but the few hundred top-level appointments requiring confirmation give the Senate a potent policy voice. Besides cabinet and subcabinet appointments, the Senate's advice and consent power covers nominees for the Supreme Court, and for the lower courts; top-level diplomatic and military appointments; and nominees for federal regulatory agencies and boards. *(See* APPOINTMENT POWER.*)*

The power to conduct INVESTIGATIONS is not mentioned in the Constitution. It is an implied power, derived from the introductory clause in Article I declaring that "all legislative Powers herein granted shall be vested" in Congress. Investigations can cover the entire range of congressional activity. They are used to review the effectiveness of existing laws, to assess the need for new ones, and to probe into government waste, inefficiency, and corruption.

Congress is also charged with making the "Rules for the Government." It can add or abolish federal agencies and departments and can even alter the size of the Supreme Court. Indeed, the entire federal court structure was established by Congress. The power to admit new states into the Union also is conferred on Congress.

Several congressional powers directly affect the presidency. Congress is given the duty, now largely ceremonial, of counting the electoral votes for president and vice president after every election and formally announcing the winners. More important is the House's power to choose the president, and the Senate's power to choose the vice president, in the event no candidate receives a clear majority of the vote. *(See* ELECTING THE PRESIDENT.*)*

The Twentieth and Twenty-fifth Amendments also give Congress powers dealing with PRESIDENTIAL DISABILITY AND SUCCESSION, including the power to confirm presidential choices to fill vacancies in the vice presidency.

The House and Senate share the power to impeach the president and other officials and remove them from office for treason, bribery, or other "high crimes and misdemeanors."

Though rarely used, IMPEACHMENT is perhaps Congress's most formidable weapon against the executive branch. The House draws up impeachment charges; the Senate acts as judge and jury.

Finally, the Constitution declares that Congress may "make all laws which shall be necessary and proper for carrying into Execution the foregoing Powers. . . ." This catchall provision was originally intended to help Congress exercise the powers specifically enumerated in the Constitution. It was broadly defined by the Supreme Court in 1819 in the case of *McCulloch v. Maryland.* In practice, the provision has allowed Congress to extend its role and has led to far-reaching debates over the scope of congressional powers.   ~

ADDITIONAL READINGS

Davidson, Roger H., and Walter J. Oleszek. *Congress and Its Members.* 2d ed. 1985.
Josephy, Alvin M., Jr. *On the Hill: A History of the American Congress.* 1981.
Wilson, Woodrow. *Congressional Government.* 1885, reprint 1981.

Subpoena Power

The power to issue subpoenas enables congressional committees to compel the cooperation of reluctant witnesses. A subpoena is a legal order that requires a witness to testify or to produce documents upon demand of a committee. A witness who refuses may be cited for CONTEMPT OF CONGRESS and prosecuted in the courts. Committees of both the Senate and the House of Representatives routinely issue subpoenas as part of their INVESTIGATIONS.

The Supreme Court has rebuffed challenges to Congress's subpoena power. "Issuance of subpoenas . . . has long been held to be a legitimate use by

Congress of its power to investigate," the court wrote in 1927. "Experience has taught that mere requests for ... information often are unavailing."   ∼

Substitute

When a motion or amendment is pending in the House or Senate, legislators can offer a substitute proposal dealing with the same subject. Under parliamentary rules, if a substitute is accepted, it supplants the original amendment, thus killing it. Also possible is an "amendment in the nature of a substitute," which replaces the entire text of a bill with a new version.

Substitute bills have been more frequent in the House, where major legislation is often handled by more than one committee. The separate committees work out their differences and draft a compromise bill, which is handled on the floor as a substitute. (See LEGISLATIVE PROCESS.)   ∼

Sumner, Charles

Charles Sumner (1811-74) served as a senator from Massachusetts at the time of the Civil War. His energies were directed toward the outlawing of slavery and later the radical reconstruction of the South. Like his Radical Republican colleagues, Sumner supported the impeachment of President Andrew Johnson. (See RECONSTRUCTION ERA.)

Sumner was a practicing lawyer when Massachusetts Democrats and Free Soilers proposed him as a candidate for the Senate. Sumner remained a Democrat until 1857, when he became a Republican. Upon entering the Senate in 1851, Sumner began speaking out against slavery. His assertion that he would not comply with the Fugitive Slave Act, which required the return of escaped slaves to their owners, provoked an unsuccessful Senate petition to expel him.

Attack in Senate

Debates in the Senate on matters pertaining to slavery were fiery and personal. In 1856, while addressing the status of Kansas, Sumner vilified many—including Illinois Sen. Stephen A. DOUGLAS, a Popular Sovereignty Democrat, whom he called a "noisome, squat and nameless animal...." Two days after the speech, while Sumner was sitting at his desk on the Senate floor, he was bludgeoned by a walking stick wielded by Rep. Preston S. Brooks, a States Rights Democrat from South Carolina, whose uncle Sumner had criticized. It took Sumner three years to recover from his injuries.

Sumner's hatred of slavery also led him to vindictiveness against the South. He believed that the Confederates had relinquished their right to constitutional protections. Disliking the more moderate Reconstruction program of Abraham Lincoln and Andrew Johnson, Sumner advocated complete congressional control over the process. He played a major role in the impeachment of Johnson, saying that he would, if he could, vote on the charges: "Guilty of all and infinitely more." (See JOHNSON IMPEACHMENT EFFORT.)

In 1861 Sumner was made chairman of the FOREIGN RELATIONS Committee. As such, he was involved in the *Trent* affair, when Confederate agents were seized from a British ship. Later, Sumner was so upset by President Ulysses S. Grant's plan to annex Santo Domingo that he was removed as chairman of the committee. Republicans felt they needed a chairman who was at least speaking to the president and the secretary of state.

Sumner died in 1874 while still a member of the Senate.   ∼

Supreme Court

Entrusted by the Constitution with "the judicial Power of the United States," the Supreme Court is the world's most influential tribunal. This power is political as well as legal, for the Supreme Court functions as both the nation's highest court of appeals and the ultimate interpreter of the Constitution. Many key parts of the Constitution are vague or ambiguous, leaving room for a wide range of opinions by Court members. As a result, the Court through its rulings has often surpassed the federal government's executive and legislative branches in shaping the course of American politics. Two such rulings among many are *Brown v. Board of Education* (1954), which outlawed racial segregation in public schools, and *Roe v. Wade* (1973), which legalized abortion in most instances.

Supreme Court justices are appointed by the president and confirmed by the Senate. Prior judicial service is not required, although most nominees in recent decades have had such experience. Indeed, some of the most highly regarded justices had never before sat on a court. The list includes five chief justices of the United States—John Marshall, Roger Brooke Taney, Charles Evans Hughes, Harlan Fiske Stone, and Earl Warren.

Of the federal government's three branches, the Supreme Court has the newest home. Its building in the Greek classical style at One First Street N.E.—facing the Capitol to the west and the Library of Congress's main Jefferson Building to the south—opened in 1935.

Early Quarters

Before 1935, however, the Court held its sessions in about a dozen different places. Some of its early courtrooms

The Supreme Court Chamber

were shared with other tribunals. After the federal government moved to Washington in 1801, the Court sat in various rooms of the Capitol—and, some sources say, in two local taverns as well.

A resolution adopted by Congress on January 23, 1801, provided that "leave be given to the Commissioners of the City of Washington to use one of the rooms on the first floor of the Capitol for holding the present session of the Supreme Court of the United States." The room chosen for the purpose was a chamber measuring only twenty-four by thirty feet. It was the first of a series of makeshift quarters assigned to the Court before the First Street building was completed more than a century later.

Because the Capitol's north wing was in need of renovation, the Court moved in 1808 into a library formerly occupied by the House of Representatives. According to Capitol Architect Benjamin H. Latrobe, the Court's 1809 sessions took place at Long's Tavern, where the main building of the Library of Congress now stands. The following year, the Court returned to the Capitol and met in a room especially designed

VISITING THE SUPREME COURT

The Supreme Court building comprises six levels, only two of which are accessible to the public. The basement contains a parking garage, a printing press, and offices for security guards and maintenance personnel. A public information office is on the ground floor, while the courtroom itself is on the main floor. The second floor contains the justices' dining rooms and library as well as various offices; the third floor, the Court library; and the fourth floor, the gym and storage areas.

From October to the end of April, the Court hears oral arguments Monday through Wednesday for about two weeks a month. These sessions begin at 10 a.m. and continue until 3 p.m., with a one-hour recess starting at noon. They are open to the public on a first-come, first-served basis.

Visitors may inspect the Supreme Court chamber at any time the Court is not in session. Historical exhibits and a free motion picture on how the Court works also are available throughout the year. The Supreme Court building is open from 9 a.m. to 4:30 p.m. Monday through Friday, except for legal holidays. When the Court is not in session, lectures are given in the courtroom every hour on the half hour between 9:30 a.m. and 3:30 p.m.

for it, beneath the Senate chamber.

There the court remained until the Capitol was burned by the British on August 24, 1814, during the War of 1812. The justices then moved to the temporary "Brick Capitol" at the site of the present Supreme Court building and then—during the two years that the Capitol was being restored—to a rented house that subsequently became Bell Tavern. The Court returned to the Capitol for its February 1817 term and occupied an undestroyed section in the north wing until 1819, when its regular quarters beneath the Senate were ready to be occupied again.

In 1860, with the Civil War imminent, the Court moved from the basement to the old Senate chamber on the first floor of the Capitol. The new courtroom was situated on the east side of the main corridor between the Rotunda and the current Senate chamber. The large room, with a dozen anterooms for office space and storage, was by far the most roomy and pleasing space the Court had occupied. The galleries had been removed after the Senate's departure, giving the room a newfound feeling of spaciousness.

Still, none of the justices had individual office space in the Capitol, and each had to provide for his own and his staff's working quarters at a time when adequate accommodations of any sort were difficult to find. The Court nonetheless conducted its business there for seventy-five years, with two minor exceptions in 1898 and 1901.

President William Howard Taft began promoting the idea of a separate building for the Supreme Court about 1912. Taft continued his campaign when he became chief justice of the United States in 1921. At his urging, Congress finally agreed in 1929 and authorized funds for the construction of a permanent home for the Court.

During the construction of the new building, the Court continued to sit in the old Senate chamber. Its last major decision announced there, handed down at the end of the 1934 term, was that striking down President Franklin D. Roosevelt's National Industrial Recovery Act. *(See* NEW DEAL.*)*

Court at Work

Cases come before the Supreme Court in three ways. First, the Constitu-

The Senate and the Court
The president nominates members of the Supreme Court, but they cannot take their seats until they are confirmed by the Senate. On occasion the Senate rejects the president's choice. In 1987 the Senate denied confirmation to Robert H. Bork, shown here as he arrived for hearings of the Senate Judiciary Committee.

tion designates two classes of cases as being in the Court's "original" jurisdiction—in other words, eligible for hearing without prior review by a lower court. Such cases, which account for only a small portion of the total number on the Supreme Court docket, are (1) those in which a state is a party and (2) those involving senior foreign diplomats.

Second, the Supreme Court has authority to hear appeals from the lower federal courts. But while the Supreme Court is required by law to hear certain types of appeals, most cases come before it through a writ of certiorari. In seeking such a writ, a litigant who has lost a case in a lower court petitions the Supreme Court to review the case, setting forth the reasons why review should be granted. The Supreme Court, under its rules, may grant a writ of certiorari by a vote of at least four justices—an exception to the rule that all business be controlled by majority decision. In general, the Court grants certiorari only if the case touches on a question of fundamental public importance. About 90 percent of petitions for certiorari fail to win approval.

Third, the Supreme Court reviews appeals from state supreme courts that present a "substantial federal question." Such questions usually arise when a U.S. constitutional right has been denied in the state courts.

The number of justices on the Supreme Court is fixed by Congress, not the Constitution. Under the Judiciary Act of 1789, Congress created a six-member Court. Congress subsequently varied the Court's size from time to time, but since 1869 the tribunal has consisted of a chief justice and eight associate justices. In early 1937 President Franklin D. Roosevelt proposed that Congress add as many as six justices to the Court, in an effort to obtain more favorable rulings on the constitutionality of New Deal legislation, but his attempt to "pack" the Court failed. (*See* COURTS AND CONGRESS.)

The Supreme Court convenes on the first Monday in October of each year. It usually hears oral arguments for two weeks at a time, at two-week intervals, but the schedule may vary. It usually recesses in late June until the following autumn.

On Friday of a week of argument (and Saturday, if need be) the nine justices meet in closed session. At the Friday conference the cases ready for decision are discussed and voted upon. If the chief justice votes with the majority, he assigns the writing of the majority opinion; if he is in the minority, the senior associate justice voting with the majority makes the assignment. Decisions usually are announced to the public on Mondays, but in recent years the press of business has meant that Tuesdays also have produced a number of important rulings.　　　　　　　～

Suspension of the Rules

The suspension of the rules is a convenient shortcut procedure that the House uses for floor action on routine legislation. By avoiding the regular, time-consuming parliamentary procedures, bills with little or no opposition can be approved quickly.

Debate on legislation considered under suspension of the rules is limited to forty minutes. Floor amendments are prohibited—another reason why this shortcut is so effective. Only one vote to pass the bill is in order; a two-thirds majority of members voting is required for passage.

Mondays and Tuesdays are set aside in the House to bring up bills by motion to suspend the rules. On "suspension" days, the Speaker has the authority to postpone recorded votes until all the bills have been debated, and then vote on them at one time, cutting voting time on each bill to as little as five minutes. A bill that fails to pass under suspension of the rules may be considered later by the regular parliamentary rules used in the House. *(See* LEGISLATIVE PROCESS.*)*

The procedure also is allowed during the last six days of a session and any time there is unanimous consent to do so. The latter route is occasionally used to pass emergency legislation, such as a bill to avert a railway or postal strike.

In the Senate, motions to suspend the rules are rare because they are debatable and thus open to FILIBUSTERS and other delaying tactics. The shortcut procedure also is considered an affront to the committee system. As in the House, a two-thirds vote is needed to pass measures by this method.　　～

Overleaf:
Congressional generations, 1988

Table, Motion to

Motions to table, or to "lay on the table," are used to block or kill amendments or other parliamentary questions. When approved, a tabling motion is considered the final disposition of that issue. One of the most widely used parliamentary procedures, the motion to table is not debatable, and adoption requires a simple majority vote.

Motions to table are used regularly in conjunction with motions to RECONSIDER to confirm a previous legislative action, be it approval or rejection of a bill, amendment, or other parliamentary question. *(See* LEGISLATIVE PROCESS.)

Members of Congress often prefer procedural votes, particularly the motion to table, to direct votes for or against a substantive proposal. By voting to table, they can avoid being recorded directly on a controversial bill or politically sensitive issue. The motion to table often will win more support than a vote to defeat the issue itself.

Motions to table are not used when the House of Representatives considers bills in the COMMITTEE OF THE WHOLE; they are used only after the Committee of the Whole is dissolved and the legislation is returned to the full House.

In the Senate, members who have the floor can use the tabling motion

415

effectively to kill unwelcome amendments without further debate.   ∼

Taft, Robert A.

Robert A. Taft (1889-1953), an Ohio Republican, entered the Senate in 1939. A leader of the conservative wing of the Republican party, Taft generally opposed President Franklin D. Roosevelt's NEW DEAL programs. Prior to the Japanese attack on Pearl Harbor in 1941, he advocated "America first" isolationism.

Taft was extremely intelligent and hard working, although he lacked charisma. In power and authority he was the leading Republican in the Senate from the 1940s to his death. However, it was not until 1953, the year he died, that Taft officially led his Senate colleagues as majority leader.

As the son of President William Howard Taft, Robert Taft was no stranger to politics. He practiced law in Cincinnati and in 1919 went to Paris to help Herbert Hoover (then head of the Food Administration) oversee the distribution of postwar aid to Europe. Shortly after his return, he entered the state legislature, where he stayed until he was elected to the U.S. Senate.

As a senator, Taft approved of only some elements of the New Deal, such as Social Security and public housing. He opposed generous farm subsidies and, until he reversed positions in 1946, federal involvement in education. Taft thought the power of organized labor had become excessive; in 1947 he cosponsored the Taft-Hartley Act, which restricted unions' right to strike.

Taft felt that Europe's problems were its own and spoke out against the lend-lease program, through which the United States helped supply the Allies during World War II. He believed that the only organization capable of pro-

moting world peace would be an international court buttressed by a body of strong international laws. He put little faith in the United Nations and objected to the North Atlantic Treaty Organization. He thought NATO would only antagonize the Soviet Union, which, he believed, had no interest in hegemony over Western Europe.

Earnest and well-briefed, Taft earned the respect of his colleagues. His power was centered in the Senate Policy Committee, which he headed from its inception in 1947. He was a candidate for the Republican presidential nomination in 1940, 1948, and 1952. In 1952 he lost to Dwight D. Eisenhower, to whom he gave his support (after Eisenhower conceded to some general conservative conditions) and his unconditional friendship.   ∼

Tax and Tariff Powers.   See
PURSE, POWER OF.

Taxation Committee, Joint

The principal function of the Joint Taxation Committee is to provide a neutral home for the nonpartisan tax experts who advise both the House WAYS AND MEANS and Senate FINANCE committees. The staff is comprised of more than sixty lawyers, economists, accountants, and other tax specialists.

The joint committee, with five senators and five representatives, is headed by the chairmen of the two tax panels, who rotate as chairman and vice chairman.

The committee, established in 1926, rarely meets. It has no legislative authority, but it does from time to time conduct investigations. One of the most notable was a probe of President Richard NIXON's taxes, undertaken at his request. The committee is also responsi-

ble for approving any tax refunds of more than $200,000, a task that consists of committee staff reviewing decisions made by the Internal Revenue Service.   ∼

Teapot Dome

Teapot Dome is the enduring legacy of Warren G. Harding's presidency (1921-23), a code name for scandal in government. After the disclosures of a long congressional investigation, one member of the president's cabinet, Interior Secretary Albert B. Fall, went to prison for accepting bribes to lease government-owned oil land to favored persons. Teapot Dome was the most prominent of several shady activities going on in Washington at that time, leaving a taint of corruption on the Harding administration.

The name Teapot Dome comes from a sandstone formation, faintly resembling a teapot, that rises well above the sagebrush plains of north-central Wyoming. Deep below the rock outcropping is a reservoir of oil that nature had formed vaguely in the shape of a dome. This underground oil and the land above it make up a tiny portion of the vast federal holdings in the West.

In 1915 President Woodrow Wilson assigned control of Teapot Dome to the Navy Department as a reserve source of fuel for American warships. It was designated Reserve No. 3; two other oil sites, Elk Hills and Buena Vista in California, had already been selected Nos. 1 and 2. The U.S. Navy, spurred by the outbreak of World War I in Europe, was converting its fleet from the use of coal to oil. But the nation's petroleum supply turned out to be far bigger than geologists envisioned at the war's onset, and Teapot Dome did not have to be tapped. However, the Navy feared that private drillers were secretly siphoning oil from the reservoir with their nearby wells.

Certainly, Teapot Dome was coveted by America's fast-growing oil industry. Oil men generally had the support of western lawmakers who clung to the frontier belief that natural resources were to be exploited. Fall was outspoken in that view. Biographer David Stratton has written of him: "His belief in the unrestrained disposition of the public lands was as typically western as his black, broad-brimmed Stetson hat and his love of fine horses." As a young Kentuckian, Fall went to the New Mexico Territory to find fame and fortune. He gained a measure of fame serving with Theodore Roosevelt's Rough Riders in the Spanish-American War. As a rancher and lawyer, his fortune-building was delayed by losses in Mexican mining ventures. In Republican politics he acquired a following and was sent to Washington as a U. S. senator when New Mexico achieved statehood in 1912. He placed Roosevelt's name in nomination for president at the Republican Convention in 1916 and handily won reelection to the Senate in 1918. Upon Harding's presidential victory in 1920, Fall was chosen to run the Interior Department.

He quickly won agreement to bring the naval reserve oil lands under Interior's control. Naval officials wanted to pump out Teapot Dome and store the oil in tanks accessible to the U.S. Pacific Fleet in the event of a war with Japan. However, the Navy had no money to build the tanks, and Congress was in no mood to appropriate it. So Fall devised a plan that was congenial to the Navy. He would lease the land to a driller who, instead of paying royalties on the oil directly to the U.S. Treasury, would issue certificates of equal value. The Navy could exchange the certificates for material to build the oil tanks. In April 1922, acting in secret and without competitive bidding—none was re-

quired—Fall awarded the Teapot Dome oil lease to Harry S. Sinclair, head of the Mammoth Oil Company. Fall had been Sinclair's guest at the Kentucky Derby the previous spring, and he had invited Sinclair to his cherished but somewhat impoverished New Mexico ranch.

To build the storage tanks, Fall received three bids and awarded the contract to Pan-American Petroleum and Transport Company, headed by Edward Doheny, a longtime friend. The contract required the construction not only of storage tanks and loading docks at Pearl Harbor in Hawaii, but also of a refinery at San Pedro, California, and a pipeline from the naval oil reserves to the refinery. Doheny, in return, would receive six million barrels of crude oil and exclusive rights to drill on about 30,000 acres of proven oil lands at Elk Hills.

In all, Fall received about $400,000 from Sinclair and Doheny, and spent most of it to enlarge and improve his ranch. The day after signing the storage-tank contract with Doheny, Fall phoned Doheny with the message that he was "prepared now to receive that loan." Doheny's son promptly delivered $100,000 in cash, in a black bag, to Fall's hotel room in Washington. From Sinclair, Fall received cash, Liberty bonds, and some expensive livestock. Fall insisted that he had accepted only loans and gifts but no bribes.

Senate Investigation

The "loans and gifts" did not come to light until after Fall resigned his Interior post in March 1923 for reasons not entirely clear. Although the first congressional hearing, by the Senate Committee on Public Lands, did not come until late October that year, the committee's investigation had been going on for nearly eighteen months and Fall was aware it was focused on him.

Sen. Reed Smoot, a Utah Republican, was nominally the committee's chairman, but the investigation was conducted by Sen. Thomas J. Walsh, a Montana Democrat, austere in manner and honest in reputation. He took on the task reluctantly but pursued it doggedly. A westerner, he did not share many of the land-policy views of conservationists who were out after Fall. Harry Slattery, a minor Washington official active in the Conservation Association and close to its founder, Gifford Pinchot, supplied Walsh much of his information. Slattery had the ear of Sen. Robert M. LA FOLLETTE, the Wisconsin Republican whose Senate resolution started the investigation. And Walsh tended to listen to La Follette in this matter.

Fall defended himself as a patriot attempting to build up the nation's naval defenses in the only way possible—and in secret lest Japan learn of them. Sinclair refused to answer many of the committee's questions, and Doheny denied any wrongdoing. Except for a blunder by Fall the hearings might have come to nothing. In a letter to Walsh, he lied about the source of the $100,000 that the Dohenys, father and son, had delivered to him. Fall said it was a loan from his millionaire friend Edward B. "Ned" McLean, publisher of the *Washington Post*. McLean initially agreed to say he had lent Fall the money but, upon being subpoenaed to testify, confessed he had not. The hearings continued into the late winter of 1924, and by then Fall's defenses had collapsed.

Trials

That summer, a District of Columbia grand jury indicted Fall, Sinclair, Doheny, and Doheny's son, but the indictments were disallowed on a technicality, and nearly a year passed before others were made. Another year elapsed—by now it was November 1926—before the first trial was held. In that trial a jury acquitted Fall and the elder Doheny of conspiracy to defraud the government. The next March Sinclair became the first defendant to draw a jail sentence—three months for contempt of Congress. That autumn he and Fall went to trial for bribery, but the judge declared a mistrial when a local newspaper reported that Sinclair had arranged to bribe a juror. For this offense he was convicted of contempt of court and sentenced to an additional six months in jail.

The Senate committee by now had obtained additional information and reopened its hearings in January 1928. They continued until May, laying out further incriminating details. Still, at his bribery retrial, Sinclair was found innocent. District of Columbia juries had a reputation for being sympathetic with defendants in government cases. Fall's trial was delayed until the following year because of his ill health, but at length he was convicted of taking a bribe from Doheny—even though Doheny in a separate trial was acquitted on charges of making the bribe. Doheny's son, who carried the black bag with $100,000 to Fall, never went to trial. He had been shot to death by an insane secretary.

Aftermath

After exhausting his appeals, Fall entered the New Mexico Penitentiary in June 1931 and served eleven months. By then the U.S. Supreme Court had nullified his contracts with Sinclair and Doheny, and jurisdiction for Teapot Dome was transferred back to the Navy Department. The Teapot Dome affair had continued under three presidents—Harding, who died in 1923, and his two successors, Calvin Coolidge and Herbert Hoover.

The memory of Teapot Dome lived on. "It is the dome we live under here at the Interior Department," Interior Secretary Stewart Udall told a congressional committee years later, in 1967, explaining that the lesson of Teapot Dome remained alive in the department's business dealings.　～

Television

Congress for years resisted live televised coverage of its daily proceedings, fearful that cameras would prompt grandstanding or erode the dignity of its operations. Now commonplace, the gavel-to-gavel broadcasts of floor action have not caused major changes in the way Congress works. Instead, television coverage has proven politically expedient, as members gain public exposure when national and local news programs air excerpts from floor debates. The broadcasts are also convenient, allowing members to follow floor action from their offices or review a debate they missed.

The House was first to open its chamber to television, in 1979. The Senate held out against the television era until 1986. Even senators who once opposed television applauded the results a year later. "It seems to be an unalloyed success at this point. . . . Our fears were unfounded," said Sen. J. Bennett Johnston, a Louisiana Democrat who had been a vocal opponent. The Senate painted its walls a new color after Kansas Republican Robert Dole complained the old backdrop made senators on TV "look like they're standing in split-pea soup."

Long before broadcasts of floor debate, television had captured dramatic events on Capitol Hill. Presidential STATE OF THE UNION messages were televised from the packed House chamber. Senate committee hearings were opened to cameras several times, enabling viewers to watch the KEFAUVER probe of organized crime and the Army-McCARTHY investigation in the 1950s, testimony on the Vietnam War in the 1960s, and the WATERGATE hearings in 1973. The House banned cameras from committee sessions until 1970; in 1974 it won a large national audience for committee sessions on impeachment of President Richard Nixon. *(See* NIXON IMPEACHMENT EFFORT.*)*

Representatives and senators have also learned to exploit television, consenting to interviews, appearing on news programs, and crafting "photo opportunities" with constituents. Legislators have used the press to lobby internally. "If you want to reach your colleagues, sometimes the best way is to let them see you on TV or read your name in the paper," said Thomas J. Downey, a Democratic representative from New York. Some legislators have even devised a video version of the press release, a prepackaged statement that can be shipped—or beamed via satellite—back to local stations.

Both the House and Senate have special studios equipped with technicians and cameras that legislators can use for interviews or statements—but not for political advertisements. The Democratic and Republican parties also operate separate Capitol Hill studios that legislators can use without restrictions; political campaign spots are often made there.

Floor Proceedings

Recordings of House and Senate floor action are not edited. Each chamber does, however, keep close control over its broadcasts, using cameras owned by Congress and operated by congressional staff. The coverage provides only a limited view of floor action, usually focusing on the rostrum or on the member who is speaking. The cameras are operated by remote control from basement studios under each chamber. Senators speak from their desks; representatives go to one of two lecterns in the House well or use the tables on each side of the central aisle. When votes are in progress, the cameras show the full chamber, with information about the vote superimposed on the screen. Recordings of House and Senate floor action cannot be used for

Window on Congress
Television coverage of floor proceedings has made Congress more accessible to the public. Gavel-to-gavel coverage is provided by the Cable Satellite Public Affairs Network (C-SPAN). House proceedings have been televised since 1979. The Senate did not enter the television era until 1986.

political or commercial purposes.

Although networks and local television stations use excerpts from the recordings, the only gavel-to-gavel coverage is on a cable network, Cable Satellite Public Affairs Network (C-SPAN). In addition to its floor coverage, C-SPAN selectively broadcasts other major congressional events—committee hearings, press conferences, and the like. By the mid-1980s more than 2,300 cable systems were carrying C-SPAN, giving Congress a potential audience of 25.5 million households. Only about 9 million of those households received the Senate coverage, however; by the time it was added in 1986, many cable television networks no longer had a channel available.

Entering the TV Era

The first formal proposal to televise floor proceedings was made in the 1940s by then-senator Claude Pepper, a Florida Democrat. But opponents resisted introducing television—or even radio—into the House and Senate chambers. They warned broadcasts would expose members to embarrassment or grandstanding by colleagues.

House The House first allowed cameras in its chamber in 1947 to record its opening session. For three decades after that, though, television coverage was permitted only for special joint sessions. A key opponent of broadcasts was Speaker Sam RAYBURN, who in 1952 banned cameras even from House committee sessions, a dictum that subsequent Speakers left in place.

Reforms of overall legislative procedure in 1970 included a new ruling that let each committee decide whether to televise its sessions. By the time Thomas P. O'NEILL, Jr., became Speaker in 1977, the House included a new generation of members who were comfortable with television and eager to invite coverage of floor debate. Members quickly agreed to a ninety-day test of a closed-circuit system.

The 1977 test, which lasted seven months, was considered successful, and the House endorsed gavel-to-gavel coverage by a lopsided vote later that year. In 1978 the House agreed to let broadcasters tap into its audio system. By early 1979 the House had invested $1.2 million in modern cameras, microphones, and lighting. Efforts by the networks to win access to the chamber for their own cameras failed. The first live House coverage occurred briefly on March 19, 1979. C-SPAN went on the air on April 3.

Controversy about the broadcasts has been rare. In 1984, however, O'Neill angered a group of militant House Republicans when he ordered cameras to pan the chamber, revealing to the television audience that the fiery GOP speakers were talking to an empty House. (House rules give the Speaker control of the broadcast system.) Now cameras routinely show the House chamber during speeches made under SPECIAL ORDERS—a period at the end of each day's session when legislators may address the often-deserted chamber.

Senate Television cameras were first allowed in the Senate chamber in December 1974, when Nelson A. Rockefeller was sworn in as vice president; in 1978 the Senate permitted radio broadcasts of its debate on the Panama Canal treaty.

Despite support from top Democratic and Republican leaders, the Senate spent several more years arguing about broadcasts. Opponents, who threatened to filibuster, argued that television would erode the Senate's historic role as the slower, more deliberative body. "My fundamental objection to television is rooted in my deep concern that [it] will result in an increase in political expediency at the expense of statesmanship," said Russell B. LONG, a veteran Louisiana Democrat and longtime opponent of Senate TV. But proponents of television prevailed, and a two-month experiment began June 2, 1986. At the end of July, the Senate voted by a four-to-one margin to keep the TV cameras rolling permanently.   ~

Terms and Sessions of Congress

The meetings of Congress are divided into two-year cycles embracing the two-year period for which representatives are elected. The system is based on constitutional requirements that members of the HOUSE OF REPRESENTATIVES must be elected "every second year" and that Congress must meet at least once each year.

A new term of Congress begins at noon on January 3 in odd-numbered years, following the election of representatives the previous November. It expires, and the next term begins, on January 3 two years later. Each two-year term is known as a "Congress." The Congress that convened in January 1987 was known as the 100th Congress because it was the 100th to convene since the founding of the Republic. It extended until January 3, 1989.

Each Congress has two regular sessions. The first begins in January of the odd-numbered year, and members elected the previous November are sworn in at that time. Because they are elected for two-year terms, all representatives must be sworn in at the beginning of each new Congress. Senators are elected for staggered six-year terms, and only about a third of the SENATE is sworn in every two years. The second regular session of a Congress begins in January of the even-numbered year and may run until a new Congress takes office the following year. (*See* ADJOURNMENT.)

Bills introduced in the first year of a Congress remain alive until that Congress ends; legislative action carries over from session to session. Unfinished measures die at the end of a Congress and must start from scratch in the next. (*See* LEGISLATIVE PROCESS.)

The modern schedule of terms and sessions was established by the Twentieth Amendment to the Constitution in 1933. Until then members of Congress took office on March 4, and Congress met annually in December. When it met in December of an even-numbered year, following the election of its successor, it could remain in session until March 4 of the next year, when the term of the new Congress began. Members who had been defeated for reelection could vote in these short—or lame-duck—sessions, which were characterized by FILIBUS-TERS and other efforts to stall legislative action. The Twentieth Amendment, known as the LAME-DUCK AMENDMENT, established January 3 as the day on which the terms of members of Congress would begin. It also provided that Congress should meet annually on January 3 "unless they shall by law appoint a different day." Congress frequently takes advantage of that option and convenes later in the month.

The Twentieth Amendment failed to eliminate postelection sessions. Seven were held between 1948 and 1988. They were called either by Congress itself or by the president, who has authority under the Constitution to convene special sessions of Congress. ∼

Tie Votes.   See VOTING.

Treaty-Making Power

Under the Constitution, the president and the Senate share the power to make treaties with other countries. Although the precise division of labor is ambiguous, the treaty clause has been interpreted to give the president the sole authority to conduct negotiations with foreign governments on treaties and other international agreements. The Senate has the power to approve, amend, or reject treaties once they are formally submitted to it by the president. The House of Representatives has no authority over treaties, although efforts are sometimes made there to block or change a treaty by withholding funds needed to carry out its terms.

For much of the nation's first 200 years, the Senate's treaty powers were a major source of congressional authority over foreign affairs. Beginning with the first treaty it approved—the Jay Treaty with Great Britain in 1795—the Senate has regularly used its approval power to force changes in international agreements. On a few occasions the Senate has rejected major treaties—notably the 1919 Treaty of Versailles, which formally concluded World War I and established the League of Nations.

Ratification Process

The Senate approves a treaty by adopting a resolution consenting to the treaty's ratification, or final confirmation, by the president. Once the president submits a treaty to the Senate, it remains before the Senate until it is approved or rejected or until the president requests its return and the Senate agrees to withdraw it. Senate consideration of a treaty is open to presidential discretion at several points. The president may refuse to submit a treaty; he may withdraw it after it has been submitted; or he may refuse to ratify it even after the Senate has given its consent.

The Foreign Relations Committee has jurisdiction over all treaties, even if an agreement covers a subject that is not under the committee's usual jurisdiction. To win Senate approval a treaty must have the support of two-thirds of voting senators. Once approved by the Senate and ratified by the president, the terms of a treaty become the law of the land, as legally valid as any legislation.

Between the founding of the Republic and 1988, the full Senate rejected outright only twenty treaties. The most recent was an agreement on international air traffic, which failed to win a two-thirds majority in 1983. The Senate, however, uses other means to thwart treaties besides rejection. One study found that between 1789 and 1929 about 900 treaties were approved by the Senate, but another 200 were

Henry Cabot Lodge

rejected or amended in ways that made them unacceptable to the president or the other parties.

Although there are no provisions in the Constitution pertaining to treaty amendments, the Senate has claimed the authority since 1795, when it consented to ratification of the Jay Treaty only on condition that an additional article be negotiated. Since then, scores of treaties have been subjected to amendments, reservations, conditions, or qualifications.

A Senate amendment to a treaty, if it is accepted by the president and the other parties to the treaty, changes it for all parties. Instead of amending a treaty, the Senate may add a reservation, which limits only the treaty obligation of the United States. A reservation, however, may be so significant that the other parties to the treaty may file similar reservations or refuse to ratify the treaty. In many cases the Senate adds relatively minor "understandings," or subtle interpretations of treaty language, which usually do not significantly affect the substance of the treaty and do not require any additional negotiations with the other parties to the treaty.

The Senate's assertion of its treaty authority sometimes is criticized by those who see it as representing excessive interference in the president's foreign policy powers. Efforts have been made over the years to amend the Constitution to reduce the two-thirds vote required for ratification to a simple majority or to include the House in the ratification process.

None of these attempts have succeeded. In the 1950s Sen. John W. Bricker, an Ohio Republican, led an effort with the opposite aim: to curb the president's treaty-making authority. Bricker's proposed constitutional amendment would have provided that a treaty's provisions take effect only when implemented through separate legislation passed by Congress. The amendment provoked heated debate during President Dwight D. Eisenhower's first term but was rejected by the Senate by a one-vote margin in 1954.

History

The division of authority over treaties was a subject of considerable debate during the Constitutional Convention. The compromise language that finally resulted was ambiguous on a number of points, which set the stage for several disputes over the treaty-making authority. The Senate established almost immediately its authority to amend treaties. But was it entitled to offer the president advice during the course of treaty negotiations? Could the Senate initiate treaty talks? Did it have the right to confirm, and thus to some extent control, presidentially appointed negotiators?

In general, most of these and similar issues have been resolved in favor of the president. The Senate's role is basically limited to considering treaties submitted by the president. However, twentieth century presidents frequently have found it politically advisable to consult informally with key senators during the course of treaty negotiations to try to ensure that the prospective agreement has broad support in the Senate.

Despite the increased use of executive agreements, disputes between the president and Congress over foreign policy issues are frequently played out during debates on treaties. Perhaps the most dramatic example was the Senate's rejection of the Treaty of Versailles, ending World War I. The treaty, worked out by President Woodrow Wilson and the leaders of the other nations that had defeated Germany, included provisions establishing a League of Nations for the resolution of international disputes. A faction of the Senate, led by Foreign Relations Committee Chairman Henry Cabot LODGE, a Massachusetts Republican, strongly opposed the part

of the treaty providing for U.S. membership in the League. Lodge proposed "reservations" making clear that membership in the League would not lead to encroachment on the sovereignty of the United States or the powers of Congress. Wilson was adamantly opposed to any changes, however, and the failure of his administration to reach a compromise with key groups of senators led to the final defeat of the treaty.

Partly as a result of the rejection of the Treaty of Versailles and partly because foreign affairs were growing more complicated, presidents began to rely with increasing frequency on the executive agreement to conduct business with other countries. Executive agreements are understandings with other countries that are not subject to Senate approval. Although most executive agreements cover routine matters such as regulation of fishing rights, some have had an important impact on U.S. foreign policy—for example, the World War II summit agreements reached by Allied leaders at Cairo, Tehran, Yalta, and Potsdam.

Some lawmakers have been alarmed at the use of executive agreements, seeing them as presidential usurpation of the Senate's treaty power. However, the treaty power continues to play a significant role in major foreign policy issues, particularly in shaping the debate on arms control agreements. ~

ADDITIONAL READINGS

Crabb, Cecil V., Jr., and Pat M. Holt. *Invitation to Struggle.* 3d. ed. 1988.
Fisher, Louis. *Constitutional Conflicts Between Congress and the President.* 1985.

Truman, Harry S

Unpretentious and unassuming, Harry S Truman (1884-1972) repre-

Harry S Truman

sented Missouri in the Senate from 1935 to 1945. Truman's diligence and honesty as the head of a Senate INVESTIGATION of defense programs drew national attention and led to his selection as President Franklin D. Roosevelt's running mate in 1944. Truman had served as VICE PRESIDENT less than four months when Roosevelt died and Truman assumed the presidency.

Truman's career began in Missouri's local Democratic politics. After years as a farmer and military service in World War I, Truman was elected to a county court judgeship. The job was nonjudicial; he was responsible for the maintenance of county roads and buildings. Truman in part owed his election to Kansas City's corrupt political machine run by Thomas Pendergast. It was Pendergast who in 1934 persuaded Truman not to run for the House of Representatives but to try instead for a Senate seat. Pendergast's support was a mixed blessing. While it made Truman's political career possible, it also alienated many supporters.

After joining the Senate in 1935, Truman served on the APPROPRIATIONS and Interstate COMMERCE committees and compiled a voting record support-

ing the NEW DEAL. In 1941 he traveled around the country to visit defense industries and concluded there were abuses in defense contracting and in the siting of defense plants. He succeeded in setting up the Senate Special Committee to Investigate the National Defense Program with himself as chairman. Known as the Truman Committee, the panel set about uncovering and correcting waste and abuse in defense preparations for World War II. Truman's role on the committee earned him national prominence and the gratitude of Roosevelt. In later years Truman said he was genuinely surprised to be selected as Roosevelt's running mate in 1944.

Truman's experience as a senator and his native good sense and diligence helped ease his transition to the presidency when Roosevelt died in 1945. After finishing Roosevelt's term, Truman was elected to the presidency in his own right in 1948. As president he oversaw the use of the atomic bomb against the Japanese, the end of World War II, the Marshall Plan for postwar European recovery, and the establishment of the North Atlantic Treaty Organization. His domestic program followed the lines of the New Deal and was named the Fair Deal. Truman retired from public life in 1953 at the end of his first full term as president.   ~

Un-American Activities Committee.   See INVESTIGATIONS.

Unanimous Consent Agreement

The Senate has no procedure equivalent to the formal House RULE that governs floor consideration of legislation, but senators often agree to restrict amendments, limit the time allowed for debate, and schedule votes for specific times. The device they use to expedite business is called a unanimous consent agreement. Senate leaders from both parties work out such agreements, which are then formally proposed on the Senate floor. Because a single objection from a senator can prevent unanimous consent, the leaders are careful to accommodate even minor objections. Once reached, an agreement is binding on senators unless it is changed by unanimous consent. For major legislation the details of a proposed agreement, which can be quite specific, are written and circulated to members in advance. *(See* LEADERSHIP; LEGISLATIVE PROCESS.*)*

In both the House and Senate, unanimous consent is frequently used for minor matters. A senator or representative will say, "I ask unanimous consent that. . ." and make the request. A legislator might ask to add additional material to the *CONGRESSIONAL RECORD*, or seek permission to have a staff aide on the floor during debate. Such requests are handled routinely, and objections are extremely rare.   ~

Underwood, Oscar W.

Alabama Democrat Oscar W. Underwood (1862-1929) served in the House of Representatives from 1895 to 1915, except for one brief interlude in 1896-97. In 1915 he moved to the Senate, where he served until 1927. Underwood benefited from a House revolt against the autocratic rule of Speaker Joseph G. CANNON, an Illinois Republican, in 1910. When rules changes weakened the Speaker's authority, Underwood became the de facto ruler of the House.

Underwood was practicing law in Birmingham, Alabama, when he first ran for the House in 1894. He won but served only until June 1896, when he was replaced by his opponent. Undaunted, he ran again that year and won.

Underwood's particular legislative interest was tariffs. The Underwood Tariff Act of 1913 reduced protective tariffs on most imported goods; it also established the modern income tax system.

In 1910, after years of suffering under Speaker Cannon's despotic rule, a coalition of Democrats and Republicans changed House rules to strip the Speaker of much of his power. The elections of that year gave the Democrats a majority in the House. Anxious to organize into a cohesive voting bloc but unwilling to risk giving power to their own Speaker, the Democrats vested new authority in the chairman of the WAYS AND MEANS COMMITTEE and in the majority leader. At the same time, they elected Underwood to both positions.

As chairman of Ways and Means, Underwood had the power to make committee assignments. He also controlled the Democratic CAUCUS, which then had the power to tell members how to vote on the floor and in committee. The House Speaker, Missouri Democrat James B. "Champ" CLARK, was only a figurehead.

In the Senate, Underwood served as Democratic floor leader from 1921 to 1923. He resigned from the Senate after two terms. Twice, in 1912 and in 1924, Underwood was considered a candidate for the presidency. In 1924 he took a courageous stand against the popular Ku Klux Klan, a move that killed any presidential hopes he may have harbored.   ~

Overleaf:
Informal moment off the floor.

To my precious friend, Jim Piersol

Vandenberg, Arthur H.

Arthur H. Vandenberg (1884-1951) was a Republican senator from Michigan from 1928 until his death in 1951. Vandenberg was an isolationist turned internationalist, and his influential position in the Senate allowed him to play a critical role in the conduct of international relations in the years following World War II.

After a long career as editor of the Grand Rapids *Herald*, Vandenberg entered the Senate in 1928 to finish an unexpired term. He also was elected to a subsequent full term in the elections of the same year. In 1929, at the beginning of his first full term, Vandenberg joined the Senate FOREIGN RELATIONS Committee. It was as a member and later as chairman of this committee that Vandenberg would make his mark in the Senate.

Although Vandenberg had supported ratification of the Treaty of Versailles and League of Nations covenant following World War I, he subsequently became a prominent isolationist. During the 1930s he supported legislation that would keep the United States free of foreign entanglements. During World War II, however, Vandenberg underwent a dramatic change of heart, stemming in part from his distrust of the Soviet Union. He took part in the planning of the United Nations and was one of eight U. S. representatives at the San Francisco Conference that drafted the UN Charter. Subsequently, he played a critical role in planning and implementing the Marshall Plan (economic aid to war-torn European countries) and Truman Doctrine (aid to Turkey and Greece). He sponsored the Vandenberg Resolution of 1948, which formed the basis of U. S. participation in the North Atlantic Treaty Organization. A bipartisan spirit characterized all his efforts in the field of foreign affairs.

Vandenberg was a colorful and emotional speaker. He enjoyed the national attention paid to him in 1947-49, when Republicans controlled the Senate and he became chairman of the Foreign Relations Committee, as well as PRESIDENT PRO TEMPORE. Vandenberg wielded an unusual amount of power in the largely ceremonial post of president pro tem; he participated in planning the legislative program and involved himself in debate while he was presiding over the chamber.   ～

Veterans' Affairs Committees, House and Senate

Federal programs for veterans, ranging from health care to job counseling, are the responsibility of the House and Senate Veterans' Affairs committees. Both committees act within Congress as advocates of improved veterans' benefits.

The House committee, set up in 1946, has been dominated by conservative southerners, who have had close ties to traditional veterans' lobbying groups, such as the American Legion and Veterans of Foreign Wars. The Senate created its committee in 1971, bucking a movement to eliminate committees with narrow jurisdictions. Its leaders have been considered more sympathetic toward Vietnam-era veterans

than their House counterparts. Despite budget constraints in the late 1980s, they were successful in passing several measures, including a new version of G.I. Bill of Rights education benefits, first provided after World War II.

Texas Democrat Olin E. Teague, a decorated World War II veteran, spent almost two decades as chairman of the House committee (1955-73). His strong support of the military was typical of committee members. That approach continued under Mississippi Democrat G. V. "Sonny" Montgomery, who became chairman in 1981. By the late 1980s, though, the committee shifted its outlook, as younger members began questioning the panel's traditional orientation. At the same time the conflict between old-line veterans' lobbying groups and those representing Vietnam veterans had eased.

California Democrat Alan Cranston chaired the Senate committee from 1977 to 1981 and took the chair again in 1987 when Democrats regained control of the Senate. Cranston, an advocate of expanded veterans' benefits, gave the committee added prestige because of his position as Democratic whip. More skeptical about expanding veterans' benefits was Wyoming Republican Alan Simpson, who led the committee until 1985, when he became the No. 2 Republican leader and, under GOP rules, had to give up the chairmanship. Republican Frank H. Murkowski of Alaska served as chairman in 1985-87.   ～

Vetoes

Article I, Section 7 of the Constitution requires the president to approve or disapprove all legislation passed by Congress. If the president opposes a bill, he vetoes it and returns the legislation, together with a message giving his reasons for disapproving it, to Congress.

Veto Pencil
President Ronald Reagan forced Congress to make cuts in federal spending by vetoing or threatening to veto annual government funding bills. Reagan shows off a "veto pencil" presented to him by Sen. William L. Armstrong, right, in 1987.

The president's veto power is not absolute, however. Section 7 gives Congress an opportunity to enact vetoed bills into law by repassing them by a two-thirds majority vote in each house. Nevertheless, the veto is the chief executive's most potent legislative power, both as a negative weapon for blocking legislation the president opposes and for persuading Congress to approve the administration's legislative priorities.

Veto Procedure

After both houses of Congress pass a bill in identical form, the measure is sent to the White House. The president has ten days, excluding Sundays, in which to sign or veto it; the ten-day period begins at midnight on the day the bill is received. If the president takes no action on the measure within ten days, and Congress is in session, the bill automatically becomes law without his signature. However, if Congress has already adjourned, and the president does not sign it within the ten-day period, the measure is killed, or "pocket vetoed."

The Constitution specifies that the president shall return a rejected bill along with his objections to the house that originated the legislation. There is no deadline by which Congress must try to override the veto. It may act any time during the Congress in which the bill is vetoed. Usually override attempts are made within weeks or even days of the veto. If the LEADERSHIP decides Congress is unlikely to override the veto, and there is no possibility of winning, it may decide not to schedule a vote. Or it may return the vetoed bill to the committee that had considered it. Occasionally, when the political climate is compatible, the committee will quickly draft a new version of the vetoed bill that satisfies the president's objections.

To override a veto, a QUORUM must be present, and the bill must be supported by two-thirds of the members voting in each chamber. If the first chamber to vote does not muster a two-thirds majority, the bill is dead and no further action is taken. If there is a two-thirds majority, the bill goes to the other chamber; a two-thirds vote there enacts the measure into law. (All LEGISLATION not enacted into law dies at the end of the Congress in which it is introduced.)

In the Senate, the question whether to override a presidential veto is debatable (it may be FILIBUSTERED, although this is rarely tried). A vetoed bill may not be amended. Only the one vote to override is permitted. And the Constitution requires recorded votes in each house on override attempts. *(See* VOTING.*)*

Historical Use

In the early years of the Republic, the veto was used infrequently. Until the administration of Andrew Jackson (1829-37), presidents usually vetoed bills only if they believed the legislation was unconstitutional or defective in some manner. Three of the first six presidents did not veto a single bill. That pattern changed under Jackson, who vetoed twelve bills, more than the combined total of all his predecessors. More important, Jackson was the first chief executive to use the veto as a political weapon to further his own legislative agenda and to kill bills he personally opposed.

After Jackson, members of Congress saw the veto as a very powerful weapon in the president's hands. The first attempt to impeach a president— John Tyler (1841-45)—resulted from his veto of a tariff bill. Proposals were introduced at the time to allow Congress to override vetoes by a simple majority rather than by a two-thirds vote. Nothing came of those attempts. President Andrew Johnson's (1865-69) struggle after the Civil War with the Radical Republicans in Congress led him to veto twenty-nine bills, a record up to that time. Congress responded with the first successful effort to override a veto on a major legislative issue.

President Grover Cleveland (1885-89, 1893-97) used the veto 584 times, a record that stood until the administration of Franklin D. Roosevelt. Many of Cleveland's vetoes were directed at preventing corruption that had mounted through the abuse of private pension bills.

Roosevelt vetoed 635 bills during his twelve years in office (1933-45). All types of bills were targeted including, for the first time, a revenue bill. Until that time it had been assumed that by precedent tax bills were immune from the presidential veto. Roosevelt dramatized his disapproval of one bill by personally delivering his veto message to a joint session of Congress.

Recent Use

Every president since World War II has made extensive use of the veto power. President Harry S TRUMAN (1945-53) used it effectively to protect organized labor until the Republicans took control of Congress in the late 1940s, making it likely that his vetoes would be overridden. Republican President Dwight D. Eisenhower (1953-61) used the veto to block or limit new social welfare programs promoted by the Democrats when they controlled Congress during his final six years in office. Eisenhower's threat to use his veto power was just as important as the veto itself in stopping legislation he opposed.

While Presidents John F. KENNEDY (1961-63) and Lyndon B. JOHNSON (1963-69) vetoed few bills (Johnson in particular had a large Democratic majority in Congress that favored his activist legislative agenda), Republican Presidents Richard NIXON (1969-74) and Gerald R. FORD (1974-77) followed Eisenhower's example in frequently vetoing social programs passed by Democratic-controlled Congresses. One of Nixon's most controversial vetoes, however, was the 1973 War Powers Act, which Congress passed near the end of the Vietnam War in an effort to limit the president's flexibility to commit U. S. forces in battle zones overseas without congressional approval. Nixon argued that the bill was unconstitutional, claiming it infringed upon the president's powers as commander in chief. But with Nixon weakened politically by an unpopular war and the Watergate scandal, the House and Senate were able to override his veto. *(See* WAR POWERS; WATERGATE SCANDAL.*)*

President Ford's use of the veto demonstrated its effectiveness. Despite large Democratic gains in Congress in 1974 after Nixon's resignation, Ford was sustained on thirteen of the seventeen bills he vetoed in 1975. Another major bill was never sent to him because Ford had threatened to veto it.

Jimmy Carter (1977-81) was the first president since Truman to have one of his vetoes overridden by a Congress controlled by the president's own party. He suffered two such ignominious defeats in 1980.

President Ronald Reagan, who took office in 1981, used the veto threat to great advantage during his two terms to deflect foreign policy and domestic initiatives of the Democratic-controlled House of Representatives. Particularly in the early years of his presidency, Reagan forced Congress to make sizable cuts in federal spending in part through his veto or threatened veto of annual appropriations bills for government departments and agencies.

Importance of Power

The veto is a powerful tool because most presidents most of the time can muster the necessary support to defeat override attempts in Congress. A president needs the support of only one-third plus one member in either house to sustain a veto. Those odds give the chief executive a great advantage. Even when Congress is controlled by the opposition political party, a president who mobilizes all the LOBBYING and public relations resources at his disposal usually can find the votes he needs. Of the six vetoes that Congress sustained during President Reagan's first six years in office, three of his victories came from the House—even though that body was controlled by the Democrats. An even more telling indicator of the power of the veto was the fact that the congressional leadership did not even schedule

veto override votes on nineteen of Reagan's thirty-seven regular vetoes cast during that period. President Woodrow Wilson (1913-21) once said the veto power made the president "a third branch of the legislature."

At each stage of the legislative process, senators and representatives, their staffs, and lobbyists for special interests must weigh the risk of a presidential veto if provisions opposed by the president are retained in legislation pending before Congress. Normally, most members of Congress would rather compromise with the president to gain his support than have a bill vetoed and face the task of trying to rally a two-thirds majority in each house to override the veto.

Decisions to veto legislation are not made in a vacuum, of course. Presidents receive advice from all sides of the issue. In the end, a president's veto decision is a collective one involving the White House staff, the heads of interested federal departments, the director of the Office of Management and Budget, key legislators of the president's party in Congress, and, when their interests are seriously affected, state and local officials, special interest groups, and influential private citizens. Some presidential vetoes are cast on principle—the legislation is diametrically opposed to the president's policies or political philosophy. Many others are close calls—the president and his advisers must balance the provisions of the bill they support against those they oppose.

Congressional Leverage

The power to override is not Congress's only leverage over presidential vetoes. Lawmakers have devised several ways to frustrate attempts by presidents to veto bills. The Senate often attaches RIDERS to legislation regarded as essential or highly desirable by the White House, forcing the president to approve provisions he strongly opposes because they are part of bills he "must" sign. Essential legislation includes APPROPRIATIONS bills to maintain and run the federal departments, measures to raise the national DEBT LIMIT, AUTHORIZATIONS for programs or activities actively promoted by the president, and various emergency measures.

In recent years Congress has relied heavily on the CONTINUING RESOLUTION—legislation incorporating many or all of the thirteen annual appropriations bills needed to run the federal government in one giant money bill, passed near the end of a session of Congress. The president is forced either to sign the bill or, if he vetoes it, to see the U. S. government run out of money and forced to shut down temporarily. In such situations, Congress often can disregard many of the president's recommendations and enact much of its own spending agenda. In 1988 President Reagan used his STATE OF THE UNION address to denounce such practices.

Congress occasionally uses the presidential veto as a foil for its own legislative goals. Particularly when the legislature is controlled by one party and the executive by the other, lawmakers who oppose the president may pass legislation with the expectation that it will be vetoed, or they may add amendments that they know will force the president to veto a particular bill. If it is an election year, they then can go home to their constituents and portray the president as heartless, indifferent, or out of touch with the public interest.

Presidents, of course, can do the same thing, by denouncing lawmakers or members of the opposition party as big spenders or the ones wanting to raise voters' taxes.

Pocket Veto Dispute

If the president does not act on a bill within the ten-day period specified in the Constitution, and Congress has adjourned, the the bill is pocket vetoed. The measure dies because the president is prevented from returning the legislation to Congress so that lawmakers can consider the vetoed bill.

Although the Constitution is more than 200 years old, the pocket veto provision continues to raise controversy. Nowhere in the veto provision is the meaning of adjournment spelled out. Presidents have given the word a very loose meaning, covering short recesses and interim adjournments within a session. Congress has applied a very narrow definition, so that the word means only the final adjournment of a two-year Congress.

James MADISON was the first president to pocket veto a bill, in 1812. In the twentieth century presidents routinely pocket vetoed bills during congressional recesses and adjournments of varying lengths. Of the 2,450 vetoes cast between 1789 and 1986, almost half (1,078) were pocket vetoes. The practice unleashed a major controversy in the late 1920s when President Calvin Coolidge's pocket veto of a bill during a four-month recess was challenged. The case went all the way to the Supreme Court, which decided in favor of the president. The Court at that time broadly interpreted the president's power, holding that he could pocket veto bills any time a congressional recess or adjournment prevented the return of a vetoed bill to Congress within the ten-day period specified in the Constitution. Another Supreme Court decision nine years later limited this interpretation somewhat, but the issue remained murky.

In the early 1970s the question arose anew. A pocket veto controversy between President Nixon and Congress in 1973 was decided by a U.S. court of appeals in favor of the lawmakers' position. The court ruled that Nixon had acted improperly in pocket vetoing a bill during a six-day congressional recess. A second case decided by the same court in 1976 broadened the ruling to prohibit the president from pocket vetoing a bill during adjournments between sessions of the same Congress.

Despite these rulings, the pocket veto remained a contentious issue between the executive and legislative branches. In 1981 and 1983 President Reagan pocket vetoed bills between the first and second sessions of the 97th and 98th Congresses. In August 1985 a U.S. federal appeals court ruled that the president's veto between sessions of Congress was unconstitutional. Reagan was not prevented from returning the bill to Congress, the court ruled, because the House and Senate had appointed agents to receive the president's veto messages during the interim. A definitive ruling on the issue awaited action by the Supreme Court.

Line-Item Veto

Like many presidents before him, Reagan asked that presidents be given a line-item veto over appropriations bills. He called for a constitutional amendment that would empower chief executives to reject the funding level approved by Congress for specific programs in an appropriations bill without being forced to veto the entire legislation. As in a regular veto, Congress could override the president's line-item veto by a two-thirds majority vote in each house.

The line-item veto idea received serious attention in the mid-1980s, a period of staggering budget deficits. Republicans in particular, and some Democrats as well, contended that the president should be given the line-item veto as a weapon to better control the federal budget. It would give presidents an effective way, they maintained, to eliminate wasteful PORK BARREL spending projects that members slip into the yearly appropriations bills.

Opponents argued that the veto might usurp the powers of Congress and would achieve limited fiscal results since some of the biggest federal spending would be beyond its reach, including programs for which spending was required by law. (See BUDGET PROCESS.)

Many experts on Congress were skeptical that the line-item veto would have much effect in reducing the budget deficit. They also expressed concern about the impact it would have on executive-legislative relations.   ~

Vice President

The vice president of the United States serves as the president of the Senate. Because the framers of the Constitution gave the position no real authority and the Senate has been disinclined to delegate power to an outsider, it is for the most part a ceremonial position.

The vice president does not participate in debates, unless permitted by a majority of the Senate, and votes only to break a tie. It is rare to see a vice president presiding over the chamber; the job usually falls to the PRESIDENT PRO TEMPORE.

When the vice president presides, it is often by design. If close votes on administration bills are expected, the vice president is on hand to break the tie in favor of the president's position. He occasionally uses his role as president of the Senate to issue parliamentary rulings that advance his party's floor strategy and to assist in the administration's legislative liaison efforts.

Origins and Development

The framers of the Constitution decided to give the vice president the Senate position to provide a job for the runner-up in the electoral vote and to give the Senate an impartial presiding officer without depriving any state of one of its two votes.

When the proposal was debated at the Constitutional Convention, there were some objections before it was

Mixed Duties

The framers of the Constitution had a hard time finding a job for the vice president. Roger Sherman pointed out that unless the vice president were made president of the Senate, he would be without employment. Others worried about mixing executive and legislative functions. In recent decades, vice presidents have been assigned to lobby on behalf of their administration's policies. Pictured here: Vice President Nelson A. Rockefeller, who held the post during the Ford administration.

adopted. George Mason complained that "it mixed too much the Legislative and the Executive." Elbridge Gerry thought it tantamount to putting the president himself at the head of the Senate because of "the close intimacy that must subsist between the president and the vice president." But Roger Sherman pointed out that "if the Vice President were not to be President of the Senate, he would be without employment."

Although the framers solved the problem of a job for the runner-up, the vice president was powerless to supply effective legislative leadership. Precedent was set by the first vice president, John Adams, who, although clearly in general agreement with the majority of the Senate during his term as vice president, perceived his role as simply that of presiding officer and made little effort to guide Senate action.

His successor, Thomas Jefferson, could not have steered the Federalist-controlled Senate had he wanted to, but he did make an important contribution by compiling a *Manual of Parliamentary Procedure.* (See JEFFERSON'S MANUAL.)

The next vice president, Aaron Burr, was so impartial that he even cost the Jefferson administration a victory or two in the Senate.

There have, of course, been vice presidents throughout history who were not content to sit on the sidelines. John C. CALHOUN, for example, was a commanding figure as vice president, and his influence was felt in the Senate before he resigned in 1832 to become a senator himself.

Examples in the twentieth century include Charles Dawes, Calvin Coolidge's vice president, who campaigned actively—albeit unsuccessfully—against Senate rules allowing FILIBUSTERS and often openly supported legislation opposed by Coolidge. John Nance Garner, a former SPEAKER of the House, helped win congressional votes for NEW DEAL legislation in Franklin D. Roosevelt's first term, although the two became estranged when Garner opposed the pace and scope of later proposals.

The most blatant power play in recent times occurred when Lyndon B. JOHNSON, a legendary Senate majority leader, sought to preside over Senate Democratic CAUCUS meetings even after he became John F. KENNEDY's vice president. The proposal was rejected.

Presiding Officers

Vice presidents have been given certain powers as presiding officers, which, for the most part, can be overridden by the chamber. The duties include: recognizing members seeking the floor; deciding points of order, subject to appeal to the full Senate; appointing senators to House-Senate conference committees, although it is customary for the presiding officer to appoint senators recommended by the floor manager of the bill; enforcing decorum; administering oaths; and appointing members to special committees.

Vice presidents occasionally become involved in parliamentary struggles while presiding over the Senate. In 1987, for example, Vice President George Bush became embroiled in the sharpest confrontation between Senate members and a vice president in at least a decade. At issue were an energy standards bill and some fairly obscure points of order under Senate rules. When the Democratic leadership began to take up the bill, which the Republicans hoped to delay, Bush rushed over from the White House to assist the Republican minority. While the Republicans succeeded in their tactics to block immediate action, Bush was chastised by Senate Majority Leader Robert C. BYRD of West Virginia for a ruling that facilitated the delay. Bush insisted that he had done nothing wrong.

Vice President Walter F. Mondale, a Democrat, got into hot water over his conduct in the chair during a prolonged battle over natural gas legislation in 1977. Byrd delivered a stinging, lengthy public lecture to Mondale, rebuking him for trying to recognize Carter administration allies ahead of Minority Leader Howard H. BAKER, Jr., a Tennessee Republican. Byrd reminded the vice president in cold, clear terms that Senate custom dictated that party leaders always be recognized when they sought the floor.

Less than two weeks later Mondale demonstrated how useful a vice president can be, when he and Byrd teamed up to bring to a halt a FILIBUSTER-by-amendment on that same gas bill. Mondale, reading from a typed script given him by Byrd, ruled a series of amendments out of order, while ignoring senators seeking to exercise their right to appeal his rulings.

Tie Votes

The vice president's constitutional authority to vote in the Senate in the event of a tie is a rarely used power, but a vital one when administration proposals are at stake.

Through mid-1988, vice presidents had cast 223 votes in the Senate. Some of these votes were recorded against questions that would have failed even if the vice president had not voted, because a question on which the Senate is evenly divided automatically dies. In such cases the vice president's negative vote is superfluous. Its only purpose is to make known his own opposition to the proposal. There are no records available showing how many of the tie-breaking votes cast by vice presidents were in the affirmative and thus decisive.

One crucial vote by a vice president was cast in 1846 when George M. Dallas broke a tie in favor of a Polk administration tariff reform bill. Among other important vice presidential votes were two cast by Woodrow Wilson's vice president, Thomas R. Marshall, on foreign policy issues. In 1916 his vote carried an amendment on a Philippines bill pledging full independence to the islands by March 4, 1921. (The amendment later was modified in conference.) In 1919 Marshall cast the deciding vote to table a resolution calling for withdrawal of U.S. troops from Russia.

In the 1980s Bush used his vote to stave off attacks on Reagan administration defense programs, including chemical weapons, the MX missile, and the Strategic Defense Initiative.

Legislative Liaison

Many vice presidents have been well suited to the job of lobbying on behalf of their administration's policies. Thirty of forty-three vice presidents previously had served in either the House or Senate, or both.

Yet it has been only in recent decades that vice presidents have been formally assigned liaison duties. Earlier, as political scientist Louis Fisher has pointed out, vice presidents were considered to be legislative officers who could not be assigned executive duties without violating the SEPARATION OF POWERS doctrine. This view was held as recently as the 1940s and 1950s, although vice presidents were used in behind-the-scenes lobbying efforts.

Lyndon Johnson, after being rebuffed by his former Senate colleagues, did little liaison work for the Kennedy administration. However, he gave his own vice president, Hubert H. HUMPHREY, substantially more tasks on Capitol Hill.

Mondale, operating out of offices in the Capitol and a Senate office building, proved to be an effective spokesman for the Carter White House on numerous occasions, as did George Bush later for the Reagan administration. ~

ADDITIONAL READINGS

Goldstein, Joel K. *The Modern American Vice Presidency.* 1982.
Light, Paul C. *Vice-Presidential Power.* 1984.
Williams, Irving G. *The Rise of the Vice Presidency.* 1956.

Voters and Congress

Members of Congress play a dual role. As legislators, they pass laws and oversee their implementation. As representatives, they voice their constituents' needs and views in Washington.

Members have grappled with the task of balancing great national issues with vital local concerns since the First Congress in 1789. But the job has become more formidable in modern times as the country has emerged as a world power and the federal government has expanded into new economic and social ventures. Serving in Congress has become a full-time, year-round job.

At the same time, constituencies have grown both in size and diversity; in the 1980s the average state numbered about four million people and the average House district more than half a million. Modern communications and travel have made members of Congress more accessible to increasingly educated constituencies and sophisticated special interest groups. They are expected to bring home federal funds and projects, respond to constituents' needs, and keep a high profile before the voters.

Election Pressures

Members of Congress always seem to be running for reelection.

This has been especially true of members of the House of Representatives, whose two-year terms leave little time for a break between campaigns. Although there are very few competitive races in the House and the incumbent reelection rate is extremely favorable—an average of about 91 percent from 1946 through 1986—many House members feel anything but secure and campaign full time to keep their seats. Even the most entrenched members remember colleagues who lost and fear that if their districts are targeted by the opposition they could be next.

The reelection rate in the Senate is much lower than in the House: An average of nearly 75 percent of senators seeking reelection kept their seats in the four decades following World War II.

'Home Style'

On their frequent trips home, members of Congress sandwich in speeches, civic meetings, ribbon-cuttings, fundraisers, district office hours, political consultations, coffees, breakfasts, luncheons, dinners, picnics, and sometimes time to just sit on the front steps trading stories. This 1973 picture shows Sen. Howard H. Baker, Jr., sharing a laugh with constituents on the courthouse steps in Huntsville, Tennessee.

At one time senators' six-year terms seemed to provide at least a modest cushion from outside pressures, allowing a senator to be a statesman in the first part of a term and a politician in the last few years. But since the mid-1970s senators have been forced to rival House members as permanent candidates.

Senate races have become highly competitive and often enormously expensive. Most senators now can expect reelection challenges next time out from candidates with the money and skill to make themselves known statewide. *(See* CAMPAIGN FINANCING.*)*

'Pork Barrel' Politics

Virtually all members try to protect their electoral bases through the time-honored PORK BARREL POLITICS by which Congress distributes federal projects, grants, and other government benefits.

Pork traditionally has been identified with public works projects such as roads, bridges, dams, and harbors. But, as the economy and country changed, it came to include environmental projects, university research, high-tech projects, defense contracts, military installations, special tax breaks, and other projects

that benefit their constituents.

A highway and mass transit reauthorization bill passed in 1987 over President Ronald Reagan's veto provided a good example of pork barrel politics. The legislation contained 120-odd special "demonstration" projects, as well as numerous small favors for particular states and districts. On the override vote, even top GOP members of Congress—including House Republican leader Robert H. MICHEL of Illinois and whip Trent Lott of Mississippi—found they could not support their president because of projects made available to their districts by the bill.

Michel knew the importance of pork barrel projects only too well. For years a fiscal purist who prided himself on resisting pork barrel temptations, Michel almost lost his congressional seat in 1982 in a close race in which his failure to "bring home the bacon" was an issue. The following year he turned on the tap and federal loans, grants, and contracts began to flow into his district. "I'm not altogether proud of it," Michel admitted in 1983. "I never perceived that the measure of my effectiveness should be how deep I could get my finger in the federal till."

Not all members share Michel's

views. Rep. Kenneth J. Gray, Democrat of Illinois, who has been called the "Prince of Pork," has said he would rather be called the "King of Pork" and that "the congressman not getting any pork is not listening to what his people are saying."

Sometimes it can backfire. For example, Missouri Rep. Robert A. Young, who campaigned on his "pork" efforts in 1986, was painted by his opponent as an old-style, deal-making pol, and he was the only Democratic incumbent in the House to lose his seat. But many members have managed to solidify their political bases with federal funds.

Constituent Casework

Members also court constituents by helping them deal with the federal government, a responsibility that is known as "casework." Congressional offices provide assistance in a broad range of areas, including Social Security benefits, military service, veterans' affairs, immigration, passports, unemployment claims, housing, health care, and Internal Revenue disputes.

While some casework involves complaints, a good deal has to do with requests for assistance in approaching federal agencies about such things as government contracts, loans, grants, jobs, and patents. One popular request from schools and organizations is for a flag that has flown over the CAPITOL building. *(See p. 286)*

The number of services performed for constituents has skyrocketed with the expansion of the federal government into many areas directly affecting the private lives of individuals. Political scientists Roger H. Davidson and Walter J. Oleszek reported studies showing that by the 1970s representatives had an average caseload of slightly more than 10,000 cases a year. Senators from small states averaged between 1,000 and 2,000 a year, while those from large states had from 8,000 to 70,000 cases.

Most casework is handled by STAFF and more and more of it is being done in members' district and state offices. Because of the volume of constituents' problems, federal agencies and the military services have special liaison offices to assist members. The Veterans Administration, military services, and Office of Personnel Management maintain offices on Capitol Hill.

Constituent Communications

Effective and frequent communications between legislators and their constituents are a key ingredient of a successful career on Capitol Hill. Members must know their constituents' views as they perform congressional duties. They also must keep voters informed on national issues and their own activities.

Election returns obviously are the best indicator of public opinion. Beyond them, members rely on constituent mail, surveys, district office reports, and trips home to measure voters' sentiments. They communicate with voters through mass mailings, personal appearances, and radio and television messages. These contacts are facilitated by special allowances to incumbent members of Congress. *(See* PAY AND PERQUISITES.*)*

Congressional Mail At one time a single clerk could handle a member's mail, but those days are long gone. Mail now consumes the largest share of congressional staff time. According to Davidson and Oleszek, the House Post Office logged more than 200 million pieces of incoming mail in 1984, while the Senate logged 41 million.

But, for all that volume, the mail remains an inexact gauge of voter sentiment. Few Americans ever write their representatives and senators. Much legislative mail—along with telegrams and telephone calls—is inspired by pressure groups through highly organized "grassroots" lobbying campaigns. *(See* LOBBYING; HOW TO WRITE YOUR CONGRESSMAN, *Appendix.)*

Outgoing mail also has mushroomed in recent years. One of members' most valuable perquisites is the FRANKING PRIVILEGE, which allows them to mail letters and packages under their signatures without being charged for postage. According to figures compiled by political scientists Norman J. Ornstein, Thomas E. Mann, and Michael J. Malbin, official congressional mailings totaled 758.7 million in fiscal 1986 at a cost of $95.7 million.

Members use the franking privilege to mail public documents, such as bills or committee hearings and reports, as well as copies of speeches or of articles reprinted in the *CONGRESSIONAL RECORD*. Legislators also use the frank to mail regular newsletters that generally paint an upbeat picture of their roles in Congress and frequently poll constituent opinion or show concern for state and district problems.

Computers have fundamentally changed the way lawmakers deal with constituent mail. The machines maintain sophisticated mailing lists organized by constituents' particular interests. Using those lists and very specific computer-generated messages, members can target letters to constituents for maximum political impact. Controversy surrounding the frank led Congress to restrict the kinds of mail that can be sent out free and to prohibit mass mailings sixty days before elections. But, despite the restrictions, the number of mailings jumps in election years.

Trips Home Only a few decades ago, most members of Congress stayed in Washington for the duration of the session. But with the ease of air travel today, home—whether it is New York or Hawaii—is accessible every week, and it is rare for any junior House member not to be publicly visible in his or her district two weekends a month. Senators and representatives are permitted to take an unlimited number of trips home and spend as much as they wish within their official expense account.

Legislative business is scheduled to accommodate members' travel. The House operates on a Tuesday-through-Thursday workweek in Washington, which allows members to spend five-day "weekends" in their home districts. Frequent "district work periods" permit longer stays. The Senate, which previously had a four-day workweek, went to a new schedule in 1988 that generally called for three full five-day workweeks and then one week off. The plan was designed to meet senators' complaints that the old schedule made it difficult to predict when they could leave town and interfered with family events, campaign fundraisers, and meetings with constituents.

On trips home, members sandwich in speeches, civic meetings, ribbon-cuttings, fundraisers, district office hours, political consultations, coffees, breakfasts, luncheons, dinners, picnics, and sometimes time to just sit on the front steps trading stories. While making the rounds, members are presenting what political scientist Richard F. Fenno, Jr., called their "home styles" to convince voters to trust them. "It is the style, not the issue content, that counts most in the reelection constituency," Fenno wrote.

Sam RAYBURN provided a good example. The legendary Democratic Speaker of the House became just a plain dirt farmer when he returned home to his east Texas district. According to Davidson and Oleszek, his drawl thickened; his suits were exchanged for khakis, old shirt, and slouch hat; and he traveled around in an old pickup truck, not the Speaker's limousine he used in Washington.

District Offices Members maintain offices in their home districts and states and sometimes even have mobile offices to make themselves more accessible to voters. The offices are funded from members' allowances.

With the aid of computers, legislators have been shifting some constituent services—such as answering letters and casework—away from Washington and back to local offices. Nearly 41 percent of House members' personal staffs were based in district offices in 1987, according to Ornstein, Mann, and Malbin. In the Senate, about 34 percent were in state offices in 1987.

Radio-TV Facilities Since 1956 Congress has operated radio and television studios for members to use to prepare programs for broadcast back in their states and districts. Studios located on Capitol Hill are available to members at subsidized fees far below the charges for private taping facilities.   ~

ADDITIONAL READINGS

Davidson, Roger H., and Walter J. Oleszek. *Congress and Its Members.* 2d ed. 1985.

Fenno, Richard F., Jr. *Home Style: House Members in Their Districts.* 1978.

Goldenberg, Edie N., and Michael W. Traugott. *Campaigning for Congress.* 1984.

Johannes, John R. *To Serve the People: Congress and Constituency Service.* 1984.

Salmore, Stephen A., and Barbara G. Salmore. *Candidates, Parties, and Campaigns: Electoral Politics in America.* 1985.

Voting in Congress

Every law must be voted on by the House and Senate. Although many votes are taken informally, with verbal "yeas" and "nays" and no record of individual positions, senators and representatives cast formal floor votes three to four hundred times a year. On those votes, each individual position is re-corded in the *CONGRESSIONAL RECORD.* Months and sometimes years of work in committees come to fruition, or fail, as the House and Senate vote.

The House and Senate have each developed their own procedures for voting. Guiding them in many cases are voting rules spelled out in the Constitution. Most specific are requirements for roll-call votes, or what the Constitution calls the "yeas and nays." One rule is aimed at preventing secret ballots: "The yeas and nays of the members of either house on any question shall, at the desire of one fifth of those present, be entered on the Journal." For votes to override presidential vetoes, the Constitution is even more specific. "In all such cases the votes of both houses shall be determined by yeas and nays, and the names of persons voting for and against the bill shall be entered on the Journal."

The ritual of voting is interesting to watch even when the question is minor, and votes on major issues can be quite dramatic. When a vote is pending, buzzers are used to summon senators and representatives from their offices to the Capitol. *(See* LEGISLATIVE PROCESS.*)*

House members stream into their chamber through several different entrances. They pull from their wallets or purses white plastic cards, which they insert into one of forty voting boxes mounted on the backs of chairs along the aisles. After each member punches a button to indicate his position, a giant electronic board behind the Speaker's desk immediately flashes green for "yes" and red for "no" next to the member's name. For those more cautious, yellow signals a "present" vote, usually changed later to reflect support or opposition. On close votes, tension builds as the fifteen minutes allowed for the vote run out. Boisterous members sometimes shout when the tally for their side hits the number needed for victory.

The House seems a bastion of high

technology when compared with the Senate, where there is no electronic voting. When the Senate takes a roll-call vote, a clerk goes through the alphabet, reading each name aloud and pausing for an answer. Most senators miss the name call; when they enter the chamber, the clerk calls their name again, and they vote. On major questions the chamber fills with senators staying to hear the final result. Although party leaders keep a tally, the official vote is not announced until voting has been completed. In contrast to the rowdier House, the noise level is kept low by the gavel of the presiding officer, who must be able to hear the clerk and the senators' replies.

Voting is a frequent target of reformers on Capitol Hill. House members complain they must interrupt other business too often to come to the floor for votes. Party leaders try to schedule several votes together and discourage members from seeking votes on unimportant questions, or when they have little chance of victory. Senators have similar complaints about time-consuming votes, which often take more than the fifteen minutes set aside because party leaders wait for late arrivals. Majority Leader Robert C. BYRD, a West Virginia Democrat, tried in 1988 to be more strict about keeping votes to fifteen minutes; often twenty or more senators would rush through the doors at the last minute.

Voting records are not a perfect measure of a member's politics. Controversial questions are often resolved without a clear up-or-down vote. The language of an AMENDMENT is often complicated, confusing members about what position to take. Local considerations can prompt a member to reject a bill he supports philosophically. Party leaders sometimes intentionally avoid a vote to protect members from having to take an unpopular stand. These shortcomings mean that voting records are, by nature, incomplete, but they are still the best available yardstick of members' views. The records are also a tool for measuring to what degree Congress is supporting the president and whether parties or regions are voting together. (See EXECUTIVE BRANCH AND CONGRESS; CONSERVATIVE COALITION.)

House Voting

Four types of votes are used regularly in the House. The vast majority of House votes are cast when the House sits as the COMMITTEE OF THE WHOLE, a type of session used often for amending legislation because rules governing it are less restrictive than those that apply to the full House.

Voice Vote The quickest method of voting is by voice vote. Even on controversial questions, voice votes may be held first, followed by more complex voting methods. The presiding officer calls first for the "ayes" and then for the "noes." A chorus of members shouts in response to each question. The chair determines the results. If the chair is in doubt, or if a single member requests a further test, a standing vote is in order.

Standing Vote In a standing—or division—vote, those in favor and then those opposed to the question stand while a head count is taken by the chair. Only the total vote on each side is recorded; no determination is made of how individual members voted. Few issues are resolved at this stage. If the issue was important enough for members to seek a standing vote, then the losing side, hoping to reverse the outcome, usually will ask for a recorded vote. The recorded vote draws many more members to the chamber.

Recorded Vote Recorded votes, which use the electronic voting system, comprise the bulk of members' voting records. Members' votes are recorded individually as they insert their voting cards in the voting boxes in the cham-

Voting, House Style
Representatives have been forced to make public their positions on many more issues since the House introduced an electronic voting system in 1973. Members insert plastic cards in voting boxes like the one shown here. Their votes are displayed on a lighted board behind the Speaker's rostrum.

ber. A recorded vote may be ordered upon demand of one-fourth of a quorum (twenty-five) when the House is meeting as the Committee of the Whole. One-fifth of a quorum (forty-four) is required when the House is meeting in regular session.

Until 1971, votes in Committee of the Whole were taken by methods that did not reveal the stands of individual members. Many questions were decided by teller votes; the chair appointed tellers representing opposite sides on a vote and directed members to pass between them up the center aisle to be counted—first the "ayes," then the "noes."

Only vote totals were announced on traditional teller votes, but the Legislative Reorganization Act of 1970 opened the way for "tellers with clerks," or recorded teller votes. This procedure, for the first time in the Committee of the Whole, made it possible to record the votes of individual members. After the electronic voting system was installed in 1973, the recorded teller vote became known simply as a recorded vote.

Yeas and Nays Until the teller vote changes of the 1970s, yeas and nays were the only votes on which House members were individually recorded. Yeas and nays are ordered upon demand of one-fifth of those present, and they are not taken in Committee of the Whole. The Constitution requires yea-and-nay votes on the question of overriding a veto.

Use of the electronic system has blurred the distinction between yeas and nays and other recorded votes. Before the electronic voting system was installed, yeas and nays were taken by calling the roll, a time-consuming process in the 435-member House; each roll call took about half an hour. The Speaker still retains the right to call the roll rather than use the electronic system. And the old-fashioned method is used when the electronic system breaks down, as it does from time to time.

During roll calls, members are required to vote "yea" or "nay." Members who do not wish to vote may answer "present." The Speaker's name is called only at his own request. He is required to vote only if his vote would be deciding.

Senate Voting
Only two types of votes are in everyday use in the Senate—voice votes and roll-call votes. Standing, or divi-

sion, votes are seldom employed. The Senate does not use the teller vote and has no electronic voting system.

As in the House, the most common method of deciding issues is by voice vote. The presiding officer determines the outcome.

To obtain a roll-call vote, the backing of one-fifth of the senators present on the floor is needed. Roll calls are required by the Constitution on attempts to override presidential vetoes; by tradition the Senate always uses roll calls when voting on treaties.

The Senate usually allows fifteen minutes for a roll-call vote, although unanimous consent requests may shorten the voting time in specific situations.

Pairs, House and Senate

Both the House and Senate permit their members to "pair" on recorded votes. Pairs are voluntary, informal arrangements by two members, usually on opposite sides of a question. In many cases the result is to subtract a vote from each side, with no effect on the outcome. Pairs are not authorized in the rules of either house, are not counted in tabulating the final result, and have no official standing. However, members pairing are identified in the *Congressional Record,* along with their positions on such votes, if known. A member who expects to be absent for a vote can pair with a member who plans to vote, with the latter agreeing to withhold his vote.

There are three types of pairs: 1) A live pair involves a member who is present for a vote and another who is absent. The member in attendance votes and then withdraws the vote, announcing that he or she has a live pair with colleague "X" and stating how the two members would have voted, one in favor, the other opposed. A live pair may affect the outcome of a closely contested vote, since it subtracts one "yea" or one "nay" vote from the final tally. A live pair may cover one or several specific issues. 2) A general pair, widely used in the House, does not entail any arrangement between two members and does not affect the vote. Members who expect to be absent notify the clerk that they wish to make a general pair. Each member then is paired with another desiring a pair, and their names are listed in the *Congressional Record,* but the stands of members pairing are not identified. 3) A specific pair is similar to a general pair, except that the opposing stands of the two members are identified and printed in the *Record.*

Informal Votes

Not all legislative or parliamentary questions are decided by formal votes. Uncontested bills, amendments, and motions, such as quorum calls, may be disposed of quickly if no one voices an objection. The terms used on the floor are "without objection" and UNANIMOUS CONSENT.   ~

Overleaf:
Earliest known photo of the Capitol, about 1846.

War Powers

One of the key powers assigned to Congress by the Constitution in Article I, Section 8 is the power to declare war. Actually, the war powers clause entails several specific grants of authority to Congress. These authorities, often collectively referred to as the war power, encompass authority to: declare war; raise and support an army; provide and maintain a navy; and make rules regulating the armed forces, which today include, by inference, the air force and all other defense agencies of the U.S. government. Supporting and maintaining the armed forces means Congress must provide the APPROPRIATIONS needed to run the military establishment.

Constitutional Background

During the drafting of the Constitution, the Founding Fathers debated whether to give the war-making power to Congress or the executive branch. Ever mindful of the excesses of the British monarchy, the Constitutional Convention decided to give Congress the power to "declare war," but to assign to the president the responsibility for conducting wars.

James MADISON expressed the majority view at the Convention when he said that government officials who wage wars are not the best judges of "whether

447

a war ought to be commenced. . . ." The Convention delegates recognized, however, that if Congress declared war, the president, as commander in chief, should conduct it. And the delegates agreed the president should have the flexibility to repel an armed attack or a sudden invasion without first seeking a declaration of war from Congress.

Declaration of War

Although the Constitution explicitly confers on Congress the power to declare war, the efficacy of that provision has not lived up to the expectations envisioned by the Founding Fathers. Over the past two centuries, U.S. armed forces have engaged in 125 major or minor conflicts overseas. But Congress exercised its power to declare war on only five occasions; only once, in the War of 1812, did Congress debate the merits of committing the nation to war.

In the 1846 fight with Mexico, and in the first and second world wars, the president committed the nation to war, and Congress merely ratified his decision. In the Civil War, the Union insisted it was putting down a rebellion in the Southern states and, technically, not waging a war with the Confederacy. By that reasoning, a declaration of war could not be considered. In the Spanish-American War in 1898, a strongly expansionist-minded Congress forced a declaration of war on President William McKinley. Only with America's entry into World War II, in response to Japan's bombing of Pearl Harbor, could it be said that the president took military action in the face of a sudden armed attack on the United States.

Congress's Other War Powers

Besides its constitutional power to declare war, Congress has three related war powers. The most important of these is the power to raise and support the armed forces of the United States—the power of the PURSE. Congress has rarely used this power to shut off funds for ongoing military operations abroad. Despite congressional complaints in recent years that the president had committed U.S. forces to trouble spots overseas without consulting Congress, lawmakers repeatedly have refused to use their power of appropriations as a way of forcing the chief executive to reverse his policy. However, early in 1988, over President Ronald Reagan's objections, Congress did refuse to continue funding Nicaraguan rebels (known as contras) in their efforts to overthrow Nicaragua's Sandinista government.

Once American forces are engaged in hostilities, the last thing members of Congress want to do is to expose themselves to accusations that they are jeopardizing the security of the country or the lives of Americans. Even during an unpopular war in Vietnam, Congress repeatedly voted funds to carry on the fighting.

Congress also retains authority to regulate the size and makeup of the armed forces. Through legislation it limits the number of personnel in the various military services. The Constitution places an important qualification on the legislature's power to raise and support the armed forces. Congress is prohibited from appropriating such funds for more than two years, ensuring that its decisions will be debated and reviewed periodically. In actual practice, Congress today appropriates the money to maintain the armed forces on an annual basis.

Presidential War Powers

The president's war powers are derived from both the Constitution and historical precedents and traditions. Article II, Section 2 designates the president commander in chief. Presidents have not hesitated to use this power to the fullest. Since the nineteenth century, presidents have sometimes sent the armed forces into battle without first consulting Congress, much less asking for a declaration of war. Even many lawmakers today acknowledge that a declaration of war is not always appropriate. Once the nation is engaged in hostilities, the Constitution leaves it up to the president when to terminate them.

Since World War II, the presidential assertion of war powers has increased. All recent presidents have justified their use of the armed forces abroad by citing: their position as commander in chief; their sworn duty to preserve, protect, and defend the Constitution; their responsibility to protect the United States against invasion or surprise attack and to protect American citizens and interests; and their claim to inherent and exclusive powers as the nation's chief executive.

Congress itself has been a party to this expansion of the president's inherent powers. It has enacted numerous open-ended authorizations and resolutions sanctioning executive actions in specific foreign crises, as well as laws conferring emergency powers on the president. The president's responsibility to defend the country and protect American citizens has been invoked to explain U.S. participation in wars in which the United States was not threatened by imminent invasion or attack. Such armed conflicts included full-scale wars in Korea and Vietnam and a multitude of limited armed actions, including President John F. KENNEDY's blockade of Cuba in 1962, President Reagan's invasion of the Caribbean island of Grenada in 1983, and military support for contra rebels in Nicaragua in the 1980s. Reagan expanded the president's inherent war powers even further by using the armed forces to counter international terrorism. This was his justification for U.S. air raids against Libya and the capture of Arab terrorists in 1986.

Although Congress from time to time has challenged the president's broad use of his war powers, the courts have sided with the executive. Generally, Congress can only react to the president's foreign policy initiatives. And such reactions usually are muted if U.S. military forces are engaged in hostilities abroad. In these situations, lawmakers have shown little inclination to repudiate the president. The public looks primarily to the president, not Congress, for effective leadership in responding to foreign crises and protecting U.S. interests abroad.

Erosion of Congress's Powers

In the twentieth century, and especially since World War II, presidential assertion of the war power has drastically eroded Congress's prerogatives. Congress's war powers were written by the Founding Fathers with a much different world in mind. In the eighteenth century, battles usually came only after formal declarations of war. That is seldom the case now. Usually, only professional armies were affected, not the general population. War was clearly defined and separate from other forms of international relations.

After 1945 the United States emerged as a superpower, with major and minor interests and commitments in every corner of the globe. Today there are well over 700 U.S. military bases or stations overseas administered by the Defense Department. Unlike the prewar period, where diplomacy and defense were distinct and separate entities, today the military establishment plays an integral, and at some levels even a dominant, role in the foreign policy process. The Cold War between Western and Soviet-bloc nations, involving a state of tension just short of armed conflict, helped to merge traditional foreign policy concerns and defense issues.

During this period came a massive arms race, United Nations "police actions" and peacekeeping forces, worldwide terrorism, round-the-clock surveillance against Soviet nuclear attack, and sophisticated intelligence gathering.

New Kinds of Conflict

In the 1780s war was clearly defined and separate from other forms of international relations. The framers of the Constitution did not contemplate the kind of armed conflict that resulted from U.S. efforts to protect Persian Gulf shipping in the 1980s.

Such a state of defense preparedness blurred the distinction between war and peace and between foreign policy and domestic policy. And unlike the prewar period, the United States today has a large armed force, global treaty obligations, and numerous foreign assistance programs. One example of how these developments have contributed to the erosion of Congress's war power is the network of military alliances that grew up to contain the Soviet Union. A provision of the treaty establishing the North Atlantic Treaty Organization states that an attack on any member nation is considered an attack on all the members, committing the United States to war in the defense of all other member states.

Although the war power has lost much of its importance for Congress, this does not mean that the legislative branch has little or no voice in foreign policy. In many ways, Congress's influence has grown immensely since World War II. More than ever before in the nation's history, the making of foreign policy is shared by both branches. (*See* STRUCTURE AND POWERS; TREATY RATIFICATION; VANDENBERG, ARTHUR H.*)*

The Nuclear Age

In the nuclear age that began toward the end of World War II, the traditional view embodied in the Constitution—that Congress is in the best position to make decisions about war and peace—no longer seems valid. As the Founding Fathers viewed it, the process of deciding whether to go to war would be carefully weighed and debated by Congress over days or perhaps even weeks. Such a procedure has become obsolete.

Many factors have altered this traditional view of Congress's war powers. Through modern means of communications and transportation and, especially, military technology and the nature of modern warfare, the world has become much smaller. Geographic remoteness no longer ensures security. If war becomes imminent, the decision of whether to counterattack with nuclear missiles may have to be made in a matter of minutes, possibly even seconds. There is no time to consult Congress, and few members of Congress would insist on consultation in such a situation.

While Congress's power to declare war may no longer be relevant to the nuclear age, that does not fully explain why the power has not been invoked in the two major "conventional" wars since World War II, in Korea and Vietnam, and on other occasions when U.S. forces have been engaged in hostilities abroad.

Undeclared Wars

The word "security" has developed a much broader meaning than was understood by the Founding Fathers. Modern-day presidents may view major economic dislocations and international terrorism as just as threatening to U.S. security as military attacks. Every battle and military operation the United States has engaged in since World War II has been "undeclared." Many labels have been given to them: police actions, peacekeeping operations, defensive wars. Nor did Congress ever debate whether to go to war or deploy American forces in combat zones. With a large standing military force, and annual defense budgets in the hundreds of billions of dollars, the president is able to make military commitments without first requesting additional funds from Congress.

Congress, on the other hand, has not always been vigilant in asserting its prerogatives. When American troops entered combat in Korea and in Vietnam, Congress did not make a serious effort to debate the merits of declaring war or to encourage the president to seek its approval. In neither war did the chief executive acknowledge that a declaration of war was warranted or required by the Constitution. In Korea, U.S. troops were sent to battle under the auspices of the United Nations; in Vietnam, Congress approved the Gulf of Tonkin resolution, which President

Lyndon B. JOHNSON insisted was equivalent to a declaration of war.

1973 War Powers Act

Efforts to redress the imbalance in war powers between the two branches began in the late 1960s as the Vietnam War was expanded despite repeated promises by both the Johnson and Nixon administrations to bring the conflict quickly to an end. At the height of U.S. involvement in the late 1960s, more than 500,000 American troops were in Southeast Asia. As the fighting dragged on, creating more fatalities and enlarging the antiwar movement, Congress challenged the executive branch's prosecution of the war. Finally, in response to its inability to limit or end the bloodshed, Congress in 1973 passed the War Powers Act over President Richard NIXON's veto.

Through this law, Congress sought to check the president's war-making powers. It required the president "in every possible instance" to consult Congress before committing U.S. forces to ongoing or imminent hostilities. If the president on his own commits military personnel to a combat situation, he must report to Congress on his action within forty-eight hours. And U.S. forces must be withdrawn from such operations within ninety (sometimes sixty) days in certain circumstances unless Congress declares war or otherwise authorizes the operation to continue, extends the withdrawal deadline, or is unable to act because of an armed attack on the United States.

Congress also can pass a concurrent resolution at any time directing the president to withdraw U.S. forces from a foreign mission. However, since concurrent resolutions are not sent to the president for his approval, this action presumably is unconstitutional under a 1983 Supreme Court decision. (See LEGISLATIVE VETO; LEGISLATION.)

Every president has refused to acknowledge the constitutionality of the

War Powers Act. Presidents Gerald R. FORD, Jimmy Carter, and Reagan contended that no act of Congress could curtail or modify their constitutional powers as commander in chief to take such actions as they alone thought necessary to protect national security or the lives of Americans. Further—with one exception—each of these chief executives was careful to avoid taking any actions that implied Congress had the authority, under the act, to control or delay any military or quasi-military action taken by the president. That exception was in 1983, when Reagan reluctantly agreed to a compromise with Congress and signed into law a time limit for the deployment of U.S. Marines in Lebanon. He continued to insist, however, that the War Powers Act was not valid. From the White House point of view, Congress has only one legitimate means of controlling the deployment of military forces overseas. That is by refusing to appropriate funds to support a foreign military operation.

Congressional Disagreement Congress itself is divided on the desirability and the constitutionality of the War Powers Act. There is disagreement about how much power and flexibility the president should have to run the military and defend the country. In September 1987 the Senate refused to approve legislation that would have invoked the act for President Reagan's Persian Gulf policy. Reagan had refused to invoke the law when he approved the use of U.S. warships to escort Kuwaiti oil tankers through the Persian Gulf, despite a series of armed confrontations with Iran. Although the Senate backed the president, some 110 members filed a lawsuit seeking to force the president to comply with the law's reporting requirement. A federal district court dismissed the suit, but the matter was appealed to a higher court.

The issue for some members, however, is chiefly political and depends more on whether they support the president and his policies. Some members have backed both sides of this question, favoring wide presidential latitude for Presidents Johnson and Nixon to conduct the war in Vietnam but calling for congressional participation in the 1970s when President Carter proposed a withdrawal of U.S. troops from South Korea.

Politics The exercise of the war power by the executive and legislative branches is governed by many factors besides the formal constitutional provisions. In the end, the effectiveness of Congress in exercising its powers, whether they are derived from the Constitution or legislation, such as the War Powers Act and other laws, depends on political factors. When Congress favors presidential policies involving the deployment of forces abroad there is little concern about constitutional or legal niceties. If there is substantial opposition by lawmakers, demands are quickly raised about the need to assert Congress's prerogatives.

Many factors can influence how and when the war power is used—the makeup of Congress between Democrats and Republicans; the influence, prestige, and popularity of the president; foreign policy successes and failures; the views of U.S. allies; and international developments, among others.

Alternatives to the War Power

In the absence of an effective war power, Congress has turned to various legislative actions as a way to participate in presidential decisions committing the armed forces to combat. In very few instances has Congress actually tried to restrain or block such presidential decisions. As one substitute for formal declarations of war, Congress since 1945 has passed at least six policy resolutions approving executive decisions either to send the armed forces to foreign trouble spots or to commit forces to hostilities if U.S. allies or interests were attacked in Taiwan (Formosa), Berlin, Cuba, the Middle East, Vietnam, or Lebanon.

One of the most controversial actions ever taken by Congress was its approval in August 1964 of the Gulf of Tonkin Resolution, which sanctioned President Johnson's prior use of American naval forces against North Vietnam. The Johnson administration subsequently called the resolution the "functional equivalent" of a declaration of war against Vietnam, although it was never presented to members of Congress in that context. Congress repealed the Tonkin resolution in 1970.

Presidents in the post-World War II period frequently have pointed to legislative actions by Congress as substitutes for declarations of war when it suited their purposes. Other congressional acts used by the Johnson and Nixon administrations to justify waging war in Southeast Asia included extension of the military draft, and military appropriations bills during the war years.

Where there is strong disagreement with the president, lawmakers tend to adopt amendments circumscribing his actions. One of the key issues in the 1987 Iran-contra hearings was the applicability and constitutionality of an amendment that prohibited the Reagan administration from giving U.S. military aid to the contra rebels in Nicaragua. In the late 1960s, hearings on the Vietnam conflict conducted by the Senate FOREIGN RELATIONS Committee helped galvanize opposition to the war. The Senate adopted a succession of antiwar amendments, but most were emasculated by the House.

Through concurrent resolutions, Congress may express its sentiment on major foreign and defense issues. In 1969 the Senate adopted a resolution expressing the sense of the Senate that national commitments involving the armed forces are entered into only from actions taken by both the legislative and executive branches—through joint resolutions, for example. However, the House did not consider the measure and it was not binding on the president. Nixon, in fact, ignored the resolution less than a year later when he ordered U.S. troops into Cambodia.

After the Vietnam War, Congress terminated several grants of emergency powers to the president that had been approved during the 1930s Depression, the Korean War, and other national crises.   ~

Watergate Scandal

Watergate is the descriptive word for political scandals in Richard NIXON's presidency. They dwarfed all others in American history. The evidence of lawbreaking led directly to the White House and even into its Oval Office, implicating the president himself. Facing IMPEACHMENT charges in Congress, Nixon became the first president ever to resign the office. His departure from the White House on August 9, 1974, ended a constitutional crisis that was marked by the president's defiance of Congress and the courts through spurious claims to EXECUTIVE PRIVILEGE and the obstruction of justice on the false grounds of national security.

Nixon was spared the likelihood of criminal prosecution when he received a pardon from his successor, Gerald R. FORD, on September 8, 1974. But nearly a score of others in government and his 1972 reelection campaign, including several close associates, drew prison sentences. Still others, including some prominent people, paid fines or—in a few instances—went to prison for Watergate-related activities. These activities included illegal contributions to Nixon's 1972 reelection campaign and

such "dirty tricks" as spying and sabotage to undermine his Democratic foes and cause trouble for "enemies" of various political stripes.

The Break-In

The chain of events that led to Nixon's disgrace was set in motion by a botched break-in at Democratic National Committee offices not far from the White House. They were on the sixth floor of a building in a posh apartment-office complex called Watergate. There at 2:30 a.m. on June 17, 1972, District of Columbia police caught and arrested five men who had forced their way in. The intruders wore surgical gloves and carried walkie-talkies and photographic and electronic eavesdropping equipment. It was later disclosed that, among other things, they intended to replace a faulty tap on the telephone of the Democratic party's national chairman, Lawrence F. O'Brien, and install a bugging device nearby.

Four of the five became known as the Cubans. They were Bernard L. Barker, Virgilio R. Gonzalez, Eugenio R. Martinez, and Frank Sturgis, all from Miami and identified with Cuban groups bitterly opposed to Fidel Castro. They had ties to the Central Intelli-

gence Agency, as did the fifth man, James W. McCord, Jr. He had been a former agent of the CIA and the Federal Bureau of Investigation before becoming director of security for the Committee for the Re-Election of the President, an organization sometimes known by the initials CRP or CREEP.

O'Brien called the break-in "an incredible act of political espionage" and on June 20 filed a $1 million civil lawsuit against the Nixon reelection committee—which was later settled out of court. He did not accept the word of John N. Mitchell, Nixon's former law partner and attorney general, who was running the reelection campaign. Mitchell said the day after the break-in, "McCord and the other four men arrested in Democratic headquarters Saturday were not operating on our behalf or with our consent in the alleged bugging." Ronald L. Ziegler, the White House press secretary, characterized the break-in as a "third-rate burglary" and nothing more. President Nixon reinforced that view at a news conference on June 22, saying: "This kind of activity . . . has no place in the electoral process. And, as Mr. Ziegler has stated, the White House has no involvement whatever in this particular incident."

Actually, the top echelon at the White House was very much involved and was busy devising a cover-up strategy. White House aides pressured the CIA to ask the FBI to call off its investigation of the case—by falsely saying intelligence operations in Mexico would be jeopardized. The Watergate schemers feared, among other things, that money "laundered" through a Mexican bank to pay the burglars would be traced to its source, the Nixon campaign headquarters. All this, and much more, would come to light only little by little over the next two years. Nixon's direct participation in the cover-up was not known with certainty until his final days in office. Once his denials were refuted, his presidency was doomed. Until then, the Watergate drama would be played out in the courts, in congressional committees, in the headlines and before the television cameras.

Without the aggressive reporting of several newspapers and magazines, the full story might never have come out. The *Washington Post* took the lead in breaching the administration's "stonewalling," as the Watergate principals called their concealment effort. The paper's reporting team of Carl Bernstein and Bob Woodward was especially adept at obtaining Watergate information from anonymous sources, including a celebrated executive-branch official identified only as Deep Throat. For its Watergate coverage, the *Post* caught the administration's wrath but won the coveted 1972 Pulitzer Prize for "meritorious service."

That summer, Rep. Wright Patman, a Texas Democrat who was chairman of the House Banking and Currency Committee, began inquiring into news reports of the Nixon campaign's money laundering. But the White House prevailed on friendly members of Patman's committee to abort his investigation. The voting public seemed little concerned that fall with the allegations of scandal. Americans

went to the polls on November 7 and gave Nixon a landslide reelection victory.

The Watergate Committee

But Watergate would not go away. At the beginning of the new Ninety-third Congress in January 1973, the Senate unanimously approved a resolution by Majority Leader Mike MANSFIELD, a Montana Democrat, to create a seven-member, bipartisan investigating committee, the Select Committee on Presidential Campaign Activities, commonly called the Watergate Committee. Its chairman was Sam J. ERVIN, Jr., an elderly North Carolina Democrat serving out his last Senate term. His courtly manner, jowly appearance, and propensity for quoting the Bible made him briefly a cult hero—and disguised his skill as a former judge and trial lawyer. That same month in a federal courtroom near the Capitol, the five break-in defendants and two others went on trial.

The two added defendants were E. Howard Hunt and G. Gordon Liddy. Hunt was an ex-CIA agent and writer of spy stories then serving as a consultant to White House aide Charles W. Colson. Liddy was a former FBI agent who later worked for John D. Ehrlichman, Nixon's chief domestic adviser, and then moved on to Nixon's reelection campaign—first under Mitchell and then under Maurice H. Stans, the former secretary of commerce, who was directing fund-raising. It would later be disclosed that Liddy and Hunt had hired two of the Cubans (Barker and Martinez) not only for that job but for another break-in, which occurred the previous year at the Beverly Hills office of a California psychiatrist, Lewis J. Fielding. His patient, Daniel Ellsberg, had earned Nixon's hatred by providing the *New York Times* and the *Washington Post* with the so-called Pentagon Papers, an official but hitherto secret study of American involvement in the

Vietnam War. The break-in at the doctor's office was an attempt to find derogatory material about Ellsberg.

The publication of the Pentagon Papers caused a group of White House aides to create a vigilante group to stop news leaks. This group, called the "plumbers," was headed by Egil Krogh, Jr., and sometimes assisted by Colson. It fell to plumbers Liddy, Hunt, and McCord to carry out the Watergate break-in. The Cubans and Hunt pleaded guilty while McCord and Liddy underwent a jury trial and were convicted January 30, 1973. The trial judge, John J. Sirica, delayed sentencing until March 23, at which time he stunned the court by reading a letter from McCord saying that others were involved in the break-in but that the defendants had been under political pressure to remain silent. Moreover, McCord said perjury had been committed during the trial. McCord was intensely loyal to his former employer, the CIA, and expressed fear that the White House might try to portray the Watergate break-in as its work.

During the trial, Sirica frequently complained that he was not getting the full story about the case. To try to make the defendants tell more of what they knew to a sitting federal grand jury or the Senate Watergate Committee, Sirica provisionally handed out maximum terms of up to forty years. "[S]hould you decide to speak freely," he said, "I would have to weigh that factor in appraising what sentence will be finally imposed. . . ." McCord, whose sentencing was delayed indefinitely, met the next day in a closed meeting with the Senate committee and testified that Mitchell, Colson, John W. Dean III, and Jeb Stuart Magruder knew in advance about the break-in. Magruder was deputy director of the reelection committee and Dean the White House counsel. Fearful of what lay ahead, Dean and Magruder agreed to tell the committee what they knew in return for

"use" (partial) IMMUNITY from prosecution. Several other Watergate figures followed suit. Sirica's key role in unraveling the Watergate cover-up brought prominence to the once-obscure jurist, now popularly known as Maximum John. *Time* magazine selected him Man of the Year in 1973.

Nixon's problems continued to grow. At Senate Judiciary Committee confirmation hearings on the nomination of L. Patrick Gray as FBI director, Gray implicated several officials of the administration in its effort to thwart the FBI's investigation of Watergate. Gray's testimony doomed his nomination, causing an irritated Ehrlichman to tell Dean on March 6: "Well, I think we ought to let him hang there. Let him twist slowly, slowly in the wind." The hapless Gray, abandoned by the White House, withdrew his nomination and resigned as acting FBI director.

At a brief news conference on April 17, Nixon said he had begun "intensive new inquiries" into the Watergate affair "as a result of serious charges which came to my attention." On April 30 the president announced Dean's firing and the resignations of White House Chief of Staff H. R. Haldeman, Ehrlichman, and Attorney General Richard G. Kleindienst. The last three, all implicated in news leaks, spoke of having difficulty carrying out their duties amid the Watergate controversies. In a television address that night, Nixon said he took full responsibility for any improper activities in his 1972 presidential campaign, and he pledged that justice would be pursued "fairly, fully, and impartially, no matter who is involved." The president named Elliot L. Richardson as the new attorney general, placing him in charge of the administration's own investigation and giving him authority to appoint a special prosecutor in the case. Richardson promptly chose Archibald Cox, a Harvard law professor who had served as solicitor general under Presidents John F. KENNEDY and

Lyndon B. JOHNSON.

The nationally televised Senate Watergate hearings opened on May 17 in the ornate Caucus Room of the Old Senate Office Building, the site of earlier famous hearings, including Sen. Joseph R. McCARTHY's inquiries into alleged communist subversion in the early 1950s and the investigation of the Teapot Dome oil-leasing scandal of President Warren G. Harding's administration. McCord, the first witness, took the stand May 18 and told of White House pressure to get him to keep silent and plead guilty to break-in charges in return for a promise of eventual executive clemency. As the hearings continued through the summer and into the fall, time and again the committee's ranking Republican, Sen. Howard H. BAKER, Jr., of Tennessee, would ask: "How much did the president know, and when did he know it?" Dean, who took the witness stand for five days, beginning June 25, became the first witness publicly to accuse the president of direct involvement in the cover-up. But it was Dean's word against the president's until tapes of some of the disputed conversations became available. In mid-July, the committee was startled to learn—almost accidentally—that the president had secretly recorded many of the Oval Office conversations.

The Tapes

From that time on, the Watergate struggle focused on the investigators' attempts to gain control of the tapes over Nixon's objections. After he refused to obey subpoenas from Cox and the Watergate Committee to produce them, Judge Sirica ruled on August 29 that the president should let him review them privately to see if the doctrine of executive privilege applied. Nixon appealed, and while the case was on the way to the Supreme Court for a historic constitutional test, he offered to prepare summaries of nine tapes Cox sought and let John C. STENNIS, a Mis-

sissippi Democrat and Senate elder known for his integrity, check their accuracy against the tapes themselves. Cox, in turn, would have to agree to request no more tapes. Cox rejected the deal, and Nixon ordered Richardson to fire him. Richardson refused and resigned, as did Deputy Attorney General William D. Ruckelshaus. Robert H. Bork, elevated to acting attorney general, complied. The resignations and firing occurred on Saturday, October 20, 1973, an event that was quickly labeled "the Saturday night massacre." It created, in the words of the new White House chief of staff, Gen. Alexander M. Haig, Jr., "a firestorm" of public outrage. According to a Gallup Poll, Nixon's popularity rating among the American people dropped to a low point of 27 percent, a plunge of 40 points during the year.

The nation's confidence in its president had also been damaged by the forced resignation of Vice President Spiro T. Agnew and by reports that Nixon had paid only nominal federal income taxes during most of his first term. He later settled the tax matter by paying $476,561 in back taxes and interest. Agnew resigned October 10 and the same day pleaded *nolo contendere*—no contest—to a charge of tax evasion. He was sentenced to three years of unsupervised probation and fined $10,000. The charge arose from an investigation into Baltimore County corruption when he was its executive and was not directly related to Watergate. But Agnew's downfall reflected on the president's judgment of men and the moral climate of the Nixon administration. Nixon promptly named Ford, the House minority leader, the new vice president. He was confirmed by the House and Senate without difficulty and sworn into office December 6, 1973.

Impeachment Drive

Jolted by the erosion of public support, Nixon said on October 23 he would surrender the tapes after all. The reversal came too late; the NIXON IM-PEACHMENT EFFORT had begun. That day forty-four Watergate bills were introduced in Congress, many of them calling for impeachment. Rep. Peter W. Rodino, Jr., a New Jersey Democrat who chaired the JUDICIARY Committee, said on October 24 he would proceed "full steam ahead" with an impeachment investigation. With only four dissenting votes, the House on February 6, 1974, gave its formal approval for the committee to report whether Nixon should be impeached.

In the meantime, Nixon's lawyers told Judge Sirica that two long-sought tapes did not exist and that an eighteen-minute segment of conversation had been erased from another tape—eliminating evidence that was expected to be damning to Nixon. Leon Jaworski, a former president of the American Bar Association who had been named the new special prosecutor, demanded more tapes. They were refused, and as he awaited a Supreme Court ruling on the tapes, his staff prepared evidence of complicity among Nixon and his associates in the cover-up for the Watergate grand jury. On March 1, the Watergate grand jury indicted Mitchell, Haldeman, Ehrlichman, and Colson. They were later convicted in federal district court and, after a long appeals process, went to prison. At the time of the indictments, Mitchell and Stans were being tried in federal court in New York on charges of interfering with a government investigation of Robert L. Vesco, an international financier, in return for a $200,000 contribution to the Nixon campaign. Both were acquitted; Vesco fled the country and never was tried.

The same grand jury named Nixon a coconspirator but at Jaworski's request did not indict him. The prosecutor explained later that an indictment would have resulted in a trial interfering with and probably delaying the im-

peachment proceedings. On July 24, 1974, hours before the House Judiciary Committee began its public debate on impeachment, the Supreme Court ruled unanimously against the president's refusal to submit sixty-four tapes to Sirica. Three in particular contained incriminating material, but the White House did not release them until August 5—until after the committee voted on impeachment. On July 27, 29, and 30, it approved three of five proposed articles of impeachment; for obstruction of justice (27-11 vote), abuse of presidential power (28-10), and contempt of Congress (21-17). Ten of the seventeen Republicans on the thirty-eight-member committee voted against all five articles. But the release of the tapes erased all doubt about Nixon's involvement from their minds. Each of the ten previously dissenting Republicans then called for his resignation or impeachment.

The president chose resignation, which came on August 9 in a tearful, televised farewell at the White House. Nixon acknowledged no wrongdoing but attributed his departure to loss of political support in Congress. Ford was immediately sworn in as the nation's thirty-eighth president. In his brief inaugural address, Ford said: "My fellow Americans, our long national nightmare is over. Our Constitution works. Our great republic is a government of laws and not of men. Here, the people rule."

The American people shared in the great sense of relief he expressed. However, not everyone was sanguine about the outcome of Watergate. Rep. John Conyers, Jr., a Michigan Democrat, said Nixon did more than anyone else or anything else to remove himself from office. "If the system has worked," Conyers continued, "it has worked by accident and good fortune." Judge Sirica later lamented that while Nixon's associates went to prison, the former president "received a large government pension and retired to his lovely home in

San Clemente [California]."

Nixon wrote his memoirs, in which he again portrayed his decision to leave office in terms of losing his political base in Congress. In May 1977, in a television interview with David Frost shown in America and Europe, Nixon said: "I have let the American people down. And I have to carry that burden with me the rest of my life." In an account of the Nixon interview, Frost wrote: "The man whose pride would not permit him to say, 'I broke the law; I violated my constitutional duty,' had come as close to admitting both as it was in his pathology to do."

Although many of Nixon's Watergate associates did indeed go to prison, they spent relatively little time behind bars. Only one, Liddy, served as long as fifty-two months. And several of them, including Liddy, found lucrative contracts and a ready audience for their books or lectures. Others found new career opportunities in business and, in the case of Colson and Magruder, the ministry.   ~

ADDITIONAL READINGS

Woodward, Bob, and Carl Bernstein. *All the President's Men.* 1987.
_____. *The Final Days.* 1987.

Ways and Means Committee, House

The House Ways and Means Committee has a pivotal role in Congress. Charged with raising revenues to run the government, the committee is also responsible for disbursing about 40 percent of the federal budget. The panel approves taxes and tariffs, and it also makes rules about public assistance, So-cial Security, health insurance, and unemployment compensation.

Though less formidable after 1970s REFORMS, Ways and Means is still one of the most powerful committees in the House. Because the House originates most tax legislation, Ways and Means usually gets to set the agenda, with the Senate FINANCE Committee reacting to House proposals.

Made a permanent committee in 1802, Ways and Means handled all aspects of federal finances until the mid-1860s, when the APPROPRIATIONS Committee was set up to oversee spending. At that time the Senate also split Appropriations away from the Finance Committee. After Social Security was set up in the 1930s, both taxing panels saw their plates fill with spending questions as Congress created welfare, health, and retirement programs financed by special federal levies. Funding of these programs has been kept separate from the regular appropriations process.

Although Ways and Means focused on tariffs in the nineteenth century, its source of revenues in the twentieth century has been taxes. Congress has spent decades manipulating tax laws, with breaks and loopholes for an endless list of causes that range from oil production to home ownership. The tax code affects every business and individual; no lobbyist can afford not to know what Ways and Means is doing.

Dan ROSTENKOWSKI, a Chicago Democrat who entered the House in 1959, became Ways and Means chairman in 1981. His background as a skillful insider in House politics was expected to help bring the chaotic committee into line. His predecessor, Oregon Democrat Al Ullman (1914-86), chairman from 1974 to 1981, had been more timid politically, and competing factions on the panel had rarely worked in harmony. But Rostenkowski's first major tax bill was rejected by the House, which instead took a substitute measure backed by President Ronald Reagan and House Republicans. That loss was eventually overshadowed by the 1986 tax "reform" bill, which Rostenkowski helped engineer. The measure eliminated many special tax breaks and lowered tax rates.

Rostenkowski's committee had thirty-seven members in the 100th Congress (1987-89), with only thirteen Republicans. That favorable ratio was a legacy of a Democratic CAUCUS vote in 1974 to expand the committee, which earlier had only twenty-five members and was split more evenly between Democrats and Republicans. The smaller group had been cohesive, at least publicly, and promoted the mystique of tax-writing as a difficult task, too complex for outsiders to understand. Arkansas Democrat Wilbur D. MILLS, chairman from 1957 to 1974, put a premium on consensus, keeping the members in closed meetings until they hashed out a bipartisan approach. An expert on the tax code, Mills was legendary for his successes on the House floor, where the united committee could resist major amendments to its tax bills. Rostenkowski resurrected the closed meetings in the mid-1980s, claiming that members worked better without public scrutiny.

Between 1910 and 1974, Democrats on Ways and Means had a special role in the party leadership. They were given responsibility for making Democratic committee assignments after a 1910 revolt by House members, which stripped that authority from the autocratic SPEAKER, Joseph G. CANNON. At the time, Majority Leader Oscar W. UNDERWOOD of Alabama was also chairman of the tax-writing panel. Controlling committee assignments gave Democratic members of Ways and Means extra clout to win votes for tax bills and made them key players in House politics.

But later critics saw the House as a closed system, dominated by older, senior members, and wanted those making committee assignments to be more accountable to the party. These reformers convinced Democrats in 1974 to shift the task to the Democratic Steering and Policy Committee, a group of about thirty members, including top party leaders and a dozen members elected by region. *(See* LEADERSHIP.*)* ~

Webster, Daniel

Daniel Webster (1782-1852) was a lawyer, a member of the House of Representatives and Senate, and twice secretary of state. Above all, however, he was an orator in an era of American politics when oratory was a high art. Webster used his skill as a debater to protect the commercial interests of his constituency, to benefit his legal clients, and to move crowds. He is best remembered for his eloquence when, putting aside special interests, he analyzed the nature of the Union and pleaded for its preservation in the years leading up to the Civil War.

Before entering the House of Representatives from his native state of New Hampshire in 1813, Webster practiced law, pamphleteering, and occasional oratory. Once in Congress, he spoke out against the War of 1812 and protective tariffs. He continued to practice law and was retained to plead before the Supreme Court in several well-known cases. He left the House in 1817 and moved to Boston to pursue his lucrative legal career. In 1823 he again entered the House as a Federalist, although this time as a representative from Boston. He remained a member of the Federalist party until 1845, when he became a Whig. In the House Webster continued his legal career and was made chairman of the JUDICIARY Committee. Reflecting the commercial interests of his constituents, he supported protec-

Legendary Orator
Sen. Daniel Webster was an orator in an era of American politics when oratory was a high art. Best known of his speeches and an example of Webster at his finest was his 1830 reply to South Carolina Sen. Robert Y. Hayne on the subject of nullification.

tive tariffs and continued to do so throughout the remainder of his career.

In 1827 he entered the Senate, where he stayed until 1850, leaving to serve as secretary of state in 1841-43 and again in 1850-52. Best known of his speeches and an example of Webster at his finest was his 1830 reply to South Carolina Sen. Robert Y. HAYNE on the subject of nullification—the right of a state to nullify an act of the federal government. Above all, Webster believed in the sanctity of the Union; he ended his oration with the words "Liberty *and* Union, now and forever, one and inseparable!"

It was his belief in the importance of maintaining the union of states that led Webster to criticize both the South and the North on the issue of slavery. He angered both sides by urging compromise on the western expansion of slavery.

Despite his large legal fees, Webster through his extravagance was often in financial difficulties. The Bank of the United States paid him a retainer while he was a senator, and eastern business interests supplemented his congressional salary to keep him in Washington. These financial arrangements did not enhance his reputation, but his devotion to the union of states and his

extraordinary eloquence put him among the most notable members in a Senate of notables that included Henry CLAY, John C. CALHOUN, and Thomas Hart BENTON.   ～

Wesberry v. Sanders.   See REAPPORTIONMENT AND REDISTRICTING.

Whips.   See LEADERSHIP.

White House

The White House, which rivals the U.S. Capitol for the distinction of being Washington's most revered building, serves three main functions. It is the president's home, the president's office, and one of the city's leading tourist attractions, drawing some 1.5 million unofficial visitors a year. Official guests at dinners and receptions swell the annual total of visitors by about 50,000.

The White House is the oldest public structure in the nation's capital; its cornerstone was laid in 1792. Called "the Palace" in the original plans, the building was designed by architect James Hoban and occupies a site chosen by George Washington.

Many persons viewing the White House for the first time express surprise at its relatively modest size. The main building, which is four stories high, is about 170 feet long and 85 feet wide. New space has been added over the years, including east and west terraces, the president's Oval Office (originally built in 1909 and moved to a different part of the West Wing twenty-five years later), the East Wing (1942), and a penthouse and a bomb shelter (1952). The colonnade at the east end of the White House is the public entrance for the daily tours of the public rooms on the main floor.

The public rooms shown to tour groups are all on the main floor. Each of the rooms is heavily used. Large receptions (and during recent administrations, presidential news conferences) usually are held in the East Room. Dinners for visiting dignitaries are held in the State Dining Room at the opposite end of the building. Three smaller rooms lie between these two large chambers. The Blue Room is the scene of many diplomatic and social receptions, while the Red Room and the Green Room are used for private and semiofficial gatherings.

Early Years

In November 1800, only four months before his single term in office ended, John Adams became the first president to live in the White House. His wife, Abigail, was not impressed by their new home. The place was "habitable," she wrote to her daughter in Massachusetts, but bells for summoning servants were "wholly wanting to assist us in this great castle." She also complained about the lack of warmth, noting that "wood is not to be had, because people cannot be found to cut and cart it!"

Fourteen years later, during the War of 1812, British troops set fire to

The President's House

The White House is the oldest public structure in the nation's capital. Like the Capitol, it was set afire by British troops during the War of 1812.

the White House as well as to the Capitol. Only a torrential rainstorm saved both buildings from being reduced to total ruin.

Among the items salvaged from the Executive Mansion by Dolley Madison, the wife of President James MADISON, was the famed full-length portrait of George Washington by Gilbert Stuart. It is the only object known to have remained in the White House since the Adamses first occupied it.

Restoration of the White House, supervised by Hoban, took three years. To hide unsightly smoke stains, the exterior walls of gray stone were painted white. Even before then, however, the building had been known as the White House. Many years later, when President Theodore Roosevelt had it engraved upon his stationery, the name became official.

The main portion of the White House looks much the same today from the outside as it did when the John Adamses moved in. But the interior has undergone many changes. In 1817, for example, Hoban added twelve new fireplaces. Nonetheless, heating the high-ceilinged public rooms remained a problem even after the addition of a central-heating system in 1853.

Plumbing was also a worry. It was not until 1833, during President Andrew Jackson's second term, that the White House was provided with hot and cold running water. A zinc-lined bathtub was installed around 1855, but the White House still had only one full bathroom when President Benjamin Harrison was inaugurated in 1889.

During the Benjamin Harrison administration, the White House was first wired for electric lighting. This change, plus others in later years, meant that floors and walls were continually being pierced to accommodate new flues, pipes, and wires. All these "improvements" eventually took their toll on the structural stability of the aging building.

Truman Restoration

Signs of serious trouble became impossible to ignore shortly after World War II. In late 1947 President Harry S TRUMAN became increasingly disturbed about vibrations in the floors of certain rooms of the White House family quarters. As a result, he ordered an engineering survey, whose findings led to follow-up studies of the condition of the entire building. The White House, it was found, was in such precarious physical shape that it needed immediate and drastic renovation.

A complete restoration of the White House followed, lasting from late 1949 to early 1952. During that time, the Trumans lived at Blair House, just across Pennsylvania Avenue from the White House. In their absence the Executive Mansion's original exterior walls were given a new underpinning of concrete, and the interior was provided with new foundations, a two-story basement, and a steel frame.

President Truman visited the reconstructed White House on March 27, 1952—two days before announcing that he would not seek reelection. The building now had fifty-four rooms instead of the previous forty-eight. On arrival, the president was given a gold key, which he held aloft for reporters and onlookers to see before he turned to enter.

Furnishing of the White House has varied greatly over the years, reflecting shifting tastes in society at large. Even today, each presidential family may decorate the second- and third-floor private quarters as it wishes.

Four rooms of the second-floor family quarters are worth special mention. The Yellow Oval Room, a formal drawing room with eighteenth century French furniture, opens onto the Truman balcony (added in 1948). The view from there of the Washington Monument and the Jefferson Memorial is regarded as one of the city's finest. Next door to the Yellow Oval Room on the east is the Treaty Room, which was

VISITING THE WHITE HOUSE

The White House ranks high on the sightseeing lists of most visitors to Washington, D. C. A free, self-guided tour takes them through the public rooms on the main floor. Visitors are welcome Tuesday through Saturday, from 10 a.m. to noon. The White House is also open for such tours on certain major public holidays, including Memorial Day and Labor Day. A special weekend garden tour is scheduled each fall and spring; dates vary.

The White House Visitor's Office uses a ticket system to minimize long lines and help visitors schedule their day's activities. On tour days, tickets for that day become available at 8 a.m. from a special kiosk on the Ellipse, the grassy area just south of the White House. Each person planning to join the tour must be present in order to get the free entrance ticket. Each ticket is valid for a particular time that same morning; visitors need not show up at the White House until the time their visit is scheduled. The supply of tickets is limited, but for most of the year the 7,000 usually available each day are enough to accommodate visitors. However, during the crush of the summer tourist season, some ticket-seekers are turned away from the kiosk.

Another route to the White House requires advance planning. Most senators and representatives will arrange for their constituents to take part in special guided White House tours conducted before 10 a.m. Write your own senator or representative and request the tour on a specific date.

used for cabinet meetings until the Theodore Roosevelt administration. Farther to the east lie the Queen's Bedroom and the Lincoln Bedroom.

Other parts of the family quarters on the second and third floors of the White House were redecorated by President Ronald Reagan and his wife Nancy in 1981-82. They themselves raised nearly $1 million from friends and supporters to have the work done. The net effect was to impart a lighter, more contemporary atmosphere to living spaces that some presidential families have found confining.

It is difficult nowadays to change the appearance of the public rooms on the main floor of the White House. These rooms have come to be regarded as almost a museum, especially since Jacqueline Kennedy—the wife of President John F. KENNEDY—launched a campaign in the early 1960s to furnish them with authentic items from the late eighteenth and early nineteenth centuries. Any major alterations to the public rooms must now be approved by the Committee for the Preservation of the White House, established by executive order in 1964.

White House Grounds

Over time, presidents and their families have left their imprint on the White House grounds as well as on the building itself. It has long been customary, for example, for each president to plant at least one tree on the grounds. In the 1820s President John Quincy ADAMS hoped to make the grounds a living museum of native American plants, particularly trees.

One of the best-known landscaping features of the White House is the Rose Garden, which lies just beyond the French doors of the Oval Office. Roses were first planted there in 1913 by Ellen Wilson, President Woodrow Wilson's first wife. But the garden as it appears today dates from 1962 when, at the request of President Kennedy, the Rose Garden was redesigned by Mrs. Paul Mellon. The Rose Garden has been the setting for many official functions. ~

Women in Congress

Women, who were not allowed to vote until 1920, always have been underrepresented in Congress. Only twenty-five women—thirteen Democrats and twelve Republicans—held seats in the 100th Congress that opened in 1987; they accounted for less than 5 percent of the total membership.

By 1987, 119 women had been elected or appointed to Congress, including two—one Senate, one House— who were never sworn in because Congress was not in session before their terms expired. Fifteen actually served in the Senate, although one sat there for just one day; 107 served in the House.

The first woman in Congress was Jeannette RANKIN, a Montana Republican who was elected to the House in 1916. Her state gave women the right to vote before a 1920 constitutional amendment mandated WOMEN'S SUFFRAGE. The first woman to serve in the Senate was Rebecca L. Felton, a Georgia Democrat. She was sworn in to fill a vacancy on November 21, 1922, but she gave up her seat the next day to the elected candidate.

Often women were appointed to fill vacancies created by the death of their husbands, allowing governors and other state leaders more time to choose a successor or hold a special election. The "widow's mandate," as such appointments are called, has been for some women the spark for a political career of their own. Margaret Chase SMITH, a Maine Republican, filled her husband's House seat when he died in 1940, and then went on to serve four terms in the Senate. Edith Nourse Rogers, a Massachusetts Republican, entered the House after her husband died in 1925 and remained there for thirty-five years, until her own death in 1960. Hattie W. Caraway, an Arkansas Democrat, took her husband's Senate seat when he died in 1931, and continued to serve until 1945.

Only three of the twenty-five women in Congress in 1987 held the seats of their late husbands, and all had been elected to the positions. Two were senators: Nancy Landon Kassebaum, a

Early Arrivals
Three pioneer women in Congress pose on the steps of the Capitol: from left, Alice M. Robertson of Oklahoma, Mae E. Nolan of California, and Winifred S. M. Huck of Illinois. All served in the House of Representatives in the early 1920s.

Number of Women Members in Congress 1947-87

Listed below by Congress is the number of women members of the Senate and House of Representatives from the 80th Congress through the beginning of the 100th Congress. The figures include women appointed to office as well as those chosen by voters in general elections and special elections. *(Women members, p. 487)*

Congress		Senate	House
100th	1987-89	2	23
99th	1985-87	2	23
98th	1983-85	2	22
97th	1981-83	2	21
96th	1979-81	1	16
95th	1977-79	2	18
94th	1975-77	0	19
93d	1973-75	0	16
92d	1971-73	2	13
91st	1969-71	1	10
90th	1967-69	1	11
89th	1965-67	2	10
88th	1963-65	2	11
87th	1961-63	2	17
86th	1959-61	1	16
85th	1957-59	1	15
84th	1955-57	1	16
83d	1953-55	3	12
82d	1951-53	1	10
81st	1949-51	1	9
80th	1947-49	1	7

Kansas Republican first elected in 1978, and Barbara A. Mikulski, a Maryland Democrat who was elected to the Senate in 1986 after one term in the House. Ironically, the Republican Mikulski defeated was also a woman, one of six seeking Senate seats that year.

No woman had chaired a full committee in either chamber since Rep. Leonor K. Sullivan, a Missouri Democrat, headed the MERCHANT MARINE AND FISHERIES Committee from 1973 to 1979. Mae Ella Nolan, a California Republican who served from 1923 to 1925, was the first woman to chair a congressional committee; she headed the House Committee on Expenditures in the Post Office Department.

Congress has been an important starting point for many women seeking national office. Shirley CHISHOLM, a Democratic representative from New York, ran for president in 1972, and Geraldine Ferraro, also a New York Democrat, was her party's vice presidential nominee in 1984.   ~

Women's Suffrage

Although several states gave women the right to vote in the nineteenth century, full voting rights were not extended to all American women until 1920, when the Nineteenth Amendment to the Constitution was ratified. That year, for the first time, women in every state had the right to participate in the November election.

The amendment states: "The right of citizens of the United States to vote shall not be denied or abridged by the United States or by any State on account of sex."

The decades-long effort for women's suffrage was under way as early as the 1830s. Women working to abolish slavery were struck by the similarity of their lot, under law, to that of slaves. A key event was the 1848 Women's Rights Convention at Seneca Falls, New York, where women passed a Declaration of Principles, a broad manifesto that included a call for the vote.

After the Civil War, some women contended they were granted equal rights, including voting privileges, by the Fourteenth Amendment, which freed slaves. Susan B. Anthony urged women to claim their right to vote at the polls; she did so in Rochester, New York, in 1872. Anthony was arrested, and later convicted of "voting without having a lawful right to vote." Anthony

Winning the Vote

American women did not win full voting rights until the Nineteenth Amendment to the Constitution was ratified in 1920. Suffragists had to battle decades-long opposition to win the franchise.

and her followers pressed Congress for a constitutional amendment granting the franchise to women, but in 1887 the Senate rejected the proposal, 16-34.

The suffragists then turned to the states, where they were more successful. By the turn of the century, four western states had extended the franchise to women: Wyoming, Colorado, Utah, and Idaho. Then, as the PROGRESSIVE movement gained influence, additional states gave women the vote: Washington in 1910, California in 1911, Arizona, Kansas, and Oregon in 1912, Montana and Nevada in 1914, New York in 1917, and Michigan, South Dakota, and Oklahoma in 1918.

Arguments for and against the vote included extravagant claims; some said women's enfranchisement would end corruption in American politics, while others cautioned it would lead to free love. By 1914 more militant tactics were being used by some advocates of wom-

en's suffrage, who were led by Alice Paul. They opposed every Democratic candidate in the eleven states where women could vote, regardless of the candidate's position on women's suffrage. They reasoned that the majority party should be held responsible for the failure of Congress to endorse a constitutional amendment. More than half of the forty-three Democrats running in those states were defeated.

Many suffragists saw President Woodrow Wilson as a major obstacle to their movement. Wilson, who endorsed women's suffrage, preferred to let the states handle voting qualifications and opposed a constitutional amendment. Women responded by demonstrating in Washington, and thousands were arrested and jailed.

In January 1918 Wilson finally announced his support for the proposed amendment. The House agreed the next day, but not until a new Congress met in 1919 did the Senate join the House in mustering the two-thirds majority required to send the amendment to the states for ratification. The amendment took effect in August 1920, when three-fourths of the states consented to ratification.

By the 1980s more than a hundred women had served as senators and representatives. The first woman in Congress was Jeannette RANKIN, a Montana Republican (1917-19, 1941-43). When Rankin first ran for the House of Representatives in 1916, only a handful of states permitted women to vote.   ~

ADDITIONAL READINGS

Flexner, Eleanor. *Century of Struggle: The Women's Rights Movement in the United States.* 1975.
Kraditor, Aileen S. *The Ideas of the Women's Suffrage Movement: 1880-1920.* 1981.

Wright, Jim

A colorful and highly visible SPEAKER of the House, Jim Wright (1922-) thrust himself onto the national scene in ways never attempted by his predecessors in the post. Wright, who became Speaker in 1987, set out to put his stamp on national policy, not just the minutiae of House procedures. But he also relished the parliamentary aspects of the job, making rulings from the chair with an oratorical flourish. When victory depended on a flexing of the Speaker's power, he never hesitated.

Wright joined the House in 1955 after a brief stint in the Texas legislature (1947-49) and four years as mayor of Weatherford, a town near Fort Worth. Impatient with the limited role of a junior House member, he bid in 1961 for the Senate seat vacated by

Jim Wright

Vice President Lyndon B. JOHNSON. The special election had a field of more than seventy candidates; the Democratic vote split, with Wright coming in third, but Texas elected Republican John G. Tower. Another Senate try in 1966 fizzled from lack of campaign funds.

Debt from the 1961 race plagued Wright for years. He was financially secure by the 1980s, though, thanks in part to a favorable book deal and to Fort Worth investments that prompted critics to charge Wright with using his influence for personal gain. His financial dealings became the subject of a House ethics investigation in 1988. *(See* STANDARDS OF OFFICIAL CONDUCT COMMITTEE, HOUSE.*)*

In the House Wright served on the PUBLIC WORKS Committee, which is responsible for roads, dams, airports, and other public works projects. He gave attention to his colleagues' needs, making sure there was a dam here or a federal building there, a courtesy that paid off later when he began his climb up the ladder of the Democratic LEADERSHIP.

When Wright ran for majority leader in 1976, he offered himself as an alternative to the bitterly antagonistic front-runners, Richard BOLLING of Missouri and Phillip Burton of California. He eliminated Bolling by three votes on the second ballot and Burton by one vote on the third. Less than a decade later, when Speaker Thomas P. O'NEILL, Jr., announced he would retire in 1987, Wright was ready; junior Democrats, whose votes would control the speakership election, would not forget the dozens of public appearances and fund-raising forays Wright had already made in their districts. Boldly, Wright announced at a February 1985 press conference that he had enough commitments to guarantee him the speakership, which would not be voted on until January 1987. The preemptive strike was effective; Wright had no challengers. The active self-promotion required by 1980s House politics, inhibiting to some legislators, was Wright's natural style.

Wright brought to the speakership a sharp mind and a willingness to do the kind of homework Speakers often left to others. He was the first to make full use of the new authority given to the Speaker by 1970s REFORMS. For example, the RULES Committee, stacked with loyalists to the leadership, often crafted limits on floor action to suit Wright; O'Neill had reserved that tactic for crucial votes.

Wright also acted independently, concerned more with results than consensus building. He raised eyebrows with his personal involvement in negotiations to end the conflict in Nicaragua, a series of moves that included endorsement of a Reagan administration plan and then praise of a regional peace proposal. Even critics, though, were impressed by his initial success in the diplomatic arena.

In October 1987 the Speaker held a key budget vote open for ten minutes until a Texas colleague could return to the floor and change his vote, making the tally 206-205 and thus reversing the outcome. Republicans and some Democrats were outraged at the move. ~

Yeas and Nays. See VOTING.

Yield

When a member of Congress has been recognized to speak, no other member may speak unless he obtains permission from the person recognized. Permission usually is requested in this form: "Will the gentleman (or gentlewoman) yield?" A legislator who has the floor, perhaps for a specified period of time to make the case for a bill or amendment, may yield some of his time to supporters who also want to speak: "I yield two minutes to the gentleman (from Arizona, Illinois, Maine)." The rules, which are enforced by the presiding officer, protect the legislator who has the floor. ~

Youth Franchise

The Twenty-sixth Amendment to the Constitution, ratified in 1971, extended voting rights to citizens eighteen years of age or older. Until then, most states required voters to be at least twenty-one years old.

The key argument for adopting the amendment linked voting rights to the military draft, which was then in effect for males aged eighteen to twenty-six, many of whom were sent to Vietnam. The same rationale had prompted Georgia in 1943 to lower its voting age

New Voters

The Twenty-sixth Amendment, ratified in 1971, extended the franchise to more than eleven million people between the ages of eighteen and twenty-one. The key argument for the amendment linked voting rights to the military draft during the Vietnam War.

to eighteen; the war-inspired slogan was "Old enough to fight, old enough to vote." But few other states extended the franchise. Kentucky lowered its voting age to eighteen in 1955, and Alaska and Hawaii, which became states in 1959, adopted minimum voting ages of nineteen and twenty, respectively.

In 1954 President Dwight D. Eisenhower proposed a constitutional amendment lowering the voting age to eighteen, but it was rejected by the Senate.

In passing the Voting Rights Act of 1970, Congress agreed to lower the voting age to eighteen years. But the Supreme Court, in a quick test of the provision's constitutionality, ruled late that year that Congress could set qualifications by law only for federal elections; a constitutional amendment was needed

to regulate voting in state and local elections.

By March 1971 Congress had sent the Twenty-sixth Amendment to the states for ratification. Moving more quickly than ever before on a proposed amendment, the states endorsed the change; the required three-fourths (thirty-eight) of the states ratified the amendment by the end of June.

More than eleven million people were given the franchise by the amendment, but the eighteen- to twenty-year-old age group has had the poorest record for voting participation.

U. S. census surveys in the 1970s and 1980s found that less than 40 percent of that age group said they voted in presidential elections, compared with a national average of about 60 percent. In congressional election years, reported turnout among the age group fell to 20 percent.

The youth franchise amendment was the fourth CONSTITUTIONAL AMENDMENT to enlarge the electorate since the Constitution was adopted in 1789:

• The Fifteenth Amendment gave the vote to blacks, although additional civil rights laws were necessary to guarantee against discrimination.

• The Nineteenth Amendment provided WOMEN'S SUFFRAGE.

• The Twenty-third Amendment gave citizens in the District of Columbia the right to vote for president.   ~

Zone Whips

Party leaders in the 435-member House of Representatives need layers of assistant leaders to help them ride herd on their members. Zone whips, the lowest level of the Democratic LEADERSHIP structure, keep in touch with party members from a particular area of the country and try to make sure they turn up for important votes. House Republicans have a similar, though less extensive, regional whip structure to perform this function.   ~

Overleaf:
Podium in the House of Representatives.

IN GOD WE TRUST

Appendix

Members of Congress

Congress at Work

Speakers of the House of Representatives, 1789-1988

Congress		Speaker
1st	(1789-91)	Frederick A. C. Muhlenberg, -Pa.
2nd	(1791-93)	Jonathan Trumbull, F-Conn.
3rd	(1793-95)	Muhlenberg
4th	(1795-97)	Jonathan Dayton, F-N.J.
5th	(1797-99)	Dayton
6th	(1799-1801)	Theodore Sedgwick, F-Mass.
7th	(1801-03)	Nathaniel Macon, D-N.C.
8th	(1803-05)	Macon
9th	(1805-07)	Macon
10th	(1807-09)	Joseph B. Varnum, -Mass.
11th	(1809-11)	Varnum
12th	(1811-13)	Henry Clay, -Ky.
13th	(1813-14)	Clay
	(1814-15)	Langdon Cheves, D-S.C.
14th	(1815-17)	Clay
15th	(1817-19)	Clay
16th	(1819-20)	Clay
	(1820-21)	John W. Taylor, D-N.Y.
17th	(1821-23)	Philip P. Barbour, D-Va.
18th	(1823-25)	Clay
19th	(1825-27)	Taylor
20th	(1827-29)	Andrew Stevenson, D-Va.
21st	(1829-31)	Stevenson
22nd	(1831-33)	Stevenson
23rd	(1833-35)	Stevenson
	(1834-35)	John Bell, W-Tenn.
24th	(1835-37)	James K. Polk, D-Tenn.
25th	(1837-39)	Polk
26th	(1839-41)	Robert M. T. Hunter, D-Va.
27th	(1841-43)	John White, W-Ky.
28th	(1843-45)	John W. Jones, D-Va.
29th	(1845-47)	John W. Davis, D-Ind.
30th	(1847-49)	Robert C. Winthrop, W-Mass.
31st	(1849-51)	Howell Cobb, D-Ga.
32nd	(1851-53)	Linn Boyd, D-Ky.
33rd	(1853-55)	Boyd
34th	(1855-57)	Nathaniel P. Banks, R-Mass.
35th	(1857-59)	James L. Orr, D-S.C.
36th	(1859-61)	William Pennington, R-N.J.
37th	(1861-63)	Galusha A. Grow, R-Pa.
38th	(1863-65)	Schuyler Colfax, R-Ind.
39th	(1865-67)	Colfax
40th	(1867-68)	Colfax
	(1868-69)	Theodore M. Pomeroy, R-N.Y.
41st	(1869-71)	James G. Blaine, R-Maine
42nd	(1871-73)	Blaine
43rd	(1873-75)	Blaine

Congress		Speaker
44th	(1875-76)	Michael C. Kerr, D-Ind.
	(1876-77)	Samuel J. Randall, D-Pa.
45th	(1877-79)	Randall
46th	(1879-81)	Randall
47th	(1881-83)	Joseph Warren Keifer, R-Ohio
48th	(1883-85)	John G. Carlisle, D-Ky.
49th	(1885-87)	Carlisle
50th	(1887-89)	Carlisle
51st	(1889-91)	Thomas Brackett Reed, R-Maine
52nd	(1891-93)	Charles F. Crisp, D-Ga.
53rd	(1893-95)	Crisp
54th	(1895-97)	Reed
55th	(1897-99)	Reed
56th	(1899-1901)	David B. Henderson, R-Iowa
57th	(1901-03)	Henderson
58th	(1903-05)	Joseph G. Cannon, R-Ill.
59th	(1905-07)	Cannon
60th	(1907-09)	Cannon
61st	(1909-11)	Cannon
62nd	(1911-13)	James B. "Champ" Clark, D-Mo.
63rd	(1913-15)	Clark
64th	(1915-17)	Clark
65th	(1917-19)	Clark
66th	(1919-21)	Frederick H. Gillett, R-Mass.
67th	(1921-23)	Gillett
68th	(1923-25)	Gillett
69th	(1925-27)	Nicholas Longworth, R-Ohio
70th	(1927-29)	Longworth
71st	(1929-31)	Longworth
72nd	(1931-33)	John Nance Garner, D-Texas
73rd	(1933-34)	Henry T. Rainey, D-Ill.[1]
74th	(1935-36)	Joseph W. Byrns, D-Tenn.
	(1936-37)	William B. Bankhead, D-Ala.
75th	(1937-39)	Bankhead
76th	(1939-40)	Bankhead
	(1940-41)	Sam Rayburn, D-Texas
77th	(1941-43)	Rayburn
78th	(1943-45)	Rayburn
79th	(1945-47)	Rayburn
80th	(1947-49)	Joseph W. Martin, Jr., R-Mass.
81st	(1949-51)	Rayburn
82nd	(1951-53)	Rayburn
83rd	(1953-55)	Martin
84th	(1955-57)	Rayburn
85th	(1957-59)	Martin
86th	(1959-61)	Rayburn
87th	(1961)	Rayburn
	(1962-63)	John W. McCormack, D-Mass.

Congress	Speaker
88th (1963-65)	McCormack
89th (1965-67)	McCormack
90th (1967-69)	McCormack
91st (1969-71)	McCormack
92nd (1971-73)	Carl Albert, D-Okla.
93rd (1973-75)	Albert
94th (1975-77)	Albert
95th (1977-79)	Thomas P. O'Neill, Jr., D-Mass.
96th (1979-81)	O'Neill
97th (1981-83)	O'Neill
98th (1983-85)	O'Neill
99th (1985-87)	O'Neill
100th (1987-89)	Jim Wright, D-Texas

Party abbreviations: (D) Democrat, (F) Federalist, (R) Republican, (W) Whig.

[1] Rainey died in 1834, but was not replaced until the next Congress.

Source: Congressional Quarterly. *American Leaders, 1789-1987.* 1987.

LONGEST-SERVING HOUSE SPEAKERS

Name	Years	Name	Years
Sam Rayburn	18	Carl Albert	6
Henry Clay	10	James G. Blaine	6
John W. McCormack	10	John G. Carlisle	6
Thomas P. O'Neill, Jr.	10	Schuyler Colfax	6
Joseph G. Cannon	8	Frederick H. Gillett	6
James B. "Champ" Clark	8	Nicholas Longworth	6
Joseph W. Martin, Jr.	8	Nathaniel Macon	6
Andrew Stevenson	7	Thomas Brackett Reed	6

Party Leadership in Congress, 1977-88

95th Congress (1977-79)

Senate

President Pro Tempore—James O. Eastland, D-Miss.
Deputy President Pro Tempore—Hubert H. Humphrey, D-Minn.
Majority Leader—Robert C. Byrd, D-W.Va.
Majority Whip—Alan Cranston, D-Calif.

Minority Leader—Howard H. Baker, Jr., R-Tenn.
Minority Whip—Ted Stevens, R-Alaska

House

Speaker—Thomas P. O'Neill, Jr., D-Mass.
Majority Leader—Jim Wright, D-Texas
Majority Whip—John Brademas, D-Ind.

Minority Leader—John J. Rhodes, R-Ariz.
Minority Whip—Robert H. Michel, R-Ill.

96th Congress (1979-81)

Senate

President Pro Tempore—Warren G. Magnuson, D-Wash.
Majority Leader—Robert C. Byrd, D-W.Va.
Majority Whip—Alan Cranston, D-Calif.

Minority Leader—Howard H. Baker, Jr., R-Tenn.
Minority Whip—Ted Stevens, R-Alaska

House

Speaker—Thomas P. O'Neill, Jr., D-Mass.
Majority Leader—Jim Wright, D-Texas
Majority Whip—John Brademas, D-Ind.

Minority Leader—John J. Rhodes, R-Ariz.
Minority Whip—Robert H. Michel, R-Ill.

97th Congress (1981-83)

Senate

Minority Leader—Robert C. Byrd, D-W.Va.
Minority Whip—Alan Cranston, D-Calif.

House

Speaker—Thomas P. O'Neill, Jr., D-Mass.
Majority Leader—Jim Wright, D-Texas
Majority Whip—Thomas S. Foley, D-Wash.

Minority Leader—Robert H. Michel, R-Ill.
Minority Whip—Trent Lott, R-Miss.

98th Congress (1983-85)

Senate

Minority Leader—Robert C. Byrd, D-W.Va.
Minority Whip—Alan Cranston, D-Calif.

House

Speaker—Thomas P. O'Neill, Jr., D-Mass.
Majority Leader—Jim Wright, D-Texas
Majority Whip—Thomas S. Foley, D-Wash.

Minority Leader—Robert H. Michel, R-Ill.
Minority Whip—Trent Lott, R-Miss.

99th Congress (1985-87)

Senate

President Pro Tempore—Strom Thurmond, R-S.C.
Majority Leader—Robert Dole, R-Kan.
Assistant Majority Leader—Alan K. Simpson, R-Wyo.

Minority Leader—Robert C. Byrd, D-W.Va.
Minority Whip—Alan Cranston, D-Calif.

House

Speaker—Thomas P. O'Neill, Jr., D-Mass.
Majority Leader—Jim Wright, D-Texas
Majority Whip—Thomas S. Foley, D-Wash.

Minority Leader—Robert H. Michel, R-Ill.
Minority Whip—Trent Lott, R-Miss.

100th Congress (1987-89)

Senate

President Pro Tempore—John C. Stennis, D-Miss.
Majority Leader—Robert C. Byrd, D-W.Va.
Majority Whip—Alan Cranston, D-Calif.

Minority Leader—Robert Dole, R-Kan.
Assistant Minority Leader—Alan K. Simpson, R-Wyo.

House

Speaker—Jim Wright, D-Texas
Majority Leader—Thomas S. Foley, D-Wash.
Majority Whip—Tony Coelho, D-Calif.

Minority Leader—Robert H. Michel, R-Ill.
Minority Whip—Trent Lott, R-Miss.

House Floor Leaders, 1899-1988

Congress	Majority	Minority
56th (1899-1901)	Sereno E. Payne, R-N.Y.	James D. Richardson, D-Tenn.
57th (1901-03)	Payne	Richardson
58th (1903-05)	Payne	John Sharp Williams, D-Miss.
59th (1905-07)	Payne	Williams
60th (1907-09)	Payne	Williams/Champ Clark, D-Mo.[1]
61st (1909-11)	Payne	Clark
62nd (1911-13)	Oscar W. Underwood, D-Ala.	James R. Mann, R-Ill.
63rd (1913-15)	Underwood	Mann
64th (1915-17)	Claude Kitchin, D-N.C.	Mann
65th (1917-19)	Kitchin	Mann
66th (1919-21)	Franklin W. Mondell, R-Wyo.	Clark
67th (1921-23)	Mondell	Claude Kitchin, D-N.C.
68th (1923-25)	Nicholas Longworth, R-Ohio	Finis J. Garrett, D-Tenn.
69th (1925-27)	John Q. Tilson, R-Conn.	Garrett
70th (1927-29)	Tilson	Garrett
71st (1929-31)	Tilson	John N. Garner, D-Texas
72nd (1931-33)	Henry T. Rainey, D-Ill.	Bertrand H. Snell, R-N.Y.
73rd (1933-35)	Joseph W. Byrns, D-Tenn.	Snell
74th (1935-37)	William B. Bankhead, D-Ala.[2]	Snell
75th (1937-39)	Sam Rayburn, D-Texas	Snell
76th (1939-41)	Rayburn/John W. McCormack, D-Mass.[3]	Joseph W. Martin Jr., R-Mass.
77th (1941-43)	McCormack	Martin
78th (1943-45)	McCormack	Martin
79th (1945-47)	McCormack	Martin
80th (1947-49)	Charles A. Halleck, R-Ind.	Sam Rayburn, D-Texas
81st (1949-51)	McCormack	Martin
82nd (1951-53)	McCormack	Martin
83rd (1953-55)	Halleck	Rayburn
84th (1955-57)	McCormack	Martin
85th (1957-59)	McCormack	Martin
86th (1959-61)	McCormack	Charles A. Halleck, R-Ind.
87th (1961-63)	McCormack/Carl Albert, D-Okla.[4]	Halleck
88th (1963-65)	Albert	Halleck
89th (1965-67)	Albert	Gerald R. Ford, R-Mich.
90th (1967-69)	Albert	Ford
91st (1969-71)	Albert	Ford
92nd (1971-73)	Hale Boggs, D-La.	Ford
93rd (1973-75)	Thomas P. O'Neill, Jr., D-Mass.	Ford/John J. Rhodes, R-Ariz.[5]
94th (1975-77)	O'Neill	Rhodes
95th (1977-79)	Jim Wright, D-Texas	Rhodes

Congress	Majority	Minority
96th (1979-81)	Wright	Rhodes
97th (1981-83)	Wright	Robert H. Michel, R-Ill.
98th (1983-85)	Wright	Michel
99th (1985-87)	Wright	Michel
100th (1987-89)	Thomas S. Foley, D-Wash.	Michel

[1] Clark became minority leader in 1908.

[2] Bankhead became Speaker of the House on June 4, 1936, after Byrns's death. The post of majority leader remained vacant until the next Congress.

[3] McCormack became majority leader on Sept. 26, 1940, filling the vacancy caused by the elevation of Rayburn to the post of Speaker of the House on Sept. 16, 1940, after Bankhead's death.

[4] Albert became majority leader on Jan. 10, 1962, filling the vacancy caused by the elevation of McCormack to the post of Speaker of the House on Jan. 10, 1962, after Rayburn's death.

[5] Rhodes became minority leader on Dec. 7, 1973, filling the vacancy caused by the resignation of Ford on Dec. 6, 1973, to become vice president.

Source: Congressional Quarterly. *American Leaders, 1789-1987.* 1987.

Senate Floor Leaders, 1911-88

Congress	Majority	Minority
62nd (1911-13)	Shelby M. Cullom, R-Ill.	Thomas S. Martin, D-Va.
63rd (1913-15)	John W. Kern, D-Ind.	Jacob H. Gallinger, R-N.H.
64th (1915-17)	Kern	Gallinger
65th (1917-19)	Thomas S. Martin, D-Va.	Gallinger/Henry Cabot Lodge, R-Mass.[1]
66th (1919-21)	Henry Cabot Lodge, R-Mass.	Martin/Oscar W. Underwood, D-Ala.[2]
67th (1921-23)	Lodge	Underwood
68th (1923-25)	Lodge/Charles Curtis, R-Kan.[3]	Joseph T. Robinson, D-Ark.
69th (1925-27)	Curtis	Robinson
70th (1927-29)	Curtis	Robinson
71st (1929-31)	James E. Watson, R-Ind.	Robinson
72nd (1931-33)	Watson	Robinson
73rd (1933-35)	Joseph T. Robinson, D-Ark.	Charles L. McNary, R-Ore.
74th (1935-37)	Robinson	McNary
75th (1937-39)	Robinson/Alben W. Barkley, D-Ky.[4]	McNary
76th (1939-41)	Barkley	McNary
77th (1941-43)	Barkley	McNary
78th (1943-45)	Barkley	McNary
79th (1945-47)	Barkley	Wallace H. White, Jr., R-Maine
80th (1947-49)	Wallace H. White, Jr., R-Maine	Alben W. Barkley, D-Ky.
81st (1949-51)	Scott W. Lucas, D-Ill.	Kenneth S. Wherry, R-Neb.
82nd (1951-53)	Ernest W. McFarland, D-Ariz.	Wherry/Styles Bridges, R-N.H.[5]
83rd (1953-55)	Robert A. Taft, R-Ohio/William F. Knowland, R-Calif.[6]	Lyndon B. Johnson, D-Texas
84th (1955-57)	Lyndon B. Johnson, D-Texas	William F. Knowland, R-Calif.
85th (1957-59)	Johnson	Knowland
86th (1959-61)	Johnson	Everett McKinley Dirksen, R-Ill.
87th (1961-63)	Mike Mansfield, D-Mont.	Dirksen
88th (1963-65)	Mansfield	Dirksen
89th (1965-67)	Mansfield	Dirksen
90th (1967-69)	Mansfield	Dirksen
91st (1969-71)	Mansfield	Dirksen/Hugh Scott, R-Pa.[7]
92nd (1971-73)	Mansfield	Scott
93rd (1973-75)	Mansfield	Scott
94th (1975-77)	Mansfield	Scott
95th (1977-79)	Robert C. Byrd, D-W.Va.	Howard H. Baker, Jr., R-Tenn.
96th (1979-81)	Byrd	Baker
97th (1981-83)	Howard H. Baker, Jr., R-Tenn.	Robert C. Byrd. D-W.Va.

Congress	Majority	Minority
98th (1983-85)	Baker	Byrd
99th (1985-87)	Robert Dole, R-Kan.	Byrd
100th (1987-89)	Byrd	Robert Dole, R-Kan.

[1] Lodge became minority leader on Aug. 24, 1918, filling the vacancy caused by the death of Gallinger on Aug. 17, 1918.

[2] Underwood became minority leader on April 27, 1920, filling the vacancy caused by the death of Martin on Nov. 12, 1919. Gilbert M. Hitchcock, D-Neb., served as acting minority leader in the interim.

[3] Curtis became majority leader on Nov. 28, 1924, filling the vacancy caused by the death of Lodge on Nov. 9, 1924.

[4] Barkley became majority leader on July 22, 1937, filling the vacancy caused by the death of Robinson on July 14, 1937.

[5] Bridges became minority leader on Jan. 8, 1952, filling the vacancy caused by the death of Wherry on Nov. 29, 1951.

[6] Knowland became majority leader on Aug. 4, 1953, filling the vacancy caused by the death of Taft on July 31, 1953. Taft's vacant seat was filled by a Democrat, Thomas Burke, on Nov. 10, 1953. The division of the Senate changed to 48 Democrats, 47 Republicans, and 1 Independent, thus giving control of the Senate to the Democrats. However, Knowland remained as majority leader until the end of the 83rd Congress.

[7] Scott became minority leader on Sept. 24, 1969, filling the vacancy caused by the death of Dirksen on Sept. 7, 1969.

Source: Congressional Quarterly. *American Leaders, 1789-1987.* 1987.

Chairman of Selected Senate and House Committees, 1947-88

Following are the names, dates, and terms of chairmen of selected Senate and House committees from 1947 to 1988. The evolution of some committees also is indicated, such as the first one listed, the Senate Agriculture, Nutrition, and Forestry Committee.

Senate

Agriculture, Nutrition and Forestry

Patrick J. Leahy, D-Vt. (1987-)
Jesse Helms, R-N.C. (1981-87)
Herman E. Talmadge, D-Ga. (1977-81)
previously named Agriculture and Forestry
Herman E. Talmadge, D-Ga. (1971-77)
Allen J. Ellender, D-La. (1955-71)
George D. Aiken, R-Vt. (1953-55)
Allen J. Ellender, D-La. (1951-53)
Elmer Thomas, D-Okla. (1949-51)
Arthur Capper, R-Kan. (1947-49)

Appropriations

John C. Stennis, D-Miss. (1987-)
Mark O. Hatfield, R-Ore. (1981-87)
Warren G. Magnuson, D-Wash. (1979-81)
John L. McClellan, D-Ark. (1972-79)
Allen J. Ellender, D-La. (1971-72)
Richard B. Russell, D-Ga. (1969-71)
Carl Hayden, D-Ariz. (1955-69)
Styles Bridges, R-N.H. (1953-55)
Kenneth McKellar, D-Tenn. (1949-53)
Styles Bridges, R-N.H. (1947-49)

Armed Services

Sam Nunn, D-Ga. (1987-)
Barry Goldwater, R-Ariz. (1985-87)
John Tower, R-Texas (1981-85)
John C. Stennis, D-Miss. (1969-81)
Richard B. Russell, D-Ga. (1955-69)
Leverett Saltonstall, R-Mass. (1953-55)
Richard B. Russell, D-Ga. (1951-53)
Millard E. Tydings, D-Md. (1949-51)
Chan Gurney, R-S.D. (1947-49)

Banking, Housing, and Urban Affairs

William Proxmire, D-Wis. (1987-)
Jake Garn, R-Utah (1981-87)
William Proxmire, D-Wis. (1975-81)

John J. Sparkman, D-Ala. (1971-75)
previously named Banking and Currency
John J. Sparkman, D-Ala. (1967-70)
A. Willis Robertson, D-Va. (1959-67)
J. W. Fulbright, D-Ark. (1955-59)
Homer E. Capehart, R-Ind. (1953-55)
Burnet R. Maybank, D-S.C. (1949-53)
Charles W. Tobey, R-N.H. (1947-49)

Budget

Lawton Chiles, D-Fla. (1987-)
Pete V. Domenici, R-N.H. (1980-87)
Edmund S. Muskie, D-Maine (1975-80)

Commerce, Science, and Transportation

Ernest F. Hollings, D-S.C. (1987-)
John C. Danforth, R-Mo. (1985-87)
Bob Packwood, R-Ore. (1981-85)
Howard W. Cannon, D-Nev. (1978-81)
previously named Commerce
Warren G. Magnuson, D-Wash. (1962-77)
previously named Interstate and Foreign Commerce
Warren G. Magnuson, D-Wash. (1955-61)
John W. Bricker, R-Ohio (1953-55)
Charles W. Tobey, R-N.H. (1953)
Edwin C. Johnson, D-Colo. (1949-53)
Wallace H. White, R-Maine (1947-49)

Energy and Natural Resources

J. Bennett Johnston, D-La. (1987-)
James A. McClure, R-Idaho (1981-87)
Henry M. Jackson, D-Wash. (1979-81)

Environment and Public Works

Quentin N. Burdick, D-N.D. (1987-)
Robert T. Stafford, R-Vt. (1981-87)
Jennings Randolph, D-W.Va. (1979-81)

Finance

Lloyd Bentsen, D-Texas (1987-)
Bob Packwood, R-Ore. (1985-87)

Robert Dole, R-Kan. (1981-85)
Russell B. Long, D-La. (1965-81)
Harry Flood Byrd, D-Va. (1955-65)
Eugene D. Millikin, R-Colo. (1953-55)
Walter F. George, D-Ga. (1949-53)
Eugene D. Millikin, R-Colo. (1947-49)

Foreign Relations

Claiborne Pell, D-R.I. (1987-)
Richard G. Lugar, R-Ind. (1985-87)
Charles Percy, R-Ill. (1981-85)
Frank Church, D-Idaho (1979-81)
John J. Sparkman, D-Ala. (1975-79)
J. W. Fulbright, D-Ark. (1959-75)
Theodore Francis Green, D-R.I. (1957-59)
Walter F. George, D-Ga. (1955-57)
Alexander Wiley, R-Wis. (1953-55)
Tom Connally, D-Texas (1949-53)
Arthur H. Vandenberg, R-Mich. (1947-49)

Intelligence, Select Committee on

David L. Boren, D-Okla. (1987-)
Lowell P. Weicker, Jr., R-Conn. (1985-87)
Barry Goldwater, R-Ariz. (1981-85)
Birch Bayh, D-Ind. (1979-81)
Daniel K. Inouye, D-Hawaii (1976-79)

Interior and Insular Affairs

renamed Energy and Natural Resources in 1977, with some jurisdiction going to Environment Committee
Henry M. Jackson, D-Wash. (1963-77)
Clinton P. Anderson, D-N.M. (1961-63)
James E. Murray, D-Mont. (1955-61)
Guy Cordon, R-Ore. (1954-55)
Hugh Butler, R-Neb. (1953-54)
Joseph C. O'Mahoney, D-Wyo. (1949-53)
Hugh Butler, R-Neb. (1947-49)

Judiciary

Joseph R. Biden, Jr., D-Del. (1987-)
Strom Thurmond, R-S.C. (1981-87)
Edward M. Kennedy, D-Mass. (1979-81)
James O. Eastland, D-Miss. (1956-79)
Harley M. Kilgore, D-W.Va. (1955-56)
William Langer, R-N.D. (1953-55)
Pat McCarran, D-Nev. (1949-53)
Alexander Wiley, R-Wis. (1947-49)

Labor and Human Resources

Edward M. Kennedy, D-Mass. (1987-)
Orrin G. Hatch, R-Utah (1981-87)
Harrison A. Williams, Jr., D-N.J. (1979-81)
previously named Human Resources
Harrison A. Williams, Jr., D-N.J. (1977-79)
previously named Labor and Public Welfare
Harrison A. Williams, Jr., D-N.J. (1971-77)
Ralph W. Yarborough, D-Texas (1969-71)
Lister Hill, D-Ala. (1955-69)
H. Alexander Smith, R-N.J. (1953-55)
James E. Murray, D-Mont. (1951-53)
Elbert D. Thomas, D-Utah (1949-51)
Robert A. Taft, R-Ohio (1947-49)

Public Works

renamed Environment and Public Works in 1977
Jennings Randolph, D-W.Va. (1966-77)
Pat McNamara, D-Mich. (1963-66)
Dennis Chavez, D-N.M. (1955-62)
Edward Martin, R-Pa. (1953-55)
Dennis Chavez, D-N.M. (1949-53)
Chapman Revercomb, R-W.Va. (1947-49)

House

Agriculture

E. "Kika" de la Garza, D-Texas (1981-)
Thomas S. Foley, D-Wash. (1975-81)
W. R. Poage, D-Texas (1967-75)
Harold D. Cooley, D-N.C. (1955-67)
Clifford R. Hope, R-Kan. (1953-55)
Harold D. Cooley, D-N.C. (1949-53)
Clifford R. Hope, R-Kan. (1947-49)

Appropriations

Jamie L. Whitten, D-Miss. (1979-)
George H. Mahon, D-Texas (1964-79)
Clarence Cannon, D-Mo. (1955-64)
John Taber, R-N.Y. (1953-55)
Clarence Cannon, D-Mo. (1949-53)
John Taber, R-N.Y. (1947-49)

Armed Services

Les Aspin, D-Wis. (1985-)
Melvin Price, D-Ill. (1975-85)

F. Edward Hébert, D-La. (1971-75)
L. Mendel Rivers, D-S.C. (1965-71)
Carl Vinson, D-Ga. (1955-65)
Dewey Short, R-Mo. (1953-55)
Carl Vinson, D-Ga. (1949-53)
Walter G. Andrews, R-N.Y. (1947-49)

Banking, Finance, and Urban Affairs

Fernand J. St Germain, D-R.I. (1981-)
Henry S. Reuss, D-Wis. (1977-81)
  *previously named Banking, Currency,
  and Housing*
Henry S. Reuss, D-Wis. (1975-77)
  previously named Banking and Currency
Wright Patman, D-Texas (1963-75)
Brent Spence, D-Ky. (1955-63)
Jesse P. Wolcott, R-Mich. (1953-55)
Brent Spence, D-Ky. (1949-53)
Jesse P. Wolcott, R-Mich. (1947-49)

Budget

William H. Gray III, D-Pa. (1985-)
James R. Jones, D-Okla. (1981-85)
Robert N. Giaimo, D-Conn. (1977-81)
Brock Adams, D-Wash. (1975-77)

Education and Labor

Augustus F. Hawkins, D-Fla. (1984-)
Carl D. Perkins, D-Ky. (1967-84)
Adam C. Powell, Jr., D-N.Y. (1961-67)
Graham A. Barden, D-N.C. (1955-61)
Samuel K. McConnell, R-Pa. (1953-55)
Graham A. Barden, D-N.C. (1950-53)
John Lesinski, D-Mich. (1949-50)
Fred A. Hartley, R-N.J. (1947-49)

Energy and Commerce

John D. Dingell, D-Mich. (1981-)
  *previously named Interstate and Foreign
  Commerce*
Harley O. Staggers, D-W.Va. (1966-81)
Oren Harris, D-Ark. (1957-66)
J. Percy Priest, D-Tenn. (1955-57)
Charles A. Wolverton, R-N.J. (1953-55)
Robert Crosser, D-Ohio (1949-53)
Charles A. Wolverton, R-N.J. (1947-49)

Foreign Affairs

Dante B. Fascell, D-Fla. (1983-)

Clement J. Zablocki, D-Wis. (1979-83)
  *previously named International
  Relations*
Clement J. Zablocki, D-Wis. (1977-79)
Thomas E. Morgan, D-Pa. (1975-77)
  previously named Foreign Affairs
Thomas E. Morgan, D-Pa. (1959-74)
Thomas S. Gordon, D-Ill. (1957-59)
James P. Richards, D-S.C. (1955-57)
Robert B. Chiperfield, R-Ill. (1953-55)
James P. Richards, D-S.C. (1951-53)
John Kee, D-W.Va. (1949-51)
Charles A. Eaton, R-N.J. (1947-49)

Intelligence, Permanent Select Committee on

Louis Stokes, D-Ohio (1987-)
Lee H. Hamilton, D-Ind. (1985-87)
Edward P. Boland, D-Mass. (1979-85)
  *previously named Select Committee on
  Intelligence*
Otis G. Pike, D-N.Y. (1975-76)
Lucien N. Nedzi, D-Mich. (1975)

Interior and Insular Affairs

Morris K. Udall, D-Ariz. (1979-)
James A. Haley, D-Fla. (1973-79)
Wayne N. Aspinall, D-Colo. (1959-73)
Clair Engle, D-Calif. (1955-59)
A. L. Miller, R-Neb. (1953-55)
John R. Murdock, D-Ariz. (1951-53)
  previously named Public Lands
J. Hardin Peterson, D-Fla. (1949-50)
Andrew L. Somers, D-N.Y. (1949)
Richard J. Welch, R-Calif. (1947-49)

Judiciary

Peter W. Rodino, Jr., D-N.J. (1973-)
Emanuel Celler, D-N.Y. (1955-73)
Chauncey W. Reed, R-Ill. (1953-55)
Emanuel Celler, D-N.Y. (1949-53)
Earl C. Michener, R-Mich. (1947-49)

Public Works and Transportation

Glenn M. Anderson, D-Calif. (1988-)
James J. Howard, D-N.J. (1981-88)
Harold T. Johnson, D-Ala. (1979-81)
Robert E. Jones, D-Ala. (1975-79)
John A. Blatnik, D-Minn. (1974-75)
  previously named Public Works

John A. Blatnik, D-Minn. (1971-73)
George H. Fallon, D-Md. (1965-71)
Charles A. Buckley, D-N.Y. (1955-65)
George A. Dondero, R-Mich. (1953-55)
Charles A. Buckley, D-N.Y. (1951-53)
William M. Whittington, D-Miss. (1949-51)
George A. Dondero, R-Mich. (1947-49)

Rules

Claude Pepper, D-Fla. (1983-)
Richard Bolling, D-Mo. (1979-83)
William M. Colmer, D-Miss. (1967-79)
Howard W. Smith, D-Va. (1955-67)

Leo E. Allen, R-Ill. (1953-55)
Adolph J. Sabath, D-Ill. (1949-53)
Leo E. Allen, R-Ill. (1947-49)

Ways and Means

Dan Rostenkowski, D-Ill. (1981-)
Al Ullman, D-Ore. (1975-81)
Wilbur D. Mills, D-Ark. (1958-75)
Jere Cooper, D-Tenn. (1955-57)
Daniel A. Reed, R-N.Y. (1953-55)
Robert L. Doughton, D-N.C. (1949-53)
Harold Knutson, R-Minn. (1947-49)

Sources: Congressional Staff Directory, 1959-76; *Congressional Quarterly Almanac,* 1947-87; *Congressional Directory,* 1947-76.

Women Members of Congress, 1917-88

As of mid-1988 a total of 120 women had been elected or appointed to Congress. One hundred five served in the House only, thirteen in the Senate, and two—Maine Republican Margaret Chase Smith and Maryland Democrat Barbara Mikulski—in both chambers. Following is a list of the women members, their parties and states, and the years in which they served. In addition, Hawaii Republican Mary E. Farrington served as a nonvoting delegate from 1954 until 1957.

Senate

Rebecca L. Felton, Ind. D-Ga.*	1922
Hattie W. Caraway, D-Ark.	1931-45
Rose McConnell Long, D-La.	1936-37
Dixie Bibb Graves, D-Ala.	1937-38
Gladys Pyle, R-S.D.†	1938-39
Vera C. Bushfield, R-S.D.	1948
Margaret Chase Smith, R-Maine	1949-73
Hazel H. Abel, R-Neb.	1954
Eva K. Bowring, R-Neb.	1954
Maurine B. Neuberger, D-Ore.	1960-67
Elaine S. Edwards, D-La.	1972
Maryon Pittman Allen, D-Ala.	1978
Muriel Buck Humphrey, D-Minn.	1978
Nancy Landon Kassebaum, R-Kan.	1979-
Paula Hawkins, R-Fla.	1981-87
Barbara Mikulski, D-Md.	1987-

House

Jeannette Rankin, R-Mont.	1917-19; 1941-43
Alice M. Robertson, R-Okla.	1921-23
Winnifred S. M. Huck, R-Ill.	1922-23
Mae E. Nolan, R-Calif.	1923-25
Florence P. Kahn, R-Calif.	1925-37
Mary T. Norton, D-N.J.	1925-51
Edith N. Rogers, R-Mass.	1925-60
Katherine G. Langley, R-Ky.	1927-31
Ruth H. McCormick, R-Ill.	1929-31
Pearl P. Oldfield, D-Ark.	1929-31
Ruth B. Owen, D-Fla.	1929-33
Ruth S. B. Pratt, R-N.Y.	1929-33
Effiegene Wingo, D-Ark.	1930-33
Willa M. B. Eslick, D-Tenn.	1932-33
Marian W. Clarke, R-N.Y.	1933-35
Virginia E. Jenckes, D-Ind.	1933-39
Kathryn O'Loughlin McCarthy D-Kan.	1933-35
Isabella S. Greenway, D-Ariz.	1934-37
Caroline L. G. O'Day, D-N.Y.	1935-43
Nan W. Honeyman, D-Ore.	1937-39
Elizabeth H. Gasque, D-S.C.†	1938-39
Clara G. McMillan, D-S.C.	1939-41
Jessie Sumner, R-Ill.	1939-47
Frances P. Bolton, R-Ohio	1940-69
Florence R. Gibbs, D-Ga.	1940-41
Margaret Chase Smith, R-Maine	1940-49
Katherine E. Byron, D-Md.	1941-43
Veronica G. Boland, D-Pa.	1942-43
Clare Boothe Luce , R-Conn.	1943-47
Winifred C. Stanley, R-N.Y.	1943-45
Willa L. Fulmer, D-S.C.	1944-45
Emily T. Douglas, D-Ill.	1945-47
Helen G. Douglas, D-Calif.	1945-51
Chase G. Woodhouse, D-Conn.	1945-47; 1949-51
Helen D. Mankin, D-Ga.	1946-47
Eliza J. Pratt, D-N.C.	1946-47
Georgia L. Lusk, D-N.M.	1947-49
Katherine P. C. St. George, R-N.Y.	1947-65
Reva Z. B. Bosone, D-Utah	1949-53
Cecil M. Harden, R-Ind.	1949-59
Edna F. Kelly, D-N.Y.	1949-69
Vera D. Buchanan, D-Pa.	1951-55
Marguerite S. Church, R-Ill.	1951-63
Maude E. Kee, D-W.Va.	1951-65
Ruth Thompson , R-Mich.	1951-57
Gracie B. Pfost, D-Idaho	1953-63
Leonor K. Sullivan, D-Mo.	1953-77
Iris F. Blitch, D-Ga.	1955-63
Edith Green, D-Ore.	1955-74
Martha W. Griffiths, D-Mich.	1955-74
Coya G. Knutson, D-Minn.	1955-59
Kathryn E. Granahan, D-Pa.	1956-63
Florence P. Dwyer, R-N.J.	1957-73
Catherine D. May, R-Wash.	1959-71
Edna O. Simpson, R-Ill.	1959-61
Jessica McC. Weis, R-N.Y.	1959-63
Julia B. Hansen, D-Wash.	1960-74
Catherine D. Norrell, D-Ark.	1961-63
Louise G. Reece, R-Tenn.	1961-63
Corinne B. Riley, D-S.C.	1962-63
Charlotte T. Reid, R-Ill.	1963-71

Irene B. Baker, R-Tenn.	1964-65	Beverly Barton Butcher Byron	
Patsy T. Mink, D-Hawaii	1965-77	D-Md.	1979-
Lera M. Thomas, D-Texas	1966-67	Geraldine Ferraro, D-N.Y.	1979-85
Margaret M. Heckler, R-Mass.	1967-83	Olympia Jean Bouchles Snowe	
Shirley Chisholm, D-N.Y.	1969-83	R-Maine	1979-
Bella S. Abzug, D-N.Y.	1971-77	Bobbi Fiedler, R-Calif.	1981-87
Ella T. Grasso, D-Conn.	1971-75	Lynn M. Martin, R-Ill.	1981-
Louise Day Hicks, D-Mass.	1971-73	Marge Roukema, R-N.J.	1981-
Elizabeth B. Andrews, D-Ala.	1972-73	Claudine Schneider, R-R.I.	1981-
Yvonne B. Burke, D-Calif.	1973-79	Jean Ashbrook, R-Ohio	1982-83
Marjorie S. Holt, R-Md.	1973-87	Barbara B. Kennelly, D-Conn.	1982-
Elizabeth Holtzman, D-N.Y.	1973-81	Sala Burton, D-Calif.	1983-87
Barbara C. Jordan, D-Texas	1973-79	Barbara Boxer, D-Calif.	1983-
Patricia Schroeder, D-Colo.	1973-	Katie Hall, D-Ind.	1983-85
Corinne C. Boggs, D-La.	1973-	Nancy L. Johnson, R-Conn.	1983-
Cardiss R. Collins, D-Ill.	1973-	Marcy Kaptur, D-Ohio	1983-
Marilyn Lloyd, D-Tenn.	1975-	Barbara Vucanovich, R-Nev.	1983-
Millicent Fenwick, R-N.J.	1975-83	Helen Delich Bentley, R-Md.	1985-
Martha E. Keys, D-Kan.	1975-79	Jan Meyers, R-Kan.	1985-
Helen S. Meyner, D-N.J.	1975-79	Cathy Long, D-La.	1985-87
Virginia Smith, R-Neb.	1975-	Constance A. Morella, R-Md.	1987-
Gladys N. Spellman, D-Md.	1975-81	Elizabeth J. Patterson, D-S.C.	1987-
Shirley N. Pettis, R-Calif.	1975-79	Patricia Saiki, R-Hawaii	1987-
Barbara A. Mikulski, D-Md.	1977-87	Louise M. Slaughter, D-N.Y.	1987-
Mary Rose Oakar, D-Ohio	1977-	Nancy Pelosi, D-N.Y.	1987-

* Felton was sworn in Nov. 21, 1922, to fill the vacancy created by the death of Thomas E. Watson, D, 1921-22. The next day she gave up her seat to Walter F. George, D, 1922-57, the elected candidate for the vacancy.
† Never sworn in because Congress was not in session between election and expiration of term.

Black Members of Congress, 1870-1988

As of mid-1988, sixty-two black Americans had served in Congress; three in the Senate and fifty-nine in the House. Following is a list of the black members, their parties and states, and the years in which they served. In addition, John W. Menard, a Louisiana Republican., won a disputed election in 1868 but was not permitted to take his seat in Congress. Walter E. Fauntroy, a Democrat, began serving in 1971 as nonvoting delegate from the District of Columbia.

Senate

Hiram R. Revels, R-Miss.	1870-71
Blanche K. Bruce, R-Miss.	1875-81
Edward W. Brooke, R-Mass.	1967-79

House

Joseph H. Rainey, R-S.C.	1870-79
Jefferson F. Long, R-Ga.	1870-71
Robert B. Elliott, R-S.C.	1871-74
Robert C. DeLarge, R-S.C.	1871-73
Benjamin S. Turner, R-Ala.	1871-73
Josiah T. Walls, R-Fla.	1871-76
Richard H. Cain, R-S.C.	1873-75; 1877-79
John R. Lynch, R-Miss.	1873-77; 1882-83
James T. Rapier, R-Ala.	1873-75
Alonzo J. Ransier, R-S.C.	1873-75
Jeremiah Haralson, R-Ala.	1875-77
John A. Hyman, R-N.C.	1875-77
Charles E. Nash, R-La.	1875-77
Robert Smalls, R-S.C.	1875-79; 1882-83; 1884-87
James E. O'Hara, R-N.C.	1883-87
Henry P. Cheatham, R-N.C.	1889-93
John M. Langston, R-Va.	1890-91
Thomas E. Miller, R-S.C.	1890-91
George W. Murray, R-S.C.	1893-95; 1896-97
George H. White, R-N.C.	1897-1901
Oscar De Priest, R-Ill.	1929-35
Arthur W. Mitchell, D-Ill.	1935-43
William L. Dawson, D-Ill.	1943-70
Adam Clayton Powell, Jr. D-N.Y.	1945-67; 1969-71

Charles C. Diggs, Jr., D-Mich.	1955-80
Robert N. C. Nix, D-Pa.	1958-79
Augustus F. Hawkins, D-Calif.	1963-
John Conyers, Jr., D-Mich.	1965-
Louis Stokes, D-Ohio	1969-
William L. Clay, D-Mo.	1969-
Shirley Chisholm, D-N.Y.	1969-83
George W. Collins, D-Ill.	1970-72
Ronald V. Dellums, D-Calif.	1971-
Ralph H. Metcalfe, D-Ill.	1971-78
Parren J. Mitchell, D-Md.	1971-87
Charles B. Rangel, D-N.Y.	1971-
Yvonne B. Burke, D-Calif.	1973-79
Cardiss Collins, D-Ill.	1973-
Barbara C. Jordan, D-Texas	1973-79
Andrew Young, D-Ga.	1973-77
Harold E. Ford, D-Tenn.	1975-
Julian C. Dixon, D-Calif.	1979-
William H. Gray III, D-Pa.	1979-
George T. Leland, D-Texas	1979-
Bennett McVey Stewart, D-Ill.	1979-81
George W. Crockett, Jr., D-Mich.	1981-
Mervin M. Dymally, D-Calif.	1981-
Gus Savage, D-Ill.	1981-
Harold Washington, D-Ill.	1981-83
Katie Hall, D-Ind.	1983-85
Charles A. Hayes, D-Ill.	1983-
Major R. Owens, D-N.Y.	1983-
Edolphus Towns, D-N.Y.	1983-
Alan Wheat, D-Mo.	1983-
Alton R. Waldon, Jr., D-N.Y.	1986-87
Mike Espy, D-Miss.	1987-
Floyd H. Flake, D-N.Y.	1987-
John Lewis, D-Ga.	1987-
Kweisi Mfume, D-Md.	1987-

Sources: Christopher Maurine, *America's Black Congressmen.* 1971; Government Printing Office. *Biographical Directory of the American Congress, 1774-1971.* 1971.

Hispanic Members of Congress, 1935-88

As of mid-1988, twenty Hispanics had served in Congress; two in the Senate and eighteen in the House. Following is a list of the Hispanic members, their parties and states, and the years in which they served. Not included are Hispanics who served as territorial delegates (ten), resident commissioners of Puerto Rico (thirteen), or nonvoting delegates of Guam (one) or the Virgin Islands (one).

Senate

Dennis Chavez, D-N.M.	1935-62
Joseph Montoya, D-N.M.	1964-77

House

Romualdo Pacheco, R-Calif.	1877-78; 1979-83
Ladislas Lazaro, D-La.	1913-27
Benigno Cardenas Hernandez, R-N.M.	1915-17; 1919-21
Nestor Montoya, R-N.M.	1921-23
Joachim Octave Fernandez, D-La.	1931-41
Antonia Manuel Fernandez, D-N.M.	1943-56
Henry B. Gonzalez, D-Texas	1961-
Edward R. Roybal, D-Calif.	1962-
E. "Kika" de la Garza, D-Texas	1965-
Manuel Lujan, Jr., R-N.M.	1969-
Herman Badillo, D-N.Y.	1971-77
Robert Garcia, D-N.Y.	1978-
Tony Coelho, D-Calif.	1979-
Matthew G. Martinez, D-Calif.	1982-
Solomon P. Ortiz, D-Texas	1983-
William B. Richardson, D-N.M.	1983-
Esteban E. Torres, D-Calif.	1983-
Albert G. Bustamante, D-Texas	1985-

Sources: Congressional Quarterly *Weekly Report;* Congressional Hispanic Caucus.

Cases of Expulsion in the House

Year	Member	Grounds	Disposition
1798	Matthew Lyon, Anti-Fed-Vt.	Assault on repre-sentative	Not expelled
1798	Roger Griswold, Fed-Conn.	Assault on repre-sentative	Not expelled
1799	Matthew Lyon, Anti-Fed-Vt.	Sedition	Not expelled
1838	William J. Graves, Whig-Ky.	Killing of representative in duel	Not expelled
1839	Alexander Duncan, Whig-Ohio	Offensive publication	Not expelled
1856	Preston S. Brooks, State Rights Dem.-S.C.	Assault on senator	Not expelled
1857	Orsamus B. Matteson, Whig-N.Y.	Corruption	Not expelled
1857	William A. Gilbert, Whig-N.Y.	Corruption	Not expelled
1857	William W. Welch, American-Conn.	Corruption	Not expelled
1857	Francis S. Edwards, American-N.Y.	Corruption	Not expelled
1858	Orsamus B. Matteson, Whig-N.Y.	Corruption	Not expelled
1861	John B. Clark, D-Mo.	Support of rebellion	*Expelled*
1861	Henry C. Burnett, D-Ky.	Support of rebellion	*Expelled*
1861	John W. Reid, D-Mo.	Support of rebellion	*Expelled*
1864	Alexander Long, D-Ohio	Treasonable utterance	Not expelled*
1864	Benjamin G. Harris, D-Md.	Treasonable utterance	Not expelled*
1866	Lovell H. Rousseau, R-Ky.	Assault on repre-sentative	Not expelled*
1870	Benjamin F. Whittemore, R-S.C.	Corruption	Not expelled*
1870	Roderick R. Butler, R-Tenn.	Corruption	Not expelled*
1873	Oakes Ames, R-Mass.	Corruption	Not expelled*
1873	James Brooks, D-N.Y.	Corruption	Not expelled*
1875	John Y. Brown, D-Ky.	Insult to representative	Not expelled*
1875	William S. King, R-Minn.	Corruption	Not expelled
1875	John G. Schumaker, D-N.Y.	Corruption	Not expelled
1884	William P. Kellogg, R-La.	Corruption	Not expelled
1921	Thomas L. Blanton, D-Texas	Abuse of leave to print	Not expelled*
1980	Michael "Ozzie" Myers, D-Pa.	Corruption	*Expelled*

* Censured after expulsion move failed or was withdrawn.

Source: Congressional Quarterly. *Guide to Congress.* 3d ed. 1982.

Cases of Expulsion in the Senate

Year	Member	Grounds	Disposition
1797	William Blount, Ind-Tenn.	Anti-Spanish conspiracy	*Expelled*
1808	John Smith, D-Ohio	Disloyalty	Not expelled
1858	Henry M. Rice, D-Minn.	Corruption	Not expelled
1861	James M. Mason, D-Va.	Support of rebellion	*Expelled*
1861	Robert M. Hunter, D-Va.	Support of rebellion	*Expelled*
1861	Thomas L. Clingman, D-N.C.	Support of rebellion	*Expelled*
1861	Thomas Bragg, D-N.C.	Support of rebellion	*Expelled*
1861	James Chestnut, Jr., States Rights-S.C.	Support of rebellion	*Expelled*
1861	Alfred O. P. Nicholson, D-Tenn.	Support of rebellion	*Expelled*
1861	William K. Sebastian, D-Ark.	Support of rebellion	*Expelled*[1]
1861	Charles B. Mitchel, D-Ark.	Support of rebellion	*Expelled*
1861	John Hemphill, State Rights D-Texas	Support of rebellion	*Expelled*
1861	Louis T. Wigfall, D-Texas[2]	Support of rebellion	Not expelled
1861	Louis T. Wigfall, D-Texas	Support of rebellion	*Expelled*
1861	John C. Breckinridge, D-Ky.	Support of rebellion	*Expelled*
1861	Lazarus W. Powell, D-Ky.	Support of rebellion	Not expelled
1862	Trusten Polk, D-Mo.	Support of rebellion	*Expelled*
1862	Jesse D. Bright, D-Ind.	Support of rebellion	*Expelled*
1862	Waldo P. Johnson, D-Mo.	Support of rebellion	*Expelled*
1862	James F. Simmons, Whig-R.I.	Corruption	Not expelled
1873	James W. Patterson, R-N.H.	Corruption	Not expelled
1893	William N. Roach, D-N.D.	Embezzlement	Not expelled
1905	John H. Mitchell, R-Ore.	Corruption	Not expelled
1907	Reed Smoot, R-Utah	Mormonism	Not expelled
1919	Robert M. La Follette, R-Wis.	Disloyalty	Not expelled
1934	John H. Overton, D-La.	Corruption	Not expelled
1934	Huey P. Long, D-La.	Corruption	Not expelled
1942	William Langer, R-N.D.	Corruption	Not expelled
1982	Harrison A. Williams, Jr., D-N.J.	Corruption	Not expelled[3]

[1] The Senate reversed its decision on Sebastian's expulsion March 3, 1877. Sebastian had died in 1865, but his children were paid an amount equal to his Senate salary between the time of his expulsion and the date of his death.

[2] The Senate took no action on an initial resolution expelling Wigfall because he represented a state that had seceded from the Union; three months later he was expelled for supporting the Confederacy.

[3] Facing probable expulsion, Williams resigned March 11, 1982.

Source: Congressional Quarterly. *Guide to Congress.* 3d ed. 1982.

Censure Proceedings in the House

Year	Member	Grounds	Disposition
1798	Matthew Lyon, Anti-Fed-Vt.	Assault on repre-sentative	Not censured
1798	Roger Griswold, Fed-Conn.	Assault on repre-sentative	Not censured
1832	William Stanbery, D-Ohio	Insult to Speaker	*Censured*
1836	Sherrod Williams, Whig-Ky.	Insult to Speaker	Not censured
1838	Henry A. Wise, Tyler Dem.-Va.	Service as second in duel	Not censured
1839	Alexander Duncan, Whig-Ohio	Offensive publication	Not censured
1842	John Q. Adams, Whig-Mass.	Treasonable petition	Not censured
1842	Joshua R. Giddings, Whig-Ohio	Offensive paper	*Censured*
1856	Henry A. Edmundson, D-Va.	Complicity in assault on senator	Not censured
1856	Laurence M. Keitt, D-S.C.		*Censured*
1860	George S. Houston, D-Ala.	Insult to representative	Not censured
1864	Alexander Long, D-Ohio	Treasonable utterance	*Censured*
1864	Benjamin G. Harris, D-Md.	Treasonable utterance	*Censured*
1866	John W. Chanler, D-N.Y.	Insult to House	*Censured*
1866	Lovell H. Rousseau, R-Ky.	Assault on repre-sentative	*Censured*
1867	John W. Hunter, Ind-N.Y.	Insult to representative	*Censured*
1868	Fernando Wood, D-N.Y.	Offensive utterance	*Censured*
1868	E. D. Holbrook, D-Idaho[1]	Offensive utterance	*Censured*
1870	Benjamin F. Whittemore, R-S.C.	Corruption	*Censured*
1870	Roderick R. Butler, R-Tenn.	Corruption	*Censured*
1870	John T. Deweese, D-N.C.	Corruption	*Censured*
1873	Oakes Ames, R-Mass.	Corruption	*Censured*
1873	James Brooks, D-N.Y.	Corruption	*Censured*
1875	John Y. Brown, D-KY.	Insult to representative	*Censured*[2]
1876	James G. Blaine, R-Maine	Corruption	Not censured
1882	William D. Kelley, R-Pa.	Offensive utterance	Not censured
1882	John D. White, R-Ky.	Offensive utterance	Not censured
1883	John Van Voorhis, R-N.Y.	Offensive utterance	Not censured
1890	William D. Bynum, D-Ind.	Offensive utterance	*Censured*
1921	Thomas L. Blanton, D-Texas	Abuse of leave to print	*Censured*
1978	Edward R. Roybal, D-Calif.	Lying to House com-mittee	Not censured
1979	Charles C. Diggs, Jr., D-Mich.	Misuse of clerk-hire funds	*Censured*
1980	Charles H. Wilson, D-Calif.	Financial misconduct	*Censured*
1983	Gerry E. Studds, D-Mass.	Sexual misconduct	*Censured*
1983	Daniel B. Crane, R-Ill.	Sexual misconduct	*Censured*

[1] Holbrook was a territorial delegate, not a representative.
[2] The House later rescinded part of the censure resolution against Brown.

Source: Congressional Quarterly. *Guide to Congress.* 3d ed. 1982.

Censure Proceedings in the Senate

Year	Member	Grounds	Disposition
1811	Timothy Pickering, Fed-Mass.	Breach of confidence	*Censured*
1844	Benjamin Tappan, D-Ohio	Breach of confidence	*Censured*
1850	Thomas H. Benton, D-Mo.	Disorderly conduct	Not censured
1850	Henry S. Foote, Unionist-Miss.	Disorderly conduct	Not censured
1902	John L. McLaurin, D-S.C.	Assault	*Censured*
1902	Benjamin R. Tillman, D-S.C.	Assault	*Censured*
1929	Hiram Bingham, R-Conn.	Bringing Senate into disrepute	*Censured*
1954	Joseph R. McCarthy, R-Wis.	Obstruction of legislative process, insult to senators, etc.	*Censured*
1967	Thomas J. Dodd, D-Conn.	Financial misconduct	*Censured*
1979	Herman E. Talmadge, D-Ga.	Financial misconduct	*Denounced*

Source: Congressional Quarterly. *Guide to Congress.* 3d ed. 1982.

Incumbents Reelected, Defeated, or Retired, 1946-86

Year	Retired*	Total seeking reelection	Defeated in primaries	Defeated in general election	Total reelected	Percentage of those seeking reelection
House						
1946	32	398	18	52	328	82.4
1948	29	400	15	68	317	79.3
1950	29	400	6	32	362	90.5
1952	42	389	9	26	354	91.0
1954	24	407	6	22	379	93.1
1956	21	411	6	16	389	94.6
1958	33	396	3	37	356	89.9
1960	26	405	5	25	375	92.6
1962	24	402	12	22	368	91.5
1964	33	397	8	45	344	86.6
1966	22	411	8	41	362	88.1
1968	23	409	4	9	396	96.8
1970	29	401	10	12	379	94.5
1972	40	390	12	13	365	93.6
1974	43	391	8	40	343	87.7
1976	47	384	3	13	368	95.8
1978	49	382	5	19	358	93.7
1980	34	398	6	31	361	90.7
1982	40	393	10	29	354	90.1
1984	22	409	3	16	390	95.4
1986	38	393	2	6	385	98.0
Senate						
1946	9	30	6	7	17	56.7
1948	8	25	2	8	15	60.0
1950	4	32	5	5	22	68.8
1952	4	31	2	9	20	64.5
1954	6	32	2	6	24	75.0
1956	6	29	0	4	25	86.2
1958	6	28	0	10	18	64.3
1960	5	29	0	1	28	96.6
1962	4	35	1	5	29	82.9
1964	2	33	1	4	28	84.8
1966	3	32	3	1	28	87.5
1968	6	28	4	4	20	71.4
1970	4	31	1	6	24	77.4
1972	6	27	2	5	20	74.1
1974	7	27	2	2	23	85.2
1976	8	25	0	9	16	64.0
1978	10	25	3	7	15	60.0
1980	5	29	4	9	16	55.2
1982	3	30	0	2	28	93.3
1984	4	29	0	3	26	89.6
1986	6	28	0	7	21	75.0

* Does not include persons who died or resigned before the election.

Source: Norman J. Ornstein et al. *Vital Statistics on Congress, 1987-1988.* 1988.

Party Affiliations in Congress and the Presidency
1789-1988

(Key to abbreviations: AD—Administration; AM—Anti-Masonic; C—Coalition; D—Democratic; DR—Democratic-Republican; F—Federalist; J—Jacksonian; NR—National Republican; Op—Opposition; R—Republican; U—Unionist; W—Whig. Figures are for the beginning of the first session of each Congress.)

Year	Congress	House Majority party	House Principal minority party	Senate Majority party	Senate Principal minority party	President
1987-1989	100th	D-258	R-177	D-55	R-45	R (Reagan)
1985-1987	99th	D-252	R-182	R-53	D-47	R (Reagan)
1983-1985	98th	D-269	R-165	R-54	D-46	R (Reagan)
1981-1983	97th	D-243	R-192	R-53	D-46	R (Reagan)
1979-1981	96th	D-276	R-157	D-58	R-41	D (Carter)
1977-1979	95th	D-292	R-143	D-61	R-38	D (Carter)
1975-1977	94th	D-291	R-144	D-60	R-37	R (Ford)
1973-1975	93rd	D-239	R-192	D-56	R-42	R (Nixon-Ford)
1971-1973	92nd	D-254	R-180	D-54	R-44	R (Nixon)
1969-1971	91st	D-243	R-192	D-57	R-43	R (Nixon)
1967-1969	90th	D-247	R-187	D-64	R-36	D (L. Johnson)
1965-1967	89th	D-295	R-140	D-68	R-32	D (L. Johnson)
1963-1965	88th	D-258	R-177	D-67	R-33	D (L. Johnson) D (Kennedy)
1961-1963	87th	D-263	R-174	D-65	R-35	D (Kennedy)
1959-1961	86th	D-283	R-153	D-64	R-34	R (Eisenhower)
1957-1959	85th	D-233	R-200	D-49	R-47	R (Eisenhower)
1955-1957	84th	D-232	R-203	D-48	R-47	R (Eisenhower)
1953-1955	83rd	R-221	D-211	R-48	D-47	R (Eisenhower)
1951-1953	82nd	D-234	R-199	D-49	R-47	D (Truman)
1949-1951	81st	D-263	R-171	D-54	R-42	D (Truman)
1947-1949	80th	R-245	D-188	R-51	D-45	D (Truman)
1945-1947	79th	D-242	R-190	D-56	R-38	D (Truman)
1943-1945	78th	D-218	R-208	D-58	R-37	D (F. Roosevelt)
1941-1943	77th	D-268	R-162	D-66	R-28	D (F. Roosevelt)
1939-1941	76th	D-261	R-164	D-69	R-23	D (F. Roosevelt)
1937-1939	75th	D-331	R-89	D-76	R-16	D (F. Roosevelt)
1935-1937	74th	D-319	R-103	D-69	R-25	D (F. Roosevelt)
1933-1935	73rd	D-310	R-117	D-60	R-35	D (F. Roosevelt)
1931-1933	72nd	D-220	R-214	R-48	D-47	R (Hoover)
1929-1931	71st	R-267	D-167	R-56	D-39	R (Hoover)
1927-1929	70th	R-237	D-195	R-49	D-46	R (Coolidge)
1925-1927	69th	R-247	D-183	R-56	D-39	R (Coolidge)
1923-1925	68th	R-225	D-205	R-51	D-43	R (Coolidge)
1921-1923	67th	R-301	D-131	R-59	D-37	R (Harding)
1919-1921	66th	R-240	D-190	R-49	D-47	D (Wilson)
1917-1919	65th	D-216	R-210	D-53	R-42	D (Wilson)
1915-1917	64th	D-230	R-196	D-56	R-40	D (Wilson)
1913-1915	63rd	D-291	R-127	D-51	R-44	D (Wilson)
1911-1913	62nd	D-228	R-161	R-51	D-41	R (Taft)
1909-1911	61st	R-219	D-172	R-61	D-32	R (Taft)
1907-1909	60th	R-222	D-164	R-61	D-31	R (T. Roosevelt)
1905-1907	59th	R-250	D-136	R-57	D-33	R (T. Roosevelt)
1903-1905	58th	R-208	D-178	R-57	D-33	R (T. Roosevelt)

Year	Congress	House Majority party	House Principal minority party	Senate Majority party	Senate Principal minority party	President
1901-1903	57th	R-197	D-151	R-55	D-31	R (T. Roosevelt)
						R (McKinley)
1899-1901	56th	R-185	D-163	R-53	D-26	R (McKinley)
1897-1899	55th	R-204	D-113	R-47	D-34	R (McKinley)
1895-1897	54th	R-244	D-105	R-43	D-39	D (Cleveland)
1893-1895	53rd	D-218	R-127	D-44	R-38	D (Cleveland)
1891-1893	52nd	D-235	R-88	R-47	D-39	R (B. Harrison)
1889-1891	51st	R-166	D-159	R-39	D-37	R (B. Harrison)
1887-1889	50th	D-169	R-152	R-39	D-37	D (Cleveland)
1885-1887	49th	D-183	R-140	R-43	D-34	D (Cleveland)
1883-1885	48th	D-197	R-118	R-38	D-36	R (Arthur)
1881-1883	47th	R-147	D-135	R-37	D-37	R (Arthur)
						R (Garfield)
1879-1881	46th	D-149	R-130	D-42	R-33	R (Hayes)
1877-1879	45th	D-153	R-140	R-39	D-36	R (Hayes)
1875-1877	44th	D-169	R-109	R-45	D-29	R (Grant)
1873-1875	43rd	R-194	D-92	R-49	D-19	R (Grant)
1871-1873	42nd	R-134	D-104	R-52	D-17	R (Grant)
1869-1871	41st	R-149	D-63	R-56	D-11	R (Grant)
1867-1869	40th	R-143	D-49	R-42	D-11	R (A. Johnson)
1865-1867	39th	U-149	D-42	U-42	D-10	R (A. Johnson)
						R (Lincoln)
1863-1865	38th	R-102	D-75	R-36	D-9	R (Lincoln)
1861-1863	37th	R-105	D-43	R-31	D-8	R (Lincoln)
1859-1861	36th	R-114	D-92	D-36	R-26	D (Buchanan)
1857-1859	35th	D-118	R-92	D-36	R-20	D (Buchanan)
1855-1857	34th	R-108	D-83	D-40	R-15	D (Pierce)
1853-1855	33rd	D-159	W-71	D-38	W-22	D (Pierce)
1851-1853	32nd	D-140	W-88	D-35	W-24	W (Fillmore)
1849-1851	31st	D-112	W-109	D-35	W-25	W (Fillmore)
						W (Taylor)
1847-1849	30th	W-115	D-108	D-36	W-21	D (Polk)
1845-1847	29th	D-143	W-77	D-31	W-25	D (Polk)
1843-1845	28th	D-142	W-79	W-28	D-25	W (Tyler)
1841-1843	27th	W-133	D-102	W-28	D-22	W (Tyler)
						W (W. Harrison)
1839-1841	26th	D-124	W-118	D-28	W-22	D (Van Buren)
1837-1839	25th	D-108	W-107	D-30	W-18	D (Van Buren)
1835-1837	24th	D-145	W-98	D-27	W-25	D (Jackson)
1833-1835	23rd	D-147	AM-53	D-20	NR-20	D (Jackson)
1831-1833	22nd	D-141	NR-58	D-25	NR-21	D (Jackson)
1829-1831	21st	D-139	NR-74	D-26	NR-22	D (Jackson)
1827-1829	20th	J-119	Ad-94	J-28	Ad-20	C (John Q. Adams)
1825-1827	19th	Ad-105	J-97	Ad-26	J-20	C (John Q. Adams)
1823-1825	18th	DR-187	F-26	DR-44	F-4	DR (Monroe)
1821-1823	17th	DR-158	F-25	DR-44	F-4	DR (Monroe)
1819-1821	16th	DR-156	F-27	DR-35	F-7	DR (Monroe)
1817-1819	15th	DR-141	F-42	DR-34	F-10	DR (Monroe)
1815-1817	14th	DR-117	F-65	DR-25	F-11	DR (Madison)
1813-1815	13th	DR-112	F-68	DR-27	F-9	DR (Madison)

| Year | Congress | House | | Senate | | President |
		Majority party	Principal minority party	Majority party	Principal minority party	
1811-1813	12th	DR-108	F-36	DR-30	F-6	DR (Madison)
1809-1811	11th	DR-94	F-48	DR-28	F-6	DR (Madison)
1807-1809	10th	DR-118	F-24	DR-28	F-6	DR (Jefferson)
1805-1807	9th	DR-116	F-25	DR-27	F-7	DR (Jefferson)
1803-1805	8th	DR-102	F-39	DR-25	F-9	DR (Jefferson)
1801-1803	7th	DR-69	F-36	DR-18	F-13	DR (Jefferson)
1799-1801	6th	F-64	DR-42	F-19	DR-13	F (John Adams)
1797-1799	5th	F-58	DR-48	F-20	DR-12	F (John Adams)
1795-1797	4th	F-54	DR-52	F-19	DR-13	F (Washington)
1793-1795	3rd	DR-57	F-48	F-17	DR-13	F (Washington)
1791-1793	2nd	F-37	DR-33	F-16	DR-13	F (Washington)
1789-1791	1st	Ad-38	Op-26	Ad-17	Op-9	F (Washington)

Source: Congressional Quarterly. *American Leaders, 1789-1987.* 1987.

Presidents and Vice Presidents of the United States

President	Term of Service	Vice President
George Washington, F (1732-1799)	April 30, 1789-March 4, 1793	John Adams
Washington	March 4, 1793-March 4, 1797	Adams
John Adams, F (1735-1826)	March 4, 1797-March 4, 1801	Thomas Jefferson
Thomas Jefferson, DR (1743-1826)	March 4, 1801-March 4, 1805	Aaron Burr
Jefferson	March 4, 1805-March 4, 1809	George Clinton
James Madison, DR (1751-1836)	March 4, 1809-March 4, 1813	Clinton
Madison	March 4, 1813-March 4, 1817	Elbridge Gerry
James Monroe, DR (1758-1831)	March 4, 1817-March 4, 1821	Daniel D. Tompkins
Monroe	March 4, 1821-March 4, 1825	Tompkins
John Q. Adams, DR (1767-1848)	March 4, 1825-March 4, 1829	John C. Calhoun
Andrew Jackson, D (1767-1845)	March 4, 1829-March 4, 1833	Calhoun
Jackson	March 4, 1833-March 4, 1837	Martin Van Buren
Martin Van Buren, D (1782-1862)	March 4, 1837-March 4, 1841	Richard M. Johnson
W. H. Harrison, W (1773-1841)	March 4, 1841-April 4, 1841	John Tyler
John Tyler, W (1790-1862)	April 6, 1841-March 4, 1845	
James K. Polk, D (1795-1849)	March 4, 1845-March 4, 1849	George M. Dallas
Zachary Taylor, W (1784-1850)	March 4, 1849-July 9, 1850	Millard Fillmore
Millard Fillmore, W (1800-1874)	July 10, 1850-March 4, 1853	
Franklin Pierce, D (1804-1869)	March 4, 1853-March 4, 1857	William R. King
James Buchanan, D (1791-1868)	March 4, 1857-March 4, 1861	John C. Breckinridge
Abraham Lincoln, R (1809-1865)	March 4, 1861-March 4, 1865	Hannibal Hamlin
Lincoln	March 4, 1865-April 15, 1865	Andrew Johnson
Andrew Johnson, R (1808-1875)	April 15, 1865-March 4, 1869	
Ulysses S. Grant, R (1822-1885)	March 4, 1869-March 4, 1873	Schuyler Colfax
Grant	March 4, 1873-March 4, 1877	Henry Wilson
Rutherford B. Hayes, R (1822-1893)	March 4, 1877-March 4, 1881	William A. Wheeler
James A. Garfield, R (1831-1881)	March 4, 1881-Sept. 19, 1881	Chester A. Arthur
Chester A. Arthur, R (1830-1886)	Sept. 20, 1881-March 4, 1885	
Grover Cleveland, D (1837-1908)	March 4, 1885-March 4, 1889	Thomas A. Hendricks
Benjamin Harrison, R (1833-1901)	March 4, 1889-March 4, 1893	Levi P. Morton
Grover Cleveland, D (1837-1908)	March 4, 1893-March 4, 1897	Adlai E. Stevenson
William McKinley, R (1843-1901)	March 4, 1897-March 4, 1901	Garret A. Hobart
McKinley	March 4, 1901-Sept. 14, 1901	Theodore Roosevelt
Theodore Roosevelt, R (1858-1919)	Sept. 14, 1901-March 4, 1905	
Roosevelt	March 4, 1905-March 4, 1909	Charles W. Fairbanks
William H. Taft, R (1857-1930)	March 4, 1909-March 4, 1913	James S. Sherman
Woodrow Wilson, D (1856-1924)	March 4, 1913-March 4, 1917	Thomas R. Marshall
Wilson	March 4, 1917-March 4, 1921	Marshall
Warren G. Harding, R (1865-1923)	March 4, 1921-Aug. 2, 1923	Calvin Coolidge
Calvin Coolidge, R (1872-1933)	Aug. 3, 1923-March 4, 1925	
Coolidge	March 4, 1925-March 4, 1929	Charles G. Dawes
Herbert Hoover, R (1874-1964)	March 4, 1929-March 4, 1933	Charles Curtis
Franklin D. Roosevelt, D (1882-1945)	March 4, 1933-Jan. 20, 1937	John N. Garner
Roosevelt	Jan. 20, 1937-Jan. 20, 1941	Garner
Roosevelt	Jan. 20, 1941-Jan. 20, 1945	Henry A. Wallace
Roosevelt	Jan. 20, 1945-April 12, 1945	Harry S Truman
Harry S Truman, D (1884-1972)	April 12, 1945-Jan. 20, 1949	
Truman	Jan. 20, 1949-Jan. 20, 1953	Alben W. Barkley
Dwight D. Eisenhower, R (1890-1969)	Jan. 20, 1953-Jan. 20, 1957	Richard Nixon
Eisenhower	Jan. 20, 1957-Jan. 20, 1961	Nixon

President	Term of Service	Vice President
John F. Kennedy, D (1917-1963)	Jan. 20, 1961-Nov. 22, 1963	Lyndon B. Johnson
Lyndon B. Johnson, D (1908-1973)	Nov. 22, 1963-Jan. 20, 1965	
Johnson	Jan. 20, 1965-Jan. 20, 1969	Hubert H. Humphrey
Richard Nixon, R (1913-)	Jan. 20, 1969-Jan. 20, 1973	Spiro T. Agnew
Nixon	Jan. 20, 1973-Aug. 9, 1974	Agnew
		Gerald R. Ford
Gerald R. Ford, R (1913-)	Aug. 9, 1974-Jan. 20, 1977	Nelson A. Rockefeller
Jimmy Carter, D (1924-)	Jan. 20, 1977-Jan. 20, 1981	Walter F. Mondale
Ronald Reagan, R (1911-)	Jan. 20, 1981-Jan. 20, 1985	George Bush
Reagan	Jan. 20, 1985-	Bush

Abbreviations: D—Democrat, DR—Democratic-Republican, F—Federalist, R—Republican, W—Whig

Vetoes and Overrides 1947-87

Congress		Total number presidential vetoes	Number of regular vetoes	Number of pocket vetoes	Vetoes overridden
80th	(1947-49)	75	42	33	6
81st	(1949-51)	79	70	9	3
82d	(1951-53)	22	14	8	3
83rd	(1953-55)	52	21	31	0
84th	(1955-57)	34	12	22	0
85th	(1957-59)	51	18	33	0
86th	(1959-61)	44	22	22	2
87th	(1961-63)	20	11	9	0
88th	(1963-65)	9	5	4	0
89th	(1965-67)	14	10	4	0
90th	(1967-69)	8	2	6	0
91st	(1969-71)	11	7	4	2
92d	(1971-73)	20	6	14	2
93rd	(1973-75)	39	27	12	5
94th	(1975-77)	37	32	5	8
95th	(1977-79)	19	6	13	0
96th	(1979-81)	12	7	5	2
97th	(1981-83)	15	9	6	2
98th	(1983-85)	24	9	15	2
99th	(1985-87)	20	13	7	2
100th	(1987 only)	3	3	0	3

Source: Adapted from Norman J. Ornstein et al., *Vital Statistics on Congress, 1977-88.* 1988.

Treaties Killed by the Senate
(As of June 1988)

Date of Vote	Country	Vote Yea-Nay	Subject
March 9, 1825	Colombia	0-40	Suppression of African Slave Trade
June 11, 1836	Switzerland	14-23	Personal and Property Rights
June 8, 1844	Texas	16-35	Annexation
June 15, 1844	German Zollverein	26-18	Reciprocity
May 31, 1860	Mexico	18-27	Transit and Commercial Rights
June 27, 1860	Spain	26-17	Cuban Claims Commission
April 13, 1869	Great Britain	1-54	Arbitration of Claims
June 1, 1870	Hawaii	20-19	Reciprocity
June 30, 1870	Dominican Republic	28-28	Annexation
Jan. 29, 1885	Nicaragua	32-23	Interoceanic Canal
April 20, 1886	Mexico	32-26	Mining Claims
Aug. 21, 1888	Great Britain	27-30	Fishing Rights
Feb. 1, 1889	Great Britain	15-38	Extradition
May 5, 1897	Great Britain	43-26	Arbitration
March 19, 1920	Multilateral	49-35	Treaty of Versailles
Jan. 18, 1927	Turkey	50-34	Commercial Rights
March 14, 1934	Canada	46-42	St. Lawrence Seaway
Jan. 29, 1935	Multilateral	52-36	World Court
May 26, 1960	Multilateral	49-30	Law of the Sea Convention
March 8, 1983	Multilateral	50-42	Montreal Aviation Protocol

Note: Two-thirds majority vote is required for Senate consent to the ratification of treaties. In many cases, treaties were blocked in committee or withdrawn before ever coming to a vote in the Senate.

Source: Compiled by Senate Historical Office from W. Stull Holt, *Treaties Defeated by the Senate* (Baltimore, Md.: Johns Hopkins University Press, 1933) and from *Senate Executive Journal.*

502

Senate Votes Cast by Vice Presidents

Following is a list of the number of votes cast by each vice president through mid-1988:

Period	Vice President	Votes Cast	Period	Vice President	Votes Cast
1789-1797	John Adams	29	1893-1897	Adlai E. Stevenson	2
1797-1801	Thomas Jefferson	3	1897-1899	Garret A. Hobart	1
1801-1805	Aaron Burr	3	1901	Theodore Roosevelt	0
1805-1812	George Clinton	11	1905-1909	Charles W. Fairbanks	0
1813-1814	Elbridge Gerry	8	1909-1912	James S. Sherman	4
1817-1825	Daniel D. Tompkins	5	1913-1921	Thomas R. Marshall	4
1825-1832	John C. Calhoun	28	1921-1923	Calvin Coolidge	0
1833-1837	Martin Van Buren	4	1925-1929	Charles G. Dawes	2
1837-1841	Richard M. Johnson	14	1929-1933	Charles Curtis	3
1841	John Tyler	0	1933-1941	John N. Garner	3
1845-1849	George M. Dallas	19	1941-1945	Henry A. Wallace	4
1849-1850	Millard Fillmore	3	1945	Harry S Truman	1
1853	William R. King	0	1949-1953	Alben W. Barkley	7
1857-1861	John C. Breckinridge	10	1953-1961	Richard M. Nixon	8
1861-1865	Hannibal Hamlin	7	1961-1963	Lyndon B. Johnson	0
1865	Andrew Johnson	0	1965-1969	Hubert H. Humphrey	4
1869-1873	Schuyler Colfax	13	1969-1973	Spiro T. Agnew	2
1873-1875	Henry Wilson	1	1973-1974	Gerald R. Ford	0
1877-1881	William A. Wheeler	5	1974-1977	Nelson A. Rockefeller	0
1881	Chester A. Arthur	3	1977-1981	Walter F. Mondale	1
1885	Thomas A. Hendricks	0	1981-1988	George Bush	7*
1889-1893	Levi P. Morton	4		Total	223

* As of July 1, 1988.

Source: Library of Congress, Congressional Research Service

CONGRESSIONAL PAY

Year	Salary [1]	Year	Salary [1]
1789-95	$6 per diem	1933-35	$8,500
1795-96	$6 per diem (House)	1935-47	$10,000
	$7 per diem (Senate)	1947-55	$12,500
1796-1815	$6 per diem	1955-65	$22,500
1815-17	$1,500	1965-69	$30,000
1817-55	$8 per diem	1969-75	$42,500
1855-65	$3,000	1975-77	$44,600
1865-71	$5,000	1977-80	$57,500
1871-73	$7,500	1980-82	$60,662
1873-1907	$5,000	1982-83	$69,800 [2]
1907-25	$7,500	1984	$72,600
1925-32	$10,000	1985-86	$75,100
1932-33	$9,000	1987-88	$89,500

[1] Annual unless otherwise indicated.
[2] Senators received the raise in 1983.

Source: Adapted from Congressional Quarterly's *Guide to Congress*, 3d ed. 1982.

Top-Level Salaries, 1987

Position	1987 Pay Level
Executive Branch	
Vice President	$115,000
Level I includes Cabinet officers	99,500
Level II includes deputy secretaries of Cabinet departments; and heads of offices and agencies such as the VA, CIA, FBI, EPA, NASA and OMB	89,500
Level III includes under secretaries of Cabinet departments; chairmen of regulatory commissions such as the FTC, FDIC and the NLRB	82,500
Level IV includes assistant secretaries of Cabinet departments; members of regulatory commissions; Cabinet department general counsels	77,500
Level V includes directors of major bureaus of Cabinet departments	72,500
Board of Governors of the U.S. Postal Service	10,000
Legislative Branch	
Speaker of the House	115,000
President pro tempore, majority and minority leaders	99,500
Senators, representatives, four delegates to Congress, resident commissioner of Puerto Rico, comptroller general	89,500
Director of CBO, deputy comptroller general, librarian of Congress and the architect of the Capitol	82,500
Deputy director of CBO; general counsel, GAO; deputy librarian of Congress; and the assistant architect of the Capitol	77,500
Judicial Branch	
Chief justice	115,000
Retired chief justice	115,000
Associate justices	110,000
Judges, circuit courts of appeal; court of military appeals	95,000
Judges, district courts; court of international trade; tax court; assistant to the chief justice; director, Administrative Office — U.S. courts; director, Federal Judicial Center	89,500
Judges, U.S. Claims Court	82,500
Deputy director, Administrative Office — U.S. Courts; circuit executives	72,500
Bankruptcy judges, U.S. magistrates	72,500

Sources: U.S. Office of Personnel Management, Administrative Office of the U.S. Courts, Office of Management and Budget.

Legislative Branch Appropriations, 1946-86

Fiscal Year	Appropriation	Fiscal Year	Appropriation
1946	$ 54,065,614	1967	$ 221,715,643
1947	61,825,020	1968	282,003,322
1948	62,119,714	1969	311,542,399
1949	62,057,678	1970	361,024,327
1950	64,313,460	1971	443,104,319
1951	71,888,244	1972	564,107,992
1952	75,673,896	1973	645,127,365
1953	77,670,076	1974	662,180,668
1954	70,925,361	1975	785,618,833
1955	86,304,923	1976	947,185,778
1956	94,827,986	1977	963,921,185
1957	120,775,798	1978	1,009,225,350
1958	107,785,560	1979	1,124,766,400
1959	136,153,580	1980	1,199,061,463
1960	131,055,385	1981	1,285,943,826
1961	140,930,781	1982	1,365,272,433
1962	136,686,715	1983	1,467,318,263
1963	150,426,185	1984	1,644,160,600
1964	168,467,869	1985	1,599,977,138
1965	221,904,318	1986	1,783,255,000
1966	197,965,307		

Note: A portion of the appropriation to the legislative branch is not spent directly on congressional operations. See detailed breakdown of fiscal 1988 appropriations, below.

Source: Norman J. Ornstein et al., *Vital Statistics on Congress, 1987-1988.* 1988.

Fiscal 1988 Legislative Appropriations

Congressional Operations

Senate	$ 337,314,000
House of Representatives	513,786,500
Joint Items	94,981,000
Office of Technology Assessment	16,901,000
Biomedical Ethics Board	100,000
Congressional Award Board	189,000
Congressional Budget Office	17,886,000
Architect of the Capitol	100,565,000
Congressional Research Service	43,022,000
Government Printing Office (congressional printing)	70,359,000
Subtotal	$1,195,103,500

Related Agencies

Botanic Garden	2,221,000
Library of Congress	191,998,000
Architect of the Capitol (library buildings)	6,741,000
Copyright Royalty Tribunal	129,000
Government Printing Office (non-congressional printing)	19,162,000
General Accounting Office	329,847,000
Subtotal	$ 550,098,000
Total	$1,745,201,500

Source: Congressional Quarterly Almanac 1987. 1987.

Congressional Workload, 1947-86

		Public bills			Private bills		
Congress		No. of bills enacted	Total pages of statutes	Average pages per statute	No. of bills enacted	Total pages of statutes	Average pages per statute
80th	(1947-49)	906	2,236	2.5	458	182	0.40
81st	(1949-51)	921	2,314	2.5	1,103	417	0.38
82nd	(1951-53)	594	1,585	2.7	1,023	360	0.35
83rd	(1953-55)	781	1,899	2.4	1,002	365	0.36
84th	(1955-57)	1,028	1,848	1.8	893	364	0.41
85th	(1957-59)	936	2,435	2.6	784	349	0.45
86th	(1959-61)	800	1,774	2.2	492	201	0.41
87th	(1961-63)	885	2,078	2.3	684	255	0.37
88th	(1963-65)	666	1,975	3.0	360	144	0.40
89th	(1965-67)	810	2,912	3.6	473	188	0.40
90th	(1967-69)	640	2,304	3.6	362	128	0.35
91st	(1969-71)	695	2,927	4.2	246	104	0.42
92nd	(1971-73)	607	2,330	3.8	161	67	0.42
93rd	(1973-75)	649	3,443	5.3	123	48	0.39
94th	(1975-77)	588	4,121	7.0	141	75	0.53
95th	(1977-79)	633	5,403	8.5	170	60	0.35
96th	(1979-81)	613	4,947	8.1	123	63	0.51
97th	(1981-83)	473	4,343	9.2	56	25	0.45
98th	(1983-85)	623	4,893	7.8	54	26	0.48
99th	(1985-87)	664	7,198	10.8	24	n.a.	n.a.

Note: n.a. = not available.

Source: Norman J. Ornstein et al., *Vital Statistics on Congress, 1987-1988.* 1988.

U.S. HOUSE OF REPRESENTATIVES

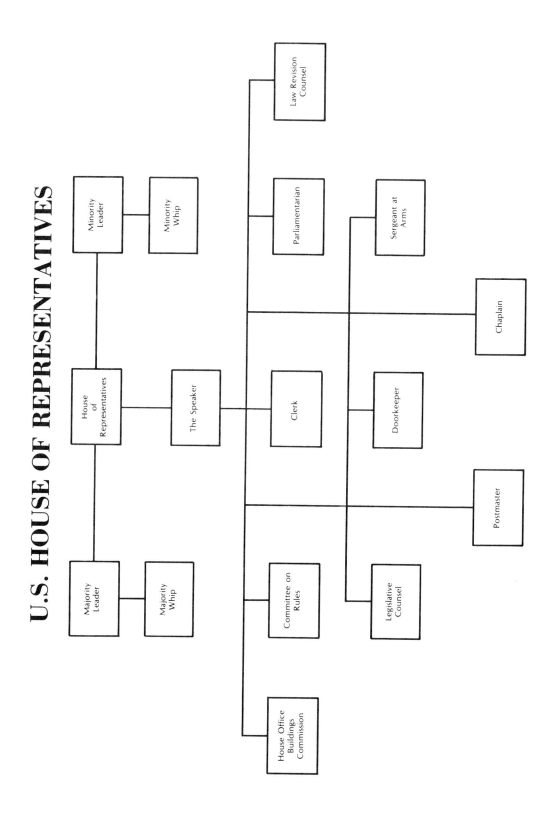

U.S. SENATE

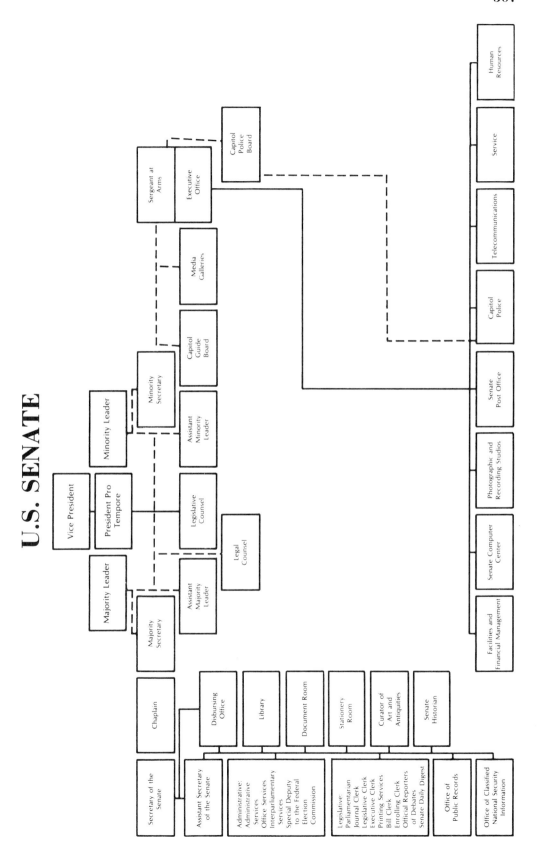

Sessions of the U.S. Congress, 1789-1987

Congress	Session	Date of beginning[1]	Date of adjournment[2]	Length in days	President pro tempore of the Senate[3]	Speaker of the House of Representatives
1st	1	Mar. 4, 1789	Sept. 29, 1789	210	John Langdon of New Hampshire[4]	Frederick A. C. Muhlenberg of Pennsylvania
	2	Jan. 4, 1790	Aug. 12, 1790	221		
	3	Dec. 6, 1790	Mar. 3, 1791	88		Jonathan Trumbull of Connecticut
2nd	1	Oct. 24, 1791	May 8, 1792	197	Richard Henry Lee of Virginia	
	2	Nov. 5, 1792	Mar. 2, 1793	119	John Langdon of New Hampshire	Frederick A. C. Muhlenberg of Pennsylvania
3rd	1	Dec. 2, 1793	June 9, 1794	190	Langdon Ralph Izard of South Carolina	
	2	Nov. 3, 1794	Mar. 3, 1795	121	Henry Tazewell of Virginia	Jonathan Dayton of New Jersey
4th	1	Dec. 7, 1795	June 1, 1796	177	Tazewell Samuel Livermore of New Hampshire	
	2	Dec. 5, 1796	Mar. 3, 1797	89	William Bingham of Pennsylvania	Dayton
5th	1	May 15, 1797	July 10, 1797	57	William Bradford Rhode Island	George Dent of Maryland[5]
	2	Nov. 13, 1797	July 16, 1798	246	Jacob Read of South Carolina Theodore Sedgwick of Massachusetts	
	3	Dec. 3, 1798	Mar. 3, 1799	91	John Laurence of New York James Ross of Pennsylvania	Theodore Sedgwick of Massachusetts
6th	1	Dec. 2, 1799	May 14, 1800	164	Samuel Livermore of New Hampshire	

Congress	Session	Convened	Adjourned	Days	President pro tempore of the Senate	Speaker of the House
	2	Nov. 17, 1800	Mar. 3, 1801	107	Uriah Tracy of Connecticut John E. Howard of Maryland James Hillhouse of Connecticut	Nathaniel Macon of North Carolina
7th	1	Dec. 7, 1801	May 3, 1802	148	Abraham Baldwin of Georgia	
	2	Dec. 6, 1802	Mar. 3, 1803	88	Stephen R. Bradley of Vermont	
8th	1	Oct. 17, 1803	Mar. 27, 1804	163	John Brown of Kentucky Jesse Franklin of North Carolina Joseph Anderson of Tennessee	Macon
	2	Nov. 5, 1804	Mar. 3, 1805	119		
9th	1	Dec. 2, 1805	Apr. 21, 1806	141	Samuel Smith of Maryland	Macon
	2	Dec. 1, 1806	Mar. 3, 1807	93		
10th	1	Oct. 26, 1807	Apr. 25, 1808	182	Smith	Joseph B. Varnum of Massachusetts
	2	Nov. 7, 1808	Mar. 3, 1809	117	Stephen R. Bradley of Vermont John Milledge of Georgia	
11th	1	May 22, 1809	June 28, 1809	38	Andrew Gregg of Pennsylvania John Gaillard of South Carolina John Pope of Kentucky	Varnum
	2	Nov. 27, 1809	May 1, 1810	156		
	3	Dec. 3, 1810	Mar. 3, 1811	91		
12th	1	Nov. 4, 1811	July 6, 1812	245	William H. Crawford of Georgia	Henry Clay of Kentucky
	2	Nov. 2, 1812	Mar. 3, 1813	122	Crawford	
13th	1	May 24, 1813	Aug. 2, 1813	71		Clay

Congress	Session	Date of beginning[1]	Date of adjournment[2]	Length in days	President pro tempore of the Senate[3]	Speaker of the House of Representatives
	2	Dec. 6, 1813	Apr. 18, 1814	134	Joseph B. Varnum of Massachusetts	
	3	Sept. 19, 1814	Mar. 3, 1815	166	John Gaillard of South Carolina	Langdon Cheves of South Carolina[6]
14th	1	Dec. 4, 1815	Apr. 30, 1816	148	Gaillard	Henry Clay of Kentucky
	2	Dec. 2, 1816	Mar. 3, 1817	92	Gaillard	
15th	1	Dec. 1, 1817	Apr. 20, 1818	141	Gaillard	Clay
	2	Nov. 16, 1818	Mar. 3, 1819	108	James Barbour of Virginia	
16th	1	Dec. 6, 1819	May 15, 1820	162	John Gaillard of South Carolina	Clay
	2	Nov. 13, 1820	Mar. 3, 1821	111	Gaillard	John W. Taylor of New York[7]
17th	1	Dec. 3, 1821	May 8, 1822	157	Gaillard	Philip P. Barbour of Virginia
	2	Dec. 2, 1822	Mar. 3, 1823	92	Gaillard	
18th	1	Dec. 1, 1823	May 27, 1824	178	Gaillard	Henry Clay of Kentucky
	2	Dec. 6, 1824	Mar. 3, 1825	88	Gaillard	
19th	1	Dec. 5, 1825	May 22, 1826	169	Nathaniel Macon of North Carolina	John W. Taylor of New York
	2	Dec. 4, 1826	Mar. 3, 1827	90	Macon	
20th	1	Dec. 3, 1827	May 26, 1828	175	Samuel Smith of Maryland	Andrew Stevenson of Virginia
	2	Dec. 1, 1828	Mar. 3, 1829	93	Smith	
21st	1	Dec. 7, 1829	May 31, 1830	176	Smith	Stevenson
	2	Dec. 6, 1830	Mar. 3, 1831	88	Littleton Waller Tazewell of Virginia	
22nd	1	Dec. 5, 1831	July 16, 1832	225	Tazewell	Stevenson
	2	Dec. 3, 1832	Mar. 2, 1833	91	Hugh Lawson White of Tennessee	

Congress	Session	Convened	Adjourned	Days	President pro tempore of the Senate	Speaker of the House
23rd	1	Dec. 2, 1833	June 30, 1834	211	George Poindexter of Mississippi	Stevenson
	2	Dec. 1, 1834	Mar. 3, 1835	93	John Tyler of Virginia	John Bell of Tennessee[8]
24th	1	Dec. 7, 1835	July 4, 1836	211	William R. King of Alabama	James K. Polk of Tennessee
	2	Dec. 5, 1836	Mar. 3, 1837	89	King	Polk
25th	1	Sept. 4, 1837	Oct. 16, 1837	43	King	
	2	Dec. 4, 1837	July 9, 1838	218	King	
	3	Dec. 3, 1838	Mar. 3, 1839	91	King	
26th	1	Dec. 2, 1839	July 21, 1840	233	King	Robert M. T. Hunter of Virginia
	2	Dec. 7, 1840	Mar. 3, 1841	87	King	
27th	1	May 31, 1841	Sept. 13, 1841	106	Samuel L. Southard of New Jersey	John White of Kentucky
	2	Dec. 6, 1841	Aug. 31, 1842	269	Willie P. Mangum of North Carolina	
	3	Dec. 5, 1842	Mar. 3, 1843	89	Mangum	
28th	1	Dec. 4, 1843	June 17, 1844	196	Mangum	John W. Jones of Virginia
	2	Dec. 2, 1844	Mar. 3, 1845	92	Mangum	
29th	1	Dec. 1, 1845	Aug. 10, 1846	253	David R. Atchison of Missouri	John W. Davis of Indiana
	2	Dec. 7, 1846	Mar. 3, 1847	87	Atchison	
30th	1	Dec. 6, 1847	Aug. 14, 1848	254	Atchison	Robert C. Winthrop of Massachusetts
	2	Dec. 4, 1848	Mar. 3, 1849	90	Atchison	
31st	1	Dec. 3, 1849	Sept. 30, 1850	302	William R. King of Alabama	Howell Cobb of Georgia
	2	Dec. 2, 1850	Mar. 3, 1851	92	King	
32nd	1	Dec. 1, 1851	Aug. 31, 1852	275	King	Linn Boyd of Kentucky
	2	Dec. 6, 1852	Mar. 3, 1853	88	David R. Atchison of Missouri	
33rd	1	Dec. 5, 1853	Aug. 7, 1854	246	Atchison	Boyd

Congress	Session	Date of beginning[1]	Date of adjournment[2]	Length in days	President pro tempore of the Senate[3]	Speaker of the House of Representatives
	2	Dec. 4, 1854	Mar. 3, 1855	90	Jesse D. Bright of Indiana Lewis Cass of Michigan	
34th	1	Dec. 3, 1855	Aug. 18, 1856	260	Jesse D. Bright of Indiana	Nathaniel P. Banks of Massachusetts
	2	Aug. 21, 1856	Aug. 30, 1856	10	Bright	
	3	Dec. 1, 1856	Mar. 3, 1857	93	James M. Mason of Virginia Thomas J. Rusk of Texas	
35th	1	Dec. 7, 1857	June 14, 1858	189	Benjamin Fitzpatrick of Alabama	James L. Orr of South Carolina
	2	Dec. 6, 1858	Mar. 3, 1859	88	Fitzpatrick	
36th	1	Dec. 5, 1859	June 25, 1860	202	Fitzpatrick Jesse D. Bright of Indiana Solomon Foot of Vermont	William Pennington of New Jersey
	2	Dec. 3, 1860	Mar. 3, 1861	93	Foot	
37th	1	July 4, 1861	Aug. 6, 1861	34	Foot	Galusha A. Grow of Pennsylvania
	2	Dec. 2, 1861	July 17, 1862	228	Foot	
	3	Dec. 1, 1862	Mar. 3, 1863	93	Foot	
38th	1	Dec. 7, 1863	July 4, 1864	209	Daniel Clark of New Hampshire	Schuyler Colfax of Indiana
	2	Dec. 5, 1864	Mar. 3, 1865	89	Clark	
39th	1	Dec. 4, 1865	July 28, 1866	237	Lafayette S. Foster of Connecticut	Colfax
	2	Dec. 3, 1866	Mar. 3, 1867	91	Benjamin F. Wade of Ohio	
40th	1	Mar. 4, 1867[9]	Dec. 2, 1867	274	Wade	Colfax

Congress	Session	Convened	Adjourned	Number	President pro tempore of Senate	Speaker of the House
	2	Dec. 2, 1867[10]	Nov. 10, 1868	345	Wade	Theodore M. Pomeroy of New York[11]
	3	Dec. 7, 1868	Mar. 3, 1869	87	Wade	
41st	1	Mar. 4, 1869	Apr. 10, 1869	38	Henry B. Anthony of Rhode Island	James G. Blaine of Maine
	2	Dec. 6, 1869	July 15, 1870	222	Anthony	
	3	Dec. 5, 1870	Mar. 3, 1871	89	Anthony	
42nd	1	Mar. 4, 1871	Apr. 20, 1871	48	Anthony	Blaine
	2	Dec. 4, 1871	June 10, 1872	190	Anthony	
	3	Dec. 2, 1872	Mar. 3, 1873	92	Anthony	
43rd	1	Dec. 1, 1873	June 23, 1874	204	Matthew H. Carpenter of Wisconsin	Blaine
	2	Dec. 7, 1874	Mar. 3, 1875	87	Carpenter / Henry B. Anthony of Rhode Island	
44th	1	Dec. 6, 1875	Aug. 15, 1876	254	Thomas W. Ferry of Michigan	Michael C. Kerr of Indiana[12] / Samuel S. Cox of New York, pro tempore[13] / Milton Sayler of Ohio, pro tempore[14]
	2	Dec. 4, 1876	Mar. 3, 1877	90	Ferry	Samuel J. Randall of Pennsylvania
45th	1	Oct. 15, 1877	Dec. 3, 1877	50	Ferry	Randall
	2	Dec. 3, 1877	June 20, 1878	200	Ferry	
	3	Dec. 2, 1878	Mar. 3, 1879	92	Ferry	
46th	1	Mar. 18, 1879	July 1, 1879	106	Allen G. Thurman of Ohio	Randall
	2	Dec. 1, 1879	June 16, 1880	199	Thurman	
	3	Dec. 6, 1880	Mar. 3, 1881	88	Thurman	
47th	1	Dec. 5, 1881	Aug. 8, 1882	247	Thomas F. Bayard of Delaware / David Davis of Illinois	J. Warren Keifer of Ohio

Congress	Session	Date of beginning[1]	Date of adjournment[2]	Length in days	President pro tempore of the Senate[3]	Speaker of the House of Representatives
	2	Dec. 4, 1882	Mar. 3, 1883	90	George F. Edmunds of Vermont	
48th	1	Dec. 3, 1883	July 7, 1884	218	Edmunds	John G. Carlisle of Kentucky
	2	Dec. 1, 1884	Mar. 3, 1885	93	Edmunds	
49th	1	Dec. 7, 1885	Aug. 5, 1886	242	John Sherman of Ohio	Carlisle
	2	Dec. 6, 1886	Mar. 3, 1887	88	John J. Ingalls of Kansas	
50th	1	Dec. 5, 1887	Oct. 20, 1888	321	Ingalls	Carlisle
	2	Dec. 3, 1888	Mar. 3, 1889	91	Ingalls	
51st	1	Dec. 2, 1889	Oct. 1, 1890	304	Ingalls	Thomas B. Reed of Maine
	2	Dec. 1, 1890	Mar. 3, 1891	93	Charles F. Manderson of Nebraska	
52nd	1	Dec. 7, 1891	Aug. 5, 1892	251	Manderson	Charles F. Crisp of Georgia
	2	Dec. 5, 1892	Mar. 3, 1893	89	Isham G. Harris of Tennessee	
53rd	1	Aug. 7, 1893	Nov. 3, 1893	89	Harris	Crisp
	2	Dec. 4, 1893	Aug. 28, 1894	268	Harris	
	3	Dec. 3, 1894	Mar. 3, 1895	97	Matt W. Ransom of North Carolina / Isham G. Harris of Tennessee	
54th	1	Dec. 2, 1895	June 11, 1896	193	William P. Frye of Maine	Thomas B. Reed of Maine
	2	Dec. 7, 1896	Mar. 3, 1897	87	Frye	
55th	1	Mar. 15, 1897	July 24, 1897	131	Frye	Reed
	2	Dec. 6, 1897	July 8, 1898	215	Frye	
	3	Dec. 5, 1898	Mar. 3, 1899	89	Frye	

Congress	Session	Convened	Adjourned	Days	President pro tempore	Speaker
56th	1	Dec. 4, 1899	June 7, 1900	186	Frye	David B. Henderson of Iowa
	2	Dec. 3, 1900	Mar. 3, 1901	91	Frye	
57th	1	Dec. 2, 1901	July 1, 1902	212	Frye	Henderson
	2	Dec. 1, 1902	Mar. 3, 1903	93	Frye	
58th	1	Nov. 9, 1903	Dec. 7, 1903	29	Frye	Joseph G. Cannon of Illinois
	2	Dec. 7, 1903	Apr. 28, 1904	144	Frye	
	3	Dec. 5, 1904	Mar. 3, 1905	89	Frye	
59th	1	Dec. 4, 1905	June 30, 1906	209	Frye	Cannon
	2	Dec. 3, 1906	Mar. 3, 1907	91	Frye	
60th	1	Dec. 2, 1907	May 30, 1908	181	Frye	Cannon
	2	Dec. 7, 1908	Mar. 3, 1909	87	Frye	
61st	1	Mar. 15, 1909	Aug. 5, 1909	144	Frye	Cannon
	2	Dec. 6, 1909	June 25, 1910	202	Frye	
	3	Dec. 5, 1910	Mar. 3, 1911	89	Frye	
62nd	1	Apr. 4, 1911	Aug. 22, 1911	141	Frye[15]	Champ Clark of Missouri
	2	Dec. 4, 1911	Aug. 26, 1912	267	Augustus O. Bacon of Georgia[16]; Frank B. Brandegee of Connecticut[17]; Charles Curtis of Kansas[18]; Jacob H. Gallinger of New Hampshire[19]; Henry Cabot Lodge of Mass.[20]	
	3	Dec. 2, 1912	Mar. 3, 1913	92	Bacon[21]; Gallinger[22]	
63rd	1	Apr. 7, 1913	Dec. 1, 1913	239	James P. Clarke of Arkansas	Clark
	2	Dec. 1, 1913	Oct. 24, 1914	328	Clarke	
	3	Dec. 7, 1914	Mar. 3, 1915	87	Clarke	
64th	1	Dec. 6, 1915	Sept. 8, 1916	278	Clarke[23]	Clark

Congress	Session	Date of beginning[1]	Date of adjournment[2]	Length in days	President pro tempore of the Senate[3]	Speaker of the House of Representatives
	2	Dec. 4, 1916	Mar. 3, 1917	90	Willard Saulsbury of Delaware	
65th	1	Apr. 2, 1917	Oct. 6, 1917	188	Saulsbury	Clark
	2	Dec. 3, 1917	Nov. 21, 1918	354	Saulsbury	
	3	Dec. 2, 1918	Mar. 3, 1919	92	Saulsbury	
66th	1	May 19, 1919	Nov. 19, 1919	185	Albert B. Cummins of Iowa	Frederick H. Gillett of Massachusetts
	2	Dec. 1, 1919	June 5, 1920	188	Cummins	
	3	Dec. 6, 1920	Mar. 3, 1921	88	Cummins	
67th	1	Apr. 11, 1921	Nov. 23, 1921	227	Cummins	Gillett
	2	Dec. 5, 1921	Sept. 22, 1922	292	Cummins	
	3	Nov. 20, 1922	Dec. 4, 1922	15	Cummins	
	4	Dec. 4, 1922	Mar. 3, 1923	90	Cummins	
68th	1	Dec. 3, 1923	June 7, 1924	188	Cummins	Gillett
	2	Dec. 1, 1924	Mar. 3, 1925	93	Cummins	
69th	1	Dec. 7, 1925	July 3, 1926	209	George H. Moses of New Hampshire	Nicholas Longworth of Ohio
	2	Dec. 6, 1926	Mar. 3, 1927	88	Moses	
70th	1	Dec. 5, 1927	May 29, 1928	177	Moses	Longworth
	2	Dec. 3, 1928	Mar. 3, 1929	91	Moses	
71st	1	Apr. 15, 1929	Nov. 22, 1929	222	Moses	Longworth
	2	Dec. 2, 1929	July 3, 1930	214	Moses	
	3	Dec. 1, 1930	Mar. 3, 1931	93	Moses	
72nd	1	Dec. 7, 1931	July 16, 1932	223	Moses	John N. Garner of Texas
	2	Dec. 5, 1932	Mar. 3, 1933	89	Moses	
73rd	1	Mar. 9, 1933	June 15, 1933	99	Key Pittman of Nevada	Henry T. Rainey of Illinois[24]
	2	Jan. 3, 1934	June 18, 1934	167	Pittman	
74th	1	Jan. 3, 1935	Aug. 26, 1935	236	Pittman	Joseph W. Byrns of Tennessee[25]

Congress	Session	Convened	Adjourned	Days	President pro tempore of the Senate	Speaker of the House
	2	Jan. 3, 1936	June 20, 1936	170	Pittman	William B. Bankhead of Alabama[26]
75th	1	Jan. 5, 1937	Aug. 21, 1937	229	Pittman	Bankhead
	2	Nov. 15, 1937	Dec. 21, 1937	37	Pittman	
	3	Jan. 3, 1938	June 16, 1938	165	Pittman	Bankhead[27]
76th	1	Jan. 3, 1939	Aug. 5, 1939	215	Pittman	
	2	Sept. 21, 1939	Nov. 3, 1939	44	Pittman[28]	
	3	Jan. 3, 1940	Jan. 3, 1941	366	William H. King of Utah[30]	Sam Rayburn of Texas[29]
77th	1	Jan. 3, 1941	Jan. 2, 1942	365	Pat Harrison of Mississippi[31]; Carter Glass of Virginia[32]	Rayburn
	2	Jan. 5, 1942	Dec. 16, 1942	346	Carter Glass of Virginia	
78th	1	Jan. 6, 1943[33]	Dec. 21, 1943	350	Glass	Rayburn
	2	Jan. 10, 1944[34]	Dec. 19, 1944	345	Glass	
79th	1	Jan. 3, 1945[35]	Dec. 21, 1945	353	Kenneth McKellar of Tennessee	Rayburn
	2	Jan. 14, 1946[36]	Aug. 2, 1946	201	McKellar	
80th	1	Jan. 3, 1947[37]	Dec. 19, 1947	351	Arthur H. Vandenberg of Michigan	Joseph W. Martin Jr. of Massachusetts
	2	Jan. 6, 1948[38]	Dec. 31, 1948	361	Vandenberg	
81st	1	Jan. 3, 1949	Oct. 19, 1949	290	Kenneth McKellar of Tennessee	Sam Rayburn of Texas
	2	Jan. 3, 1950[39]	Jan. 2, 1951	365	McKellar	
82nd	1	Jan. 3, 1951[40]	Oct. 20, 1951	291	McKellar	Rayburn
	2	Jan. 8, 1952[41]	July 7, 1952	182	McKellar	
83rd	1	Jan. 3, 1953[42]	Aug. 3, 1953	213	Styles Bridges of New Hampshire	Joseph W. Martin Jr. of Massachusetts
	2	Jan. 6, 1954[43]	Dec. 2, 1954	331	Bridges	
84th	1	Jan. 5, 1955[44]	Aug. 2, 1955	210	Walter F. George of Georgia	Sam Rayburn of Texas

Congress	Session	Date of beginning[1]	Date of adjournment[2]	Length in days	President pro tempore of the Senate[3]	Speaker of the House of Representatives
	2	Jan. 3, 1956[45]	July 27, 1956	207	George	
85th	1	Jan. 3, 1957[46]	Aug. 30, 1957	239	Carl Hayden of Arizona	Rayburn
	2	Jan. 7, 1958[47]	Aug. 24, 1958	230	Hayden	
86th	1	Jan. 7, 1959[48]	Sept. 15, 1959	252	Hayden	Rayburn
	2	Jan. 6, 1960[49]	Sept. 1, 1960	240	Hayden	
87th	1	Jan. 3, 1961[50]	Sept. 27, 1961	268	Hayden	Rayburn[51]
	2	Jan. 10, 1962[52]	Oct. 13, 1962	277	Hayden	John W. McCormack of Massachusetts[53]
88th	1	Jan. 9, 1963[54]	Dec. 30, 1963	356	Hayden	McCormack
	2	Jan. 7, 1964[55]	Oct. 3, 1964	270	Hayden	
89th	1	Jan. 4, 1965	Oct. 23, 1965	293	Hayden	McCormack
	2	Jan. 10, 1966[56]	Oct. 22, 1966	286	Hayden	
90th	1	Jan. 10, 1967[57]	Dec. 15, 1967	340	Hayden	McCormack
	2	Jan. 15, 1968[58]	Oct. 14, 1968	274	Hayden	
91st	1	Jan. 3, 1969[59]	Dec. 23, 1969	355	Richard B. Russell of Georgia	McCormack
	2	Jan. 19, 1970[60]	Jan. 2, 1971	349	Russell	
92nd	1	Jan. 21, 1971[61]	Dec. 17, 1971	331	Russell[62]; Allen J. Ellender of Louisiana[63]	Carl Albert of Oklahoma
	2	Jan. 18, 1972[64]	Oct. 18, 1972	275	Ellender[65]; James O. Eastland of Mississippi[66]	
93rd	1	Jan. 3, 1973[67]	Dec. 22, 1973	354	Eastland	Albert
	2	Jan. 21, 1974[68]	Dec. 20, 1974	334	Eastland	
94th	1	Jan. 14, 1975[69]	Dec. 19, 1975	340	Eastland	Albert
	2	Jan. 19, 1976[70]	Oct. 2, 1976	258	Eastland	
95th	1	Jan. 4, 1977[71]	Dec. 15, 1977	346	Eastland	Thomas P. O'Neill Jr. of Massachusetts
	2	Jan. 19, 1978[72]	Oct. 15, 1978	270	Eastland	
96th	1	Jan. 15, 1979[73]	Jan. 3, 1980	354	Warren G. Magnuson of Washington	O'Neill

Congress	Session				President pro tempore	Speaker
	2	Jan. 3, 1980[74]	Dec. 16, 1980	349	Magnuson	
97th	1	Jan. 5, 1981[75]	Dec. 16, 1981	347	Strom Thurmond of South Carolina	O'Neill
	2	Jan. 25, 1982[76]	Dec. 23, 1982	333	Thurmond	O'Neill
98th	1	Jan. 3, 1983[77]	Nov. 18, 1983	320	Thurmond	
	2	Jan. 23, 1984[78]	Oct. 12, 1984	264	Thurmond	
99th	1	Jan. 3, 1985[79]	Dec. 20, 1985	352	Thurmond	O'Neill
	2	Jan. 21, 1986[80]	Oct. 18, 1986	271	Thurmond	O'Neill
100th	1	Jan. 6, 1987	Dec. 22, 1987	351	John C. Stennis of Mississippi	Jim Wright of Texas

1. The Constitution (art. I, sec. 4) provided that "The Congress shall assemble at least once in every year . . . on the first Monday in December, unless they shall by law appoint a different day." Pursuant to a resolution of the Continental Congress, the first session of the First Congress convened March 4, 1789. Up to and including May 20, 1820, 18 acts were passed providing for the meeting of Congress on other days in the year. After 1820 Congress met regularly on the first Monday in December until 1934, when the Twentieth Amendment to the Constitution became effective changing the meeting date to Jan. 3. [Until then, brief special sessions of the Senate only were held at the beginning of each presidential term to confirm Cabinet and other nominations—and occasionally at other times for other purposes. The Senate last met in special session from March 4 to March 6, 1933.]

The first and second sessions of the First Congress were held in New York City. Subsequently, including the first session of the Sixth Congress, Philadelphia was the meeting place; since then, Congress has convened in Washington.

2. Until adoption of the Twentieth Amendment, the deadline for adjournment of Congress in odd-numbered years was March 3. However, the expiring Congress often extended the "legislative day" of March 3 up to noon of March 4, when the new Congress came officially into being. After ratification of the Twentieth Amendment, the deadline for adjournment of Congress in odd-numbered years was noon on Jan. 3.

3. Until recent years the appointment or election of a president pro tempore was considered by the Senate to be for the occasion only, so that more than one appears in several sessions and in others none was chosen. Since March 12, 1890, they have served until "the Senate otherwise ordered."

4. Elected to count the vote for president and vice president, which was done April 6, 1789, because there was a quorum of the Senate for the first time. John Adams, vice president, appeared April 21, 1789, and took his seat as president of the Senate.

5. Elected Speaker pro tempore for April 20, 1798, and again for May 28, 1798.

6. Elected Speaker Jan. 19, 1814, to succeed Henry Clay, who resigned Jan. 19, 1814.

7. Elected Speaker Nov. 15, 1820, to succeed Henry Clay, who resigned Oct. 28, 1820.

8. Elected Speaker June 2, 1834, to succeed Andrew Stevenson of Virginia, who resigned.

9. There were recesses in this session from Saturday, Mar. 30, to Wednesday, July 1, and from Saturday, July 20, to Thursday, Nov. 21.

10. There were recesses in this session from Monday, July 27, to Monday, Sept. 21, to Friday, Oct. 16, and to Tuesday, Nov. 10. No business was transacted subsequent to July 27.

11. Elected Speaker Mar. 3, 1869, and served one day.

12. Died Aug. 19, 1876.

13. Appointed Speaker pro tempore Feb. 17, May 12, June 19.

14. Appointed Speaker pro tempore June 4.

15. Resigned as president pro tempore Apr. 27, 1911.

16. Elected to serve Jan. 11-17, Mar. 11-12, Apr. 8, May 10, May 30 to June 1 and 3, June 13 to July 5, Aug. 1-10, and Aug. 27 to Dec. 15, 1912.

17. Elected to serve May 25, 1912.

18. Elected to serve Dec. 4-12, 1911.

19. Elected to serve Feb. 12-14, Apr. 26-27, May 7, July 6-31, Aug. 12-26, 1912.

20. Elected to serve Mar. 25-26, 1912.

21. Elected to serve Aug. 27 to Dec. 15, 1912, Jan. 5-18, and Feb. 2-15, 1913.

22. Elected to serve Dec. 16, 1912, to Jan. 4, 1913, Jan. 19 to Feb. 1, and Feb. 16 to Mar. 3, 1913.

23. Died Oct. 1, 1916.

24. Died Aug. 19, 1934.

25. Died June 4, 1936.

26. Elected June 4, 1936.

27. Died Sept. 15, 1940.

28. Died Nov. 10, 1940.

29. Elected Sept. 16, 1940.

30. Elected Nov. 19, 1940.

31. Elected Jan. 6, 1941; died June 22, 1941.

32. Elected July 10, 1941.

33. There was a recess in this session from Thursday, July 8, to Tuesday, Sept. 14.

34. There were recesses in this session from Saturday, Apr. 1, to Wednesday, Apr. 12; from Friday, June 23, to Tuesday, Aug. 1; and from Thursday, Sept. 21, to Tuesday, Nov. 14.

35. The House was in recess in this session from Saturday, July 21, 1945, to Wednesday, Sept. 5, 1945, and the Senate from Wednesday, Aug. 1, 1945, to Wednesday, Sept. 5, 1945.

36. The House was in recess in this session from Thursday, Apr. 18, 1946, to Tuesday, Apr. 30, 1946.

37. There was a recess in this session from Sunday, July 27, 1947, to Monday, Nov. 17, 1947.

38. There were recesses in this session from Sunday, June 20, 1948, to Monday, July 26, 1948, and from Saturday, Aug. 7, 1948, to Friday, Dec. 31, 1948.

39. The House was in recess in this session from Thursday, Apr. 6, 1950, to Tuesday, Apr. 18, 1950, and both the Senate and the House were in recess from Saturday, Sept. 23, 1950, to Monday, Nov. 27, 1950.

40. The House was in recess in this session from Thursday, Mar. 22, 1951, to Monday, Apr. 2, 1951, and from Thursday, Aug. 23, 1951, to Wednesday, Sept. 12, 1951.

41. The House was in recess in this session from Thursday, Apr. 10, 1952, to Tuesday, Apr. 22, 1952.

42. The House was in recess in this session from Thursday, Apr. 2, 1953, to Monday, Apr. 13, 1953.

43. The House was in recess in this session from Thursday, Apr. 15, 1954, to Monday, Apr. 26, 1954, and adjourned sine die Aug. 20, 1954. The Senate was in recess in this session from Friday, Aug. 20, 1954, to Monday, Nov. 8, 1954; from Thursday, Nov. 18, 1954, to Monday, Nov. 29, 1954, and adjourned sine die Dec. 2, 1954.

44. There was a recess in this session from Monday, Apr. 4, 1955, to Wednesday, Apr. 13, 1955.

45. There was a recess in this session from Thursday, Mar. 29, 1956, to Monday, Apr. 9, 1956.

46. There was a recess in this session from Thursday, Apr. 18, 1957, to Monday, Apr. 29, 1957.

47. There was a recess in this session from Thursday, Apr. 3, 1958, to Monday, Apr. 14, 1958.

48. There was a recess in this session from Thursday, Mar. 26, 1959, to Tuesday, Apr. 7, 1959.

49. The Senate was in recess in this session from Thursday, Apr. 14, 1960, to Monday, Apr. 18, 1960; from Friday, May 27, 1960, to Tuesday, May 31, 1960, and from Sunday, July 3, 1960, to Monday, Aug. 8, 1960. The House was in recess in this session from Thursday, Apr. 14, 1960, to Monday, Apr. 18, 1960; from Friday, May 27, 1960, to Tuesday, May 31, 1960, and from Sunday, July 3, 1960, to Monday, Aug. 15, 1960.

50. The House was in recess in this session from Thursday, Mar. 30, 1961, to Monday, Apr. 10, 1961.

51. Died Nov. 16, 1961.

52. The House was in recess in this session from Thursday, Apr. 19, 1962, to Monday, Apr. 30, 1962.

53. Elected Jan. 10, 1962.

54. The House was in recess in this session from Thursday, Apr. 11, 1963, to Monday, Apr. 22, 1963.

55. The House was in recess in this session from Thursday, Mar. 26, 1964, to Monday, Apr. 6, 1964; from Thursday, July 2, 1964, to Monday, July 20, 1964; from Friday, Aug. 21, 1964, to Monday, Aug. 31, 1964. The Senate was in recess in this session from Friday, July 10, 1964, to Monday, July 20, 1964; from Friday, Aug. 21, 1964, to Monday, Aug. 31, 1964.

56. The House was in recess in this session from Thursday, Apr. 7, 1966, to Monday, Apr. 18, 1966; from Thursday, June 30, 1966, to Monday, July 11, 1966. The Senate was in recess in this session from Thursday, Apr. 7, 1966, to Wednesday, Apr. 13, 1966; from Thursday, June 30, 1966, to Monday, July 11, 1966.

57. There was a recess in this session from Thursday, Mar. 23, 1967, to Monday, Apr. 3, 1967; from Thursday, June 29, 1967, to Monday, July

10, 1967; from Thursday, Aug. 31, 1967, to Monday, Sept. 11, 1967; and from Wednesday, Nov. 22, 1967, to Monday, Nov. 27, 1967.

58. The House was in recess this session from Thursday, Apr. 11, 1968, to Monday, Apr. 22, 1968; from Wednesday, May 29, 1968, to Monday, June 3, 1968; from Wednesday, July 3, 1968, to Monday, July 8, 1968; from Friday, Aug. 2, 1968, to Wednesday, Sept. 4, 1968. The Senate was in recess this session from Thursday, Apr. 11, 1968, to Wednesday, Apr. 17, 1968; from Wednesday, May 29, 1968, to Monday, June 3, 1968; from Wednesday, July 3, 1968, to Monday, July 8, 1968; from Friday, Aug. 2, 1968, to Wednesday, Sept. 4, 1968.

59. The House was in recess this session from Friday, Feb. 7, 1969, to Monday, Feb. 17, 1969; from Thursday, Apr. 3, 1969, to Monday, Apr. 14, 1969; from Wednesday, May 28, 1969, to Monday, June 2, 1969; from Wednesday, July 2, 1969, to Monday, July 7, 1969; from Wednesday, Aug. 13, 1969, to Wednesday, Sept. 3, 1969; from Thursday, Nov. 6, 1969, to Wednesday, Nov. 12, 1969; from Wednesday, Nov. 26, 1969, to Monday, Dec. 1, 1969. The Senate was in recess this session from Friday, Feb. 7, 1969, to Monday, Feb. 17, 1969; from Thursday, Apr. 3, 1969, to Monday, Apr. 14, 1969; from Wednesday, July 2, 1969, to Monday, July 7, 1969; from Wednesday, Aug. 13, 1969, to Wednesday, Sept. 3, 1969; from Wednesday, Nov. 26, 1969, to Monday, Dec. 1, 1969.

60. The House was in recess this session from Tuesday, Feb. 10, 1970, to Monday, Feb. 16, 1970; from Thursday, Mar. 26, 1970, to Tuesday, Mar. 31, 1970; from Wednesday, May 27, 1970, to Monday, June 1, 1970; from Wednesday, July 1, 1970, to Monday, July 6, 1970; from Friday, Aug. 14, 1970, to Wednesday, Sept. 9, 1970; from Wednesday, Oct. 14, 1970, to Monday, Nov. 16, 1970; from Wednesday, Nov. 25, 1970, to Monday, Nov. 30, 1970; from Tuesday, Dec. 22, 1970, to Tuesday, Dec. 29, 1970. The Senate was in recess this session from Tuesday, Feb. 10, 1970, to Monday, Feb. 16, 1970; from Thursday, Mar. 26, 1970, to Tuesday, Mar. 31, 1970; from Wednesday, Sept. 2, 1970, to Tuesday, Sept. 8, 1970; from Wednesday, Oct. 14, 1970, to Monday, Nov. 16, 1970; from Wednesday, Nov. 25, 1970, to Monday, Nov. 30, 1970; from Tuesday, Dec. 22, 1970, to Monday, Dec. 28, 1970.

61. The House was in recess this session from Wednesday, Feb. 10, 1971, to Wednesday, Feb. 17, 1971; from Wednesday, Apr. 7, 1971, to Monday, Apr. 19, 1971; from Thursday, May 27, 1971, to Tuesday, June 1, 1971; from Thursday, July 1, 1971, to Tuesday, July 6, 1971; from Friday, Aug. 6, 1971, to Wednesday, Sept. 8, 1971; from Thursday, Oct. 7, 1971, to Tuesday, Oct. 12, 1971; from Thursday, Oct. 21, 1971, to Monday, Nov. 29, 1971. The Senate was in recess this session from Thursday, Feb. 11, 1971, to Wednesday, Feb. 17, 1971; from Wednesday, Apr. 7, 1971, to Wednesday, Apr. 14, 1971; from Wednesday, May 26, 1971, to Tuesday, June 1, 1971; from Wednesday, June 30, 1971, to Tuesday, July 6, 1971; from Friday, Aug. 6, 1971, to Wednesday, Sept. 8, 1971; from Thursday, Oct. 21, 1971, to Tuesday, Oct. 26, 1971; from Wednesday, Nov. 24, 1971, to Monday, Nov. 29, 1971.

62. Died Jan. 21, 1971.

63. Elected Jan. 22, 1971.

64. The House was in recess this session from Wednesday, Feb. 9, 1972, to Wednesday, Feb. 16, 1972; from Wednesday, Mar. 29, 1972, to Monday, Apr. 10, 1972; from Wednesday, May 24, 1972, to Tuesday, May 30, 1972; from Friday, June 30, 1972, to Monday, July 17, 1972; from Friday, Aug. 18, 1972, to Tuesday, Sept. 5, 1972. The Senate was in recess this session from Wednesday, Feb. 9, 1972, to Monday, Feb. 14, 1972; from Thursday, Mar. 30, 1972, to Tuesday, Apr. 4, 1972; from Thursday, May 25, 1972, to Tuesday, May 30, 1972; from Friday, June 30, 1972, to Monday, July 17, 1972; from Friday, Aug. 18, 1972, to Tuesday, Sept. 5, 1972.

65. Died July 27, 1972.

66. Elected July 28, 1972.

67. The House was in recess this session from Thursday, Feb. 8, 1973, to Monday, Feb. 19, 1973; from Thursday, Apr. 19, 1973, to Monday, Apr. 30, 1973; from Thursday, May 24, 1973, to Tuesday, May 29, 1973; from Saturday, June 30, 1973, to Tuesday, July 10, 1973; from Friday, Aug. 3, 1973, to Wednesday, Sept. 5, 1973; from Thursday, Oct. 4, 1973, to Tuesday, Oct. 9, 1973; from Thursday, Oct. 18, 1973, to Tuesday, Oct. 23, 1973; from Thursday, Nov. 15, 1973 to Monday, Nov. 26, 1973. The Senate was in recess this session from Thursday, Feb. 8, 1973, to Thursday, Feb. 15, 1973; from Wednesday, Apr. 18, 1973, to Monday, Apr. 30, 1973; from Wednesday, May 23, 1973, to Tuesday, May 29, 1973; from Saturday, June 30, 1973, to Monday, July 9, 1973; from Friday, Aug. 3, 1973, to Wednesday, Sept. 5, 1973; from Thursday, Oct. 18, 1973, to Tuesday, Oct. 23, 1973; from Wednesday, Nov. 21, 1973, to Monday, Nov. 26, 1973.

68. The House was in recess this session from Thursday, Feb. 7, 1974, to Wednesday, Feb. 13, 1974; from Thursday, Apr. 11, 1974, to Monday, Apr. 22, 1974; from Thursday, May 23, 1974, to Tuesday, May 28, 1974; from Thursday, Aug. 22, 1974, to Wednesday, Sept. 11, 1974; from Thursday, Oct. 17, 1974, to Monday, Nov. 18, 1974; from Tuesday, Nov. 26, 1974, to Tuesday, Dec. 3, 1974. The Senate was in recess this session from Friday, Feb. 8, 1974, to Monday, Feb. 18, 1974; from Wednesday, Mar. 13, 1974, to Tuesday, Mar. 19, 1974; from Thursday,

Apr. 11, 1974, to Monday, Apr. 22, 1974; from Wednesday, May 23, 1974, to Tuesday, May 28, 1974; from Thursday, Aug. 22, 1974, to Wednesday, Sept. 4, 1974; from Thursday, Oct. 17, 1974, to Monday, Nov. 18, 1974; from Tuesday, Nov. 26, 1974, to Monday, Dec. 2, 1974.

69. The House was in recess this session from Wednesday, Mar. 26, 1975, to Monday, Apr. 7, 1975; from Thursday, May 22, 1975, to Monday, June 2, 1975; from Thursday, June 26, 1975, to Tuesday, July 8, 1975; from Friday, Aug. 1, 1975, to Wednesday, Sept. 3, 1975; from Thursday, Oct. 9, 1975, to Monday, Oct. 20, 1975; from Thursday, Oct. 23, 1975, to Tuesday, Oct. 28, 1975; from Thursday, Nov. 20, 1975, to Monday, Dec. 1, 1975. The Senate was in recess this session from Wednesday, Mar. 26, 1975, to Monday, Apr. 7, 1975; from Thursday, May 22, 1975, to Monday, June 2, 1975; from Friday, June 27, 1975, to Monday, July 7, 1975; from Friday, Aug. 1, 1975, to Wednesday, Sept. 3, 1975; from Thursday, Oct. 9, 1975, to Monday, Oct. 20, 1975; from Thursday, Oct. 23, 1975, to Tuesday, Oct. 28, 1975; from Thursday, Nov. 20, 1975, to Monday, Dec. 1, 1975.

70. The House was in recess this session from Wednesday, Feb. 11, 1976, to Monday, Feb. 16, 1976; from Wednesday, Apr. 14, 1976, to Monday, Apr. 26, 1976; from Thursday, May 27, 1976, to Tuesday, June 1, 1976; from Friday, July 2, 1976, to Monday, July 19, 1976; from Tuesday, Aug. 10, 1976, to Monday, Aug. 23, 1976; from Wednesday, Sept. 8, 1976. The Senate was in recess this session from Friday, Feb. 6, 1976, to Monday, Feb. 16, 1976; from Wednesday, Apr. 14, 1976, to Monday, Apr. 26, 1976; from Friday, May 28, 1976, to Wednesday, June 2, 1976; from Friday, July 2, 1976, to Monday, July 19, 1976; from Tuesday, Aug. 10, 1976, to Monday, Aug. 23, 1976; from Wednesday, Sept. 1, 1976, to Tuesday, Sept. 7, 1976.

71. The House was in recess this session from Wednesday, Feb. 9, 1977, to Wednesday, Feb. 16, 1977; from Wednesday, Apr. 6, 1977, to Monday, Apr. 18, 1977; from Thursday, May 26, 1977, to Wednesday, June 1, 1977; from Thursday, June 30, 1977, to Monday, July 11, 1977; from Friday, Aug. 5, 1977, to Wednesday, Sept. 7, 1977; from Thursday, Oct. 6, 1977, to Tuesday, Oct. 11, 1977. The Senate was in recess this session from Friday, Feb. 11, 1977, to Monday, Feb. 21, 1977; from Thursday, Apr. 7, 1977, to Monday, Apr. 18, 1977; from Friday, May 27, 1977, to Monday, June 6, 1977; from Friday, July 1, 1977, to Monday, July 11, 1977; from Saturday, Aug. 6, 1977, to Wednesday, Sept. 7, 1977.

72. The House was in recess this session from Thursday, Feb. 9, 1978, to Tuesday, Feb. 14, 1978; from Wednesday, Mar. 22, 1978, to Monday, Apr. 3, 1978; from Thursday, May 25, 1978, to Wednesday, May 31, 1978; from Thursday, June 29, 1978, to Monday, July 10, 1978; from Thursday, Aug. 17, 1978, to Wednesday, Sept. 6, 1978. The Senate was in recess this session from Friday, Feb. 10, 1978, to Monday, Feb. 20, 1978; from Thursday, Mar. 23, 1978, to Monday, Apr. 3, 1978; from Friday, May 26, 1978, to Monday, June 5, 1978; from Thursday, June 29, 1978, to Monday, July 10, 1978; from Friday, Aug. 25, 1978, to Wednesday, Sept. 6, 1978.

73. The House was in recess this session from Thursday, Feb. 8, 1979, to Tuesday, Feb. 13, 1979; from Tuesday, Apr. 10, 1979, to Monday, Apr. 23, 1979; from Thursday, May 24, 1979, to Wednesday, May 30, 1979; from Friday, June 29, 1979, to Monday, July 9, 1979; from Thursday, Aug. 2, 1979, to Wednesday, Sept. 5, 1979; from Tuesday, Nov. 20, 1979, to Monday, Nov. 26, 1979. The Senate was in recess this session from Friday, Feb. 9, 1979, to Monday, Feb. 19, 1979; from Tuesday, Apr. 10, 1979, to Monday, Apr. 23, 1979; from Friday, May 25, 1979, to Monday, June 4, 1979; from Friday, Aug. 3, 1979, to Wednesday, Sept. 5, 1979; from Tuesday, Nov. 20, 1979, to Monday, Nov. 26, 1979.

74. The House was in recess this session from Wednesday, Feb. 13, 1980, to Tuesday, Feb. 19, 1980; from Wednesday, Apr. 2, 1980, to Tuesday, Apr. 15, 1980; from Thursday, May 22, 1980, to Wednesday, May 28, 1980; from Wednesday, July 2, 1980, to Monday, July 21, 1980; from Friday, Aug. 1, 1980, to Monday, Aug. 18, 1980; from Thursday, Aug. 28, 1980, to Wednesday, Sept. 13, 1980. The Senate was in recess this session from Monday, Feb. 11, 1980, to Thursday, Feb. 14, 1980; from Thursday, Apr. 3, 1980, to Tuesday, Apr. 15, 1980; from Thursday, May 22, 1980, to Wednesday, May 28, 1980; from Wednesday, Aug. 6, 1980, to Monday, Aug. 18, 1980; from Wednesday, Aug. 27, 1980, to Wednesday, Sept. 3, 1980; from Wednesday, Oct. 1, 1980, to Wednesday, Nov. 12, 1980; from Monday, Nov. 24, 1980, to Monday, Dec. 1, 1980.

75. The House was in recess this session from Friday, Feb. 6, 1981, to Tuesday, Feb. 17, 1981; from Friday, Apr. 10, 1981, to Monday, Apr. 27, 1981; from Friday, June 26, 1981, to Wednesday, July 8, 1981; from Tuesday, Aug. 4, 1981, to Wednesday, Sept. 9, 1981; from Wednesday, Oct. 7, 1981, to Tuesday, Oct. 13, 1981; from Monday, Nov. 23, 1981, to Monday, Nov. 30, 1981. The Senate was in recess this session from Friday, Feb. 6, 1981, to Monday, Feb. 16, 1981; from Friday, Apr. 10, 1981, to Monday, Apr. 27, 1981; from Thursday, June 25, 1981, to Wednesday, July 8, 1981; from Monday, Aug. 3, 1981, to Wednesday, Sept. 9, 1981; from Wednesday, Oct. 7, 1981, to Wednesday, Oct. 14, 1981; from Tuesday, Nov. 24, 1981, to Monday, Nov. 30, 1981.

76. The House was in recess this session from Wednesday, Feb. 10, 1982, to Monday, Feb. 22, 1982; from Tuesday, Apr. 6, 1982, to Tuesday,

523

Apr. 20, 1982; from Thursday, May 27, 1982, to Wednesday, June 2, 1982; from Thursday, July 1, 1982, to Monday, July 12, 1982; from Friday, Aug. 20, 1982, to Wednesday, Sept. 8, 1982; from Friday, Oct. 1, 1982, to Monday, Nov. 29, 1982. The Senate was in recess this session Thursday, Feb. 11, 1982, to Monday, Feb. 22, 1982; from Thursday, Apr. 1, 1982, to Tuesday, Apr. 13, 1982; from Thursday, May 27, 1982, to Tuesday, June 8, 1982; from Thursday, July 1, 1982, to Monday, July 12, 1982; from Friday, Aug. 20, 1982, to Wednesday, Sept. 8, 1982; from Friday, Oct. 1, 1982, to Monday, Nov. 29, 1982.

77. The House adjourned for recess this session Friday, Jan. 7, 1983, to Tuesday, Jan. 25, 1983; Thursday, Feb. 17, 1983, to Tuesday, Feb. 22, 1983; Thursday, March 24, 1983, to Tuesday, Apr. 5, 1983; Thursday, May 26, 1983, to Wednesday, June 1, 1983; Thursday, June 30, 1983, to Monday, July 11, 1983; Friday, Aug. 5, 1983, to Monday, Sept. 12, 1983; Friday, Oct. 7, 1983, to Monday, Oct. 17, 1983. The Senate adjourned for recess this session Monday, Jan. 3, 1983, to Tuesday, Jan. 25, 1983; Friday, Feb. 4, 1983, to Monday, Feb. 14, 1983; Friday, March 25, 1983, to Tuesday, Apr. 5, 1983; Friday, May 27, 1983, to Monday, June 6, 1983; Friday, July 1, 1983, to Monday, July 11, 1983; Friday, Aug. 5, 1983, to Monday, Sept. 12, 1983; Monday Oct. 10, 1983, to Monday, Oct. 17, 1983.

78. The House adjourned for recess this session Thursday, Feb. 9, 1984, to Tuesday, Feb. 21, 1984; Friday, Apr. 13, 1984, to Tuesday, Apr. 24, 1984; Friday, May 25, 1984, to Wednesday, May 30, 1984; Friday, June 29, 1984, to Monday, July 23, 1984; Wednesday, Sept. 5, 1984. The Senate adjourned for recess this session Friday, Feb. 10, 1984, to Monday, Feb. 20, 1984; Friday, Apr. 13, 1984, to Tuesday, Apr. 24, 1984; from Friday, May 25, 1984, to Thursday, May 31, 1984; from Friday, June 29, 1984, to Monday, July 23, 1984; Friday, Aug. 10, 1984, to Wednesday, Sept. 5, 1984.

79. The House adjourned for recess this session Monday, Jan. 7, 1985, to Monday, Jan. 21, 1985; Thursday, Feb. 7, 1985, to Tuesday, Feb. 19, 1985; Thursday, March 7, 1985, to Tuesday, March 19, 1985; Thursday, April 4, 1985, to Monday, April 15, 1985; Thursday, May 23, 1985, to Monday, June 3, 1985; Thursday, June 27, 1985, to Monday, July 8, 1985; Thursday, Aug. 1, 1985, to Wednesday, Sept. 4, 1985; Thursday, Nov. 21, 1985, to Monday, Dec. 2, 1985. The Senate adjourned for recess this session Monday, Jan. 7, 1985, to Monday, Jan. 21, 1985; Thursday, Feb. 7, 1985, to Monday, Feb. 18, 1985; Tuesday, March 12, 1985, to Thursday, March 14, 1985; Thursday, April 4, 1985, to Monday, April 15, 1985; Friday, May 24, 1985, to Monday, June 3, 1985; Thursday, June 27, 1985, to Monday, July 8, 1985; Thursday, Aug. 1, 1985, to Monday, Sept. 9, 1985; Saturday, Nov. 23, 1985, to Monday, Dec. 2, 1985.

80. The House adjourned for recess this session Tuesday, Jan. 7, 1986, to Tuesday, Jan. 21, 1986; Friday, Feb. 7, 1986, to Tuesday, Feb. 18, 1986; Tuesday, March 25, 1986, to Tuesday, April 8, 1986; Thursday, May 22, 1986, to Tuesday, June 3, 1986; Thursday, June 26, 1986, to Monday, July 14, 1986; Friday, Aug. 15, 1986, to Monday, Sept. 8, 1986. The Senate adjourned for recess this session Tuesday, Jan. 7, 1986, to Tuesday, Jan. 21, 1986; Friday, Feb. 7, 1986, to Monday, Feb. 17, 1986; Thursday, March 27, 1986, to Tuesday, April 8, 1986; Wednesday, May 21, 1986, to Monday, June 2, 1986; Thursday, June 26, 1986, to Monday, July 14, 1986; Friday, Aug. 15, 1986, to Monday, Sept. 8, 1986.

Source: Congressional Directory.

REPORT OF THE

NATIONAL COMMISSION

ON

SOCIAL SECURITY

REFORM

JANUARY 1983

Executive Proposals

In 1983 Congress enacted legislation designed to save the Social Security system from threatened insolvency. The measure was based on recommendations of the National Commission on Social Security Reform, which issued its report early that year. The commission had been established by President Ronald Reagan in 1981.

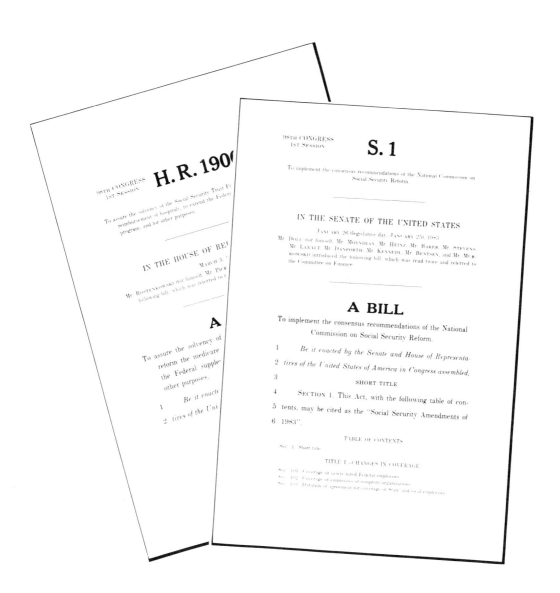

Introduction of Bills

In the Senate, Finance Committee Chairman Robert Dole introduced S 1, to carry out the commission's recommendations, on January 26. In the House, Ways and Means Committee Chairman Dan Rostenkowski introduced HR 1900, a companion bill, on March 3, 1983.

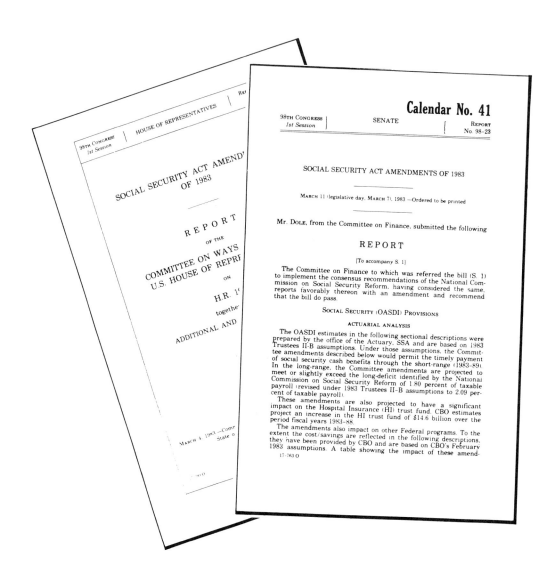

98TH CONGRESS
1st Session | HOUSE OF REPRESENTATIVES

SOCIAL SECURITY ACT AMEND'
OF 1983

REPORT
OF THE
COMMITTEE ON WAYS
U.S. HOUSE OF REPRI

ON

H.R. 1

togethe'

ADDITIONAL AND

MARCH 4, 1983—Comr
State o

98TH CONGRESS
1st Session | SENATE | Calendar No. 41
REPORT
No. 98-23

SOCIAL SECURITY ACT AMENDMENTS OF 1983

MARCH 11 (legislative day, MARCH 7), 1983 —Ordered to be printed

Mr. DOLE, from the Committee on Finance, submitted the following

REPORT

[To accompany S. 1]

The Committee on Finance to which was referred the bill (S. 1) to implement the consensus recommendations of the National Commission on Social Security Reform, having considered the same, reports favorably thereon with an amendment and recommend that the bill do pass.

SOCIAL SECURITY (OASDI) PROVISIONS

ACTUARIAL ANALYSIS

The OASDI estimates in the following sectional descriptions were prepared by the office of the Actuary, SSA and are based on 1983 Trustees II-B assumptions. Under those assumptions, the Committee amendments described below would permit the timely payment of social security cash benefits through the short-range (1983–89). In the long-range, the Committee amendments are projected to meet or slightly exceed the long-deficit identified by the National Commission on Social Security Reform of 1.80 percent of taxable payroll (revised under 1983 Trustees II-B assumptions to 2.09 percent of taxable payroll).

These amendments are also projected to have a significant impact on the Hospital Insurance (HI) trust fund. CBO estimates project an increase in the HI trust fund of $14.6 billion over the period fiscal years 1983–88.

The amendments also impact on other Federal programs. To the extent the cost/savings are reflected in the following descriptions, they have been provided by CBO and are based on CBO's February 1983 assumptions. A table showing the impact of these amend-

17-763 O

Committee Reports

The Ways and Means Committee reported HR 1900 to the full House on March 4. The report included an explanation of the purpose and scope of the bill, a summary of principal provisions, cost estimates, committee votes, and additional and dissenting views by committee members. The Finance Committee reported S 1 to the Senate on March 11.

98TH CONGRESS
1ST SESSION

H. R. 1900

AN ACT

To assure the solvency of the Social Security Trust Funds, to reform the medicare reimbursement of hospitals, to extend the Federal supplemental compensation program, and for other purposes.

1   *Be it enacted by the Senate and House of Representa-*

2 *tives of the United States of America in Congress assembled.*

3   SHORT TITLE

4   SECTION 1. This Act, with the following table of con-

5 tents, may be cited as the "Social Security Act Amendments

6 of 1983".

TABLE OF CONTENTS

Sec. 1. Short title.

MARCH 9, 1983
Considered, amended and passed

Passage of Bills

The House passed HR 1900 on March 9. The Senate never passed S 1. Instead, on March 29 it passed HR 1900, after substituting the text of S 1 for the text of the House-passed bill.

98TH CONGRESS }   HOUSE OF REPRESENTATIVES   {   REPORT
1st Session }   No. 98-47

SOCIAL SECURITY AMENDMENTS OF 1983

MARCH 24, 1983.—Ordered to be printed

Mr. ROSTENKOWSKI, from the committee of conference,
submitted the following

CONFERENCE REPORT

[To accompany H.R. 1900]

The committee of conference on the disagreeing votes of the two Houses on the amendment of the Senate to the bill (H.R. 1900) to assure the solvency of the Social Security Trust Funds, to reform the medicare reimbursement of hospitals, to extend the Federal supplemental compensation program, and for other purposes, having met, after full and free conference, have agreed to recommend and do recommend to their respective Houses as follows:

That the House recede from its disagreement to the amendment of the Senate and agree to the same with an amendment as follows:

In lieu of the matter proposed to be inserted by the Senate amendment insert the following:

SHORT TITLE

SECTION 1. *This Act, with the following table of contents, may be cited as the "Social Security Amendments of 1983".*

TABLE OF CONTENTS

18-370 O

Conference Report

A joint Senate-House conference committee worked out a compromise version of the bill, which required approval by each chamber. Conferees filed their report March 24. The House and Senate quickly approved the report, and HR 1900 was sent to the White House for the president's signature.

PUBLIC LAW 98-21—APR. 20, 1983   97 STAT. 65

Public Law 98-21
98th Congress

An Act

To assure the solvency of the Social Security Trust Funds, to reform the medicare reimbursement of hospitals, to extend the Federal supplemental compensation program, and for other purposes.

Be it enacted by the Senate and House of Representatives of the United States of America in Congress assembled,

Apr. 20, 1983
[H.R. 1900]

Social Security Amendments of 1983

SHORT TITLE

SECTION 1. This Act, with the following table of contents, may be cited as the "Social Security Amendments of 1983"

42 USC 1305 note

TABLE OF CONTENTS

11-119 O - 83 (21)

Public Law

The president signed the bill into law on April 23, 1983, and it became PL 98-21. Public laws are first presented in a pamphlet called a "slip law."

HOW TO WRITE YOUR MEMBER OF CONGRESS

Citizens with complaints, suggestions, and comments on how the government is being run can voice their views directly to Congress and the executive branch.

Writing Tips

The following hints on how to write a member of Congress were suggested by congressional sources and the League of Women Voters.

• Write to your own senators or representative. Letters sent to other members will end up on the desk of members from your state.

• Write at the proper time, when a bill is being discussed in committee or on the floor.

• Use your own words and your own stationery. Avoid signing and sending a form or mimeographed letter.

• Don't be a pen pal. Don't try to instruct the representative or senator on every issue that comes up.

• Don't demand a commitment before all the facts are in. Bills rarely become law in the same form as introduced.

• Whenever possible, identify all bills by their number.

• If possible, include pertinent editorials from local papers.

• Be constructive. If a bill deals with a problem you admit exists but you believe the bill is the wrong approach, tell what you think the right approach is.

• If you have expert knowledge or wide experience in particular areas, share it with the member. But don't pretend to wield vast political influence.

• Write to the member when he does something you approve of. A note of appreciation will make him remember you more favorably the next time.

• Feel free to write when you have a question or problem dealing with procedures of government departments.

• Be brief, write legibly and be sure to use the proper form of address. Feminine forms of address should be substituted as appropriate.

Correct Form for Letters

President

The President
The White House
Washington, D.C. 20500

Dear Mr. President:

Very respectfully yours,

Vice President

The Vice President
Old Executive Office Bldg.
17th St. and Pennsylvania Ave., N.W.
Washington, D.C. 20510

Dear Mr. Vice President:

Sincerely yours,

Senator

Honorable _____
United States Senate
Washington, D.C. 20510

Dear Senator _____

Sincerely yours,

Representative

Honorable _____
House of Representatives
Washington, D.C. 20515

Dear Mr. _____

Sincerely yours,

Member of the Cabinet

Honorable _____
The Secretary of State
Washington, D.C. 20520

Dear Mr. Secretary:

Sincerely yours,

CAPITOL FLOOR PLAN
Principal Floor

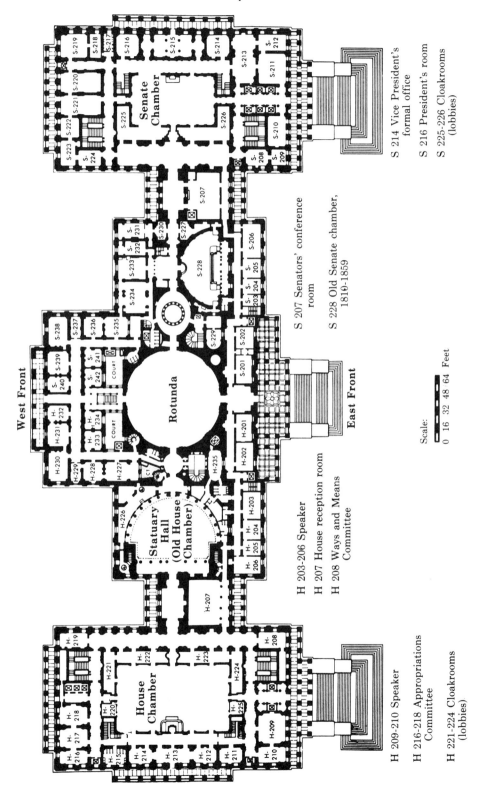

West Front

Senate Chamber

S-219 S-218 S-217 S-216 S-215 S-214 S-213 S-212 S-211 S-220 S-221 S-222 S-225 S-226 S-210 S-208 S-209 S-223 S-224 S-207 S-230 S-231 S-232 S-233 S-234 S-235 S-227 S-228 S-229 S-206 S-205 S-204 S-203 S-202 S-201 S-236 S-237 S-238 S-239 S-240 S-241 S-242

Rotunda

COURT

House Chamber

Statuary Hall (Old House Chamber)

H-226 H-227 H-228 H-229 H-230 H-231 H-232 H-233 H-234 H-235 H-201 H-202 H-203 H-204 H-205 H-206 H-207 H-208 H-209 H-210 H-211 H-212 H-213 H-214 H-215 H-216 H-217 H-218 H-219 H-220 H-221 H-222 H-223 H-224 H-225

East Front

Scale:

0 16 32 48 64 Feet

S 207 Senators' conference room

S 228 Old Senate chamber, 1810–1859

S 214 Vice President's formal office

S 216 President's room

S 225–226 Cloakrooms (lobbies)

H 203–206 Speaker

H 207 House reception room

H 208 Ways and Means Committee

H 209–210 Speaker

H 216–218 Appropriations Committee

H 221–224 Cloakrooms (lobbies)

PLAN OF SENATE CHAMBER

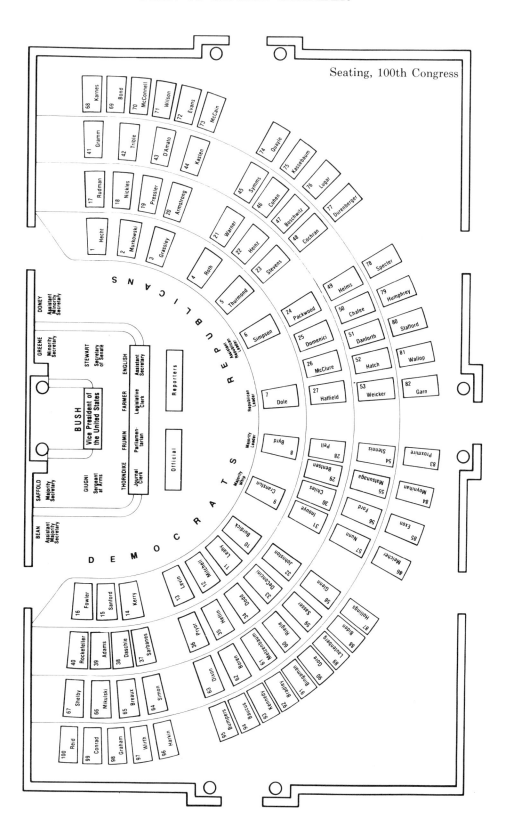

Seating, 100th Congress

PLAN OF HOUSE CHAMBER

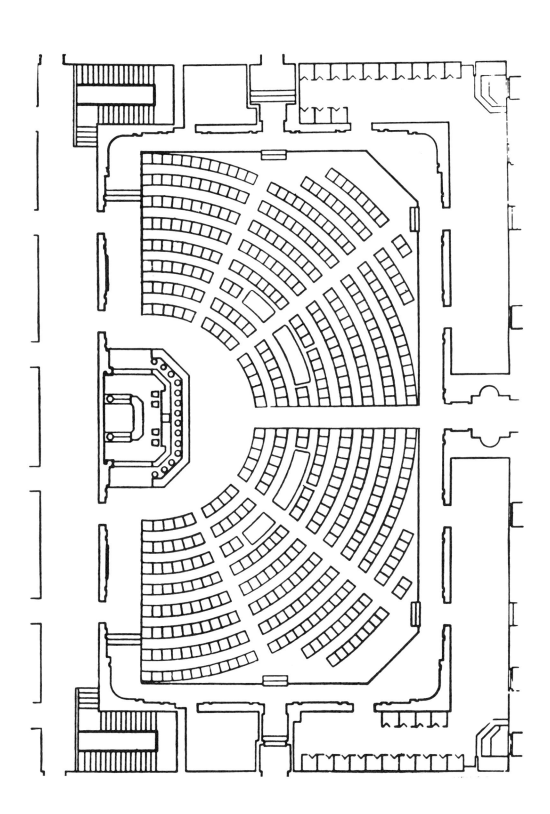

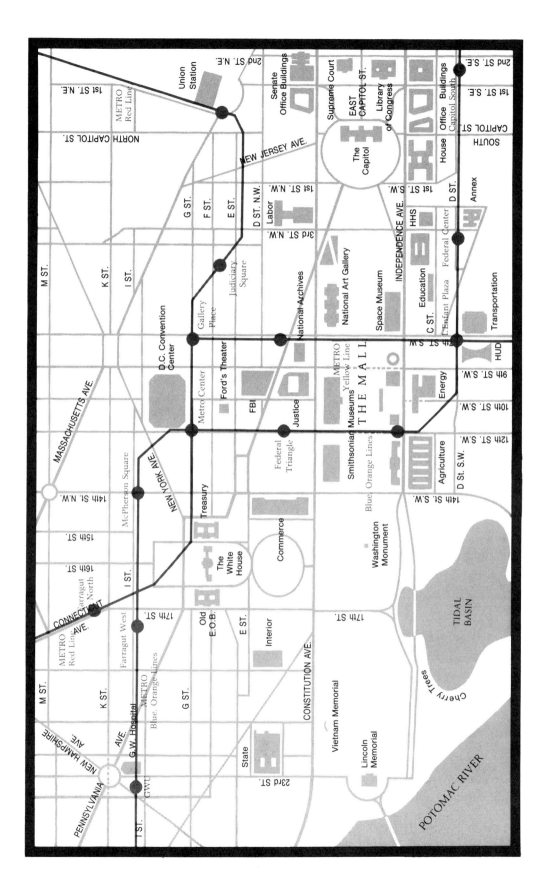

Capital Attractions

Many of Washington's foremost sightseeing attractions are clustered around the Mall, the grassy strip that stretches from the Capitol east to the Lincoln Memorial.

TOURMOBILE shuttle buses provide narrated sightseeing service to eighteen sites in the Mall area and to nearby Arlington National Cemetery. Passengers pay a single daily fee; they may board and reboard the buses as often as they like. For information, call 554-7950. For information on METRO bus and subway service in the D.C. area, call 637-7000. The Washington, D.C., area code is 202.

The sites listed below are open daily unless otherwise noted.

Capitol
224-3121, 225-6827 (tours)

North side of the Mall:

National Gallery of Art
Constitution Avenue at Sixth Street NW
737-4215

National Archives
Constitution Avenue at Eighth Street NW
523-3220

Washington Monument
Constitution Avenue at Fifteenth Street
  NW
426-6839

Vietnam Veterans Memorial
Constitution Avenue at Twenty-first Street
  NW

Lincoln Memorial
Constitution Avenue at Twenty-third Street
  NW
426-6985

Smithsonian Institution

Smithsonian museums line both sides of the
  Mall between Seventh and Fourteenth
  Streets. General information: 357-2700

National Museum of Natural History
Constitution Avenue at Tenth Street NW

National Museum of American History
Constitution Avenue at Fourteenth Street
  NW

South side of the Mall:

National Air and Space Museum
Independence Avenue at Seventh Street SW

Hirshhorn Museum and Sculpture Garden
Independence Avenue at Seventh Street SW

Arts and Industries Building
900 Jefferson Drive SW

Smithsonian Castle
1000 Jefferson Drive SW

National Museum of African Art
950 Independence Ave SW

Arthur M. Sackler Gallery
1050 Independence Avenue SW

Freer Gallery of Art
Jefferson Drive at Twelfth Street SW

Beyond the Mall:
White House
1600 Pennsylvania Avenue
Open Tuesday-Saturday
456-7041

Jefferson Memorial
Tidal Basin SW
426-6821

Library of Congress
10 1st Street SE
287-5108

Ford's Theatre
511 Tenth Street NW
Museum/tours: 426-6924

Arlington National Cemetery
Arlington, Virginia
695-3175

National Zoological Park (Smithsonian)
3000 Connecticut Avenue NW
673-4800

U.S. GOVERNMENT ORGANIZATION

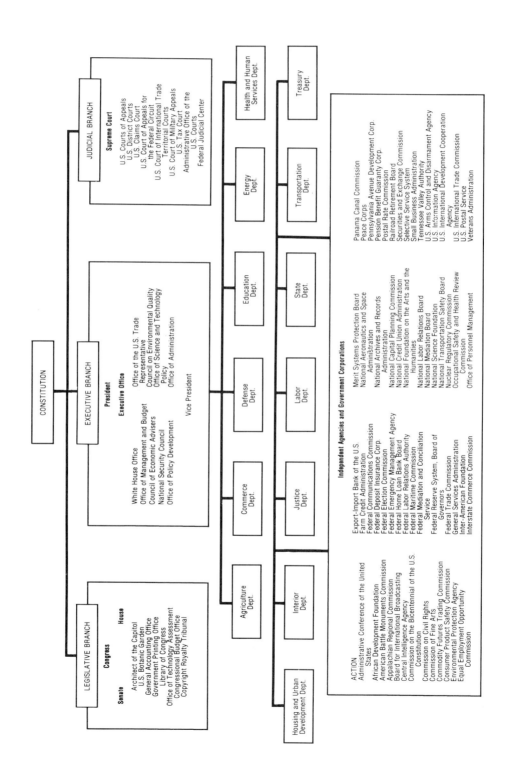

CONSTITUTION

LEGISLATIVE BRANCH

Congress

Senate

House

Architect of the Capitol
U.S. Botanic Garden
General Accounting Office
Government Printing Office
Library of Congress
Office of Technology Assessment
Congressional Budget Office
Copyright Royalty Tribunal

EXECUTIVE BRANCH

President

Executive Office

White House Office
Office of Management and Budget
Council of Economic Advisers
National Security Council
Office of Policy Development

Office of the U.S. Trade Representative
Council on Environmental Quality
Office of Science and Technology Policy
Office of Administration

Vice President

JUDICIAL BRANCH

Supreme Court

U.S. Courts of Appeals
U.S. District Courts
U.S. Claims Court
U.S. Court of Appeals for the Federal Circuit
U.S. Court of International Trade
Territorial Courts
U.S. Court of Military Appeals
U.S. Tax Court
Administrative Office of the U.S. Courts
Federal Judicial Center

Agriculture Dept.
Commerce Dept.
Defense Dept.
Education Dept.
Energy Dept.
Health and Human Services Dept.

Housing and Urban Development Dept.
Interior Dept.
Justice Dept.
Labor Dept.
State Dept.
Transportation Dept.
Treasury Dept.

Independent Agencies and Government Corporations

ACTION
Administrative Conference of the United States
African Development Foundation
American Battle Monuments Commission
Appalachian Regional Commission
Board for International Broadcasting
Central Intelligence Agency
Commission on the Bicentennial of the U.S. Constitution
Commission on Civil Rights
Commission of Fine Arts
Commodity Futures Trading Commission
Consumer Product Safety Commission
Environmental Protection Agency
Equal Employment Opportunity Commission

Export-Import Bank of the U.S.
Farm Credit Administration
Federal Communications Commission
Federal Deposit Insurance Corp.
Federal Election Commission
Federal Emergency Management Agency
Federal Home Loan Bank Board
Federal Labor Relations Authority
Federal Maritime Commission
Federal Mediation and Conciliation Service
Federal Reserve System, Board of Governors
Federal Trade Commission
General Services Administration
Inter-American Foundation
Interstate Commerce Commission

Merit Systems Protection Board
National Aeronautics and Space Administration
National Archives and Records Administration
National Capital Planning Commission
National Credit Union Administration
National Foundation on the Arts and the Humanities
National Labor Relations Board
National Mediation Board
National Science Foundation
National Transportation Safety Board
Nuclear Regulatory Commission
Occupational Safety and Health Review Commission
Office of Personnel Management

Panama Canal Commission
Peace Corps
Pennsylvania Avenue Development Corp.
Pension Benefit Guaranty Corp.
Postal Rate Commission
Railroad Retirement Board
Securities and Exchange Commission
Selective Service System
Small Business Administration
Tennessee Valley Authority
U.S. Arms Control and Disarmament Agency
U.S. Information Agency
U.S. International Development Cooperation Agency
U.S. International Trade Commission
U.S. Postal Service
Veterans Administration

Constitution of the United States

We the People of the United States, in Order to form a more perfect Union, establish Justice, insure domestic Tranquility, provide for the common defence, promote the general Welfare, and secure the Blessings of Liberty to ourselves and our Posterity, do ordain and establish this Constitution for the United States of America.

Article I

Section 1. All legislative Powers herein granted shall be vested in a Congress of the United States, which shall consist of a Senate and House of Representatives.

Section 2. The House of Representatives shall be composed of Members chosen every second Year by the People of the several States, and the Electors in each State shall have the Qualifications requisite for Electors of the most numerous Branch of the State Legislature.

No Person shall be a Representative who shall not have attained to the age of twenty five Years, and been seven Years a Citizen of the United States, and who shall not, when elected, be an Inhabitant of that State in which he shall be chosen.

[Representatives and direct Taxes shall be apportioned among the several States which may be included within this Union, according to their respective Numbers, which shall be determined by adding to the whole Number of free Persons, including those bound to Service for a Term of Years, and excluding Indians not taxed, three fifths of all other Persons.] [1] The actual Enumeration shall be made within three Years after the first Meeting of the Congress of the United States, and within every subsequent Term of ten Years, in such Manner as they shall by Law direct. The Number of Representatives shall not exceed one for every thirty Thousand, but each State shall have at Least one Representative; and until such enumeration shall be made, the State of New Hampshire shall be entitled to chuse three, Massachusetts eight, Rhode-Island and Providence Plantations one, Connecticut five, New-York six, New Jersey four, Pennsylvania eight, Delaware one, Maryland six, Virginia ten, North Carolina five, South Carolina five, and Georgia three.

When vacancies happen in the Representation from any State, the Executive Authority thereof shall issue Writs of Election to fill such Vacancies.

The House of Representatives shall chuse their Speaker and other Officers; and shall have the sole Power of Impeachment.

Section 3. The Senate of the United States shall be composed of two Senators from each State, [chosen by the Legislature thereof,] [2] for six Years; and each Senator shall have one Vote.

Immediately after they shall be assembled in Consequence of the first Election, they shall be divided as equally as may be into three Classes. The Seats of the Senators of the first Class shall be vacated at the Expiration of the second Year, of the second Class at the Expiration of the fourth Year, and of the third Class at the Expiration of the sixth Year, so that one third may be chosen every second Year; [and if Vacancies happen by Resignation, or otherwise, during the Recess of the Legislature of any State, the Executive thereof may make temporary Appointments until the next Meeting of the Legislature, which shall then fill such Vacancies.] [3]

No Person shall be a Senator who shall not have attained to the Age of thirty Years, and been nine Years a Citizen of the United States, and who shall not, when elected, be an Inhabitant of that State for which he shall be chosen.

The Vice President of the United States shall be President of the Senate, but shall have no Vote, unless they be equally divided.

The Senate shall chuse their other Officers, and also a President pro tempore, in the Absence of the Vice President, or when he shall exercise the Office of President of the United States.

The Senate shall have the sole Power to try all Impeachments. When sitting for that Purpose, they shall be on Oath or Affirmation. When the President of the United States is tried the Chief Justice shall preside: And no Person shall be convicted without the Concurrence of two thirds of the Members present.

Judgment in Cases of Impeachment shall not extend further than to removal from Office, and disqualification to hold and enjoy any Office of honor, Trust or Profit under the United

States: but the Party convicted shall nevertheless be liable and subject to Indictment, Trial, Judgment and Punishment, according to Law.

Section 4. The Times, Places and Manner of holding Elections for Senators and Representatives, shall be prescribed in each State by the Legislature thereof; but the Congress may at any time by Law make or alter such Regulations, except as to the Places of chusing Senators.

The Congress shall assemble at least once in every Year, and such Meeting shall [be on the first Monday in December],[4] unless they shall by Law appoint a different Day.

Section 5. Each House shall be the Judge of the Elections, Returns and Qualifications of its own Members, and a Majority of each shall constitute a Quorum to do Business; but a smaller Number may adjourn from day to day, and may be authorized to compel the Attendance of absent Members, in such Manner, and under such Penalties as each House may provide.

Each House may determine the Rules of its Proceedings, punish its Members for disorderly Behaviour, and, with the Concurrence of two thirds, expel a Member.

Each House shall keep a Journal of its Proceedings, and from time to time publish the same, excepting such Parts as may in their Judgment require Secrecy; and the Yeas and Nays of the Members of either House on any question shall, at the Desire of one fifth of those Present, be entered on the Journal.

Neither House, during the Session of Congress, shall, without the Consent of the other, adjourn for more than three days, nor to any other Place than that in which the two Houses shall be sitting.

Section 6. The Senators and Representatives shall receive a Compensation for their Services, to be ascertained by Law, and paid out of the Treasury of the United States. They shall in all Cases, except Treason, Felony and Breach of the Peace, be privileged from Arrest during their Attendance at the Session of their respective Houses, and in going to and returning from the same; and for any Speech or Debate in either House, they shall not be questioned in any other Place.

No Senator or Representative shall, during the Time for which he was elected, be appointed to any civil Office under the Authority of the United States, which shall have been created, or the Emoluments whereof shall have been encreased during such time; and no Person holding any Office under the United States, shall be a Member of either House during his Continuance in Office.

Section 7. All Bills for raising Revenue shall originate in the House of Representatives; but the Senate may propose or concur with amendments as on other Bills.

Every Bill which shall have passed the House of Representatives and the Senate, shall, before it become a Law, be presented to the President of the United States; If he approve he shall sign it, but if not he shall return it, with his Objections to that House in which it shall have originated, who shall enter the Objections at large on their Journal, and proceed to reconsider it. If after such Reconsideration two thirds of that House shall agree to pass the Bill, it shall be sent, together with the Objections, to the other House, by which it shall likewise be reconsidered, and if approved by two thirds of that House, it shall become a Law. But in all such Cases the Votes of both Houses shall be determined by yeas and Nays, and the Names of the Persons voting for and against the Bill shall be entered on the Journal of each House respectively. If any Bill shall not be returned by the President within ten Days (Sundays excepted) after it shall have been presented to him, the Same shall be a Law, in like Manner as if he had signed it, unless the Congress by their Adjournment prevent its Return, in which Case it shall not be a Law.

Every Order, Resolution, or Vote to which the Concurrence of the Senate and House of Representatives may be necessary (except on a question of Adjournment) shall be presented to the President of the United States; and before the Same shall take Effect, shall be approved by him, or being disapproved by him, shall be repassed by two thirds of the Senate and House of Representatives, according to the Rules and Limitations prescribed in the Case of a Bill.

Section 8. The Congress shall have Power To lay and collect Taxes, Duties, Imposts and Excises, to pay the Debts and provide for the common Defence and general Welfare of the

United States; but all Duties, Imposts and Excises shall be uniform throughout the United States;

To borrow Money on the credit of the United States;

To regulate Commerce with foreign Nations, and among the several States, and with the Indian Tribes;

To establish an uniform Rule of Naturalization, and uniform Laws on the subject of Bankruptcies throughout the United States;

To coin Money, regulate the Value thereof, and of foreign Coin, and fix the Standard of Weights and Measures;

To provide for the Punishment of counterfeiting the Securities and current Coin of the United States;

To establish Post Offices and post Roads;

To promote the Progress of Science and useful Arts, by securing for limited Times to Authors and Inventors the exclusive Right to their respective Writings and Discoveries;

To constitute Tribunals inferior to the supreme Court;

To define and punish Piracies and Felonies commited on the high Seas, and Offences against the Law of Nations;

To declare War, grant Letters of Marque and Reprisal,and make Rules concerning Captures on Land and Water;

To raise and support Armies, but no Appropriation of Money to that Use shall be for a longer Term than two Years;

To provide and maintain a Navy;

To make Rules for the Government and Regulation of the land and naval Forces;

To provide for calling forth the Militia to execute the Laws of the Union, suppress Insurrections and repel Invasions;

To provide for organizing, arming, and disciplining, the Militia, and for governing such Part of them as may be employed in the Service of the United States, reserving to the States respectively, the Appointment of the Officers, and the Authority of training the Militia according to the discipline prescribed by Congress;

To exercise exclusive Legislation in all Cases whatsoever, over such District (not exceeding ten Miles square) as may, by Cession of Particular States, and the Acceptance of Congress, become the Seat of the Government of the United States, and to exercise like Authority over all Places purchased by the Consent of the Legislature of the State in which the Same shall be, for the Erection of Forts, Magazines, Arsenals, dock-Yards, and other needful Buildings; — And

To make all Laws which shall be necessary and proper for carrying into Execution the foregoing Powers, and all other Powers vested by this Constitution in the Government of the United States, or in any Department or Officer thereof.

Section 9. The Migration or Importation of such Persons as any of the States now existing shall think proper to admit, shall not be prohibited by the Congress prior to the Year one thousand eight hundred and eight, but a Tax or duty may be imposed on such Importation, not exceeding ten dollars for each Person.

The Privilege of the Writ of Habeas Corpus shall not be suspended, unless when in Cases of Rebellion or Invasion the public Safety may require it.

No Bill of Attainder or ex post facto Law shall be passed.

No capitation, or other direct, Tax shall be laid, unless in Proportion to the Census of Enumeration herein before directed to be taken.[5]

No Tax or Duty shall be laid on Articles exported from any State.

No Preference shall be given by any Regulation of Commerce or Revenue to the Ports of one State over those of another; nor shall Vessels bound to, or from, one State, be obliged to enter, clear or pay Duties in another.

No Money shall be drawn from the Treasury, but in Consequence of Appropriations made by Law; and a regular Statement and Account of the Receipts and Expenditures of all public Money shall be published from time to time.

No Title of Nobility shall be granted by the United States: And no Person holding any

Office of Profit or Trust under them, shall, without the Consent of the Congress, accept of any present, Emolument, Office, or Title, of any kind whatever, from any King, Prince or foreign State.

Section 10. No State shall enter into any Treaty, Alliance, or Confederation; grant Letters of Marque and Reprisal; coin Money; emit Bills of Credit; make any Thing but gold and silver Coin a Tender in Payment of Debts; pass any Bill of Attainder, ex post facto Law, or Law impairing the Obligation of Contracts, or grant any Title of Nobility.

No State shall, without the Consent of the Congress, lay any Imposts or Duties on Imports or Exports, except what may be absolutely necessary for executing it's inspection Laws: and the net Produce of all Duties and Imposts, laid by any State on Imports or Exports, shall be for the Use of the Treasury of the United States; and all such Laws shall be subject to the Revision and Controul of the Congress.

No State shall, without the Consent of Congress, lay any Duty of Tonnage, keep Troops, or Ships of War in time of Peace, enter into any Agreement or Compact with another State, or with a foreign Power, or engage in War, unless actually invaded, or in such imminent Danger as will not admit of delay.

Article II

Section 1. The executive Power shall be vested in a President of the United States of America. He shall hold his Office during the Term of four Years, and, together with the Vice President, chosen for the same Term, be elected, as follows.

Each State shall appoint, in such Manner as the Legislature thereof may direct, a Number of Electors, equal to the whole Number of Senators and Representatives to which the State may be entitled in the Congress: but no Senator or Representative, or Person holding an Office of Trust or Profit under the United States, shall be appointed an Elector.

[The Electors shall meet in their respective States, and vote by Ballot for two Persons, of whom one at least shall not be an Inhabitant of the same State with themselves. And they shall make a List of all the Persons voted for, and of the Number of Votes for each; which List they shall sign and certify, and transmit sealed to the Seat of the Government of the United States, directed to the President of the Senate. The President of the Senate shall, in the Presence of the Senate and House of Representatives, open all the Certificates, and the Votes shall then be counted. The Person having the greatest Number of Votes shall be the President, if such Number be a Majority of the whole Number of Electors appointed; and if there be more than one who have such Majority, and have an equal Number of Votes, then the House of Representatives shall immediately chuse by Ballot one of them for President; and if no Person have a Majority, then from the five highest on the list the said House shall in like Manner chuse the President. But in chusing the President, the Votes shall be taken by States, the Representation from each State having one Vote; a quorum for this Purpose shall consist of a Member or Members from two thirds of the States, and a Majority of all the States shall be necessary to a Choice. In every Case, after the Choice of the President, the Person having the greatest Number of Votes of the Electors shall be the Vice President. But if there should remain two or more who have equal Votes, the Senate shall chuse from them by Ballot the Vice President.] [6]

The Congress may determine the Time of chusing the Electors, and the Day on which they shall give their Votes; which Day shall be the same throughout the United States.

No Person except a natural born Citizen, or a Citizen of the United States, at the time of the Adoption of this Constitution, shall be eligible to the Office of President; neither shall any Person be eligible to that Office who shall not have attained to the Age of thirty five Years, and been fourteen Years a Resident within the United States.

In Case of the Removal of the President from Office, or of his Death, Resignation, or Inability to discharge the Powers and Duties of the said Office,[7] the Same shall devolve on the Vice President, and the Congress may by Law provide for the Case of Removal, Death, Resignation or Inability, both of the President and Vice President, declaring what Officer shall then act as President, and such Officer shall act accordingly, until the Disability be removed, or a President shall be elected.

The President shall, at stated Times, receive for his Services, a Compensation, which shall neither be encreased nor diminished during the Period for which he shall have been elected, and he shall not receive within that Period any other Emolument from the United States, or any of them.

Before he enter on the Execution of his Office, he shall take the following Oath or Affirmation: — "I do solemnly swear (or affirm) that I will faithfully execute the Office of President of the United States, and will to the best of my Ability, preserve, protect and defend the Constitution of the United States."

Section 2. The President shall be Commander in Chief of the Army and Navy of the United States, and of the Militia of the several States, when called into the actual Service of the United States; he may require the Opinion, in writing, of the principal Officer in each of the executive Departments, upon any Subject relating to the Duties of their respective Offices, and he shall have Power to grant Reprieves and Pardons for Offenses against the United States, except in Cases of Impeachment.

He shall have Power, by and with the Advice and Consent of the Senate, to make Treaties, provided two thirds of the Senators present concur; and he shall nominate, and by and with the Advice and Consent of the Senate, shall appoint Ambassadors, other public Ministers and Consuls, Judges of the supreme Court, and all other Officers of the United States, whose Appointments are not herein otherwise provided for, and which shall be established by Law: but the Congress may by Law vest the Appointment of such inferior Officers, as they think proper, in the President alone, in the Courts of Law, or in the Heads of Departments.

The President shall have Power to fill up all Vacancies that may happen during the Recess of the Senate, by granting Commissions which shall expire at the End of their next Session.

Section 3. He shall from time to time give to the Congress Information of the State of the Union, and recommend to their Consideration such Measures as he shall judge necessary and expedient; he may, on extraordinary Occasions, convene both Houses, or either of them, and in Case of Disagreement between them, with Respect to the Time of Adjournment, he may adjourn them to such Time as he shall think proper; he shall receive Ambassadors and other public Ministers; he shall take Care that the Laws be faithfully executed, and shall Commission all the Officers of the United States.

Section 4. The President, Vice President and all Civil Officers of the United States, shall be removed from office on Impeachment for, and Conviction of, Treason, Bribery, or other high Crimes and Misdemeanors.

Article III

Section 1. The judicial Power of the United States, shall be vested in one supreme Court, and in such inferior Courts as the Congress may from time to time ordain and establish. The Judges, both of the supreme and inferior Courts, shall hold their Offices during good Behaviour, and shall, at stated Times, receive for their Services, a Compensation, which shall not be diminished during their Continuance in Office.

Section 2. The judicial Power shall extend to all Cases, in Law and Equity, arising under this Constitution, the Laws of the United States, and Treaties made, or which shall be made, under their Authority; — to all Cases affecting Ambassadors, other public Ministers and Consuls; — to all Cases of admiralty and maritime Jurisdiction; — to Controversies to which the United States shall be a Party; — to Controversies between two or more States; — between a State and Citizens of another State;[8] — between Citizens of different States; — between Citizens of the same State claiming Lands under Grants of different States, and between a State, or the Citizens thereof, and foreign States, Citizens or Subjects.[8]

In all Cases affecting Ambassadors, other public Ministers and Consuls, and those in which a State shall be Party, the supreme Court shall have original Jurisdiction. In all the other Cases before mentioned, the supreme Court shall have appellate Jurisdiction, both as to Law and Fact, with such Exceptions, and under such Regulations as the Congress shall make.

The Trial of all Crimes, except in cases of Impeachment, shall be by Jury; and such Trial shall be held in the State where the said Crimes shall have been committed; but when not committed within any State, the Trial shall be at such Place or Places as the Congress may by Law have directed.

Section 3. Treason against the United States, shall consist only in levying War against them, or in adhering to their Enemies, giving them Aid and Comfort. No Person shall be convicted of Treason unless on the Testimony of two Witnesses to the same overt Act, or on Confession in open Court.

The Congress shall have Power to declare the Punishment of Treason, but no Attainder of Treason shall work Corruption of Blood, or Forfeiture except during the Life of the Person attainted.

Article IV

Section 1. Full Faith and Credit shall be given in each State to the public Acts, Records, and judicial Proceedings of every other State. And the Congress may by general Laws prescribe the Manner in which such Acts, Records and Proceedings shall be proved, and the Effect thereof.

Section 2. The Citizens of each State shall be entitled to all Privileges and Immunities of Citizens in the several States.

A Person charged in any State with Treason, Felony, or other Crime, who shall flee from Justice, and be found in another State, shall on Demand of the executive Authority of the State from which he fled, be delivered up, to be removed to the State having Jurisdiction of the Crime.

[No Person held to Service or Labour in one State, under the Laws thereof, escaping into another, shall, in Consequence of any Law or Regulation therein, be discharged from such Service or Labour, but shall be delivered up on Claim of the Party to whom such Service or Labour may be due.] [9]

Section 3. New States may be admitted by the Congress into this Union; but no new State shall be formed or erected within the Jurisdiction of any other State; nor any State be formed by the Junction of two or more States, or Parts of States, without the Consent of the Legislatures of the States concerned as well as of the Congress.

The Congress shall have Power to dispose of and make all needful Rules and Regulations respecting the Territory or other Property belonging to the United States; and nothing in this Constitution shall be so construed as to Prejudice any Claims of the United States, or of any particular State.

Section 4. The United States shall guarantee to every State in this Union a Republican Form of Government, and shall protect each of them against Invasion; and on Application of the Legislature, or of the Executive (when the Legislature cannot be convened) against domestic Violence.

Article V

The Congress, whenever two thirds of both Houses shall deem it necessary, shall propose Amendments to this Constitution, or, on the Application of the Legislatures of two thirds of the several States, shall call a Convention for proposing Amendments, which, in either Case, shall be valid to all Intents and Purposes, as Part of this Constitution, when ratified by the Legislatures of three fourths of the several States, or by Conventions in three fourths thereof, as the one or the other Mode of Ratification may be proposed by the Congress; Provided [that no Amendment which may be made prior to the Year One thousand eight hundred and eight shall in any Manner affect the first and fourth Clauses in the Ninth Section of the first Article; and] [10] that no State, without its Consent, shall be deprived of its equal Suffrage in the Senate.

Article VI

All Debts contracted and Engagements entered into, before the Adoption of this Constitution, shall be as valid against the United States under this Constitution, as under the Confederation.

This Constitution, and the Laws of the United States which shall be made in Pursuance thereof; and all Treaties made, or which shall be made, under the Authority of the United States, shall be the supreme Law of the Land; and the Judges in every State shall be bound thereby, any Thing in the Constitution or Laws of any State to the Contrary notwithstanding.

The Senators and Representatives before mentioned, and the Members of the several State Legislatures, and all executive and judicial Officers, both of the United States and of the several States, shall be bound by Oath or Affirmation, to support this Constitution; but no religious Test shall ever be required as a Qualification to any Office or public Trust under the United States.

Article VII

The Ratification of the Conventions of nine States, shall be sufficient for the Establishment of this Constitution between the States so ratifying the Same. Done in Convention by the Unanimous Consent of the States present the Seventeenth Day of September in the Year of our Lord one thousand seven hundred and Eighty seven and of the Independence of the United States of America the Twelfth In witness whereof We have hereunto subscribed our Names, George Washington, President and deputy from Virginia.

New Hampshire:	John Langdon, Nicholas Gilman.
Massachusetts:	Nathaniel Gorham, Rufus King.
Connecticut:	William Samuel Johnson, Roger Sherman.
New York:	Alexander Hamilton
New Jersey:	William Livingston, David Brearley, William Paterson, Jonathan Dayton.
Pennsylvania:	Benjamin Franklin, Thomas Mifflin, Robert Morris, George Clymer, Thomas FitzSimons, Jared Ingersoll, James Wilson, Gouverneur Morris.
Delaware:	George Read, Gunning Bedford Jr., John Dickinson, Richard Bassett, Jacob Broom.
Maryland:	James McHenry, Daniel of St. Thomas Jenifer, Daniel Carroll.
Virginia:	John Blair, James Madison Jr.
North Carolina:	William Blount, Richard Dobbs Spaight, Hugh Williamson.
South Carolina:	John Rutledge, Charles Cotesworth Pinckney, Charles Pinckney, Pierce Butler.
Georgia:	William Few, Abraham Baldwin.

[The language of the original Constitution, not including the Amendments, was adopted by a convention of the states on September 17, 1787, and was subsequently ratified by the states on the following dates: Delaware, December 7, 1787; Pennsylvania, December 12, 1787; New Jersey, December 18, 1787; Georgia, January 2, 1788; Connecticut, January 9, 1788; Massachusetts, February 6, 1788; Maryland, April 28, 1788; South Carolina, May 23, 1788; New Hampshire, June 21, 1788.

Ratification was completed on June 21, 1788.

The Constitution subsequently was ratified by Virginia, June 25, 1788; New York, July 26, 1788; North Carolina, November 21, 1789; Rhode Island, May 29, 1790; and Vermont, January 10, 1791.]

Amendments

Amendment I

(First ten amendments ratified December 15, 1791.)

Congress shall make no law respecting an establishment of religion, or prohibiting the free exercise thereof; or abridging the freedom of speech, or of the press; or the right of the people peaceably to assemble, and to petition the Government for a redress of grievances.

Amendment II

A well regulated Militia, being necessary to the security of a free State, the right of the people to keep and bear Arms, shall not be infringed.

Amendment III

No Soldier shall, in time of peace be quartered in any house, without the consent of the Owner, nor in time of war, but in a manner to be prescribed by law.

Amendment IV

The right of the people to be secure in their persons, houses, papers, and effects, against unreasonable searches and seizures, shall not be violated, and no Warrants shall issue, but upon probable cause, supported by Oath or affirmation, and particularly describing the place to be searched, and the persons or things to be seized.

Amendment V

No person shall be held to answer for a capital, or otherwise infamous crime, unless on a presentment or indictment of a Grand Jury, except in cases arising in the land or naval forces, or in the Militia, when in actual service in time of War or public danger; nor shall any person be subject for the same offence to be twice put in jeopardy of life or limb; nor shall be compelled in any criminal case to be a witness against himself, nor be deprived of life, liberty, or property, without due process of law; nor shall private property be taken for public use, without just compensation.

Amendment VI

In all criminal prosecutions, the accused shall enjoy the right to a speedy and public trial, by an impartial jury of the State and district wherein the crime shall have been committed, which district shall have been previously ascertained by law, and to be informed of the nature and cause of the accusation; to be confronted with the witnesses against him; to have compulsory process for obtaining witnesses in his favor, and to have the Assistance of Counsel for his defence.

Amendment VII

In Suits at common law, where the value in controversy shall exceed twenty dollars, the right of trial by jury shall be preserved, and no fact tried by a jury, shall be otherwise re-examined in any Court of the United States, than according to the rules of the common law.

Amendment VIII

Excessive bail shall not be required, nor excessive fines imposed, nor cruel and unusual punishments inflicted.

Amendment IX

The enumeration in the Constitution, of certain rights, shall not be construed to deny or disparage others retained by the people.

Amendment X
The powers not delegated to the United States by the Constitution, nor prohibited by it to the States, are reserved to the States respectively, or to the people.

Amendment XI *(Ratified February 7, 1795)*
The Judicial power of the United States shall not be construed to extend to any suit in law or equity, commenced or prosecuted against one of the United States by Citizens of another State, or by Citizens or Subjects of any Foreign State.

Amendment XII *(Ratified June 15, 1804)*
The Electors shall meet in their respective states and vote by ballot for President and Vice-President, one of whom, at least, shall not be an inhabitant of the same state with themselves; they shall name in their ballots the person voted for as President, and in distinct ballots the person voted for as Vice-President, and they shall make distinct lists of all persons voted for as President, and of all persons voted for as Vice-President, and of the number of votes for each, which lists they shall sign and certify, and transmit sealed to the seat of the government of the United States, directed to the President of the Senate; — The President of the Senate shall, in the presence of the Senate and House of Representatives, open all the certificates and the votes shall then be counted; — The person having the greatest number of votes for President, shall be the President, if such number be a majority of the whole number of Electors appointed; and if no person have such majority, then from the persons having the highest numbers not exceeding three on the list of those voted for as President, the House of Representatives shall choose immediately, by ballot, the President. But in choosing the President, the votes shall be taken by states, the representation from each state having one vote; a quorum for this purpose shall consist of a member or members from two-thirds of the states, and a majority of all the states shall be necessary to a choice. [And if the House of Representatives shall not choose a President whenever the right of choice shall devolve upon them, before the fourth day of March next following, then the Vice-President shall act as President, as in the case of the death or other constitutional disability of the President —] [11] The person having the greatest number of votes as Vice-President, shall be the Vice-President, if such number be a majority of the whole number of Electors appointed, and if no person have a majority, then from the two highest numbers on the list, the Senate shall choose the Vice-President; a quorum for the purpose shall consist of two-thirds of the whole number of Senators, and a majority of the whole number shall be necessary to a choice. But no person constitutionally ineligible to the office of President shall be eligible to that of Vice-President of the United States.

Amendment XIII *(Ratified December 6, 1865)*
Section 1. Neither slavery nor involuntary servitude, except as a punishment for crime whereof the party shall have been duly convicted, shall exist within the United States, or any place subject to their jurisdiction.

Section 2. Congress shall have power to enforce this article by appropriate legislation.

Amendment XIV
Section 1. All persons born or naturalized in the United States and subject to the jurisdiction thereof, are citizens of the United States and of the State wherein they reside. No State shall make or enforce any law which shall abridge the privileges or immunities of citizens of the United States; nor shall any State deprive any person of life, liberty, or property, without due process of law; nor deny to any person within its jurisdiction the equal protection of the laws.

Section 2. Representatives shall be apportioned among the several States according to their respective numbers, counting the whole number of persons in each State, excluding Indians not taxed. But when the right to vote at any election for the choice of electors for President and Vice President of the United States, Representatives in Congress, the Executive and Judicial officers of a State, or the members of the Legislature thereof, is denied to any of the male inhabitants of such State, being twenty-one years of age,[12] and citizens of the United States, or in any way abridged, except for participation in rebellion, or other crime, the basis of representation therein shall be reduced in the proportion which the number of such male citizens shall bear to the whole number of male citizens twenty-one years of age in such State.

Section 3. No person shall be a Senator or Representative in Congress, or elector of President and Vice President, or hold any office, civil or military, under the United States, or under any State, who, having previously taken an oath, as a member of Congress, or as an officer of the United States, or as a member of any State legislature, or as an executive or judicial officer of any State, to support the Constitution of the United States, shall have engaged in insurrection or rebellion against the same, or given aid or comfort to the enemies thereof. But Congress may by a vote of two-thirds of each House, remove such disability.

Section 4. The validity of the public debt of the United States, authorized by law, including debts incurred for payment of pensions and bounties for services in suppressing insurrection or rebellion, shall not be questioned. But neither the United States nor any State shall assume or pay any debt or obligation incurred in aid of insurrection or rebellion against the United States, or any claim for the loss or emancipation of any slave; but all such debts, obligations and claims shall be held illegal and void.

Section 5. The Congress shall have power to enforce, by appropriate legislation, the provisions of this article.

Amendment XV *(Ratified February 3, 1870)*
Section 1. The right of citizens of the United States to vote shall not be denied or abridged by the United States or by any State on account of race, color, or previous condition of servitude.

Section 2. The Congress shall have power to enforce this article by appropriate legislation.

Amendment XVI *(Ratified February 3, 1913)*
The Congress shall have power to lay and collect taxes on incomes, from whatever source derived, without apportionment among the several States, and without regard to any census or enumeration.

Amendment XVII *(Ratified April 8, 1913)*
The Senate of the United States shall be composed of two Senators from each State, elected by the people thereof, for six years; and each Senator shall have one vote. The electors in each State shall have the qualifications requisite for electors of the most numerous branch of the State legislatures.

When vacancies happen in the representation of any State in the Senate, the executive authority of such State shall issue writs of election to fill such vacancies: *Provided,* That the legislature of any State may empower the executive thereof to make temporary appointments until the people fill the vacancies by election as the legislature may direct.

This amendment shall not be so construed as to affect the election or term of any Senator chosen before it becomes valid as part of the Constitution.

[Amendment XVIII *(Ratified January 16, 1919)*
Section. 1. After one year from the ratification of this article the manufacture, sale, or transportation of intoxicating liquors within, the importation thereof into, or the exportation thereof from the United States and all territory subject to the jurisdiction thereof for beverage purposes is hereby prohibited.

Section 2. The Congress and the several States shall have concurrent power to enforce this article by appropriate legislation.

Section 3. This article shall be inoperative unless it shall have been ratified as an amendment to the Constitution by the legislatures of the several States, as provided in the Constitution, within seven years from the date of the submission hereof to the States by the Congress.] [13]

Amendment XIX *(Ratified August 18, 1920)*
The right of citizens of the United States to vote shall not be denied or abridged by the United States or by any State on account of sex.

Congress shall have power to enforce this article by appropriate legislation.

Amendment XX *(Ratified January 23, 1933)*

Section 1. The terms of the President and Vice President shall end at noon on the 20th day of January, and the terms of Senators and Representatives at noon on the 3d day of January, of the years in which such terms would have ended if this article had not been ratified; and the terms of their successors shall then begin.

Section 2. The Congress shall assemble at least once in every year, and such meeting shall begin at noon on the 3d day of January, unless they shall by law appoint a different day.

Section 3.[14] If, at the time fixed for the beginning of the term of the President, the President elect shall have died, the Vice President elect shall become President. If a President shall not have been chosen before the time fixed for the beginning of his term, or if the President elect shall have failed to qualify, then the Vice President elect shall act as President until a President shall have qualified; and the Congress may by law provide for the case wherein neither a President elect nor a Vice President elect shall have qualified, declaring who shall then act as President, or the manner in which one who is to act shall be selected, and such person shall act accordingly until a President or Vice President shall have qualified.

Section 4. The Congress may by law provide for the case of the death of any of the persons from whom the House of Representatives may choose a President whenever the right of choice shall have devolved upon them, and for the case of the death of any of the persons from whom the Senate may choose a Vice President whenever the right of choice shall have devolved upon them.

Section 5. Sections 1 and 2 shall take effect on the 15th day of October following the ratification of this article.

Section 6. This article shall be inoperative unless it shall have been ratified as an amendment to the Constitution by the legislatures of three-fourths of the several States within seven years from the date of its submission.

Amendment XXI *(Ratified December 5, 1933)*

Section 1. The eighteenth article of amendment to the Constitution of the United States is hereby repealed.

Section 2. The transportation or importation into any State, Territory or possession of the United States for delivery or use therein of intoxicating liquors, in violation of the laws thereof, is hereby prohibited.

Section 3. This article shall be inoperative unless it shall have been ratified as an amendment to the Constitution by conventions in the several States, as provided in the Constitution, within seven years from the date of the submission hereof to the States by the Congress.

Amendment XXII *(Ratified February 27, 1951)*

Section 1. No person shall be elected to the office of the President more than twice, and no person who has held the office of President, or acted as President, for more than two years of a term to which some other person was elected President shall be elected to the office of the President more than once. But this Article shall not apply to any person holding the office of President when this Article was proposed by the Congress, and shall not prevent any person who may be holding the office of President, or acting as President, during the term within which this Article become operative from holding the office of President or acting as President during the remainder of such term.

Section 2. This Article shall be inoperative unless it shall have been ratified as an amendment to the Constitution by the legislatures of three-fourths of the several States within seven years from the date of its submission to the States by the Congress.

Amendment XXIII *(Ratified March 29, 1961)*

Section 1. The District constituting the seat of Government of the United States shall appoint in such manner as the Congress may direct:

A number of electors of President and Vice President equal to the whole number of Senators and Representatives in Congress to which the District would be entitled if it were a State, but in no event more than the least populous State; they shall be in addition to those appointed by the States, but they shall be considered, for the purposes of the election of President and Vice President, to be electors appointed by a State; and they shall meet in the District and perform such duties as provided by the twelfth article of amendment.

Section 2. The Congress shall have power to enforce this article by appropriate legislation.

Amendment XXIV *(Ratified January 23, 1964)*

Section 1. The right of citizens of the United States to vote in any primary or other election for President or Vice President, for electors for President or Vice President, or for Senator or Representative in Congress, shall not be denied or abridged by the United States or any State by reason of failure to pay any poll tax or other tax.

Section 2. The Congress shall have power to enforce this article by appropriate legislation.

Amendment XXV *(Ratified February 10, 1967)*

Section 1. In case of the removal of the President from office or of his death or resignation, the Vice President shall become President.

Section 2. Whenever there is a vacancy in the office of the Vice President, the President shall nominate a Vice President who shall take office upon confirmation by a majority vote of both Houses of Congress.

Section 3. Whenever the President transmits to the President pro tempore of the Senate and the Speaker of the House of Representatives his written declaration that he is unable to discharge the powers and duties of his office, and until he transmits to them a written declaration to the contrary, such powers and duties shall be discharged by the Vice President as Acting President.

Section 4. Whenever the Vice President and a majority of either the principal officers of the executive departments or of such other body as Congress may by law provide, transmit to the President pro tempore of the Senate and the Speaker of the House of Representatives their written declaration that the President is unable to discharge the powers and duties of his office, the Vice President shall immediately assume the powers and duties of the office as Acting President.

Thereafter, when the President transmits to the President pro tempore of the Senate and the Speaker of the House of Representatives his written declaration that no inability exists, he shall resume the powers and duties of his office unless the Vice President and a majority of either the principal officers of the executive department or of such other body as Congress may by law provide, transmit within four days to the President pro tempore of the Senate and the Speaker of the House of Representatives their written declaration that the President is unable to discharge the powers and duties of his office. Thereupon Congress shall decide the issue, assembling within forty-eight hours for that purpose if not in session. If the Congress, within twenty-one days after receipt of the latter written declaration, or, if Congress is not in session, within twenty-one days after Congress is required to assemble, determines by two-thirds vote of both houses that the President is unable to discharge the powers and duties of his office, the Vice President shall continue to discharge the same as Acting President; otherwise, the President shall resume the powers and duties of his office.

Amendment XXVI *(Ratified July 1, 1971)*

Section 1. The right of citizens of the United States, who are eighteen years of age or older, to vote shall not be denied or abridged by the United States or by any State on account of age.

Section 2. The Congress shall have power to enforce this article by appropriate legislation.

Footnotes

1. The part in brackets was changed by section 2 of the Fourteenth Amendment.
2. The part in brackets was changed by section 1 of the Seventeenth Amendment.
3. The part in brackets was changed by the second paragraph of the Seventeenth Amendment.

4. The part in brackets was changed by section 2 of the Twentieth Amendment.
5. The Sixteenth Amendment gave Congress the power to tax incomes.
6. The material in brackets has been superseded by the Twelfth Amendment.
7. This provision has been affected by the Twenty-fifth Amendment.
8. These clauses were affected by the Eleventh Amendment.
9. This paragraph has been superseded by the Thirteenth Amendment.
10. Obsolete.
11. The part in brackets has been superseded by section 3 of the Twentieth Amendment.
12. See the Twenty-sixth Amendment.
13. This Amendment was repealed by section 1 of the Twenty-first Amendment.
14. See the Twenty-fifth Amendment.

BIBLIOGRAPHY

Aikman, Lonelle M. *We the People: The Story of the United States Capitol.* 13th ed. Washington, D.C.: United States Capitol Historical Society, 1985.

Alexander, Herbert E. *Financing Politics: Money, Elections, and Political Reform.* 3d ed. Washington, D.C.: CQ Press, 1984.

Arnold, Douglas R. *Congress and the Bureaucracy: A Theory of Influence.* New Haven: Yale University Press, 1980.

Asbell, Bernard. *The Senate Nobody Knows.* New York: Doubleday, 1978.

Ashworth, William. *Under the Influence: Congress, Lobbies, and the American Pork Barrel System.* New York: Hawthorn/Dutton, 1981.

Bailey, Stephen K. *Congress Makes a Law.* New York: Columbia University Press, 1950.

Baker, Ross K. *Friend and Foe in the U.S. Senate.* New York: Free Press, 1980.

Barone, Michael, and Grant Ujifusa. *The Almanac of American Politics 1988.* Washington, D.C.: National Journal, 1987.

Baum, Lawrence. *The Supreme Court.* Washington, D.C.: CQ Press, 1985.

Berger, Raoul. *Congress versus the Supreme Court.* Cambridge: Harvard University Press, 1969.

———. *Executive Privilege.* Cambridge: Harvard University Press, 1974.

Berman, Daniel M. *How a Bill Becomes a Law: Congress Enacts Civil Rights Legislation.* 2d ed. New York: Macmillan, 1966.

———. *In Congress Assembled: The Legislative Process in the National Government.* New York: Macmillan, 1964.

Bibby, John E., ed. *Congress Off the Record: The Candid Analyses of Seven Members.* Washington, D.C.: American Enterprise Institute, 1983.

Binkley, Wilfred. *President and Congress.* New York: Vintage Books, 1962.

Birnbaum, Jeffrey H., and Alan S. Murray. *Showdown at Gucci Gulch.* New York: Random House, 1987.

Blanchard, Robert O., ed. *Congress and the News Media.* New York: Hastings House, 1974.

Bocchus, William I. *Inside the Legislative Process: The Passage of the Foreign Service Act of 1980.* Boulder, Colo.: Westview, 1983.

Bolling, Richard. *House Out of Order.* New York: E. P. Dutton, 1965.

———. *Power in the House: A History of the Leadership of the House of Representatives.* New York: Capricorn Books, 1974.

Brenner, Phillip. *The Limits and Possibilities of Congress.* New York: St. Martin's, 1983.

Brinkley, Joel, and Stephen Engelberg, eds. *Report of the Congressional Committees Investigating the Iran-Contra Affair. With the Minority View.* Abridged edition. New York: Random House, 1988.

Brown, Glenn. *History of the United States Capitol.* Washington, D.C.: U.S. Government Printing Office, 1903. Reprint. New York: Da Capo, 1970.

Burdette, Franklin L. *Filibustering in the Senate.* Princeton, N.J.: Princeton University Press, 1940.

Caro, Robert A. *The Years of Lyndon Johnson: The Path to Power.* New York: Alfred A. Knopf, 1982.

Chamberlain, Lawrence H. *The President, Congress and Legislation.* New York: Columbia University Press, 1946.

Chambers, W. N., and Walter D. Burnham, eds. *The American Party System.* 2d ed. Cambridge: Oxford University Press, 1975.

Champagne, Anthony. *Congressman Sam Rayburn.* New Brunswick, N.J.: Rutgers University Press, 1984.

Cheney, Richard B., and Lynne V. Cheney. *Kings of the Hill: Power and Personality in the House of Representatives.* New York: Cross Road, 1983.

Cigler, Allan J., and Burdett A. Loomis. *Interest Group Politics.* 2d ed. Washington, D.C.: CQ Press, 1986.

Cohen, William S. *Roll Call: One Year in the United States Senate.* New York: Simon and Schuster, 1981.

Congressional Quarterly. *Congressional Districts in the 1980s.* Washington, D.C.: Congressional Quarterly, 1983.

_____. *Congressional Ethics.* Washington, D.C.: Congressional Quarterly, 1980.

_____. *Guide to Congress.* 3d ed. Washington, D.C.: Congressional Quarterly, 1982.

_____. *Guide to the U.S. Supreme Court.* Washington, D.C.: Congressional Quarterly, 1979.

_____. *Guide to U.S. Elections.* 2d ed. Washington, D.C.: Congressional Quarterly, 1985.

_____. *The Iran-Contra Puzzle.* Washington, D.C.: Congressional Quarterly, 1988.

_____. *Watergate: Chronology of a Crisis.* Washington, D.C.: Congressional Quarterly, 1975.

Cooper, Joseph, and Calvin G. Mackenzie. *The House at Work.* Austin: University of Texas Press, 1981.

Corwin, Edward S., *The Commerce Power versus States' Rights.* Princeton, N.J.: Princeton University Press, 1936.

Crabb, Cecil V., Jr., and Pat M. Holt. *Invitation to Struggle: Congress, the President, and Foreign Policy.* 2d ed. Washington, D.C.: CQ Press, 1984.

Craig, Barbara H. *Chadha.* New York: Oxford University Press, 1988.

_____. *The Legislative Veto: Congressional Control of Regulation.* Boulder, Colo.: Westview Press, 1983.

Crawford, Kenneth. *The Pressure Boys: The Inside Story of Lobbying in America.* 1939. Reprint. New York: Arno Press, 1974.

Cummings, Frank. *Capitol Hill Manual.* 2d ed. Washington, D.C.: Bureau of National Affairs, 1984.

Davidson, Roger H., and Walter J. Oleszek. *Congress Against Itself.* Bloomington: Indiana University Press, 1979.

_____. *Congress and Its Members.* 2d ed. Washington, D.C.: CQ Press, 1985.

_____. *Governing: Readings and Cases in American Politics.* Washington, D.C.: CQ Press, 1987.

Deakin, James. *The Lobbyists.* Washington, D.C.: Public Affairs Press, 1966.

deKeiffer, Donald. *How to Lobby Congress: A Guide for the Citizen Lobbyist*. New York: Dodd, Mead, 1981.

Dodd, Lawrence C., and Bruce I. Oppenheimer. *Congress Reconsidered*. 3d ed. Washington, D.C.: CQ Press, 1985.

Dodd, Lawrence C., and Richard L. Schott. *Congress and the Administrative State*. New York: John Wiley and Sons, 1979.

Drew, Elizabeth. *Politics and Money: The New Road to Corruption*. New York: Macmillan, 1983.

_____. *Senator*. New York: Simon and Schuster, 1979.

Ehrenhalt, Alan, ed. *Politics in America: The 100th Congress*. Washington, D.C.: Congressional Quarterly, 1987.

Elazar, Daniel J. *American Federalism: A View from the States*. New York: Harper and Row, 1984.

Evans, Rowland, and Robert Novak. *Lyndon B. Johnson: The Exercise of Power*. New York: New American Library, 1966.

The Federalist Papers. Intro. by Clinton Rossiter. New York: Mentor, 1961.

Fenno, Richard F., Jr. *Congressmen in Committees*. Boston: Little, Brown, 1973.

_____. *Home Style: House Members in their Districts*. Boston: Little, Brown, 1978.

_____. *The Power of the Purse: Appropriations Politics in Congress*. Boston: Little, Brown, 1966.

Fiorina, Morris P. *Congress: Keystone of the Washington Establishment*. New Haven: Yale University Press, 1977.

Fisher, Louis. *Constitutional Conflicts Between Congress and the President*. Princeton, N.J.: Princeton University Press, 1985.

_____. *The Politics of Shared Power: Congress and the Executive Branch*. Washington, D.C.: CQ Press, 1987.

Flexner, Eleanor. *Century of Struggle: The Women's Rights Movement in the United States*. Rev. ed. Cambridge: Harvard University Press, 1975.

Follet, Mary P. *The Speaker of the House of Representatives*. 1902. Reprint. New York: Burt Franklin, 1974.

Fox, Harrison W., and Susan W. Hammond. *Congressional Staff: The Invisible Force in American Lawmaking*. New York: Free Press, 1979.

Franck, Thomas M., and Edward Weisband. *Foreign Policy by Congress*. New York: Oxford University Press, 1979.

Frantzich, Stephen E. *Write Your Congressman: Constituent Communications and Representation*. New York: Praeger, 1986.

Froman, Lewis A., Jr. *The Congressional Process: Strategies, Rules, and Procedures*. Boston: Little, Brown, 1967.

Galloway, George B. *History of the House of Representatives*. Rev. ed. by Sidney Wise. New York: Thomas Y. Crowell, 1976.

_____. *The Legislative Process in Congress*. New York: Thomas Y. Crowell, 1953.

Gavit, Bernard C. *The Commerce Clause of the United States Constitution*. New York: AMS Press, 1970.

Gertzog, Irwin N. *Congressional Women: Their Recruitment, Treatment, and Behavior*. New York: Praeger, 1984.

Goehlert, Robert U., and John R. Sayre. *The United States Congress: A Bibliography*. New York: Free Press, 1982.

Goldenberg, Edie N., and Michael W. Traugott. *Campaigning for Congress*. Washington, D.C.: CQ Press, 1984.

Goldstein, Joel K. *The Modern American Vice Presidency*. Princeton, N.J.: Princeton University Press, 1982.

Goodwin, George. *The Little Legislatures: Committees of Congress.* Amherst, Mass.: University of Massachusetts Press, 1970.

Graber, Doris A. *Mass Media and American Politics.* 2d ed. Washington, D.C.: CQ Press, 1984.

____. *Media Power in Politics.* Washington, D.C.: CQ Press, 1984.

Gross, Bertram M. *The Legislative Struggle.* New York: McGraw-Hill, 1953.

Hale, Dennis, ed. *The United States Congress: Proceedings of the Thomas P. O'Neill, Jr. Symposium, Boston College.* Boston: Transaction, 1982.

Hamilton, James. *The Power to Probe: A Study of Congressional Investigations.* New York: Random House, 1976.

Hansen, Orval, and Ellen Miller. *Congressional Operations: The Role of Mail in Decisionmaking in Congress.* Washington, D.C.: Center for Responsive Politics, 1987.

Hardeman, D. B., and Donald Bacon. *Rayburn: A Biography.* Austin: Texas Monthly Press, 1987.

Harris, Joseph P. *The Advice and Consent of the Senate: A Study of the Confirmation of Appointments by the United States Senate.* 1953. Reprint. Westport, Conn.: Greenwood, 1968.

Havemann, Joel. *Congress and the Budget.* Bloomington: Indiana University Press, 1978.

Haynes, George H. *The Senate of the United States: Its History and Practice.* 2 vols. Boston: Houghton Mifflin, 1938.

Heclo, Hugh. *A Government of Strangers.* Washington, D.C.: Brookings Institution, 1977.

Hess, Stephen. *The Ultimate Insiders: U.S. Senators in the National Media.* Washington, D.C.: Brookings Institution, 1986.

____. *The Washington Reporters.* Washington, D.C.: Brookings Institution, 1981.

Hinckley, Barbara. *Congressional Elections.* Washington, D.C.: CQ Press, 1981.

____. *Stability and Change in Congress.* New York: Harper and Row, 1988.

Hunter, Robert E., Wayne L. Berman, and John F. Kennedy, eds. *Making Government Work: From White House to Congress.* Boulder, Colo.: Westview, 1986.

Ippolito, Dennis S. *Congressional Spending.* Ithaca, N.Y.: Cornell University Press, 1981.

Jacobson, Gary C. *Money in Congressional Elections.* New Haven: Yale University Press, 1980.

____. *The Politics of Congressional Elections.* Boston: Little, Brown, 1983.

Jewell, Malcolm E., and Samuel C. Patterson. *The Legislative Process in the United States.* 3d ed. New York: Random House, 1977.

Johannes, John. *To Serve the People: Congress and Constituency Service.* Lincoln: University of Nebraska Press, 1984.

Johnson, Lyndon B. *The Vantage Point: Perspective on the Presidency, 1963-69.* New York: Holt, Rinehart and Winston, 1971.

Jones, Charles O. *Every Second Year: Congressional Behavior and the Two-Year Term.* Washington, D.C.: Brookings Institution, 1967.

____. *The Minority Party in Congress.* Boston: Little, Brown, 1970.

____. *The United States Congress: People, Place, and Policy.* Chicago: Dorsey, 1982.

Jones, Rochelle, and Peter Woll. *The Private World of Congress.* New York: Free Press, 1979.

Josephy, Alvin M., Jr. *On the Hill: A History of the American Congress from 1789 to the Present.* New York: Simon and Schuster, 1979. (Originally published as *The American Heritage History of the Congress of the United States.* New York:

American Heritage Publishing Co., 1975.)

Kau, James B., and Paul H. Rubin. *Congressmen, Constituents, and Contributors.* Boston: Martinus Nijhoff, 1982.

Keefe, William J. *Parties, Politics, and Public Policy in America.* 3d ed. Washington, D.C.: CQ Press, 1987.

——, and Morris S. Ogul. *The American Legislative Process: Congress and the States.* 5th ed. Englewood Cliffs, N.J.: Prentice-Hall, 1981.

——, and Samuel Kernell. *Strategy and Choice in Congressional Elections.* New Haven: Yale University Press, 1981.

——, et al. *American Democracy.* 2d ed. Chicago: Dorsey, 1986.

Kennon, Donald R., ed. *The Speakers of the U.S. House of Representatives.* Baltimore: Johns Hopkins University Press, 1986.

King, Anthony, ed. *Both Ends of the Avenue: The Presidency, the Executive Branch, and Congress in the 1980s.* Washington, D.C.: American Enterprise Institute, 1983.

Kingdon, John W. *Congressmen's Voting Decisions.* 2d ed. New York: Harper and Row, 1980.

Kozak, David C., and John D. Macartney, eds. *Congress and Public Policy.* 2d ed. Chicago: Dorsey, 1987.

Kraditor, Aileen S. *The Ideas of the Women's Suffrage Movement: 1880-1920.* New York: Norton, 1981.

Levitan, Sar, and Martha R. Cooper. *Business Lobbies: The Public Good and the Bottom Line.* Baltimore: Johns Hopkins University Press, 1984.

Light, Paul C. *Vice Presidential Power.* Baltimore: Johns Hopkins University Press, 1984.

Livingston, William S., et al, eds. *The Presidency and the Congress: A Shifting Balance of Power?* Austin: University of Texas Press, 1979.

Loomis, Burdett A. *Setting Course: A Congressional Management Guide.* Washington, D.C.: American University, 1984.

Maass, Arthur. *Congress and the Common Good.* New York: Basic Books, 1983.

Mackaman, Frank H., ed. *Understanding Congressional Leadership.* Washington, D.C.: CQ Press, 1981.

MacKenzie, G. Calvin. *The Politics of Presidential Appointments.* New York: Free Press, 1981.

MacNeil, Neil. *Forge of Democracy: The House of Representatives.* New York: David Mckay, 1963.

Maisel, Louis Sandy. *From Obscurity to Oblivion: Running in the Congressional Primary.* Knoxville: University of Tennessee Press, 1982.

——, and Joseph Cooper, eds. *Congressional Elections.* Beverly Hills, Calif.: Sage Publications, 1981.

Malbin, Michael. *Unelected Representatives: Congressional Staff and the Future of Representative Government.* New York: Basic Books, 1982.

——, ed. *Money and Politics in the United States.* Chatham, N.J.: Chatham House, 1984.

——, ed. *Parties, Interest Groups, and Campaign Finance Laws.* Washington, D.C.: American Enterprise Institute, 1980.

Mann, Thomas E., and Norman J. Ornstein, eds. *The New Congress.* Washington, D.C.: American Enterprise Institute, 1981.

Mansbridge, Jane J. *Why We Lost the Equal Rights Amendment.* Chicago: University of Chicago Press, 1986.

Marbut, F. B. *News from the Capital: The Story of Washington Reporting*. Carbondale: Southern Illinois University Press, 1971.

Marcuss, Stanley J. *Effective Washington Representation*. New York: Harcourt Brace Jovanovich, 1983.

Matsunaga, Spark M., and Ping Chen. *Rulemakers of the House*. Urbana: University of Illinois Press, 1976.

Matthews, Donald R. *U.S. Senators and Their World*. 1960. Reprint ed. New York: W. W. Norton, 1980.

Mayhew, David R. *Congress: The Electoral Connection*. New Haven: Yale University Press, 1974.

McCubbins, Mathew D. and Terry Sullivan, eds. *Congress: Structure and Policy*. New York: Cambridge University Press, 1987.

McGeary, M. Nelson. *The Development of Congressional Investigative Power*. New York: Octagon Books, 1966.

Mencken, H. L. *A Carnival of Buncombe: Writings on Politics*. 1956. Reprint. Chicago: University of Chicago Press, 1984.

Miller, Clem. *Member of the House: Letters of a Congressman*. New York: Charles Scribner's Sons, 1962.

Miller, James. *Running in Place: Inside the Senate*. New York: Simon and Schuster, 1986.

Miller, Merle. *Lyndon: An Oral Biography*. New York: G. P. Putnam's Sons, 1980.

Miller, Stephen. *Special Interest Groups in American Politics*. New Brunswick, N.J.: Transaction, 1983.

National Security Archive. *The Chronology*. New York: Warner Books, 1987.

Oleszek, Walter J. *Congressional Procedures and the Policy Process*. 3d ed. Washington, D.C.: CQ Press, 1988.

O'Neill, Thomas P., Jr., and William Novak. *Man of the House: The Life and Political Memoirs of Speaker Tip O'Neill*. New York: Random House, 1987.

Ornstein, Norman J., Thomas E. Mann, Michael J. Malbin. *Vital Statistics on Congress, 1987-1988*. Washington, D.C.: Congressional Quarterly, 1987.

Oshinsky, David M. *A Conspiracy So Immense: The World Of Joe McCarthy*. New York: Free Press, 1983.

O'Toole, Lawrence J., Jr., ed. *American Intergovernmental Relations*. Washington, D.C.: CQ Press, 1985.

Parker, Glenn R. *Studies of Congress*. Washington, D.C.: CQ Press, 1985.

_____, and Suzanne L. Parker. *Factions in House Committees*. Knoxville: University of Tennessee Press, 1985.

Peabody, Robert L. *Leadership in Congress: Stability, Succession and Change*. Boston: Little, Brown, 1976.

Peirce, Neal, and Lawrence D. Longley. *The People's President*. rev. ed. New Haven: Yale University Press, 1981.

Plano, Jack C., and Milton Greenberg. *The American Political Dictionary*. 7th ed. New York: Holt, Rinehart and Winston, 1985.

Redman, Eric. *The Dance of Legislation*. New York: Simon and Schuster, 1974.

Reedy, George E. *The U.S. Senate*. New York: Crown, 1986.

Reid, T. R. *Congressional Odyssey: Saga of a Senate Bill*. San Francisco: W. H. Freeman, 1980.

Riddick, Floyd M. *The Organization and Procedure of the United States Congress*. Manassas, Va.: National Capitol Publishers, 1949.

_____. *Senate Procedure: Precedents and Practices*. Washington, D.C.: Government Printing Office, 1981.

Rieselbach, Leroy N. *Congressional Reform*. Washington, D.C.: CQ Press, 1986.

Ripley, Randall B. *Congress: Process and Policy*. 3d ed. New York: W. W. Norton, 1983.

_____. *Majority Party Leadership in Congress*. Boston: Little, Brown, 1969.

_____. *Power in the Senate*. New York: St. Martin's, 1969.

Ripley, Randall B., and Grace A. Franklin. *Congress, the Bureaucracy, and Public Policy*. 3d ed. Chicago: Dorsey, 1984.

Rothman, David J. *Politics and Power: The United States Senate, 1869-1901*. Cambridge: Harvard University Press, 1966.

Sabato, Larry J. *PAC Power*. New York: W. W. Norton, 1984.

Salmore, Stephen A., and Barbara G. Salmore. *Candidates, Parties, and Campaigns: Electoral Politics in America*. Washington, D.C.: Congressional Quarterly, 1985.

Schick, Allen. *Congress and Money: Budgeting, Spending, and Taxing*. Washington, D.C.: Urban Institute, 1980.

_____. *Reconciliation and the Congressional Budget Process*. Washington, D.C.: American Enterprise Institute, 1981.

_____, ed. *Making Economic Policy in Congress*. Washington, D.C.: American Enterprise Institute, 1983.

Schlesinger, Arthur M., ed. *History of U.S. Political Parties*. 4 vols. 1973. Reprint. New York: Chelsea House, 1981.

Schneider, Jerrold E. *Ideological Coalitions in Congress*. Westport, Conn.: Greenwood Press, 1979.

Shafritz, Jay M. *The Dorsey Dictionary of American Government and Politics*. Chicago: Dorsey, 1988.

Sheppard, Burton D. *Rethinking Congressional Reform: The Reform Roots of the Special Interest Congress*. Cambridge, Mass.: Schenkman, 1985.

Shuman, Howard E. *Politics and the Budget*. Englewood Cliffs, N.J.: Prentice-Hall, 1984.

Siff, Ted, and Alan Weil. *Ruling Congress: How House and Senate Rules Govern the Legislative Process*. New York: Grossman, 1975.

Simon, Paul. *The Glass House*. New York: Continuum, 1984.

Sinclair, Barbara. *Majority Leadership in the U.S. House*. Baltimore: Johns Hopkins University Press, 1983.

Smith, Gene. *High Crimes and Misdemeanors: The Impeachment and Trial of Andrew Johnson*. New York: McGraw-Hill, 1985.

Smith, Hedrick. *The Power Game: How Washington Works*. New York: Random House, 1988.

Smith, Steven S., and Christopher J. Deering. *Committees in Congress*. Washington, D.C.: CQ Press, 1984.

Stern, Philip M. *The Best Congress Money Can Buy*. New York: Pantheon, 1988.

Stockman, David. *The Triumph of Politics: The Inside Story of the Reagan Revolution*. New York: Harper and Row, 1986.

Sullivan, Terry. *Procedural Structure: Success and Influence in Congress*. New York: Praeger, 1984.

Sundquist, James L. *Constitutional Reform and Effective Government*. Washington, D.C.: Brookings Institution, 1986.

_____. *The Decline and Resurgence of Congress*. Washington, D.C.: Brookings Institution, 1981.

Swisher, Carl Brent. *American Constitutional Development*. 1954. Reprint. Westport, Conn.: Greenwood, 1978.

Tacheron, Donald G. and Morris K. Udall. *The Job of the Congressman: An Introduction to Service in the U.S. House of Representatives*. 2d ed. Indianapolis: Bobbs-Merrill, 1970.

Taylor, Telford. *Grand Inquest: The Story of Congressional Investigations*. New York: Simon and Schuster, 1955.

Tobin, Maurice B. *Hidden Power: The Seniority System and Other Customs of Congress*. New York: Greenwood, 1986.

Truman, David B. *The Governmental Process: Political Interests and Public Opinion*. New York: Alfred A. Knopf, 1981.

Udall, Morris. *Too Funny to Be President: Notes from the Life of a Politician*. New York: Henry Holt, 1987.

Unekis, Joseph K., and Leroy N. Rieselbach. *Congressional Committee Politics: Continuity and Change*. New York: Praeger, 1984.

Vogler, David. *The Politics of Congress*. 4th ed. Boston: Allyn and Bacon, 1983.

Vogler, David J. *The Third House: Conference Committees in the U.S. Congress*. Evanston, Ill.: Northwestern University Press, 1971.

———, and Sidney R. Waldman. *Congress and Democracy*. Washington, D.C.: CQ Press, 1985.

Walker, David B. *Toward a Functioning Federalism*. Cambridge, Mass.: Winthrop, 1981.

Wander, Thomas W., Ted F. Hebert, and Gary W. Copeland, eds. *Congressional Budgeting*. Baltimore: Johns Hopkins University Press, 1984.

Warren, Charles. *Congress as Santa Claus*. 1932. Reprint. New York: Arno, 1978.

———. *Congress, the Constitution, and the Supreme Court*. Boston: Little, Brown, 1925.

———. *The Supreme Court in United States History*. 1926. Reprint. Littleton, Colo.: Rothman, 1987.

Wattenberg, Martin P. *The Decline of American Political Parties, 1952 to 1980*. Cambridge: Harvard University Press, 1984.

Weatherford, J. McIver. *Tribes on the Hill: The U.S. Congress—Rituals and Realities*. South Hadley, Mass.: Bergin and Garvey, 1985.

Whalen, Charles. *The House and Foreign Policy: The Irony of Congressional Reform*. Chapel Hill: University of North Carolina Press, 1982.

———, and Barbara Whalen. *The Longest Debate: A Legislative History of the 1964 Civil Rights Act*. Washington, D.C.: Seven Locks Press, 1985.

White, William Smith. *The Professional: Lyndon B. Johnson*. Boston: Houghton Mifflin, 1964.

Wildavsky, Aaron. *The Politics of the Budgetary Process*. 4th ed. Boston: Little, Brown, 1984.

Williams, Irving G. *The Rise of the Vice Presidency*. Washington, D.C.: Public Affairs Press, 1956.

Wilson, Woodrow. *Congressional Government*. 1885. Reprint. Baltimore: Johns Hopkins University Press, 1981.

Woodward, Bob, and Carl Bernstein. *All the President's Men*. New York: Simon and Schuster, 1987.

———. *The Final Days*. Simon and Schuster, 1987.

Wright, Gerald C., Jr., Leroy N. Rieselbach, and Lawrence C. Dodd, eds. *Congress and Policy Change*. New York: Agathon, 1966.

Indexes

MEMBERS INDEX

Listed below are current or former members of Congress who are mentioned in this book. Biographical essays are designated by boldface type.

GENERAL INDEX

Text entries are designated by boldface type.

Abel, Hazel H., 487
Abolition. *See* Slavery and antislavery
Abortion
    committee jurisdiction, 221-222
    constitutional amendment, 95
    and debt-limit bill, 349, 359
    Hyde amendment, 9
    legalization protest, 263
    opposition PAC, 310
    special caucuses, 69
    Supreme Court decision, 410
Abourezk, James, 160, 161, 201
Abscam scandal, 1-2, 112, 132, 184, 282
Abzug, Bella S., 488
Acid rain, 126, 128
Adams, Abigail, 462
Adams, Brock, 39-40, 485
Adams, Henry, 340
Adams, John, 2, 13, 61, 180, 243, 324, 393,
    436, 462, 502
Adams, John G., 278
Adams, John Quincy, 2-3
    biography, 2-3
    Calhoun career, 53
    Clay career, 74
    election, 1824, 74, 124, 177, 340
    service in Congress, 325, 326
    White House grounds, 464
Adams, Sherman, 125, 207
Adams, William, 273
Adamson Act, 333
Adjournment, 3
    Christmas tree bills, 73
    continuing resolutions, 100
    legislative day, 245
    morning hour, 284-285
    motions for, 285
    pocket veto issue, 431, 434-435
    special orders, 388
Administrative assistants, 391
Adolescents and youth
    franchise, 469-471

Great Society programs, 172
    hazardous occupations, 290
    sub-minimum wage, 231
Adult education, 172
Advertising
    campaign financing, 57-59, 183
    Post Office Committee, 321
    regulation, 79
Advice and consent. *See* Appointment
    power; Treaties and international agree-
    ments
Affirmative action, 398
Afghanistan, 370
AFL-CIO Committee on Political Educa-
    tion, 310
Age. *See also* Elderly persons
    characteristics of members, 190, 279, 375
    qualifications for office, 404
    youth franchise, 469-471
**Aging Committees, House and Senate,
3**
Agnew, Spiro T., 124, 133, 154, 155, 183, 323,
    324, 457, 502
Agricultural Adjustment Act of 1933, 245,
    290
Agriculture and farming
    Estes investigation, 171
    export shipping rules, 282
    farm bill, 116
    farmers' protest, 261, 263
    Foley career, 154
    irrigation, 203
    Morrill Act, 398
    New Deal programs, 288, 290
    price supports, 4-6, 45, 268, 406
    railroad regulation, 78
    seed distribution, 163
    Whitten expertise, 18
Agriculture Committee, House, 4-5
    chairmen, 1947-88, 484
    history and jurisdiction, 4-5, 203
Agriculture Department, U.S., 163

contra aid
  committee jurisdiction, 20
  debate record, 92
  Republican leadership, 116, 283
  war powers, 448, 449, 453
  Wright role, 469
Nicholson, Alfred O. P., 492
Night sessions, 144, 146
Nineteenth Amendment, 97, 333, 340, 466, 471
92 Group, 70
Nix, Robert N. C., 489
Nixon, Richard
  biography, 192, 227, **290-292**
  congressional service, 325
    anticommunism investigations, 182, 204, 209
  impeachment effort, 292-294
  executive privilege, 140
  Ford career, 154
  historic milestones, 183
  impeachment power, 196-200
  Judiciary Committee investigation, 204, 206, 210, 222
  removal power, 358
  television, 420
  Watergate scandal, 453, 457-458
  presidency
    appropriations, impoundment, 43, 200, 334
    federal-state relations, 399
    legislative veto, 255
    patronage, 306
    pocket vetoes, 434-435
    resignation, 124, 154, 183, 197, 210, 292-293, 394, 453, 458
    social programs, 173
    State of the Union report, 394
    Supreme Court nominations, 15, 224
    vetoes, 432-433
    vice presidents, 124, 154-155, 183, 323, 324, 325
    Vietnam policies, 147, 164, 275, 432, 451-453
    war powers, 400, 407, 432-433, 451-453
  vice presidency, 502
  Watergate scandal, 453-459
    Baker career, 27
    campaign financing, 57-58
    Ervin career, 129-130
    ethics issues, 133
    executive privilege, 140
    historic milestones, 183
    impeachment power, 197
    income tax issue, 416, 457
    investigations, oversight power, 204, 206, 210, 301
    pardon, 155, 198, 294, 453
    removal power, 358
Nofziger, Lyn, 265
Nolan, Mae E., 465, 466, 487

Nongermane amendments. *See* Riders
Nonpartisanship. *See* Bipartisanship
Norrell, Catherine D., 487
Norris, George W., 61, 232, 233, **294-295**, 332
North, Oliver L., 205, 211-215, 300
North Atlantic Assembly, 159
North Atlantic Treaty, 93
North Atlantic Treaty Organization, 416, 426, 430, 450
North Carolina
  Senate election, 1984, 54
North Dakota
  House representation, 191
Northeast-Midwest Congressional Coalition, 70, 71
Norton, Mary T., 487
Novak, Robert, 139, 240
Nuclear energy
  committee jurisdiction, 87, 125, 203
  waste disposal, 365
Nuclear weapons. *See also* Arms control
  committee jurisdiction, 21
  Smith career, 384
  Truman career, 426
  war powers of Congress, 407, 450-451
Nullification, 53, 175-176, 177-178, 396-397, 461
Nunn, Sam, 24, 163, 171, 483
Nurses, 230
Nye, Gerald P., 208

Oakar, Mary Rose, 488
Oath of office, 297-298, 422
Obey, David R., 133
Objectors, 93
O'Brien, Lawrence F., 454
Obscenity, 102
Occupational health and safety
  committee jurisdiction, 120, 230
  congressional hiring practices, 390
  Progressive Era, 332
  teenager limits, 290
Oceans policy, 81, 282
O'Day, Caroline L. G., 487
Office of Management and Budget, 16, 43, 48, 167, 245, 433
O'Hara, James E., 489
Ohio
  House representation, 345
Oil industry
  jurisdiction, 125, 127
  lobbying, 263
  Long career, 149, 269
  mergers, 127
  Persian Gulf war, 452
  Teapot Dome scandal, 208, 417-419
Oklahoma
  women's suffrage, 467
Old Bullion. *See* Benton, Thomas H.

Randolph, Jennings, 128-129, 483-484
Randolph, John, 77, **339-340**
Rangel, Charles B., 35, 287, 489
Rankin, Jeannette, 180, **340-341**, 465, 468, 487
Ransier, Alonzo J., 489
Rapler, James T., 489
Rayburn, Sam, **341-342**
  associates, 7, 37, 276, 279, 284, 305
  biography, 341-342
  disciplining members, 132
  home style, 441
  House power centers, 188-190
  House rules, 186
  leadership, 240, 476-477, 479
  length of service, 281, 282
  Rules Committee reform, 356, 384
  Speaker history, 387
  television opposition, 421
Rayburn Securities Act, 333
Read, John M., 102
Readings of bills, **342**
Reagan, Nancy, 464
Reagan, Ronald
  agriculture programs, 6
  appointments, 203, 275
    staff, 28, 161, 265
    Supreme Court nominations, 15, 224, 370
  appropriations
    continuing resolutions, 99, 434
    line-item veto, 435
  banking, 28
  budget policies, 44-45, 70, 139, 330, 387, 431
  congressional-executive relations, 27-28, 40, 49, 98, 283, 299, 319, 381, 393, 438
  congressional pay, 307
  defense programs, 21, 22-23, 24, 437
  education policies, 120-121
  energy policies, 127
  environmental policy, 128
  federal-state relations, 399
  foreign policy, 156, 158, 449
  housing programs, 29, 30
  Iran-contra affair, 184, 211-214, 300
  legislative veto, 255
  movie industry investigation, 209
  Nicaraguan contra aid, 448
  pocket veto, 435
  pork-barrel politics, 320, 321, 439
  presidential disability, 324
  riders, 359
  social programs, 42, 120-121
  taxation, 44-45, 149, 460
  television expertise, 139
  uniform drinking age, 264
  vetoes, 433
  war powers, 452
  White House renovation, 464

Real estate
  banking deregulation, 28
Realtors Political Action Committee, 261-262, 311
Reapportionment and redistricting, **342-348**, 405
Recess, 3, 245, 434-435
Recess appointments, 13, 232
Reciprocal Trade Agreements Act of 1934, 335
Reclamation Bureau, 203
Recommittal motion, **349**
Reconsider, motion to, **349-350**, 415
Reconstruction Committee, House, 220
Reconstruction Era, **350-353**
  blacks in Congress, 34
  filibusters, 144
  historic milestones, 179
  judicial review, 244
  party caucuses, 67
  Stevens career, 400-401
  Sumner career, 409
Recorded votes
  bells, 31-32
  in Committee of the Whole, 83
  House procedures, 443-444
  pairs, 445
  veto overrides, 442, 444, 445
Reece, Louise G., 487
Reed, Chauncey W., 485
Reed, Daniel A., 486
Reed, Thomas Brackett, 179, 188-190, **353-355**, 386, 476
Reed rules, 179, 354
Reform, **355-357**. *See also* Constitutional amendments; Progressive Era
  Albert career, 7
  Appropriations subcommittees, 19
  campaign financing, 54-59
  committee staff, 187
  direct election of senators, 106-109
  ethics, 133-134
  filibusters and cloture rule, 143-147
  historic milestones, 184
  Johnson rule, 219
  McCormack ouster attempt, 278
  Mills career, 284
  open sessions, 328
  party organizations, 64-68, 86, 319
  Rules Committee expansion, 384
  Senate development, 374
  Senate Rules and Administration Committee, 360
  seniority system, 377-378
Regulation and deregulation
  commerce power, 75-80
  committee jurisdiction, 81-82, 87, 125
  legislative veto, 255, 256
  removal power, 358
Reid, Charlotte T., 487
Reid, John W., 491

committee relationships
  Appropriations, 18
  Budget, 39
  Joint Taxation, 85, 416
floor leadership of chairman, 190, 236,
  317, 427
history and jurisdiction, 29, 86, 87, 126,
  459-460
House origins and development, 188
power of the purse, 334
status, 35-36, 83, 87, 187, 333
tax bills
  closed rules, 248
  discharge, 110
  origination, 148
Waxman, Henry A., 126
Weaver, James, 132, 151
Webster, Daniel, 460-461
antislavery, 372
biography, 157, 161, 460-461
Calhoun career, 53
Clay career, 74
Compromise of 1850, 178
ethics, 130
Hayne debate, 175-176, 178, 396
House origins and development, 187-188
Senate leadership, 373
Wednesday Group, 69
Weicker, Lowell P., Jr., 230-231, 383, 484
Weights and measures, 406
Weis, Jessica McC., 487
Welch, Richard J., 485
Welfare and social services
  committee jurisdiction, 87, 120-121, 147-
    149, 229-231, 459
  Eisenhower policies, 432
  Great Society programs, 172-173, 218
  Progressive Era, 331-332
Wendell, Cornelius, 170
Wesberry v. Sanders, 182, 347, 347
West Germany
  congressional travel, 159
West Virginia
  public works projects, 128-129
Western states
  Energy and Natural Resources Commit-
    tee, 127
  Interior Committee, 203
Wheat, Alan, 489
Wheeler, William A., 502
Whig party, 315-316
Whips
  election, 190
  House leadership, 236-238
  Senate leadership, 238
  zones, 471
White, George H., 489
White, George M., 63
White, James, 106
White, John, 475
White, John D., 493

White, Wallace H., Jr., 481, 483
White, William Allen, 341
White House (Executive Mansion), **461-
464**
  visiting (box), 464
  War of 1812, 177
Whittemore, Benjamin F., 491, 493
Whitten, Jamie L., 17, 281, 282, 484
Whittington, William M., 486
Widow's mandate, 465
Wigfall, Louis T., 492
Wilderness Act of 1964, 203
Wilderness protection, 127, 202-203
  Alaska, 265
Wildlife
  committee jurisdiction, 203, 282
Wiley, Alexander, 484
Williams, George H., 102
Williams, Harrison A., Jr., 1-2, 112, 136, 230,
  484, 492
Williams, John Sharp, 479
Williams, Sherrod, 493
Wilmot, David, 178
Wilmot Proviso, 178
Wilson, Charles H., 113, 151, 493
Wilson, Ellen, 464
Wilson, Henry, 502
Wilson, Woodrow
  Borah career, 37-38
  Clark career, 73
  congressional committees, 86
  filibusters, 144-145, 180
  lame-duck sessions, 233
  Lodge career, 158, 425
  naval oil reserves, 417
  New Deal origins, 288
  Norris career, 294
  party caucuses, 66
  presidential addresses to Congress, 180,
    393
  presidential disability, 324
  Progressive Era, 332-333
  special interests, 262
  veto power, 433
  vice president, 437
  women's suffrage, 467
Wingo, Effiegene, 487
Winthrop, Robert C., 475
Wisconsin Idea, 231
Wise, Henry A., 493
Wizard of Ooze. *See* Dirksen, Everett M.
Wolcott, Alexander, 102
Wolcott, Jesse P., 485
Wolverton, Charles A., 485
Women
  congressional hiring practices, 390
  Equal Rights Amendment, 95
  members of Congress, 465-466
    blacks, 35
    characteristics, 191, 279, 375
    cloakrooms, 75